Microsoft®
Visual Basic® 2005: RELOADED
Advanced

Richard Johnson, Diane Zak

THOMSON
COURSE TECHNOLOGY

Australia • Canada • Mexico • Singapore • Spain • United Kingdom • United States

Microsoft® Visual Basic® 2005: RELOADED, Advanced

by Richard Johnson and Diane Zak

Vice President, Technology and Trades ABU:
Dave Garza

Director of Learning Solutions:
Sandy Clark

Acquisitions Editor:
Amy Jollymore

Managing Editor:
Tricia Coia

Developmental Editor:
Ann Shaffer

Editorial Assistant:
Erin Kennedy

Quality Assurance tester:
Green Pen Quality Assurance

Production Editor:
GEX Publishing Services

Art Director:
Beth Paquin

Compositor:
Gex Publishing Services

Manufacturing Coordinator:
Julio Esperas

Cover Designer:
Steve Deschene

Printed in the United States of America

1 2 3 4 5 6 7 8 9 TW 07 06 05 04 03

For more information, contact Thomson Course Technology, 25 Thomson Place, Boston, Massachusetts, 02210.

Or find us on the World Wide Web at: www.course.com

ISBN 13: 978-1-4188-3643-6
ISBN 10: 1-4188-3643-5

Contents

CHAPTER 11
Arrays, Collections, and Generics 527

CHAPTER 12
Multithreading in Visual Basic 573

Preface

Welcome to *Microsoft Visual Basic 2005: RELOADED, Advanced*. This book is intended for use in either a second course in Visual Basic or a first course in Visual Basic for those who already have programming experience in another language. It is a continuation of *Microsoft Visual Basic 2005: RELOADED, Second Edition* by Diane Zak, providing additional depth in topics such as object-orientation, user interface design, and ADO .NET. This book also presents new topics such as exception handling, ASP .NET, database and SQL, generics, and multithreading.

Microsoft Visual Basic 2005: RELOADED, Advanced assumes you are already quite familiar with computers and computer programming. The first two chapters of *RELOADED, Advanced* are intended as a quick review of several fundamental Visual Basic programming topics. If you are already very proficient with Visual Basic, you may be able to skip these first two chapters entirely. However, if you feel you may be somewhat rusty, you may find these review chapters helpful in getting back up to speed with Visual Basic.

ORGANIZATION AND COVERAGE

Microsoft Visual Basic 2005: RELOADED, Advanced contains 12 chapters and 2 appendices. As mentioned earlier, the first two chapters are a concise yet complete review of the first text in this series, *Microsoft Visual Basic 2005: RELOADED*. The reason for this comprehensive review is twofold: (1) students may be rusty on fundamentals if there has been a significant time lapse since their first exposure to Visual Basic; and (2) students who have studied another programming language (such as Java or C++) will find the review a great way to jumpstart their study of Visual Basic.

Chapters 3 and 4 provide an in-depth look at the object-oriented features of Visual Basic, including the fundamentals of objects and classes, as well as the more advanced topics of inheritance and polymorphism. Chapter 5 explores input validation, classic error handling, and structured error handling. Chapter 6 examines advanced Windows user interfaces including tabbed pages, menus, and MDI (multiple document interface). Chapter 7 covers database and SQL using both Microsoft Access and Microsoft SQL Server. Chapter 8 applies the concepts of Chapter 7 using ADO.NET to add database functionality to Windows applications. Chapter 9 introduces another important Microsoft technology, ASP.NET, which is used to create dynamic Web sites. Chapter 10 continues the exploration of ASP.NET including coverage of database, XML, and Web services. Chapter 11 presents important coverage of advanced arrays, collections, and generics. Chapter 12 discusses the interesting world of multithreading in an easy to understand and unique way. Appendix A covers the important topic of deployment concisely yet completely. Finally, Appendix B provides many useful suggestions for debugging Windows applications.

APPROACH

Like *Microsoft Visual Basic 2005: RELOADED,* this advanced text focuses on important programming concepts in many key areas, such as exception handling, object-orientation, generics, and multithreading. However, *RELOADED, Advanced* also presents extremely valuable hands-on techniques in working with user interfaces, databases, SQL, Web application development, XML, and Web services.

Each chapter of *RELOADED, Advanced* has many helpful pedagogical features. Important How To boxes throughout the book make sure students clearly understand Visual Basic .NET programming syntax and development techniques. This book also employs pseudocode, flow charts, and UML (Unified Modeling Language). Frequent tips provide a wealth of useful information. Complete programs are presented and explained in a way that makes them much easier to understand than code snippets. A plethora of screen shots help to illustrate important concepts and techniques.

At the end of each chapter is a complete programming example using TOE charts, pseudocode, and a full listing of program code. Also included at the end of each chapter is a comprehensive Quick Review; an alphabetized Key Terms listing with definitions; 20 multiple-choice Review Questions (good for self-testing or for creating short quizzes); 7 well-designed, real-world Computer Exercises; and 3 additional challenging Case Projects. Complete solutions to all exercises and projects are provided in instructor materials and at *www.course.com* (password protected).

FEATURES

Microsoft Visual Basic 2005: RELOADED, Advanced is an exceptional textbook because it also includes the following features:

- **Read This Before You Begin:** This section is consistent with Thomson Course Technology's unequaled commitment to helping instructors introduce technology into the classroom. Technical considerations and assumptions about hardware, software, and default settings are listed in one place to help instructors save time and eliminate unnecessary aggravation.
- **Learning Objectives:** Each chapter begins with a list of objectives so you know the topics that will be presented in the chapter. In addition to providing a quick reference to topics covered, this feature provides a useful study aid.
- **How To boxes:** The How To boxes in each chapter summarize important concepts and provide a quick reference for students. For example, How To boxes show the steps for performing a task, such as starting Microsoft Visual Studio 2005 or Microsoft SQL Server. Additionally, each time a new statement or method is covered, its syntax is shown in a How To box along with examples of using the syntax.
- **Tip:** Tips provide additional information for example, an alternate method of performing a procedure or where to look for additional information.
- **Programming Examples:** A complete Programming Example at the end of each chapter allows students to see the concepts they have learned and how they are applied.
- **Quick Review:** Following the Programming Example in each chapter is a Quick Review, which recaps the concepts covered in the chapter.
- **Key Terms:** Following the Quick Review in each chapter is an alphabetized collection of all the key terms found throughout the chapter. Definitions are also included in sentence format.
- **Review Questions:** This section provides meaningful questions that test students' understanding of what they learned in the chapter.
- **Computer Exercises:** Following the Review Questions are seven Computer Exercises that provide students with additional practice of the skills and concepts they learned in the chapter.

- **Case Projects:** At the end of each chapter are three Case Projects. The Case Projects give the student the opportunity to independently synthesize and evaluate information, examine potential solutions, and make recommendations.
- **Glossary:** A glossary is included at the end of the book listing all the key terms in alphabetical order, along with definitions.

TEACHING TOOLS

The following supplemental materials are available when this book is used in a classroom setting. All of the teaching tools available with this book are provided to the instructor on a single CD-ROM. Many can also be found at the Thomson Course Technology Web site (*www.course.com*).

- **Electronic Instructor's Manual:** The Instructor's Manual that accompanies this textbook includes additional instructional material to assist in class preparation, including Sample Syllabi, Chapter Outlines, Technical Notes, Lecture Notes, Quick Quizzes, Teaching Tips, Discussion Topics, and Additional Case Projects.
- **ExamView®:** This textbook is accompanied by ExamView, a powerful testing software package that allows instructors to create and administer printed, computer (LAN-based), and Internet exams. ExamView includes hundreds of questions that correspond to the topics covered in this text, enabling students to generate detailed study guides that include page references for further review. The computer-based and Internet testing components allow students to take exams at their computers, and also save time for the instructor by grading each exam automatically.
- **Microsoft® PowerPoint® Presentations:** This book comes with Microsoft PowerPoint slides for each chapter. These are included as a teaching aid for classroom presentation, to make available to students on the network for chapter review, or to be printed for classroom distribution. Instructors can add their own slides for additional topics they introduce to the class.
- **Data Files:** Data Files, which are necessary for completing many of the Exercises, are provided on the Teaching Tools CD-ROM and may also be found on the Thomson Course Technology Web site at *www.course.com*.
- **Solution Files:** Solutions to end-of-chapter Questions and Exercises are provided on the Teaching Tools CD-ROM and may also be found on the Thomson Course Technology Web site at *www.course.com*. The Solution Files also include the applications that appear in the concepts section in each chapter; these applications are used to illustrate the concepts being taught. The solutions are password protected.
- **Distance Learning:** Thomson Course Technology is proud to present online test banks in WebCT and Blackboard to provide the most complete and dynamic learning experience possible. Instructors are encouraged to make the most of the course, both online and offline. For more information on how to access the online test bank, contact your local Thomson Course Technology sales representative.

ACKNOWLEDGMENTS

Writing a book is a team effort rather than an individual one. We would like to take this opportunity to thank our team, especially Tricia Coia (Senior Product Manager), Ann Shaffer (Development Editor), and the Quality Assurance testers at Green Pen Quality Assurance who carefully tested each chapter multiple times. Thank you for your support, enthusiasm, patience, and hard work. We could not have completed this project without you. Last, but certainly not least, we want to thank the following reviewers for their invaluable suggestions and comments: Henry Bojack, Farmingdale State University; Larry Langellier, Moraine Valley Community College; and Jill Slater, University of Denver.

Richard Johnson, Diane Zak

Read This Before You Begin

TO THE USER

Thomson Course Technology Data Files

To complete some of the tutorials and exercises, you will need the data files created for this book. Your instructor will provide the data files to you. You also can obtain the files electronically from *www.course.com*. (Once there, you'll need to navigate to the page for this book.)

Each chapter in this book has its own set of data files, which are stored in a separate folder within the VbReloadedAdvanced folder. For example, the files for Chapter 1 are stored in the VbReloadedAdvanced\Chap01 folder. Similarly, the files for Chapter 2 are stored in the VbReloadedAdvanced\Chap02 folder. Throughout this book, you will be instructed to open files from, or save files to, these folders.

You can use a computer in your school lab or your own computer to complete the Programming Examples, Computer Exercises, and Case Projects in this book.

Using Your Own Computer

To use your own computer to complete the material in this book, you will need the following:

- A Pentium II-class processor, 600 MHz or higher, personal computer running Microsoft Windows. This book was written and Quality Assurance tested using Microsoft Windows XP.
- Microsoft Visual Studio 2005 Professional Edition installed on your computer. Also, you will need Microsoft Access and Microsoft SQL Server 2005 Express Edition installed for Chapters 7-10.
- Data files: You will not be able to complete some of the Exercises in this book using your own computer unless you have the necessary data files. You can get the data files from your instructor, or you can obtain them electronically from *www.course.com*. (Once there, you'll need to navigate to the page for this book.)

Figures

The figures in this book reflect how your screen will look if you are using Microsoft Visual Studio 2005 Professional Edition and a Microsoft Windows XP system. Your screen may appear slightly different in some instances if you are using another version of Microsoft Visual Studio, Microsoft Visual Basic, or Microsoft Windows.

TO THE INSTRUCTOR

To complete some of the Programming Tutorials and Computer Exercises in this book, your users must use a set of data files. These files are included on the Instructor's Resource CD-ROM. They also may be obtained electronically through the Thomson Course Technology Web site at *www.course.com*. Follow the instructions in the Help file to copy the data files to your server or standalone computer. You can view the Help file using a text editor such as WordPad or Notepad. Once the files are copied, you should instruct your users how to copy the files to their own computers or workstations.

The Programming Examples, Computer Exercises, and Case Projects in this book were Quality Assurance tested using Microsoft Visual Studio 2005 Professional Edition and Microsoft Visual Basic Express Edition on a Microsoft Windows XP operating system.

Thomson Course Technology Data Files

You are granted a license to copy the data files to any computer or computer network used by individuals who have purchased this book.

CHAPTER

Reviewing Microsoft Visual Basic 2005 Reloaded: Part 1

After studying Chapter 1, you should be able to:

- Design and create a user interface for an application
- Use variables and constants in methods to perform calculations
- Create pseudocode, flowcharts, and program code for the sequence, selection, and repetition structures
- Create a project, solution, and application in Visual Basic 2005

If you are reading this book, you are probably quite familiar with computers and computer programming. The first two chapters of this book are intended as a quick review of several fundamental Visual Basic programming topics. It is very important that you thoroughly understand the material in these review chapters before proceeding with the more challenging material in the remainder of the book.

AN INTRODUCTION TO VISUAL BASIC 2005

This section introduces some basic terms associated with programming and shows you how to get started using the Visual Studio 2005 integrated development environment (IDE).

Programmers and Programming Languages

As you know, computers need programs (sets of computer instructions) to operate, and programs must be written by programmers like you. Well-written programs are not created haphazardly—instead, they are developed with great care. There are two main categories of programmers, **systems programmers** who write and maintain programs that help the computer carry out its basic operating functions and **applications programmers** who write and maintain programs that handle specific real-world tasks. This text is concerned with applications programming.

Programmers communicate with computers via programming languages. Examples of popular programming languages are the series of .NET languages (such as Visual Basic and Visual C#), Java, and C++. (Also, many legacy languages, such as FORTRAN and COBOL, which were important in years past, are still used today.) However, computers cannot directly understand any of these kinds of programming languages. Computer processors can understand only their own special **machine languages** where instructions are represented in binary code (groups of 0s and 1s). The very first computer programs, dating back to the 1940s, were written in machine languages (also called first-generation languages).

By the early 1950s, programming languages evolved into **assembly languages** where the codes of 0s and 1s were replaced with mnemonics, which are simple codes (such as ADD and MOV) that are easier for programmers to remember. Assembly languages (also called second-generation languages) require an assembler, software that translates assembly language into machine language.

By the late 1950s, programming languages evolved into **high-level languages** (also called third-generation languages) that use complete English-like programming statements (such as total = price + tax). Programs written in high-level languages require either an interpreter or a compiler to convert the English-like instructions into machine language. Figure 1.1 illustrates the three generations of programming languages.

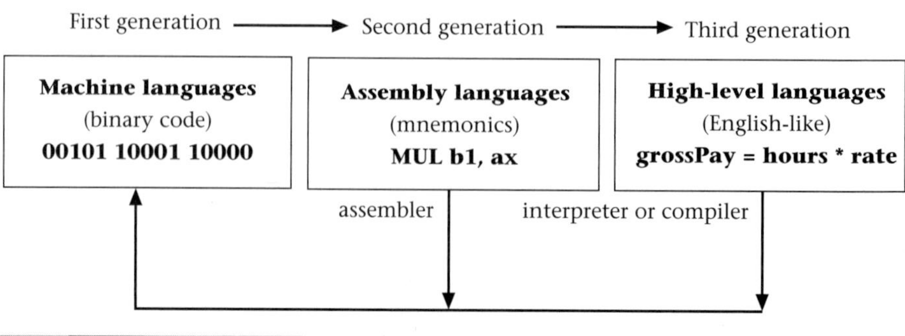

FIGURE 1.1 Three generations of programming languages

Procedure-Oriented and Object-Oriented Programming

There are basically two ways of writing computer programs in a high-level language: procedure-oriented and object-oriented.

Procedure-Oriented Programming

Until the 1990s, nearly all programs were created using **procedure-oriented programming**. This means that program code is broken down into groups of procedures (also called functions, methods, or modules) designed to receive certain pieces of data, perform specialized tasks using that data, and return new kinds of useful information. Programming languages such as FORTRAN, Pascal, and C were developed specifically for procedure-oriented programming.

Object-Oriented Programming

On the other hand, **object-oriented programming (OOP)** has been around since the 1960s but gained a great deal of popularity in the 1990s. OOP is radically different from procedure-oriented programming. Instead of focusing on procedural code that receives input, performs processes, and provides output, the object-oriented (OO) programmer gives greater attention to various kinds of interacting objects that use their own internal data and procedures to accomplish application objectives. Special object-oriented programming languages, such as Visual Basic, Java, and C++, enable programmers to create OO applications.

Object-Oriented Terminology

OOP is very different from procedure-oriented programming. In the world at large, an object is anything that can be seen, touched, or used. However, in a programming context, the term "object" has a very specific meaning. An **object** is an instance of a class in computer memory, where a **class** is a unit of program code that defines a category of objects. A programming object typically represents something in the real world such as a text box in a program window or a student in a university. An object has **attributes** (also called properties), which are the characteristics that describe an object. An object also has **behaviors** (also called procedures or methods), which are the operations that an object is capable of performing. An object is said to encapsulate (enclose or contain) both its attributes and behaviors.

In OOP, you begin by creating a class, such as student class or movie class. The class defines what an object is (its attributes) and what an object does (its behaviors). **Instantiation** is the process of creating an object in computer memory. The object is thus called an instance of a class and becomes a software representation of its real-world counterpart. For example, a student class may define student objects as things having an ID number, a name, and a grade point average (GPA). In a computer application, you would be represented by a student object, a specific instance of the student class, with a specific ID number, a specific name, and a specific GPA.

Other aspects of object orientation include abstraction, inheritance, and polymorphism. **Abstraction** means focusing only on the relevant aspects of something. In object orientation, this means using the properties and methods of objects without worrying about how the properties and methods are implemented in program code. Examples of abstraction would be driving a car without concern for the details of how the engine and transmission work, or calculating a student's GPA without worrying about the formula used. **Inheritance** is the process by which a derived class (also called a subclass) can automatically reuse (inherit) the properties and methods of a base class (or superclass). For example, both a student class and a faculty class can inherit certain properties and methods from a person class because students and faculty have things in common, such as Social Security numbers and names.

Finally, **polymorphism** enables one method (such as one called "print") to have several different implementations depending on the type of object calling the method. For example, printing a student object may produce different kinds of output than printing a faculty object, but both kinds of output are produced with the same method called "print".

While learning OOP can be challenging, creating a complicated OOP application is ultimately much easier than creating a similar application via procedure-oriented programming. Object-oriented design (OOD) is a methodology that helps developers carefully plan their object-oriented programming projects; OOD will be explored later in this book. Figure 1.2 illustrates many of these object-oriented terms in the context of a university information system.

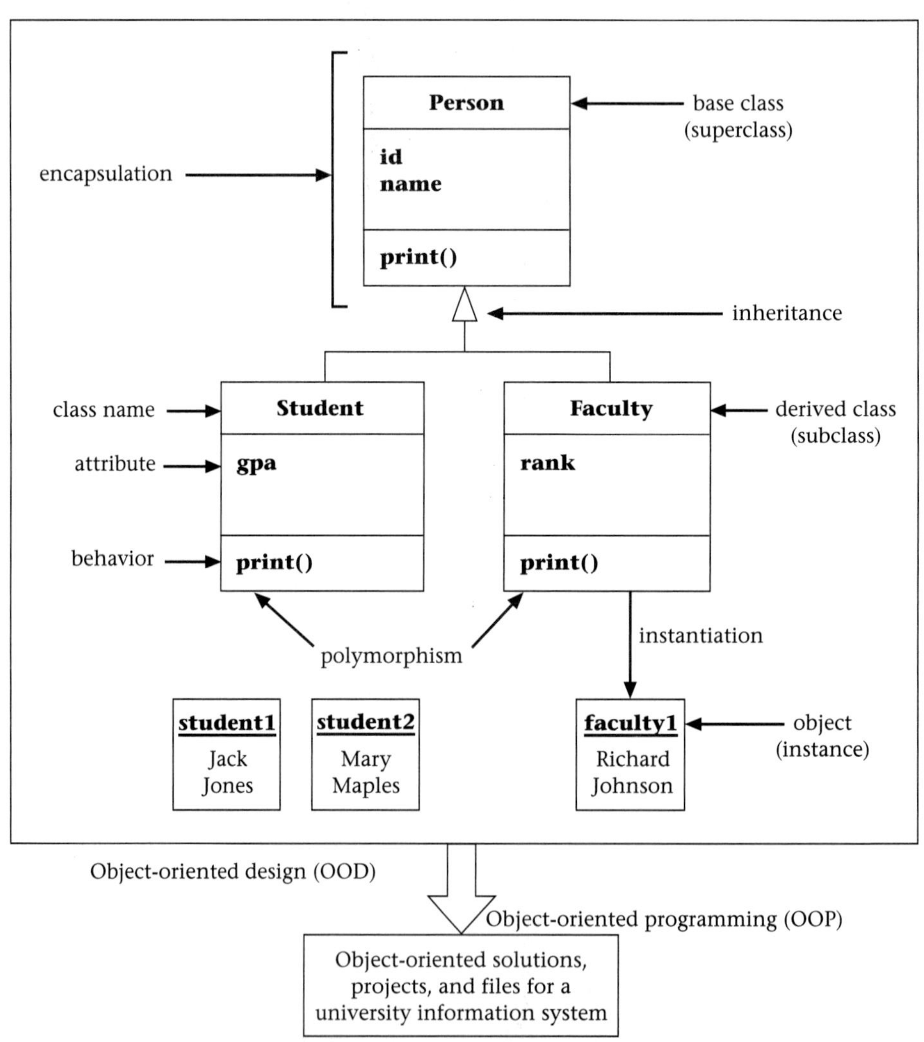

FIGURE 1.2 Illustration of object-oriented terms

Visual Studio 2005

Visual Studio 2005 is Microsoft's integrated development environment (IDE) for creating an object-oriented computer application using languages such as Visual Basic, Visual C++, Visual C#, and Visual J#. An **IDE** contains many tools for creating, compiling, and testing programs. As a start, all applications must have a **user interface**—the means by which the user interacts with the application. Visual Studio 2005 can be used to create a console application (using the text-based command prompt), a Windows-based application (using a Windows user interface) on a desktop computer, or a Web-based application (using a Web user interface) that runs on a Web server.

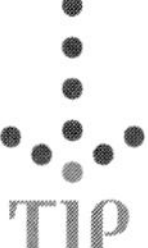

.NET is pronounced "dot net." You may obtain information about Visual Studio 2005 at *http://msdn.microsoft.com/vstudio/*.

The programming languages in Visual Studio 2005 run in the Microsoft .NET Framework 2.0, a development and execution environment that allows different programming languages and libraries (groups of predefined classes) to work together to create applications. The programming languages are often referred to as .NET languages, and applications created using the .NET languages are commonly called .NET applications. This application development environment includes the .NET Framework class library, which contains an extensive set of classes that provide prepackaged functionality.

Microsoft also provides various free, "lightweight" versions of Visual Studio 2005 called Visual Studio 2005 Express Editions for the Visual Basic, C#, C++, and J# languages (see *http://msdn.microsoft.com/vstudio/express/* for more information). Note that some of the menu commands for Express Editions may be slightly different than for the full versions of Visual Studio.

You are strongly encouraged to explore topics in the .NET Framework by visiting *http://msdn.microsoft.com/library/*, the Web site of the Microsoft Developers Network (MSDN) Library. You can browse through an extensive set of topics or enter text in the Search for text box and click the Search button. Performing a search will result in a list of links within the site with helpful tutorials as well as detailed specifications for all the .NET Framework namespaces, classes, methods, and programming statements. For example, if you search for "inheritance" you will find an excellent general discussion on this topic. On the other hand, if you search for "form" you will find the detailed specs of the Form class in the .NET Framework.

The Common Language Runtime

Each .NET language has its own compiler that translates .NET program instructions into a language called Intermediate Language (IL). Next, the **Common Language Runtime (CLR)**, the core runtime engine of the Microsoft .NET Framework, takes over to compile (using a just-in-time compiler) and execute the IL for a wide variety of computer platforms, such as Windows, Unix, and Macintosh. Figure 1.3 illustrates the role of the CLR.

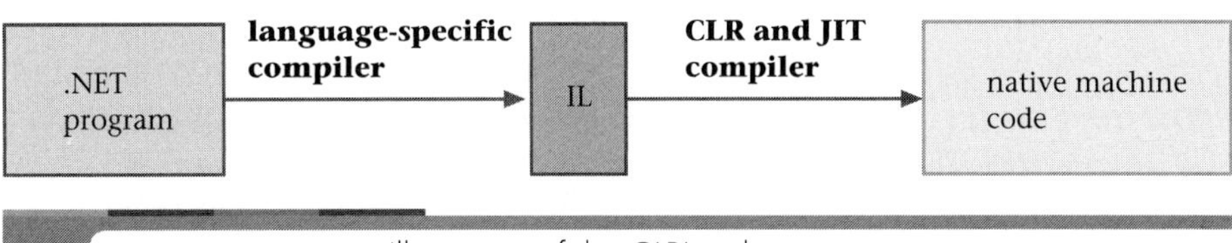

FIGURE 1.3 Illustration of the CLR's role

When running Visual Studio 2005 for the first time, choose Visual Basic Development Settings (not General Development Settings) to match the steps presented in this text. You can change development settings from the Visual Studio menu by clicking Tools and then clicking Import and Export Settings.

Solutions, Projects, and Files

A Visual Studio 2005 application consists of solutions, projects, and files. A solution contains projects and files for an entire application, while a project contains files for a specific part of the solution. You can think of a solution, its projects, and its files as a filing cabinet, folders, and reports, respectively. This approach to software development represents a well-designed system for keeping your software projects organized.

Starting Microsoft Visual Studio 2005

To start Microsoft Visual Studio 2005 you perform the steps in Figure 1.4. (If you are using a previous version of Visual Studio or Visual Studio 2005 Express Editions, your steps may be slightly different.)

HOW TO...

Start Microsoft Visual Studio 2005

1. Click the Start button on the taskbar.
2. Point to All Programs, then point to Microsoft Visual Studio 2005.
3. Click Microsoft Visual Studio 2005.

FIGURE 1.4 How to start Microsoft Visual Studio 2005

TIP

A solution may contain several projects written in different .NET languages.

Creating a Visual Basic Windows-Based Application

Figure 1.5 contains the steps to begin creating a Visual Basic Windows-based application. (Again, if you are using a previous version of Visual Studio or Visual Studio 2005 Express Editions, your steps may be slightly different.)

HOW TO...

Create a Visual Basic Windows-based Application

1. Start Microsoft Visual Studio 2005, then click File on the menu bar.
2. Click New Project. The New Project dialog box opens.
3. If necessary, expand the Visual Basic node in the Project types list, then click Windows.
4. If necessary, click Windows Application in the Visual Studio installed templates section of the Templates list.
5. Enter an appropriate name in the Name box.
6. Click the OK button.

FIGURE 1.5 How to create a Visual Basic Windows-based application

When you click the OK button in the New Project dialog box, Visual Studio 2005 creates a Visual Basic project, as shown in Figure 1.6 (named XYZ Project as an example). If the Solution Explorer window or the Properties window are not visible in the Visual Studio IDE, click View in the Visual Studio menu and select Solution Explorer or Properties Window.

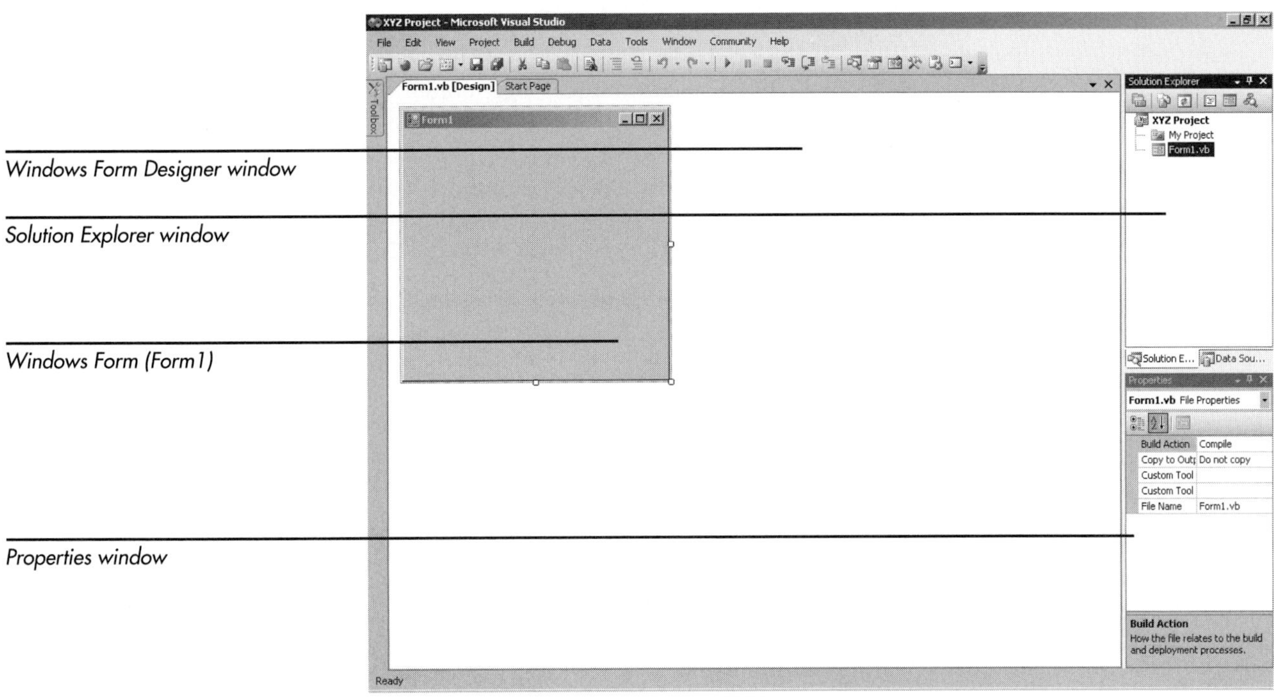

FIGURE 1.6 Visual Basic project created by Visual Studio 2005

Managing the Windows in the IDE

Several windows are available in the Visual Studio IDE. You may decide to close those that you are not using, but you can always open various windows by clicking View in the menu bar. Another useful technique is to click the Auto Hide button of a window (just to the left of its Close button). This hides the window but displays a tab for the window on the left or right side of the IDE. Moving the mouse over this tab causes the window to temporarily appear, and clicking the Auto Hide button again causes the window to remain open. Finally, you can undock a window by double-clicking its title bar and redock it by dragging it to various sides or corners of the IDE, as desired.

The Windows Form Designer Window

The **Windows Form Designer window** contains a Windows Form object (that is, a form) with a title bar and the minimize/maximize/close buttons. The form (named Form1 by default) is used to create a graphical user interface (GUI) for the application and holds other objects, such as labels, buttons, or text boxes, with which the user interacts. At the top of the Windows Form Designer window is the name of the file for this form, such as the default file name Form1.vb.

The Solution Explorer Window

The **Solution Explorer window** lists the projects, folders, and files within a solution. Within each project are a My Project node and one or more folders or files for that project. Double-clicking the My Project node opens the Project Designer window, which contains a wide variety of project management tools that will be covered in this text when necessary.

The .vb files listed in the Solution Explorer are Visual Basic source files that contain program code. This code is either written by you or automatically created by the IDE. The automatically generated Form1.vb source file is also referred to as a form file, because it contains the code associated with a Windows Form object. If you create a new form, it will be named Form2.vb by default. To make the various parts of the project easier to understand at a glance, you should rename these files with more meaningful names. To do this you will right-click on the file in the Solution Explorer and click Rename.

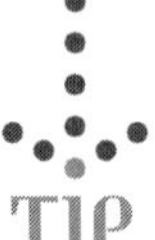

TIP

Right-click a file name, such as Form1.vb, in the Solution Explorer window, and then click Rename on the context menu to give a file a more meaningful name.

The Properties Window

Recall that objects have attributes or properties. A Visual Basic file is an object and therefore has properties, which are displayed in the **Properties window**. In the Solution Explorer window, click the Form1.vb file to display the properties and default property values in the Properties window. Just below the Properties window title bar is the Object box, which displays the name of the object (Form1.vb by default). Just below the Object box are various buttons to alter the display as desired. Below these buttons is the Properties list that displays the property names (left column) and the Settings box that lists the current values of the properties (right column). The Settings box enables you to change the value of a property.

TIP

In this text, special code font (for example, `TextBox`) is used to designate text that could appear within program code, such as Visual Basic keywords or identifiers that you create for program variables and methods.

Properties of a Windows Form Object

If you click on the form in the Windows Form Designer window, it becomes selected and the properties of the form are displayed in the Properties window. In the Object box you see the name of the object (Form1) followed immediately by this series of words connected with periods: `System.Windows.Forms.Form`. This indicates that `Form1` is an object instantiated from the `Form` class, which is in the `System.Windows.Forms` namespace. A **namespace** is simply a name given to a collection of related classes. The `System` namespace contains all the basic classes for creating Visual Basic applications. The `System.Windows.Forms` namespace contains additional classes for creating Windows-based applications. This namespace also contains classes such as `Button` and `TextBox`.

TIP

Go to *http://msdn.microsoft.com/* to obtain additional reference material on how to use the .NET framework class library. Use the Search text box on this site for specific searches. For general searches, click the Library link at the top of this page and expand the .NET Development link on the left.

As you know, an object may have dozens of properties that you can set to serve the purposes of your application. For a form object, a few of the important properties that you will find in the Properties window are `Name` (a meaningful name given to the form), `Text` (the text that appears in the form's title bar), and `StartPosition` (where the form will be positioned on the screen).

In the past, object names were written in Hungarian notation, in which the object name begins with a three-letter lowercase prefix denoting the type of object followed by a word that explains the purpose of the object. For example, the main form in an application might be called `frmMain` in Hungarian notation. Recently, a new naming convention for program identifiers has emerged, and this is the naming convention used in this book. In this new naming convention, the name begins with the form's purpose, followed by the form's class (`Form`). The name of the main form then becomes `MainForm`. Note that `MainForm` is written in Pascal case, which means that each word in the name begins with an uppercase letter.

The Toolbox Window

The **Toolbox window**, also called the Toolbox, contains tools for building an application. The Toolbox shown in Figure 1.7 is for the Windows Form Designer and the list of objects contains Windows Forms controls (labels, text boxes, buttons, etc.). Controls (another name for objects added to a form) can be dragged from the Toolbox to the form and then manipulated to meet the needs of the application.

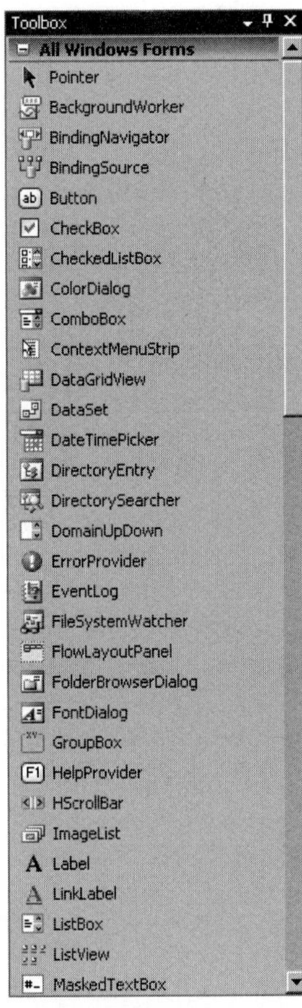

FIGURE 1.7 Toolbox window

TIP

The term camel case refers to the fact that the taller uppercase letters appear in the middle of the name, like humps in the middle of a camel.

The `Label` Tool

The `Label` tool can create a label control on a form. The purpose of a label is simply to display text in the form for either input or output purposes. Clicking the `Label` control will cause its properties to be displayed in the Properties window. You will usually want to change the name of a label to something more meaningful and, of course, change the text of the label to fit the application. Figure 1.8 shows a sample form with four labels (along with two buttons, a text box, and a list box). An appropriate name for the label that contains the program output (the empty rectangle to the left of the Exit button) would be `commissionLabel`. Note that `commissionLabel` is written in camel case, which means that the first letter is lowercase, but each new word in the name begins with an uppercase letter.

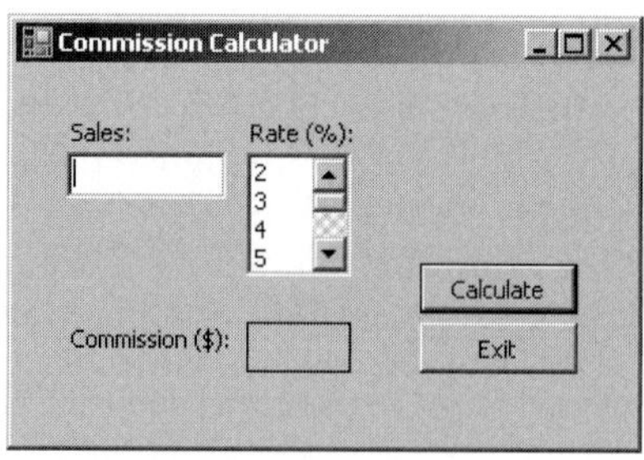

FIGURE 1.8 Label controls (among other controls) on a form

The `Button` Tool

You use the `Button` tool to create a button control on a form. When the user clicks a button on a form, a specific action (as defined by the programmer) occurs. Figure 1.8 has two buttons, Calculate and Exit. The corresponding names of these `Button` controls, using camel case, could be defined as `calculateButton` and `exitButton`.

TIP

In Figure 1.9, the keyword `Public` in the `Class` declaration indicates that the class can be used by code defined outside of the class.

The Code Editor Window

Clicking a button in a form is an example of an **event**. The set of instructions (program code) that tells the application what to do when an event occurs is called an **event procedure**. You, the programmer, are responsible for writing event procedure code in the Code Editor window of the Visual Studio IDE. You can open the Code Editor window by right-clicking the form and then clicking the View Code option. You can also click View and then Code in the menu. Figure 1.9 shows the Code Editor window for the form `MainForm` (renamed from the default `Form1`). Don't worry if you don't understand all the code in Figure 1.9 just yet.

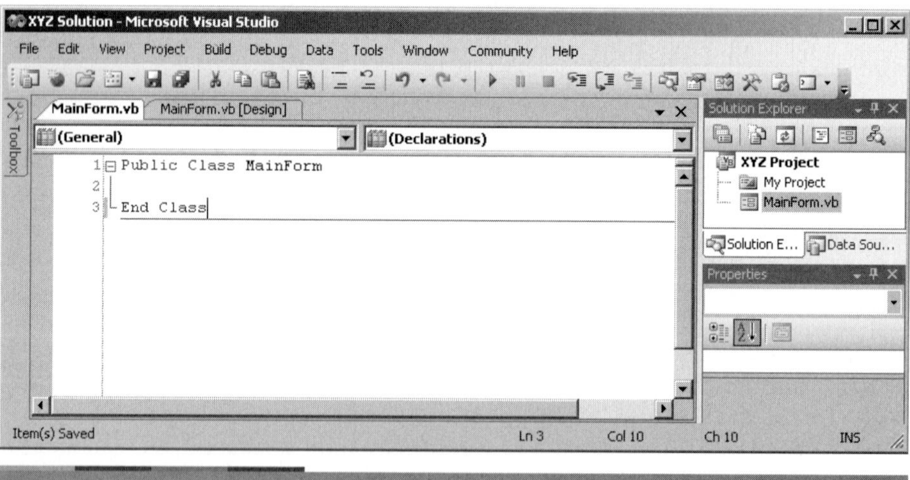

FIGURE 1.9 Code Editor window opened in the IDE

The class that defines the form object called `MainForm` begins with the code `Public Class MainForm` and ends with the code `End Class`. To make a program easier to read, you can hide code from view by clicking the minus box next to each section of code in the Code Editor and display code by clicking the plus box.

Creating a `Sub` Procedure for a Control

The key to creating useful applications in Visual Basic is creating a **`Sub` procedure** (a block of code that performs specific tasks) associated with a form control. You can begin creating a `Sub` procedure using the two list boxes at the top of the Code Editor window, the Class Name list box on the left and the Method Name list box on the right. You can select an object from the Class Name list box (such as a `Button` control) and an event from the Method Name list box (such as `Click`). When you do so, a code template appears in the editor to help you get started, as shown in Figure 1.10.

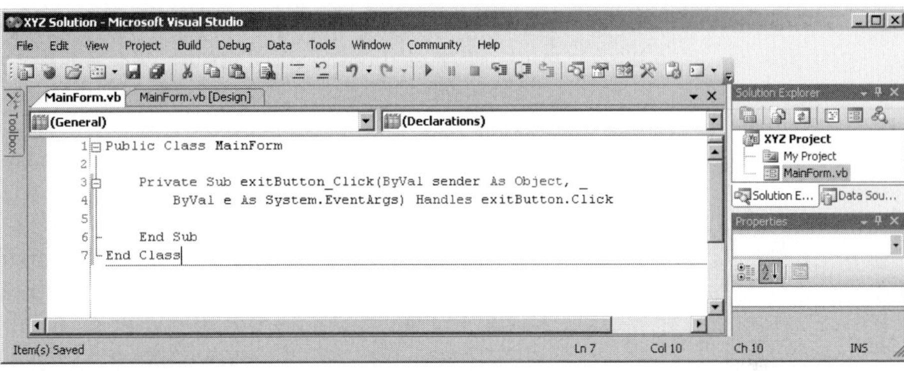

FIGURE 1.10 Code template for the `exitButton` object's `Click` event procedure

TIP

To display line numbers in the Code Editor window, click Tools, then click Options. Expand the Text Editor node, then expand the Basic node and click General. Select the Line numbers check box, then click the OK button.

This code template represents the beginning of a `Sub` procedure. The first line of the procedure is called the procedure header and the last line is called the procedure footer. The procedure header begins with the two keywords `Private Sub`. A keyword (also called a reserved word) is a word that has a special meaning in a programming language and can be used only in certain situations. The `Private` keyword indicates that the procedure can be used only within the class in which it is defined—in this case, only within the `MainForm` class. The `Sub` keyword identifies the procedure as a special kind of procedure that is at a sub-level within a class.

Following `Private Sub` in Figure 1.10 (Line 3) is the name of the object (`exitButton`), an underscore (_), the name of the event (`Click`), and parentheses containing the following code: `ByVal sender As Object, _ ByVal e As System.EventArgs`. The two items separated by a comma within the parentheses are called parameters and represent information that is required by the procedure to perform its task when it is invoked (called). The object `sender` stores information about the control that is sending information to the procedure and the `EventArgs` object `e` contains specific event data needed by the procedure to execute properly.

The underscore character following the first parameter (Line 3) is called a line-continuation character—it must be preceded by a space and followed immediately by a carriage return. The line-continuation character is used to break up long lines of code for better program readability.

Following the two parameters in parentheses in the procedure header is the code `Handles exitButton.Click` (Line 4). This part of the procedure header indicates that the procedure handles (responds to) the `Click` event for the `exitButton` control. The code `exitButton.Click` means that the object `exitButton` calls the `Click` event. In other words, the `Sub` procedure named `exitButton_Click` handles a `Click` event called by the `exitButton` control.

The `Me.Close` Method

If you enter the code `Me.Close()` within the `Sub` procedure shown in Figure 1.10, the form will close and the application will terminate when `exitButton` is clicked. The keyword `Me` refers to the specific instance of a class or structure in which the code is currently executing, which in this case is `MainForm`. Therefore, `Me.Close()` is calling the `Close` procedure for `MainForm`.

Debugging an Application

To test an application properly, you must specify a **startup form**, the form that is automatically displayed when an application is started. To do so, right-click the project name in the Solution Explorer window and click Properties. If necessary, click the Application tab on the left. Click the Startup form list arrow and then click the desired form name for startup (in the case of the XYZ Project in Figure 1.10, `MainForm` is the only form). Then close the Properties window.

To save an application, click the Save All button in the Standard toolbar or click File on the menu bar and then click Save All. To test an application, click the Start Debugging button in the Standard toolbar (the green arrow) or press the F5 key on the keyboard. This saves the application and creates an executable file with the same name as the project and an extension of .exe. This .exe file is stored in the project's bin folder. The executable file is the file provided to the user to run the application. See Appendix A, Deployment, for more information on deploying a completed application.

TIP

In most cases, you give the user only the executable file (with the .exe extension) instead of the complete solution folder, thus ensuring that the user cannot modify the application's code. To allow someone to modify the code, you need to provide the entire solution.

You end an application by clicking the Stop Debugging button in the Standard toolbar (the blue square) or clicking the Close button in the application's title bar. See Appendix B, Debugging, for more detailed information on how to debug your programs.

Printing Your Code

It's a good idea to print your code for debugging purposes. To do so, make sure the Code Editor window is active by clicking on it. Click the plus boxes only for the code that you want to print. Then click File on the menu bar, click Print, and click the OK button.

Closing and Opening a Solution

To close the current solution, click File on the menu bar and click Close. To open a solution that you have previously saved, click File on the menu bar, then click Open File. Locate the solution filename (with the .sln extension) and double-click it. Click View on the menu bar to display the desired windows (such as Solution Explorer, Properties Window, or Toolbox). Note that only one solution can be open in a single Visual Studio IDE at any one time, but you can open several applications in separate Visual Studio IDEs.

CREATING A USER INTERFACE

Now you will explore how to plan an application and design a user interface using the Visual Studio 2005 IDE.

Planning an Application

Carefully planning an application (always in cooperation with the users of the application) is an absolute requirement for successful application development.

One way of planning a Visual Basic application is through the use of a TOE (Task, Object, Event) chart. The TOE chart helps you identify the tasks that the application should perform, identify the objects to which the tasks will be assigned, and identify the events that will trigger these objects to perform the tasks. After the TOE chart is completed, you can design the GUI (graphical user interface).

To review the process of creating a user interface, you will use the example of the Skate-Away Sales Company. Skate-Away sells skateboards over the telephone. Salespeople record information on a paper form (Figure 1.11) and then manually calculate the total.

Skate-Away Sales Order Form:

Customer name: ____________

Address: ____________

City: ________ State: ______ ZIP: ______

Number of blue skateboards ordered:	Number of yellow skateboards ordered:	Total number of skateboards ordered:	Total price:
		Grand total:	

FIGURE 1.11 Current order form used by Skate-Away Sales

Identifying the Application Tasks

The first step in developing an application is identifying the tasks you want the application to perform. To identify the application tasks, you start by talking to the users. The following questions will help you zero in on the required tasks:

1. *What information should be displayed in the interface and/or printed to the printer?* For Skate-Away, printing information to the printer is not required. However, several labels must be displayed in the interface, such as "Customer name:", "Address:", and "Number of blue skateboards ordered:".
2. *What information will the user need to enter into the user interface?* The user will need to enter the customer name, address, etc., as well as the number of blue and yellow skateboards ordered.
3. *What information will the application need to calculate?* The application needs to calculate the total number of skateboards and the total price of the order.
4. *How will the user end the application?* This application will use an Exit button.
5. *Will previous information need to be cleared from the screen before new information is entered?* Users should be able to clear previously entered data so that incorrect values are not displayed.

Identifying the Objects

After you identify the application tasks, you must identify the objects that will perform these tasks. Just as a paper order form collects information from a salesperson, a Visual Basic `Form` object in the Skate-Away application will collect information on the screen. This form should include text boxes in which the user will enter data. You instantiate (create) a text box using the `TextBox` tool in the Toolbox. Some important properties of a `TextBox` object are `Name`, `Multiline` (if more than one line of input is needed), and `Text` (text that should automatically appear in the text box).

For starters, the Skate-Away application requires text boxes for entering the customer name, address, city, state, and zip. (The names of the text boxes should begin with a descriptive term and end with `TextBox`. For example, the state text box could be given the name `stateTextBox`.) You also need text boxes for entering the number of blue skateboards and the number of yellow skateboards ordered. All of these text boxes require labels so the user knows what is to be entered in each text box. `Label` controls in the form can also be used to display the total number of skateboards ordered and the total price of the order. As with text boxes, the names of labels should begin with a descriptive term and end with `Label`. For example, the label that displays the total number of skateboards in the order can be called `totalBoardsLabel`. Recall that control names (identifiers) use camel case, not Pascal case.

`Button` controls are needed to perform specific actions, such as calculating the total order price, clearing all text boxes, and exiting the application. Buttons are named similarly to labels and text boxes. For example, the calculate button might be called `calcButton`.

TIP

You can draw a TOE chart by hand, or you can use software such as an electronic spreadsheet or word processor.

Identifying the Events

In the Skate-Away application, no special events are needed for the `Label` and `TextBox` objects. Visual Basic automatically handles data entry for text boxes, as well as data display for text boxes and labels. However, you must identify events for the three buttons required for calculating, clearing, and exiting. In this case, the application will use the `Click` event for these three buttons. Table 1.1 is a TOE chart for this application. For a larger application, you may want to alphabetically list objects in the first column and then identify the tasks and events for each object.

Task	Object	Event
Get the following order information from the user:		
Customer's name	nameTextBox	None
Street address	addressTextBox	None
City	cityTextBox	None
State	stateTextBox	None
ZIP code	zipTextBox	None
Number of blue skateboards ordered	blueTextBox	None
Number of yellow skateboards ordered	yellowTextBox	None
(Table is continued on next page)		

Calculate the total skateboards ordered and the total price	calcButton	Click
Display the following information: Customer's name Street address City State ZIP code Number of blue skateboards ordered Number of yellow skateboards ordered Total skateboards ordered Total price	 nameTextBox addressTextBox cityTextBox stateTextBox zipTextBox blueTextBox yellowTextBox calcButton, totalBoardsLabel calcButton, totalPriceLabel	 None None None None None None None Click, None Click, None
End the application	exitButton	Click
Clear the screen for the next order	clearButton	Click

TABLE 1.1 Completed TOE chart ordered by task

Designing the User Interface

Now that you have created the TOE chart (tasks, objects, and events), you need to design exactly where the controls will be located within the form. Most Windows applications have a resizable **primary window**, the main user interface, with a title bar and a Close button. An application may also have **dialog boxes** (non-resizable windows) that support and supplement a user's activities in the primary window. You can control the appearance and functionality of an application's primary window using the `FormBorderStyle` property of the `Form` object. For example, if you don't want the user to be able to resize a window, you could select the value `FixedSingle` for the `FormBorderStyle` property (instead of the default value `Sizable`). Recall that you can view the properties and their settings in the Properties window after selecting the object in the Designer.

Arranging the Controls

In Western countries, information is usually organized in a left-to-right and/or top-to-bottom arrangement, with the most important information coming first. An example of a user interface for Skate-Away is shown in Figure 1.12. Notice the neat appearance, organization, and consistent spacing. Many features, such as button size, font selection, spacing, choice of words, capitalization, etc., are governed by generally accepted rules (and common sense). For example, the first three text boxes in Figure 1.12 are all the same size, as are the three buttons, resulting in a neat appearance. Also, the labels use sentence capitalization (only the first letter of the first word is capitalized) and the form title uses book capitalization (the first letters of all words are capitalized).

Related controls can be grouped together using a `GroupBox` control, a `Panel` control, or a `TableLayoutPanel` control. You instantiate these controls using the `GroupBox`, `Panel`, and `TableLayoutPanel` tools, respectively, in the Toolbox. A `GroupBox` creates a border around a group of controls and a caption for the group. A `Panel` can have scroll bars, and a `TableLayoutPanel` provides a table structure for controls. These controls are found in the Containers section of the Toolbox. To use a `Container` control, select it from the Toolbox and drag the pointer around the controls in the form that are to be contained. Then the properties of the `Container` control can be altered to meet the specific needs of the application. Individual controls, such as `Label`, `TextBox`, and `Button` controls, can be dragged and dropped within a `GroupBox`, `Panel`, or cells of a `TableLayoutPanel`.

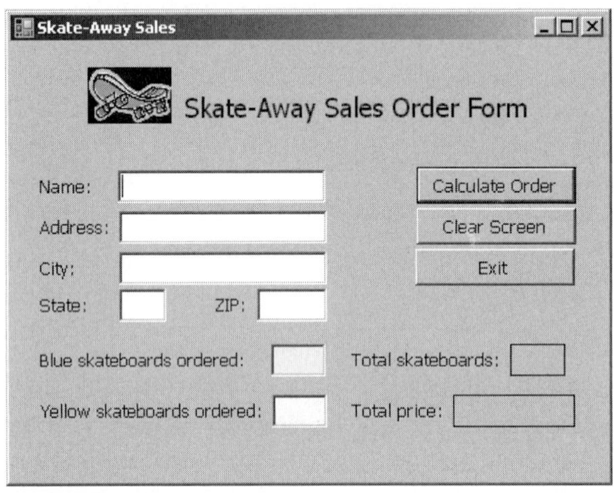

FIGURE 1.12 The Skate-Away Sales interface

Aligning and Sizing Controls

To align and size controls, select them, click Format in the menu bar, and then choose one of several options in the Format menu. For consistency among a group of controls, you can select several controls at once using Control-click or dragging the mouse pointer around the controls. Keep in mind that a user interface should be simple and easy to use, so try to refrain from making an interface particularly "snazzy" with lots of different colors and/or graphics. This may impress users at first, but it can soon become annoying.

Including Graphics in the User Interface

Graphics in a user interface should be limited, reserved mostly for quickly drawing attention to certain parts of the interface, presenting a company logo (as in Figure 1.12), or occasionally serving an aesthetic purpose. Of course, games would be an exception, since they ordinarily make heavy use of graphics. Figure 1.13 explains how to add a graphic to a user interface.

HOW TO...

Add a Graphic to a User Interface

1. Create or obtain the graphics file (with formats such as GIF, JPG, PNG, TIF, etc.).
2. Create a Resources folder in the project to contain the graphics file by right-clicking the project in the Solution Explorer, pointing to Add, clicking New Folder, and typing the name of the folder.
3. Drag a `PictureBox` control from the Toolbox to the form.
4. Click the ellipsis button for the `Image` property of the `PictureBox` and click the Import... button in the Select Resource dialog box. Navigate to the desired graphics file, double-click it, and then click OK.
5. Select `StretchImage` for the `SizeMode` property of the `PictureBox` to fill the `PictureBox.`
6. Adjust the size of the `PictureBox` using its handles and position it in the form.

FIGURE 1.13 How to add a graphic to a user interface

Including Different Fonts in the User Interface

An object's `Font` property controls the object's text type, style, and size. You may want to change the `Font` property for the form object first, as this change will then be applied to all controls added later. You should use no more than two different fonts in a form. Avoid using italic or underline, which makes text harder to read. You should limit bold font to places where emphasis is really needed.

TIP

The graphics, font, and color guidelines do not apply to game programs.

Including Color in the User Interface

The human eye is attracted to color but, again, use this feature sparingly. Black text on a white, off-white, or light gray background is recommended; don't use dark text on a dark background. If you must use colors, limit them to three that are complementary. Color is used in the Skate-Away Sales application to assist the user in entering the number of blue and yellow skateboards.

TIP

To display access keys in Windows XP, click Start on the Windows taskbar, click Control Panel, click Appearance and Themes, and then click Display to open the Display Properties dialog box. Click the Appearance tab, and then click the Effects button. Click the Hide underlined letters for keyboard navigation until I press the Alt key check box to remove the check mark. Click the OK button twice, then close the Appearance and Themes window.

Assigning Access Keys

An **access key** allows an object to be selected using a combination of the Alt key with a letter or number. For example, Alt-F is often used to access a file menu. For the Skate-Away application, you could use Alt-C to calculate or Alt-X to exit. This is sometimes recommended as an option for people who prefer not to have to use the mouse so much. To assign an access key, enter an ampersand (&) just before the desired letter in the control's `Text` property (such as &Calculate for the Calculate button, or E&xit for the Exit button).

Setting the `TabIndex` Property

The `TabIndex` property determines the order in which a control receives **focus** (that is, the ability of an object to accept user input) when the Tab key or an access key is used. For example, if a `TextBox` has focus, it contains an insertion point signifying it is ready to accept input from the keyboard. By default, the `TabIndex` property for a control is set by Visual Basic in the order in which the control is added to a form (starting with the value 0 for the first control, 1 for the second, and so on).

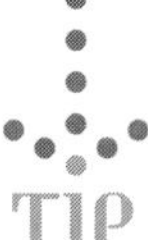

TIP

When a text box has the focus, an insertion point appears inside it. When a button has the focus, its border is highlighted and a dotted rectangle appears around its caption.

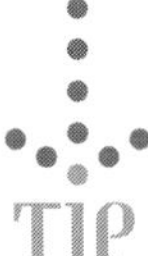

TIP

If you make a mistake when specifying the tab order, you can press the Esc key and start over again.

You can change the tab order by selecting a control and changing its `TabIndex` property in the Properties window (values for `TabIndex` are 0, 1, 2, ...). An easier way is to click View in the menu bar, then click Tab Order (see Figure 1.14). Then use the mouse to click the controls in the desired tab order. Note that a label for a `TextBox` must have a `TabIndex` value one less than its accompanying text box for the `TextBox` access key (defined in the label) to work properly.

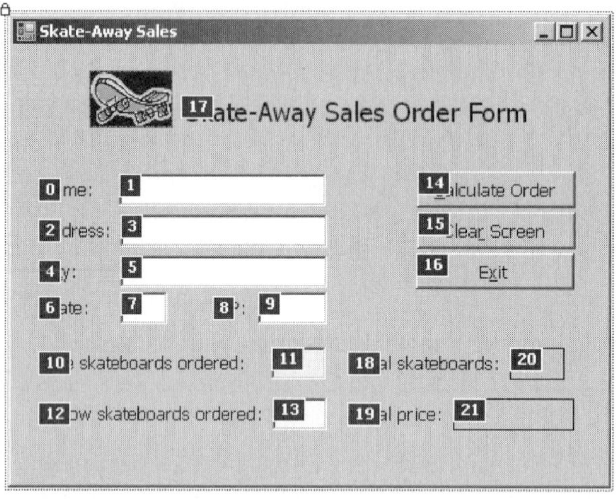

FIGURE 1.14 `TabIndex` values in the Skate-Away Sales form

Defining Default and Cancel Buttons

If a button in a form is the one that is used most frequently, you can make it a default button, one that is always selected when the user presses the Enter key. This saves the user from having to click it with the mouse every time. A default button is created by setting the form's `AcceptButton` property to the name of the button.

A button can also be designated as a cancel button, which closes the application. For example, a form's Exit button can be made a cancel button by setting the form's `CancelButton` property to the name of the button.

VARIABLES, CONSTANTS, METHODS, AND CALCULATIONS

This section discusses how to work with variables, create arithmetic expressions, and provide application output. It also presents techniques for planning, creating, testing, and debugging an application.

Variables

Variables are simply computer memory locations that can store specific types of data and are given special names. Various data values may be stored in these locations while an application is running, hence the term "variable."

Selecting a Data Type for a Variable

To improve the program's performance and reduce the program's size in memory, a variable should be assigned a specific **data type**, the specific kind of data a variable can store. In Visual Basic, the integer data types (positive or negative whole numbers and zero) are `Integer`, `Short`, and `Long`. The floating-point data types (numbers with decimals expressed in scientific notation) are `Single` and `Double`. Other special data types are `Boolean` (values `True` or `False`), `Byte` (binary number), `Char` (one character expressed by a standard numeric code called Unicode), `Date` (containing date and time information), `Decimal` (numbers with fixed decimal points), and `String` (text, or a "string" of characters).

If you don't specify a data type, Visual Basic assigns a variable the `Object` data type. A variable with an `Object` data type can thus store different kinds of data (such as `Integer` or `String`) at different times during program execution. Because of this flexibility, using the `Object` data type is very inefficient when running applications and should be avoided. (You will see later in this section how to use the statement `Option Explicit On` to force the programmer to assign data types to variables.) In this book, the most commonly used data types are `Integer`, `Decimal`, and `String`.

Selecting a Name for a Variable

Variables must have names (also called **identifiers**) and the names should be very descriptive, indicating the variable's purpose. Remember that you should also use camel case for variable names (such as `totalCost` or `employeeName`). According to Visual Basic's **syntax** (rules of a programming language), variable names must begin with a letter or an underscore; can contain only letters, numbers, and the underscore (no spaces); and must not be a Visual Basic keyword word (such as `Me`, `Nothing`, or `True`).

TIP

`Dim` comes from the word "dimension," which is how programmers in the 1960s referred to the process of allocating the computer's memory. "Dimension" refers to the "size" of something, and when you declare a variable, you are indicating its data type, which is related to the amount of memory the variable will use.

Declaring a Variable

You should declare variables in a program before using them. Doing so gives you more control over how a variable is used in an application. Declaring a variable creates space for it in computer memory, but doesn't load or populate the variable with a value. The syntax of a variable declaration statement is shown in Figure 1.15.

HOW TO...

Declare a Variable

Syntax

[**Dim** | **Private** | **Static**] *variablename* [**As** *datatype*][= *initialvalue*]

Example

```
Dim totalCost As Integer
```

FIGURE 1.15 How to declare a variable

Referring to Figure 1.15, the italicized words in the syntax statement are replaced with valid Visual Basic code when writing a program. The bold print represents specific keywords or symbols and the square brackets ([]) indicate optional code. The pipeline character (|) means that only one of a group of items can be selected. [`Dim` | `Private` | `Static`] refers to the accessibility of a variable where `Dim` is the usual choice within a Visual Basic procedure. (The accessibility keywords `Private` and `Static` will be discussed later.) Technically, *datatype* is optional, but if it is omitted, Visual Basic assigns the variable the `Object` data type. *Initialvalue* is the value assigned to the variable at declaration, when the program is said to **initialize** the variable. If a variable is not initialized, Visual Basic gives it a default value: `0` for numeric data types, `False` for the `Boolean` data type, or `Nothing` for `Object` or `String` data types.

Assigning Data to an Existing Variable

An assignment statement assigns a value to a variable while the application is running. The terms "load" or "populate" are also used for this assignment operation. The syntax for an assignment statement is simply *variablename = value* where the equal sign (=) is called the **assignment operator.** (The equal sign does not denote algebraic equality; it literally means "is assigned the value of.")

A variable may be assigned a literal constant (a value does not change while an application is running). For example, the following assignment statements are valid: `itemCost = 19.95` and `firstName = "Mary"`. (Note that a string literal must be enclosed in double quotation marks.) Variables must be assigned values of the correct data type. For example, `itemCost = "Mary"` or `firstName = 19.95` would result in a build (compilation) error if the data type for `itemCost` is `Decimal` and the data type for `firstName` is `String`. You can change a numeric literal constant's data type to match that of a variable by adding a **literal type character** as a suffix to the constant. For example, `rate = .0005D` converts the `Double` literal constant .0005 into a `Decimal` data type before storing it in `rate`. The statement `initial = "A"C` converts the literal string "A" to a `Character` data type.

TIP

The word "parse" means to analyze something by separating it into individual elements. The **`TryParse`** method analyzes a string by separating it into individual characters, determining whether each character can be converted to a number.

Using the `TryParse` Method

A data type in Visual Basic is defined by a class, which is a set of program instructions used to create an object—in this case, the object is a variable that you declare. Most classes in the .NET Framework have methods. A **method** is a part of a class that performs a specific task. For example, every numeric data type in Visual Basic has a `TryParse` method that can be used to convert a string of numeric characters into an actual numeric value of a particular numeric data type. The syntax of the `TryParse` method is shown in Figure 1.16.

HOW TO...

Use the `TryParse` Method

Syntax

datatype.**`TryParse`**(*string*, [*numberStyles*, *IFormatProvider*,] *variable*)

Example 1

```
Dim sales As Decimal
Dim isConverted As Boolean
isConverted = Decimal.TryParse(salesTextBox.Text, sales)
```

Example 2

```
Dim sales As Decimal
Dim isConverted As Boolean
isConverted = Decimal.TryParse(salesTextBox.Text, _
    NumberStyles.Currency, _
    NumberFormatInfo.CurrentInfo, sales)
```

FIGURE 1.16 How to use the **`TryParse`** method

TIP

The Customize Regional Options dialog box resides outside of Visual Studio .NET and is part of the Windows operating system. To open the Customize Regional Options dialog box (using the Classic style of Windows), click Start, and then click Control Panel. Double-click Regional and Language Options, and then click the Customize button.

In Figure 1.16, *datatype* is the numeric type to which the *string* is to be converted. If parsing is successful, the value will be stored in the *variable*—if not, zero will be stored in the *variable*. *NumberStyles* is one of several number formatting styles used by the *string*, such as `NumberStyles.Currency` or `NumberStyles.Float`.

The *IFormatProvider* argument specifies the characters used by your computer system to format numbers, dates, and times. Examples of such characters for the United States include the currency symbol (`$`), thousands separator (`,`), decimal point indicator (`.`), date separator (/), and time separator (`:`). Although the *IFormatProvider* argument can take on many different values, in this book you will use the value `NumberFormatInfo.CurrentInfo`, which tells the `TryParse` method to use the formatting characters specified in the Customize Regional Options dialog box. To open the dialog box, click Start on the taskbar, and then click Control Panel. When the Control Panel dialog box opens, click Date, Time, Language, and Regional Options. When the Date, Time, Language, and Regional Options dialog box opens, click Regional and Language Options. Finally, click the Customize button in the Regional and Language Options dialog box.

The `TryParse` method returns the `Boolean` value `True` if the parsing was successful, and otherwise returns `False`. In the first example of Figure 1.16, the last line of code takes the string in `salesTextBox`, tries to convert it to a `Decimal` data type, and (if successful) stores the value in the variable `sales`. The second example does the same thing, but uses the *numberStyles* and *IFormatProvider* arguments. Notice the use of the line continuation character (_), which allows the programmer to break up a long program statement across several lines in the Code Editor window, making the program easier to read.

Before you can use the *numberStyles* and *IFormatProvider* values shown in Example 2 of Figure 1.16, you first need to enter the `Imports System.Globalization` statement in the General Declarations section of the Code Editor window. The General Declarations section appears above the `Public Class` statement in the Code Editor window, as shown in Figure 1.17. The `Imports System.Globalization` statement imports the `System.Globalization` namespace, which contains classes that define culture-related information, including the language, the country/region, the calendars in use, the format patterns for dates, currency, and numbers, and the sort order for strings.

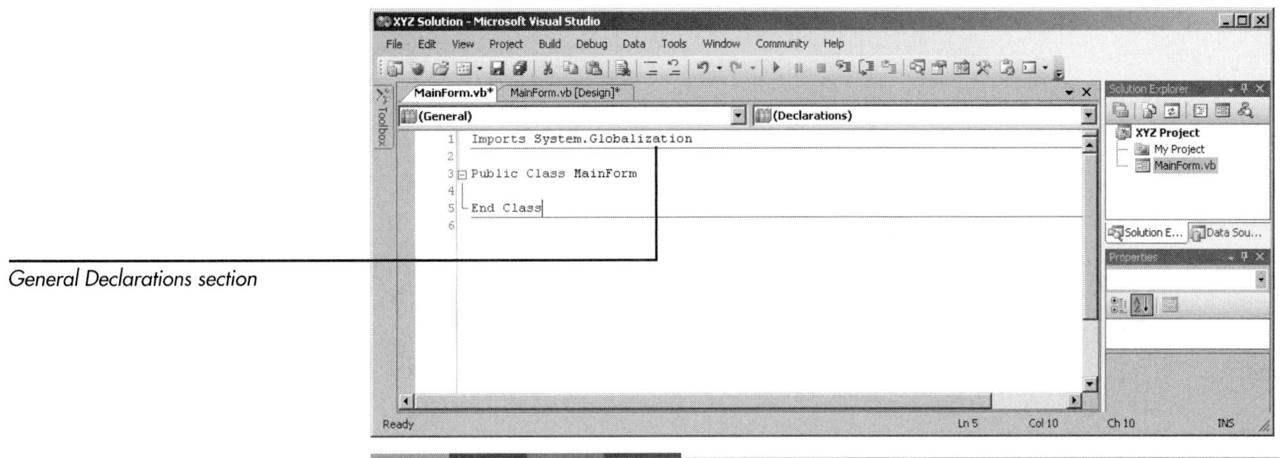

FIGURE 1.17 Statement entered in the General Declarations section

Using the `Convert` Class

The `Convert` class has methods for converting numbers from one data type to another or for converting a string to a number. The most commonly used methods in the `Convert` class are `ToDecimal`, `ToDouble`, `ToInt32`, and `ToString`. Figure 1.18 shows an example of how to use the `ToDouble` method to convert the `Integer` value in `sales` to a `Double` value, storing that in the variable `newSales`:

HOW TO...

Use the Methods in the `Convert` Class

Syntax

```
Convert.ToBoolean(value)
Convert.ToChar(value)
Convert.ToDateTime(value)
Convert.ToDecimal(value)
Convert.ToDouble(value)
Convert.ToInt16(value)
Convert.ToString(value)
```

Example 1

```
Dim sales As Integer = 4500
Dim newSales As Double
newSales = Convert.ToDouble(sales)
```

Example 2

```
Dim dateStr As String = "1/1/2008"
Dim newYears As DateTime
newYears = Convert.ToDateTime(dateStr)
```

Example 3

```
Dim newYears As DateTime = #1/1/2008#
Dim dateStr As String
dateStr = Convert.ToDateTime(newYears)
```

FIGURE 1.18 How to use the methods contained in the `Convert` class

Writing Arithmetic Expressions

Calculations in a Visual Basic program are performed using arithmetic expressions that contain arithmetic operators. These operators have **precedence numbers**, the order in which the computer performs an operation in an expression. Table 1.2 shows the precedence numbers for arithmetic operators. When operators have the same precedence numbers, operators are applied from left to right.

TIP

The difference between the negation and subtraction operators shown in Table 1.2 is that the negation operator is unary, whereas the subtraction operator is binary. Unary and binary refer to the number of operands required by the operator. Unary operators require one operand, whereas binary operators require two operands. The expression –7 uses the negation operator to turn the positive number 7 into a negative number. The expression 9 – 4 uses the subtraction operator to subtract the number 4 from the number 9.

Operator	Operation	Precedence number
^	exponentiation (raises a number to a power)	1
–	negation	2
*, /	multiplication and division	3
\	integer division	4
Mod	modulus arithmetic	5
+, –	addition and subtraction	6
Important Note: You can use parentheses to override the order of precedence. Operations within parentheses are always performed before operations outside parentheses.		

TABLE 1.2 Most commonly used arithmetic operators and their order of precedence

Parentheses can be used to override normal operator precedence. For example, in the expression 3 + 12 / 3 – 1, division is performed first, then addition, then subtraction, resulting in 6. In the expression (3 + 12) / 3 – 1, the addition (in parentheses) is performed first, then division, then subtraction, yielding the result of 4.

Note that the integer division operator results in the integer part of a division result. For example, `211 \ 4` is 52 (the .75 is dropped or truncated). The modulus arithmetic operator does the opposite—it keeps the remainder upon division and drops the integer part. For example, `211 Mod 4` evaluates to 3, the remainder after dividing 211 by 4. This can be used, for example, to determine if a year is a leap year—`2007 Mod 4` is 3 but `2008 Mod 4` is 0, so 2008 is a leap year. Examples of statements involving arithmetic expressions are `value = currentYear Mod 4` and `bonus = annualSalary * (1 + .05D)`.

Remember that assigning a value to a variable causes the variable's previously existing value to be replaced. A statement such as `totalCost = totalCost + itemCost` means to take the current value of `totalCost`, add to it the value in `itemCost`, and store the result back in `totalCost`.

The Scope and Lifetime of a Variable

The **scope** of a variable is the context or boundary within an application where the variable is declared and can be used. For example, variables can be declared (and hence, used) for the entire form or for just a block of code within the form. The **lifetime** of a variable is the length of time the variable remains in computer memory.

To give a variable **module scope,** begin the declaration with the keyword `Private` within a module, class, or structure. (You already know that a class is a unit of program used for Windows applications; a module is a unit of code for a console application; and a structure is a unit of code for defining a group of variables.) A variable with module scope can be used by all procedures in the module, class, or structure. The lifetime of a module-level variable lasts as long as the application is running.

A variable declared within a procedure has **procedure scope.** Other procedures in the application have no way of knowing that a procedure-level variable exists. A procedure-level variable is declared beginning with the keyword `Dim` and has a lifetime only as long as its procedure is running. The same variable

TIP

Procedure-level variables are also called local variables, and their scope is sometimes referred to as local scope.

name used in two different procedures will not conflict because each is removed from memory (destroyed) when its procedure ends.

A `Static` **variable** is a procedure-level variable that retains its value even when the procedure in which it is declared ends. Similar to a module-level variable, a `Static` variable is not removed from the computer's internal memory until the application ends.

A variable can also have **block scope** if it is declared within a block of code, such as within an `If...Then...Else` statement or a `For...Next` statement. (You will learn about these statements shortly.) Block-level variables are also declared beginning with the keyword `Dim`. When the block finishes executing, the block-level variable is destroyed.

Comments are indicated in program code by the apostrophe (`'`). Comments provide internal documentation–useful information and reminders–to a program. All text following a `'` character on a line is considered a comment and won't be executed by Visual Basic. Figure 1.19 shows a Code Editor window for a `MainForm` class with several variables of different scope.

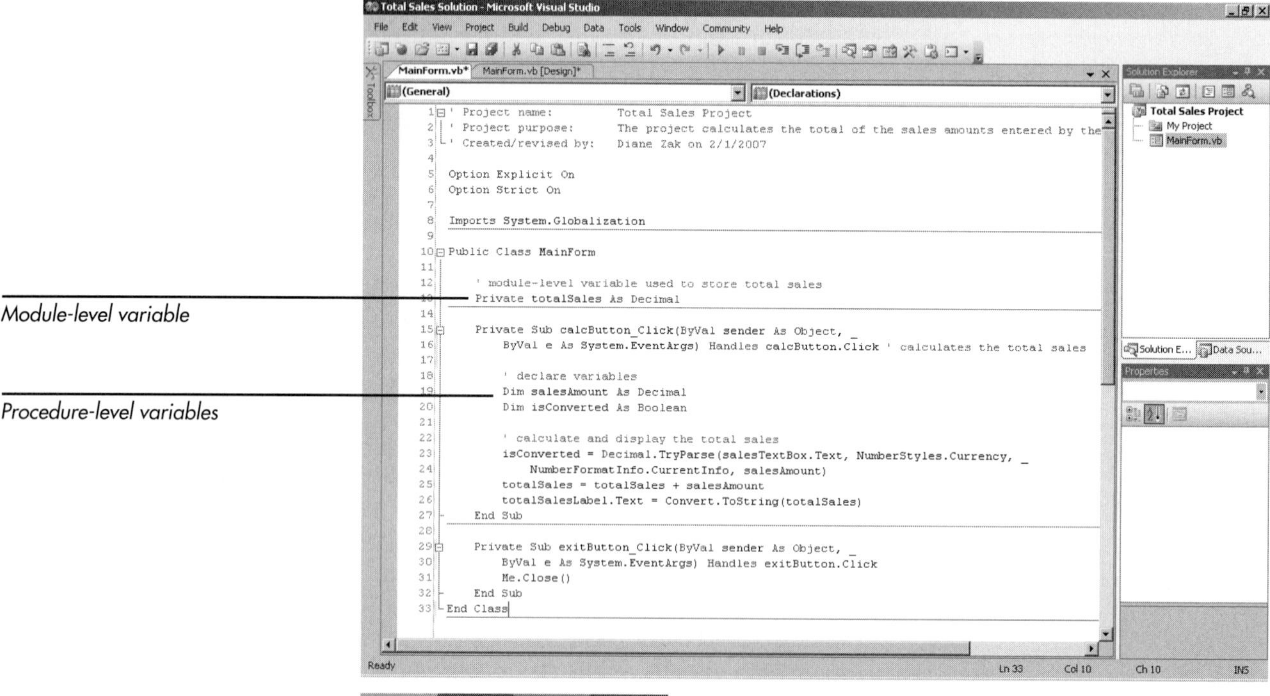

FIGURE 1.19 `MainForm` code using module-level and procedure-level variables

Named Constants

A **named constant**, like a variable, is a named memory location. But unlike the value of a variable, the value of a named constant cannot be changed while the application is running. Named constants are useful for holding constants that are used repeatedly throughout an application or that may need to be changed by the programmer over a period of time. An example of the latter would be interest rates in financial applications. A named constant is declared and initialized with a `Const` statement using the syntax in Figure 1.20.

HOW TO...

Declare a Named Constant

Syntax

`Const` *constantname* [`As` *datatype*] = *expression.*

Examples

```
Private Const Title As String = "ABC Company"
Dim Const InterestRate As Decimal = .0625
```

FIGURE 1.20 How to declare a named constant

Note that the initialization of a named constant is always required. In Figure 1.20, the first example declares the module-level variable `Title` while the second example declares the procedure-level variable `InterestRate`. Also note that it is a convention to use Pascal case for named constants instead of camel case.

Providing for Application Output

An application needs to produce output, and this output is often provided in the user interface (other options for output would be a printer or a file). This section discusses various aspects of providing application output to the user interface.

Assigning a Value to the Property of a Control

The syntax for assigning a value to the property of a control in a form is given in Figure 1.21.

HOW TO...

Assign a Value to the Property of a Control

Syntax

[`Me.`]*object.property* = *expression.*

Examples

```
Me.totalPriceLabel.Text = Convert.ToString(totalPrice)
nameTextBox.Text = ""
nameTextBox.Text = String.Empty
```

FIGURE 1.21 How to assign a value to the property of a control

In providing output, you will often want to display results of calculations in a form control. In the first example of Figure 1.21, the value of the variable `totalPrice` is converted to a string and then assigned to the `Text` property of `totalPriceLabel` (`Me.` refers to the current form and is optional). The second example clears the contents of `nameTextBox` using `""` (the empty string). The final example uses the `String.Empty` field to accomplish the same thing.

Using the Focus Method

Part of the output of an application may involve moving the focus to a certain control to begin a new process. The **Focus** method moves the focus to a specified control while the application is running. After an application clears text boxes in the form and outputs data to other controls, you may want the application to give focus to a specific text box so the user can begin typing additional input without using the mouse. The syntax for using the **Focus** method is displayed in Figure 1.22.

HOW TO...

TIP

If you can anticipate the control the user will employ next, you can use the **Focus** method to send the focus to the control. Doing this gives the user immediate access to the control, and it saves the user the time and effort needed to either click the control or tab to it.

Use the Focus Method

Syntax

[**Me.**]*object*.**Focus()**

Example

```
nameTextBox.Focus()
```

FIGURE 1.22 How to use the **Focus** method

Formatting Numeric Output

Numbers that represent currency often display dollar signs, a comma for a thousands separator, and possibly two decimal places. Percentages are usually displayed with a percent sign. Displaying numbers in this way is called formatting. Figure 1.23 gives the syntax for formatting numbers.

HOW TO...

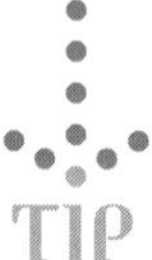

TIP

To learn how to create custom format strings, click Help on the menu bar, and then click Index. Click Visual Basic in the Filtered By list box, then type "custom numeric format strings" in the Look For text box, and then press Enter. You can also search for "custom numeric format strings" at *http://msdn.microsoft.com/library*.

Format Numeric Output

Syntax

variablename.**ToString**(*formatString*)

Examples

```
Dim interestRate As Decimal = 0.05D
interestRate.ToString("P") ' returns the string 5.00 %
Dim totalCost As Decimal = 5000D
totalCost.ToString("C0") 'returns the string $5,000
```

FIGURE 1.23 How to format numeric output

In Figure 1.23, the argument *formatString* is a special string that contains formatting information. The *formatString* contains a **format specifier**, which is a letter (either uppercase or lowercase) that signifies the type of formatting. The possible format specifiers are: C for currency, D for decimal, F for fixed-point, N for number, or P for percent. Following the format specifier is the precision specifier, the optional number of decimal places to display. (If no precision specifier is included, the default is two decimal places.)

`Option Explicit` and `Option Strict`

As stated earlier, you *should* declare variables before they are used. Unfortunately, Visual Basic does not absolutely require you to do so. If your program uses an undeclared variable, Visual Basic will assign it an inefficient `Object` data type. To guard against this, you can add the statement `Option Explicit On` in the General Declarations section of the Code Editor window. Using an undeclared variable will then result in an error.

Another problem can occur when assigning values to variables. Visual Basic uses **implicit type conversion** when assigning values of one data type to variables of a different data type. For example, if the integer value 9 is assigned to a `Decimal` variable `number1`, Visual Basic will implicitly change the 9 to 9.0. However, if your program tries to store a `Double` value 3.2 in an `Integer` variable `number2`, Visual Basic will implicitly convert the 3.2 to an integer, 3, causing a loss of precision and possibly erroneous results. To prevent this, you can add the statement `Option Strict On` in the General Declarations. When you do so, implicit type conversions will take place only if there is no loss of precision. A 9 will be converted to 9.0, but a 3.2 will not be converted to a 3 (instead, a syntax error will occur). Also, strings will not implicitly be converted to numbers with `Option Strict On`.

Coding the Skate-Away Sales Application

You will now continue to develop the Skate-Away Sales application. As you recall, planning the application involves (1) creating a TOE (Task, Object, Event) chart (see Table 1.1) and then (2) designing the user interface (see Figure 1.12). The next steps are (3) planning the code for the event procedures and then (4) writing the code.

Using Pseudocode to Plan a Procedure

Pseudocode is text (which may look similar to programming code) that describes a procedure. Before creating a procedure, it's a good idea to start by writing it in pseudocode. This is especially true for very simple procedures. For the `calcButton` control's `Click` event procedure, you could write the following pseudocode:

1. get blue skateboards ordered and yellow skateboards ordered
2. calculate total skateboards ordered = blue skateboards ordered + yellow skateboards ordered
3. calculate total price = total skateboards ordered * skateboard price * (1 + sales tax rate)
4. display total skateboards ordered and total price

Using a Flowchart to Plan a Procedure

A **flowchart** uses standard symbols to graphically depict a procedure. Flowcharts may be helpful for more complex procedures. Flowcharts for the Skate-Away Sales application are shown in Figure 1.24. Note that the oval is used for start/stop symbols, the rectangle for a process symbol, and a parallelogram for input/output symbols. The lines connecting the flowchart symbols are called flowlines.

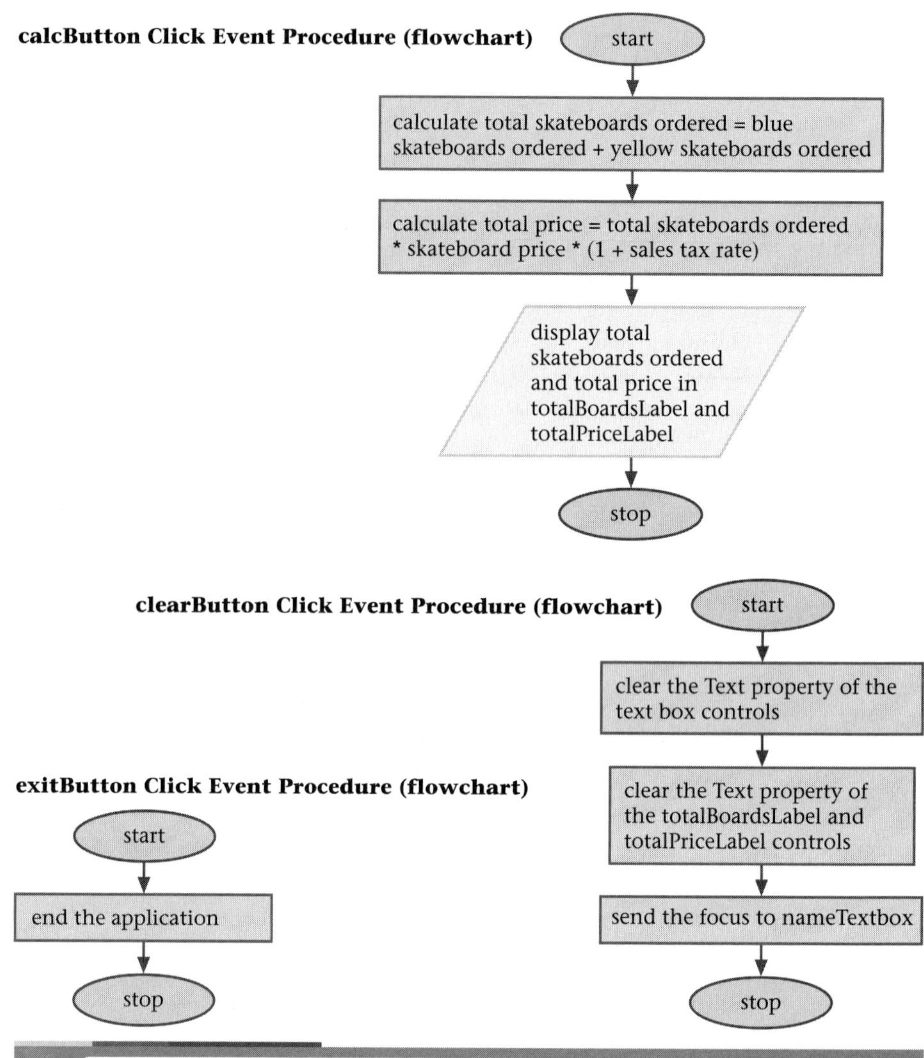

FIGURE 1.24 Flowcharts for the Skate-Away Sales application

Coding the `calcButton`, `clearButton`, and `exitButton` Controls' `Click` Event Procedures

After planning the event procedures for the Skate-Away Sales application, it's time to begin writing program code. After a fair amount of work, Figure 1.25 presents the finished code followed by some brief comments.

```
' Project name:       Skate Away Project
' Project purpose:    The project allows the user to enter a name,
'                     address, city, state, ZIP code, the number
'                     of blue skateboards ordered, and the number of
'                     yellow skateboards ordered. The project
'                     calculates the total number of skateboards
'                     ordered and the total price.
' Created/revised by: <your name> on <current date>

```

(Figure is continued on next page)

```
Option Explicit On
Option Strict On

Imports System.Globalization

Public Class MainForm

    Private Sub exitButton_Click(ByVal sender As Object, _
        ByVal e As System.EventArgs) Handles exitButton.Click
        Me.Close()
    End Sub

    Private Sub clearButton_Click(ByVal sender As Object, _
        ByVal e As System.EventArgs) Handles clearButton.Click
        ' prepare the screen for the next order

        ' clear the text boxes and labels, then set the focus
        nameTextBox.Clear()
        addressTextBox.Clear()
        cityTextBox.Clear()
        stateTextBox.Clear()
        zipTextBox.Clear()
        blueTextBox.Clear()
        yellowTextBox.Clear()
        totalBoardsLabel.Text = ""
        totalPriceLabel.Text = ""
        nameTextBox.Focus()
    End Sub

    Private Sub calcButton_Click(ByVal sender As Object, _
        ByVal e As System.EventArgs) Handles calcButton.Click
        ' calculates the total skateboards ordered and total price

        ' declare constants and variables
        Const TaxRate As Decimal = 0.05D
        Const SkateboardPrice As Decimal = 100D
        Dim blueBoards As Integer
        Dim yellowBoards As Integer
        Dim totalSkateboards As Integer
        Dim totalPrice As Decimal
        Dim isConverted As Boolean

        ' convert input
        isConverted = Integer.TryParse(blueTextBox.Text, _
            NumberStyles.AllowThousands, _
            NumberFormatInfo.CurrentInfo, blueBoards)
        isConverted = Integer.TryParse(yellowTextBox.Text, _
            NumberStyles.AllowThousands, _
            NumberFormatInfo.CurrentInfo, yellowBoards)

        ' calculate total skateboards and total price
        totalSkateboards = blueBoards + yellowBoards
        totalPrice = _
            (totalSkateboards * SkateboardPrice) * (1 + TaxRate)

        ' display calculated results
        totalBoardsLabel.Text = Convert.ToString(totalSkateboards)
        totalPriceLabel.Text = Convert.ToString(totalPrice)
    End Sub
End Class
```

FIGURE 1.25 Program code for the Skate-Away Sales application

Figure 1.25 begins with several comments about the project, followed by the statements `Option Explicit On`, `Option Strict On`, and `Imports System.Globalization` (all of which were explained earlier in this chapter).

The public class called `MainForm` contains three procedures: `exitButton_Click`, `clearButton_Click`, and `calcButton_Click`. The `exitButton_Click` procedure contains only one statement, `Me.Close()`. The `clearButton_Click` procedure uses the `Clear` method, the `Focus` method, and the `Text` property of various controls to clear the form of data. Note that all these statements will be executed in sequence from first to last when the Clear button is clicked. This is known as sequential processing.

Finally, the `calcButton_Click` procedure declares several variables, converts the text entered in the `blueTextBox` and `yellowTextBox` controls to integers, performs the required calculations for `totalSkateboards` and `totalPrice`, and displays these values as strings in their respective labels. Again, all the statements in this procedure are executed sequentially from first to last when the Calculate button is clicked.

Testing and Debugging the Application

After an application is coded, it must be thoroughly tested and debugged (corrected). An application should run properly as long as valid data are entered. Invalid data (such as letters entered when numbers are expected) will cause an application to display an error message and terminate. You will learn how to handle such errors later. To continue working on an application that has generated errors, you should read the error message window carefully, then close the window and click the Stop Debugging button in the Standard toolbar.

Debugging is the process of locating and correcting errors in a program. **Syntax errors** are violations of a programming language's syntax, such as entering `Me.Clse()` instead of `Me.Close()`. Visual Basic will find syntax errors for you. **Logic errors** are not syntax errors; they result when an application provides output that is incorrect due to mistakes made in defining the logic of an application. An example is in the code `average = number1 + number2 / 2` where `average` is supposed to be the average of the two numbers. The correct code is `average = (number1 + number2) / 2` . You will have to carefully ferret out logic errors and correct them. The result of testing the Skate-Away Sales application is shown in Figure 1.26.

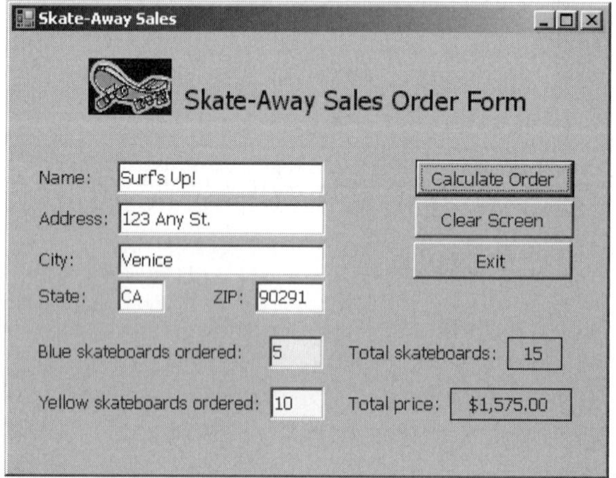

FIGURE 1.26 Result of testing the application using valid data

MAKING DECISIONS IN PROGRAMS

The ability of an application to make decisions is an extremely vital part of program functionality. This section investigates how to use the selection structure in Visual Basic to make decisions.

The Selection Structure

Three basic structures are used in computer programming: the sequence structure, selection structure, and repetition structure. The procedures that you coded in the Skate-Away Sales application all used the **sequence structure**, in which each statement is processed, one after another, each time the procedure is called. This section explores the **selection structure** (also called the decision structure), in which different sets of instructions are processed depending on certain conditions in the program. The repetition structure will be discussed in the next section.

Suppose a program uses the following logic: if income is greater than $50,000, use the 20% tax rate; otherwise, use the 10% tax rate. This is an example of selection logic. In this case, *income > 50000* is the condition that is either true or false, resulting in performing the statement `taxRate = .20` or `taxRate = .10`. Visual Basic uses four forms of the selection structure: `If`, `If` / `Else`, `If` / `ElseIf` / `Else`, and `Case`.

Writing Pseudocode for the `If` and `If` / `Else` Selection Structures

The `If` selection structure executes just one set of tasks (follows the true path) if a condition is true and does nothing if the condition is false. The `If / Else` selection structure executes one set of tasks (the true path) if a condition is true and a different set of tasks (the false path) if the condition is false. Pseudocode for each is shown in Figure 1.27. Note in this pseudocode example that the selection structures begin with the word *if* and end with the words *end if*. The true and false paths for the `If` / `Else` structure are separated by *else*.

If selection structure

Condition — True path

1. get the part number and price
2. if the part number is "AB203"
   calculate the price by multiplying the price by 1.1
   display "Price increase" message
   end if
3. display the part number and price

If/Else selection structure

Condition — True path — False path

1. get the sales amount
2. if the sales amount is greater than 1500
   calculate the commission by multiplying the sales amount by .02
   else
   calculate the commission by multiplying the sales amount by .01
   end if
3. display the commission

FIGURE 1.27 Examples of the `If` and `If/Else` selection structures expressed in pseudocode

Flowcharting the `If` and `If / Else` Selection Structures

Figure 1.28 shows flowcharts for the `If` and `If / Else` selection structures. This figure introduces the diamond shape, which is the selection/repetition symbol. Note that this symbol is used for both the selection and repetition structures.

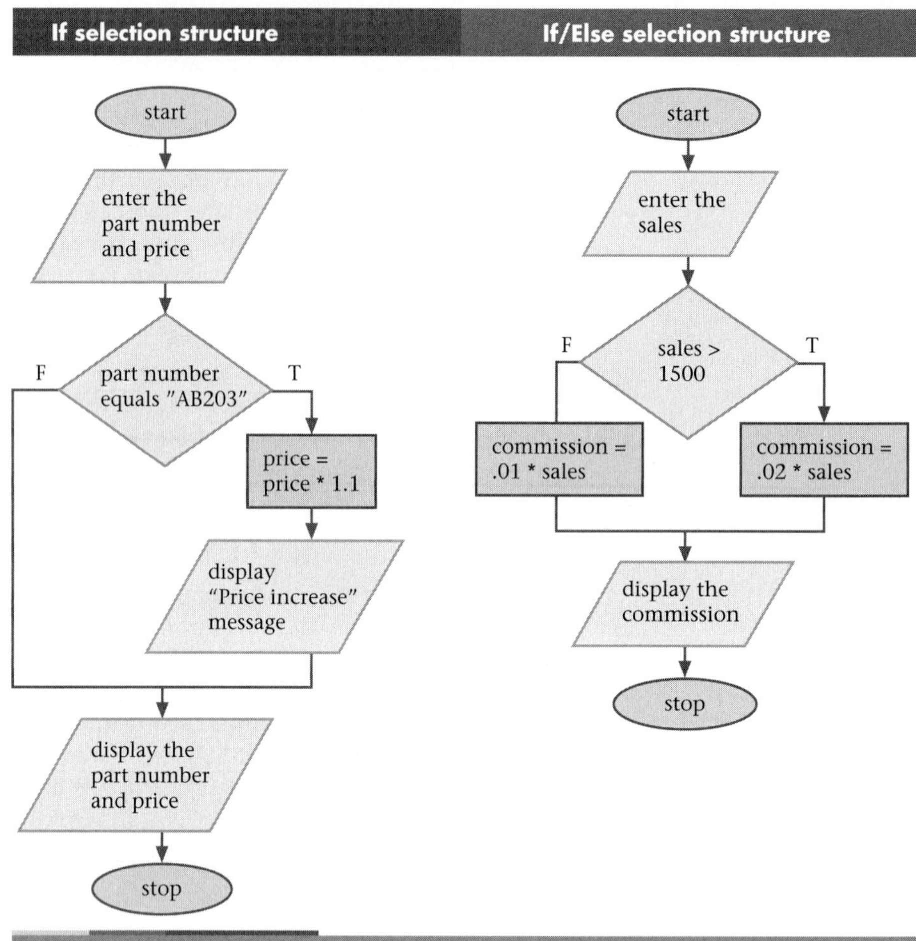

FIGURE 1.28 Examples of the `If` and `If/Else` selection structures drawn in flowchart form

Coding the `If` and `If / Else` Selection Structures

Visual Basic uses the `If...Then...Else` statement to code the `If` and `If / Else` selection structures. The syntax for this statement is shown in Figure 1.29.

HOW TO...

Use the If...Then...Else Statement

Syntax

```
If condition Then
    statement block to be processed when the condition is true
[Else
    statement block to be processed when the condition is false]
End If
```

Example 1

```
If partNumber = "AB203" Then
     price = price * 1.1
     messageLabel.Text = "Price increase"
End If
```

Example 2

```
If sales > 1500D Then
     commission = .02D * sales
Else
     commission = .01D * sales
End If
```

FIGURE 1.29 How to use the `If...Then...Else` statement

In Figure 1.29, the condition is a `Boolean` expression (an expression that evaluates to `True` or `False`). The **statement block** is a set of statements terminated by an `Else`, `End If`, `Loop`, or `Next` statement. (The keywords `Loop` and `Next` relate to the repetition structure, explained in the next section.) In the first example, `price` is multiplied by 1.1 *and* the text of `messageLabel` is assigned `"Price increase"` only if `partNumber` is `"AB203"`. In the second example, `commission` will be 2% of `sales` if `sales` exceeds 1500, 1% otherwise.

Comparison Operators

In Visual Basic, there are six comparison operators (or relational operators): =, >, >=, <, <=, and <>. You are probably familiar with these from algebra (except <>, which means *not equal to*). These comparison operators are used in logical expressions (expressions that are either `True` or `False`), such as `age >= 21` or `state <> "CA"`. These logical expressions are used as conditions in `If` and `If` / `Else` selection structures.

A logical expression can contain both arithmetic operators and comparison operators. Arithmetic operators always take precedence over comparison operators (arithmetic operations are performed first). However, all comparison operators have the same precedence—they are executed from left to right unless parentheses are used (operators within parentheses are interpreted first). For example, 12 / 2 * 3 < 7 + 4 evaluates to 18 < 11, which is `False`. The example in Figures 1.30, 1.31, and 1.32 illustrates the use of `If` / `Else`.

Flowchart

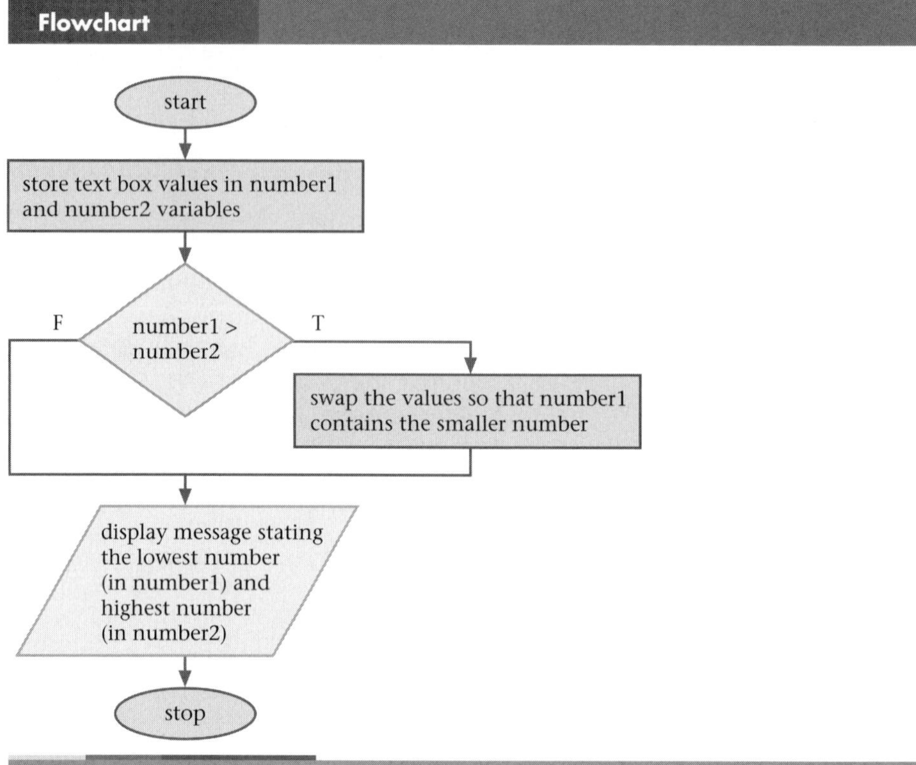

FIGURE 1.30 Flowchart showing the `If` selection structure

Procedure-level variables

```
' Project name:          Number Swap Project
' Project purpose:       The project displays the lowest and highest
'                        of two numbers entered by the user.
' Created/revised by:    <your name> on <current date>

Option Explicit On
Option Strict On

Public Class MainForm

    Private Sub exitButton_Click(ByVal sender As Object, _
        ByVal e As System.EventArgs) Handles exitButton.Click
        Me.Close()
    End Sub

    Private Sub displayButton_Click(ByVal sender As Object, _
        ByVal e As System.EventArgs) Handles displayButton.Click
        ' displays the lowest and highest of two numbers

        Dim number1 As Integer
        Dim number2 As Integer
        Dim isConverted1 As Boolean
        Dim isConverted2 As Boolean

        ' convert input to integers
        isConverted1 = Integer.TryParse(firstTextBox.Text, number1)
        isConverted2 = Integer.TryParse(secondTextBox.Text, number2)
```

(Figure is continued on next page)

Block-level variable

Concatenation operator

`NewLine` *method in* `ControlChars` *class*

```
        ' swap numbers, if necessary
        If number1 > number2 Then
            Dim temp As Integer
            temp = number1
            number1 = number2
            number2 = temp
        End If

        ' display message stating lowest and highest number
        messageLabel.Text = "Lowest: " & _
            Convert.ToString(number1) & ControlChars.NewLine & _
            "Highest: " & Convert.ToString(number2)
    End Sub

End Class
```

FIGURE 1.31 Program code for the Number Swap application

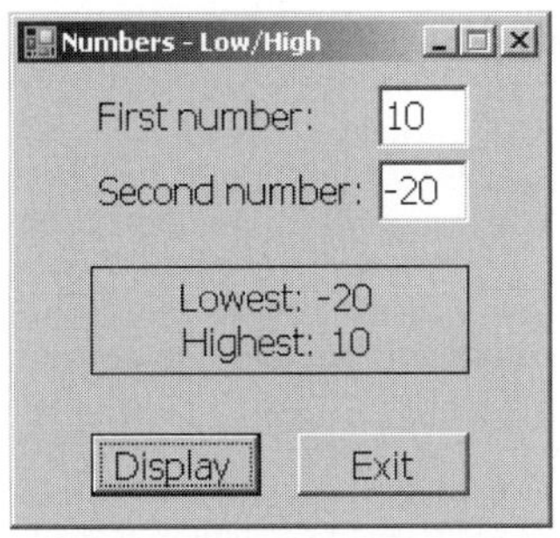

FIGURE 1.32 Sample run of the Number Swap application

The flowchart of Figure 1.30 illustrates a simple `If` selection structure. The Visual Basic code in Figure 1.31 is for the `MainForm` class. Notice that `number1` and `number2` are procedure-level variables while `temp` is a block-level variable. Two numbers are entered in the text boxes of Figure 1.32. If the first is greater than the second, then it is placed in the variable `temp`, the second number is placed in `number1`, and the first (larger) number is placed in `number2`. This is done to display the lowest number first in the output of the user interface. Note that if the first number entered is less than the second, the `If` statement is not executed.

Also note two new features in the last statement of the procedure in Figure 1.31. First is the use of the ampersand (`&`), which is the concatenation operator. This character allows you to combine (concatenate) strings with other strings or variables to form a new string. Also note the `ControlChars.NewLine` method used to move the insertion point of the string to the next line. You can see how these features work in Figure 1.32.

Figures 1.33 and 1.34 provide an example of an `If` / `Else` selection structure. If the variable `operation` contains "A", then addition of `number1` and `number2` is performed; otherwise, subtraction is performed (`number1` – `number2`).

```
' Project name:          AddSub Project
' Project purpose:       The project calculates either the sum of or
'                        the difference between two numbers.
' Created/revised by:    <your name> on <current date>

Option Explicit On
Option Strict On

Public Class MainForm

    Private Sub exitButton_Click(ByVal sender As Object, _
        ByVal e As System.EventArgs) Handles exitButton.Click
        Me.Close()
    End Sub

    Private Sub calcButton_Click(ByVal sender As Object, _
        ByVal e As System.EventArgs) Handles calcButton.Click
        ' calculates the sum of or difference between two numbers

        Dim operation As String
        Dim number1 As Integer
        Dim number2 As Integer
        Dim answer As Integer
        Dim isConverted1 As Boolean
        Dim isConverted2 As Boolean

        ' assign operation input to a variable
        operation = operationTextBox.Text

        ' convert number input to integers
        isConverted1 = Integer.TryParse(num1TextBox.Text, number1)
        isConverted2 = Integer.TryParse(num2TextBox.Text, number2)

        ' calculate and display the sum or the difference
        If operation = "A" Then
            answer = number1 + number2
            answerLabel.Text = "Sum: " & Convert.ToString(answer)
        Else
            answer = number1 - number2
            answerLabel.Text = "Difference: " & _
                Convert.ToString(answer)
        End If
    End Sub

End Class
```

FIGURE 1.33 Program code for the AddSub application

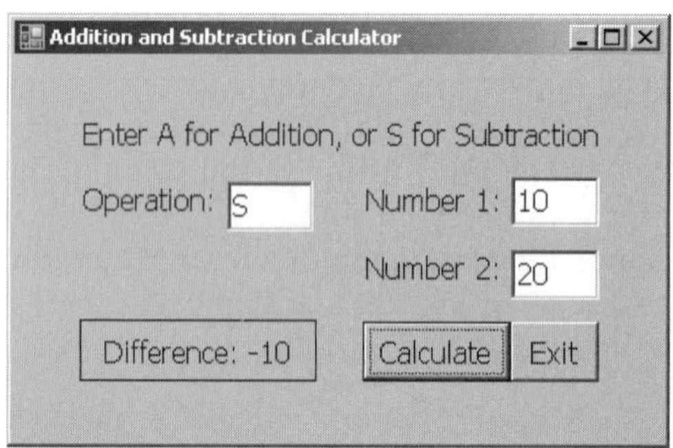

FIGURE 1.34 Sample run of the AddSub application

Using the ToUpper and ToLower Methods

When comparing strings in Visual Basic, case is important. The string "Yes" is not the same as "yes". Since users may not always enter input with the same case (or you may not know the case of data read from a file), you may want your program to convert input to either uppercase or lowercase before processing. Visual Basic has the methods `ToUpper` and `ToLower` to convert the case of text, as demonstrated in Figure 1.35.

HOW TO...

Use the ToUpper and ToLower Methods

Syntax

string.**ToUpper()**
string.**ToLower()**

Example 1

```
If state.ToLower() = "ca"
```

Example 2

```
state = state.ToUpper()
```

FIGURE 1.35 How to use the `ToUpper` and `ToLower` Methods

The first example in Figure 1.35 compares the contents of `state` (after being converted to lowercase) to `"ca"`—the true path will be followed if `state` contains `"Ca"`, `"CA"`, `"cA"`, or `"ca"`. The second example actually converts the string in `state` to uppercase and reassigns that new value to `state`.

Logical Operators

Logical operators (or Boolean operators) allow you to create compound logical expressions, which can be used as conditions in `If` and `If / Else` selection structures. The logical operators in Visual Basic are (in order of precedence) `Not`, `And`, and `AndAlso`; `Or` and `OrElse`; and `Xor`. Using `Not` with a logical expression changes its value from `True` to `False`, or vice versa. Combining two logical expressions with `And` makes the compound expression `True` only if both parts are `True`. Combining two logical expressions with `Or` makes the compound expression `False` only if both parts are `False`.

Combining several logical expressions with `Xor` (exclusive or) makes the entire expression `True` if and only if exactly one of the parts is `True`. `AndAlso` and `OrElse` work like `And` and `Or`, respectively, except that they perform short-circuit evaluation. This means that as soon as Visual Basic determines the logical outcome of a compound expression, it will cease to evaluate the other parts of the expression, since such evaluation is then unnecessary. For example, several logical expressions combined with `AndAlso` will be deemed `False` as soon as just one part is determined to be `False`. If `And` is used instead, Visual Basic would evaluate each part before determining the expression to be `False`. This makes `AndAlso` and `OrElse` more efficient than `And` and `Or`, respectively, and they are therefore preferred.

Keep in mind that in a complex expression involving arithmetic operators, comparison operators, and logical operators, arithmetic operators have the highest precedence (Visual Basic performs the arithmetic first), comparison operators have the next highest precedence, and logical operators have the lowest precedence (they are executed last).

Performing Data Validation

It is extremely important for programmers to ensure that users are entering valid data in an application. Verifying this input data within an application is called data validation. For example, if a user is entering hours worked in an application and the hours must be between 0 and 40, the following code could help perform data validation:

```
If hoursWorked >= 0D AndAlso hoursWorked <= 40D Then
     grossPay = hoursWorked * 15.50D
     grossLabel.Text = grossPay.ToString("C2")
Else
     grossLabel.Text = "Error"
End If
```

You can also perform data validation by checking to see if a text box contains data before proceeding with processing. To do this, you can use the `String.IsNullOrEmpty` method. The syntax for this method is **String.IsNullOrEmpty**(*string*) and it returns either `True` or `False`. For example, the following code will check to see if a text box contains data. If it does, the statement block following the `If` clause will execute (`StringIsNullOrEmpty` will return `False` and `Not False` is `True`). If the text box is empty, the following statement block will be ignored.

```
If Not String.IsNullOrEmpty(quantityTextBox.Text) Then
    ' statement block
End If
```

Modifying the Skate-Away Sales Application

The Skate-Away Sales application (Figure 1.12) has a slight problem: if the user enters a non-numeric character in either the `blueTextBox` or the `yellowTextBox`, zeros will appear for the total skateboards and total price. This unexpected result may take the user by surprise. Your goal is to solve this problem. You plan to do so by having the program display an error message to the user if one of these text boxes does not contain an integer. The code for the modified Skate-Away Sales application is presented in Figure 1.36 with the new code shaded.

```
' Project name:         Skate Away Project
' Project purpose:      The project allows the user to enter a name,
'                       address, city, state, ZIP code, the number
'                       of blue skateboards ordered, and the number of
'                       yellow skateboards ordered. The project
'                       calculates the total number of skateboards
'                       ordered and the total price.
' Created/revised by: <your name> on <current date>

Option Explicit On
Option Strict On

```

(Figure is continued on next page)

```
Imports System.Globalization

Public Class MainForm

    Private Sub exitButton_Click(ByVal sender As Object, _
        ByVal e As System.EventArgs) Handles exitButton.Click
        Me.Close()
    End Sub

    Private Sub clearButton_Click(ByVal sender As Object, _
        ByVal e As System.EventArgs) Handles clearButton.Click
        ' prepare the screen for the next order

        ' clear the text boxes and labels, then set the focus
        nameTextBox.Clear()
        addressTextBox.Clear()
        cityTextBox.Clear()
        stateTextBox.Clear()
        zipTextBox.Clear()
        blueTextBox.Clear()
        yellowTextBox.Clear()
        totalBoardsLabel.Text = ""
        totalPriceLabel.Text = ""
        nameTextBox.Focus()
    End Sub

    Private Sub calcButton_Click(ByVal sender As Object, _
        ByVal e As System.EventArgs) Handles calcButton.Click
        ' calculates the total skateboards ordered and total price

        ' declare constants and variables
        Const TaxRate As Decimal = 0.05D
        Const SkateboardPrice As Decimal = 100D
        Dim blueBoards As Integer
        Dim yellowBoards As Integer
        Dim totalSkateboards As Integer
        Dim totalPrice As Decimal
        Dim isConverted1 As Boolean
        Dim isConverted2 As Boolean

        ' if a skateboards ordered text box is empty, then
        ' display 0 in it
        If String.IsNullOrEmpty(blueTextBox.Text) Then
            blueTextBox.Text = "0"
        End If
        If String.IsNullOrEmpty(yellowTextBox.Text) Then
            yellowTextBox.Text = "0"
        End If

        ' convert input
        isConverted1 = Integer.TryParse(blueTextBox.Text, _
            NumberStyles.AllowThousands, _
            NumberFormatInfo.CurrentInfo, blueBoards)
        isConverted2 = Integer.TryParse(yellowTextBox.Text, _
            NumberStyles.AllowThousands, _
            NumberFormatInfo.CurrentInfo, yellowBoards)

        ' if the input is converted to Integer, then
        ' calculate and display total skateboards and total price
        ' otherwise, display an error message
```

(Figure is continued on next page)

```
        If isConverted1 = True AndAlso isConverted2 = True Then
            totalSkateboards = blueBoards + yellowBoards
            totalPrice = _
                (totalSkateboards * SkateboardPrice) * (1 + TaxRate)
            totalBoardsLabel.Text = Convert.ToString(totalSkateboards)
            totalPriceLabel.Text = totalPrice.ToString("C2")
        Else
            MessageBox.Show( _
                "The skateboards ordered entries must be numbers.", _
                "Skate-Away Sales", _
                MessageBoxButtons.OK, MessageBoxIcon.Information)
        End If
    End Sub

End Class
```

FIGURE 1.36 Program code for the Modified Skate-Away Sales application

The only changes to the earlier version of the Skate-Away Sales application are in the `calcButton_Click` procedure. Note that the `String.IsNullOrEmpty` method is used to replace an empty text box with 0. Then the `Integer.TryParse` method works on `blueTextBox.Text` and `yellowTextBox.Text` to store `True` in the `Boolean` variables `isConverted1` and `isConverted2`, respectively, if indeed the text boxes contain integers. Finally, the `If` ... `Else` ... `EndIf` structure uses these `Boolean` variables and the `AndAlso` operator (the more efficient shortcut version of `And`) to either process the valid data (integers) or display an error message. The error message is displayed using the `MessageBox.Show` method, which is explained next.

The `MessageBox.Show` Method

The `Else` statement in Figure 1.36 uses the `MessageBox.Show` method to display a dialog box that contains text, an OK button, and an `Information` icon. The syntax for this method is **`MessageBox.Show(`***text*, [*caption*, *buttons*, *icon*[, *defaultButton*]]`)`. The first parameter, *text* is the text displayed in the dialog pane, *caption* is the text displayed in the dialog title bar, *buttons* are the types of buttons (`OK`, `Cancel`, `Yes`, `No`, etc.), *icon* is the graphic displayed (`Information`, `Warning`, etc.), and *defaultButton* is the highlighted button selected automatically when the Enter key is pressed.

Figure 1.37 shows the members of various enumerations associated with the `MessageBox` class. In Visual Basic, an enumeration is simply a list of related values. Thus, the values of the `MessageBoxButtons` enumeration include `OK` and `YesNo`, while the values of the `MessageBoxDefaultButtons` enumeration are `Button1`, `Button2`, and `Button3` (the first, second, and third buttons displayed in the `MessageBox`). Figure 1.38 provides the program code for a MessageBoxTest application and Figure 1.39 shows a sample run.

```
MessageBoxButtons.AbortRetryIgnore
MessageBoxButtons.OK
MessageBoxButtons.OKCancel
MessageBoxButtons.RetryCancel
MessageBoxButtons.YesNo
MessageBoxButtons.YesNoCancel
```

FIGURE 1.37(a) `MessageBoxButtons` Enumeration

```
DialogResult.Abort
DialogResult.Cancel
DialogResult.Ignore
DialogResult.No
DialogResult.None
DialogResult.OK
DialogResult.Retry
DialogResult.Yes
```

FIGURE 1.37(b) `DialogResult` Enumeration

```
MessageBoxIcon.Asterisk
MessageBoxIcon.Error
MessageBoxIcon.Exclamation
MessageBoxIcon.Hand
MessageBoxIcon.Information
MessageBoxIcon.None
MessageBoxIcon.Question
MessageBoxIcon.Stop
MessageBoxIcon.Warning
```

FIGURE 1.37(c) `MessageBoxIcon` Enumeration

```
MessageBoxDefaultButton.Button1
MessageBoxDefaultButton.Button2
MessageBoxDefaultButton.Button3
```

FIGURE 1.37(d) `MessageBoxDefaultButton` Enumeration

```
Public Class MainForm
    Private result As DialogResult
    Private message As String
    Private caption1 As String = "Message Box Test"
    Private caption2 As String = "Result of Test"

```

(Figure is continued on next page)

```
    Private Sub abortRetryIgnoreButton_Click( _
        ByVal sender As System.Object, ByVal e As System.EventArgs) _
        Handles abortRetryIgnoreButton.Click

        message = "Choose wisely!"
        result = MessageBox.Show(message, caption1, _
            MessageBoxButtons.AbortRetryIgnore, _
            MessageBoxIcon.Asterisk, _
            MessageBoxDefaultButton.Button1)

        If result = Windows.Forms.DialogResult.Abort Then
            MessageBox.Show("Abort! Abort!", caption2)
        ElseIf Windows.Forms.DialogResult.Retry Then
            MessageBox.Show("Persistence pays off", caption2)
        Else
            MessageBox.Show("Ignore me?!", "Result of Test")
        End If
    End Sub

    Private Sub okCancelButton_Click(ByVal sender As System.Object, _
        ByVal e As System.EventArgs) Handles okCancelButton.Click

        message = "How are you?"
        result = MessageBox.Show(message, caption1, _
            MessageBoxButtons.OKCancel, MessageBoxIcon.Stop, _
            MessageBoxDefaultButton.Button2)

        If Windows.Forms.DialogResult.OK Then
            MessageBox.Show("Glad to hear it", caption2)
        Else
            MessageBox.Show("Cancel this!", caption2)
        End If

    End Sub

    Private Sub yesNoButton_Click(ByVal sender As System.Object, _
        ByVal e As System.EventArgs) Handles yesNoButton.Click

        message = "Will you marry me?"
        result = MessageBox.Show(message, caption1, _
            MessageBoxButtons.YesNo, MessageBoxIcon.Question, _
            MessageBoxDefaultButton.Button3)

        If result = Windows.Forms.DialogResult.Yes Then
            MessageBox.Show("That's wonderful!", caption2)
        Else
            MessageBox.Show("I'm heartbroken :(", caption2)
        End If

    End Sub

    Private Sub exitButton_Click(ByVal sender As System.Object, _
        ByVal e As System.EventArgs) Handles exitButton.Click
        Me.Close()
    End Sub
End Class
```

FIGURE 1.38 Program code for the MessageBoxTest application

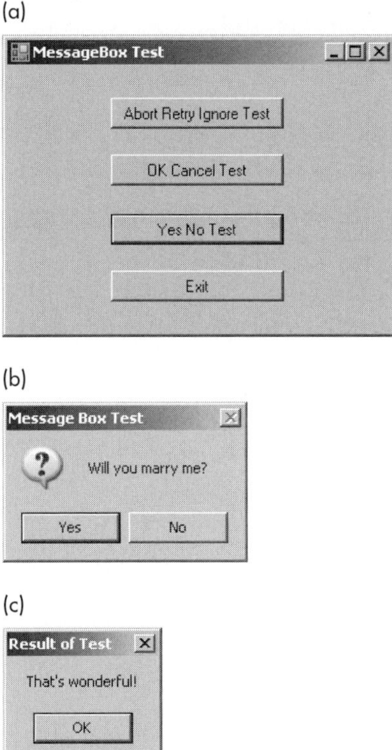

FIGURE 1.39 Sample run of the MessageBoxTest application

In Figure 1.38, the variable `result` is declared as a `DialogResult` enumeration (one of eight possible values) in Line 2. The three event procedures in `MainForm` (Lines 7, 26, and 42) produce different kinds of `MessageBox` objects demonstrating the use of captions, buttons, icons, and default buttons. Keep in mind that many of the parameters for a `MessageBox` are optional. If you do not specify buttons, Visual Basic uses `MessageBoxButtons.OK` by default.

Nested Selection Structures

When creating an `If` or `If / Else` selection structure, you will sometimes need to allow for multiple decisions by including additional selection structures within either the true path or the false path. Such a selection structure, located within an outer selection structure, is called a **nested selection structure**. The outer selection structure represents the primary decision, and the inner (or nested) selection structure represents a secondary decision. For example, in order to vote, you must first be at least 18 years of age (primary decision). If you meet this criterion, then you must also be registered to vote (secondary decision). Figures 1.40 and 1.41 present a flowchart and program code, respectively, that illustrate nested selection structures.

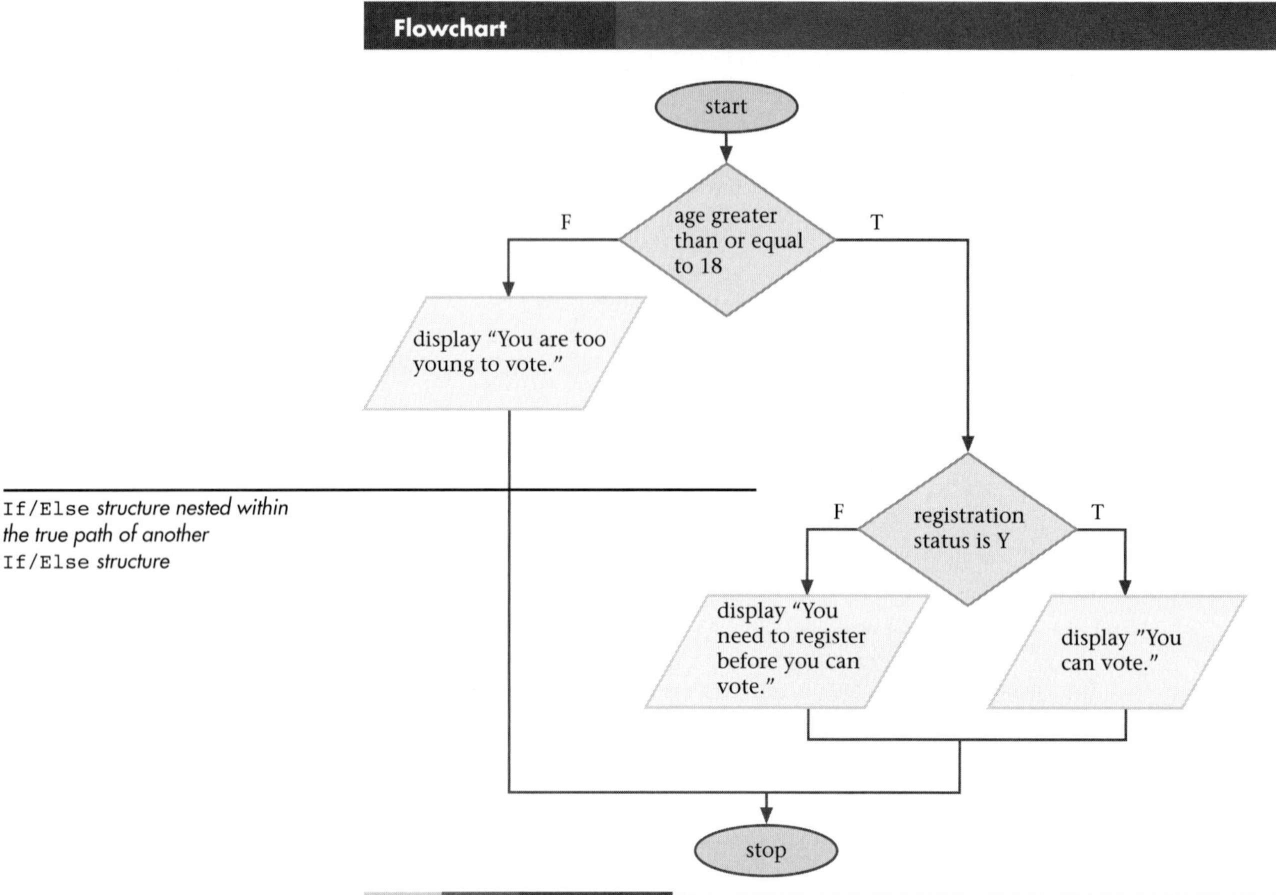

FIGURE 1.40 Flowchart showing the nested selection structure

```
' Project name:         Voter Project
' Project purpose:      The project displays a message that
'                       indicates whether a person can vote.
' Created/revised by:   <your name> on <current date>

Option Explicit On
Option Strict On

Public Class MainForm
    Private Sub exitButton_Click(ByVal sender As Object, _
        ByVal e As System.EventArgs) Handles exitButton.Click
        Me.Close()
    End Sub

    Private Sub displayButton_Click(ByVal sender As Object, _
        ByVal e As System.EventArgs) Handles displayButton.Click
        ' displays a message based on a person's age and voter status

        Dim age As Integer
        Dim status As String
        Dim isConverted As Boolean

        ' convert age input to Integer
        isConverted = Integer.TryParse(ageTextBox.Text, age)
```

(Figure is continued on next page)

```

        ' display appropriate message
        If age >= 18 Then
            status = statusTextBox.Text
            If status = "Y" Then
                messageLabel.Text = "You can vote."
            Else
                messageLabel.Text = _
                    "You need to register before you can vote."
            End If
        Else
            messageLabel.Text = "You are too young to vote."
        End If
    End Sub
End Class
```

FIGURE 1.41 Program code for the Voter project

The `If` / `ElseIf` / `Else` Structure

The `If...Then` statement in Visual Basic allows you to make a decision in a program with only a true path. The `If...Then...Else` statement allows a decision with exactly two alternatives: the true path and the false (`else`) path. If you need to make a decision in a program with more than two alternatives, you can use the special `If` / `ElseIf` / `Else` selection structure. Figure 1.42 provides code from the Grade Calculator application, which uses the `If` / `ElseIf` / `Else` selection structure. Figure 1.43 displays a sample run.

```
' Project name:       Grade Calculator Project
' Project purpose:    The project allows the user to enter total points
'                       to determine a letter grade.
' Created/revised by: <your name> on <current date>

Option Explicit On
Option Strict On

Public Class MainForm
    Private Sub exitButton_Click(ByVal sender As Object, _
        ByVal e As System.EventArgs) Handles exitButton.Click
        Me.Close()
    End Sub

    Private Sub assignButton_Click(ByVal sender As Object, _
        ByVal e As System.EventArgs) Handles assignButton.Click

        Dim grade As String
        Dim totalPoints As Integer
        Dim isConverted As Boolean = _
            Integer.TryParse(totalPointsTextBox.Text, totalPoints)

        ' If / ElseIf / Else structure
        If totalPoints >= 360 Then
            grade = "A"
        ElseIf totalPoints >= 320 Then
            grade = "B"
        ElseIf totalPoints >= 280 Then
            grade = "C"
```

(Figure is continued on next page)

```
30          ElseIf totalPoints >= 240 Then
31              grade = "D"
32          Else
33              grade = "F"
34          End If
35
36          'display the grade
37          gradeLabel.Text = grade
38      End Sub
39  End Class
```

FIGURE 1.42 Program code for the Grade Calculator application

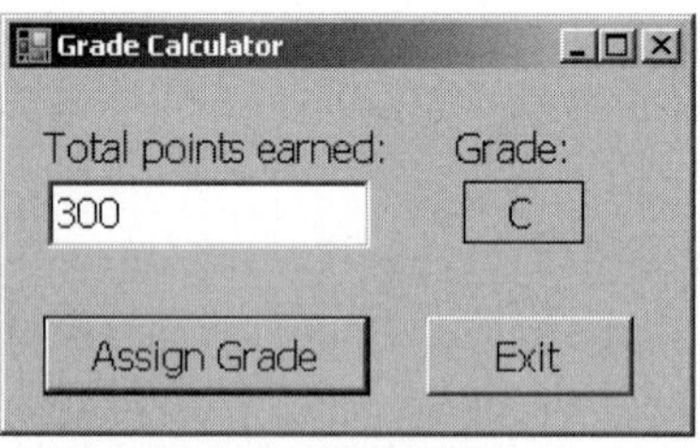

FIGURE 1.43 Sample run of the Grade Calculator application

In Figure 1.42, if the first condition isn't met (`totalPoints >= 360`), program flow proceeds to the next condition (`totalPoints >= 320`) because of the keyword `ElseIf` (Line 26). All conditions in the structure are tested until one is found to be true. Then the corresponding code block (such as `grade = "C"`) is executed and flow leaves the structure. If no conditions are true, the `Else` block (Line 32) is executed. Note that the `If / ElseIf / Else` structure is equivalent to multiple nested `If / Else` structures. For example, the following code could serve as a substitute for the `If...ElseIf...Else...EndIf` statement in Figure 1.42, but it is much more complicated at first glance:

```
If totalPoints >= 360 Then
    grade = "A"
Else
    If totalPoints >= 320 Then
        grade = "B"
    Else
        If totalPoints >= 280 Then
            grade = "C"
        Else
            If totalPoints >= 240 Then
                grade = "D"
            Else
                grade = "F"
            End If
        End If
    End If
End If
```

The `Case` Selection Structure

While the `If` / `ElseIf` / `Else` selection structure is very effective for handling multiple decisions, some programmers prefer the special `Case` selection structure. The syntax for the `Select Case` statement is shown in Figure 1.44.

HOW TO...

Use the `Select Case` Statement

Syntax

`Select Case` *selectorExpression*
    `Case` *expressionList1*
        [statements for the first Case]
    [**`Case`** *expressionList2*
        [statements for the second Case]]
    [**`Case`** *expressionListn*]
        [statements for the nth case]]
    [**`Case Else`**
        [statements for when the selectorExpression does not match any of the expressionLists]]
`End Select`

Example 1

```
Select Case grade
    Case "A"
        MessageBox.Show("Excellent")
    Case "B"
        MessageBox.Show("Very Good")
    Case "C"
        MessageBox.Show("OK")
    Case "D"
        MessageBox.Show("Needs Work")
    Case "F"
        MessageBox.Show("Sorry")
    Case Else
        MessageBox.Show("Not a valid grade")
End Select
```

Example 2

```
Select Case numberOrdered
    Case 1 To 5
        itemPrice = 25
    Case 6 To 10
        itemPrice = 23
    Case Is > 10
        itemPrice = 20
    Case Else
        itemPrice = 0
End Select
```

(Figure is continued on next page)

Example 3
```
Select Case totalPoints
    Case Is >= 360
        grade = "A"
    Case Is >= 320
        grade = "B"
    Case Is >= 280
        grade = "C"
    Case Is >= 240
        grade = "D"
    Case Else
        grade = "F"
End Select
```

FIGURE 1.44 How to use the `SelectCase` Statement

The syntax in Figure 1.44 looks a little complicated at first, but it is actually very simple in practice. The *selectorExpression* within the `Select Case` clause is a single variable or expression that can have one of several possible values. If its value equals one in an *expressionList* following the `Case` keywords (starting with the first `Case` clause and proceeding down), the set of program statements in that particular `Case` clause is executed; immediately after this the entire selection structure is exited. (Note that the *expressionList* can contain more than one expression separated by commas, and that the data type of these expressions must match the data type of the *selectorExpression*.) If the value of the *selectorExpression* is not found in any of the *expressionLists*, the instructions in the `Case Else` clause are executed. Thus, the `Case` selection structure is essentially equivalent to the `If` / `ElseIf` / `Else` selection structure.

Example 1 in Figure 1.44 shows the simplest way of using the `Case` structure. The *selectorExpression* is the `String` variable `grade`. If the value of `grade` is "A", a `MessageBox` appears with the text "Excellent", and so on. Note that if `grade` doesn't contain a valid letter grade, the `Case Else` clause displays an error message. Example 2 shows how to use the `Case` structure with the keyword `To` when upper and lower bounds of a range of values are known. Example 3 uses the keyword `Is` when only one of the bounds is known. Note that Example 3 is equivalent to the `If...Then...ElseIf...Endif` statement in Figure 1.42.

TIP

Pseudo-random numbers are chosen with equal probability from a finite set of numbers. The chosen numbers are not completely random because a definite mathematical algorithm is used to select them, but they are sufficiently random for practical purposes. That's why they are called "pseudo" random.

Sometimes you want a program to select among several alternatives at random, such as in simulations or games. This requires the ability to generate random numbers, as discussed in the next section.

Generating Random Numbers

Visual Basic provides a **pseudo-random number generator**, which is a device that produces a sequence of numbers that meet certain statistical requirements for randomness. The syntax for creating a random number generator in Visual Basic is shown in Figure 1.45.

HOW TO...

Generate Random Numbers

Syntax

Dim *randomObjectName* As New Random
randomObjectName.Next(*minValue, maxValue*)

Example

```
Dim number As Integer
Dim randomGenerator As New Random
number = randomGenerator.Next(0, 51)
```

FIGURE 1.45 How to generate random numbers

TIP

The `Random.NextDouble` method is used to generate a random floating-point number.

The first line in the syntax of Figure 1.45 creates a `Random` object called *randomObjectName* that will generate the random numbers. In the second line, the `Random` object *randomObjectName* calls the `Next` method to create a random integer within the range beginning with the integer *minValue* up to (but not including) the integer *maxValue*. The example in Figure 1.45 generates a random integer from 0 to 50, inclusive.

REPEATING PROGRAM INSTRUCTIONS

This section reviews how to perform looping and work with several different kinds of Visual Basic controls related to the repetition structure.

The Repetition Structure

As discussed earlier, the three programming structures are sequence, selection, and repetition. The **repetition structure** (also called a loop) is used when a program needs to repeat a block of code (called the loop body) while a certain condition is true. There are two types of repetition structures. A pretest loop evaluates the condition before the loop body is executed. A posttest loop evaluates the condition after the loop body has been executed once.

You code a repetition structure (loop) in Visual Basic using one of the following statements: `For...Next`, `Do...Loop`, and `For Each...Next`. The `For...Next` and `Do...Loop` statements are reviewed in this chapter. The `For Each...Next` statement is reviewed in Chapter 2 because it applies to arrays, which are also reviewed in Chapter 2.

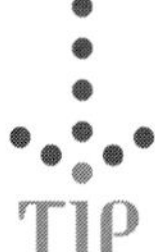

TIP

You can use the `Exit For` statement to exit the `For...Next` statement prematurely—in other words, exit it before it has finished processing. You may need to do so if the loop encounters an error when processing its instructions.

The `For...Next` Statement

The `For...Next` statement is used to execute a loop when the number of repetitions to be performed is known. The syntax of the `For...Next` statement is shown in Figure 1.46.

HOW TO...

Use the For...Next Statement

Syntax

For *counter* [**As** *datatype*] = *startvalue* **To** *endvalue* [**Step** *stepvalue*]
  [*statements*]
Next *counter*

Example 1

```
Dim numberSquared As Integer
For number As Integer = 1 To 3
     numberSquared = number * number
     MessageBox.Show(Convert.ToString(number) & " squared is " _
        & Convert.ToString(numberSquared), "Number Squared", _
        MessageBoxButtons.OK, MessageBoxIcon.Information)
Next number
```

Example 2

```
Dim x As Decimal
For x = .05D To .1D Step .01D
     rateLabel.Text = rateLabel.Text & x.ToString("P0") _
          & ControlChars.NewLine
Next x
```

FIGURE 1.46 How to use the `For...Next` statement

TIP

You can nest `For...Next` statements, which means that you can place one `For...Next` statement within another `For...Next` statement.

As you can see in Figure 1.46, the `For...Next` statement begins with a `For` clause, continues with *statements* to be executed (called the loop body), and closes with a `Next` clause. The *counter* is a variable that controls how many times the loop body will be executed. The *counter* can be declared using `As` *datatype*, which gives this variable block scope. Alternatively, the *counter* can be declared before the `For...Next` statement using `Dim` and have procedure scope. The *counter* is initialized with the `Integer` *startvalue*. When *counter* exceeds the *endvalue*, the loop is terminated (the *statements* will not be executed and the program continues after the `Next` clause). The *stepvalue* is the amount the *counter* increases with each iteration of the loop (*stepvalue* is 1 by default). Note that *stepvalue* can be a negative number, so *counter* will begin with a *startvalue* and count down to a smaller *endvalue*. The *statements* are all the program statements in a statement block (the loop body) that are to be repeated in the loop.

Figure 1.47 presents a flowchart for the first example in Figure 1.46. The flowchart uses a hexagon to denote the beginning of a `For...Next` loop. In this example, `number` is the counter variable (an `Integer`), which begins with a *startvalue* of 1. The *statements* (the rectangle and parallelogram) execute three times, corresponding to the values of `number` (1, 2, and 3). Three different message boxes are displayed with the strings "1 squared is 1", "2 squared is 4", and "3 squared is 9". When `number` becomes 4, the loop is exited.

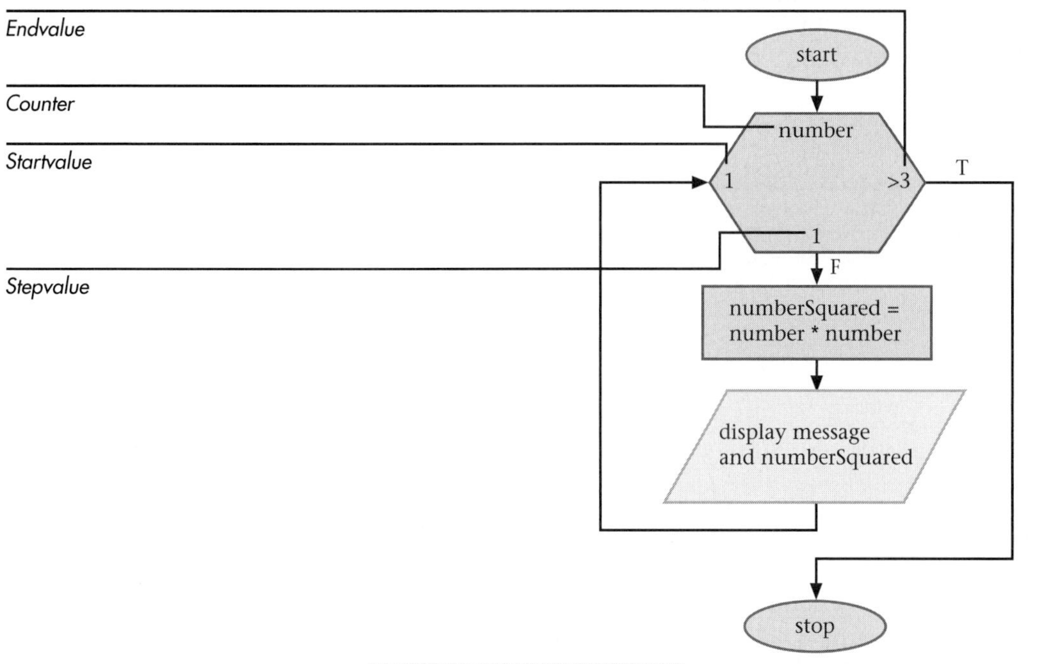

FIGURE 1.47 Flowchart that includes a `For...Next` loop

The second example in Figure 1.46 uses the keyword `Step`. In this example, `x` is the counter variable, .05 is the starting value of `x`, and .10 is the ending value of `x`. With each iteration, `x` increases by .01. (The suffix `D` converts each number of `Double` data type to `Decimal` data type.) This code will produce the output 5 %, 6 %, 7 %, 8 %, 9 %, and 10 % in a label with each value displayed on a new line.

The `Financial.Pmt` Method

You can use the `Financial.Pmt` method to calculate a periodic payment on either a loan or an investment. This method is often used with a loop to calculate monthly loan payments for a series of different interest rates. The syntax of this method is

`Financial.Pmt(`*Rate, NPer, PV*[*, FV, Due*]**`)`**

where *Rate* is the interest rate per period, *NPer* is the number of periods, *PV* is the present value of a loan or investment, *FV* is the future value of a loan or investment, and *Due* is the due date of payments. For example, `Financial.Pmt(.06, 3, 10000, 0, DueDate.EndOfPeriod)` returns the `Double` type value –3741.09812790551, which is the annual payment on a loan of $10,000 at 6% annual interest for 3 years. The rounded value –$3741.10 is negative, indicating a payment instead of income. To avoid this negative sign in the result, you can begin the expression with a minus sign, as follows:

```
-Financial.Pmt(.06, 3, 10000, 0, DueDate.EndOfPeriod)
```

The Monthly Payment Calculator Application

Figures 1.48 and 1.49 show the code and output, respectively, for a monthly payment calculator application that illustrates the use of a `For...Next` loop. In Figure 1.48, a `For...Next` loop causes the variable `rate` to store six different values (.05, .06, .07, .08, .09, and .1). For each different value, the variable `monthlyPayment` is calculated and displayed in the `paymentsLabel` control.

```
' Project name:       Payment Calculator Project
' Project purpose:    Displays monthly payments on a loan.
' Created/revised by: <your name> on <current date>

Option Explicit On
Option Strict On

Imports System.Globalization

Public Class MainForm

    Private Sub exitButton_Click(ByVal sender As Object, _
        ByVal e As System.EventArgs) Handles exitButton.Click
        Me.Close()
    End Sub

    Private Sub calcButton_Click(ByVal sender As Object, _
        ByVal e As System.EventArgs) Handles calcButton.Click
        ' calculates the monthly payments on a loan
        ' using interest rates of 5% through 10%, w/ a term of 5 years
        Const Term As Decimal = 5D
        Dim principal As Decimal
        Dim monthlyPayment As Decimal
        Dim isConverted As Boolean

        paymentsLabel.Text = String.Empty
        isConverted = Decimal.TryParse( _
            principalTextBox.Text, NumberStyles.Currency, _
            NumberFormatInfo.CurrentInfo, principal)

        If isConverted Then
            ' calculate and display payments
            For rate As Decimal = 0.05D To 0.1D Step 0.01D
                monthlyPayment = _
                    Convert.ToDecimal( _
                    -Financial.Pmt(rate / 12D, Term * 12D, principal))
                paymentsLabel.Text = paymentsLabel.Text _
                    & rate.ToString("P0") & " -> " _
                    & monthlyPayment.ToString("C2") _
                    & ControlChars.NewLine
            Next rate
        Else    ' principal cannot be converted to a number
            MessageBox.Show("Please re-enter the principal.", _
                "Payment Calculator", _
                 MessageBoxButtons.OK, MessageBoxIcon.Information)
        End If

        principalTextBox.Focus()
        principalTextBox.SelectAll()
    End Sub


     Private Sub principalTextBox_TextChanged(ByVal sender As Object, _
         ByVal e As System.EventArgs) _
```

(Figure is continued on next page)

```
        Handles principalTextBox.TextChanged
        paymentsLabel.Text = String.Empty
    End Sub
End Class
```

FIGURE 1.48 Program code for the Payment Calculator application

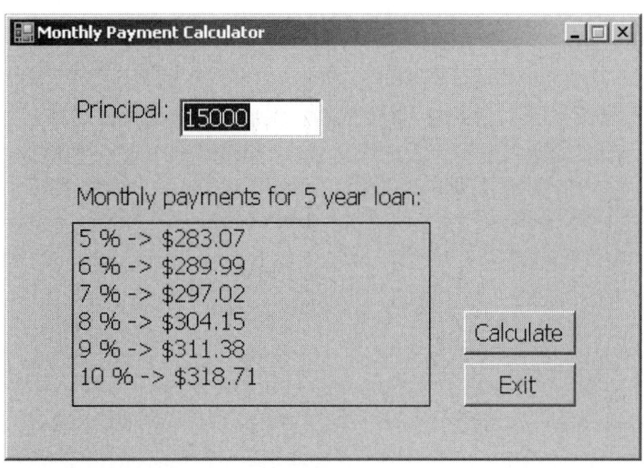

FIGURE 1.49 Sample run of the Payment Calculator application

Selecting the Existing Text in a Text Box

As a convenience to the user, it is often helpful to set up a text box so that the text it contains is already selected. This allows the user to simply begin entering data in the text box, which replaces the selected text. This is accomplished in Figure 1.48 by the last two statements in the `calcButton_Click` event procedure. The statement `principalTextBox.Focus()` gives this text box focus. The statement `principalTextBox.SelectAll()` selects the contents of the text box.

Coding a Control's `TextChanged Event` Procedure

The payment calculator as it is now coded has a potential problem. If the user enters a new principal in the `principalTextBox` control, the `paymentsLabel` control will still contain the data from the previous calculation. This could lead to confusion if the user is not sure if the displayed payments apply to the old principal or new principal. A human error here could be costly to a company.

To solve this problem, you can clear the contents of the `paymentsLabel` control whenever the contents of the `principalTextBox` control are changed. This simply requires a `TextChanged` event procedure for the `principalTextBox` control. In the Code Editor window, select the `principalTextBox` control (from the Class Name list, top left) and the `TextChanged` method (from the Method Name list, top right). This action creates the `Sub` procedure. Then, within this procedure, enter the code `paymentsLabel.Text = String.Empty` as follows. Thus, whenever the contents of the `principalTextBox` control change, the `paymentsLabel` control is cleared.

Using a `ListBox` Control in an Interface

You use the `ListBox` tool in the Toolbox to add a list box to an interface. You can use a list box to display a list of choices from which the user can select zero choices, one choice, or more than one choice. The `ListBox` class is the class that defines the `ListBox` control, while the `ListBox.ObjectCollection` class defines the collection of items contained in the `ListBox`. The most important properties of a `ListBox` are `Items`, `SelectedItems`, `SelectedIndex`, and `SelectionMode`.

The `Items` property contains a collection of all items in the list box. To add items to a list box, click the `Items` property in the Properties list and click the ellipsis button. Then enter the list items in the String Collection Editor dialog box and click OK. These items are then displayed in the list box. Within the program, add items to a list box using the syntax *listBoxName*`.Items.Add(`*itemName*`)`. You can also determine the number of items in a list box with the syntax *listBoxName*`.Items.Count`.

The size of the list box can be changed to display one or more of the items. (A scroll bar will appear if there are more items than can be displayed in the list box.) By default, the items appear in the order they were entered, or you can use the Sorted property to list them alphabetically.

The `SelectedItem` and `SelectedIndex` Properties

Each item in a list box has an index starting with 0 and continuing with 1, 2, and so forth. When an item in a list box is selected, the `SelectedItems` property of the list box equals the item name and the `SelectedIndex` property equals the item index. If no item is selected from the list box, the `SelectedItem` property is the empty string `""` and the `SelectedIndex` is -1. The following examples show how to use the `SelectedItem` and `SelectedIndex` properties:

```
If codeListBox.SelectedItem = "Dog" Then …
If codeListBox.SelectedIndex = 0 Then …
```

The `SelectionMode` property can be set in the Properties window to `One`, `MultiSimple`, or `MultiExtended`. (`One` will be used for now while the others will be explained later.) A `SelectionMode` of `One` is the default and allows the user to select only one item from the list box.

The `SelectedValueChanged` and `SelectedIndexChanged` Events

Each time the user or a program statement selects an item in a list box, the list box's `SelectedValueChanged` and `SelectedIndexChanged` events occur. You can use procedures associated with these events to perform one or more tasks when the selected item has changed, as shown in the List Box Example application (Figure 1.50). The `SelectedValueChanged` procedure shown in the figure displays the value of the selected item in a `MessageBox`. The `SelectedIndexChanged` event procedure displays a `MessageBox` that contains the index of the selected item. A sample run is provided in Figure 1.51.

```
' Project name:       List Box Example Project
' Project purpose:    Demonstrates the use of the SelectedValueChanged
'                     and SelectedIndexChanged events.
' Created/revised by: <your name> on <current date>

Option Explicit On
Option Strict On

```

(Figure is continued on next page)

```
Public Class MainForm
    Private Sub MainForm_Load(ByVal sender As Object, _
        ByVal e As System.EventArgs) Handles Me.Load
        ' add items to the animalListBox
        animalListBox.Items.Add("Dog")
        animalListBox.Items.Add("Cat")
        animalListBox.Items.Add("Horse")

        ' add items to the codeListBox
        For code As Integer = 100 To 105
            codeListBox.Items.Add(code.ToString)
        Next code
    End Sub

    Private Sub animalListBox_SelectedValueChanged( _
        ByVal sender As Object, _
        ByVal e As System.EventArgs) _
        Handles animalListBox.SelectedValueChanged

        MessageBox.Show(animalListBox.SelectedItem.ToString, _
            "List Box Examples", _
            MessageBoxButtons.OK, MessageBoxIcon.Information)
    End Sub

    Private Sub codeListBox_SelectedIndexChanged( _
        ByVal sender As Object, _
        ByVal e As System.EventArgs) _
        Handles codeListBox.SelectedIndexChanged

        MessageBox.Show(codeListBox.SelectedIndex.ToString, _
            "List Box Examples", _
            MessageBoxButtons.OK, MessageBoxIcon.Information)
    End Sub

    Private Sub exitButton_Click(ByVal sender As Object, _
    ByVal e As System.EventArgs) Handles exitButton.Click
        Me.Close()
    End Sub
End Class
```

FIGURE 1.50 Program code for the List Box Example application

(a)

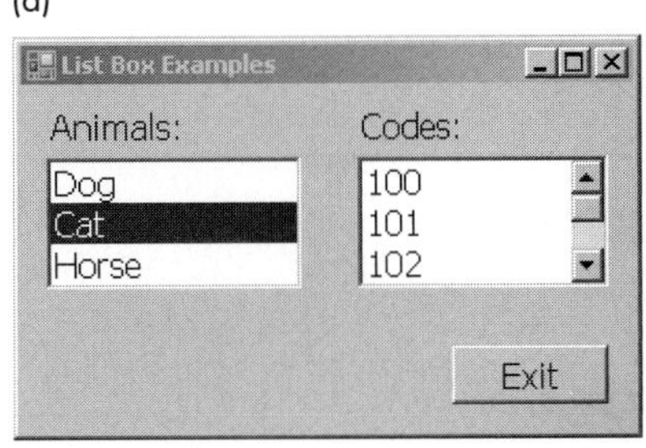

(b)

FIGURE 1.51 Sample run of the List Box Example application

Modifying the Monthly Payment Calculator Application

The Payment Calculator application (Figure 1.48) is now modified to use a list box that contains the possible terms of 2, 3, 4, or 5 years for the loan. Figure 1.52 shows the application's code and Figure 1.53 displays a sample run of the modified application. Changes made to the original code are shaded in Figure 1.52.

```
' Project name:    Modified Payment Calculator Project
' Project purpose: The project displays the monthly payments on a loan.
' Created/revised by: <your name> on <current date>

Option Explicit On
Option Strict On

Imports System.Globalization

Public Class MainForm
    Private Sub exitButton_Click(ByVal sender As Object, _
        ByVal e As System.EventArgs) Handles exitButton.Click
        Me.Close()
    End Sub

    Private Sub MainForm_Load(ByVal sender As Object, _
        ByVal e As System.EventArgs) Handles Me.Load
        ' fills the termListBox with terms of 2, 3, 4, and 5 years
        For term As Integer = 2 To 5
            termListBox.Items.Add(term.ToString)
        Next term

        ' select the 4-year term
        termListBox.SelectedItem = "4"
    End Sub

    Private Sub calcButton_Click(ByVal sender As Object, _
        ByVal e As System.EventArgs) Handles calcButton.Click
        ' calculates the monthly payments on a loan
        ' using interest rates of 5% through 10%
        ' and terms of 2, 3, 4, or 5 years
        Dim term As Decimal
        Dim principal As Decimal
        Dim monthlyPayment As Decimal
        Dim isConverted As Boolean

        paymentsLabel.Text = String.Empty
        isConverted = Decimal.TryParse( _
            principalTextBox.Text, NumberStyles.Currency, _
            NumberFormatInfo.CurrentInfo, principal)

        If isConverted Then
            ' calculate and display payments
            term = Convert.ToDecimal(termListBox.SelectedItem)
            For rate As Decimal = 0.05D To 0.1D Step 0.01D
                monthlyPayment = Convert.ToDecimal( _
                    -Financial.Pmt(rate / 12D, term * 12D, principal))
                paymentsLabel.Text = paymentsLabel.Text _
                    & rate.ToString("P0") & " -> " _
                    & monthlyPayment.ToString("C2") _
                    & ControlChars.NewLine
            Next rate
        Else    ' principal cannot be converted to a number
            MessageBox.Show( _
                "Please re-enter the principal.", _
```

(Figure is continued on next page)

```
56                 "Payment Calculator", _
57                 MessageBoxButtons.OK, MessageBoxIcon.Information)
58         End If
59 
60         principalTextBox.Focus()
61         principalTextBox.SelectAll()
62     End Sub
63 
64     Private Sub principalTextBox_TextChanged(ByVal sender As Object, _
65         ByVal e As System.EventArgs) _
66         Handles principalTextBox.TextChanged
67         ' clears the contents of the paymentsLabel
68         paymentsLabel.Text = String.Empty
69     End Sub
70 
71     Private Sub termListBox_SelectedValueChanged( _
72         ByVal sender As Object, _
73         ByVal e As System.EventArgs) _
74         Handles termListBox.SelectedValueChanged
75         ' clears the contents of the paymentsLabel
76         paymentsLabel.Text = String.Empty
77     End Sub
78 End Class
```

FIGURE 1.52 Program code for the Modified Payment Calculator application

FIGURE 1.53 Sample run of the Modified Payment Calculator application

Some of the changes in Figure 1.52 require additional explanation. Instead of adding items to the `termListBox` control using the Properties window, this application has a `MainForm_Load` procedure (Line 16). (Select the `MainForm` class and the `Load` method in the Code Editor window.) The procedure uses the `Add` method for a list box object in a `For...Next` loop. Then the default `SelectedItem` for the `termListBox` is set to `"4"` in the `MainForm_Load` procedure.

In the `calcButton_Click` procedure of Figure 1.52 (Line 27), the variable `term` is declared and then assigned the value of the `SelectedItem` property of the `termTextBox` after converting it to a `Decimal` (Line 44). Finally, the `termListBox_SelectedValueChanged` procedure clears the `paymentsLabel` control.

Using a Combo Box in an Interface

You use the ComboBox tool in the Toolbox to add a combo box to an interface. A combo box is similar to a list box in that it allows the user to select from a list of choices. However, unlike a list box, a combo box also can contain a text field that allows the user to type an entry that is not on the list.

There are three styles of combo boxes in Visual Basic. The style is controlled by the combo box's `DropDownStyle` property, which can be set to `Simple`, `DropDown` (the default), or `DropDownList`. A `Simple` combo box displays the editable text field and the complete list. A `DropDown` combo box displays only the first item in the list (with a list arrow), and the text field is editable. A `DropDownList` combo box is like a `DropDown` combo box, but the text field is not editable.

Items can be added to combo boxes in the same way as with list boxes, using either the `Items` property or the `Add` method. Also, the key properties of a combo box (such as `Item.Count`, `SelectedItem`, and `SelectedText`) are the same as for list boxes. However, the `Text` property of the combo box is the text entered in the box's text field, which does not exist in a list box.

If the Monthly Payment Calculator application uses a combo box for the term of the loan instead of a list box, the code would be nearly identical to that in Figure 1.52 except that `termListBox.SelectedItem` would be replaced by `termComboBox.SelectedText`. Because the user can enter text in a combo box text field, the procedure would need to verify that the user had indeed entered a positive number for the term using code such as `isTermConverted = Decimal.TryParse(termComboBox.Text, term)`.

The `Do...Loop` Statement

Use a `For...Next` statement for a repetition structure when you know beforehand exactly how many iterations of the loop should be performed, such as for loan terms of 2, 3, 4, and 5 years. However, the number of iterations that a loop performs will often depend on user input or other program conditions that are not known before the program is executed. In this case, you need to use a `Do...Loop` statement.

Unlike the `For...Next` statement, the `Do...Loop` statement can be used to code both a pretest loop and a posttest loop. The syntax for the pretest loop is shown in Figure 1.54.

HOW TO...

Use a Do...Loop Statement

Syntax for a pretest loop

`Do` {`While` | `Until`} *condition*
    [*instructions to be processed either while the condition is true or until the condition becomes true*]
`Loop`

(Figure is continued on next page)

TIP

You can use the `Exit Do` statement to exit the `Do...Loop` statement prematurely—in other words, exit it before the loop has finished processing. You may need to do this if the loop encounters an error when processing its instructions.

Example of a pretest loop

```
Dim number As Integer = 1
Do While number <= 3
    MessageBox.Show(number.ToString, "Numbers", _
        MessageBoxButtons.OK, MessageBoxIcon.
Information)
    number = number + 1
Loop
```

Syntax for a posttest loop

`Do`

[instructions to be processed either while the condition is true or until the condition becomes true]

`Loop` {`While` | `Until`} *condition*

Example of a posttest loop

```
Dim number As Integer = 10
Do
    MessageBox.Show(number.ToString, "Numbers", _
    MessageBoxButtons.OK, MessageBoxIcon.Information)
    number = number + 1
Loop Until number > 3
```

FIGURE 1.54 How to use a `Do...Loop` statement

As shown in Figure 1.54, the `Do...Loop` statement begins with a `Do` clause and ends with a `Loop` clause, with the loop body in between. You must choose either `While` or `Until` (not both). The posttest version of `Do...Loop` executes the loop body at least once, regardless of the value of the condition. The instructions in the loop body must cause the condition to change from true to false, or vice versa. Otherwise the loop body either will never execute or will execute continuously in an infinite loop.

Figure 1.54 contains an example of a pretest loop. This example first declares a counter variable `number` and initializes it to 1. Because this is a pretest version of `Do...Loop`, the condition in the `Do` clause, `number <= 3`, is tested before the loop body is executed. If the condition is true, the loop body is executed. The last statement in the loop body is `number = number + 1` and the condition in the `Do` clause is tested again.

Figure 1.54 also contains an example of a posttest loop. This code does exactly the same thing as the previous example by using slightly different logic. First, `number` is declared and initialized. Because this is a posttest loop, the loop body (displaying a message box) will always execute at least once. The last statement in the loop body is `number = number + 1`. The `Loop` clause tests the condition `number > 3`. If it is false, the loop body will execute again. Figure 1.55 shows flowcharts for these two examples.

(a) Pretest loop

Pseudocode for the pretest loop example

1. assign 1 to the number variable
2. repeat while the value in the number variable is less than or equal to 3
   display the contents of the number variable
   add 1 to the number variable
   end repeat

Flowchart for the pretest loop example

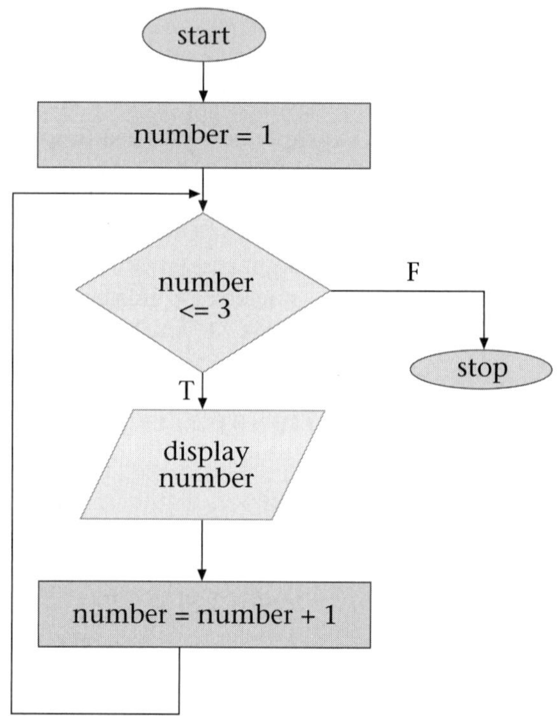

(b) Posttest loop

Pseudocode for the posttest loop example

1. assign 1 to the number variable
2. repeat
        display the contents of the number variable
        add 1 to the number variable
   end repeat until the value in the number variable is greater than 3

Flowchart for the posttest loop example

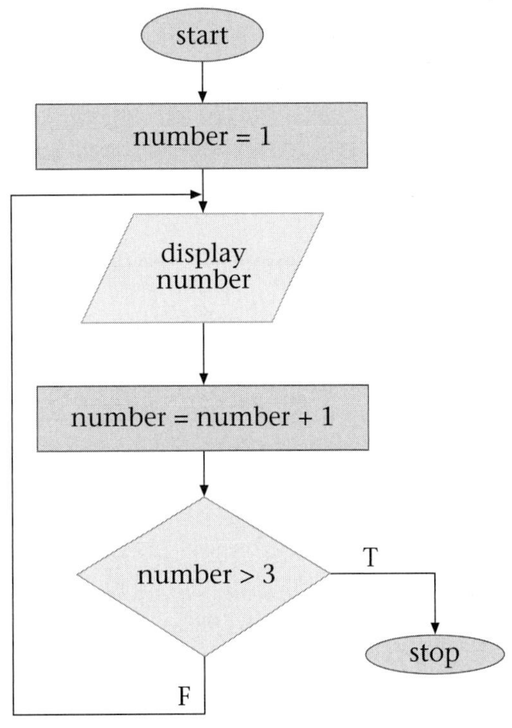

FIGURE 1.55 Pseudocode and flowcharts for pretest and posttest loops

TIP

Counters are used to answer the question "How many?" For example, "How many salespeople live in Virginia?" Accumulators are used to answer the question "How much?" For example, "How much did the salespeople sell this quarter?"

Using Counters and Accumulators

The repetition structure is often used for counting things or summing values. A **counter** is a numeric variable used for counting something—such as the number of employees paid in a week. An **accumulator** is a numeric variable used for accumulating (adding) items—such as the total dollar amount of a week's payroll. Counters and accumulators are usually initialized by setting their initial values to zero. Then they are updated (or incremented) by adding values to them for each iteration of a loop.

The `InputBox` Function

A **function** is a predefined procedure that performs a specific task and then returns a value after completing the task. The `InputBox` function displays a predefined dialog box that contains a message, along with an OK button, a Cancel button, and an input area in which the user can enter information. If the user clicks the OK button, the `InputBox` function returns the value contained in the input area of the dialog box; this value is always treated as a string. However, if the user clicks either the Cancel button in the dialog box or the Close button on the dialog box's title bar, the `InputBox` function returns an empty (or zero-length) string.

Figure 1.56 shows an example of a dialog box created by the `InputBox` function.

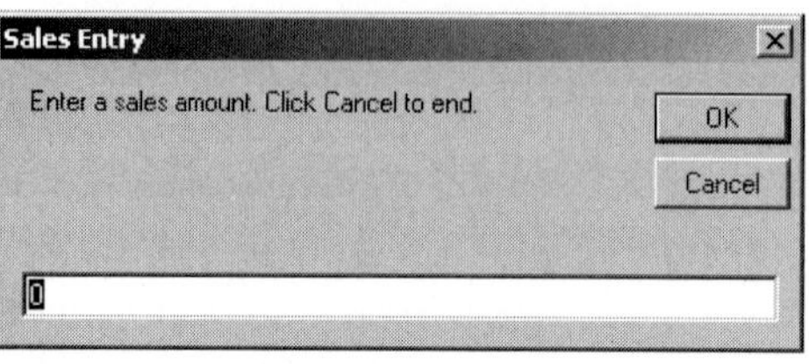

FIGURE 1.56 Example of a dialog box created by the `InputBox` function

Figure 1.57 provides the syntax for the `InputBox` function.

HOW TO...

Use the `InputBox` Function

Syntax

`InputBox(`*prompt*[, *title*][, *defaultResponse*]`)`

Example

```
Const Prompt As String = _
  "Enter a sales amount. Click Cancel to end."
Const Title As String = "Sales Entry"
Dim inputSales As String
inputSales = InputBox(Prompt, Title, "0")
```

FIGURE 1.57 How to use the `InputBox` function

In Figure 1.57, *prompt* is the message displayed in the dialog box, *title* is the text in the title bar of the box, and *defaultResponse* is the text initially displayed in the text box of the dialog box. The code that would create the input box in Figure 1.56 and store the input in a variable called `hoursWorked` can be found in the example of Figure 1.57.

The Sales Express Application

The Sales Express Company wants to enter the sales for all of its salespersons and then calculate the average sales per salesperson. Figure 1.58 displays the code for this application and Figure 1.59 provides some sample output.

```
' Project name:         Sales Express Project
' Project purpose:      The project calculates the average sales
'                       amount entered by the user.
' Created/revised by:   <your name> on <current date>

Option Explicit On
Option Strict On

Imports System.Globalization

Public Class MainForm
    Private Sub exitButton_Click(ByVal sender As Object, _
        ByVal e As System.EventArgs) Handles exitButton.Click
        Me.Close()
    End Sub

    Private Sub calcButton_Click(ByVal sender As Object, _
        ByVal e As System.EventArgs) Handles calcButton.Click
        ' calculates and displays the average sales amount
        Const Prompt As String = _
            "Enter a sales amount. Click Cancel to end."
        Const Title As String = "Sales Entry"
        Dim inputSales As String
        Dim sales As Decimal
        Dim salesCounter As Integer
        Dim salesAccumulator As Decimal
        Dim salesAverage As Decimal
        Dim isConverted As Boolean

        ' get first sales amount
        inputSales = InputBox(Prompt, Title, "0")

        ' repeat as long as the user enters a sales amount
        Do While inputSales <> String.Empty
            ' try to convert the sales amount to a number
            isConverted = Decimal.TryParse( _
                inputSales, NumberStyles.Currency, _
                        NumberFormatInfo.CurrentInfo, sales)

            ' if the sales amount can be converted to a number, then
            ' update the counter and accumulator;
            ' otherwise, display a message
            If isConverted = True Then
                salesCounter = salesCounter + 1
                salesAccumulator = salesAccumulator + sales
            Else
                MessageBox.Show("Please re-enter the sales amount.", _
                    "Sales Express", MessageBoxButtons.OK, _
                    MessageBoxIcon.Information)
            End If

            ' get the next sales amount
            inputSales = InputBox(Prompt, Title, "0")
        Loop

        ' if salesCounter is greater than 0, then calculate and
        ' display the average sales amount; otherwise, display 0 as
        ' the average sales amount
        If salesCounter > 0 Then
            salesAverage = _
                salesAccumulator / Convert.ToDecimal(salesCounter)
            averageLabel.Text = salesAverage.ToString("C2")
```

(Figure is continued on next page)

```
        Else
            averageLabel.Text = "0"
        End If
    End Sub
End Class
```

FIGURE 1.58 Program code for the Sales Express application

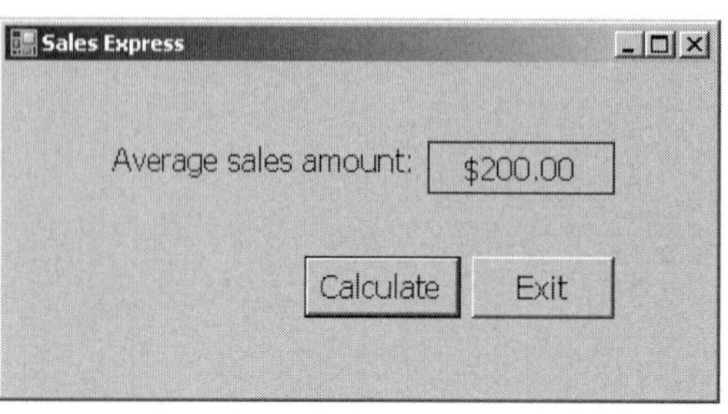

FIGURE 1.59 Sample run of the Sales Express application

The `calcButton_Click` procedure in Figure 1.58 begins by declaring several variables. Then an input box is displayed with the value `"0"` stored in `inputSales` (see Figure 1.56). This step is called a **priming read** because it primes (or prepares) the loop that follows, which has a condition based on the value of `inputSales`. The `Do...Loop` statement first converts the `String` entered in the input box to a `Decimal`, then counts the number of sales and accumulates the sales amounts. Note that at the end of the `Do...Loop` statement, the input box is displayed again. Once out of the loop, an `If` / `Else` selection structure calculates and displays the average. For the sample run in Figure 1.59, the three sales values of 100, 200, and 300 were entered, resulting in an average sales value of $200.

PROGRAMMING EXAMPLE

Modified Grade Calculator

This section presents a Visual Basic application called Modified Grade Calculator. It is similar to the Grade Calculator application of Figure 1.42, but this project allows the user to enter the points a student earns on four projects and two tests. Each project is worth 50 points, and each test is worth 100 points. The application should total the points earned and then assign the appropriate grade, using the following chart:

Total points earned	Grade
360 – 400	A
320 – 359	B
280 – 319	C
240 – 279	D
below 240	F

After assigning the grade, the application should display the total points earned and the grade. Name the solution Grade Calculator Solution. Name the project Grade Calculator Project. Name the form file MainForm.vb. Save the application in the \VbReloadedAdv\Chap01 folder. Various aspects of the application, including the user interface, pseudocode, and program code, are shown in in the following tables and figures:

TOE Chart

Task	Object	Event
1. Get points earned on four projects and two tests 2. Display an appropriate message if the points earned cannot be converted to a number 3. Calculate the total points earned 4. Display the total points earned in the totalPointsLabel 5. Display the grade in the gradeLabel	assignButton	Click
End the application	exitButton	Click
Display the total points earned (from assignButton)	totalPointsLabel	None
Display the grade (from assignButton)	gradeLabel	None

FIGURE 1.60

User Interface

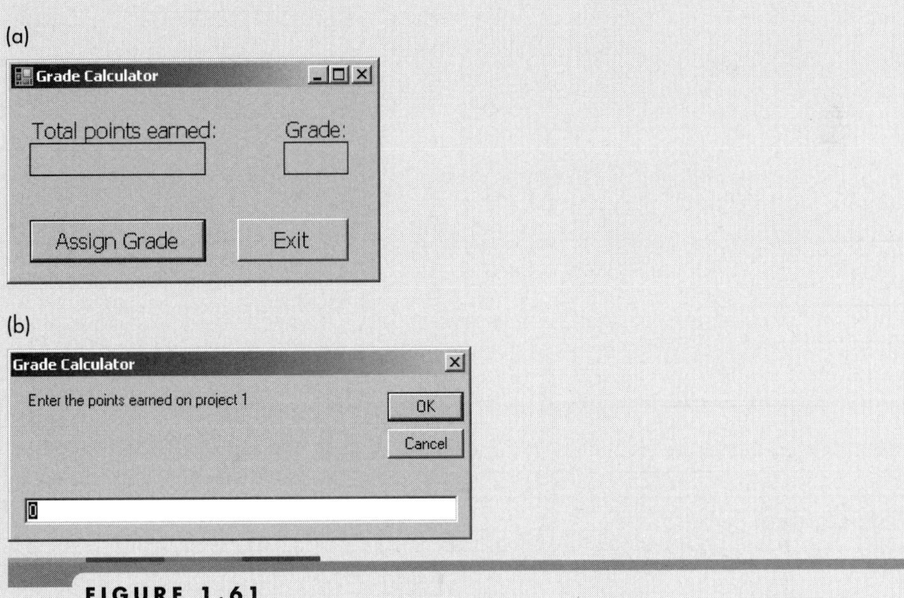

FIGURE 1.61

Objects, Properties, and Settings

Object	Property	Setting
Form1	Name Font Size StartPosition Text	MainForm Tahoma, 12 point 288, 176 CenterScreen Grade Calculator
Label1	Location Text	12, 21 Total points earned:
Label2	Location Text	207, 21 Grade:
Label3	Name AutoSize BorderStyle Location Size Text TextAlign	totalPointsLabel False FixedSingle 14, 40 135, 25 (empty) MiddleCenter
Label4	Name AutoSize BorderStyle Location Size Text TextAlign	gradeLabel False FixedSingle 209, 40 50, 25 (empty) MiddleCenter
Button1	Name Location Size Text	assignButton 14, 98 135, 32 &Assign Grade
Button2	Name Location Size Text	exitButton 173, 98 86, 32 E&xit

FIGURE 1.62

Tab Order

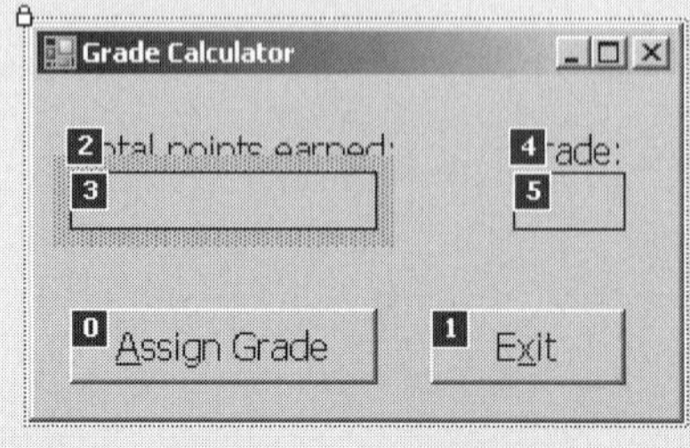

FIGURE 1.63

Pseudocode

exitButton_Click event procedure

1. close application

assignButton_Click event procedure

```
1. repeat while the number of projects counter is less than 5
       get the points earned on the project
       if the points earned can be converted to a number
             add 1 to the number of projects counter
             add the project points to the total points accumulator
       else
             display an appropriate message in a message box
             end if
   end repeat
2. repeat while the number of tests counter is less than 3
       get the points earned on the test
       if the points earned can be converted to a number
             add 1 to the number of tests counter
             add the test points to the total points accumulator
       else
             display an appropriate message in a message box
       end if
   end repeat
3. assign the grade based on the total points earned value:
   >= 360 assign A as the grade
   >= 320 assign B as the grade
   >= 280 assign C as the grade
   >= 240 assign D as the grade
   < 240 assign F as the grade
4. display the total points earned in the totalPointsLabel
5. display the grade in the gradeLabel
```

Code

```
' Project name:          Grade Calculator Project
' Project purpose:       The project allows the user to enter the points
'                        a student earns on 4 projects and 2 tests.
'                        It then totals the points earned and displays
'                        the appropriate grade.
' Created/revised by:    <your name> on <current date>

Option Explicit On
Option Strict On

Public Class MainForm
    Private Sub exitButton_Click(ByVal sender As Object, _
        ByVal e As System.EventArgs) Handles exitButton.Click
        Me.Close()
    End Sub

    Private Sub assignButton_Click(ByVal sender As Object, _
        ByVal e As System.EventArgs) Handles assignButton.Click
```

(Figure is continued on next page)

```
        ' calculates the total points earned, then displays the
        ' total (points) earned and the appropriate grade
        Dim inputProjectPoints As String
        Dim inputTestPoints As String
        Dim grade As String
        Dim projectPoints As Integer
        Dim testPoints As Integer
        Dim totalPointsAccumulator As Integer
        Dim projectCounter As Integer = 1
        Dim testCounter As Integer = 1
        Dim isConverted As Boolean

        ' get and accumulate the project points
        Do While projectCounter < 5
            inputProjectPoints = _
                InputBox("Enter the points earned on project " _
                    & projectCounter, "Grade Calculator", "0")
            isConverted = Integer.TryParse( _
                inputProjectPoints, projectPoints)
            If isConverted Then
                projectCounter = projectCounter + 1
                totalPointsAccumulator = _
                    totalPointsAccumulator + projectPoints
            Else
                MessageBox.Show( _
                    "Please enter a number.", "Grade Calculator", _
                    MessageBoxButtons.OK, MessageBoxIcon.Information)
            End If
        Loop

        ' get and accumulate the test points
        Do While testCounter < 3
            inputTestPoints = InputBox( _
                "Enter the points earned on test " _
                & testCounter, "Grade Calculator", "0")
            isConverted = Integer.TryParse(inputTestPoints, testPoints)
            If isConverted Then
                testCounter = testCounter + 1
                totalPointsAccumulator = _
                    totalPointsAccumulator + testPoints
            Else
                MessageBox.Show("Please enter a number.", _
                    "Grade Calculator", _
                    MessageBoxButtons.OK, MessageBoxIcon.Information)
            End If
        Loop

        If totalPointsAccumulator >= 360 Then
            grade = "A"
        ElseIf totalPointsAccumulator >= 320 Then
            grade = "B"
        ElseIf totalPointsAccumulator >= 280 Then
            grade = "C"
        ElseIf totalPointsAccumulator >= 240 Then
            grade = "D"
        Else
            grade = "F"
        End If

```

(Figure is continued on next page)

```
        'display the total points earned and the grade
        totalPointsLabel.Text = _
            Convert.ToString(totalPointsAccumulator)
        gradeLabel.Text = grade
    End Sub
End Class
```

FIGURE 1.64

Quick Review

- Programming languages have progressed from machine languages to assembly languages, and then to high-level languages. Procedure-oriented programs focus on tasks, whereas object-oriented programs focus on objects.
- In the world at large, an object is anything that can be seen, touched, or used. All objects have attributes (properties) and behaviors (methods and events). A class is a pattern from which an object can be instantiated (created). A class encapsulates the object's attributes and behaviors. Some attributes and behaviors are hidden (private), while others are exposed (public).
- The Microsoft .NET Framework 2.0 is a platform on which .NET applications are created. The .NET Framework contains a class library and the Common Language Runtime, which manages execution of an intermediate language MSIL.
- Applications created in Visual Studio are composed of solutions, projects, and files.
- Create your application's GUI in the Windows Form Designer window. A form is the foundation for the user interface in a Windows-based application. The forms you create inherit the attributes and behaviors of the `Form` class.
- The Solution Explorer window displays the names of projects and files contained in the current solution. The Project Designer window contains panes that display project settings. The Properties window exposes an object's properties to the programmer. The Toolbox window contains the tools you use when creating your application's GUI.
- Tell an object how to respond to an event by coding an event procedure. Use the Class Name and Method Name list boxes in the Code Editor window to select the object and event, respectively, that you want to code. The Code Editor then provides a code template for each of an object's event procedures, beginning with `Private Sub` and ending with `End Sub`. Enter your Visual Basic program code between those lines.
- When you start a Visual Basic application, the computer automatically creates an executable file (extension .exe). When you are finished with the application, this is the file given to the user.
- Identifying labels and button captions should be meaningful. Button captions should be entered using book title capitalization. When buttons are positioned horizontally on the screen, all the buttons should be the same height; their widths, however, may vary if necessary. When buttons are stacked vertically on the screen, all the buttons should be the same height and the same width.

- Graphics and color should be used sparingly in an interface. You should assign access keys to each of the interface controls, such as text boxes and buttons, that can accept user input. Assign an access key by including an ampersand (&) in the control's caption or identifying label.
- The `TabIndex` property determines the order in which a control receives the focus when the user presses either the Tab key or an access key. The `TabIndex` property of a text box should be set to a value that is one number more than the value stored in the `TabIndex` property of its identifying label.
- If you want code processed before a form is displayed, place the code in the form's `Load` event procedure.
- Variables and named constants are computer memory locations that store data. The contents of a variable can change while the application is running. However, the contents of a named constant cannot change while the application is running. All variables and named constants have a name, data type, scope, and lifetime.
- Use a declaration statement to declare a variable. If the variable has either block or procedure scope, begin the declaration statement with the keyword `Dim`. If the variable has module scope, begin the declaration statement with the keyword `Private`.
- A procedure-level memory location can be used only by the procedure in which it is declared. A module-level memory location can be used by all of the procedures in the form. A block-level memory location can be used only within the block of code in which it is declared. A static variable is a procedure-level variable that retains its value even when the procedure ends.
- You can use the `TryParse` method to convert a string to a number. If the string can be converted, the method converts the string to a number and stores the number in a numeric variable; it also returns the `Boolean` value `True`. If the string cannot be converted, the method stores the number zero in the numeric variable and returns the `Boolean` value `False`. The `Convert` class contains methods that convert values to a specified data type.
- The `Option Explicit On` statement tells the computer to warn you if your code contains the name of an undeclared variable. The `Option Strict On` statement tells the computer not to perform any implicit type conversions that may lead to a loss of data. The computer also should not implicitly convert strings to numbers, and vice versa.
- The selection structure allows a program to make a decision or comparison and then select one of two paths, depending on the result of that decision or comparison. Visual Basic provides four forms of the selection structure: `If`, `If` / `Else`, `If` / `ElseIf` / `Else`, and `Case`. Variables declared in either the true or false path of a selection structure have block scope.
- Connect (or link) strings together using the concatenation operator (`&`). The `ControlChars.NewLine` constant advances the insertion point to the next line in a control.
- You can nest selection structures, which means that you can place one selection structure in either the true or false path of another selection structure. The primary decision is always made by the outer selection structure. The secondary decision is always made by the inner (nested) selection structure. Typically, you use the `If` / `ElseIf` / `Else` and `Case` forms of the selection structure when the structure must choose from several alternatives.
- The repetition structure, also called a loop, allows a program to repeatedly process one or more program instructions. A repetition structure can be either a pretest loop or a posttest loop. A variable declared in a `For` clause has block scope and can be used only by the `For...Next` loop.

- Use a label control to provide keyboard access to a list box. Set the label control's `TabIndex` property to a value that is one number less than the list box's `TabIndex` value.
- To add an item to a list box, use the `Add` method of the `Items` collection. When the user selects an item in a list box, the item appears highlighted in the list. The item's value is stored in the list box's `SelectedItem` property, and the item's index is stored in the list box's `SelectedIndex` property.
- Combo boxes are similar to list boxes in that they allow the user to select from a list of choices. However, combo boxes can also have a text field to enter data not in the list. A combo box's `SelectedItem` property contains the value of the item selected in the list portion of the combo box. A combo box's `Text` property contains the value that appears in the text portion of the combo box.
- You can use the `Do...Loop` statement to code either a pretest loop or a posttest loop. When used in the `Do...Loop` statement, the keyword `While` indicates that the loop instructions should be processed *while* the condition is true. The keyword `Until`, on the other hand, indicates that the loop instructions should be processed *until* the condition becomes true.
- Use a counter and/or an accumulator to calculate subtotals, totals, and averages. A counter determines "how many," while an accumulator determines "how much." Counters and accumulators must be initialized and updated. The initialization is done outside of the loop that uses the counter, and the updating is done within the loop.

Key Terms

abstraction—The act of focusing only on the relevant aspects of something.

access key—The underlined character in an object's identifying label or caption. An access key allows the user to select the object by using the Alt key in combination with the character.

accumulator—A numeric variable used for accumulating (adding) items; it allows you to answer the question "How much?"

applications programmers—Programmers who write and maintain programs that handle a specific task.

assembly languages—Programming languages that allow the programmer to use mnemonics in place of the 0s and 1s in a program.

assignment operator—The equal sign (=) in an assignment statement.

attributes—The characteristics that describe an object.

behaviors—The operations (actions) that an object is capable of performing.

block scope—Scope confined to the code block in which a variable is declared (using the keyword `Dim`).

Boolean operators—see **logical operators**

class—A unit of program code that defines a category of objects.

Common Language Runtime (CLR)—The core runtime engine of the Microsoft .NET Framework.

counter—A numeric variable used for counting something; it allows you to answer the question "How many?"

data type—The type of data a variable can store.

debugging—The process of locating errors in a program.

dialog box—A window that supports and supplements a user's activities in the primary window.

event—An action (such as clicking, double-clicking, and scrolling) to which an object can respond.

event procedure—The set of instructions (program code) that tells the application what to do when an event occurs.

flowchart—An arrangement of standard graphic symbols used to plan a procedure.

focus—The ability of an object to accept user input.

format specifier—A letter (either uppercase or lowercase) that signifies the type of formatting. The possible format specifiers are: `C` for currency, `D` for decimal, `F` for fixed-point, `N` for number, or `P` for percent.

function—A predefined procedure that performs a specific task and then returns a value after completing the task.

high-level languages—Programming languages that allow the programmer to use computer instructions that more closely resemble the English language.

IDE—An acronym for integrated development environment (an example is Visual Studio 2005).

identifier—The descriptive name given to an object.

implicit type conversion—Automatically assigning values of one data type to variables of a different data type.

inheritance—The process by which a derived class can use the properties and methods of a base class.

initialize—To assign an initial value to a variable when it is first declared.

instantiation—The process of creating an object in computer memory.

lifetime—The amount of time a variable remains in computer memory.

literal type character—A suffix character that forces a literal constant to assume a data type other than the one its form indicates.

logic error—An error in a syntactically correct program that produces unexpected results.

logical operators—Operators (also called Boolean operators) such as `Not`, `And`, and `Or`, that allow you to combine two or more conditions into one compound condition.

machine languages—Computer instructions consisting of 0s and 1s.

method—Part of a class that performs a task.

module scope—Scope confined to the module, class, or structure in which a variable is declared (using the keyword `Private`).

named constant—A computer memory location whose contents cannot be changed while the application is running.

namespace—A name given to a group of related classes.

nested selection structure—A selection structure (the inner selection structure) within another selection structure (the outer selection structure).

object—An instance of a class that consists of data and the operations associated with that data.

object-oriented programming—A method of programming in which the programmer concentrates on the objects that the program can use to accomplish its goal.

polymorphism—The object-oriented feature that enables one method to have several different implementations depending on the type of object calling the method.

precedence numbers—The order in which the computer performs an operation in an expression.

primary window—The main user interface of an application.

priming read—A program statement that initializes a variable used in the condition of a `Do...Loop`.

procedure-oriented programming—A method of programming in which the programmer concentrates on the major tasks that the program needs to perform.

procedure scope—Scope confined to the procedure in which a variable is declared (using the keyword `Dim`).

Properties window—The window that displays an object's attributes (properties).

pseudo-random number generator—A device that produces a sequence of numbers that meet certain statistical requirements for randomness.

pseudocode—Text (which may look similar to programming code) that is used to plan a procedure.

repetition structure—A basic programming structure (also called a loop) that allows the program to repeatedly process one or more program instructions until some condition is met.

scope—The part of a program where a variable is declared and can be used.

selection structure—A basic programming structure (also called the decision structure) that allows a program to make a decision or comparison and then select the appropriate path.

sequence structure—A basic programming structure in which each statement is processed, one after another, each time the procedure is called.

Solution Explorer window—The window in the Visual Studio 2005 IDE that displays a list of the projects contained in the current solution, and the items contained in each project.

startup form—The form that is automatically displayed when an application is started.

statement block—A set of statements terminated by an `Else`, `End If`, `Loop`, or `Next` statement.

static variable—A special type of procedure-level variable that retains its value even when the procedure ends.

sub procedure—A block of code that performs a specific task.

syntax—The rules of a programming language.

syntax error—An error resulting from violating the programming language's syntax.

systems programmers—Programmers who write and maintain programs that help the computer carry out its basic operating functions.

Toolbox window—The window in the Visual Studio 2005 IDE that contains the tools you use when creating an application. Each tool represents a class.

user interface—The means by which the user interacts with the application.

variable—A computer memory location where the programmer can temporarily store data while an application is running.

Windows Form Designer window—The window in the Visual Basic IDE that contains a Windows Form object (or form) that serves as the application's graphical user interface.

Review Questions

1. Both systems programmers and applications programmers write programs that handle specific real-world tasks, but use different kinds of programming languages.
   a. True
   b. False
2. Inheritance is the term that relates to base classes and derived classes.
   a. True
   b. False
3. It is usually a good idea to use several different colors in the interface of a business application to keep the user's attention.
   a. True
   b. False
4. The `Group` control draws a border around a group of controls.
   a. True
   b. False
5. In Visual Basic, identifiers can begin with the underscore (_) character.
   a. True
   b. False
6. The `TryParse` method requires two arguments.
   a. True
   b. False
7. In Visual Basic, 12 / 2 * 3 = 7 + 4 is a logical expression.
   a. True
   b. False
8. A logical operator is also called a Boolean operator.
   a. True
   b. False
9. A user can make several selections from a single list box.
   a. True
   b. False
10. A `Do...Loop` is preferred over a `For...Next` loop when the number of iterations to be performed is known before the program is run.
    a. True
    b. False

11. Which type of programming language makes heavy use of mnemonics?
    a. assembly language
    b. machine language
    c. high-level language
    d. none of the above
12. Which of the following languages is not an object-oriented programming language?
    a. Visual Basic
    b. C
    c. C++
    d. Java
13. Which of the following is not part of a TOE chart?
    a. Task
    b. Object
    c. Event
    d. all of the above are found in a TOE chart
14. An access key is enabled by changing a control's ____ property.
    a. `Name`
    b. `Text`
    c. `Size`
    d. `TabIndex`
15. Which of the following data types is most likely to result in slow performance?
    a. `Decimal`
    b. `Integer`
    c. `Object`
    d. `String`
16. Which of the following key words is not used when declaring a variable?
    a. `Dim`
    b. `Public`
    c. `Private`
    d. `Static`
17. A procedure-level variable is declared using the key word ____.
    a. `Dim`
    b. `Public`
    c. `Private`
    d. `Static`
18. Which type of programming structure uses the key word `If`?
    a. sequence
    b. selection
    c. repetition
    d. loop
19. A statement block is terminated by ____.
    a. `Else`
    b. `End If`
    c. `Next`
    d. All of the above
20. Which of the following key words is not used with the repetition structure?
    a. `For`
    b. `If`
    c. `Do`
    d. `Loop`

Computer Exercises

When you create user interfaces, follow all conventions for an attractive, organized form with meaningful names for controls. When you create event procedures, use the `TryParse` method to ensure that valid data are entered, use named constants when appropriate, and use format specifiers for output requiring special formatting. Your instructor may also request that you use TOE charts, pseudocode, and/or flowcharts as planning aids.

1. In this exercise, you create an application that calculates an employee's payroll deductions and net pay.
    a. Create a project called **Employee Payroll**. Save the application in the \VBReloadedAdvanced\Chap01 folder.
    b. Design and create a user interface that accepts an employee's ID number, name, weekly hours worked, and hourly wage in separate text boxes.
    c. Add a list box with three entries: Health insurance, Dental insurance, and Life insurance (all are optional for an employee).
    d. Add a single label that displays the weekly gross earnings, the total deduction for all insurance, the deduction for tax (10% of gross earnings), and the net pay.
    e. Add a Calculate button and a Clear button.
    f. Add event procedures for the Calculate and Clear buttons. Health insurance is $25 per week, dental insurance is $5 per week, and life insurance is 5% of gross earnings. However, if an employee has all three kinds of insurance, he or she receives an additional 20% discount on the total insurance cost.
    g. Save the solution, test the application, and modify as necessary.

2. In this exercise, you create an application that calculates the areas and volumes of various geometric shapes. Hint: To find the square root of *number*, use the `Math` class and the `Sqrt` function as follows: `Math.Sqrt(`*number*`)`.
    a. Create a project called **Geometric Shapes**. Save the application in the \VBReloadedAdvanced\Chap01 folder.
    b. Design and create a user interface that calculates the area of a square, a circle, or an equilateral triangle. The interface also allows the user to calculate the volume of a cube, a sphere, or a tetrahedron (a three-dimensional figure with four sides, each an equilateral triangle).
    c. Add two list boxes, one containing Square, Circle, Triangle, the other containing Cube, Sphere, Tetrahedron. Nothing is selected initially in either list box. Only one item from each list box can be selected.
    d. Add a text box for entering the appropriate dimension: the side of a square (s), the radius of a circle (r), or the side of a triangle (a).
    e. Add a Calculate button, a Clear button, and a Close button.
    f. The area output should be located in a label with a colored background, and the volume output should be located in a label with a different colored background.
    g. Add event procedures for all buttons. Use one `Case` selection structure for choosing the correct type of area calculation, and use another `Case` selection structure for choosing the correct type of volume calculation.

The formulas for areas and volumes of the various shapes are as follows. (Note that in Visual Basic, π is defined by the field `Math.PI`.)

Square	Circle	Equilateral Triangle
$A = s^2$	$A = \pi * r^2$	$A = (\sqrt{3} / 4) * a^2$
Cube	**Sphere**	**Tetrahedron**
$V = s^3$	$V = (4 / 3) * \pi * r^3$	$V = (\sqrt{2} / 12) * a^3$

h. If the user does not select any shape and clicks the Calculate button, display a dialog box with an appropriate message, such as "No shape was selected." Whenever the user changes the value of the dimension text box, display empty strings in the output labels.

i. Save the solution, test the application, and modify as necessary.

3. In this exercise, you create an application that displays total credit hours and GPA for a student during one semester.

   a. Create a project called **Grade Point Average**. Save the application in the \VBReloadedAdvanced\Chap01 folder.

   b. Design and create a user interface that displays a student's total credit hours and grade point average (GPA) for a semester.

   c. The interface uses three labels for output: one for the total credit hours, one for the GPA, and one for the number of grades entered.

   d. The form has an Enter Data button, a Clear button, and a Close button.

   e. When the user clicks the Enter Data button, two input boxes appear in succession, one for the number of credit hours (such as 3) and the next for the corresponding letter grade (such as A). One credit hour of A is worth 4 grade points, an hour of B is worth 3 grade points, and so on.

   f. The labels on the form are updated after the user supplies each set of credit hours and grade points.

   g. If the user clicks the Cancel button on either of the input boxes, the application will end.

   h. Save the solution, test the application, and modify as necessary.

4. In this exercise, you create an application that calculates monthly car payments.

   a. Create a project called **Car Payments**. Save the application in the \VBReloadedAdvanced\Chap01 folder.

   b. Design and create a user interface that allows the user to enter a loan amount in one text box, an annual interest rate in another, and the term (in years) of the loan in a third.

   c. Place these three text boxes in a `GroupBox` control.

   d. Use a label to display the payments to be made at the beginning of each month.

   e. Provide Calculate, Reset, and Exit buttons with access keys.

   f. Use the `Financial.Pmt` method to calculate the payment.

   g. Save the solution, test the application, and modify as necessary.

5. In this exercise, you create an application that selects lottery numbers at random.
   a. Create a project called **Fat Chance Lottery**. Save the application in the \VBReloadedAdvanced\Chap01 folder.
   b. In a popular lottery game, the player chooses five different numbers (each ranging from 1 through 55) plus a special sixth number ranging from 1 through 42 (the sixth number can repeat any of the other five numbers). Design and create a user interface that has six labels to display the six random numbers.
   c. Arrange the labels horizontally using the `TableLayoutPanel` tool.
   d. The first five labels have a blue background but the sixth label has a red background. Use a bold 24-point font to display the numbers.
   e. The user clicks a Select button to generate each number individually, going from left to right.
   f. Clicking the Select button after all numbers have already been selected creates a dialog box with an appropriate ending message for the user. A Clear button clears all labels.
   g. Save the solution, test the application, and modify as necessary.

6. In this exercise, you modify the solution of Exercise 1 to allow for multiple employees.
   a. Call the project **Company Payroll**. Save the application in the \VBReloadedAdvanced\Chap01 folder.
   b. Add another set of labels to display the cumulative totals for gross pay, insurance, taxes, and net pay for all employee data entered.
   c. Each time the user clicks the Calculate button, data for another employee may be entered.
   d. Add a list box to display the name and net pay for all employees entered.
   e. Add an Exit button to end the application.
   f. Save the solution, test the application, and modify as necessary.

7. In this exercise, you create an application that calculates the future value of a monthly investment.
   a. Create a project called **Monthly Savings**. Save the application in the \VBReloadedAdvanced\Chap01 folder.
   b. Design and create a user interface that allows the user to enter a monthly savings amount in a text box.
   c. Add a `ComboBox` control with a list of possible annual interest rates. The user can select an interest rate or enter one that is not in the list.
   d. Place these two controls in a `Panel` control.
   e. Use a label to display the future value of the investments at the end 1, 2, 3, 4, and 5 years. Use a `For...Next` loop to determine these values.
   f. The form has Calculate, Reset, and Exit buttons with access keys. Use the `Financial.FV` method to calculate the future value.
   g. Save the solution, test the application, and modify as necessary.

Case Projects

Interest Rate

Visit *http://msdn.microsoft.com/* and search for "Financial.Rate". Create an application that allows the user to enter all the required and optional values specified in the `Financial.Rate` method in an organized user interface. If required values are not entered, provide a message box to inform the user that they must be entered. If optional values are entered, use them in the calculations. The interface will display the return value, the interest rate per period for an annuity.

ATM Simulator

Create an application that simulates an ATM (automated teller machine). A label should simulate the monitor that displays messages and data to the user. For example, the opening message could be, "Welcome to the <bank name> ATM." Number buttons (1, 2, ..., 9, 0) should be arranged below this "monitor" to serve as a keypad, along with an Enter button and a Clear button. Additional buttons should be arranged to the right of the monitor for the functions Deposit, Withdraw, Inquire, and Exit. The application should begin by requesting and recognizing a four-digit PIN of an existing bank customer who already has a balance in a checking account. Then the ATMs allow the user to select a function and enter numeric data. Make the ATM application as realistic as possible, using the techniques presented in this chapter.

Tic-Tac-Toe

Using three different kinds of graphics (to represent an unselected position, a position selected by the X player, and a position selected by the O player), create an application that allows two players to engage in a game of Tic-Tac-Toe. Create a 3x3 grid of graphics in a user interface. If the first player clicks an originally unselected graphic, it turns into the X graphic. The next unselected graphic will turn into the O graphic when clicked, and so on. (Use any three graphics of your choice.) If a player clicks a graphic that is already an X or O, do not allow a change. If either the X or O player gets three positions in a row (vertically, horizontally, or diagonally), he or she wins the game and a message box should appear to proclaim the victory. Include a Clear button that resets the game. (Hint: Go to *http://msdn.microsoft.com/* and search for "PictureBox Control" and "SetBounds Method" to investigate how to add graphics to and position graphics in a form. You can also use the `TableLayoutPanel` control to create the 3x3 grid.)

CHAPTER

2

Reviewing Microsoft Visual Basic 2005 Reloaded: Part II

After studying Chapter 2, you should be able to:

- Manipulate characters within strings
- Add radio buttons and check boxes to user interfaces
- Create `Sub` procedures and `Function` procedures within applications
- Create and manipulate one-dimensional and two-dimensional arrays
- Create a structure and manipulate structure variables
- Read information from and write information to sequential access files

In Chapter 1 you reviewed Chapters 1–5 of *Microsoft Visual Basic 2005: Reloaded* by Diane Zak. This chapter continues the review by surveying Chapters 6–9 of the *Reloaded* text. After you are up to speed on the basics of Microsoft Visual Basic 2005, the remaining 10 chapters of this text will explore new, advanced topics including object orientation, ADO.NET, ASP.NET, collections, generics, and multithreading.

If you are already proficient with Visual Basic, you may skip these first two chapters entirely. However, if you feel you need the review, these chapters should be extremely helpful.

STRING MANIPULATION AND MORE CONTROLS

This section explores ways of examining and manipulating strings, a very common requirement in applications that deal with textual data.

Determining the Number of Characters Contained in a String

The number of characters contained in a string is stored in the string's `Length` property. The syntax of the `Length` property is provided in Figure 2.1.

HOW TO...

Use the Length Property of a String

Syntax

***string*.Length.**

Example

```
Dim cityChars As Integer
Dim cityName As String = "Los Angeles"
cityChars = cityName.Length ' returns 11
```

FIGURE 2.1 How to use the Length property of a string

Figure 2.1 demonstrates that the length of the string "Los Angeles" is 11 (note that the space is also considered a character). To further illustrate the `Length` property, the ZIP Codes application in Figure 2.2 adds a ZIP code entered by the user to the list box only if the ZIP code has exactly five characters. If not, a message is displayed to the user. Figure 2.3 shows a sample run of this application (a) when a ZIP code is entered correctly and (b) when it is not.

```
' Project name:         Zip Codes Project
' Project purpose:      The project fills a list box with ZIP codes.
' Created/revised by:   <your name> on <current date>

Option Explicit On
Option Strict On

Public Class MainForm
    Private Sub addButton_Click(ByVal sender As Object, _
        ByVal e As System.EventArgs) Handles addButton.Click
```

(Figure is continued on next page)

```
        ' fills the list box with only 5-digit ZIP codes

        If zipTextBox.Text.Length = 5 Then
            zipListBox.Items.Add(zipTextBox.Text)
        Else
            MessageBox.Show("The ZIP code must contain 5 digits.", _
                "ZIP Codes", MessageBoxButtons.OK, _
                MessageBoxIcon.Information)
        End If

        zipTextBox.Focus() ' set input focus to zipTextBox
    End Sub

    Private Sub zipTextBox_Enter(ByVal sender As Object, _
        ByVal e As System.EventArgs) Handles zipTextBox.Enter
        zipTextBox.SelectAll() ' select all when zipTextBox is entered
    End Sub

    Private Sub exitButton_Click(ByVal sender As Object, _
        ByVal e As System.EventArgs) Handles exitButton.Click
        Me.Close()
    End Sub
End Class
```

FIGURE 2.2 Program code for the ZIP Codes application

(a) ZIP code entered with 5 digits

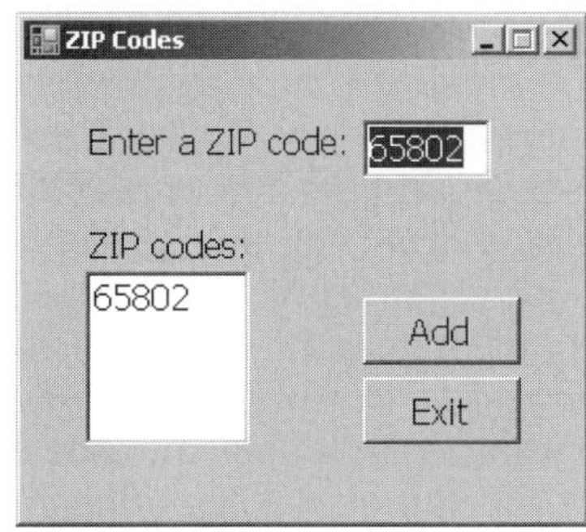

(b) ZIP code entered with 4 digits

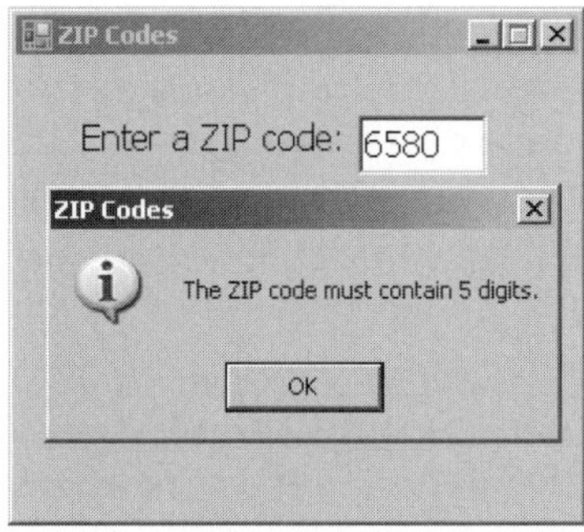

FIGURE 2.3 Sample run of the ZIP Codes application

Removing Characters from a String

At times, a user may inadvertently enter unwanted characters (such as spaces) at the beginning or end of a string within a text box. Such characters may be removed within an application using the `TrimStart` method, the `TrimEnd` method, or the `Trim` method. Figure 2.4 shows the syntax for these methods.

HOW TO...

Use the `TrimStart`, `TrimEnd` and `Trim` Methods

Syntax

string`.TrimStart(`[*trimChars*]`)`
string`.TrimEnd(`[*trimChars*]`)`
string`.Trim(`[*trimChars*]`)`

Example 1

```
Dim name As String
name = InputBox("Name:", "Name")
name = name.TrimStart() ' trim spaces from start
```

Example 2

```
Dim number As String
number = InputBox("Number:", "Number")
number = number.Trim("$"c, " "c, "%"c) 'trim $, space, %
```

FIGURE 2.4 How to use the `TrimStart`, `TrimEnd`, and `Trim` Methods

`TrimStart` removes certain kinds of characters from the beginning of a string, `TrimEnd` from the end of a string, and `Trim` from both the beginning and end of a string. In each syntax, *trimChars* is a comma-separated list of characters that you want removed (trimmed) from the string. If you omit the optional *trimChars* argument, Visual Basic assumes you want to remove only spaces from the beginning and/or end of the string. For example, the code in Example 1 of Figure 2.4 removes only white space (spaces) from the beginning of the `String` variable called `name` and re-stores the trimmed string in `name`. Example 2 of Figure 2.4 removes any leading and trailing dollar signs, spaces, and percent signs from the `number` variable. The character `c` following `"$"`, `" "`, and `"%"` is the literal type character that converts these strings to the `Char` data type (*trimChars* must be `Char` data types).

The City Names application in Figure 2.5 adds city names to a list box after removing leading and trailing spaces. A sample run is shown in Figure 2.6, where leading and trailing spaces are removed from the string "St. Louis".

```
' Project name:         City Names Project
' Project purpose:      The project allows the user to add
'                       city names to a combo box.
' Created/revised by:   <your name> on <current date>

Option Explicit On
Option Strict On

```

(Figure is continued on next page)

```
Public Class MainForm
    Private Sub MainForm_Load(ByVal sender As Object, _
        ByVal e As System.EventArgs) Handles Me.Load
        ' fills the combo box with initial values
        cityComboBox.Items.Add("Chicago")
        cityComboBox.Items.Add("Nashville")
        cityComboBox.Items.Add("Atlanta")
        cityComboBox.SelectedIndex = 0
    End Sub

    Private Sub addButton_Click(ByVal sender As Object, _
        ByVal e As System.EventArgs) Handles addButton.Click
        ' trims any leading and trailing spaces from the
        ' city name before adding it to the combo box
        cityComboBox.Items.Add(cityComboBox.Text.Trim())
        cityComboBox.Focus()
    End Sub

    Private Sub exitButton_Click(ByVal sender As Object, _
        ByVal e As System.EventArgs) Handles exitButton.Click
        Me.Close()
    End Sub
End Class
```

FIGURE 2.5 Program code for the City Names application

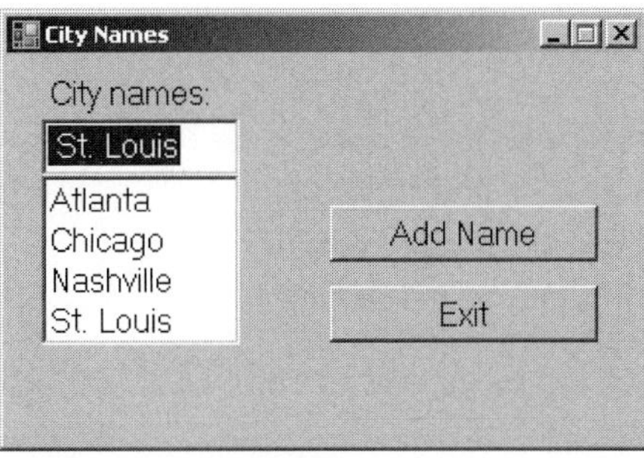

FIGURE 2.6 Sample run of the City Names application

The `Remove` Method

The `Remove` method allows you to remove one or more characters located anywhere in a string, not just the beginning or end. The syntax for the `Remove` method is given in Figure 2.7.

HOW TO...

Use the `Remove` Method

Syntax

string`.Remove(`*startIndex, count*`)`

Example

```
Dim zipCode As String = "65802-3345"
zipCodeTextBox.Text = zipCode.Remove(5, 5) ' returns 65802
```

FIGURE 2.7 How to use the `Remove` method

The argument *startIndex* is the position of a character in a string (beginning with index 0 for the first character) and the argument *count* is the number of characters to be removed beginning at the *startIndex*. The hyphen in 65802-3345 is at index 5 and five characters will be removed (-3345).

The code for the Social Security application is shown in Figure 2.8. This application removes the hyphens (-) from a Social Security number. For example, 123-45-6789 becomes 123456789, as illustrated in a sample run in Figure 2.9.

```
' Project name:         Social Security Project
' Project purpose:      The project removes the dashes
'                       from a Social Security number.
' Created/revised by:   <your name> on <current date>

Option Explicit On
Option Strict On

Public Class MainForm
    Private Sub removeButton_Click(ByVal sender As Object, _
        ByVal e As System.EventArgs) Handles removeButton.Click
        ' removes the dashes from a Social Security number
        Const message As String = _
            "The Social Security number must contain 11 characters."
        Dim socSecNumber As String

        socSecNumber = numberTextBox.Text

        If socSecNumber.Length = 11 Then
            socSecNumber = socSecNumber.Remove(3, 1)
            socSecNumber = socSecNumber.Remove(5, 1)
            numberLabel.Text = socSecNumber
        Else
            MessageBox.Show(message, "Social Security", _
                MessageBoxButtons.OK, MessageBoxIcon.Information)
        End If

        numberTextBox.Focus()
    End Sub

    Private Sub numberTextBox_Enter(ByVal sender As Object, _
        ByVal e As System.EventArgs) Handles numberTextBox.Enter
        numberTextBox.SelectAll()
    End Sub

    Private Sub exitButton_Click(ByVal sender As Object, _
    ByVal e As System.EventArgs) Handles exitButton.Click
        Me.Close()
    End Sub
End Class
```

FIGURE 2.8 Program code for the Social Security application

FIGURE 2.9 Sample run of the Social Security application

Replacing Characters in a String

Instead of removing characters, you may often need to replace existing characters in a string with new characters. The `Replace` method and `Mid` statement accomplish this.

The `Replace` Method

You can use the `Replace` method to replace a sequence of characters in a string with another sequence of characters. For example, you can use the `Replace` method to replace area code "800" with area code "866" in a phone number. The syntax is provided in Figure 2.10.

HOW TO...

Use the `Replace` Method

Syntax

string`.Replace(`*oldValue, newValue* `)`

Example

```
Dim name As String = "Emily Johnson"
Dim newName As String
newName = name.Replace("Johnson", "Smith")
```

FIGURE 2.10 How to use the `Replace` method

The example in Figure 2.10 assigns "Emily Smith" to the `newName` variable.

The `Mid` Statement

You can use the `Mid` statement to replace a specified number of characters in an existing string with characters from another string by using the syntax shown in Figure 2.11.

HOW TO...

Use the `Mid` Method

Syntax

`Mid(`*targetString*`,` *start* `[,` *count*`])` = *replacementString*

Example

```
Dim phoneNumber As String = "800 555-1212"
Mid(phoneNumber, 8, 1) = " " ' returns "800 555 1212"
```

FIGURE 2.11 How to use the `Mid` method

In Figure 2.11, *replacementString* will replace all characters in the argument *targetString* beginning with the position *start* for the number of characters *count*. Keep in mind that *start* is a position beginning with the number 1, not an index that begins with 0.

Figure 2.12 provides the code for the Phone application that replaces the existing area code 800 of a phone number (entered in a text box) with a new area code 866 (note that the 1 refers to the starting position of the 8 in 800 and the 3 refers to the three characters to be replaced). A sample run is shown in Figure 2.13.

```
' Project name:          Phone Project
' Project purpose:       The project changes the area code
'                        in a phone number to 877.
' Created/revised by:    <your name> on <current date>

Option Explicit On
Option Strict On

Public Class MainForm
    Private Sub reformatButton_Click(ByVal sender As Object, _
        ByVal e As System.EventArgs) Handles reformatButton.Click
        ' changes an area code to 866
        Dim newPhone As String

        newPhone = originalTextBox.Text

        ' reformat and display
        Mid(newPhone, 1, 3) = "866"
        newLabel.Text = newPhone

        originalTextBox.Focus()
    End Sub

    Private Sub originalTextBox_Enter(ByVal sender As Object, _
        ByVal e As System.EventArgs) Handles originalTextBox.Enter
        originalTextBox.SelectAll()
    End Sub

    Private Sub exitButton_Click(ByVal sender As Object, _
    ByVal e As System.EventArgs) Handles exitButton.Click
        Me.Close()
    End Sub
End Class
```

FIGURE 2.12 Program code for the Phone application

FIGURE 2.13 Sample run of the Phone application

Inserting Characters in a String

In addition to removing and replacing characters in a string, you also can insert characters within a string using the methods explained next.

The `PadLeft` and `PadRight` Methods

If you want to insert characters at either the beginning or end of the string, you can use the `PadLeft` and `PadRight` methods, respectively. Both methods pad the string with a character until the entire string is a specified length, then they return the new padded string. The syntax for the `PadLeft` and `PadRight` methods is given in Figure 2.14.

HOW TO...

Use the `PadLeft` and `PadRight` Methods

Syntax

string`.PadLeft(`*length*[`,` *character*]`)`
string`.PadRight(`*length*[`,` *character*]`)`

Example 1

```
Dim netPay As Decimal = 667.50D
Dim formattedNetPay As String
' assigns "********$667.50" to the formattedNetPay variable
formattedNetPay = netPay.ToString("C2").PadLeft(15, "*"c)
```

Example 2

```
Dim firstName As String = "Nicole"
' assigns "Nicole    " to the firstName variable
firstName = firstName.PadRight(10)
```

FIGURE 2.14 How to use the `PadLeft` and `PadRight` methods

In Figure 2.14, the argument *length* is the total length of the returned string and the argument *character* is the character used for padding. In Example 1 of Figure 2.14, the contents of the variable `netPay` are first converted to a string using the `ToString` method (with currency formatting), and then the `PadLeft` method is applied using the * character. Note that `PadLeft` results in right justifying the currency amount within the field of 15 spaces. In Example 2, the default space character is used for padding (no *character* argument), adding four spaces to the right of `"Nicole"`. This padding in effect left justifies the string within a total field of 10 spaces.

Figure 2.15 presents code for the Item Prices application. This application updates prices entered or selected in the combo boxes, adding 10% to Price 1 and 15% to Price 2. The key feature, however, is found in the `MainForm_Load` event procedure. There, the prices listed in the `rightComboBox` are right justified using the code `PadLeft(5)`. Figure 2.16 shows a sample run of the Item Prices application.

```
' Project name:          Item Prices Project
' Project purpose:       The project increases the price
'                        selected or entered in each
'                        combo box.
' Created/revised by:    <your name> on <current date>

Option Explicit On
Option Strict On

Public Class MainForm
    Private Sub MainForm_Load(ByVal sender As Object, ByVal e As System.EventArgs) Handles Me.Load
        ' fills the combo boxes with values
        For price As Decimal = 9.45D To 11.45D Step 0.25D
            leftComboBox.Items.Add(price.ToString("N2"))
        Next price
        leftComboBox.SelectedIndex = 0

        For price As Decimal = 9.45D To 11.45D Step 0.25D
            rightComboBox.Items.Add(price.ToString("N2").PadLeft(5))
        Next price
        rightComboBox.SelectedIndex = 0
    End Sub

    Private Sub updateButton_Click(ByVal sender As Object, _
        ByVal e As System.EventArgs) Handles updateButton.Click
        ' increases the prices by 10% and 15%
        Const Percent1 As Decimal = 0.1D
        Const Percent2 As Decimal = 0.15D
        Dim leftPrice As Decimal
        Dim rightPrice As Decimal
        Dim leftNewPrice As Decimal
        Dim rightNewPrice As Decimal

        leftPrice = Convert.ToDecimal(leftComboBox.Text)
        rightPrice = Convert.ToDecimal(rightComboBox.Text)

        ' calculate and display new prices
        leftNewPrice = leftPrice + leftPrice * Percent1
        rightNewPrice = rightPrice + rightPrice * Percent2
        leftUpdatedLabel.Text = leftNewPrice.ToString("N2")
        rightUpdatedLabel.Text = rightNewPrice.ToString("N2")
    End Sub

    Private Sub leftComboBox_TextChanged(ByVal sender As Object, _
        ByVal e As System.EventArgs) Handles leftComboBox.TextChanged
        leftUpdatedLabel.Text = String.Empty
    End Sub

```

(Figure is continued on next page)

```
    Private Sub rightComboBox_TextChanged(ByVal sender As Object, _
        ByVal e As System.EventArgs) Handles rightComboBox.TextChanged
        rightUpdatedLabel.Text = String.Empty
    End Sub

    Private Sub exitButton_Click(ByVal sender As Object, _
     ByVal e As System.EventArgs) Handles exitButton.Click
        Me.Close()
    End Sub
End Class
```

FIGURE 2.15 Program code for the Item Prices application

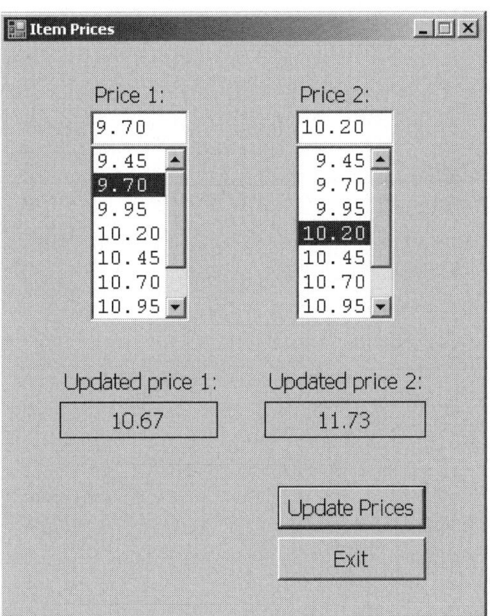

FIGURE 2.16 Sample run of the Item Prices application

The `Insert` Method

Visual Basic provides the `Insert` method for inserting characters anywhere within a string. The syntax for the `Insert` method is shown in Figure 2.17.

HOW TO...

Use the `Insert` Method

Syntax

string`.Insert(`*startIndex*`,` *value*`)`

(Figure is continued on next page)

Example

```
Dim name As String = "Richard Johnson"
Dim fullName As String
' inserts "A. " in name at index 8 returning "Richard A. Johnson"
fullName = name.Insert(8, "A. ")
```

FIGURE 2.17 How to use the `Insert` method

The `Insert` method inserts a *value* in a *string* at location *startIndex* in *string*. The example in Figure 2.17 inserts the string literal `"A. "` in the string contained within the variable `name` beginning at index 8 (the location of the character `'J'` in the string `"Richard Johnson"`) resulting in `"Richard A. Johnson"` assigned to `fullName`. (Recall that index numbers begin with 0.)

The Date project code in Figure 2.18 converts a date entered in the format mm/dd/yy to a date in the format mm/dd/20yy. A sample run of this application is shown in Figure 2.19.

```
' Project name:          Date Project
' Project purpose:       The project changes the year
'                        number in a date from "yy" to
'                        "20yy".
' Created/revised by:    <your name> on <current date>

Option Explicit On
Option Strict On

Public Class MainForm
    Private Sub changeButton_Click(ByVal sender As Object, _
        ByVal e As System.EventArgs) Handles changeButton.Click
        ' changes a year number from "yy" to "20yy"
        Dim newDate As String

        newDate = dateTextBox.Text
        dateLabel.Text = newDate.Insert(newDate.Length - 2, "20")

        dateTextBox.Focus()
    End Sub

    Private Sub dateTextBox_Enter(ByVal sender As Object, _
        ByVal e As System.EventArgs) Handles dateTextBox.Enter
        dateTextBox.SelectAll()
    End Sub

    Private Sub exitButton_Click(ByVal sender As Object, _
    ByVal e As System.EventArgs) Handles exitButton.Click
        Me.Close()
    End Sub
End Class
```

FIGURE 2.18 Program code for the Date application

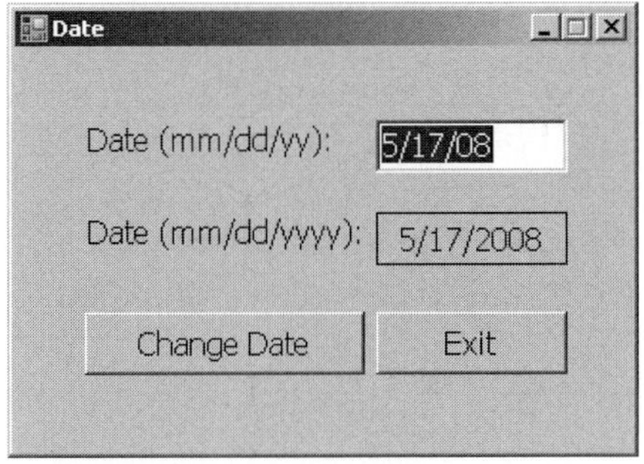

FIGURE 2.19 Sample run of the Date application

Searching a String for Characters

In some applications, you may need to determine whether a string begins or ends with a specific character or characters.

The `StartsWith` and `EndsWith` Methods

A **substring** is a contiguous (adjacent) sequence of characters taken from a string. For example, the string "world" is a substring of "Hello world!". You can use the `StartsWith` method to determine whether a specific substring occurs at the beginning of a string, and the `EndsWith` method to determine whether a specific substring occurs at the end of a string. The syntax for these methods can be found in Figure 2.20.

HOW TO...

Use the `StartsWith` and `EndsWith` Methods

Syntax

string.`StartsWith(`*subString*`)`
string.`EndsWith(`*subString*`)`

Example

```
Dim pay As String
pay = InputBox("Pay rate:", "Pay")
' if the user enters value with a leading $, it will be trimmed
If pay.StartsWith("$") Then
    pay = pay.TrimStart("$"c)
End If
```

FIGURE 2.20 How to use the `StartsWith` and `EndsWith` methods

In Figure 2.20, the argument *subString* is a string that may be a part of *string*. The example uses the `StartsWith` method to remove the `$` from the beginning of a string, if it exists. In the Sales Tax application (Figure 2.21), the `EndsWith` method is used to remove a trailing `%` if the user enters one with the tax rate, as demonstrated in the sample run in Figure 2.22.

```
' Project name:        Sales Tax Project
' Project purpose:     The project calculates a sales tax amount.
' Created/revised by:  <your name> on <current date>

Option Explicit On
Option Strict On

Public Class MainForm
    Private Sub calcButton_Click(ByVal sender As Object, _
        ByVal e As System.EventArgs) Handles calcButton.Click
        ' calculates a sales tax amount
        Const Message As String = _
            "The sales amount and tax rate must be numeric."
        Dim sales As Decimal
        Dim rate As Decimal
        Dim tax As Decimal
        Dim taxRate As String
        Dim isConvertedSales As Boolean
        Dim isConvertedRate As Boolean

        ' if necessary, remove the percent sign
        If rateTextBox.Text.EndsWith("%") Then
            taxRate = rateTextBox.Text.TrimEnd("%"c)
        Else
            taxRate = rateTextBox.Text
        End If

        isConvertedSales = Decimal.TryParse(salesTextBox.Text, sales)
        isConvertedRate = Decimal.TryParse(taxRate, rate)

        If isConvertedSales AndAlso isConvertedRate Then
            If rate > 1 Then
                rate = rate / 100
            End If
            tax = sales * rate
            taxLabel.Text = tax.ToString("C2")
        Else
            MessageBox.Show(Message, "Sales Tax Calculator", _
                MessageBoxButtons.OK, MessageBoxIcon.Information)
        End If

        salesTextBox.Focus()
    End Sub

    Private Sub salesTextBox_Enter(ByVal sender As Object, _
        ByVal e As System.EventArgs) Handles salesTextBox.Enter
        salesTextBox.SelectAll()
    End Sub

    Private Sub rateTextBox_Enter(ByVal sender As Object, _
        ByVal e As System.EventArgs) Handles rateTextBox.Enter
        rateTextBox.SelectAll()
    End Sub

    Private Sub salesTextBox_TextChanged(ByVal sender As Object, _
        ByVal e As System.EventArgs) Handles salesTextBox.TextChanged
        taxLabel.Text = String.Empty
    End Sub

    Private Sub rateTextBox_TextChanged(ByVal sender As Object, _
        ByVal e As System.EventArgs) Handles rateTextBox.TextChanged
```

(Figure is continued on next page)

```
            taxLabel.Text = String.Empty
        End Sub

        Private Sub exitButton_Click(ByVal sender As Object, _
        ByVal e As System.EventArgs) Handles exitButton.Click
            Me.Close()
        End Sub
    End Class
```

FIGURE 2.21 Program code for the Sales Tax application

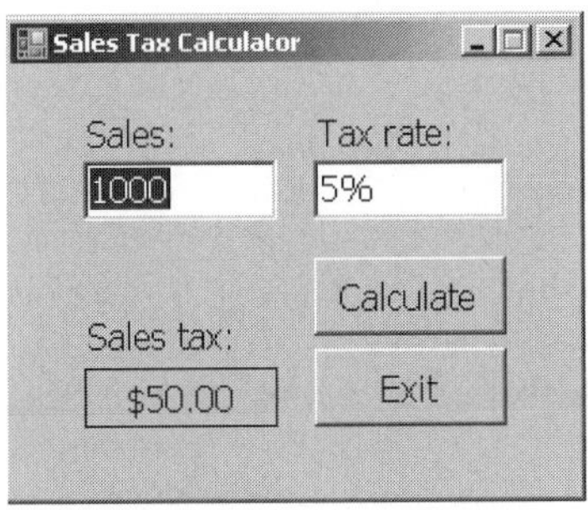

FIGURE 2.22 Sample run of the Sales Tax application

The `Contains` Method

You can use the `Contains` method to determine whether a string contains a specific sequence of characters. The syntax for the `Contains` method and an example are shown in Figure 2.23.

HOW TO...

Use the `Contains` Method

Syntax

string.`Contains(`*subString*`)`

Example

```
Dim zipCode As String
zipCode = InputBox("Zip code:", "Zip")
' if 65802-3345 is entered, 65802 is assigned to zipCode
If zipCode.Contains("-")Then
    zipCode = zipCode.Remove(5, 5)
End If
```

FIGURE 2.23 How to use the `Contains` method

In Figure 2.23, *string* is the original string and the argument *subString* is the string that may be contained in *string*. The example uses an `If` statement to test whether the ZIP code is entered in the format 99999-9999. If so, the last five characters are removed.

The `IndexOf` Method

Sometimes you want to know not only if a substring exists within a string (True or False), but exactly where the substring might be found in a string. The `IndexOf` method accomplishes this goal. The syntax for the `IndexOf` method is presented in Figure 2.24.

HOW TO...

Use the `IndexOf` Method

Syntax

string`.IndexOf(`*subString*`[, `*startIndex*`])`

Example 1

```
Dim message As String = "Have a nice day"
Dim indexNum As Integer
indexNum = message.IndexOf("Nice") ' returns -1, "Nice" not found
```

Example 2

```
Dim message As String = "Have a nice day"
Dim indexNum As Integer
indexNum = message.ToUpper.IndexOf("NICE") ' returns index number 7
```

Example 3

```
Dim message As String = "Have a nice day"
Dim indexNum As Integer
indexNum = message.IndexOf("a", message.IndexOf("a") + 1) ' returns 5
```

FIGURE 2.24 How to use the `IndexOf` method

Referring to the syntax in Figure 2.24, the `IndexOf` method returns the index of the first occurrence of *subString* within *string*. You can use the optional *startIndex* argument to specify the starting point for the search within *string* (other than index 0). If the `IndexOf` method does not find the *subString*, it returns the number –1; otherwise, it returns the index of the starting position of *subString* within *string*. Example 1 in Figure 2.24 assigns –1 to `indexNum` because `"Nice"` does not occur in the variable `message` (`"nice"` does, however). Example 2 returns 7 because the contents of the `message` are first converted to uppercase before a search is made for `"NICE"`. Example 3 returns 5 because the *startIndex* parameter `(message.IndexOf("a") + 1)` is 2, so the first occurrence of "a" beginning with index 2 is at index 5 (the letter "a" following the word "Have").

Figure 2.25 contains code for a Count application that determines how many times a given substring (entered in an input box) appears in the original string (entered in `MainForm`). Note that if the substring is indeed found in the string, the value of `startIndex` is set to one more than the `searchIndex` within the loop, which starts the search anew just after the index where the substring was found. Figure 2.26 displays a sample run of the Count application.

```
' Project name:        Count Project
' Project purpose:     The project determines the number
'                      of times a sequence of characters
'                      appears in a string.
' Created/revised by:  <your name> on <current date>
```

(Figure is continued on next page)

```
Option Explicit On
Option Strict On

Public Class MainForm
    Private Sub stringTextBox_Enter(ByVal sender As Object, _
        ByVal e As System.EventArgs) Handles originalTextBox.Enter
        originalTextBox.SelectAll()
    End Sub

    Private Sub stringTextBox_TextChanged(ByVal sender As Object, _
        ByVal e As System.EventArgs) _
        Handles originalTextBox.TextChanged
        countLabel.Text = String.Empty
    End Sub

    Private Sub searchButton_Click(ByVal sender As Object, _
        ByVal e As System.EventArgs) Handles searchButton.Click
        ' displays a message that indicates the number
        ' of times a sequence of characters appears
        ' in the string entered in the stringTextBox
        Dim origString As String
        Dim searchFor As String
        Dim startIndex As Integer
        Dim searchIndex As Integer
        Dim counter As Integer

        origString = originalTextBox.Text

        ' get the subString
        searchFor = InputBox("Search for:", "Count")

        ' search for the subString
        ' continue the search until the subString
        ' can no longer be located
        searchIndex = origString.IndexOf(searchFor, startIndex)
        Do Until searchIndex = -1
            ' update the counter, then begin the next search
            ' with the character located immediately
            ' after where the subString was last located
            counter = counter + 1
            startIndex = searchIndex + 1
            searchIndex = origString.IndexOf(searchFor, startIndex)
        Loop

        ' display the results of the search
        countLabel.Text = "'" & searchFor _
            & "' appears in the string " _
            & counter.ToString & " time(s)."
    End Sub

    Private Sub exitButton_Click(ByVal sender As Object, _
    ByVal e As System.EventArgs) Handles exitButton.Click
        Me.Close()
    End Sub
End Class
```

FIGURE 2.25 Program code for the Count application

(a) Input

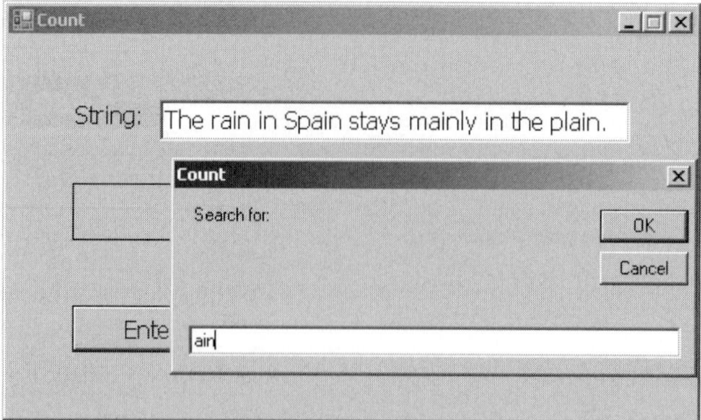

(b) Output

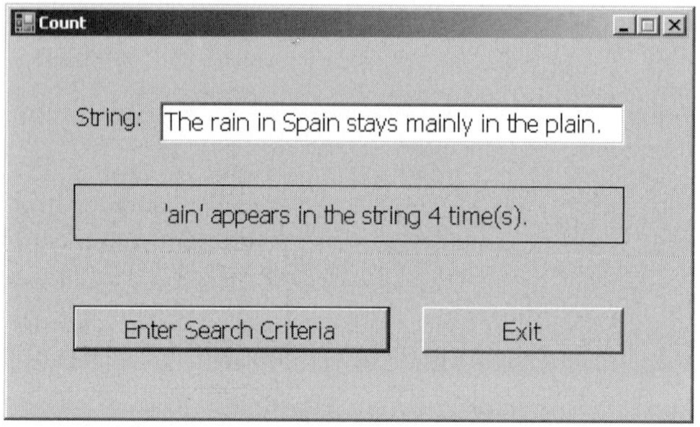

FIGURE 2.26 Sample run of the Count application

Accessing Characters Contained in a String

Visual Basic provides the `Substring` method to return any part of a string. The syntax for the `Substring` method is given in Figure 2.27.

HOW TO...

Use the `Substring` Method

Syntax

string`.Substring(`*startIndex*`[, `*count*`])`

Example

```
' the original string is "Napoleon Bonaparte"
Dim fullName As String = "Napoleon Bonaparte"
Dim firstName As String
Dim lastName As String

' index of space is 8
Dim indexOfSpace As Integer = fullName.IndexOf(" ")
```

(Figure is continued on next page)

```
' returns "Napoleon"
firstName = fullName.Substring(0, indexOfSpace)

' returns "Bonaparte"
lastName  = fullName.Substring(indexOfSpace + 1)
```

FIGURE 2.27 How to use the `Substring` method

The `Substring` method returns the substring contained within *string* that is *count* characters long beginning with *startIndex*. Note that *count* is optional, in which case the substring goes to the end of the *string*. The example in Figure 2.27 uses the `IndexOf` and `Substring` methods to determine the first and last names of a name in the variable `fullName`. The execution can be a little tricky. First, the index of the space in `"Napoleon Bonaparte"` is 8 (beginning index is 0). Therefore, `fullName.Substring(0, indexOfSpace)` returns the substring starting with index 0 up to (but not including) index 8 (the first name, `"Napoleon"`, which is assigned to `firstName`). The last line of code in the example returns the substring that begins at `indexOfSpace + 1` (9, in this case) to the end of the string. Thus, the remaining substring that begins with index 9 is `"Bonaparte"` and is assigned to `lastName`.

Comparing Strings

You have already learned that strings can be compared with comparison operators such as =, >, and <>. However, there are additional ways of comparing strings in Visual Basic.

The `String.Compare` Method

To compare strings you can use the `String.Compare` method. The syntax is provided in Figure 2.28.

HOW TO...

Use the `String.Compare` Method

Syntax

`String.Compare(`*string1*`,` *string2*[`,` *ignoreCase*]`)`

Examples

```
Dim result1 As Integer
result1 = String.Compare("Dallas", "DALLAS") ' returns -1

Dim result2 As Integer
result2 = String.Compare("Dallas", "DALLAS", True) ' returns 0

Dim result3 As Integer
result3 = String.Compare("Dallas", "Boston") ' returns 1
```

FIGURE 2.28 How to use the `String.Compare` method

In Figure 2.28, the `String.Compare` method returns an integer that indicates the result of comparing *string1* and *string2*. (The optional *ignoreCase* argument can be set to `True`, making the comparison case-insensitive). When both strings are equal, the method returns the number 0. When *string1* is greater than *string2* (alphabetically speaking), the method returns the number 1. When *string1* is less than *string2*, the method returns the number –1. The `String.Compare` method uses rules called **word sort rules** when comparing the strings. Following these rules, numbers are considered less than lowercase letters, which are considered less than uppercase letters. The three examples in Figure 2.28 assign the values of –1, 0, and 1 to the variables `result1`, `result2`, and `result3`, respectively.

The Word Sort application in Figure 2.29 makes use of the `String.Compare` method to determine how characters are ordered according to word sort rules. Figure 2.30 shows a sample run of the Word Sort application.

```
' Project name:          Word Sort Project
' Project purpose:       The project displays a message that
'                        indicates whether a character is equal
'                        to another character, or comes before
'                        or after the other letter.
' Created/revised by:    <your name> on <current date>

Option Explicit On
Option Strict On

Public Class MainForm
    Private Sub compareButton_Click(ByVal sender As Object, _
        ByVal e As System.EventArgs) Handles compareButton.Click
        ' displays the result of comparing two letters
        Dim character1 As String
        Dim character2 As String
        Dim result As Integer

        character1 = firstTextBox.Text
        character2 = secondTextBox.Text

        result = String.Compare(character1, character2)

        Select Case result
            Case 0
                messageLabel.Text = "Both letters are the same."
            Case 1
                messageLabel.Text = "The character " & character1 _
                    & " comes after the character " _
                    & character2
            Case -1
                messageLabel.Text = "The character " & character1 _
                     & " comes before the character " _
                     & character2
        End Select

        firstTextBox.Focus()
    End Sub

    Private Sub firstTextBox_Enter(ByVal sender As Object, _
    ByVal e As System.EventArgs) Handles firstTextBox.Enter
        firstTextBox.SelectAll()
    End Sub
```

(Figure is continued on next page)

```
    Private Sub firstTextBox_TextChanged(ByVal sender As Object, _
        ByVal e As System.EventArgs) Handles firstTextBox.TextChanged
        messageLabel.Text = String.Empty
    End Sub

    Private Sub secondTextBox_Enter(ByVal sender As Object, _
        ByVal e As System.EventArgs) Handles secondTextBox.Enter
        secondTextBox.SelectAll()
    End Sub

    Private Sub secondTextBox_TextChanged(ByVal sender As Object, _
        ByVal e As System.EventArgs) Handles secondTextBox.TextChanged
        messageLabel.Text = String.Empty
    End Sub

    Private Sub exitButton_Click(ByVal sender As Object, _
    ByVal e As System.EventArgs) Handles exitButton.Click
        Me.Close()
    End Sub
End Class
```

FIGURE 2.29 Program code for the Word Sort application

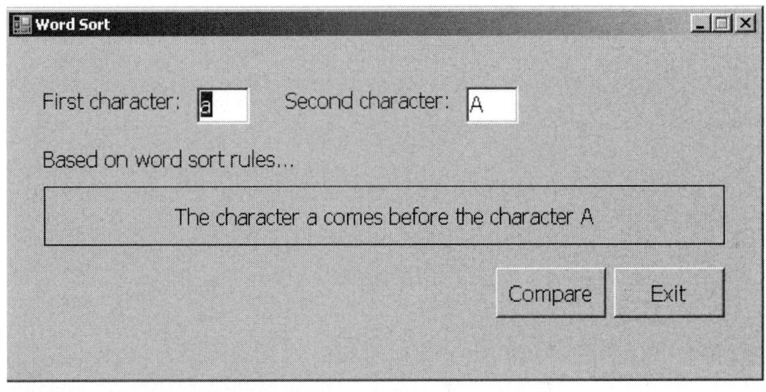

FIGURE 2.30 Sample run of the Alphabet application

The `Like` Operator

The `String.Compare` method is used to determine if one string is less than, the same, or greater than another. The `Like` operator allows you to use pattern-matching characters to determine whether a string matches a specified pattern. The syntax is shown in Figure 2.31. Several examples in Figure 2.31 present snippets of code illustrating how to use the `Like` operator.

HOW TO...

Use the `Like` Operator

Syntax

`Like` *patternString*

(Figure is continued on next page)

Example 1

```
' condition is True if state begins with K (* is a wildcard)
If state Like "K*" Then
```

Example 2

```
' condition is True if idNum begins with 3 numbers
Do While idNum Like "###*"
```

Example 3

```
' condition is True if firstName is Tom or Tim, ignoring case
If firstName.ToUpper() Like "T[OI]M" Then
```

Example 4

```
' isLowercase is True if letter contains just one lowercase letter
isLowercase = letter Like "[a-z]"
```

Example 5

```
' the loop counts the number of nonletters in name
Dim nonLetter As Integer = 0
For indexNum As Integer = 0 to name.Length - 1
       If name.Substring(indexNum, 1) Like "[!a-zA-Z]" Then
              nonLetter = nonLetter + 1
       End If
Next indexNum
```

FIGURE 2.31 How to use the `Like` operator

In Figure 2.31, *patternString* contains characters including the following special pattern-matching characters: ? (any single character), * (zero or more characters), and # (any single digit, 0–9). The *patternString* can also be of the form [*charlist*] where *charlist* is a list of characters, such as [a–z] or [*!charlist*], meaning not in the *charlist* (such as [!a–z]).

Table 2.1 summarizes the string-manipulation techniques you learned in this section.

Technique	Syntax	Purpose
Length property	*string*.**Length**	determine the number of characters in a string
Trim method	*string*.**Trim(**[*trimChars*]**)**	remove characters from both the beginning and end of a string
TrimStart method	*string*.**TrimStart(**[*trimChars*]**)**	remove characters from the beginning of a string
TrimEnd method	*string*.**TrimEnd(**[*trimChars*]**)**	remove characters from the end of a string
Remove method	*string*.**Remove(***startIndex*, *count***)**	remove characters from anywhere in a string
Replace method	*string*.**Replace(***oldValue*, *newValue***)**	replace all occurrences of a sequence of characters in a string with another sequence of characters
Mid statement	**Mid(***targetString*, *start* [, *count*]**)** = *replacementString*	replace a specific number of characters in a string with characters from another string

(Table is continued on next page)

PadLeft method	*string*.**PadLeft(***length*[, *character*]**)**	pad the beginning of a string with a character until the string is a specified length
PadRight method	*string*.**PadRight(***length*[, *character*]**)**	pad the end of a string with a character until the string is a specified length
Insert method	*string*.**Insert(***startIndex*, *value***)**	insert characters within a string
StartsWith method	*string*.**StartsWith(***subString***)**	determine whether a string begins with a specific sequence of characters
EndsWith method	*string*.**EndsWith(***subString***)**	determine whether a string ends with a specific sequence of characters
Contains method	*string*.**Contains(***subString***)**	determine whether a string contains a specific sequence of characters; returns a Boolean value
IndexOf method	*string*.**IndexOf(***subString*[, *startIndex*]**)**	determine whether a string contains a specific sequence of characters; returns an integer
Substring method	*string*.**Substring(***startIndex*[, *count*]**)**	access one or more characters contained in a string
String.Compare method	**String.Compare(***string1*, *string2*[, *ignoreCase*]**)**	compare two strings
Like operator	*string* **Like** *pattern*	use pattern-matching characters to determine whether one string is equal to another string

TABLE 2.1 String-manipulation techniques

More Controls

Most of the applications presented so far in this book have used text boxes to get user input. A disadvantage of using a text box is that it requires the application to perform data validation to ensure that the data are entered in the required format. In applications where the user is expected to enter one or more specific values, it is better to use other controls—such as list boxes, combo boxes, radio buttons, or check boxes—to display the possible values. Then, rather than typing the desired value in a text box, the user can select the appropriate value from one of these other controls. You learned how to use list boxes and combo boxes in Chapter 1. In this chapter, you learn how to use radio buttons and check boxes.

Using Radio Buttons

The `RadioButton` tool is used to add a **radio button** to an interface. A `RadioButton` control allows you to limit the user to only one choice in a group of two or more choices. `GroupBox` controls are used so that only one radio button can be selected in each group.

Important properties of a radio button are `Checked` (indicating whether the radio button is selected or not), `Name` (a meaningful name given to the radio button), and `Text` (the text that appears with the radio button). Figure 2.32 displays the code for the Gentry Supplies application. When the appropriate state and delivery methods are selected, clicking the Display Shipping Charge button will cause the correct shipping charge to display in the label. Figure 2.33 shows the result for shipping to Louisiana overnight.

```
' Project name:         Gentry Supplies Project
' Project purpose:      The project displays a shipping charge
'                       based on the state and delivery method.
' Created/revised by:   <your name> on <current date>

Option Explicit On
Option Strict On

Public Class MainForm
    Private Sub displayButton_Click(ByVal sender As Object, _
        ByVal e As System.EventArgs) Handles displayButton.Click
        ' displays the appropriate shipping charge
        Dim shipCharge As Integer

        ' determine state shipping charge
        If alabamaRadioButton.Checked Then
            shipCharge = 20
        ElseIf georgiaRadioButton.Checked Then
            shipCharge = 35
        ElseIf louisianaRadioButton.Checked Then
            shipCharge = 30
        Else
            shipCharge = 28
        End If

        ' add $10 for overnight delivery
        If overnightRadioButton.Checked Then
            shipCharge = shipCharge + 10
        End If

        ' display shipping charge
        shipLabel.Text = shipCharge.ToString("C2")
    End Sub

    Private Sub exitButton_Click(ByVal sender As Object, _
    ByVal e As System.EventArgs) Handles exitButton.Click
        Me.Close()
    End Sub
End Class
```

FIGURE 2.32 Program code for the Gentry Supplies application

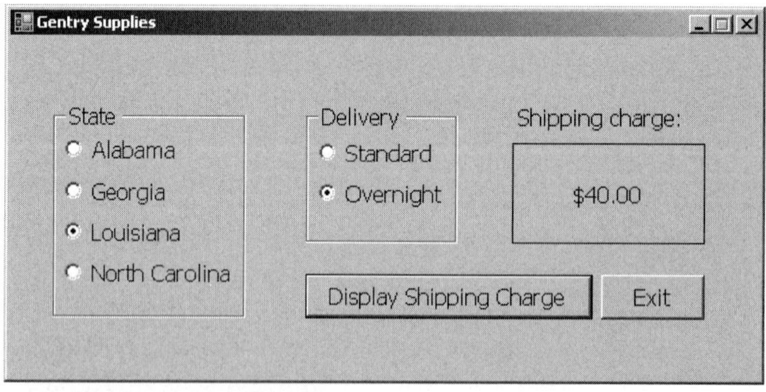

FIGURE 2.33 Sample run of the Gentry Supplies application

It is a common practice in Windows applications to have one of the radio buttons in each group already selected when the user interface first appears. The selected button is called the default radio button and is either the radio button that represents the user's most likely choice or the first radio button in the group. If you don't want to bias the user's selection, you may decide to have all radio buttons in the group deselected initially.

Using Check Boxes

The `CheckBox` tool in the toolbox adds a **check box** to an interface. Check boxes allow the user to select any number of choices from a group of one or more choices (not just one choice, as with radio buttons). Figure 2.34 displays a different interface for the Gentry Supplies application that uses a single check box if special overnight delivery is required. The code for this interface is identical to that in Figure 2.32 except that the expression `overnightRadioButton.Checked` is replaced by `overnightCheckBox.Checked`.

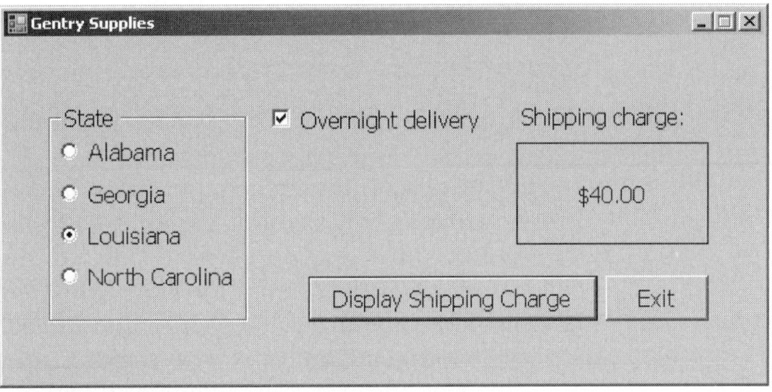

FIGURE 2.34 Sample run of the modified Gentry Supplies application

Sub AND Function PROCEDURES

Recall that a Visual Basic **procedure** is a block of program code that performs a specific task. Most procedures are either `Sub` procedures or `Function` procedures. The only difference between the two is that a **`Function` procedure** returns a value after performing its assigned task while a **`Sub` procedure** does not return a value.

Sub Procedures

There are two types of `Sub` procedures in Visual Basic: event procedures and independent `Sub` procedures. An **event procedure** is a `Sub` procedure that is associated with a specific object and event, such as a button's `Click` event or a text box's `TextChanged` event. (Event procedures are reviewed in Chapter 1.) An **independent `Sub` procedure** is a section of code that can be invoked (called) from one or more places in an application and is independent of any object and event—it is processed only when invoked from code. Figure 2.35 provides the syntax for an independent `Sub` procedure (which is identical to the syntax of an event procedure).

HOW TO...

Create an Independent Sub Procedure

Syntax

```
Private Sub procedureName([parameterList])
   [statements]
End Sub
```

Example

```
Private Sub ClearLabels()
    ' removes the contents of the labels that
    ' display the regular, overtime, and gross pay
    regularLabel.Text = String.Empty
    overtimeLabel.Text = String.Empty
    grossLabel.Text = String.Empty
End Sub
```

FIGURE 2.35 How to create an independent `Sub` procedure

In most cases, the independent `Sub` procedure header begins with the keyword `Private`, which indicates that the procedure can be used only by the other procedures in the current class (or form). A procedure must have a *procedureName*—the convention is to use Pascal case, where the first letter in each word is capitalized. The name should be descriptive and should begin with a verb denoting action (`CalculateTotal`, for example).

Following the procedure name in the procedure header is a set of parentheses that contains an optional *parameterList*. The parameter list consists of the data type and name of one or more variables. This combination of data type and variable name in a parameter list is called a **parameter**. The parameters store the information passed to the procedure when it is called. The parameter list also specifies how each parameter is passed—either by value or by reference. You learn more about the parameter list, and about passing information by value and by reference, later in this section.

The independent `Sub` procedure in Figure 2.35 does not have a parameter list because it does not need to receive any data to do its job. When the procedure `clearLabels()` is called from elsewhere in an application, it will assign empty strings to the `Text` property of three labels.

You can invoke an independent `Sub` procedure using the `Call` statement. Figure 2.36 shows the syntax for a `Call` statement.

HOW TO...

Call an Independent Sub Procedure

Syntax

```
Call procedureName([argumentList])
```

Example

```
Call ClearLabels()
```

FIGURE 2.36 How to call an independent `Sub` procedure

In Figure 2.36, *procedureName* is the name of the procedure you are invoking. (calling). The *argumentList* is a comma-separated list of arguments you want passed to the procedure. An argument list is required only if the called `Sub` procedure has a parameter list. In that case, the number and type of arguments in the argument list must exactly match the number and type of parameters in the parameter list.

The Gadis Antiques application in Figure 2.37 uses an independent `Sub` procedure called `ClearLabels` to clear the contents of three labels. Note that the `ClearLabels` procedure is called by three different event procedures. Doing so saves the code in `ClearLabels` from being repeated within each of these event procedures. (This is a better way of writing code.) Note in Figure 2.37 that the `ClearLabels Sub` procedure is written first. By convention, the independent `Sub` procedures go either before or after the event procedures within a form. Figure 2.38 shows a sample run of this application.

```
' Project name:          Gadis Antiques Project
' Project purpose:       The project calculates an employee's
'                        regular, overtime, and gross pay
' Created/revised by:    <your name> on <current date>

Option Strict On
Option Explicit On

Public Class MainForm
    Private Sub ClearLabels() ' independent Sub procedure
        ' clears the labels that display the
        ' regular, overtime, and gross pay
        regularLabel.Text = String.Empty
        overtimeLabel.Text = String.Empty
        grossLabel.Text = String.Empty
    End Sub

    Private Sub MainForm_Load(ByVal sender As Object, _
        ByVal e As System.EventArgs) Handles Me.Load
        ' fills the combo boxes with values
        For hours As Decimal = 30D To 50D Step 0.5D
            hoursComboBox.Items.Add(hours.ToString("N1"))
        Next hours

        For rates As Decimal = 7.75D To 12.5D Step 0.25D
            rateComboBox.Items.Add(rates.ToString("N2"))
        Next rates
    End Sub

    Private Sub calcButton_Click(ByVal sender As Object, _
        ByVal e As System.EventArgs) Handles calcButton.Click
        ' calculates the regular pay, overtime pay,
        ' and gross pay

        Const Message As String = _
            "The hours and rate entries must be numeric."
        Dim hoursWorked As Decimal
        Dim payRate As Decimal
        Dim regularPay As Decimal
        Dim overtimePay As Decimal
        Dim grossPay As Decimal
        Dim isConvertedHours As Boolean
        Dim isConvertedRate As Boolean

```

(Figure is continued on next page)

```
        ' convert input to Decimal
        isConvertedHours = _
            Decimal.TryParse(hoursComboBox.Text, hoursWorked)
        isConvertedRate = _
            Decimal.TryParse(rateComboBox.Text, payRate)

        ' if input can be converted to a number,
        ' perform calculations and display results
        ' otherwise, clear labels and display message
        If isConvertedHours AndAlso isConvertedRate Then
            If hoursWorked <= 40D Then
                ' calculate regular pay only
                regularPay = hoursWorked * payRate
            Else
                ' calculate regular and overtime pay
                regularPay = 40 * payRate
                overtimePay = (hoursWorked - 40) * payRate * 1.5D
            End If

            ' calculate gross pay
            grossPay = regularPay + overtimePay

            ' display calculated results
            regularLabel.Text = regularPay.ToString("N2")
            overtimeLabel.Text = overtimePay.ToString("N2")
            grossLabel.Text = grossPay.ToString("N2")
        Else
            MessageBox.Show(Message, "Gadis Antiques", _
                MessageBoxButtons.OK, MessageBoxIcon.Information)
        End If

    End Sub

    Private Sub exitButton_Click(ByVal sender As Object, _
        ByVal e As System.EventArgs) Handles exitButton.Click
        Me.Close()
    End Sub

    Private Sub clearButton_Click(ByVal sender As Object, _
        ByVal e As System.EventArgs) Handles clearButton.Click
        Call ClearLabels()
    End Sub

    Private Sub hoursComboBox_TextChanged(ByVal sender As Object, _
        ByVal e As System.EventArgs) Handles hoursComboBox.TextChanged
        Call ClearLabels()
    End Sub

    Private Sub rateComboBox_TextChanged(ByVal sender As Object, _
        ByVal e As System.EventArgs) Handles rateComboBox.TextChanged
        Call ClearLabels()
    End Sub
End Class
```

FIGURE 2.37 Program code for the Gadis Antiques application

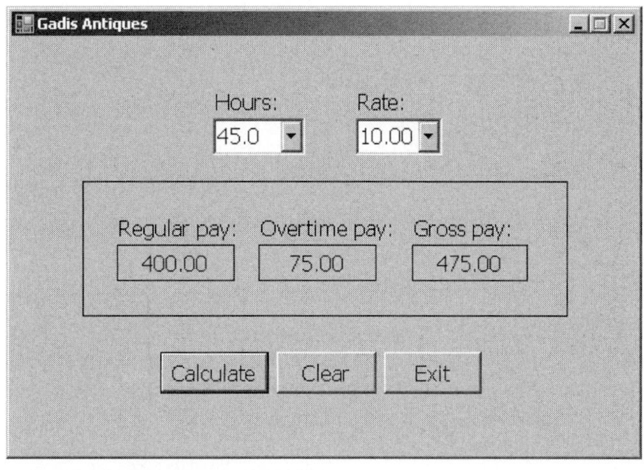

FIGURE 2.38 Sample run of the Gadis Antiques application

Including Parameters in an Independent `Sub` Procedure

The `Call` statements in Figure 2.37 do not have an argument list (the parentheses following the procedure name are empty). However, many `Call` statements do have an argument list, as you will see in the following examples. A `Call` statement uses the argument list to pass information to a procedure when necessary. Recall that the number of arguments listed in the argument list must agree with the number of parameters listed in the parameter list in the procedure header. In addition, the data type and position of each parameter in the parameter list must agree with the data type and position of its corresponding argument in the parameter list. You can pass a literal constant, named constant, keyword, or variable to an independent `Sub` procedure; in most cases, you will pass a variable. You will see an example of `Sub` procedure parameters shortly.

Passing Variables to a `Sub` Procedure

Each variable declared in an application has both a value and a unique memory address. A procedure call allows you to pass either the variable's value or its address to the receiving procedure. Passing a variable's value is referred to as **passing by value**, while passing a variable's memory address is referred to as **passing by reference**. Passing by value simply gives a procedure a value with which to work, but does not grant it access to the variable where the value is stored. Passing by reference gives a procedure access to the variable, which includes the ability to change its contents. Further explanation of this important point follows.

Passing by Value

To pass a variable by value in Visual Basic, you include the keyword `ByVal` before the variable's corresponding parameter in the procedure's parameter list. When you pass a variable by value, the computer passes only the contents of the variable (its value) to the receiving procedure. Figure 2.39 provides an example of passing by value and Figure 2.40 shows a sample run.

```
' Project name:         Pet Information Project
' Project purpose:      The project displays a message
'                       that contains a pet's name and age.
' Created/revised by:   <your name> on <current date>

Option Explicit On
Option Strict On

Public Class MainForm
    ' independent Sub procedure
    Private Sub DisplayMessage(ByVal pet As String, _
        ByVal years As String)
        ' displays the pet information passed to it
        messageLabel.Text = "Your pet " & pet & " is " _
            & years & " years old."
    End Sub

    Private Sub getInfoButton_Click(ByVal sender As Object, _
        ByVal e As System.EventArgs) Handles getInfoButton.Click
        ' gets the pet information, then displays the
        ' information in a message
        Dim petName As String
        Dim petAge As String

        petName = InputBox("Pet's name:", "Name Entry")
        petAge = InputBox("Pet's age (years):", "Age Entry")

        Call DisplayMessage(petName, petAge) ' procedure call
    End Sub

    Private Sub exitButton_Click(ByVal sender As Object, _
        ByVal e As System.EventArgs) Handles exitButton.Click
        Me.Close()
    End Sub
End Class
```

FIGURE 2.39 Program code for the Pet Information application

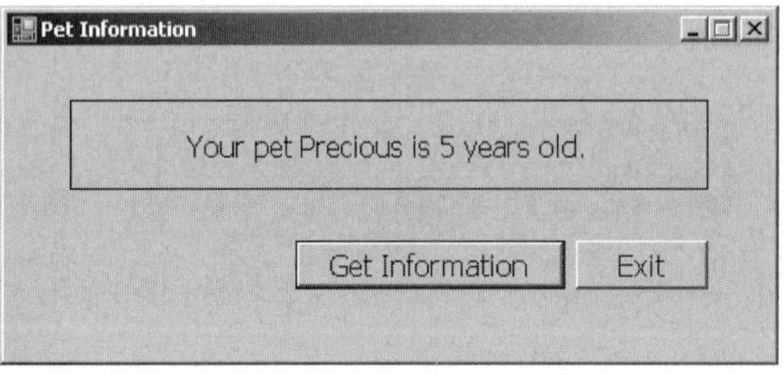

FIGURE 2.40 Sample run of the Pet Information application

Note that the `getInfoButton_Click` event procedure gets the pet's name and age using two input boxes. Then the `Call` statement calls the `DisplayMessage` procedure with arguments `petName` and `petAge` (both are `String` variables). The `DisplayMessage` procedure has two parameters with `String` variables `pet` and `age` that receive the values of `petName` and `petAge`, respectively (because of the keyword `ByVal`). The `DisplayMessage` procedure then simply displays this information in a label.

Note that the variables in the argument list of the procedure that call for `DisplayMessage` (`petName` and `petAge`) do not have the same name as the variables in the parameter list of `DisplayMessage` (`pet` and `age`). All these variables have only local scope, so the corresponding variables (`pet/petName` and `age/petAge`) could use the same name without conflict. They would have the same name but actually would be different memory locations. However, different names are often used in procedure calls and procedure definitions to avoid confusion.

TIP

When a program passes a variable by value, it is not really passing the variable (a memory location); it is passing a value (Integer, Decimal, Char, Boolean, etc.), leaving the variable unchanged. When a program passes a variable by reference, it is actually passing the entire variable (memory location), so changes made to the variable are permanent.

Passing Variables by Reference

Passing a variable's memory address, not the variable's value, is referred to as passing by reference, and it gives the receiving procedure total access to the variable being passed. To pass a variable by reference in Visual Basic, you include the keyword `ByRef` before the variable's corresponding parameter in the receiving procedure's header. The `ByRef` keyword tells the program to pass the variable's address rather than its value.

It is very important to understand what happens when a variable is passed by reference. Figure 2.41 has code for an independent `Sub` procedure called `CalcGrossPay` and an event procedure called `calcButton_Click`. When `calcButton` is clicked, three variables are declared, user input is received, and a `Call` statement passes three variables to the `CalcGrossPay` procedure. This procedure receives `hoursWkd` and `rateOfPay` by value, storing these values in the variables `hours` and `rate`, respectively. But the variable `grossPay` is passed by reference. This means that the variable `gross` in the `CalcGrossPay` procedure refers to the same memory address as `grossPay` in `calcButton_Click`. Thus, any change made to `gross` in `CalcGrossPay` will also be reflected in the variable `grossPay` in `calcButton_Click`. After the `Call` statement in `calcButton_Click` executes, the content of `grossPay` is displayed in `grossLabel`, which is the value assigned to `gross` in `CalcGrossPay`. Figure 2.42 shows a sample run of the Gross Pay application.

```
' Project name:         Gross Pay Project
' Project purpose:      The project calculates gross pay.
' Created/revised by:   <your name> on <current date>

Option Explicit On
Option Strict On

Public Class MainForm
    ' CalcGrossPay has one purpose: calculate gross pay
    Private Sub CalcGrossPay(ByVal hours As Decimal, _
                             ByVal rate As Decimal, _
                             ByRef gross As Decimal)
        ' calculates gross pay
        If hours <= 40D Then
            gross = hours * rate
        Else
            gross = hours * rate + (hours - 40D) * rate / 2D
        End If
    End Sub

    Private Sub MainForm_Load(ByVal sender As Object, _
        ByVal e As System.EventArgs) Handles Me.Load
        ' fills list boxes with values, then
        ' selects a default item
        For hours As Decimal = 0.5D To 50D Step 0.5D
            hoursListBox.Items.Add(hours.ToString)
```

(Figure is continued on next page)

```
        Next hours

        For rates As Decimal = 7.25D To 10.5D Step 0.25D
            rateListBox.Items.Add(rates.ToString)
        Next rates

        hoursListBox.SelectedItem = "40.0"
        rateListBox.SelectedIndex = 0
    End Sub

    Private Sub calcButton_Click(ByVal sender As Object, _
        ByVal e As System.EventArgs) Handles calcButton.Click
        ' calculates and displays a gross pay amount
        Dim hoursWkd As Decimal
        Dim rateOfPay As Decimal
        Dim grossPay As Decimal

        hoursWkd = Convert.ToDecimal(hoursListBox.SelectedItem)
        rateOfPay = Convert.ToDecimal(rateListBox.SelectedItem)

        Call CalcGrossPay(hoursWkd, rateOfPay, grossPay)

        grossLabel.Text = grossPay.ToString("C2")
    End Sub

    Private Sub hoursListBox_SelectedValueChanged( _
        ByVal sender As Object, _
        ByVal e As System.EventArgs) _
        Handles hoursListBox.SelectedValueChanged
        grossLabel.Text = String.Empty
    End Sub

    Private Sub rateListBox_SelectedValueChanged( _
        ByVal sender As Object, _
        ByVal e As System.EventArgs) _
        Handles rateListBox.SelectedValueChanged
        grossLabel.Text = String.Empty
    End Sub

    Private Sub exitButton_Click(ByVal sender As Object, _
        ByVal e As System.EventArgs) Handles exitButton.Click
        Me.Close()
    End Sub
End Class
```

FIGURE 2.41 Program code for the Gross Pay application

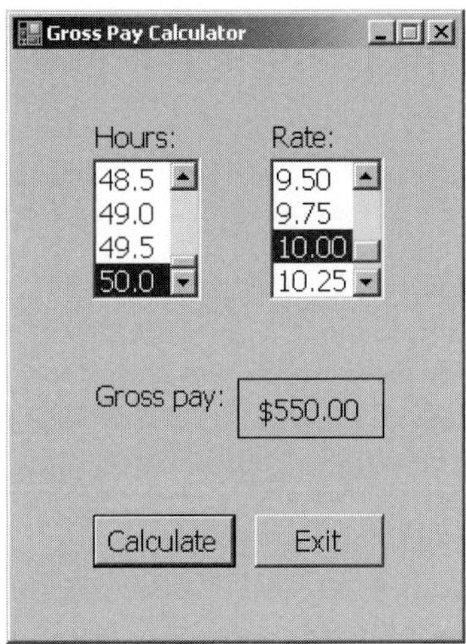

FIGURE 2.42 Sample run of the Gross Pay application

Associating a Procedure with Multiple Events

You may have noticed that the procedure header for an event procedure contains some strange-looking code. For example, the event procedure header for the `exitButton_Click` procedure in Figure 2.41 is as follows:

```
Private Sub exitButton_Click(ByVal sender As Object, _
    ByVal e As System.EventArgs) Handles exitButton.Click
```

The argument list contains the variables `sender` and `e`. The variable `sender` is an object that receives the memory address of the object that raised the event, in this case the `exitButton` control. The variable `e` contains additional event data (required by the event procedure) provided by the object that raised the event.

The event procedure header also contains a `Handles` clause, which consists of the `Handles` keyword followed by the button name, the dot operator, and the event name. In the previous example, the `exitButton_Click` event procedure header ends with the code `Handles exitButton.Click`. This indicates that the event procedure is associated with the object `exitButton` when the `Click` event occurs for this object. The name of the event procedure, `exitButton_Click` in this case, can be anything the programmer desires, although it is a convention to use the button name (`exitButton`) and the event (`Click`) separated by the underscore (_). The `Handles` clause adds the required functionality to the event procedure.

A `Handles` clause in a procedure can include several objects and events, as shown in the following code. (Compare this `ClearLabels` procedure to the one in Figure 2.37.) This `ClearLabels` procedure will be executed whenever the `clearButton` is clicked, the `hoursComboBox`'s text is changed, *or* the `rateComboBox`'s text is changed.

```
Private Sub ClearLabels(ByVal sender As Object, _
    ByVal e As System.EventArgs) _
    Handles clearButton.Click, hoursComboBox.TextChanged, _
    rateComboBox.TextChanged

    ' clears the labels that display the
    ' regular, overtime, and gross pay
    regularLabel.Text = String.Empty
```

```
        overtimeLabel.Text = String.Empty
        grossLabel.Text = String.Empty
    End Sub
```

The last three event procedures in Figure 2.37 would not be necessary if this code is used for the `ClearLabels` `Sub` procedure, making the Gadis Antiques application much simpler.

`Function` Procedures

Recall that a `Sub` procedure is a block of code that performs a specific task. A `Function` procedure, which is typically referred to simply as a **function**, is also a block of code that performs a specific task. However, unlike a `Sub` procedure, a function returns a value after completing its task.

Visual Basic has many built-in functions, such as the `InputBox` function, but you can write your own functions. The syntax for a function is similar to that for a `Sub` procedure but includes the keyword `Function` (instead of `Sub`), a return data type in the `As` *datatype* clause, a `Return` statement, and the footer `End Function`, as shown in Figure 2.43.

HOW TO...

Create a `Function` Procedure

Syntax

Private Function *procedurename*(*[parameterlist]*) **As** *datatype*
  [statements]
  Return *expression*
End Function

Example

```
Private Function CalcPriceWithTax(ByVal price As Decimal) As
Decimal
    ' calculates and returns a new price using the current
    ' price passed to it and a 5% price increase rate
    Return price * 1.05D
End Function
```

FIGURE 2.43 How to create a `Function` procedure

Figure 2.43 demonstrates a function called `CalcPriceWithTax`, which receives a value into the variable `price` and returns the `Decimal` value `price * 1.05D`. The `Return` statement alerts the application that the function has completed its task and ends the function after returning the value of its *expression*.

Note that the function `CalcPriceWithTax` would be called in an application by code such as the following:

```
priceAfterTax = CalcPriceWithTax(priceBeforeTax)
```

The *value* of the variable `priceBeforeTax` is passed to the `CalcPriceWithTax` function, which increases the value by 5% (the tax rate), assigning the result of the function call to the variable `priceAfterTax`. Note that it is the convention to use nouns when naming variables and to use verbs when naming procedures and functions. This is because variables usually represent things, and procedures/functions usually represent actions.

The Pine Lodge Application

The Pine Lodge application in Figure 2.44 demonstrates the two techniques just presented: (1) associating a procedure with multiple events, and (2) using a `Function` procedure. The owner of the Pine Lodge needs to calculate an employee's new hourly pay using the employee's current hourly pay and raise rate. Figure 2.44 presents the application's code and Figure 2.45 shows a sample run of the Pine Lodge application. You should study this application carefully to make sure you understand the differences between `Sub` procedures and `Function` procedures.

```
' Project name:         Pine Lodge Project
' Project purpose:      The project calculates an employee's
'                       new pay amount.
' Created/revised by:   <your name> on <current date>

Option Explicit On
Option Strict On

Public Class MainForm
    Private Function GetNewPay(ByVal current As Decimal, _
        ByVal rate As Decimal) As Decimal
        ' calculates and returns the new hourly pay based on
        ' the current hourly pay and raise rate passed to it
        Dim raise As Decimal
        Dim newPay As Decimal

        raise = current * rate
        newPay = current + raise

        Return newPay
    End Function

    Private Sub ClearLabel(ByVal sender As Object, _
        ByVal e As System.EventArgs) _
        Handles currentListBox.SelectedValueChanged, _
        rateListBox.SelectedValueChanged
        newPayLabel.Text = String.Empty
    End Sub

    Private Sub calcButton_Click(ByVal sender As Object, _
        ByVal e As System.EventArgs) Handles calcButton.Click
        ' calls a function to calculate an employee's new
        ' hourly pay, then displays the new hourly pay
        Dim currentPay As Decimal
        Dim rateChoice As String
        Dim raiseRate As Decimal
        Dim newHourlyPay As Decimal

        currentPay = Convert.ToDecimal(currentListBox.SelectedItem)
        rateChoice = rateListBox.SelectedItem.ToString.TrimEnd("%"c)
        raiseRate = Convert.ToDecimal(rateChoice) / 100D
        ' function call
        newHourlyPay = GetNewPay(currentPay, raiseRate)

        newPayLabel.Text = newHourlyPay.ToString("C2")
    End Sub

    Private Sub MainForm_Load(ByVal sender As Object, _
        ByVal e As System.EventArgs) Handles Me.Load
        ' fills the list boxes with values, then selects
        ' the first value

```

(Figure is continued on next page)

```
        For pay As Decimal = 7D To 12D Step 0.5D
            currentListBox.Items.Add(pay.ToString("N2"))
        Next pay

        For rate As Decimal = 0.02D To 0.11D Step 0.01D
            rateListBox.Items.Add(rate.ToString("P0"))
        Next rate

        currentListBox.SelectedIndex = 0
        rateListBox.SelectedIndex = 0
    End Sub

    Private Sub exitButton_Click(ByVal sender As Object, _
        ByVal e As System.EventArgs) Handles exitButton.Click
        Me.Close()
    End Sub
End Class
```

FIGURE 2.44 Program code for the Pine Lodge application

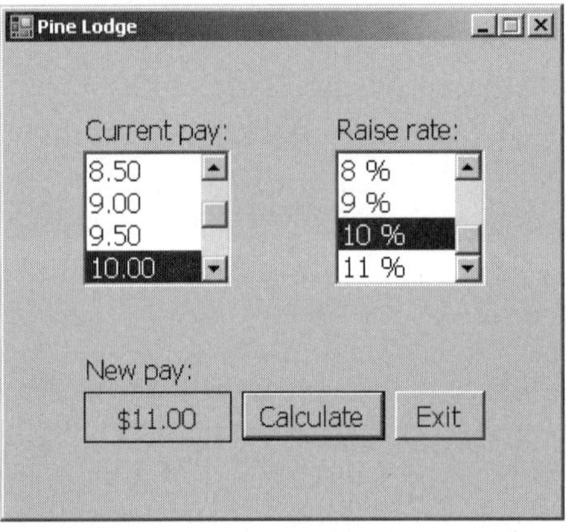

FIGURE 2.45 Sample run of the Pine Lodge application

ARRAYS

Recall that a variable is a location in memory. A **simple variable**, also called a **scalar variable**, is one that is unrelated to any other variable. In many applications, however, it is very useful to have a group of related variables, referred to as an array.

Using Arrays

An **array** is a group of variables that is given a name (the name of the array), and all variables in the group have the same data type. The variables in the array usually represent the same kind of entity, such as stock prices or people's names. It is convenient to temporarily store related data (such as tax tables or price lists) in arrays (in main memory) when an application needs to access such data many times. Accessing data in arrays is much faster than repeatedly accessing the data in a file on disk (secondary storage).

The two most common types of arrays are one-dimensional and two-dimensional, both of which are discussed in this section.

One-Dimensional Arrays

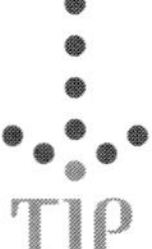

TIP

The variables in an array are stored in consecutive memory locations in the computer's internal memory.

You can think of a **one-dimensional** array as a column (or row) of variables. A unique number called a **subscript** identifies each variable (referred to as an **element**) in a one-dimensional array. It may be helpful to picture a one-dimensional array as a group of small, adjacent (consecutive) boxes inside the computer's memory, where each box is assigned a number starting with 0. Figure 2.46 illustrates these concepts with an array called `stockPrice` that has five variables, all of data type `Decimal`. These five elements could represent the closing price of a stock over five consecutive days.

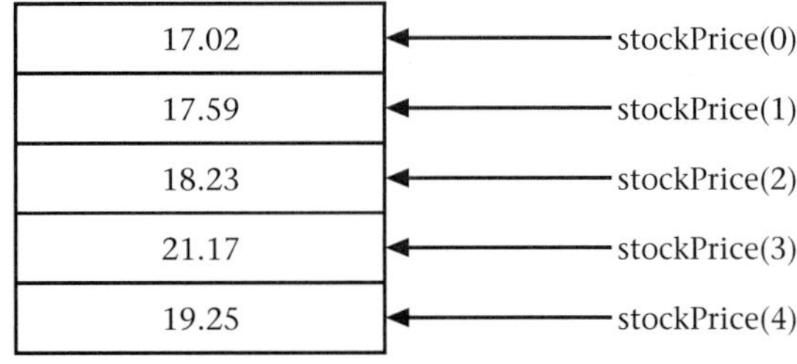

FIGURE 2.46 A `Decimal` array called `stockPrice` with five elements

TIP

A subscript is also called an index.

The computer assigns the subscripts to the array elements when the array is created. The first element in a one-dimensional array has a subscript of 0 (zero), the second a subscript of 1 (one), and so on. You refer to each element in an array by the array's name and the element's subscript. For example, to refer to the first element in a one-dimensional array named `stockPrice`, you use `stockPrice(0)`—read "stockPrice sub zero." Similarly, to refer to the fourth element in the array, you use `stockPrice(3)`.

Before you can use an array, you first must declare (create) it. The syntax for declaring an array is shown in Figure 2.47.

HOW TO...

Declare a One-Dimensional Array

Syntax – Version 1

{**Dim** | **Private**} *arrayName*(*highestSubscript*) **As** *datatype*

Example 1

```
' four String elements that contain Nothing
Dim cities(3) As String
```

Syntax – Version 2

{**Dim** | **Private**} *arrayName*() **As** *datatype* = {*initialValues*}

Example 2

```
' four Decimal elements that contain the values in the braces
Dim sales() As Decimal = {75.33D, 9.65D, 23.55D, 6.89D}
```

FIGURE 2.47 How to declare a one-dimensional array

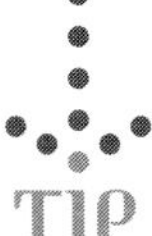

TIP

Assigning initial values to an array is often referred to as populating the array.

Version 1 of the syntax in Figure 2.47 declares an array called *arrayName* and reserves space in memory for a total number of *highestSubscript* + 1 elements, all of which have the same *datatype*. Version 2 declares the array and assigns the values within the braces to the array variables. The keyword `Dim` is used for procedure-level arrays while `Private` is used for module-level arrays.

In the case of the `String` array `cities` in Figure 2.47, the four elements are initialized with the value `Nothing`. The elements of numeric arrays declared with Version 1 are initialized with the value zero.

Storing Data in a One-Dimensional Array

Example 2 in Figure 2.47 shows the way to populate an array when it is first declared. However, you will often need to store data in an array after it has been declared. Figure 2.48 presents the syntax for assigning values to array elements.

HOW TO...

Store Data in a One-Dimensional Array

Syntax

arrayName(*subscript*) = *value*

Example 1

```
cities(0) = "Madrid"
cities(1) = "Paris"
cities(2) = "Rome"
```

Example 2

```
For x As Integer = 1 To 6
    numbers(x - 1) = x * x
Next x
```

Example 3

```
isConverted = Decimal.TryParse(salesTextBox.Text, sales(0))
```

FIGURE 2.48 How to store data in a one-dimensional array

In Example 1 in Figure 2.48, the array `cities` has each array element assigned a literal string value individually. In Example 2, a `For...Next` loop is used to assign the squared values of the integers 1 through 6 to the elements of the `squares` array. Note that if `x` is 1, the first array element is `numbers(x - 1)` or `numbers(0)`. In Example 3, the `TryParse` method assigns the string in `salesTextBox` (converted to `Decimal`) to the first element of the `sales` array.

Manipulating One-Dimensional Arrays

The variables (elements) in an array can be used just like any other variables. In many cases, the key to accessing these array elements is in using the subscripts. In the next several sections, you view sample procedures that demonstrate how one-dimensional arrays are used in applications.

Displaying the Contents of a One-Dimensional Array

Figure 2.49 shows the code for the Months application and Figure 2.50 displays a sample run. Note that the `For...Next` loop uses a variable called `subscript` to access the elements of the `String` array `months`. The `monthsListBox.Items.Add` method adds a value from the array to the list box with each iteration of the loop. Also note that populating the list box is performed in the `MainForm_Load` event procedure.

```
' Project name:         Months Project
' Project purpose:      The project displays the contents of an
'                       array in a list box. It also displays
'                       the item selected in the list box.
' Created/revised by:   <your name> on <current date>

Option Explicit On
Option Strict On

Public Class MainForm
    Private Sub MainForm_Load(ByVal sender As Object, _
        ByVal e As System.EventArgs) Handles Me.Load
        ' fills the list box with array values, then selects
        ' the first item
        Dim months() As String = {"JAN", "FEB", "MAR", _
               "APR", "MAY", "JUN", "JUL", "AUG", "SEP", _
               "OCT", "NOV", "DEC"}

        For subscript As Integer = 0 To 11
            monthListBox.Items.Add(months(subscript))
        Next subscript

        monthListBox.SelectedIndex = 0
    End Sub

    Private Sub exitButton_Click(ByVal sender As Object, _
        ByVal e As System.EventArgs) Handles exitButton.Click
        Me.Close()
    End Sub

    Private Sub displayButton_Click(ByVal sender As Object, _
        ByVal e As System.EventArgs) Handles displayButton.Click
        selectedItemLabel.Text = monthListBox.SelectedItem.ToString
    End Sub

    Private Sub monthListBox_SelectedValueChanged( _
        ByVal sender As Object, _
        ByVal e As System.EventArgs) _
        Handles monthListBox.SelectedValueChanged
        selectedItemLabel.Text = String.Empty
    End Sub
End Class
```

FIGURE 2.49 Program code for the Months application

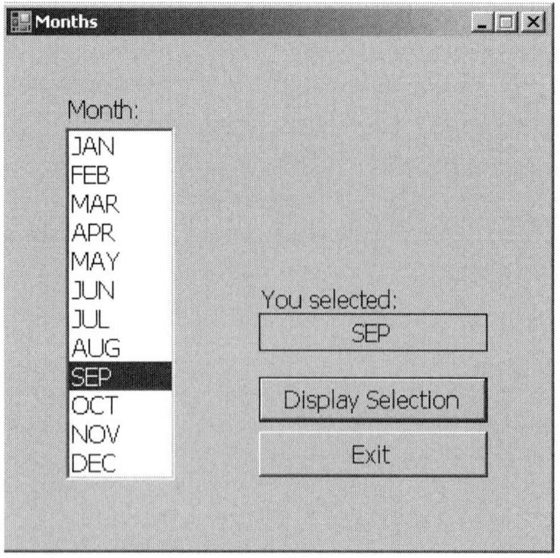

FIGURE 2.50 Sample run of the Months application

The `For Each...Next` Statement

You can use the `For Each...Next` statement to access each element in a group (such as an array) without explicitly using the subscripts of the group elements, making the process a little easier. The syntax of `For Each...Next` is shown in Figure 2.51.

HOW TO...

Use the `For Each...Next` Statement

Syntax

`For Each` *element* [**`As`** *datatype*] **`In`** *group*
  [*statements*]
`Next` *element*

Example

```
Dim monthName As String

For Each monthName In months
    monthListBox.Items.Add(monthName)
Next monthName
```

FIGURE 2.51 How to use the **`For Each...Next`** statement

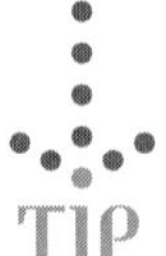

TIP

You can nest `For Each...Next` statements, which means that you can place one `For Each...Next` statement within another `For Each...Next` statement.

As Figure 2.51 shows, the `For Each...Next` statement begins with a `For Each` clause and ends with a `Next` clause. *Element* is the name of a variable that holds the contents of each array element, and *group* is the name of the array. The optional syntax **As** *datatype* is used if the *element* is to have block scope only (that is, scope only within the loop). In this case, the data type of the *element* must match the data type of the *group*. The code in Figure 2.51 could replace the `For...Next` loop in Figure 2.49. Note that in Figure 2.51, `monthName` will have procedure scope because it is declared in a `Dim` statement, not in the `For Each` clause.

Calculating the Average of One-Dimensional Numeric Array Elements

Summing the elements of a numeric array and finding their average is very straightforward using a `For Each...Next` statement, an accumulator variable, and the `Length` property of an array. The syntax *arrayName*.`Length` returns the number of elements in *arrayName*. The Average application in Figures 2.52 and 2.53 demonstrates these techniques. Note that the array `scores` is declared and values are assigned in the first statement of the `calcButton_click` procedure. A `For Each...Next` statement sums each value of scores in the variable `scoresAccumulator`. After the loop, `scoresAccumulator` and `scores.Length` are used to calculate `averageScore`, which is then displayed in `averageLabel`.

```
' Project name:          Average Project
' Project purpose:       The project calculates and displays
'                        the average of the test scores stored
'                        in an array.
' Created/revised by:    <your name> on <current date>

Option Explicit On
Option Strict On

Public Class MainForm
    Private Sub calcButton_Click(ByVal sender As Object, _
        ByVal e As System.EventArgs) Handles calcButton.Click
        ' calculates and displays the average test score
        Dim scores() As Integer = {98, 100, 56, 74, 35}
        Dim scoresAccumulator As Integer
        Dim averageScore As Double

        ' accumulate scores
        For Each score As Integer In scores
            scoresAccumulator += score
        Next score

        ' calculate and display the average score
        averageScore = scoresAccumulator / scores.Length
        averageLabel.Text = Convert.ToString(averageScore)
    End Sub

    Private Sub exitButton_Click(ByVal sender As Object, _
        ByVal e As System.EventArgs) Handles exitButton.Click
        Me.Close()
    End Sub
End Class
```

FIGURE 2.52 Program code for the Average application

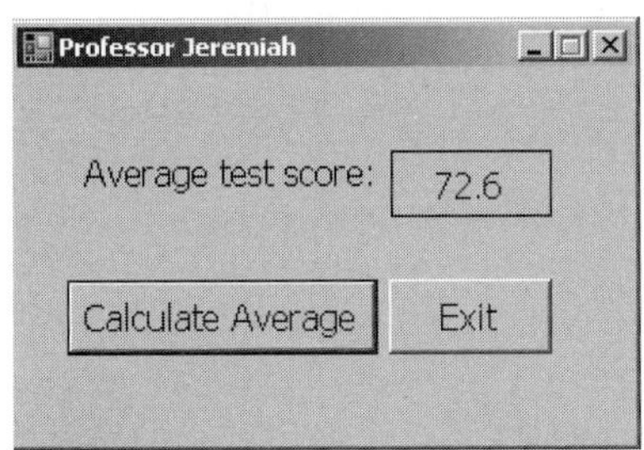

FIGURE 2.53 Sample run of the Average application

Determining the Highest Value Stored in a One-Dimensional Array

The Pay application in Figures 2.54 and 2.55 demonstrates how to find the maximum value of an array using array subscripts. (Note that you could accomplish the same thing without subscripts using the `For Each...Next` statement.) In the `displayHighButton_Click` procedure, the array `pays` is declared and initialized with five values. Then the variable `highestPay` is initially assigned `pay(0)`. The `For...Next` loop then compares `pay(1)` with `highestPay`. If it is greater than the current value of `highestPay`, then `highestPay` is assigned `pay(1)`, and the loop continues. Notice that the loop shown in Figure 2.54 begins with subscript 1, not 0. The first element is not included in the search because it is already stored in the `highestPay` variable.

```
' Project name:          Pay Project
' Project purpose:       The project displays the highest pay
'                        amount stored in an array.
' Created/revised by:    <your name> on <current date>

Option Explicit On
Option Strict On

Public Class MainForm
    Private Sub displayHighButton_Click(ByVal sender As Object, _
        ByVal e As System.EventArgs) Handles displayHighButton.Click
        ' displays the highest amount stored in an array
        Dim pays() As Decimal = {25.6D, 30.25D, 50D, 20D, 25.45D}
        Dim highestPay As Decimal = pays(0)

        ' search the array, beginning with the second element
        For subscript As Integer = 1 To pays.Length - 1
            If pays(subscript) > highestPay Then
                ' store the higher value in the highestPay variable
                highestPay = pays(subscript)
            End If
        Next subscript

        ' displays the highest value
        highestLabel.Text = highestPay.ToString("C2")
    End Sub

    Private Sub exitButton_Click(ByVal sender As Object, _
        ByVal e As System.EventArgs) Handles exitButton.Click
        Me.Close()
    End Sub
End Class
```

FIGURE 2.54 Program code for the Pay application

TIP

When writing code that accesses an array element, you should always verify that the subscript will be valid—in other words, that it will be in range. If the procedure uses a subscript that is not in range, Visual Basic displays an error message and the procedure ends abruptly.

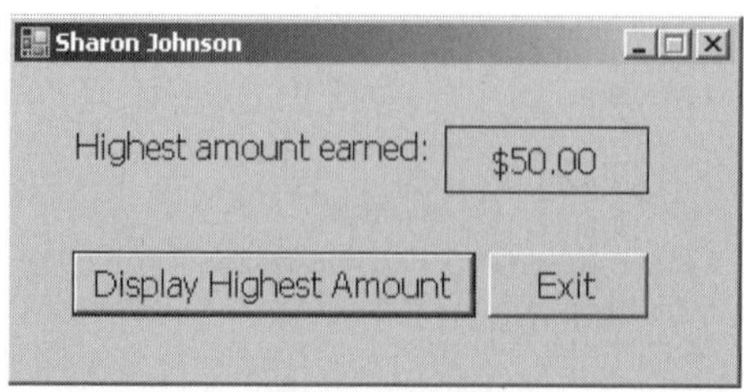

FIGURE 2.55 Sample run of the Pay application

Sorting the Data Stored in a One-Dimensional Array

In some applications, you may need to sort the contents of an array in either ascending or descending order. You use the `Array.Sort` method to sort the elements in a one-dimensional array in ascending order. The method's syntax is `Array.Sort(`*arrayName*`)`, where *arrayName* is the name of the one-dimensional array to be sorted. To sort a one-dimensional array in descending order, you first use the `Array.Sort` method to sort the array in ascending order, and then use the `Array.Reverse` method to reverse the array elements. The syntax of the `Array.Reverse` method is `Array.Reverse(`*arrayName*`)`.

The State application shown in Figures 2.56 and 2.57 allows the user to enter five state names (in input boxes), and then sort them in either ascending or descending order. Note that the array `stateNames` is declared as a module-level variable, which allows it to be used in both the `sortAscendButton_Click` and the `sortDescendButton_Click` event procedures.

```
' Project name:          State Project
' Project purpose:       The project allows the user to enter
'                        state names. It then sorts the names
'                        in ascending or descending order and
'                        displays them in the stateLabel.
' Created/revised by:    <your name> on <current date>

Option Explicit On
Option Strict On

Public Class MainForm
    ' module-level array contains 5 elements
    Private stateNames(4) As String

    Private Sub enterButton_Click(ByVal sender As Object, _
        ByVal e As System.EventArgs) Handles enterButton.Click
        ' allows the user to enter five state names
        ' stores the state names in the module-level
        ' stateNames array
        For subscript As Integer = 0 To stateNames.Length - 1
            stateNames(subscript) = _
                InputBox("State name", "State Names")
        Next subscript
    End Sub

    Private Sub sortAscendButton_Click(ByVal sender As Object, _
        ByVal e As System.EventArgs) Handles sortAscendButton.Click
        ' sorts the array values in ascending order, then
        ' displays them in the stateLabel
        Array.Sort(stateNames)

        stateLabel.Text = String.Empty
        For Each name As String In stateNames
            stateLabel.Text = _
                stateLabel.Text & name & ControlChars.NewLine
        Next name
    End Sub

    Private Sub sortDescendButton_Click(ByVal sender As Object, _
        ByVal e As System.EventArgs) Handles sortDescendButton.Click
        ' sorts the array values in descending order, then
        ' displays them in the stateLabel
        Array.Sort(stateNames)
        Array.Reverse(stateNames)

```

(Figure is continued on next page)

```
        stateLabel.Text = String.Empty
        For Each name As String In stateNames
            stateLabel.Text = _
                stateLabel.Text & name & ControlChars.NewLine
        Next name
    End Sub

    Private Sub exitButton_Click(ByVal sender As Object, _
        ByVal e As System.EventArgs) Handles exitButton.Click
        Me.Close()
    End Sub
End Class
```

FIGURE 2.56 Program code for the State application

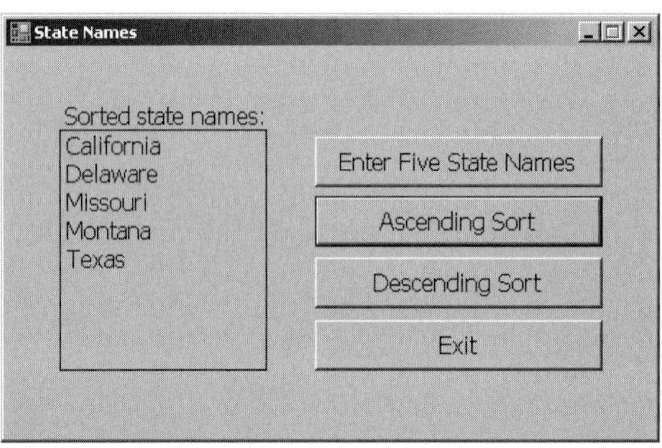

FIGURE 2.57 Sample run of the State application

Parallel One-Dimensional Arrays

TIP

Recall that an array's `Length` property stores the number of elements in the array and is always one number more than the highest subscript in the array.

Many times an application needs to keep track of two or more kinds of information for each of several different entities. For example, a company may have several employees (entities) and needs to keep records of each employee's ID number, name, and address. Such information about employees could be stored in three different but parallel arrays, such as `employeeID`, `employeeName`, and `employeeAddress`. **Parallel arrays** are two or more arrays whose elements are related by their positions in the arrays. Arrays are said to be parallel because each corresponding element of the separate arrays belongs to a single entity—for example, the third element of `employeeID`, `employeeName`, and `employeeAddress` must all refer to the same employee.

The Price List application in Figure 2.58 contains two parallel arrays, `ids` and `prices`, both referring to various products. Obviously, these arrays must be parallel in order for the correct price to be associated with a particular product ID. The `Do Until` loop iterates through the entire `ids` array if the ID entered by the user is not found, or terminates when the desired ID is found. If the user enters a valid product ID in the text box and clicks the Display Price button, the price will appear in the label, as shown in Figure 2.59(a). If the product ID is not valid, a message will be displayed, as seen in Figure 2.59(b).

```
' Project name:          Price List Project
' Project purpose:       The project displays the price
'                        associated with a product ID.
' Created/revised by:    <your name> on <current date>

Option Explicit On
Option Strict On

Public Class MainForm
    Private Sub displayButton_Click(ByVal sender As Object, _
        ByVal e As System.EventArgs) Handles displayButton.Click
        ' displays the price associated with the product
        ' ID entered by the user
        Dim ids() As String = {"BX35", "CR20", "FE15", "KW10", "MM67"}
        Dim prices() As Integer = {13, 10, 12, 24, 4}
        Dim searchFor As String
        Dim subscript As Integer

        ' assign the product ID to a variable
        searchFor = idTextBox.Text

        ' search the ids array for the product ID;
        ' continue searching until there are no more array
        ' elements to search or the product ID is found
        Do Until subscript = ids.Length _
            OrElse searchFor = ids(subscript)
            subscript = subscript + 1
        Loop

        ' determine whether the product ID
        ' was found in the ids array
        If subscript < ids.Length Then
            priceLabel.Text = prices(subscript).ToString("C0")
        Else
            MessageBox.Show("Invalid product ID.", _
                "Treasures Gift Shop", MessageBoxButtons.OK, _
                MessageBoxIcon.Information)
        End If

        idTextBox.Focus()
    End Sub

    Private Sub exitButton_Click(ByVal sender As Object, _
        ByVal e As System.EventArgs) Handles exitButton.Click
        Me.Close()
    End Sub

    Private Sub idTextBox_Enter(ByVal sender As Object, _
        ByVal e As System.EventArgs) Handles idTextBox.Enter
        idTextBox.SelectAll()
    End Sub

    Private Sub idTextBox_TextChanged(ByVal sender As Object, _
        ByVal e As System.EventArgs) Handles idTextBox.TextChanged
        priceLabel.Text = String.Empty
    End Sub
End Class
```

FIGURE 2.58 Program code for the Price List application

(a)

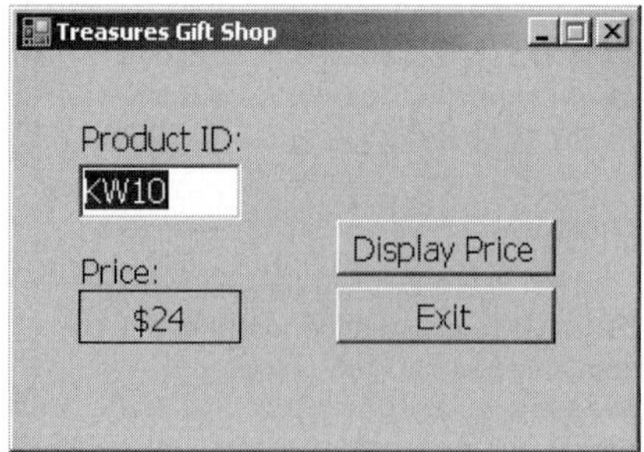

(b)

FIGURE 2.59 Sample run of the Price List application

Two-Dimensional Arrays

Recall that a one-dimensional array can represent data listed as a column of values. A **two-dimensional array**, however, can be viewed as a table of values with a fixed number of rows and columns. Figure 2.60 represents data in a table.

	Column 1: Product ID	Column 2: Product Description	Column 3: Product Color
Row 1	AC34	Shirt	Red
Row 2	BD12	Coat	White
Row 3	CP14	Blouse	Blue

FIGURE 2.60 Data displayed in a table format

The first column in Figure 2.60 represents product ID, the second column product description, and the third product color. Three different products have been added to the table, resulting in three rows (with each row representing a different product). You could use two subscripts to identify any particular value in a table. If the table is called "clothing", then clothing(1, 3)—read "clothing sub one comma three"—could represent the value in row 1, column 3, or "Red". The value in clothing(2, 2) is "Coat".

The data in Figure 2.60 can also be stored in a two-dimensional array called `clothing` that uses subscripts (however, subscripts in Visual Basic must begin with 0, not 1). The syntax for declaring two-dimensional arrays is shown in Figure 2.61.

HOW TO...

Declare a Two-Dimensional Array

Syntax - Version 1

{**`Dim`** | **`Private`**} *arrayName*`(`*highestRowSubscript, highestColumnSubscript*`)` **`As`** *datatype*

Example 1

```
Dim clothing(2, 2) As String
```

Syntax - Version 2

{**`Dim`** | **`Private`**} *arrayName*`(,)` **`As`** *datatype* `=` `{{`*initialValues*`}`,...`{`*initialValues*`}}`

Example 2

```
Dim clothing (,) As String = {{"AC34", "Shirt", "Red"}, _
                              {"BD12", "Coat", "Blue"}, _
                              {"CP14", "Blouse", "White"}}
```

FIGURE 2.61 How to declare a two-dimensional array

In Figure 2.61, the keywords **`Dim`** and **`Private`** are used to declare the array as either procedure-level or module-level, respectively. (Note that the data type for all elements in a two-dimensional array must be the same.) Example 1 of Figure 2.61 simply reserves space in memory for a three-row, three-column table of `String` values. Example 2 of Figure 2.61 indicates that a two-dimensional array is really a one-dimensional array whose elements are themselves one-dimensional arrays. Each of the three one-dimensional arrays in Example 2 represents a row in the clothing table. Also note that `clothing(0)` is a one-dimensional array with elements `{"AC34", "Shirt", "Red"}`.

Storing Data in a Two-Dimensional Array

After a two-dimensional array is declared (and possibly initialized), an application may need to store new data in the array. The syntax for assigning a value to a two-dimensional array element is *arrayName(rowSubscript, columnSubscript = value.* For example, if the shirt product in the array `clothing` now comes in only pink instead of red, the value of that array element would be changed using the following code (the first row has subscript 0 and the third column has subscript 2):

```
clothing(0, 2) = "Pink"
```

The following `For Each...Next` statement can be used to assign the empty string to each value in the clothing array:

```
For Each item As String In clothing
    item = String.Empty
Next item
```

Searching a Two-Dimensional Array

Figure 2.58 presents a Price List application that stores product IDs and product prices in two separate parallel arrays. Figure 2.62 shows the code for a modified Price List application that uses a two-dimensional array called `products` to store the same data. Note, however, that prices must be stored as the `String` data type—a single array must store all data using only one data type.

```
' Project name:        Price List Project
' Project purpose:     The project displays the price
'                      associated with a product ID.
' Created/revised by:  <your name> on <current date>

Option Explicit On
Option Strict On

Public Class MainForm
    Private Sub displayButton_Click(ByVal sender As Object, _
        ByVal e As System.EventArgs) Handles displayButton.Click
        ' displays the price associated with the product
        ' ID entered by the user
        Dim products(,) As String = {{"BX35", "13"}, _
                                     {"CR20", "10"}, _
                                     {"FE15", "12"}, _
                                     {"KW10", "24"}, _
                                     {"MM67", "4"}}
        Dim searchFor As String
        Dim row As Integer

        ' assign the product ID to a variable
        searchFor = idTextBox.Text

        ' search for the product ID in the first column
        ' of the products array; continue searching until
        ' there are no more array elements to search or
        ' the product ID is found
        Do Until row = 5 OrElse searchFor = products(row, 0)
            row = row + 1
        Loop

        ' determine whether the product ID
        ' was found in the ids array
        If row < 5 Then
            priceLabel.Text = "$" & products(row, 1)
        Else
            MessageBox.Show("Invalid product ID.", _
                "Treasures Gift Shop", MessageBoxButtons.OK, _
                MessageBoxIcon.Information)
        End If

        idTextBox.Focus()
    End Sub

    Private Sub idTextBox_Enter(ByVal sender As Object, _
        ByVal e As System.EventArgs) Handles idTextBox.Enter
        idTextBox.SelectAll()
    End Sub

    Private Sub idTextBox_TextChanged(ByVal sender As Object, _
        ByVal e As System.EventArgs) Handles idTextBox.TextChanged
        priceLabel.Text = String.Empty
    End Sub

    Private Sub exitButton_Click(ByVal sender As Object, _
        ByVal e As System.EventArgs) Handles exitButton.Click
        Me.Close()
    End Sub
End Class
```

FIGURE 2.62 Program code for the modified Price List application

The Do `Until loop` in Figure 2.62 now iterates through the different row values and terminates if the product ID in `products(row, 0)` matches the one stored in the variable `searchFor` (column 0 is the first column in the `products` array and contains product IDs). The `If...Then...Else` statement will display the price found in `products(row, 1)`—the subscript 1 corresponds to the second column in the array—or will display a message to the user if the product ID is not found. The output of the applications in Figures 2.58 and 2.62 will be the same.

STRUCTURES AND SEQUENTIAL ACCESS FILES

In these first two chapters, you use only the data types built into Visual Basic, such as the `Integer`, `Decimal`, and `String` data types. You also can create your own custom data types in Visual Basic using the `Structure` statement. Custom data types give the programmer more control and flexibility in defining and describing entities used in a program. For example, an application may need to define a `Student` data type or a `Product` data type, which cannot be expressed using Visual Basic's built-in data types alone.

Structures

A **structure** (also called a **user-defined data type**) is a data type consisting of a group of different members. The **structure members** can be variables, constants, or procedures. However, in most cases the members will be variables and are referred to as member variables.

You create a structure in Visual Basic with the `Structure` statement. The syntax for the `Structure` statement is provided in Figure 2.63.

HOW TO...

Create a `Structure` (User-Defined Data Type)

Syntax

`Structure` *structureName*
  `Public` *memberVariable1* **`As`** *datatype*
  [**`Public`** *memberVariableN* **`As`** *datatype*]
`End Structure`

Example

```
Structure Employee
    Public number As String
    Public firstName As String
    Public lastName As String
    Public salary As Decimal
End Structure
```

FIGURE 2.63 How to create a structure (user-defined data type)

In Figure 2.63, the members of the structure are declared between the `Structure` and `End Structure` clauses. The example in Figure 2.63 is an `Employee` structure with four member variables.

In most applications, you enter the `Structure` statement in the form's Declarations section in the Code Editor window. Recall that the form's Declarations section begins with the `Public Class` clause and ends with the `End Class` clause. After entering the `Structure` statement, you then can use the structure to declare a variable.

Using a Structure to Declare a Variable

Variables declared using a structure are often referred to as **structure variables**. The syntax for declaring a structure variable is very similar to that for declaring other variables, as follows:

`{Dim | Private}` *structureVariableName* **`As`** *structureName*

As always, the keyword `Dim` is used for procedure-level variables and `Private` is used for module-level variables. The only difference in this syntax is that *structureName* replaces the predefined *datatype*. This code declares the variable `manager` to be an `Employee` structure.

```
Dim manager As Employee
```

To refer to an individual member variable within a structure variable, you precede the member variable's name with the name of the structure variable in which it is defined. You use the dot member access operator (a period) to separate the structure variable's name from the member variable's name. For instance, the names of the member variables within the `manager` structure variable are `manager.number`, `manager.firstName`, `manager.lastName`, and `manager.salary`. Structure member variables can be used in the same way as any other variables.

Structures (user-defined data types) are used to group related items into one unit. The advantages of using structures will become more apparent as you read through the next two sections.

Passing a Structure Variable to a Procedure

This section discusses how to use structures in an application that calculates the volume of a rectangular swimming pool. Such a pool has the properties of `length`, `width`, and `depth`. The volume of the pool is determined by the formula `volume = length * width * depth`. Figure 2.64 provides the program code for the Pool application and Figure 2.65 shows a sample run.

```
' Project name:          Pool Project
' Project purpose:       The project calculates the volume
'                        of a rectangular pool.
' Created/revised by:    <your name> on <current date>

Option Explicit On
Option Strict On

Public Class MainForm
    Structure Dimensions
        Public length As Decimal
        Public width As Decimal
        Public depth As Decimal
    End Structure

    Private Sub calcButton_Click(ByVal sender As Object, _
    ByVal e As System.EventArgs) Handles calcButton.Click
```

(Figure is continued on next page)

```
        ' validates the user's input, then displays either
        ' the volume or an error message
        Dim poolDims As Dimensions
        Dim isValid As Boolean
        Dim poolVolume As Decimal

        isValid = ValidateInput(poolDims)

        If isValid = True Then
            poolVolume = CalcVolume(poolDims)
            volumeLabel.Text = Convert.ToString(poolVolume)
        Else
            MessageBox.Show("The pool measurements must be numeric.", _
                "Willow Pools", MessageBoxButtons.OK, _
                MessageBoxIcon.Information)
        End If
    End Sub

    Private Function ValidateInput(ByRef pool As Dimensions) As Boolean
        Dim isLenValid As Boolean
        Dim isWidValid As Boolean
        Dim isDepValid As Boolean
        ' convert strings in textboxes to Decimal
        isLenValid = Decimal.TryParse(lengthTextBox.Text, pool.length)
        isWidValid = Decimal.TryParse(widthTextBox.Text, pool.width)
        isDepValid = Decimal.TryParse(depthTextBox.Text, pool.depth)

        If isLenValid AndAlso isWidValid AndAlso isDepValid Then
            Return True
        Else
            Return False
        End If
    End Function

    Private Function CalcVolume(ByVal pool As Dimensions) As Decimal
        Return pool.length * pool.width * pool.depth
    End Function

    Private Sub SelectText(ByVal sender As Object, _
        ByVal e As System.EventArgs) _
        Handles lengthTextBox.Enter, widthTextBox.Enter, _
        depthTextBox.Enter
        Dim currentTextBox As TextBox
        currentTextBox = TryCast(sender, TextBox)
        currentTextBox.SelectAll()
    End Sub

    Private Sub ClearVolume(ByVal sender As Object, _
        ByVal e As System.EventArgs) _
        Handles lengthTextBox.TextChanged, widthTextBox.TextChanged, _
        depthTextBox.TextChanged
        volumeLabel.Text = String.Empty
    End Sub

    Private Sub exitButton_Click(ByVal sender As Object, _
        ByVal e As System.EventArgs) Handles exitButton.Click
        Me.Close()
    End Sub
End Class
```

FIGURE 2.64 Program code for the Pool application

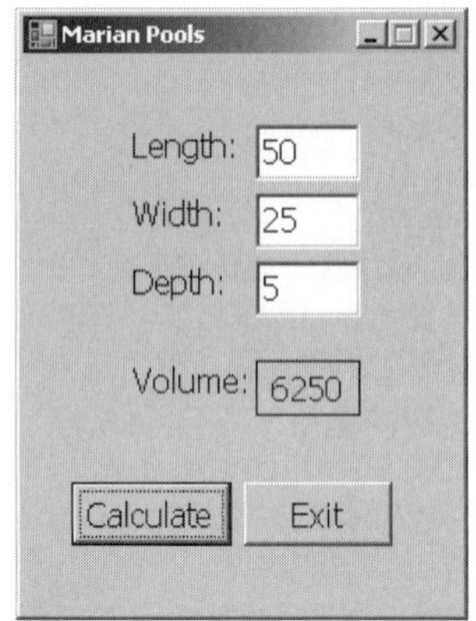

FIGURE 2.65 Sample run of the Pool application

Note first that the class `MainForm` begins by declaring a structure called `Dimensions` consisting of three `Decimal` member variables: `length`, `width`, and `depth`. Next, focus on the `calcButton_Click` procedure. It begins by declaring a `Dimensions` structure variable called `poolDims`. This variable is passed to the `ValidateInput` function by reference (that is, the actual variable is passed, not just the values in the variable), and the result of that function is stored in the `Boolean` variable `isValid`.

The `ValidateInput` function receives the reference to `poolDims`, naming it `pool`. Then the values entered by the user in `lengthTextBox`, `widthTextBox`, and `depthTextBox` are assigned to the `pool` member variables `pool.length`, `pool.width`, and `pool.depth`, respectively. If all three values are valid `Decimal` numbers (as determined by the `TryParse` method), the `ValidateInput` function returns the value `True` (`False`, otherwise) and control returns to the `calcButton_Click` procedure.

Within the `calcButton_Click` procedure, an `If / Else` statement tests the variable `isValid`. If it is `True`, the `poolDims` structure variable (which now contains valid values of `length`, `width`, and `depth`) is passed by value (that is, just the values are passed) to the `CalcVolume` function; otherwise, a message is displayed to the user. Within the `CalcVolume` function, the values of `poolDims.length`, `poolDims.width`, and `poolDims.depth` are stored in the `pool` structure variable and the product of the three member variables is returned to the `calcButton_Click` procedure, which displays the product in the `volumeLabel`.

Creating an Array of Structure Variables

Earlier in this chapter a Price List application was created using parallel arrays for product IDs and product prices (Figure 2.58). Then this application was modified to use one two-dimensional array instead (Figure 2.62). Parallel arrays and multi-dimensional arrays (arrays with two or more dimensions) can at times be awkward and/or confusing to use. Figure 2.66 shows how to code the Price List application using a simple one-dimensional array of structure variables. The output of this application will look the same as in previous versions, such as that displayed in Figure 2.59.

```
' Project name:         Price List Project
' Project purpose:      The project displays the price
'                       associated with a product ID.
' Created/revised by:   <your name> on <current date>

Option Explicit On
Option Strict On

Public Class MainForm
    Structure Item
        Public id As String
        Public price As Integer
    End Structure

    Private Sub displayButton_Click(ByVal sender As Object, _
        ByVal e As System.EventArgs) Handles displayButton.Click
        ' displays the price associated with the product
        ' ID entered by the user
        Dim searchFor As String
        Dim subscript As Integer

        ' declare an array of structure variables
        Dim gifts(4) As Item

        ' assign product IDs and prices to the array
        gifts(0).id = "BX35"
        gifts(0).price = 13
        gifts(1).id = "CR20"
        gifts(1).price = 10
        gifts(2).id = "FE15"
        gifts(2).price = 12
        gifts(3).id = "KW10"
        gifts(3).price = 24
        gifts(4).id = "MM67"
        gifts(4).price = 4

        ' assign the product ID to a variable
        searchFor = idTextBox.Text

        ' search the gifts array for the product ID
        ' continue searching until there are
        ' no more array elements to search or
        ' the product ID is found
        Do Until subscript = gifts.Length _
            OrElse searchFor = gifts(subscript).id
            subscript = subscript + 1
        Loop

        ' determine whether the product ID
        ' was found in the gifts array
        If subscript < gifts.Length Then
            priceLabel.Text = gifts(subscript).price.ToString("C0")
        Else
            MessageBox.Show("Invalid product ID.", _
                "Treasures Gift Shop", MessageBoxButtons.OK, _
                MessageBoxIcon.Information)
        End If

        idTextBox.Focus()
    End Sub

    Private Sub idTextBox_Enter(ByVal sender As Object, _
        ByVal e As System.EventArgs) Handles idTextBox.Enter
```

(Figure is continued on next page)

```
            idTextBox.SelectAll()
        End Sub

        Private Sub idTextBox_TextChanged(ByVal sender As Object, _
            ByVal e As System.EventArgs) Handles idTextBox.TextChanged
            priceLabel.Text = String.Empty
        End Sub

        Private Sub exitButton_Click(ByVal sender As Object, _
            ByVal e As System.EventArgs) Handles exitButton.Click
            Me.Close()
        End Sub
    End Class
```

FIGURE 2.66 Program code for the Price List application using an array of structure variables

Within the `MainForm` class, an `Item` structure variable, consisting of member variables `id` and `price`, is declared. The `displayButton_Click` event procedure declares a one-dimensional array called `gifts` that will hold five values of the `Item` data type. Then this array `gifts` is loaded using code such as `gifts(0).id = "BX35"` and `gifts(0).price = 13`. Notice that the `Do...Until` loop iterates through each of the `gifts` elements, trying to match the value of `id` with the value entered by the user and stored in the `searchFor` variable. The `If / Else` statement displays the price of the product if a valid ID is found. This application demonstrates how using structure variables can be easier than using parallel arrays or multidimensional arrays.

File Types

So far in this book, applications have received information from the keyboard or mouse and have sent information to the computer screen. However, an application may also need to get information from and send information to a file on a disk. Getting information from an **input file** is referred to as "reading the file," and sending information to an **output file** is referred to as "writing to the file."

Visual Basic can perform input and output with three kinds of files: sequential, random, and binary. Data in a **sequential access file** are always accessed in sequence from the beginning of the file through the end of the file. The data stored in a **random access file** (also called direct access) can be accessed directly without going from beginning to end. Information about where data are located is stored with the file. The data in a **binary access file** can be accessed by byte location in the file. This section deals only with sequential access files. Random access and binary access files are covered later in this book.

Sequential Access Files

A sequential access file is also referred to as a **text file**, because it is composed of lines of human-readable text. For example, the following employee list could be stored in a text file:

```
Bonnel, Jacob
Carlisle, Donald
Eberg, Jack
Hou, Chang
```

If these data are stored in a sequential access file, a fifth employee could be added to the file only after the fourth. It could not be inserted at the beginning or in the middle. If an application needs to retrieve the third employee from the file, it must begin by reading the first and second employees. Data can be accessed only sequentially.

Writing Information to a Sequential Access File

You can use the `WriteAllText` method to write information to a sequential access file. The syntax for this method is found in Figure 2.67.

HOW TO...

Write Information to a Sequential Access File

Syntax

`My.Computer.FileSystem.WriteAllText(`*file*`, `*text*`, `*append*`)`

Example

```
Dim file As String = "C:\VbReloadedAdv\Chap02\report.txt"
Dim price As Decimal = 5.6D
My.Computer.FileSystem.WriteAllText(file, "Total price: ", False)
My.Computer.FileSystem.WriteAllText(file, _
    Strings.Space(5) & price.ToString("C2") & _
    ControlChars.NewLine, True)
```

FIGURE 2.67 How to write information to a sequential access file

The `My` in the syntax shown in Figure 2.67 is a new feature in Visual Basic 2005. The `My` feature (actually, the `My` namespace) exposes a set of commonly used objects to the programmer. One of the objects exposed by the `My` feature is the `My.Computer` object. Using the `My.Computer` object, you can easily access the host computer and its resources, such as files. For example, the `My.Computer.FileSystem` object is used to call the `WriteAllText` method in Figure 2.67.

For the `WriteAllText` method, the argument *file* is a string containing the file path and name of the sequential access file to which the string *text* is written. If the file doesn't exist, the computer will create the file. You use the argument *append* with the value `True` if you want the text to be appended at the end of any existing data in the file. If *append* is `False`, any existing data in *file* are erased before the new data are written to the file.

In the example of Figure 2.67, the variables `file` and `price` are declared. Then the string `"Total price: "` is written to the file specified by the absolute path contained in the variable `file`. Because the *append* argument is `False`, all existing data in `report.txt` are erased. Then five spaces are written to the file using the `Strings.Space` method, followed by the value of `price` in currency format and a newline character. Because the *append* argument is `True`, the price is appended after the existing data in the file (which is the text `Total price:`). The file will then contain the following text:

```
Total price: $5.60
```

Aligning Columns of Information in a Sequential Access File

Earlier in this chapter, you learned how to use the PadLeft and PadRight methods to pad a string with a character until the string is a specified length. These methods also apply to strings written to sequential access files, as shown in the following example:

```
Dim name As String
Dim age As String
Dim path As String = "C:\VbReloadedAdv\Chap02\"
Dim heading As String = "Name" & Strings.Space(11) & "Age"

My.Computer.FileSystem.WriteAllText(path & "info.txt", _
    heading & ControlChars.NewLine, True)

name = InputBox("Enter name:", "Name")

Do While name <> String.Empty
    age = InputBox("Enter age:", "Age")
    My.Computer.FileSystem.WriteAllText( _
path & "info.txt", _
        name.PadRight(15) & age _
        & ControlChars.NewLine, True)
    name = InputBox("Enter name:", "Name")
Loop
```

The previous code declares four variables and then writes a heading to the file called info.txt. Then, the code requests a name from the user with an input box. If the variable name is not empty, the Do...While loop asks for an age and writes the name (justified left with the PadRight method) followed by the age. The last statement in the Do...While loop asks for the next name. The output from this code in the file info.txt would appear as follows:

```
[t/ch]

Name           Age
[t/tx]
Janice         23
Sue            67
```

Reading Information from a Sequential File

The ReadAllText method can be used to read the information stored in a sequential access file. The syntax for this method is shown in Figure 2.68.

HOW TO...

Read Information from a Sequential Access File

Syntax

My.Computer.FileSystem.ReadAllText(*file*)

Example

```
Dim path As String = "C:\VbReloadedAdv\Chap02\"
reportTextBox.Text = _
    My.Computer.FileSystem.ReadAllText(path & "info.txt")
```

FIGURE 2.68 How to read information from a sequential access file

The code in Figure 2.68 stores the path to the file in a string and uses that string with the file name `info.txt` to read the file contents and display them in a text box.

Determining Whether a File Exists

An error occurs when the computer attempts to read a sequential access file that does not exist in the specified location. You can prevent this error from occurring by determining whether the file exists before attempting to read from it using the `FileExists` method. The syntax of this method is `My.Computer.FileSystem.FileExists(`*file*`)` and is demonstrated by the following code:

```
Dim text As String
If My.Computer.FileSystem.FileExists("prices.txt") Then
    text = My.Computer.FileSystem.ReadAllText("prices.txt")
Else
    MessageBox.Show("File does not exist", "Prices", _
        MessageBoxButtons.OK, MessageBoxIcon.Information)
End If
```

This code indicates that data from the file `prices.txt` will be read only if the application first determines that the file exists. If the file does not exist, a message is displayed to the user.

The `FormClosing` Event

A form's `FormClosing` event occurs just before a form is about to be closed. This happens when the computer processes the `Me.Close()` statement in the form's code or when the user clicks the Close button on the form's title bar. The following two examples in Figure 2.69 show how you might want to use the `FormClosing` event in an application:

HOW TO...

Use the `FormClosing` Event Procedure

Example 1

```
Private Sub MainForm_FormClosing(ByVal sender As Object, _
    ByVal e As System.Windows.Forms.FormClosingEventArgs) _
    Handles Me.FormClosing

    My.Computer.FileSystem.WriteAllText("date.txt", _
        dateLabel.Text, True)
End Sub
```

Example 2

```
Private Sub MainForm_FormClosing(ByVal sender As Object, _
    ByVal e As System.Windows.Forms.FormClosingEventArgs) _
    Handles Me.FormClosing

    Dim button As DialogResult
    button = MessageBox.Show("Do you want to exit?", "Payroll", _
        MessageBoxButtons.YesNo, MessageBoxIcon.Exclamation, _
        MessageBoxDefaultButton.Button2)
```

(Figure is continued on next page)

```
        If button = DialogResult.No Then
            ' stop the form from closing
            e.Cancel = True
        End If
    End Sub
```

FIGURE 2.69 How to use the `FormClosing` event procedure

This code in Example 1 of Figure 2.69 writes the contents of `dateLabel` to the file `date.txt` before the file is closed. Example 2 displays a message box to verify that the user really wants to close the application. If the user selects No, then the code `e.Cancel = True` is executed, which cancels the form closing. The following programming example demonstrates many of the techniques presented in this section.

The Friends Application

The application in Figure 2.70 allows you to store the names of your friends in a sequential file. A sample run in Figure 2.71 shows (a) the user interface and (b) the contents of the `friends.txt` file.

```
' Project name:          Friends Project
' Project purpose:       The project writes information to
'                        and reads information from a
'                        sequential access file.
' Created/revised by:    <your name> on <current date>

Option Explicit On
Option Strict On

Public Class MainForm
    Private path As String = "C:\Friends Project\"

    Private Sub MainForm_Load(ByVal sender As Object, _
        ByVal e As System.EventArgs) Handles Me.Load
        ' reads names from a sequential access file and displays
        ' the names in a list box
        Dim text As String
        Dim name As String
        Dim newLineIndex As Integer
        Dim nameIndex As Integer
        ' clear the contents of the list box
        friendListBox.Items.Clear()

        If My.Computer.FileSystem.FileExists(path & "friends.txt") Then
            ' if the file exists, assign its contents to a variable
            text = _
                My.Computer.FileSystem.ReadAllText(path & _
                    "friends.txt")
            ' search for the newline character that separates
            ' each name; continue the search until there are
            ' no more newline characters
            newLineIndex = _
                text.IndexOf(ControlChars.NewLine, nameIndex)
```

(Figure is continued on next page)

```
            Do Until newLineIndex = -1
                ' the name begins with the character located in the
                ' nameIndex position; its length is the difference
                ' between the location of the newline
                ' character (newLineIndex) and the location of the
                ' first character in the name (nameIndex)
                name = _
                    text.Substring(nameIndex, newLineIndex - nameIndex)
                ' add the name to the list box
                friendListBox.Items.Add(name)
                ' start the next search after the newline
                ' character, which has a length of 2
                nameIndex = newLineIndex + 2
                newLineIndex = _
                    text.IndexOf(ControlChars.NewLine, nameIndex)
            Loop
        End If
    End Sub

    Private Sub MainForm_FormClosing(ByVal sender As Object, _
        ByVal e As System.Windows.Forms.FormClosingEventArgs) _
        Handles Me.FormClosing
        ' writes contents of the list box to a sequential access file

        If My.Computer.FileSystem.FileExists(path & "friends.txt") Then
            My.Computer.FileSystem.WriteAllText(path & "friends.txt", _
            String.Empty, False)
        End If

        For Each item As String In friendListBox.Items
            My.Computer.FileSystem.WriteAllText(path & "friends.txt", _
            item & ControlChars.NewLine, True)
        Next item
    End Sub

    Private Sub nameTextBox_Enter(ByVal sender As Object, _
        ByVal e As System.EventArgs) Handles nameTextBox.Enter
        nameTextBox.SelectAll()
    End Sub

    Private Sub addButton_Click(ByVal sender As Object, _
        ByVal e As System.EventArgs) Handles addButton.Click
        ' adds a name to the list box
        friendListBox.Items.Add(nameTextBox.Text)
        nameTextBox.Focus()
    End Sub

    Private Sub removeButton_Click(ByVal sender As Object, _
        ByVal e As System.EventArgs) Handles removeButton.Click
        ' removes a name from the list box
        If friendListBox.SelectedIndex > -1 Then
            friendListBox.Items.RemoveAt(friendListBox.SelectedIndex)
        End If
    End Sub

    Private Sub exitButton_Click(ByVal sender As Object, _
        ByVal e As System.EventArgs) Handles exitButton.Click
        Me.Close()
    End Sub
End Class
```

FIGURE 2.70 Program code for the Friends application

(a) User interface for the Friends application

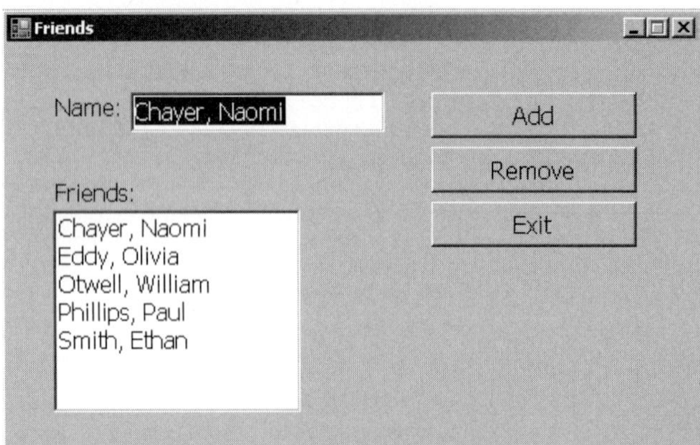

(b) Text file for the Friends application

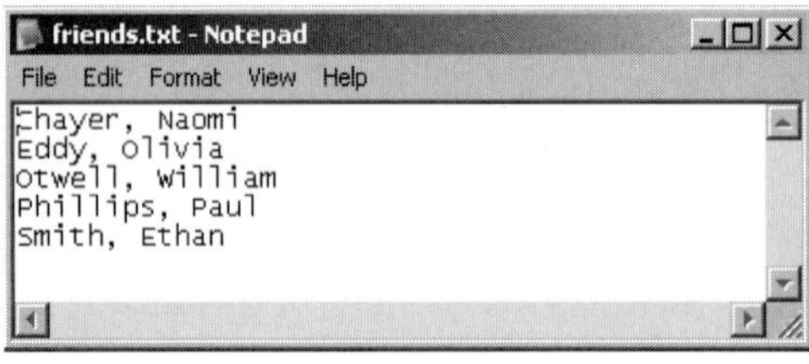

FIGURE 2.71 Sample run of the Friends application

The first statement in the `MainForm` class assigns a string to the module-level variable `path`, which is the location of the sequential access file used in this application.

The `addButton_Click` procedure simply adds a name entered in the text box to the list box and gives `nameTextBox` focus. The `removeButton_Click` procedure removes a selected name from the list box.

File processing occurs in the `MainForm_Load` event procedure and the `MainForm_FormClosing` event procedure. If the file `friends.txt` exists at the specified location, the `ReadAllText` method retrieves all the text in `friends.txt` and assigns the string to the variable `text`. Then `text.IndexOf` finds the index of the first newline character, storing that index in `newLineIndex`.

The `Do Until...Loop` repeats as long as there are new lines (names) in `friends.txt`. If a line of text exists in `friends.txt`, the `text.Substring` method gets the appropriate substring and stores it in the variable `name`. Then the `name` is added to `friendListBox`. After increasing `nameIndex` by 2 (the length of a newline character), the index of the next newline character is determined in the last statement of the loop. The result of the loop is populating the list box with the names contained in the file `friends.txt`.

Next, examine the `MainForm_FormClosing` event procedure. If the file `friends.txt` exists, the `WriteAllText` method writes the empty string to the file (to remove the file's current contents). Then the `For Each...Next` statement writes each name in `friendsListBox` (along with a newline character) to the file.

PROGRAMMING EXAMPLE

Glovers Application

Glovers Industries stores the item numbers and prices of the items it sells in a sequential access file named `itemInfo.txt`. Opal Jacoby, the company's sales manager, wants an application that allows her to display the price of an item. Open the Glovers Solution (`Glovers Solution.sln`) file, which is contained in the \VbReloadedAdv\Chap02\Glovers Solution\Glovers Project folder. Open the `itemInfo.txt` file, which is contained in the \VbReloadedAdv\Chap02\Glovers Solution\Glovers Project folder. Notice that each item's number and price appear on a separate line in the file. Close the `itemInfo.txt` window and complete the Glovers Industries application.

TOE Chart

Task	Object	Event
1. Fill the items array with the item numbers and prices stored in the itemInfo.txt file 2. Fill the numbersListBox with the item numbers 3. Select the first item in the numbersListBox	MainForm	Load
Display the price of the item whose number is selected in the numbersListBox	numbersListBox	SelectedIndexChanged
End the application	exitButton	Click

FIGURE 2.72

User Interface

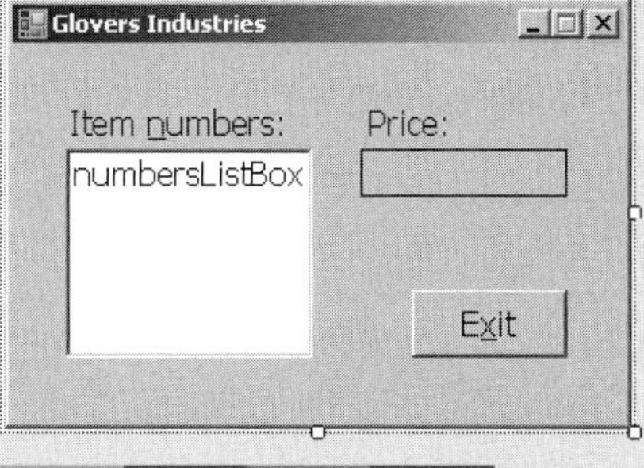

FIGURE 2.73

Objects, Properties, and Settings

Object	Property	Setting
MainForm	Size	305, 212
Label1	Location Text	24, 27 Item &numbers:
Label2	Location Text	169, 27 Price:
Label3	Name AutoSize BorderStyle Location Size Text TextAlign	priceLabel False FixedSingle 169, 49 100, 23 (empty) MiddleCenter
ListBox1	Name Location Size Sorted	numbersListBox 26, 49 120, 99 False
Button1	Name Location Size Text	exitButton 194, 116 75, 32 E&xit

FIGURE 2.74

Tab Order

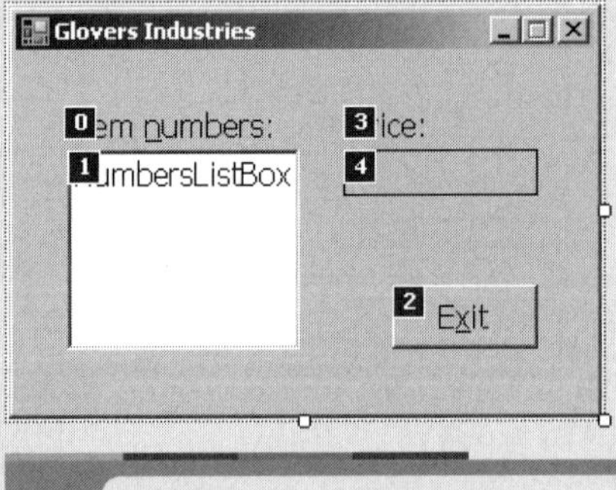

FIGURE 2.75

Pseudocode

`exitButton Click` **event procedure**

1. close the application

`MainForm Load` event procedure

1. if the itemInfo.txt file exists
   - assign the file's contents to the `text` variable
   - repeat for subscripts of 0 through 4
     - search for the newline character in the text variable and assign its index to the `newLineIndex` variable
     - assign a line from the text variable to the `record` variable; the line begins with the first character in the item number and ends with the character immediately before the newline character
     - locate the comma in the `record` variable and assign its index to the `commaIndex` variable
     - assign all of the characters that appear to the left of the comma in the `record` variable to the `number` member of the `items` array
     - assign all of the characters that appear to the right of the comma in the `record` variable to the `price` member of the `items` array
     - add the item number to the `numbersListBox`
     - add 2 (which is the length of the newline character) to the `recordIndex`, which keeps track of where the next search for the newline character should begin
   - end repeat

   end if

`numbersListBox SelectedIndexChanged` event procedure

1. display the price associated with the item number selected in the list box

Code

```
' Project name:          Glovers Project
' Project purpose:       The project displays the price of an item.
' Created/revised by:    <your name> on <current date>

Option Explicit On
Option Strict On

Public Class MainForm
    ' define the Product structure
    Structure Product
        Public number As String
        Public price As Decimal
    End Structure

    ' declare module-level array
    Private items(4) As Product

    Private Sub MainForm_Load(ByVal sender As Object, _
        ByVal e As System.EventArgs) Handles Me.Load
        ' fills the items array and numbersListBox
        ' with the data stored in a sequential access file
        Dim path As String = _
            "C:\VbReloadedAdv\Chap02\Glovers Solution\Glovers Project\"
        Dim text As String
        Dim newLineIndex As Integer
        Dim recordIndex As Integer
        Dim record As String
        Dim commaIndex As Integer
```

(Figure is continued on next page)

```

        If My.Computer.FileSystem.FileExists(path & "itemInfo.txt") _
            Then
            ' if the file exists, assign its contents to a variable
            text = My.Computer.FileSystem.ReadAllText( _
                path & "itemInfo.txt")

            For subscript As Integer = 0 To 4
                ' locate the newline character in the text variable
                newLineIndex = _
                    text.IndexOf(ControlChars.NewLine, recordIndex)

                ' assign a line from the text variable
                ' to the record variable
                record = _
                    text.Substring(recordIndex, _
                        newLineIndex - recordIndex)

                ' locate the comma in the record variable
                commaIndex = record.IndexOf(",", 0)

                ' assign the item number and price to the array
                items(subscript).number = _
                    record.Substring(0, commaIndex)
                items(subscript).price = _
                    Convert.ToDecimal(record.Substring(commaIndex + 1))

                ' add the item number to the list box
                numbersListBox.Items.Add(items(subscript).number)

                ' update the record index by 2, which is the
                ' length of the ControlChars.NewLine constant
                recordIndex = newLineIndex + 2
            Next subscript
        End If

        ' select the first item in the list box
        numbersListBox.SelectedIndex = 0
    End Sub

    Private Sub numbersListBox_SelectedIndexChanged( _
        ByVal sender As Object, _
        ByVal e As System.EventArgs) _
        Handles numbersListBox.SelectedIndexChanged
        ' displays the price corresponding to the item selected
        ' in the list box
        priceLabel.Text = _
            items(numbersListBox.SelectedIndex).price.ToString("N2")
    End Sub

    Private Sub exitButton_Click(ByVal sender As Object, _
        ByVal e As System.EventArgs) Handles exitButton.Click
        Me.Close()
    End Sub
End Class
```

FIGURE 2.76

Quick Review

- You can use a string's `Length` property to determine the number of characters contained in the string.
- The `TrimStart` method removes one or more characters from the beginning of a string, and the `TrimEnd` method removes one or more characters from the end of a string. The `Trim` method removes one or more characters from both the beginning and end of a string. The `TrimStart`, `TrimEnd`, and `Trim` methods return a string with the appropriate characters removed (trimmed).
- You can use the `Remove` method to remove one or more characters from anywhere in a string. The `Remove` method returns a string with the appropriate characters removed. You can use the `Replace` method to replace all occurrences of a sequence of characters in a string with another sequence of characters. The method returns a string with all occurrences of the old value replaced with the new value.
- The `Mid` statement allows you to replace a specific number of characters in a string with characters from another string.
- The `PadLeft` method allows you to insert characters at the beginning of a string, until the string is a specified length. The `PadRight` method allows you to insert characters at the end of a string, until the string is a specified length. Both methods return a string with the appropriate characters inserted.
- You can use the `Insert` method to insert characters within a string. The method returns a string with the appropriate characters inserted.
- The `StartsWith` method determines whether a string begins with a specific sequence of characters. The method returns either the `Boolean` value `True` or the `Boolean` value `False`. The `EndsWith` method determines whether a string ends with a specific sequence of characters. The method returns either the `Boolean` value `True` or the `Boolean` value `False`.
- You can use the `Contains` method to search a string to determine whether it contains a specific sequence of characters. The method returns either the `Boolean` value `True` or the `Boolean` value `False`.
- The `IndexOf` method allows you to search a string to determine whether it contains a specific sequence of characters. The method returns the number –1 when the sequence of characters is not contained in the portion of the string being searched; otherwise, it returns the index of the starting position of the characters within the string.
- The `Substring` method allows you to access one or more characters contained in a string. The method returns a string that contains the specified number of characters.
- You can use the `String.Compare` method to determine whether one string is equal to another string. The method returns the number 0 when both strings are equal. It returns the number –1 when *string1* is less than *string2*, and returns the number 1 when *string1* is greater than *string2*.
- The `Like` comparison operator allows you to use pattern-matching characters to determine whether one string is equal to another string.
- Use radio buttons when you want to limit the user to one of two or more related and mutually exclusive choices. The minimum number of radio buttons in a group is two, and the recommended maximum is seven. The label in the radio button's `Text` property should be entered using sentence capitalization. Assign a unique access key to each radio button in an interface.
- Use a container (such as a group box, panel, or table layout panel) to create separate groups of radio buttons. Only one button in each group can be selected at a time. Designate a default radio button in each group of radio buttons.

- Use check boxes when you want to allow the user to select any number of choices from a group of one or more independent and nonexclusive choices. The label in the check box's `Text` property should be entered using sentence capitalization. Assign a unique access key to each check box in an interface.
- The difference between a `Sub` procedure and a `Function` procedure is that a `Function` procedure returns a value, whereas a `Sub` procedure does not return a value.
- An event procedure is a `Sub` procedure that is associated with one or more objects and events. Independent `Sub` procedures and `Function` procedures are not associated with any specific object or event. The names of independent `Sub` procedures and `Function` procedures typically begin with a verb.
- Procedures allow programmers to avoid duplicating code in different parts of a program. Procedures also allow a team of programmers to work on large and complex programs. You enter `Sub` and `Function` procedures in the Code Editor window.
- You can use the `Call` statement to invoke an independent `Sub` procedure. The `Call` statement allows you to pass arguments to the `Sub` procedure. You invoke a `Function` procedure by including its name and any arguments in a statement.
- When calling a procedure, the number of arguments listed in the *argumentlist* should agree with the number of parameters listed in the *parameterlist* in the procedure header. Also, the data type and position of each parameter in the *parameterlist* should agree with the data type and position of its corresponding argument in the *argumentlist*.
- You can pass information to a `Sub` or `Function` procedure either by value or by reference. To pass a variable by value, you precede the variable's corresponding parameter with the keyword `ByVal`. To pass a variable by reference, you precede the variable's corresponding parameter with the keyword `ByRef`.
- The procedure header indicates whether a variable is being passed by value or by reference. When you pass a variable by value, only the contents of the variable are passed. When you pass a variable by reference, the variable's address is passed.
- Variables that appear in the *parameterlist* in a procedure header are procedure-level, which means they can be used only by the procedure.
- Programmers use arrays to temporarily store related data in the internal memory of the computer. All of the variables in an array have the same name and data type.
- Each element in a one-dimensional array is identified by a unique subscript, which appears in parentheses after the array's name. Each element in a two-dimensional array is identified by a unique combination of two subscripts: a row subscript and a column subscript. The subscripts appear in parentheses after the array's name. You list the row subscript first, followed by a comma and the column subscript.
- The first subscript in a one-dimensional array is 0 (zero). The first row subscript in a two-dimensional array is 0 (zero). Likewise, the first column subscript also is 0 (zero).
- When declaring a one-dimensional array, you provide either the highest subscript or the initial values. When declaring a two-dimensional array, you provide either the highest row and column subscripts or the initial values.
- The number of elements in a one-dimensional array is one number more than its highest subscript. The number of rows in a two-dimensional array is one number more than its highest row subscript. Likewise, the number of columns is one number more than its highest column subscript.

- You usually use an assignment statement to store data in an array. You refer to an element in a one-dimensional array using the array's name followed by the element's subscript. You refer to an element in a two-dimensional array using the array's name followed by the element's row and column subscripts, which are separated by a comma.
- You can use the `For Each...Next` statement to code a loop whose instructions you want processed for each element in an array. You also can use the `For...Next` statement or the `Do...Loop` statement. You can use the `Length` property to determine the number of elements in an array.
- You use the `Array.Sort` method to sort the elements in a one-dimensional array in ascending order. You use the `Array.Reverse` method to reverse the order of the elements in a one-dimensional array.
- The elements in parallel arrays are related by their subscript (or position) in the arrays.
- You can use the `Structure` statement to define a user-defined data type (or structure) in Visual Basic. You typically enter the `Structure` statement in the form's Declarations section in the Code Editor window.
- After defining a structure, you can use the structure to declare a structure variable. A structure variable contains one or more member variables. You access a member variable using the structure variable's name, followed by the dot member access operator and the member variable's name. The member variables contained in a structure variable can be used just like any other variables. A structure variable can be passed to procedures.
- You can create a one-dimensional array of structure variables. You access a member variable in an array element using the array's name, followed by the element's subscript enclosed in parentheses, the dot member access operator, and the member variable's name.
- An application can write information to a file and can also read information from a file. The information in a sequential access file is always accessed in consecutive order (sequentially) from the beginning of the file through the end of the file.
- In Visual Basic, you can use the `WriteAllText` method to write text to a sequential access file. You can use the `ReadAllText` method to read the text contained in a sequential access file.
- You can use the `Strings.Space` method to write a specific number of spaces to a file. You can use the `PadLeft` and `PadRight` methods to align the text stored in a sequential access file.
- An error occurs when the computer attempts to read a nonexistent file. You can use the `FileExists` method to determine whether a file exists. The method returns the `Boolean` value `True` if the file exists; otherwise, it returns the `Boolean` value `False`.
- The `FormClosing` event occurs when a form is about to be closed. You can use the `FormClosing` event procedure to prevent a form from being closed. To do so, you set the `Cancel` property of the procedure's `e` parameter to `True`.

Key Terms

array—A group of variables where the group is given a name, all variables in the group have the same data type, and the variables are accessed using the group name with a subscript.

binary access file—A file that contains data accessed by byte location in the file.

check box—A control in an interface that allows the user to select any number of choices from a group of one or more choices.

element—One of the variables in an array.

event procedure—A `Sub` procedure that is associated with a specific object and event.

function—A procedure that returns a value after completing its task.

independent `Sub` procedure—A procedure that can be invoked from one or more places in an application and that is independent of any object and event.

input file—A file that is read to provide data input to an application.

one-dimensional array—An array that logically represents a single column (or row) that contains the array variables.

output file—A file to which data from an application is written.

parallel arrays—Two or more arrays whose elements are related by their positions in the arrays.

parameter—The data type and name of a variable within the parentheses of a procedure header.

passing by reference—Passing a variable's memory address from a procedure call to a receiving procedure.

passing by value—Passing a variable's value from a procedure call to a receiving procedure.

procedure—A block of program code that performs a specific task.

radio button—A control in an interface that allows the user to make only one choice in a group of two or more buttons.

random access file—A file that contains data that are accessed directly using information stored with the file.

scalar variable—See **simple variable**.

sequential access file—A file that contains lines of human-readable text that are accessed in sequence from the beginning of the file through the end of the file. Also called a text file.

simple variable—A variable that is unrelated to any other variable. Also known as a scalar variable.

structure—A single data type consisting of a logical grouping of simple variables, each variable having possibly different data types. Also called a user-defined data type.

structure members—The variables, constants, or procedures contained within a structure.

structure variables—Structure members of which all members are variables.

`Sub` **procedure**—A procedure that does not return a value.

subscript—An integer, beginning with 0, that serves as an index number for all elements in an array.

substring—A contiguous sequence of characters taken from a string.

text file—See **sequential access file**.

two-dimensional array—An array that logically represents a fixed number of rows and columns that contain the array variables.

user-defined data type—See **structure**.

word sort rules—A set of rules for comparing strings where numbers are considered less than lowercase letters, which are considered less than uppercase letters.

Review Questions

1. You use the `PadLeft` method to right justify the output.
   a. True
   b. False
2. In word sort rules, the number 0 comes before the letter a.
   a. True
   b. False
3. `"Lord of the Rings" Like "[a-z]"` returns `False`.
   a. True
   b. False
4. A `Function` procedure must include the keyword `Return`.
   a. True
   b. False
5. A `Call` statement may include an argument list.
   a. True
   b. False
6. A `Call` statement may include the keyword `ByVal`.
   a. True
   b. False
7. Array subscripts begin with the value 1.
   a. True
   b. False
8. The keyword `Private` is used to declare module-level arrays.
   a. True
   b. False
9. The `For Each...Next` statement uses a subscript to access array elements.
   a. True
   b. False
10. A structure can contain variables of differing data types.
    a. True
    b. False
11. Which of the following is returned by the expression `"Don't tread on me.".Length`?
    a. 4
    b. 15
    c. 16
    d. 18
12. Which method would you use to insert characters in the middle of a string?
    a. `Replace`
    b. `Mid`
    c. `Insert`
    d. `Trim`
13. Which type of control does not allow multiple selections from a group?
    a. radio button
    b. check box
    c. list box
    d. combo box

14. Which of the following is returned by the expression `"To be, or not to be".IndexOf("be")`?
    a. -1
    b. 0
    c. 1
    d. 3

15. Which of the following is returned by the expression `"To be, or not to be".Substring(7, 9)`?
    a. To be
    b. or not
    c. or not to
    d. or not to be

16. A single `Sub` procedure can at most handle ____ event(s).
    a. 0
    b. 1
    c. 5
    d. any number of

17. Which of the following types of variables is not related to other variables?
    a. simple
    b. array
    c. scalar
    d. structure

18. The data in a ____ access file can be accessed by byte location in the file.
    a. binary
    b. random
    c. sequential
    d. none of the above

19. Which method can erase the existing contents of a file?
    a. `ReadAllText`
    b. `WriteAllText`
    c. `Replace`
    d. `Remove`

20. A member of a structure can be a ____.
    a. variable
    b. constant
    c. procedure
    d. all the above

Computer Exercises

When creating user interfaces, follow all conventions for an attractive, organized form with meaningful names for controls. When creating event procedures, use the `TryParse` method to ensure valid data are entered, use named constants when appropriate, and use format specifiers for output requiring special formatting. Your instructor may also request that you use TOE charts, pseudocode, or flowcharts as planning aids.

1. In this exercise, you create an application that reformats a person's full name.
    a. Create a project called **Name Formatting**. Save the application in the \VBReloadedAdvanced\Chap02 folder.

b. Design and create a user interface that accepts a person's full name (first, middle, and last) in a single text box.
c. Add a single label that will display the person's name in the format: lastname, firstname middle_initial. (for example, John James Smith becomes Smith, John J.).
d. Add a Format Name button and a Clear button.
e. Add event procedures for the Format Name button and the Clear button so that the reformatted name appears in the label when the Format Name button is clicked and all fields are cleared when the Clear button is clicked.
f. Save the solution, test the application, and modify as necessary.

2. In this exercise, you create an application that reformats a date.
   a. Create a project called **Date Formatting**. Save the application in the \VBReloadedAdvanced\Chap02 folder.
   b. Design and create a user interface that accepts a month, date, and year in one text box in the format: month date, year (for example, January 15, 2008).
   c. Add a single label that displays the date in the format mm/dd/yy (for example, January 15, 2008 becomes 01/15/08).
   d. Add a Format Date button and a Clear button.
   e. Add event procedures for the Format Date button and the Clear button so that the reformatted date appears in the label when the Format Name button is clicked and all fields are cleared when the Clear button is clicked. The event procedure for Format Date should verify that the entered month, date, and year are all valid.
   f. Save the solution, test the application, and modify as necessary.

3. In this exercise, you create an application that converts from feet to meters and vice versa.
   a. Create a project called **English and Metric Length**. Save the application in the \VBReloadedAdvanced\Chap02 folder.
   b. The interface should include two text boxes, one for meters and the other for feet. If one text box is clicked, the contents of both text boxes should be cleared.
   c. The interface should also have a Convert button and a Clear button.
   d. If a number is entered in one of the text boxes (for either feet or meters) and the Convert button is clicked, the converted number should appear in the other text box (1 foot = 0.3048 meter). Use two independent `Sub` procedures to perform the required calculations.
   e. Save the solution, test the application, and modify as necessary.

4. In this exercise, you create an application that displays air fares to five different international destinations from New York City.
   a. Create a project called **Globe Trotting**. Save the application in the \VBReloadedAdvanced\Chap02 folder.
   b. The interface should include five check boxes with identifying labels, one check box for each of the destinations. The user should be able to select any or all of the check boxes.
   c. Store the destinations and the air fares in two parallel arrays.
   d. Each check box should also have an output label that displays the air fare only if the check box is selected. If the check box is deselected, the output label is cleared.
   e. Add a Clear button that clears all the output labels and deselects all check boxes.
   f. Save the solution, test the application, and modify as necessary.

5. In this exercise, you modify the application in Exercise 4 above to use a two-dimensional array.
   a. Create a project called **Two-Dimensional Globe Trotting**. Save the application in the \VBReloadedAdvanced\Chap02 folder.
   b. Instead of using two parallel arrays, use one two-dimensional array that stores all destinations and air fares.
   c. Instead of providing the total air fare in an output label for each destination, output the list of selected destinations and air fares within a separate dialog box when a Display button is clicked.
   d. Save the solution, test the application, and modify as necessary.
6. In this exercise, you use structures to determine flight information for a point of origin to a destination.
   a. Create a project called **Structured Globe Trotting**. Save the application in the \VBReloadedAdvanced\Chap02 folder.
   b. The user interface should have a list box with three departure cities in the United States and a list box with three arrival cities outside the United States.
   c. The application should use a structure called `Flight`. The member variables of `Flight` should be: `flightNumber`, `departureCity`, `arrivalCity`, `flightTime` (in decimal hours), and `airFare` (in dollars).
   d. The application should use a two-dimensional array with three rows (for the origination cities) and three columns (for the destination cities).
   e. Allow the user to select only one item in each list box. When the user selects the cities and clicks the Calculate button, all flight information should be displayed in a separate dialog box.
   f. Save the solution, test the application, and modify as necessary.
7. In this exercise, you modify the application in Exercise 6 above to use sequential input and output files.
   a. Create a project called **Sequential Globe Trotting**. Save the application in the \VBReloadedAdvanced\Chap02 folder.
   b. This application should have the same functionality required in Exercise 6. However, when the form loads, all data should be loaded into the array of structure variables from a sequential access file called `input.txt`.
   c. When the user clicks the Calculate button, the data for that flight should be appended in a sequential access file called `output.txt` as well as displayed in a dialog box. In addition, the current date and time should be included in the record stored in the file (Hint: Use the `Now` function).
   d. Save the solution, test the application, and modify as necessary.

Case Projects

Financial Calculator

The Visual Basic `Financial` class has three functions: `Pmt`, `FV`, and `PV` (payment, future value, and present value, respectively). Research these functions by searching for the `Financial` class at *http://msdn.microsoft.com/library*. Create a project called **Financial Calculator**. Design and create a user interface that has three radio buttons, one for each of these functions. The interface should also have a label that briefly explains the function selected by the user. The interface should contain text boxes (with appropriate labels) for inputting the arguments required by each function. Finally, the interface should include a label that displays the result of each function and two buttons, Calculate and Clear. Initially (and when the Clear button is clicked), no radio button should be selected. When a radio button is selected, appropriate text should be displayed in all labels. The user should then enter values in the five text boxes and click Calculate. All financial calculations and label changes should be performed within three separate user-defined functions that return the result of the `Pmt`, `FV`, and `PV` functions.

Password Checker

Develop an application called **Password Checker** that allows the user to enter a possible password in a text box. When the user clicks the Check Password button, the application should check the password to determine if it meets certain requirements for validity. The requirements are: (1) the password must be between 8 and 15 characters in length, no spaces; (2) the password must contain at least one nonnumeric uppercase character and one nonnumeric lowercase character; (3) the password must contain at least one numeric digit. Use a dialog box to display a message to the user explaining whether or not the password is acceptable.

Student Scores

Develop an application called **Student Scores** that uses a sequential file for input. Each record in the file should contain a student ID, a student last name, a student first name, and five test scores. When the application runs, the data should be stored in an array of student structures. The student names should be displayed in a list box in the format *lastname, firstname*, in alphabetical order. When the student is selected in the list box, a dialog box should display the five scores and the average score.

CHAPTER

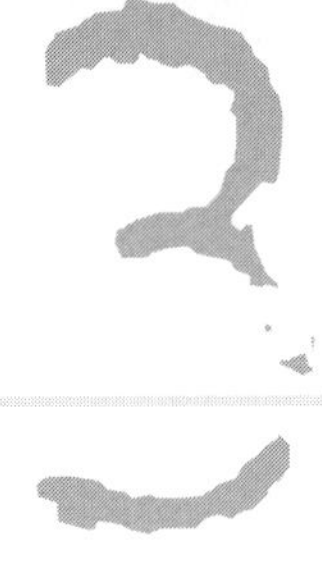

Objects and Classes

After studying Chapter 3, you should be able to:

- Compare real-world classes and objects, and software classes and objects
- Create simple UML class diagrams
- Code object-defining classes and application classes
- Create overloaded constructors in classes
- Apply the dependency and composition relationships between classes

The program code you wrote in the first two chapters of this text was not truly object-oriented (**OO**)—it was procedure-oriented instead. Yes, you wrote this procedure-oriented code using an OO programming language (Visual Basic 2005). You even used many predefined Visual Basic classes (such as `Form`, `Label`, and `Button`) to create objects (such as `MainForm`, `nameLabel`, and `calculateButton`). However, at this point you have not yet created your own custom classes and objects. A truly **object-oriented application** is one in which the programmer uses an object-oriented programming language to create special classes that are used to represent objects in the real world for the purpose of solving a particular real-world problem. You will be creating such OO applications in this and following chapters.

UNDERSTANDING OBJECTS AND CLASSES

TIP

In procedure-oriented programming, the basic unit of program code is the procedure. However, in object-oriented programming, the basic unit of program code is the class, which is used to define and create objects.

In Chapter 1, you learned about some of the differences between procedure-oriented programming and object-oriented programming (OOP). You learned that OOP is radically different from procedure-oriented programming. You also learned that an object (anything that can be seen, touched, or used) has attributes (also called properties) and behaviors (also called methods). Next, you learned that a class is program code that can be used to define an entire category of objects, such as student objects or movie objects. The class is the program code that defines what an object is (its attributes) and what an object does (its behaviors). The class is then used to create these objects that make applications work.

An object is a specific instance of a class—for example, you are an instance of the student class. In a Visual Basic application, `MainForm` is an instance of the `Form` class. You learned that there are four basic foundations to object orientation: *abstraction* (defining the relevant aspects of something), *encapsulation* (enclosing the abstractions within a class), *inheritance* (creating new classes from an existing class), and *polymorphism* (using one method name to implement different behaviors for different kinds of objects). In this chapter and the next you will learn much more about the details of truly object-oriented application development.

Real-World Objects and Classes

In the real world, you are surrounded by things: people, cars, buildings, trees, clouds, and so on. Real-world things are often considered parts of **real-world systems**. The things within the systems are called **system components**, which relate and interact in predictable ways. A real-world system is often represented and managed through the use of a computer-based **information system**. For example, a space shuttle mission or a university is a complex real-world system that can be effectively and efficiently operated only via a sophisticated information system. The things that make up such systems (astronauts, space shuttles, engineers, students, teachers, and courses) are usually modeled (that is, represented) within the information system through the use of data and methods. The information system keeps the real-world system organized and running smoothly.

You can divide real-world things such as actual students, teachers, and courses into groups, or categories, called classes. As mentioned earlier, you belong to the student group or class. Your professor belongs to the teacher class. History 101 belongs to the course class. If you use the term *object* instead of *thing*, then you could say that a **real-world object** (a thing in the real world that has attributes and behaviors) belongs to a particular **real-world class** (a category to which similar real-world objects belong). Figure 3.1 shows examples of specific objects that belong to the people, car, and tree classes. For example, Albert Einstein belongs to the people class.

FIGURE 3.1 Objects in the real world

TIP

From now on in this book, the terms "object" and "class" will refer to the software versions, not their real-world counterparts.

Software Objects

An application developer creates a representation of a real-world object that belongs to a real-world class using a **software object** (a representation of a real-world object in computer memory). A software object is created from a **software class** (program code that defines software objects). An object has two primary features: attributes and behaviors.

Object Attributes

Object **attributes** are the characteristics (or data) that define what an object is at any point in time. Take for example a student object in the context of a university information system. Student objects can have many attributes including student ID number, name, gender, address, date of birth, and GPA. These attributes define what a student object is as far as the university information system is concerned. Also note that attribute values for a given student object, such as the value of GPA, can change with time.

A student object in a university system has another important attribute: a course schedule. A course schedule can in turn be considered an object created from the course schedule class, with attributes, such as semester, year, and a list of courses. Each course within a schedule can also be considered an object. A course has attributes such as course number, course title, and section. A course section is an object that has attributes such as a section number, meeting time, room number, and instructor. An instructor is an object that has attributes such as a faculty ID number, name, gender, and date of birth.

You can see that analyzing and designing an information system using so many objects can become very involved. The point is that all these objects (student, schedule, course, section, and instructor) have attributes, and these objects are closely related to each other. Some of these objects even contain other objects. For example, a student object has (contains) a schedule object. An object-oriented programming language such as Visual Basic is extremely useful for modeling complex real-world systems (such as a university) because it allows you to create software objects that correspond to real-world objects, and it allows you to express the real-world relationships among these objects.

Object Behaviors

Not only do objects have attributes—they also exhibit behaviors. While an object's attributes define what an object *is*, object **behaviors** are the actions or operations that define what an object *does*. A student object can exhibit some important behaviors in our university information system, such as *register* for a particular course or *pay tuition*. An instructor object can *assign a grade* to a student or *enroll in a health insurance plan*. You are undoubtedly aware that a complex university system needs an information system to keep track of all students, courses, and instructors with such a wide range of attributes and behaviors. To define all the attributes and behaviors of the many objects in an information system requires the creation of many software classes.

Software Classes

This section discusses some of the basic concepts behind software classes and introduces a notation for diagramming such classes. The notation is called the Unified Modeling Language, which will be used throughout this chapter and the next to explain many OO concepts.

Class Concepts

A software class is a unit of program code that defines the attributes and behaviors of a specific group of objects. For example, a student class defines student objects and a faculty class defines faculty objects. In Visual Basic, these attributes and behaviors are called variables and methods.

Not only does a class define objects, it also provides the means for creating objects in computer memory. Thus, a class is something like a blueprint or template from which you can create specific software objects, just as a builder uses a blueprint to create real-world buildings.

A class is said to contain **class members**. Class members can be divided into two types—data members that define attributes and method members that define behaviors. Essentially, the **data members** are the class's variables. The **method members** are the class's methods. When the variables and methods relate directly to the attributes and behaviors of objects created from the class, they are called **instance variables** and **instance methods** (because objects are called instances of a class). When the variables and methods relate to the entire class in general (not to individual objects), they are called **class variables** and **class methods**. For example, `gpa` is an instance variable of the `Student` class because it is used to describe an individual student, and `calculateGpa` is the instance method of the `Student` class used to set the value of `gpa`. On the other hand, `numberOfStudents` is a class variable that applies to the entire `Student` class (not an individual `Student` object) and `countStudents` is a class method that determines the value of `numberOfStudents`.

So, essentially, a software class is a unit of program code that declares:

- the variables that define both the attributes of the objects derived from the class and the attributes that apply to the class in general (for example, the `gpa` of individual students and the `numberOfStudents` for the entire class)
- the methods that define both the behaviors of the objects derived from the class and the behaviors that apply to the class in general (for example, `calculateGpa` to determine `gpa` and `countStudents` to determine `numberOfStudents`)

Visual Basic contains thousands of predefined classes, such as `Form` and `Label`, but Visual Basic enables you to create your own custom programmer-defined classes as well, which is the basis of true object-oriented programming.

The Class Diagram

The **Unified Modeling Language** (UML) is a standardized, graphical notation for specifying, visualizing, constructing, and documenting a software system. The UML is programming language independent. It doesn't care what kind of programming language (OO or non-OO) you use to implement the software system, although the UML is primarily based on the OO paradigm or way of thinking. The UML was created by the "Three Amigos" of object orientation (Grady Booch, James Rumbaugh, and Ivar Jacobson) in the mid-1990s. It is now maintained by the **Object Management Group** (OMG), a not-for-profit computer industry specifications consortium dedicated to the standardization of software-modeling techniques (*http://www.omg.org*).

One of the most important diagrams that a software developer can create using the UML is the class diagram. The simplest type of class diagram is one that specifies a single class. A class diagram consists of a box divided into three sections, as shown in Figure 3.2. The first section holds the class name, the second holds the class data members (variables or properties), and the third holds the class method members (methods or procedures). Figure 3.2 displays a class diagram for a `Student` class with private instance variables `studentId`, `studentName`, and `studentGpa`. It also contains public instance methods `getStudentId`, `getStudentName`, `getStudentGpa`, `setStudentId`, `setStudentName`, `setStudentId`, and `printStudent`. The private members of a class are preceded with a minus sign (–), while the public members are preceded with a plus sign (+). The diagram also shows the data types of the variables and the return types of the procedures. In Visual Basic, a procedure with a return type is a `Function` procedure, while a procedure without a return type (`"void"`) is a `Sub` procedure.

Student
–studentId:String –studentName:String –studentGpa:Decimal
+getStudentId( ):String +getStudentName( ):String +getStudentGpa( ):Decimal +setStudentId( ):void +setStudentName( ):void +setStudentGpa( ):void +printStudent( ):void

FIGURE 3.2 UML class diagram for the Student class

TIP

In smaller organizations, the planner and the programmer are often the same person.

A software planner could create such class diagrams to help plan an application and document those plans. Then a programmer could use the class diagrams to write the OO application. Now that you have a good understanding of software objects and classes, it's time to learn how to implement these important constructs in Visual Basic.

IMPLEMENTING CLASSES

So far, you have been learning about objects and classes from a theoretical point of view. In this section, you will learn how to implement classes in Visual Basic. In the following section, you will learn how to create objects from classes and use them in programs.

Implementing Classes

In an OO application, objects do most of the work. But before you can understand how to use objects in Visual Basic, you must first understand how to implement the classes that are needed to define and create objects. Figure 3.3 demonstrates how to define a class in Visual Basic.

HOW TO...

Define a Class

Syntax

Public Class *ClassName*
    attributes section
    behaviors section
End Class

Example

```
Public Class Square
    ' attributes section
    Private _side As Decimal

    ' behaviors section
    Public Property Side() As Decimal
        Get
            Return _side
        End Get

        Set(ByVal value As Decimal)
            _side = value
        End Set
    End Property

    Public Sub New()
        Side = 0
    End Sub

    Public Function CalculateArea() As Decimal
        Return _side * _side
    End Function

End Class
```

FIGURE 3.3 How to define a class

The `Class` statement in Figure 3.3 begins with the keywords `Public Class`, followed by the name of the class; it ends with the keywords `End Class`. Although it is not required by the syntax, the convention is to enter the class name using Pascal case, which means that you capitalize the first letter in the name and the first letter in any subsequent words in the name. The names of predefined Visual Basic classes (for example, `String` and `TextBox`) also follow this naming convention.

When you add a class to an application, you are actually creating a new custom data type. The example in Figure 3.3 creates a new data type called `Square`, which is also called an abstract data type. An **abstract data type (ADT)** is a programmer-defined type with a set of values and a collection of operations (methods) that may be performed on those values. An ADT is defined by a class. Within the `Class` statement, you define the attributes and behaviors of the class. The attributes are represented by variables, and the behaviors are represented by `Property`, `Sub`, and `Function` procedures. The ADT called `Square` is thus an abstraction (that is, a representation of the relevant characteristics) of what this application considers to be a square. You will learn what the program code in Figure 3.3 means in the next section, but notice that the code is neatly divided into an attributes section and a behaviors section.

Visual Basic begins creating a `Class` statement for you when you add a class file to an existing project. Figure 3.4 shows you how to do this.

HOW TO...

Add a Class File to a Project

1. With a project open, click Project on the menu bar.
2. Click Add Class. The Add New Item dialog box opens with Class selected in the Visual Studio installed templates box.
3. Type the name of the class followed by a period and the letters vb in the Name box.
4. Click the Add button.

FIGURE 3.4 How to add a class file to a project

Figure 3.5 shows a new project called Shapes that contains only a form named `MainForm`. If you perform the steps in Figure 3.4 for the Shapes application and add a `Square` class, the code for the file Square.vb (generated automatically by Visual Basic) will appear as shown in Figure 3.6. It is now your job to supply the specific attributes and behaviors to the `Square` class, as shown in the example of Figure 3.3.

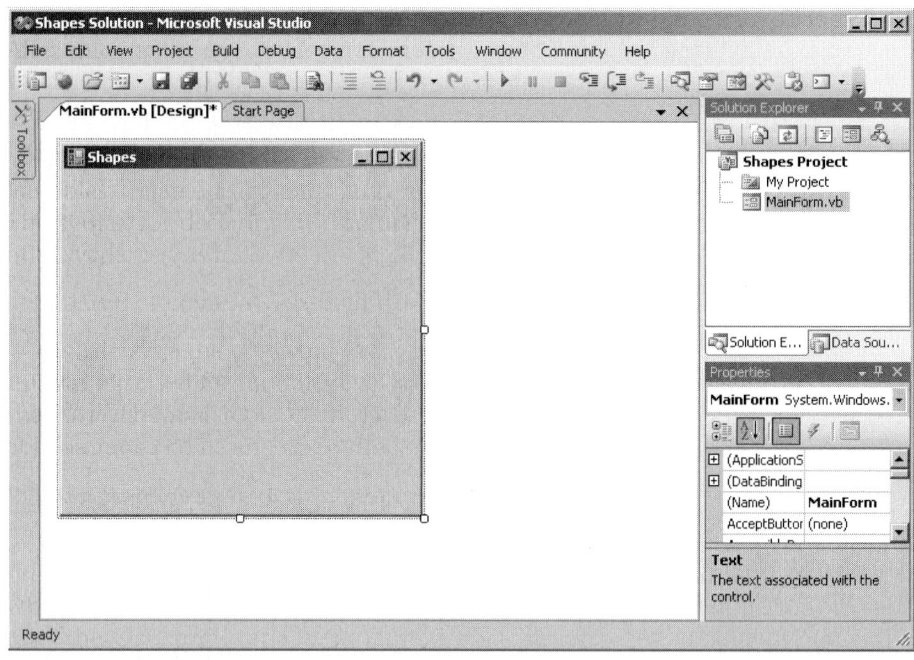

FIGURE 3.5 A new project named Shapes

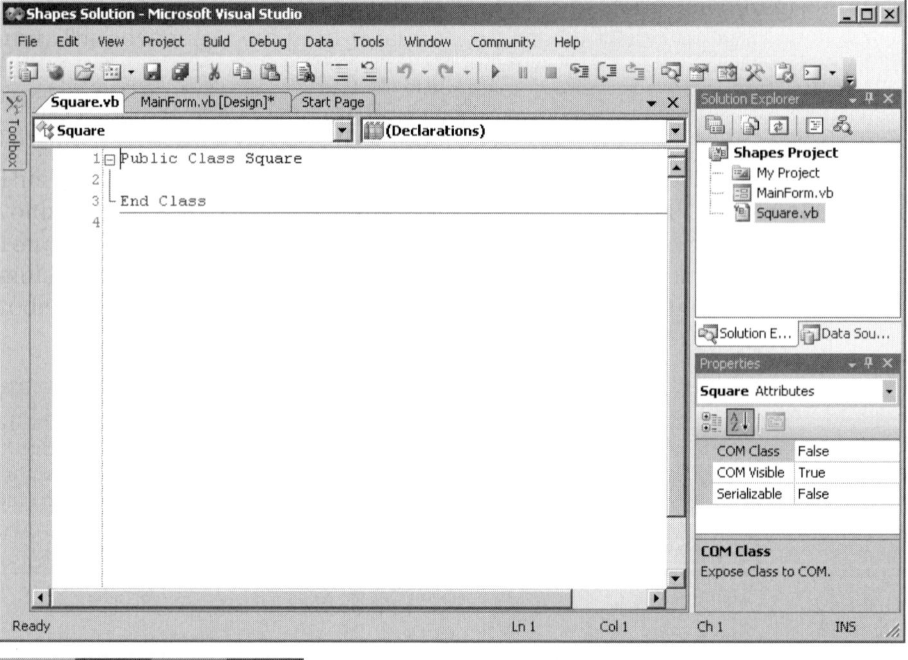

FIGURE 3.6 A class named Square in Square.vb

Implementing Attributes in Classes

In this section, you will learn how to define the attributes of objects created from a class. Recall that object attributes are defined by instance variables. In Visual Basic, instance variables are also called properties. As you will see, these instance variables are considered so important in Visual Basic that you can gain access to them only by following very strict procedures.

Properties of Objects

The attributes of an object are defined by the instance variables included in the object's class. This process of defining an object's attributes involves abstraction—focusing only on the relevant details, one of the foundational principles of OO. For example, the Shapes application in Figure 3.6 has a class named `Square` from which `Square` objects will be created in computer memory. For the purpose of this application, you will specify the defining characteristic (attribute) of a square to be an instance variable called `_side`. (See the following Tip to learn why the underscore character is used.) The code in Figure 3.7 accomplishes this objective.

```
' Class name:          Square
' Class purpose:       Defines Square objects
' Created/revised by:  <your name> on <current date>

Public Class Square
    Private _side As Integer
End Class
```

`Private` *instance variable* `_side` *in class* `Square`

FIGURE 3.7 Program code for class `Square` with a `Private` instance variable

TIP

A convention for naming instance variables (properties) in classes is to begin with the underscore character, as in `_side`, to distinguish them from other variables in classes.

Thus, `_side` is defined as a data member of the class `Square`. In general, you would call `_side` an attribute of a `Square` object. Because the length of a square's side is a special defining characteristic of a `Square` object, you would also call `_side` an instance variable. (Recall that an object is an instance of a class, hence the term instance variable.) Some would also call `_side` a field of the `Square` object. In the context of Visual Basic, you would call the instance variable `_side` a property of the `Square` object.

TIP

In OO terminology, there are often several different names for the same thing depending on the context. For example, when discussing object orientation in general, you might refer to `_side` as an instance variable of the class `Square`. However, when working with the Visual Basic language, you would refer to `_side` as a property of the class `Square`.

Member Access Modifiers

Notice that the first statement within the `Square` class in Figure 3.7 begins with the keyword `Private`. Members of a class (whether data members or method members) are identified with the following member access modifiers: `Private`, `Public`, `Protected`, `Friend`, or `Protected Friend`. Access modifiers determine the access level of class members. `Private` means that only code within the class itself has direct access to the member. Direct access means that the member can be accessed by its simple name, such as `_side`, instead of using more indirect ways of gaining access to the member, which will be explained later. `Public` means that any program code in the application (inside or outside the class) has direct access to the member. The other access modifiers will be explained in the next chapter after certain key OO concepts are introduced.

Instance variables or properties of a class (the basic attributes of objects created from the class) are almost always made `Private`. This is because the developer wants to closely control access to these very important object attributes. This `Private` access thus supports encapsulation (enclosing data and behavior within objects), one of the foundational principles of OO. Thus, the properties

TIP

The access level of a declared programming element (such as a variable or a method) is the extent of the ability of code to read or write to a variable or call a method.

of critical system objects cannot be changed except through the use of `Public` methods within the class, as you will soon see.

Other Data Members in Classes

Recall that a class has two types of members—data members and method members. Data members can be instance variables (variables that relate directly to individual objects created from the class) or general class variables (variables that relate to the class as a whole). To demonstrate a class variable, suppose you are working with a class called `Circle`. To calculate the area of a circle you would use the formula $Area = \pi * radius^2$. The `Circle` class will need a data member for the value of π, but π should not be an instance variable—it is a classwide variable that all `Circle` objects can use. In fact, π is a constant with a value of approximately 3.14159265. Thus, you could use the following code in a `Circle` class to declare and initialize a constant called `PI`:

```
Public Const PI As Double = 3.14159265
```

Note that the access modifier `Public` is used because `PI` does not require any special protection. It is not a special instance variable of an object and should be available to all code throughout the application. Next observe that the optional keyword `Const` is used because `PI` is a fixed value that should not be changed by a **client program** (a program that uses the members of a class). Using the keyword `Const` prevents `PI` from being changed while the application is running. Finally, note that the variable name `PI` is all uppercase. By convention, names of constants are uppercase in Visual Basic.

Implementing Behaviors in Classes

A class defines both attributes and behaviors of objects. The attributes define what objects are and the behaviors define what objects do. In Visual Basic, there are three kinds of methods that define object behaviors: `Property` procedures, constructors, and general methods.

`Property` Procedures in Classes

As you have seen, a property of the `Square` class is the variable `_side`. If an application needs to have `Square` objects increase or decrease in size, a behavior can be added to the `Square` class to change the value of `_side`. (For example, a game program may need to change the size, shape, or color of various geometric shapes.) Also, because an application may often need to retrieve the size of a particular `Square` object, another behavior can be added to get the value of `_side`. These behaviors are usually called **set methods** and **get methods** in a class—methods that assign values to and retrieve values from instance variables, respectively. It is very common to have set and get methods for many or all the instance variables in a class. Because a class contains set and get methods, you would say that `Square` objects have certain behaviors. They know how to change their sizes (using set methods) and report their sizes (using get methods). Note that the terms "change" and "report" (or set and get) are verbs, denoting action or behavior. All method names should begin with a verb.

Visual Basic uses a special procedure to implement the set and get methods—the **`Property` procedure**. Thus, `Property` procedures permit access to the `Private` data members of a class. Figure 3.8 demonstrates how to create a `Property` procedure.

HOW TO...

Create a Property Procedure

Syntax

```
Public [ReadOnly | WriteOnly] Property propertyName( ) As datatype
    Get
      [instructions]
        Return privateVariable
    End Get
    Set(ByVal value As datatype)
      [instructions]
      privateVariable = {value | defaultValue}
    End Set
End Property
```

Example 1—Uses both Get and Set statements

```
Public Property Side() As Integer
    Get
        Return _side
    End Get

    Set(ByVal value As Integer)
        _side = value
    End Set
End Property
```

Example 2—Uses ReadOnly and Get statement

```
Public ReadOnly Property Name() As String
    Get
        Return _name
    End Get
End Property
```

Example 3—Uses WriteOnly, Set statement, and performs validation

```
Public WriteOnly Property Cost() As Decimal
    Set(ByVal value As Decimal)
        If value > 0 Then
            _cost = value
        Else
            _cost = 0
        End If
    End Set
End Property
```

FIGURE 3.8 How to create a **Property** procedure

Figure 3.8 contains the syntax for the `Property` procedure and three examples. Note that the `Property` procedure is declared using the access modifier `Public`. Procedures are usually `Public` because you want client programs to have full access to them. The `Public Property` procedure within a class gives a client program access to the `Private` instance variables of the class's objects. Access to `Private` instance variables from outside the class must go through proper channels, that is, the `Public` methods, thus enforcing encapsulation.

The `Property` procedure header can contain the optional keywords `ReadOnly` or `WriteOnly`, which allow an application to only get a property value or only set a property value, respectively. Thus, these keywords help the programmer to enforce the desired level of security and integrity of the application. The `Property` procedure header also contains *propertyName* (a name that the programmer supplies) and *datatype* (the type of variable that is addressed by the `Property` procedure).

Within the `Property` procedure are special `Get` and `Set` procedures. A `Get` procedure allows an application to retrieve the value of *privateVariable* and the `Set` procedure allows an application to assign a value to *privateVariable*. Example 1 allows a client program to both `Get` and `Set` the `Side` property, which accesses the instance variable `_side`. Notice how the underscore in the variable name `_side` distinguishes this variable from the `Property` name `Side`. The underscore is essential because Visual Basic is not case sensitive. Example 2 makes the property `Name` read-only, so its `Property` procedure only has a `Get` procedure. (It would be impossible for a client program to assign a value to `_cost`.) Example 3 makes the property `Cost` write-only, so its `Property` procedure only has a `Set` procedure. (A client program would not be able to retrieve `_cost`.) Note that the `Set` procedure in Example 3 does some validation before assigning a value to `_cost`. Figure 3.9 shows the code for the class `Square` with a `Private` instance variable `_side` and a `Public Property` procedure called `Side`.

`Public Property` procedure `Side` with `Get` and `Set` procedures for instance variable `_side`

```
' Class name:          Square
' Class purpose:       Defines Square objects
' Created/revised by:  <your name> on <current date>

Public Class Square
    Private _side As Decimal

    Public Property Side() As Decimal
        Get
            Return _side
        End Get
        Set(ByVal value As Decimal)
            If value >= 0 Then
                _side = value
            Else
                _side = 0
            End If
        End Set
    End Property
End Class
```

FIGURE 3.9 Program code for class `Square` with a `Public Property` procedure

Constructors in Classes

Accessing instance variables of objects is an important behavior provided by `Property` procedures in classes. Of course, objects can't do anything in an application unless they are first created (instantiated) in computer memory. **Instantiation** is the formal term for creating an object. An application instantiates an object by calling a special method member of a class known as a **constructor**, so called because this method creates or constructs objects. When a constructor is called by a client program, two very important actions take place: (1) an object is created in computer memory and (2) values are assigned to the object's instance variables. Figure 3.10 shows how to create a constructor in a class.

HOW TO...

Create a Constructor

Syntax

`Public Sub New(`[*parameterlist*]**`)`**
  instructions to initialize the class's `Private` *variables*
`End Sub`

Example 1—default constructor

```
Public Sub New()
     _side = 0
End Sub
```

Example 2—parameterized constructor

```
Public Sub New(ByVal length As Decimal)
     _side = length
End Sub
```

Example 3—optional parameterized constructor

```
Public Sub New(Optional ByVal length As Decimal = 0)
     _side = length
End Sub
```

FIGURE 3.10 How to create a constructor

Referring to Figure 3.10, note that a constructor is a `Sub` procedure with the special name `New`. This `Sub` procedure is also `Public` because you want client programs in your application to be able to call the constructor and create needed objects. The optional *parameterList* can be used to receive values from the application to populate the instance variables of the object. If the *parameterList* is omitted, the constructor is called a **default constructor** and default values are used for the instance variables. If the *parameterList* is present, then the constructor is called a **parameterized constructor**.

Example 1 in Figure 3.10 contains an example of a default constructor that assigns 0 to `_side`. Example 2 is a parameterized constructor that receives a value in the variable `length` and then uses that variable to assign a value to the instance variable `_side`. Finally, Example 3 uses the keyword `Optional`, which means that the parameter `length` is optional, enabling the constructor to serve as either a default constructor or a parameterized constructor. You will read more about these different constructors shortly.

There are many factors to consider when creating constructors in a class. If any instance variables are omitted from the constructor, they are automatically initialized to their default values (0 for numeric variables, `""` for string variables). If no constructors are coded in a class, Visual Basic will provide a default constructor implicitly. You won't see the constructor in the code, but Visual Basic provides it. However, if you do add a parameterized constructor in a class, Visual Basic will not provide a default constructor. These are important points that you must consider when creating a class. In the class shown in Figure 3.11, both a default constructor and a parameterized constructor are added. Note that these two constructors could be replaced by the single constructor shown in Example 3 of Figure 3.10.

```
' Class name:           Square
' Class purpose:        Defines Square objects
' Created/revised by:   <your name> on <current date>

Public Class Square
    Private _side As Decimal

    Public Property Side() As Decimal
        Get
            Return _side
        End Get
        Set(ByVal value As Decimal)
            If value >= 0 Then
                _side = value
            Else
                _side = 0
            End If
        End Set
    End Property

    Public Sub New()
        _side = 0
    End Sub

    Public Sub New(ByVal length As Decimal)
        Side = length
    End Sub

End Class
```

Default constructor (Public Sub New())

Parameterized constructor (Public Sub New(ByVal length As Decimal))

FIGURE 3.11 Program code for class `Square` with constructors

Overloaded Constructors

As previously mentioned, Figure 3.11 contains both a default constructor and a parameterized constructor. Placing both of these constructors in the same class is an example of **overloaded constructors**—that is, two or more constructors in the same class but with different parameter lists. The **signature** of a constructor is the combination of the constructor's name (`New`) and its parameter list. Thus, you would say that overloaded constructors have different signatures. For example, the default constructor `New()`and the parameterized constructor `New(ByVal length As Decimal)` in Figure 3.11 have different signatures because their parameter lists are different. An application may need to use one constructor under certain conditions and another constructor under other conditions. In fact, a class can have as many overloaded constructors as an application needs. You will see how to use overloaded constructors later in this chapter.

As an alternative to providing several overloaded constructors, you can code a single constructor with `Optional` parameters. The code in Example 3 of Figure 3.10

uses the keyword `Optional` to create a constructor. This constructor makes the parameter `length` optional. Thus, if this constructor is called and `length` is provided by the constructor call, the value of `length` will be stored in `_side`. If no `length` is provided by the constructor call, the value 0 will be stored in `_side`. Using a single constructor with `Optional` parameters may be convenient at times, but you might still need to use overloaded constructors in some applications.

General Methods in Classes

The third category of behaviors for classes is represented by general methods. These methods are simply ordinary `Sub` procedures or `Function` procedures that add to the functionality of your application. (You studied `Sub` and `Function` procedures in Chapter 1.) Suppose that in the Shapes application, you want `Square` objects to be able to calculate their areas and perimeters. You could add general methods to accomplish this as shown in Figure 3.12.

```
' Class name:           Square
' Class purpose:        Defines Square objects
' Created/revised by:   <your name> on <current date>

Option Explicit On
Option Strict On

Public Class Square
    Private _side As Decimal

    Private Shared squareCount As Integer

    Public Property Side() As Decimal
        Get
            Return _side
        End Get
        Set(ByVal value As Decimal)
            If value >= 0 Then
                _side = value
            Else
                _side = 0
            End If
        End Set
    End Property

    Public Sub New()
        _side = 0
    End Sub

    Public Sub New(ByVal length As Decimal)
        Side = length
    End Sub

    Public Function CalculatePerimeter() As Decimal
        Return 4 * _side
    End Function

    Public Function CalculateArea() As Decimal
        Return _side * _side
    End Function

End Class
```

FIGURE 3.12 Program code for class `Square` with general methods `CalculateArea` and `CalculatePerimeter`

The functions `CalculateArea` and `CalculatePerimeter` both use the value in the instance variable `_side` to calculate the area of a square (`_side * _side`) and the perimeter of a square (`4 * _side`). Note that the code in Figure 3.12 constitutes a complete `Square` class, which defines all the attributes and behaviors of `Square` objects. The `Square` class is thus a blueprint for creating `Square` objects in computer memory. However, the `Square` class can't do anything by itself. It must be used by a client program to be of value.

To review what you have learned so far about implementing classes, the `Square` class has the attribute side (implemented with the instance variable `_side`) and the behaviors get side, set side, instantiate a square, calculate area, and calculate perimeter (implemented with the `Property` procedure `Side`, the constructor `New`, and the general procedures `CalculateArea` and `CalculatePerimeter`, respectively). This code exists within a class called `Square`, which is in a file called Square.vb. This file is part of the Shapes application, which also contains the class `MainForm` in the file MainForm.vb. A user-defined class such as `Square` that specifies the attributes and behaviors of objects is called an **object-defining class**. A class such as `MainForm` in the file MainForm.vb that contains the user interface and uses object-defining classes is called an **application class.** An application class can also be considered a client program (a client or user of the `Square` class). Next you will see how an application class uses the `Square` class to create `Square` objects.

INSTANTIATING AND USING OBJECTS

In the previous section, you learned how to implement an object-defining class in Visual Basic. In this section, you will learn how to instantiate (create) objects using such a class and how to use these objects to achieve the goals of an application.

Instantiating Objects

Recall that objects are instances of classes in computer memory. To instantiate objects, you must first have an object-defining class, the blueprint for creating objects. An application class can then be coded to use the object-defining class for creating objects. The application class can subsequently use those objects to meet the objectives of the application. Figure 3.13 demonstrates how to instantiate an object from a class.

HOW TO...

Instantiate an Object

Syntax - Version 1

{`Dim` | `Private`} *objectVariable* `As` *class*
objectVariable = `New` *class*

Syntax - Version 2

{`Dim` | `Private`} *objectVariable* `As New` *ClassName*

Example 1

```
Private employeeTimeCard As TimeCard
employeeTimeCard = New TimeCard()
```

Example 2

```
Dim employeeTimeCard As New TimeCard()
```

FIGURE 3.13 How to instantiate an object

Figure 3.13 provides the syntax and examples for instantiating an object. First, assume that an object-defining class called *ClassName* exists in the application. The *objectVariable* is the identifier or **reference variable** that stores the memory address of the object. The *objectVariable* may also be loosely referred to as the **object name**. The keyword `Dim` is used to declare a procedure-level *objectVariable* while the `Private` keyword is used to declare a module-level *objectVariable*. If an object must be accessed by several methods in an application class, you should declare the object as module-level.

Version 1 of the syntax in Figure 3.13 uses two statements to instantiate an object. The first declares the *objectVariable* while the second populates the object variable with the memory address where the object is located. Version 2 of the syntax accomplishes both steps with just one statement. Example 1 and Example 2 illustrate versions 1 and 2 of the syntax, respectively. Note that both examples use the expression `New Timecard()`, which calls a default constructor `New` in the `Timecard` class.

The Shapes application, which you view next, uses the `Square` class to instantiate and manipulate a `Square` object. Figure 3.14 shows the application's code.

```
' Project name:         Shapes Project
' Project purpose:      Displays the area and perimeter of a square.
' Created/revised by:   <your name> on <current date>

Option Explicit On
Option Strict On

Public Class MainForm
    ' declare instance variables of MainForm
    Private mySquare As Square
    Private isConverted As Boolean

    ' Sub procedure for loading MainForm
    Private Sub MainForm_Load(ByVal sender As Object, _
        ByVal e As System.EventArgs) Handles Me.Load
        ' instantiate an object
        mySquare = New Square()
    End Sub

    ' Sub procedure for Calculate Area button
    Private Sub calcAreaButton_Click(ByVal sender As Object, _
        ByVal e As System.EventArgs) Handles calcAreaButton.Click
        ' calculates and displays the area of a square
        Dim area As Decimal

        ' assign side measurement to the Square object's property
        isConverted = _
            Decimal.TryParse(sideTextBox.Text, mySquare.Side)

        If isConverted Then
            ' calculate and display the area
            area = mySquare.CalculateArea()
            areaLabel.Text = Convert.ToString(area)
            perimeterLabel.Text = String.Empty
        Else
            displayMessage()
        End If

        sideTextBox.Focus()
    End Sub

```

The object `mySquare` *is declared as a module-level variable*

The object `mySquare` *is instantiated when* `MainForm` *loads using the default constructor*

Assigns a value to the `Side` *property of object* `mySquare`

Object `mySquare` *calls its* `CalculateArea` *method*

(Figure is continued on next page)

The object `mySquare` *is instantiated using the parameterized constructor*

Object `mySquare` *calls its* `Calculate-Perimeter` *method*

```
    ' Sub procedure for Calculate Perimeter button
    Private Sub calcPerimeterButton_Click(ByVal sender As Object, _
        ByVal e As System.EventArgs) Handles calcPerimeterButton.Click
        ' calculates and displays the perimeter of a square
        Dim perimeter As Decimal
        Dim length As Decimal

        isConverted = _
            Decimal.TryParse(sideTextBox.Text, length)

        mySquare = New Square(length)

        If isConverted Then
            ' calculate and display the perimeter
            perimeter = mySquare.CalculatePerimeter()
            perimeterLabel.Text = Convert.ToString(perimeter)
            areaLabel.Text = String.Empty
        Else
            displayMessage()
        End If

        sideTextBox.Focus()
    End Sub

    ' Sub procedure for displaying error message
    Private Sub displayMessage()
        MessageBox.Show("The side measurement must be numeric.", _
            "Square Calculator", MessageBoxButtons.OK, _
            MessageBoxIcon.Information)
    End Sub

    ' Sub procedures for various controls
    Private Sub sideTextBox_Enter(ByVal sender As Object, _
    ByVal e As System.EventArgs) Handles sideTextBox.Enter
        sideTextBox.SelectAll()
    End Sub

    Private Sub sideTextBox_TextChanged(ByVal sender As Object, _
        ByVal e As System.EventArgs) Handles sideTextBox.TextChanged
        areaLabel.Text = String.Empty
        perimeterLabel.Text = String.Empty
    End Sub

    Private Sub exitButton_Click(ByVal sender As Object, _
        ByVal e As System.EventArgs) Handles exitButton.Click
        Me.Close()
    End Sub

End Class
```

FIGURE 3.14 Program code for the `MainForm` class in the Shapes application (see Figure 3.12 for the program code for the `Square` class)

The code in Figure 3.14 is for the `MainForm` class, which is the application class that uses the `Square` class. (The code for the Square class is in Figure 3.12.) Note that the `MainForm` class has its own data members and method members. For example, `MainForm` has `Private` instance variables `mySquare` (a reference variable for a `Square` object) and `isConverted` (a `Boolean` variable for data validation). The statement `Private mySquare As Square` declares a `Square` object called `mySquare` and reserves memory for it. The object `mySquare` is declared as a module-level variable (in the class `MainForm`) so that all methods in `MainForm` will be able to access it.

The `MainForm` class also has method members, nearly all of which are event procedures. The `Sub` procedure `MainForm_Load` instantiates the `Square` object called `mySquare` using the statement `mySquare = New Square()`. Thus, when the form loads, the default constructor `New` in the `Square` class is called, a `Square` object is created in memory (with instance variable `_side` initialized to 0), and the reference variable `mySquare` stores the location of this object in memory.

Using Objects in Applications

Once an object, such as `mySquare`, has been instantiated, it can be used by an application class, such as `MainForm`. Essentially, you use an object to call methods contained in its class. (The methods provide the functionality of the application.) The syntax for an object calling a method is simply *objectVariable.methodName*. The period is known as the **member access operator** or **dot operator.** An object can call its `Property` procedure or an object can call a general procedure in its class. Note that an object can't call a constructor because the object doesn't exist yet. (That's what makes constructors "special.")

Objects Calling a Property Procedure

Objects have instance variables, which are usually given `Private` access. Therefore, a client program will need to use the `Public Property` procedure to get or set the value of an instance variable. For example, look at the `MainForm_Load` procedure in Figure 3.14. First, `mySquare.Side` is the object `mySquare` calling the `Property` procedure `Side` for the purpose of getting the value of the instance variable `_side` and displaying it in the `sideLabel` control. In this context, Visual Basic knows that the `Get` statement within the `Side` procedure should be used. This happens because the `Convert.ToString` method is called; the method is trying to retrieve data and convert it to a `String`.

The Set method of a `Property` procedure is called in the same way. In the `calcAreaButton_Click` procedure of Figure 3.14 is a call to the `TryParse` method that takes the text in `sideTextBox`, converts it to a `Decimal`, and assigns that number to the instance variable `_side` using the expression `mySquare.Side`. In this context of assigning a value, Visual Basic knows to use the `Set` statement in the `Property` procedure `Side`.

Objects Calling a General Procedure

Objects can not only call `Property` procedures, they can also call general procedures (`Sub` procedures or `Function` procedures) in their class. Take another look at the `calcAreaButton_Click` and `calcPerimeterButton_Click` event procedures in Figure 3.14. The procedure `calcAreaButton_Click` takes the value in `sideTextBox`, converts it to a `Decimal`, and assigns it to the `Side` property of `mySquare` using the code `mySquare.Side`. Then the area of `mySquare` is calculated using the code `mySquare.CalculateArea()`, and this area is displayed in `areaLabel`. The object `mySquare` is calling the general procedure `CalculateArea()` using the dot operator (`.`). A similar process is performed in the event procedure `calcPerimeterButton_Click`. However, for illustration purposes, a new `mySquare` object is instantiated in this event procedure using the parameterized constructor via the code `mySquare = New Square(length)`.

Figure 3.15(a) shows the result of entering 7.5 for the side measurement of the square and clicking the Calculate Area button, while Figure 3.15(b) shows the result of entering 5 for the side measurement and clicking the Calculate Perimeter button.

(a) Sample run calculating area

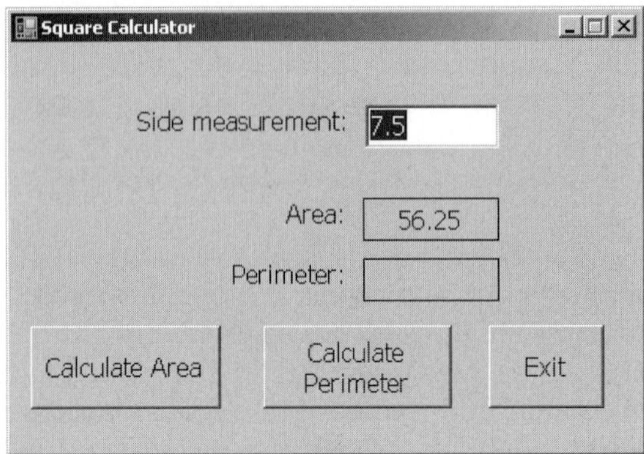

(b) Sample run calculating perimeter

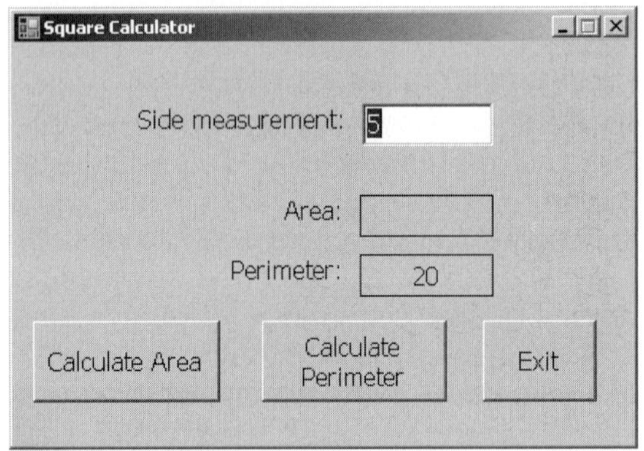

FIGURE 3.15 Sample run of the Shapes application

Shared Class Members

The class members you have examined so far have been instance variables and instance methods—that is, variables and methods that related directly to specific, individual objects created from a class. An object created from a class carries with it in computer memory a copy of all the instance variables of the class. The instance methods of a class are those that must be called by specific individual objects because these methods deal with object-specific information. For example, the object `mySquare` will have its own copy of `_side` with a specific `Decimal` value (such as 5.5), and the instance method `CalculateArea` can be called only by a `Square` object such as `mySquare` using the code `mySquare.CalculateArea()`, returning the area of that particular `Square` object. (An area of 30.25 for `mySquare` would result from a `_side` value of 5.5.)

However, some variables and methods relate to the class as a whole, not just to individual objects. These class members were defined earlier as class variables and class methods. In Visual Basic, these class members are identified with the keyword `Shared`, so they are often called `Shared` class members. That means they are shared by all objects of the class. `Shared` class members exist independently of any class objects—they even exist when no objects of that class have been created.

Figure 3.16 shows revisions to the Shapes application that demonstrate `Shared` class members. In the figure, the revised `Square` class has a `Private Shared` variable called `squareCount` and a `Shared Property` procedure called `Count`. Note that the variable `squareCount` is not an instance variable since it does not relate to specific objects. It is a classwide `Shared` variable that holds the count of all `Square` objects created by the application. The `Property` procedure `Count` must be denoted as `Shared` in order to access the `Shared` variable `squareCount`. The value of `squareCount` is incremented by one within the `Square` constructor using the code `squareCount += 1`. Each time a new `Square` object is created, `squareCount` increases by 1.

`Shared` *variable* `squareCount` *declared*

`Shared Property` *procedure for* `Shared` *variable* `squareCount`

`Shared` *variable* `squareCount` *incremented by 1 when* `Square` *object instantiated*

```
' Class name:          Square
' Class purpose:       Defines Square objects
' Created/revised by:  <your name> on <current date>

Option Explicit On
Option Strict On

Public Class Square
    Private _side As Decimal

    Private Shared squareCount As Integer

    Public Property Side() As Decimal
        Get
            Return _side
        End Get
        Set(ByVal value As Decimal)
            If value >= 0 Then
                _side = value
            Else
                _side = 0
            End If
        End Set
    End Property

    Public Shared ReadOnly Property Count() As Integer
        Get
            Return squareCount
        End Get
    End Property

   Public Sub New(ByVal length As Decimal)
        Side = length
        squareCount += 1
    End Sub

    Public Function CalculatePerimeter() As Decimal
        Return 4 * _side
    End Function

    Public Function CalculateArea() As Decimal
        Return _side * _side
    End Function

End Class
```

FIGURE 3.16 Modified `Square` class with `Shared` variable `squareCount`

The `MainForm` class now undergoes several changes, as shown in Figure 3.17. Instead of creating a new `Square` object when `MainForm` loads or when `sideTextBox` changes, this application has a `createSquareButton` that instantiates a `Square` object; calculates area, perimeter, and count for squares; and displays the results in various labels. A sample run after creating three different `Square` objects is shown in Figure 3.18 (the Create Square button was clicked three times). Note that although the same name is used for all new `Square` objects (`mySquare`), each of these objects is created at a new location in computer memory, so they are different squares even if they have the same side measurement. Also note that each of the squares could be placed in an array if desired.

Separate procedure for creating `square` *objects*

Calculate and display area, perimeter, and count of Square objects

```
' Project name:          Shapes Project with Shared variable
' Project purpose:       Displays the area, perimeter, count of squares.
' Created/revised by:    <your name> on <current date>

Option Explicit On
Option Strict On

Public Class MainForm
    ' Sub procedure for instantiating Square objects
    Private Sub createSquareButton_Click( _
        ByVal sender As System.Object, _
        ByVal e As System.EventArgs) Handles createSquareButton.Click
        ' declare variables
        Dim mySquare As Square
        Dim length As Decimal
        Dim area As Decimal
        Dim perimeter As Decimal
        Dim isConverted As Boolean

        ' try to convert sideTextBox contents to Decimal
        isConverted = _
            Decimal.TryParse(sideTextBox.Text, length)

        If isConverted Then
            mySquare = New Square(length) ' instantiate Square object
            area = mySquare.CalculateArea()
            areaLabel.Text = Convert.ToString(area)
            perimeter = mySquare.CalculatePerimeter()
            perimeterLabel.Text = Convert.ToString(perimeter)
            countLabel.Text = Convert.ToString(Square.Count)
            sideTextBox.Focus()
        Else
            displayMessage()
        End If
    End Sub

    ' Sub procedure for displaying error message
    Private Sub displayMessage()
        MessageBox.Show("The side measurement must be numeric.", _
            "Square Calculator", MessageBoxButtons.OK, _
            MessageBoxIcon.Information)
    End Sub

    ' Sub procedures for various controls
    Private Sub sideTextBox_Enter(ByVal sender As Object, _
    ByVal e As System.EventArgs) Handles sideTextBox.Enter
        sideTextBox.SelectAll()
    End Sub
```

(Figure is continued on next page)

```
    Private Sub sideTextBox_TextChanged(ByVal sender As Object, _
         ByVal e As System.EventArgs) Handles sideTextBox.TextChanged
        areaLabel.Text = String.Empty
        perimeterLabel.Text = String.Empty
    End Sub

    Private Sub exitButton_Click(ByVal sender As Object, _
        ByVal e As System.EventArgs) Handles exitButton.Click
        Me.Close()
    End Sub
End Class
```

FIGURE 3.17 Modified `MainForm` class with `Shared` variable `squareCount`

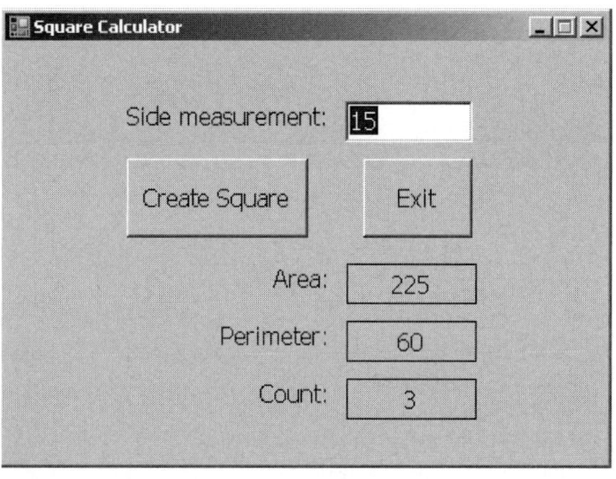

FIGURE 3.18 Sample run of the Shapes application with a `Shared` variable

So far, this chapter has been devoted to defining and implementing classes and objects. Figure 3.19 summarizes the progression of events in creating and using objects.

```
' this code is in the MainForm class, instantiates mySquare
mySquare = New Square(5.5) ' passes 5.5 to Square constructor

' this code is in the Square class
Public Sub New(ByVal length As Decimal) ' length receives 5.5
    _side = length ' instance variable _side stores length value
End Sub

' this code is in the MainForm class
area = mySquare.CalculateArea() ' mySquare calls CalculateArea

' this code is in the Square class
Public Function CalculateArea() As Decimal
    Return _side * _side ' value in _side used in area calculation
End Function

' this code is in the MainForm class
areaLabel.Text = Convert.ToString(area) ' displays area of square
```

FIGURE 3.19 Progression of events in creating and using an object

EXPLORING CLASS RELATIONSHIPS

Figure 3.2 presented a UML class diagram containing just one class called Student. However, class diagrams can contain several classes used within an application. Additionally, you can use a class diagram to express the relationships among these classes.

The Dependency Relationship

As you have already seen, classes contain variables and methods that can be used by other classes within the same application. This implies that two classes can be related to each other. For example, the Shapes application of Figures 3.16 and 3.17 has two classes that are related: `Square` and `MainForm`. The type of relationship between these two classes is called a **dependency relationship**, meaning that one class simply uses the members of another class. The usage is often in the form of method calls. For the Shapes application, the class `MainForm` creates an object called `mySquare`. Then the `mySquare` object uses the `CalculateArea` method in the `Square` class when the code `mySquare.CalculateArea()` is executed. Thus, class `MainForm` uses class `Square`. This UML diagram for the Shapes application that illustrates dependency is shown in Figure 3.20.

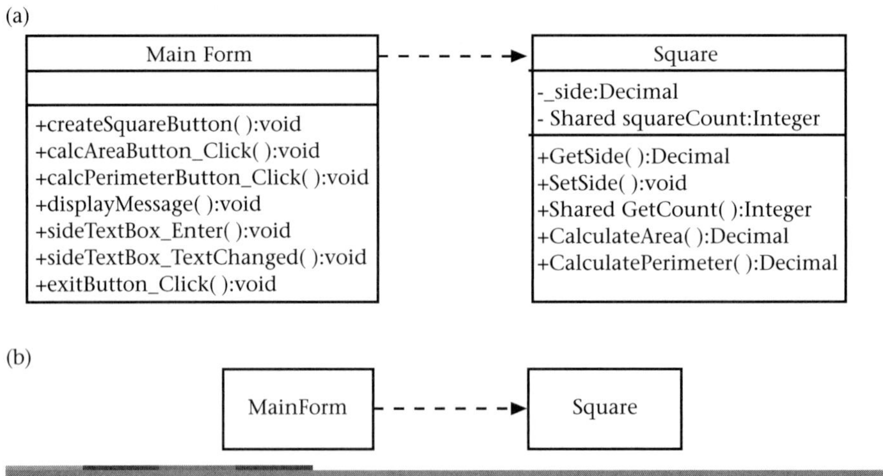

FIGURE 3.20 UML diagrams for the Shapes application

Figure 3.20(a) shows the class `MainForm` with no instance variables but several methods. The figure also shows the class `Square` with its variables `_side` (an instance variable) and `squareCount` (a `Shared` variable), as well as its methods for getting and setting `_side`, getting `squareCount`, and calculating the square's area and perimeter. The dashed arrow illustrates the dependency relationship between `MainForm` and `Square`. A simpler version of the class diagram is shown in Figure 3.20(b) using only the class names. You could illustrate class relationships using a diagram like Figure 3.20(b) and provide the details of each individual class separately in another class diagram.

The Composition Relationship

Another important relationship between two classes is an **association**, in which one class contains variables that are references to objects of another class. An association is also known as a **has-a relationship** because one class has or contains a reference to an object of another class. This type of relationship is important because it is often found in the real world. For example, a Person can be viewed as an object with many attributes such as Social Security number, name, and address. However, an Address can itself be viewed as an object with the attributes street, city, state, and ZIP code. Thus, a Person object can have as one of its attributes an Address object. Therefore, there is an association between the Person class and the Address class.

TIP

When we talk about the object in a composition relationship, we often say that one object has another. For example, a person has an address, a house has a window, a dog has a tail. Thus, a composition relationship is sometimes referred to as a has-a relationship.

This section focuses on a particular type of association between classes: the composition relationship. The **composition relationship** is a type of association between two classes in which the contained object would not normally exist apart from the containing object. For example, the Person-Address relationship described above is a composition relationship because an Address object would not normally exist in an information system without a corresponding Person object. The composition relationship is expressed in the UML with a solid line going from the contained class to the containing class. A solid diamond shape is added on the side of the containing class, as shown in Figure 3.21.

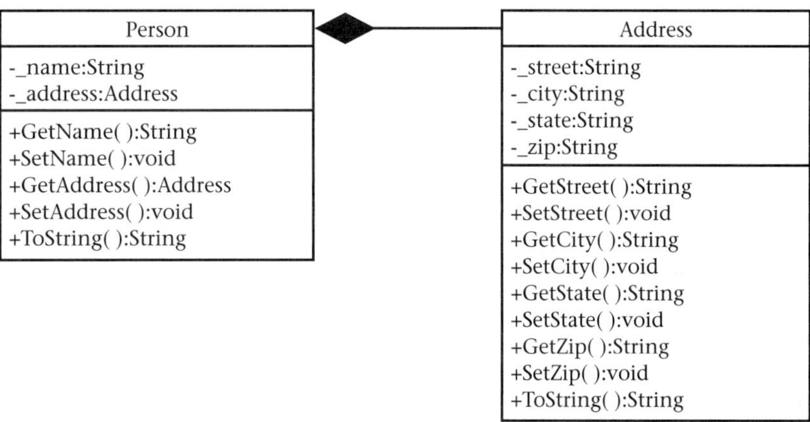

FIGURE 3.21 UML diagram for a composition relationship

To implement a composition relationship in Visual Basic, you must create two classes, such as `Person` and `Address`, and reference an object of one class as an instance variable of the other. The simple Human Resources application shown in Figures 3.22, 3.23, and 3.24 demonstrates this. Figure 3.22 includes a `Person` class, Figure 3.23 includes an `Address` class, and Figure 3.24 includes a `MainForm` class. A sample run of this application is shown in Figure 3.25, where information about a person is entered in the interface and a complete mailing address is displayed in a label.

Note that the `Person` class in Figure 3.22 has two instance variables: `_name` and `_address`. The data type for `_name` is `String`, but the data type for `_address` is something more—a new abstract data type defined by the class `Address`. Thus, a `Person` object is defined as something with a name and an address. The `Person` class has an `Address` object as an instance variable, so there is a composition relationship between `Person` and `Address`. Note that the

`Person` constructor assigns an empty string to the `_name` instance variable and `Nothing` to the `_address` instance variable. (`Nothing` is used, not `""` or `String.Empty`, because `_address` is a general reference variable, not a `String`.)

The `Person` class also has a special `ToString` method (a `Function` procedure) that returns the `Name` property of the `Person` object followed by a new line character. Note that you can use the keyword `Overrides` to replace or override the default `ToString` method found in Visual Basic's `Object` class. Providing your own custom `ToString` method is a common practice in OO programming. An object can call its `ToString` method to create a string to represent itself, using it for display purposes or for writing to a file.

```
' Class name:          Person
' Class purpose:       Defines Person objects
' Created/revised by:  <your name> on <current date>

Option Explicit On
Option Strict On

Public Class Person
    ' instance variables
    Private _name As String
    Private _address As Address

    ' constructor
    Public Sub New(Optional ByVal theName As String = "", _
        Optional ByVal theAddress As Address = Nothing)
        Name = theName
        Address = theAddress
    End Sub

    ' Property procedures
    Public Property Name() As String
        Get
            Return _name
        End Get
        Set(ByVal Value As String)
            _name = Value
        End Set
    End Property

    Public Property Address() As Address
        Get
            Return _address
        End Get
        Set(ByVal Value As Address)
            _address = Value
        End Set
    End Property

    ' ToString function displays Name property
    Public Overrides Function ToString() As String
        Return Name & ControlChars.CrLf
    End Function

End Class
```

New abstract data type called `Address`

The `Address` *object is instantiated with* `Nothing` *in its memory location*

`ToString` *function here overrides the* `ToString` *function in the* `Object` *class*

FIGURE 3.22 Program code for `Person` class

The `Address` class in Figure 3.23 has several instance variables: `_street`, `_city`, `_state`, and `_zip`, all of which are simple variables (not objects). A constructor is provided, and each instance variable has a `Property` procedure. The `Address` class also has its own `ToString` method for outputting the data contained in an `Address` object.

`Optional` constructor parameters: If any are omitted in a constructor call, `""` is stored in the instance variable

```
' Class name:           Address
' Class purpose:        Defines Address objects
' Created/revised by:   <your name> on <current date>

Option Explicit On
Option Strict On

Public Class Address
    ' instance variables
    Private _street As String
    Private _city As String
    Private _state As String
    Private _zip As String

    ' constructor
    Public Sub New(Optional ByVal theStreet As String = "", _
                   Optional ByVal theCity As String = "", _
                   Optional ByVal theState As String = "", _
                   Optional ByVal theZip As String = "")
        _street = theStreet
        _city = theCity
        _state = theState
        _zip = theZip
    End Sub

    ' Property procedures
    Public Property Street() As String
        Get
            Return _street
        End Get
        Set(ByVal Value As String)
            _street = Value
        End Set
    End Property

    Public Property City() As String
        Get
            Return _city
        End Get
        Set(ByVal Value As String)
            _city = Value
        End Set
    End Property

    Public Property State() As String
        Get
            Return _state
        End Get
        Set(ByVal Value As String)
            _state = Value
        End Set
    End Property

```

(Figure is continued on next page)

```
    Public Property Zip() As String
        Get
            Return _zip
        End Get
        Set(ByVal Value As String)
            _zip = Value
        End Set
    End Property

    ' ToString function displays Address properties
    Public Overrides Function ToString() As String
        Return Street & ControlChars.CrLf _
             & City & ", " & State & " " & Zip
    End Function

End Class
```

FIGURE 3.23 Program code for `Address` class

The Human Resources application is driven by the `MainForm` application class in Figure 3.24. This class declares two objects (a `Person` object and an `Address` object) as module-level variables. When `MainForm_Load` executes, the objects `aPerson` and `anAddress` are instantiated without any data. When the Display button is clicked, `MainForm` gets the data from the `TextBox` controls and assigns them to the properties of the respective objects. Then the `ToString` methods are called by their respective objects. Figure 3.25 shows a sample run of the Human Resources application.

```
' Project name:          Human Resources Project
' Project purpose:       The project displays a mailing address.
' Created/revised by:    <your name> on <current date>

Option Explicit On
Option Strict On

Public Class MainForm
    ' declare objects
    Private aPerson As Person
    Private anAddress As Address

    Private Sub MainForm_Load(ByVal sender As System.Object, _
        ByVal e As System.EventArgs) Handles MyBase.Load
        ' instantiate objects
        aPerson = New Person
        anAddress = New Address
    End Sub

```

Objects declared

Objects instantiated

(Figure is continued on next page)

Stored contents of text boxes in instance variables of `anAddress`

Stored object `anAddress` *in instance variable of* `aPerson`

```
    Private Sub displayButton_Click(ByVal sender As System.Object, _
        ByVal e As System.EventArgs) Handles displayButton.Click
        ' get data from form, load into objects
        anAddress.Street = streetTextBox.Text
        anAddress.City = cityTextBox.Text
        anAddress.State = stateTextBox.Text
        anAddress.Zip = zipTextBox.Text

        aPerson.Name = nameTextBox.Text
        aPerson.Address = anAddress

        ' display mailing address
        mailingLabel.Text = aPerson.ToString()
    End Sub

    Private Sub exitButton_Click(ByVal sender As System.Object, _
        ByVal e As System.EventArgs) Handles exitButton.Click
        Me.Close()
    End Sub

End Class
```

FIGURE 3.24 Program code for `MainForm` class

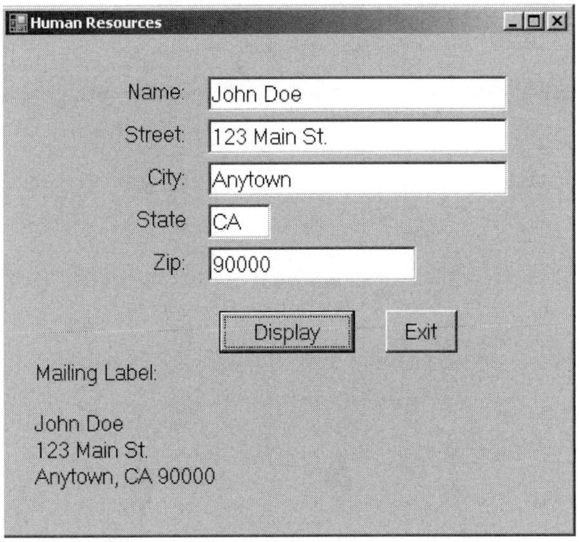

Human Resources

Name: John Doe
Street: 123 Main St.
City: Anytown
State CA
Zip: 90000

Display Exit

Mailing Label:

John Doe
123 Main St.
Anytown, CA 90000

FIGURE 3.25 Sample run of the Human Resources application

In the next chapter, you will learn about the powerful inheritance relationship between classes and how to use more advanced OO features such as polymorphism.

PROGRAMMING EXAMPLE

College Course Information

In this section we will create a Visual Basic application that allows the user to enter information about college courses using four different kinds of objects: `Course`, `Section`, `Instructor`, and `Student`. After receiving specific pieces of data (such as course ID and department, semester and year, instructor name and student names), the application should display a summary of the information in a message dialog. Name the solution and the project College Course. Name the form file MainForm.vb. Name the class files Course.vb, Section.vb, Instructor.vb, and Student.vb. Save the application in the \VbReloadedAdv\Chap03 folder.

Class Diagram

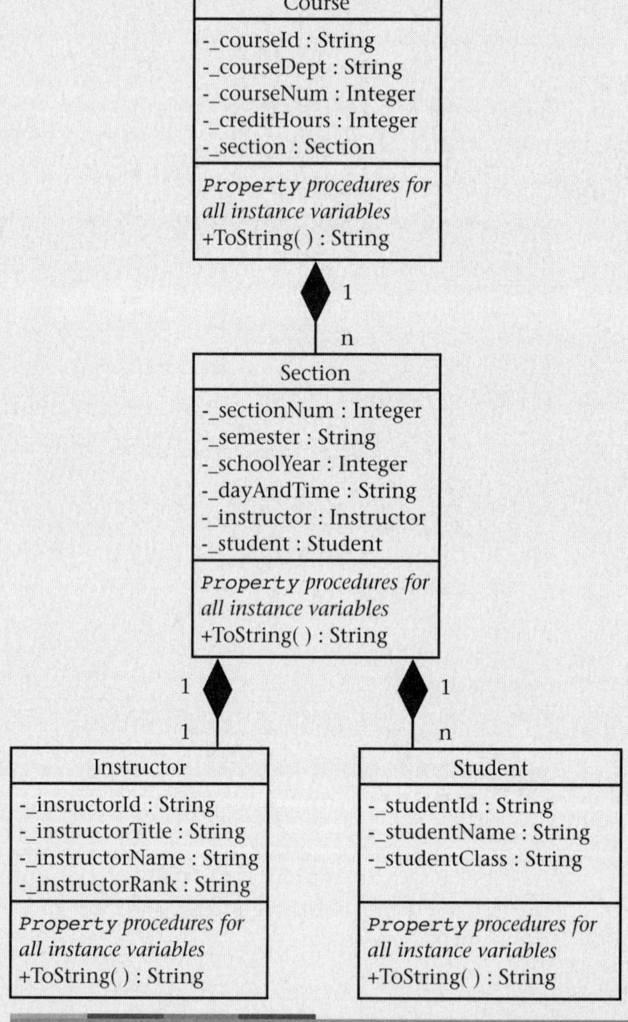

FIGURE 3.26 Class diagram for the College Course application

TOE Chart

Task	Object	Event
1. instantiate Course object 2. instantiate Section object 3. instantiate Instructor object 4. instantiate Student object	MainForm	Load
1. assign values to Course object 2. assign values to Section object 3. assign values to Instructor object 4. assign values to Student object 5. display the Course object	displayButton	Click
End the application	exitButton	Click
Get the course ID	courseIdTextBox	None
Get the course department	courseDeptListBox	None
Get the course number	courseNumTextBox	None
Get the course credit hours	creditHoursTextBox	None
Get the section number	secNumTextBox	None
Get the semester	secSemesterListBox	None
Get the calendar year	secYearTextBox	None
Get the day/time of section	secDayTimeTextBox	None
Get the instructor ID	instructorIdTextBox	None
Get the instructor title	instructorTitleListBox	None
Get the instructor name	instructorNameTextBox	None
Get the instructor Rank	instructorRankListBox	None
Get the student ID	studentIdTextBox	None
Get the student name	studentNameTextBox	None
Get the student class	studentClassListBox	None

FIGURE 3.27 TOE Chart for College Course application

User Interface

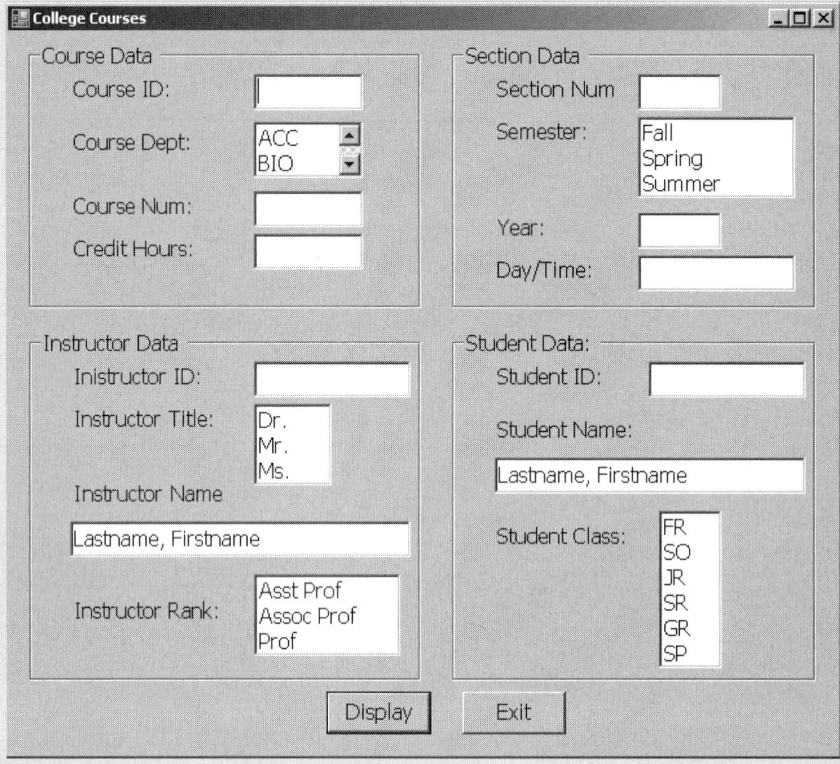

FIGURE 3.28 User interface for College Course application

Pseudocode

`MainForm Load` event procedure

1. instantiate `Course` object
2. instantiate `Section` object
3. instantiate `Instructor` object
4. instantiate `Student` object

`exitButton Click` event procedure

1. close application

`displayButton Click` event procedure

1. assign values from `Course` fields in interface to `Course` object instance variables
2. assign values from `Section` fields in interface to `Section` object instance variables
3. assign values from `Instructor` fields in interface to `Instructor` object instance variables
4. assign values from `Student` fields in interface to `Student` object instance variables
5. display the `Course` object in a message dialog

Program Code

```
' Class name:           Course
' Class purpose:        Defines Course objects
' Created/revised by:   <your name> on <current date>

Public Class Course
    ' instance variables
    Private _courseId As String
    Private _courseDept As String
    Private _courseNum As Integer
    Private _creditHours As Integer
    Private _section As Section

    ' constructor
    Public Sub New(Optional ByVal theCourseId As String = "", _
                   Optional ByVal theCourseDept As String = "", _
                   Optional ByVal theCourseNum As Integer = 0, _
                   Optional ByVal theCreditHours As Integer = 0, _
                   Optional ByRef theSection As Section = Nothing)
        _courseId = theCourseId
        _courseDept = theCourseDept
        _courseNum = theCourseNum
        _creditHours = theCreditHours
        _section = theSection
    End Sub

    ' Property procedures
    Public Property CourseId() As String
        Get
            Return _courseId
        End Get
        Set(ByVal Value As String)
            _courseId = Value
        End Set
    End Property

    Public Property CourseDept() As String
        Get
            Return _courseDept
        End Get
        Set(ByVal Value As String)
            _courseDept = Value
        End Set
    End Property

    Public Property CourseNum() As Integer
        Get
            Return _courseNum
        End Get
        Set(ByVal Value As Integer)
            _courseNum = Value
        End Set
    End Property

```

(Figure is continued on next page)

```
    Public Property CreditHours() As Integer
        Get
            Return _creditHours
        End Get
        Set(ByVal Value As Integer)
            _creditHours = Value
        End Set
    End Property

    Public Property Section() As Section
        Get
            Return _section
        End Get
        Set(ByVal Value As Section)
            _section = Value
        End Set
    End Property

    ' ToString function
    Public Overrides Function ToString() As String
        Return "Course: " & CourseId & " " & CourseDept _
             & " " & CourseNum & "-" & Section.SectionNum _
             & " (" & CreditHours & ")" _
             & ControlChars.CrLf & Section.ToString()
    End Function

End Class
```

FIGURE 3.29 Program code for the Course.vb file

```
' Class name:           Section
' Class purpose:        Defines Section objects
' Created/revised by:   <your name> on <current date>

Public Class Section
    ' instance variables
    Private _sectionNum As Integer
    Private _semester As String
    Private _schoolYear As Integer
    Private _dayAndTime As String
    Private _instructor As Instructor
    Private _student As Student

    ' constructor
    Public Sub New(Optional ByVal theSectionNum As Integer = 1, _
                   Optional ByVal theSemester As String = "", _
                   Optional ByVal theSchoolYear As Integer = 1900, _
                   Optional ByVal theDayAndTime As String = "", _
                   Optional ByRef theInstructor As Instructor = _
                       Nothing, _
                   Optional ByRef theStudent As Student = Nothing)
        _sectionNum = theSectionNum
        _semester = theSemester
        _schoolYear = theSchoolYear
        _dayAndTime = theDayAndTime
        _instructor = theInstructor
        _student = theStudent
    End Sub

```

(Figure is continued on next page)

```
    ' Property procedures
    Public Property SectionNum() As Integer
        Get
            Return _sectionNum
        End Get
        Set(ByVal Value As Integer)
            _sectionNum = Value
        End Set
    End Property

    Public Property Semester() As String
        Get
            Return _semester
        End Get
        Set(ByVal Value As String)
            _semester = Value
        End Set
    End Property

    Public Property SchoolYear() As Integer
        Get
            Return _schoolYear
        End Get
        Set(ByVal Value As Integer)
            _schoolYear = Value
        End Set
    End Property

    Public Property DayAndTime() As String
        Get
            Return _dayAndTime
        End Get
        Set(ByVal Value As String)
            _dayAndTime = Value
        End Set
    End Property

    Public Property Instructor() As Instructor
        Get
            Return _instructor
        End Get
        Set(ByVal Value As Instructor)
            _instructor = Value
        End Set
    End Property

    Public Property Student() As Student
        Get
            Return _student
        End Get
        Set(ByVal Value As Student)
            _student = Value
        End Set
    End Property

    ' ToString function
    Public Overrides Function ToString() As String
        Return "Meets: " & Semester & " " & " " & SchoolYear & " " _
             & DayAndTime _
             & ControlChars.CrLf & Instructor.ToString() _
             & ControlChars.CrLf & Student.ToString()
    End Function

End Class
```

FIGURE 3.30 Program code for the Section.vb file

```
' Class name:           Instructor
' Class purpose:        Defines Instructor objects
' Created/revised by:   <your name> on <current date>

Public Class Instructor
    ' instance variables
    Private _instructorId As String
    Private _instructorTitle As String
    Private _instructorName As String
    Private _instructorRank As String

    ' constructor
    Public Sub New(Optional ByVal theInstructorId As String = "", _
                   Optional ByVal theInstructorTitle As String = "", _
                   Optional ByVal theInstructorName As String = "", _
                   Optional ByVal theInstructorRank As String = "")
        _instructorId = theInstructorId
        _instructorTitle = theInstructorTitle
        _instructorName = theInstructorName
        _instructorRank = theInstructorRank
    End Sub

    ' Property procedures
    Public Property InstructorId() As String
        Get
            Return _instructorId
        End Get
        Set(ByVal Value As String)
            _instructorId = Value
        End Set
    End Property

    Public Property InstructorTitle() As String
        Get
            Return _instructorTitle
        End Get
        Set(ByVal Value As String)
            _instructorTitle = Value
        End Set
    End Property

    Public Property InstructorName() As String
        Get
            Return _instructorName
        End Get
        Set(ByVal Value As String)
            _instructorName = Value
        End Set
    End Property

```

(Figure is continued on next page)

```
    Public Property InstructorRank() As String
        Get
            Return _instructorRank
        End Get
        Set(ByVal Value As String)
            _instructorRank = Value
        End Set
    End Property

    ' ToString function
    Public Overrides Function ToString() As String
        Return "Instructor: " & InstructorTitle & " " & InstructorName
    End Function

End Class
```

FIGURE 3.31 Program code for the Instructor.vb file

```
' Class name:           Student
' Class purpose:        Defines Student objects
' Created/revised by:   <your name> on <current date>

Public Class Student
    ' instance variables
    Private _studentId As String
    Private _studentName As String
    Private _studentClass As String

    ' constructor
    Public Sub New(Optional ByVal theStudentId As String = "", _
                   Optional ByVal theStudentName As String = "", _
                   Optional ByVal theStudentClass As String = "")
        _studentId = theStudentId
        _studentName = theStudentName
        _studentClass = theStudentClass
    End Sub

    ' Property procedures
    Public Property StudentId() As String
        Get
            Return _studentId
        End Get
        Set(ByVal Value As String)
            _studentId = Value
        End Set
    End Property

    Public Property StudentName() As String
        Get
            Return _studentName
        End Get
        Set(ByVal Value As String)
            _studentName = Value
        End Set
    End Property

```

(Figure is continued on next page)

```
    Public Property StudentClass() As String
        Get
            Return _studentClass
        End Get
        Set(ByVal Value As String)
            _studentClass = Value
        End Set
    End Property

    ' ToString function
    Public Overrides Function ToString() As String
        Return "Student: " & StudentId & " " & StudentName _
             & " " & " (" & StudentClass & ")"
    End Function

End Class
```

FIGURE 3.32 Program code for the Student.vb file

```
' Project name:          College Course Project
' Project purpose:       Displays information about a college course.
' Created/revised by:    <your name> on <current date>

Option Explicit On
Option Strict On

Public Class MainForm
    ' declare all application objects
    Private aCourse As Course
    Private aSection As Section
    Private anInstructor As Instructor
    Private aStudent As Student

    Private Sub MainForm_Load(ByVal sender As System.Object, _
        ByVal e As System.EventArgs) Handles MyBase.Load

        ' instantiate objects when form loads using default values
        aCourse = New Course
        aSection = New Section
        anInstructor = New Instructor
        aStudent = New Student
    End Sub

    Private Sub displayButton_Click(ByVal sender As System.Object, _
        ByVal e As System.EventArgs) Handles displayButton.Click

        ' get data from form, set instance variables for objects
        aCourse.CourseId = courseIdTextBox.Text
        aCourse.CourseDept = courseDeptListBox.Text
        aCourse.CourseNum = Convert.ToInt16(courseNumTextBox.Text)
        aCourse.CreditHours = Convert.ToInt16(courseCreditTextBox.Text)
        aCourse.Section = aSection

        aSection.SectionNum = Convert.ToInt16(secNumTextBox.Text)
        aSection.Semester = secSemesterListBox.Text
        aSection.SchoolYear = Convert.ToInt16(secYearTextBox.Text)
        aSection.DayAndTime = secDayTimeTextBox.Text
        aSection.Instructor = anInstructor
        aSection.Student = aStudent

```

(Figure is continued on next page)

```
        anInstructor.InstructorId = instructorIdTextBox.Text
        anInstructor.InstructorTitle = instructorTitleListBox.Text
        anInstructor.InstructorName = instructorNameTextBox.Text
        anInstructor.InstructorRank = instructorRankListBox.Text

        aStudent.StudentId = studentIdTextBox.Text
        aStudent.StudentName = studentNameTextBox.Text
        aStudent.StudentClass = studentClassListBox.Text

        ' display all course information
        MessageBox.Show(aCourse.ToString(), _
            "College Course Information", _
            MessageBoxButtons.OK, MessageBoxIcon.Information)
    End Sub

    Private Sub exitButton_Click(ByVal sender As System.Object, _
        ByVal e As System.EventArgs) Handles exitButton.Click
        Me.Close()
    End Sub
End Class
```

FIGURE 3.33 Program code for the MainForm.vb file

Input/Output

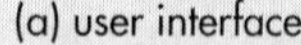

(a) user interface

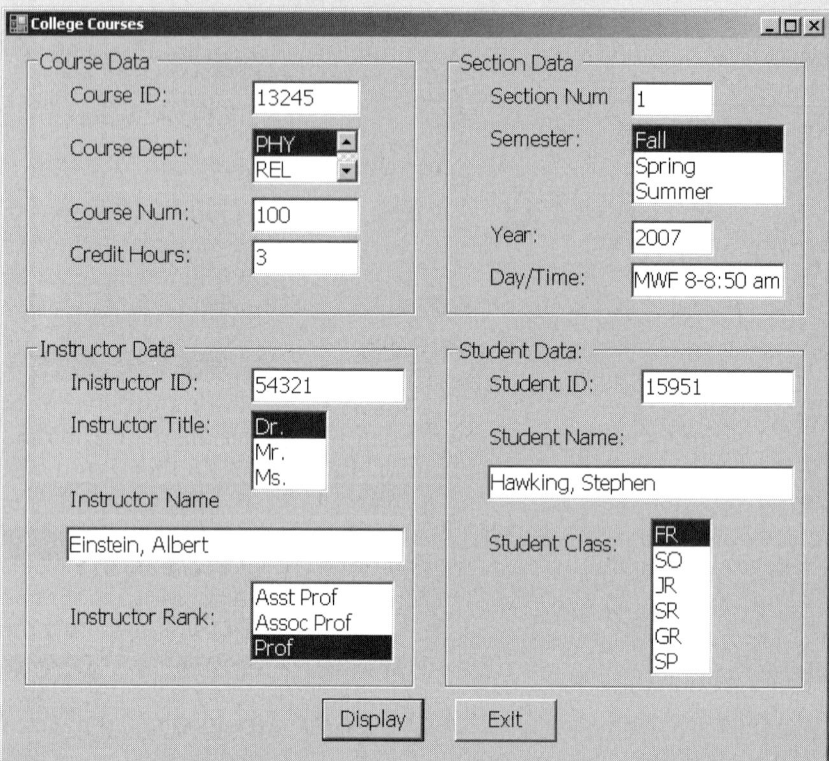

(b) output

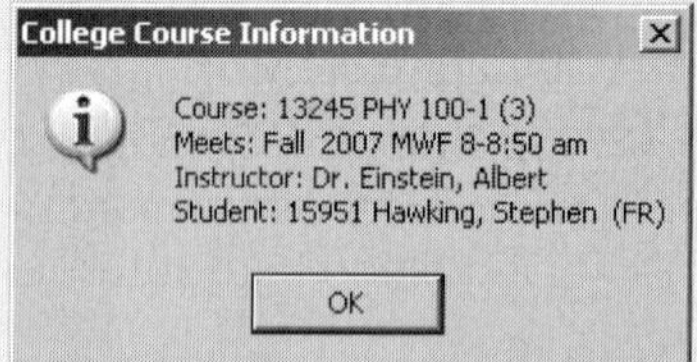

FIGURE 3.34 Completed user interface and output for College Course application

Quick Review

- Real-world things are often considered parts of real-world systems. The things within the systems are called system components, which relate and interact in predictable ways. A real-world system is often represented by and managed with a computer-based information system. The information system keeps the real-world system organized and running smoothly.
- A real-world object (a thing in the real world that has attributes and behaviors) belongs to a particular real-world class (a category to which similar real-world objects belong). As an application developer, you create a representation of a real-world object that belongs to a real-world class using a software object, A

software object is a representation of a real-world object in computer memory and is created from a software class (program code that defines software objects).

- An object has two primary features: attributes and behaviors. Object attributes are the characteristics (or data) that define what an object is at any point in time. While an object's attributes define what an object *is*, object behaviors are the actions or operations that define what an object *does*.
- A software class is a unit of program code that defines the attributes and behaviors of a specific group of objects. Not only does a class define objects, it also provides the means for creating objects in computer memory. Thus, a class is something like a blueprint or template from which specific software objects can be created.
- A class is said to contain class members. Class members can be divided into two types—data members that define attributes and method members that define behaviors. Essentially, the data members are the class's variables. The method members are the class's methods.
- When the variables and methods relate directly to the attributes and behaviors of objects created from the class, they are called instance variables and instance methods (because objects are called instances of a class). When the variables and methods relate to the entire class in general (not individual objects), they are called class variables and class methods.
- The Unified Modeling Language (UML) is a standardized, graphical notation for specifying, visualizing, constructing, and documenting a software system. The UML is programming language independent.
- One of the most important diagrams that a software developer can create using the UML is the class diagram. The simplest type of class diagram is one that specifies a single class.
- The `Class` statement begins with the keywords `Public Class`, followed by the name of the class; it ends with the keywords `End Class`. Within the `Class` statement, you define the attributes and behaviors of the class. The attributes are represented by variables, and the behaviors are represented by `Property`, `Sub`, and `Function` procedures.
- An abstract data type (ADT) is a programmer-defined type with a set of values and a collection of operations (methods) that may be performed on those values. An ADT is defined by a class.
- The attributes of an object are defined by the instance variables included in the object's class. This process of defining an object's attributes involves abstraction—that is, focusing only on the relevant details. Abstraction is one of the foundational principles of OO. Instance variables or properties of a class (the basic attributes of objects created from the class) are almost always made `Private`.
- In Visual Basic, three kinds of methods define object behaviors: `Property` procedures, constructors, and general methods. `Property` procedures permit access to the `Private` data members of a class. A constructor is a special method used to create objects from the class. General methods are simply ordinary `Sub` procedures or `Function` procedures that add to the functionality of your application.
- Instantiation is the formal term for creating an object. An application instantiates an object by calling a special method member of a class known as a constructor, so called because this method creates or constructs objects. A constructor is a `Sub` procedure with the special name `New`.
- A default constructor does not contain a parameter list, while a parameterized constructor does. Placing both of these constructors in the same class is an example of overloaded constructors—that is, two or more constructors in the same class but with different parameter lists.

- The signature of a constructor is the combination of the constructor's name (`New`) and its parameter list, so you would say that overloaded constructors have different signatures. As an alternative to providing several overloaded constructors, you can code a single constructor with `Optional` parameters.
- A user-defined class that specifies the attributes and behaviors of objects is called an object-defining class. A class such as `MainForm` in the file MainForm.vb that contains the user interface and uses object-defining classes is called an application class, which can also be considered a client program.
- To instantiate objects, you must first have an object-defining class, the blueprint for creating objects. An application class (such as `MainForm`) can then be coded to use the object-defining class for creating objects. The application class can subsequently use those objects to call methods contained in its class.
- The instance methods of a class are those that must be called by specific individual objects because these methods deal with object-specific information. However, some variables and methods relate to the class as a whole, not just to individual objects. These class members are defined as class variables and class methods. These class members are identified with the keyword `Shared`.
- Classes contain variables and methods that can be used by other classes within the same application. This implies that two classes can be related to each other. One class that uses the members of another class has a dependency relationship.
- Another important relationship between two classes is an association, in which one class contains variables that are references to objects of another class. The composition relationship is a type of association between two classes in which the contained object would not normally exist apart from the containing object.

Key Terms

abstract data type (ADT)—A programmer-defined type with a set of values and a collection of operations that may be performed on those values.

application class—A class that defines the application and that usually contains the user interface.

association—A relationship between classes in which one class contains variables that are references to objects of another class.

attributes—The characteristics (or data) that define what an object is at any point in time.

behaviors—The actions or operations that define what an object does.

class members—The data members and method members of a class.

class methods—Method members that define classwide behaviors.

class variables—Data members that define classwide attributes.

client program—A program that uses the members of a class.

composition relationship—A special type of association between two classes, in which the contained object would not normally exist apart from the containing class.

constructor—A special method that performs instantiation.

data members—The variables defined within a class.

default constructor—A constructor that contains no parameters.

dependency relationship—A relationship between two classes in which one class uses the members of another class (usually with method calls).

dot operator—see **member access operator**.

get methods—Methods that retrieve values of instance variables.

has-a relationship—see **association**.

information system—A system designed to provide needed information.

initialize—To assign an initial value to a variable when it is first declared.

instance methods—Method members that define the behaviors of class objects.

instance variables—Data members that define the attributes of class objects.

instantiation—The process of creating an object in computer memory.

member access operator—The period character (`.`) used to access a data member or call a method member of a class. Sometimes referred to as a dot operator.

method members—The methods defined within a class.

Object Management Group (OMG)—A not-for-profit computer industry specifications consortium dedicated to the standardization of software-modeling techniques (*http://www.omg.org*).

object name—The identifier of an object, which is a reference variable.

object-defining class—A class used to define object attributes and behaviors.

object-oriented (OO) application—An application in which the programmer uses an object-oriented programming language to create special classes that are used to represent objects in the real world for the purpose of solving a particular real-world problem.

OO—Abbreviation for "object-oriented."

overloaded constructors—Constructors within a single class (all having the same name, `New`) with different parameter lists.

parameterized constructor—A constructor that has one or more parameters.

`Property` **procedure**—A Visual Basic procedure designed to implement set and get methods.

real-world class—A category to which similar real-world objects belong.

real-world object—A thing in the real world that has attributes and behaviors.

real-world system—A system that exists in the real world.

reference variable—A variable that stores the memory address of an object.

set methods—Methods that assign values to instance variables.

signature—The combination of the method's name and its parameter list.

software class—Program code that defines and creates software objects.

software object—A representation of a real-world object in computer memory.

system components—The parts of a system that interact to meet system objectives.

Unified Modeling Language (UML)—A standardized, graphical notation for specifying, visualizing, constructing, and documenting a software system.

Review Questions

1. A truly object-oriented application is one that uses predefined Visual Basic classes and objects.
   a. True
   b. False
2. Instance variables in classes are used to represent object attributes.
   a. True
   b. False
3. Visual Basic is an example of a Unified Modeling Language.
   a. True
   b. False
4. An object-defining class is an example of an abstract data type.
   a. True
   b. False
5. Instance variables should be `Private` and instance methods should be `Public`.
   a. True
   b. False
6. Variables whose values should not be changed during program execution are identified in Visual Basic with the keyword `Static`.
   a. True
   b. False
7. A `ReadOnly Property` procedure should have only a `Get` statement.
   a. True
   b. False
8. The object-defining class called `Square` in this chapter would be considered to be a client program.
   a. True
   b. False
9. A constructor must always be defined in an object-defining class.
   a. True
   b. False
10. A reference variable could not have data type `String`.
    a. True
    b. False
11. Which of the following classes in the Human Resources application (presented in this chapter) would not be considered a client program?
    a. `MainForm`
    b. `Person`
    c. `Address`
    d. all the above are client programs
12. Which is the correct way for the object `mySquare` to access the property `Side`?
    a. `mySquare(Side)`
    b. `mySquare.Side`
    c. `Side.mySquare`
    d. `mySquare._side`

13. Which of the following variables in an `Employee` class should be a `Shared` variable?
    a. `_employeeName`
    b. `employeeCount`
    c. `_employeeAge`
    d. none of the above
14. Which of the following relationships is least like the others?
    a. has-a
    b. association
    c. dependency
    d. composition
15. Which access modifier is best for an instance method?
    a. `Public`
    b. `Private`
    c. `Protected`
    d. `Friend`
16. Which keyword should most obviously be used in the declaration of a variable named `TaxRate`?
    a. `Property`
    b. `Private`
    c. `WriteOnly`
    d. `Const`
17. Which of the following is the correct syntax for beginning a default constructor?
    a. `Public Sub New(ByVal value = 0)`
    b. `Private Sub New()`
    c. `Public Sub New()`
    d. none of the above
18. Which type of symbol is used to connect classes in a dependency relationship?
    a. solid arrow
    b. dashed arrow
    c. solid line with a diamond tip
    d. dashed line with a diamond tip
19. A constructor would not use which of these keywords?
    a. `New`
    b. `Sub`
    c. `Optional`
    d. all the above could be used
20. Which of the following is least like the other three?
    a. `Sub`
    b. `Property`
    c. `Shared`
    d. `Function`

Computer Exercises

When creating user interfaces, follow all conventions to create an attractive, organized form with meaningful names for controls. When creating event procedures, use the `TryParse` method to ensure valid data are entered, use named constants when appropriate, and use format specifiers for output requiring special formatting. Your instructor may also request that you use TOE charts, pseudocode, flowcharts, and/or UML diagrams as planning aids.

1. In this exercise, you create an application that displays the citation of a book.
   a. Create a project called **Citation**. Save the application in the \VBReloadedAdvanced\Chap03 folder.
   b. Design and create a user interface that accepts the author, title, copyright year, and publisher for a book in separate text boxes. Copyright year should be an integer.
   c. Create a class called `Book` with instance variables for the data items specified in part (b) of this exercise. The `Book` class should have instance variables, `Property` procedures, a single constructor with four `Optional` parameters, and a `ToString` method that creates the formatted citation.
   d. Add a label that will display a citation of the book in the format *author, title, publisher:year*.
   e. Add a Display Citation button, a Clear button, and an Exit button.
   f. Save the solution, test the application, and modify as necessary.

2. In this exercise, you create an application that displays time in hours, minutes, and seconds.
   a. Create a project called **Time**. Save the application in the \VBReloadedAdvanced\Chap03 folder.
   b. Design and create a user interface that accepts hours, minutes, and seconds in three separate text boxes. The values entered can be any integer.
   c. Add a label that will display the time in the format HH:MM:SS, but both MM and SS cannot be larger than 59.
   d. Add a Display Time button and an Exit button.
   e. Clicking the Display Time button will cause hours and minutes to be displayed in the output with values less than 60, adding the extra time to the next highest time variable. For example, if the user enters hours = 1, minutes = 70, and seconds = 100, the displayed time will be 2:11:40.
   f. Create a `Clock` class with instance variables `_hours`, `_minutes`, and `_seconds`. Add a default constructor and a constructor that accepts hours, minutes, and seconds. Add `Property` procedures for all instance variables. Add a `CalculateTime` method to calculate the correct number of hours, minutes, and seconds. Add a `ToString` method to create an output string. The `CalculateTime` method in the class `Clock` is called when the Display Time button is clicked.
   g. Save the solution, test the application, and modify as necessary.

3. In this exercise, you modify the Shapes application presented earlier in this chapter.
   a. Make a copy of the Shapes Solution folder (for Figures 3.12–14), which is contained in the \VBReloadedAdvanced\Chap03 folder. Rename the copy **Shapes2 Solution**.
   b. Add a class called `Circle` with instance variable `radius` and a constant called `PI` that is equal to 3.14159265. The `Circle` class should also have `CalculateArea` and `CalculatePerimeter` functions.

c. Modify the user interface so that the user can select either a circle or square using radio buttons. The user can enter a number in the text box (called `sideTextBox` in the original Shapes application) and select a circle or square. The area and perimeter will be displayed as usual.
d. Save the solution, test the application, and modify as necessary.

4. In this exercise, you modify the Human Resources application presented earlier in this chapter.
   a. Make a copy of the Human Resources Solution folder, which is contained in the \VBReloadedAdvanced\Chap03 folder. Rename the copy **Human Resources 2** Solution.
   b. Add a class called `Phone` with instance variables `_landline`, `_cell`, and `_fax`. Add `Property` procedures, one or more constructors, and a `ToString` method. The `ToString` method should display all phone numbers for an individual in an attractive format.
   c. The user should enter phone numbers as ten numeric digits with no other characters.
   d. The `Get` statements for the phone numbers should return phone number with parentheses around the area code, a space after the right parenthesis, and a hyphen between the sixth and seventh digit. For example, 1234567890 should be displayed as (123) 456-7890.
   e. The output label in the interface should display all the contact information for the person (mailing address and phone information).
   f. Save the solution, test the application, and modify as necessary.

5. In this exercise, you create an application that calculates the annual interest on a savings account.
   a. Create a project called **Savings Account**. Save the application in the \VBReloadedAdvanced\Chap03 folder.
   b. Design and create a user interface that receives an investment amount and an annual interest rate from the user. The interface will output the future value of the investment at yearly intervals.
   c. The interface will have a Calculate Future Value button. Each time the user clicks the button, one year's interest is added to the previous value. The interface will display the number of years represented by the total amount displayed (the number of times the button has been clicked).
   d. Create a `SavingsAccount` class with instance variables `_initialInvestment`, `_numberOfYears`, `_totalInterest`, and `_totalValue`. The interest rate is stored in a constant.
   e. Save the solution, test the application, and modify as necessary.

6. In this exercise, you redesign a solution to Exercise 4 in Chapter 1 to make it object-oriented.
   a. Create a project called **OO Car Payments**. Save the application in the \VBReloadedAdvanced\Chap03 folder.
   b. Design and create a user interface that allows the user to enter a loan amount in one text box, an annual interest rate in another, and the term (in years) of the loan in a third. Place these three text boxes in a `GroupBox` control.
   c. Use a class called `Loan` with instance variables for loan amount, interest rate, and term.
   d. A label is used to display the payments to be made at the beginning of each month.
   e. The form has Calculate, Reset, and Exit buttons with access keys.
   f. Use the `Financial.Pmt` method to calculate the payment.
   g. Save the solution, test the application, and modify as necessary.

7. In this exercise, you redesign the application you created in Exercise 5 of Chapter 1 to make it object-oriented.
   a. Create a project called **OO Lottery**. Save the application in the \VBReloadedAdvanced\Chap03 folder.
   b. A popular lottery game has the player choose five different numbers (each ranging from 1 through 55) plus a special sixth number ranging from 1 through 42. The sixth number can repeat any of the other five numbers. Design and create a user interface that has six labels to display the six random numbers.
   c. Arrange the labels horizontally using the `TableLayoutPanel` tool.
   d. The first five labels have a blue background but the sixth label has a red background. Use a bold 24-point font to display the numbers.
   e. A Select button is clicked to generate each number individually, going from left to right.
   f. Clicking the Select button after all numbers have already been selected creates a dialog box with an appropriate message for the user. A Clear button clears all labels.
   g. Use a `LotteryTicket` class in this application with instance variables for each lottery number.
   h. Save the solution, test the application, and modify as necessary.

Case Projects

Drag Race

Create an application called **Drag Race.** The application should contain the class `RaceCar`. The instance variables should be `_horsePower`, `_weight`, `_zeroTo60`, and `_milesPerGal`. The value of `_zeroTo60` (in seconds) is determined by the formula `_zeroTo60 = horsePower / weight / .7` where `_horsePower` can range from 200 to 700 hp and `_weight` can range from 1000 to 3000 pounds. Include a constructor and all `Property` procedures. Create a user interface that allows the user to enter data for two competing cars. When the Race button is clicked, the application should create two `RaceCar` objects. The application should then calculate the time it takes both cars to drag race for .25 miles using a method called `CalculateTime`. The formula for time (in seconds) is *t = sqrt(2 * distance / acceleration)* where acceleration is `.0167/_zeroTo60`. The application should display the time required for each car to complete the race and indicate whether car #1 or car #2 won the race. Save the application in the \VBReloadedAdvanced\Chap03 folder.

ATM Simulator

Refer to the ATM Simulator project in the Case Projects for Chapter 1. Redesign this project so that it uses a `BankAccount` class.

Retail Sales

Create an application called Retail Sales that uses a `Customer` class, a `CreditCardAccount` class, and a `RetailOrder` class. The customer should have a credit card account and a retail order. The credit card account should have a credit balance. The retail order has an amount. When the appropriate data are entered into the user interface, the output should indicate whether the transaction is approved or rejected.

CHAPTER

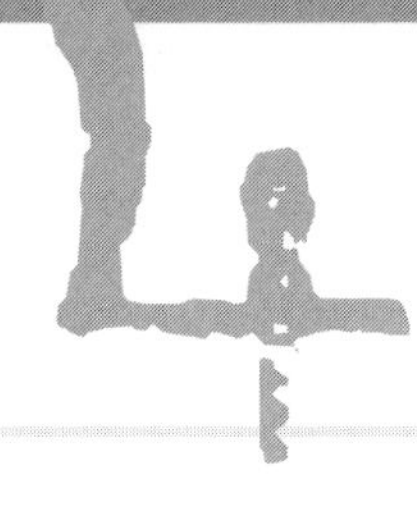

Object Orientation: Inheritance and Polymorphism

After studying Chapter 4, you should be able to:

- Explain how Visual Basic predefined classes use inheritance
- Create overloaded methods in a class
- Override methods in a base class with methods in a derived class
- Create Visual Basic classes that have inheritance relationships
- Create abstract classes and methods in an application
- Use overtyped variables through polymorphism
- Use the Class Designer to create and modify applications

The first two chapters of this text are a review of basic, procedure-oriented programming with Visual Basic 2005. Chapter 3 introduces the concepts and procedures behind simple object-oriented programming (OOP) with Visual Basic. OOP involves creating classes that define objects, which includes writing code for instance variables, constructors, and procedures. OOP also includes creating application classes that instantiate objects to solve real-world problems.

This chapter continues to explore OOP by investigating two major features of object orientation: inheritance and polymorphism. Both concepts are crucial to true OO application development, and they enable you to improve code reuse, application flexibility, and application extensibility. Inheritance allows you to write code once and make it available to many other related (inheriting) classes. Polymorphism, based on inheritance, allows you to write code once and apply it to many different kinds of objects.

INHERITANCE AMONG VISUAL BASIC PREDEFINED CLASSES

The concept of inheritance is vital to OO application development. **Inheritance** is a special relationship between two classes in which one class (called the **base class**) gives to another class (called the **derived class**) direct access to all of its `Public` (not `Private`) members. (Recall that the members of a class include data members and method members.)

TIP

In some OO programming contexts (such as Java), a base class is called a superclass and a derived class is called a subclass.

Just as people inherit many of the attributes and behaviors of their parents or grandparents, Visual Basic predefined classes inherit attributes and behaviors from other Visual Basic predefined classes. You choose from hundreds of such predefined classes when creating applications. Additionally, you can create your own classes that inherit from predefined Visual Basic classes or other programmer-defined classes. The whole idea behind inheritance is to promote code reuse by making code that already exists in a base class automatically available to a derived class, thus reducing the need to duplicate code in new classes.

An Inheritance Hierarchy for Predefined .NET Framework Classes

Recall that in Visual Basic .NET, a namespace is a grouping or library of classes. Visual Basic comes with many namespaces, each containing hundreds of predefined classes, and inheritance is used extensively throughout these namespaces. For example, the `System` namespace contains fundamental classes that provide much of the functionality of your .NET applications. One class in the `System` namespace is `System.Object`, which is the ultimate base class of all classes in the .NET Framework. You could say that `Object` is the mother of all classes. Figure 4.1 shows just a very small segment of the **inheritance hierarchy** for predefined Visual Basic classes used to create a user interface in a windows application. An inheritance hierarchy is a treelike structure showing how classes inherit the members of other classes. Figure 4.1 uses the UML (Unified Modeling Language, introduced in Chapter 3) to display some of the data members and method members of the classes. Only a very small fraction of the members of these classes are shown. (See *http://msdn.microsoft.com/library/* for complete documentation of the .NET Framework class library.)

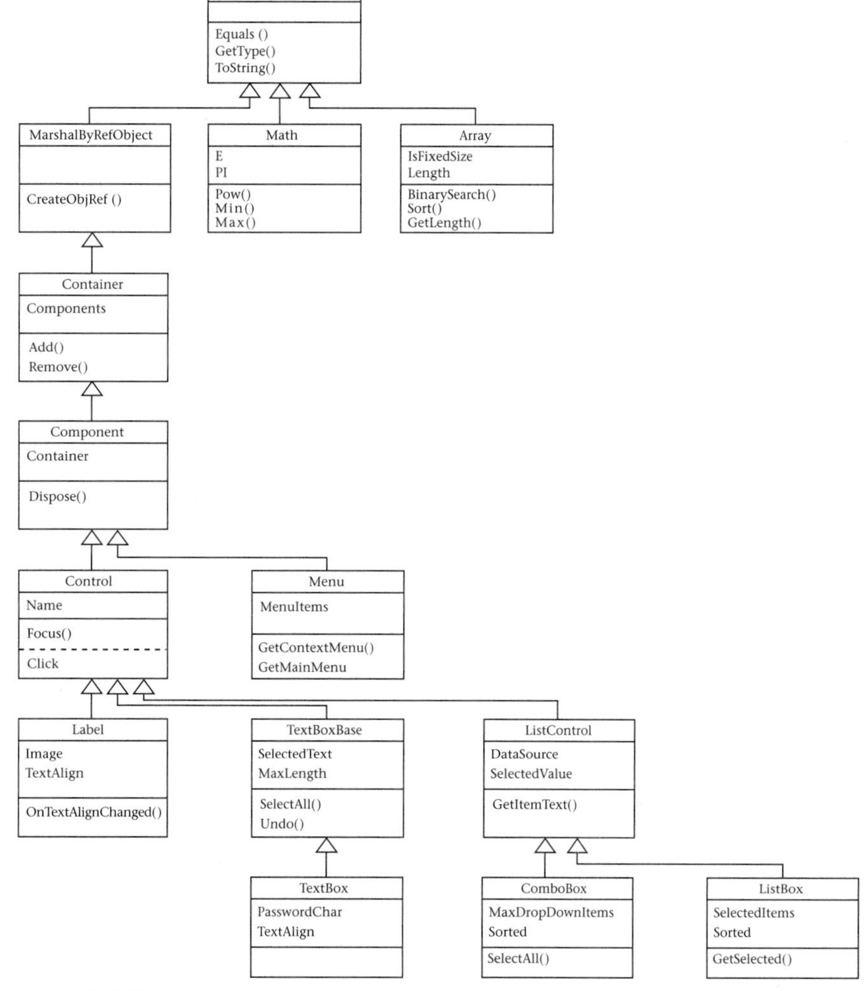

FIGURE 4.1 A partial inheritance hierarchy for .NET Framework classes

TIP

Do not confuse the `Object` class with the general term "object." The `Object` class is the name given to the ultimate base class for all classes in the .NET Framework. An object is a specific instance of a specific class in computer memory. An application can create an `Object` object or a `TextBox` object.

TIP

The open arrowheads in a UML class diagram indicate inheritance. The derived class points to the base class and thus inherits the `Public` members of the base class.

Recall that in a UML class diagram, the box represents a class. The class name is in the top section of the box, class attributes (data members) are in the middle section, and class behaviors (method members) are in the bottom section. As Figure 4.1 indicates, `System.Object` (namespace `System`, class name `Object`) is the ultimate base class of all classes in the .NET Framework, the root of Visual Basic's abstract data type (ADT) hierarchy. All predefined .NET classes and classes that you create in applications derive from `Object.` This means that such classes inherit all the `Public` data members and method members of `Object`. The `Object` class has no attributes (properties), but it does have three `Public` methods: `Equals`, `GetType`, and `ToString`. These methods do the following, respectively: (1) determine if two objects are equal; (2) return the type or class from which an object was instantiated; and (3) create a `String` representation of the object.

You will now focus on several different inheritance relationships in Figure 4.1. You should proceed through this discussion very deliberately, realizing that many of the details about these predefined .NET Framework classes are beyond the scope of the present discussion.

Beginning at the top of the inheritance hierarchy, note that three of Object's derived classes are MarshalByRefObject, Math, and Array. The Math and Array classes may be familiar to you, and you have probably used some of their properties and methods. The MarshalByRefObject class is much less intuitive but is required for objects in one application domain to communicate with objects in another application domain using object references. This is why the method CreateObjRef is needed. Of particular importance is that the MarshalByRefObject class inherits the Public methods Equals, GetType, and ToString from Object, so these methods do not need to be defined again in the MarshalByRefObject class.

Much more familiar to you is the Container class that derives (inherits) from MarshalByRefObject. While Object and MarshalByRefObject are in the System namespace, the Container class is in the System.ComponentModel namespace, so it is properly referred to as System.ComponentModel.Container. The Container class is used to logically "encapsulate" (that is, contain) components, so it makes sense that Components is a property of Container and that Add and Remove are methods of Container. Note that a Container "knows" about its Components (an attribute) and "knows how to" Add and Remove its Components (behaviors).

TIP

Recall that attributes are what objects know. Behaviors are what objects know how to do.

Continuing with Figure 4.1, the Component class inherits from Container and represents any kind of object enclosed within a Container. A Component knows the Container to which it belongs and knows how to Dispose (release) the resources used by the Component.

Both the Control and Menu classes derive from Component—a Control is a Component with a visual representation. A Control has a Name property, a Focus method, and a Click event associated with it. That is, a Control object knows how to receive focus and how to listen for a mouse click. A Label object is a Control with a unique property TextAlign. Because Label inherits from Control, a Label object can also have a Name property and it knows how to receive Focus and listen for a Click. The TextBoxBase and ListControl classes both inherit from Control. These classes are base classes of the familiar TextBox, ComboBox, and ListBox classes, with their own unique properties and methods.

The Is-A Class Relationship

You may find this quick tour of some of the inheritance features involved in predefined Visual Basic classes a little confusing. At this point, all you really need to grasp is that inheritance is widely used to provide the necessary functionality of the user interfaces you create with Visual Basic. Note that a TextBox object that you place in a form is a Control, that a Control is a Component, and that a Component is an Object. Also, a TextBox object can directly access the SelectAll method in the TextBoxBase class, the Name property in the Control class, the Add method in the Container class, and even the Equals method in the Object class. You can do all this without writing any duplicate code in the Visual Basic language. Notice the repeated use of the term "is a" in this discussion. Inheritance is called an **is-a relationship** between classes because an instance of a derived class "is a" (or rather, is an) instance of any of its base classes. (Little did you know all that was involved when you dragged and dropped a text box onto a Windows form.) Next, you will turn your attention to implementing inheritance in your own applications.

TIP

Another term for an inheritance relationship (or an "is-a" relationship) is a generalization relationship. This term derives from the fact that the base class is more general than the derived class (or, inversely, the derived class is more specific than the base class).

INHERITANCE AMONG PROGRAMMER-DEFINED CLASSES

Not only is inheritance extremely useful for the predefined classes in the .NET Framework, it can prove equally helpful when you are creating your own classes within applications.

Creating an Inheritance Relationship

When you create a new Windows Application project in Visual Studio 2005 (by launching Visual Studio 2005 and clicking File, then New Project..., and then OK), the form that appears (for example, `Form1` in Figure 4.2) uses inheritance, perhaps without your knowledge. To illustrate this you can view the code behind the form. To do so, click View and then click Code in the Visual Studio menu, resulting in the window in Figure 4.3. This code is in the file Form1.vb, which is the file that you, the programmer, will modify as you develop the application.

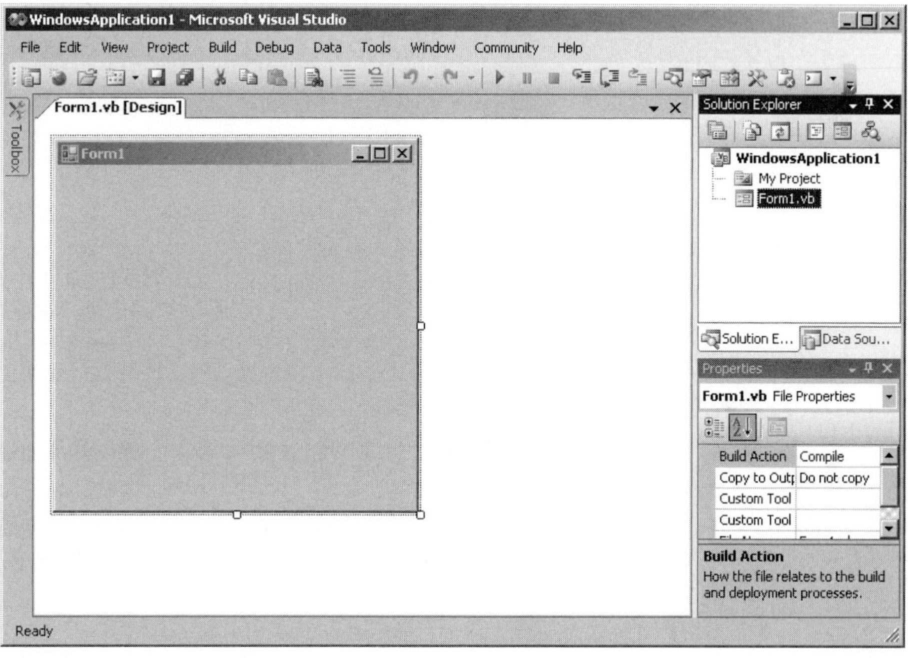

FIGURE 4.2 `Form1` created in a new Windows Application project

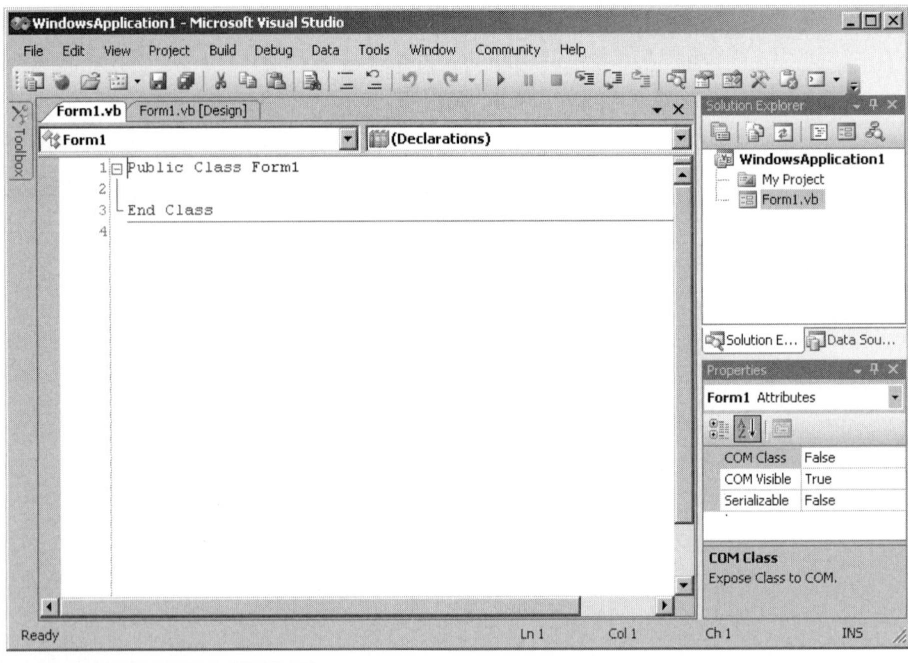

FIGURE 4.3 Code view for `Form1`

However, if you want to view all the code generated behind the scenes by Visual Basic for this form, you need to take a few additional steps. For example, click the Show All Files button in the Solution Explorer, click the plus sign next to the file Form1.vb, and double-click the Form1.Designer.vb file to reveal all the code behind the form as shown in Figure 4.4. (Remember that this code is generated by Visual Basic and should never be modified by the programmer.)

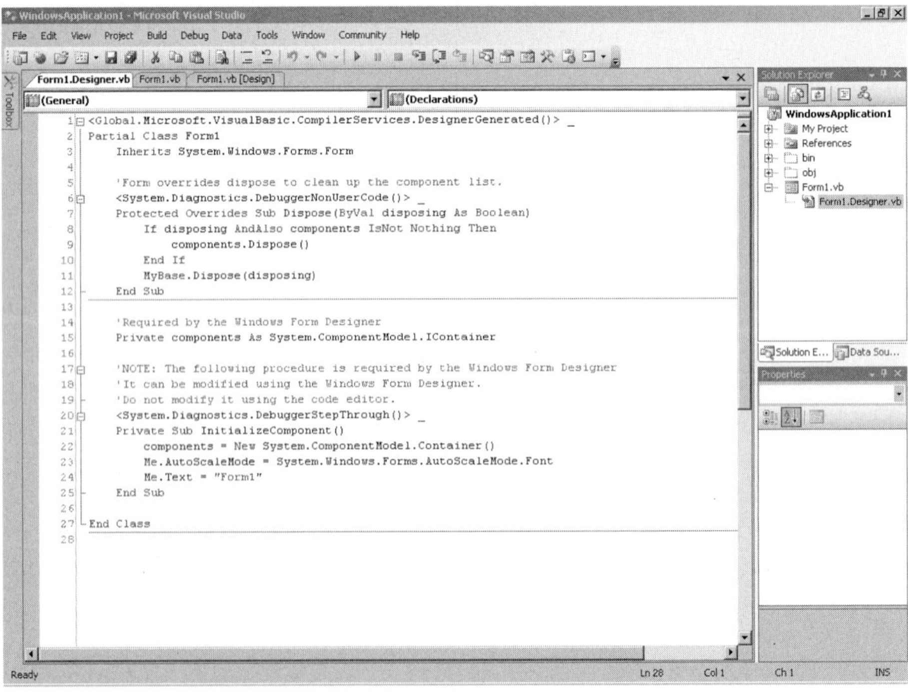

FIGURE 4.4 Program code for Form1.Designer.vb

The code in Figure 4.4 may look a little complicated, but notice Line 3. It indicates that `Form1` inherits from the class `Form` in the namespace `System.Windows.Forms`. Thus, the fully qualified name for the `Form` class is `System.Windows.Forms.Form`. The `Form` class is used to create windows for user interfaces in a Windows application and `Form1` is a class that inherits the members of the `Form` class, giving it much of the functionality it requires to serve as a user interface. To hide these Windows-generated files, click the Show All Files button in the Solution Explorer.

The point of viewing the file Form1.Designer.vb in Figure 4.4 is to illustrate that you will create similar code when you want the classes that you create to use inheritance. Figure 4.5 shows how to create an inheritance relationship between user-defined classes in Visual Basic.

HOW TO...

Create an Inheritance Relationship

Syntax

```
Public Class DerivedClass
    Inherits BaseClass
      attributes section
      behaviors section
End Class
```

Example

```
Public Class Square
    Inherits Rectangle

    ' attributes section
    Private _side As Decimal

    ' behaviors section
    Public Sub New()
        Side = 0
    End Sub

    Public Property Side() As Decimal
        Get
            Return _side
        End Get

        Set(ByVal value As Decimal)
            _side = value
        End Set
    End Property

End Class
```

FIGURE 4.5 How to create an inheritance relationship

The syntax of Figure 4.5 shows that to create a class that inherits from another class you simply add an `Inherits` clause specifying the base class from which it inherits. The base class must be within the current namespace, must be

TIP

If you are familiar with the Java programming language, you will realize that instead of using the keyword **Inherits**, Java uses the keyword **extends** to implement inheritance. This is because the derived class (subclass in Java) **extends** the attributes and behaviors of the base class (superclass in Java).

within a namespace imported by the program, or must be a fully qualified class name. (Remember that a fully qualified class name includes the namespace, such as `System.Windows.Forms.Form`, as seen in Figure 4.4.)

The example in Figure 4.5 shows that the class `Square` inherits from the class `Rectangle`. Thus, a `Square` "is a" `Rectangle`. That is, a `Square` is a more specialized version of a `Rectangle` (all sides are equal) and a `Rectangle` is a more general version of a `Square`. A `Rectangle` class (not shown) would have instance variables `_length` and `_width` and could also contain a `Public` method called `CalculateArea`, which would return the value of `_length * _width`. The class `Square` would not need to contain a `CalculateArea` method because that method is inherited from `Rectangle`, thus requiring less code. A `Square` object would just need to pass the value of its side to the length and width parameters of `CalculateArea` in the `Rectangle` class to determine its area. Thus, the `Square` class reuses code in the `Rectangle` class, making the application simpler. Note that every `Square` is a `Rectangle`, but a `Rectangle` is not always a `Square`. Is-a relationships work in only one direction.

More About Access Modifiers

As you have seen so far, the access modifier `Public` is very important when using inheritance. In Chapter 3, you learned that two access modifiers are frequently used in object-oriented programming: `Public` and `Private`. `Public` means that there are no restrictions on access to a class member. Any other class in any other application has direct access to such members. You could say that `Public` provides interapplication access. Most methods in an object-oriented application are `Public`. By contrast, `Private` means that class members can be directly accessed only within the class in which the members are declared. That is, `Private` provides only intraclass access. Instance variables are usually `Private`, which means that they can be accessed outside the class only by using `Public` methods within the class, such as a `Public Property` procedure (with `Get` and `Set` statements).

In Chapter 3, you also learned that there are other access modifiers: `Friend`, `Protected`, and `Protected Friend`. The first of these access modifiers, `Friend`, means that a class member can be directly accessed from anywhere within the application in which it is defined. Thus, `Friend` is what you could call intra-application access and it is a little more restrictive than `Public`. A `Protected` class member is directly accessible within the declaring class and classes that inherit from the declaring class. Thus, if an instance variable is given `Protected` access (such as `Protected _name` in a class called `Person`), any class that inherits from the declaring class (`Person`, in this case) can directly refer to that variable without using any `Public` procedures. `Protected` access is thus more restrictive than `Friend`. Finally, you can use the combination of access modifiers `Protected Friend`, which is the union of `Protected` and `Friend`. `Protected Friend` grants access anywhere within an application and within any derived classes.

Using these access modifiers appropriately is a demonstration of the **principle of least privilege**, which states that elements in a computing environment should be granted only information and resources that are immediately necessary. The principle of least privilege thus enhances protection of data and functionality from faults and malicious behavior. As computer scientists Jerome Saltzer and Michael Schroeder first stated in 1975, "Every program and every user of the system should operate using the least set of privileges necessary to complete the job." These access modifiers are summarized in Table 4.1 in order of most to least restrictive.

Access Modifier	Level of Access (most to least restrictive)
`Private`	Only within the class in which the member is declared
`Protected`	Within the declaring class and within any derived classes
`Friend`	Anywhere within an application in which the member is declared
`Protected Friend`	Within an application and within any derived classes
`Public`	Across all applications (no restrictions)

TABLE 4.1 Summary of Visual Basic access modifiers

INHERITANCE: OVERLOADING AND OVERRIDING

As a final requirement for using inheritance in applications, you need to understand how inheritance relates to the topics of overloading and overriding methods in Visual Basic.

Overloaded Methods in the Same Class

In Chapter 3 you learned about overloading constructors. To review, an overloaded constructor is one of two or more constructors in the same class that has a different parameter list. Figure 4.6 shows (a) a default constructor for the `Address` class and (b) a parameterized constructor for the `Address` class. These two overloaded constructors could coexist and replace the parameterized constructor for the `Address` class with `Optional` parameters found in Figure 3.23. These constructors could be called by the code shown in part (c) of Figure 4.6.

(a)

```
' default Address constructor
Public Sub New()
    _street = ""
    _city = ""
    _state = ""
    _zip = ""
End Sub
```

(b)

```
' parameterized Address constructor
Public Sub New(ByVal theStreet As String, _
               ByVal theCity As String, _
               ByVal theState As String, _
               ByVal theZip As String)
    _street = theStreet
    _city = theCity
    _state = theState
    _zip = theZip
End Sub
```

(Figure is continued on next page)

(c)

```
' uses default Address constructor
Dim address1 As New Address

' uses parameterized Address constructor
Dim address2 As New Address("123 Main St.", "Anytown", "CA", "90001")
```

FIGURE 4.6 Defining and using overloaded constructors

Constructors are very specialized methods that are used to construct (create or instantiate) objects. However, any method in a class (not just constructors) can be overloaded. An **overloaded method** in a class is one of two or more methods in the same class or inheritance hierarchy with the same name but an otherwise different method signature. A **method signature** is the combination of the method name and its parameter list. Thus, if two methods have the same name but different signatures, they must have different parameter lists. For example, a method named `MyMethod` declared using the code `MyMethod()` does not have a parameter list (the parentheses are empty). However, `MyMethod(ByVal x As Integer)` has a single `Integer` parameter and `MyMethod(ByVal x As Integer, ByVal y As String)` has two parameters (an `Integer` parameter first, then a `String` parameter). The method `MyMethod(ByVal x As String, ByVal y As Integer)` has yet a different parameter list (`String` first, then `Integer`). Thus, a parameter list can differ by the number of parameters, the types of parameters, and/or the order of its parameters. Note that two parameter lists are identical if they have the same number of parameters and corresponding parameters have the same data types—the variable names used in the parameter lists are immaterial. Therefore, `MyMethod(ByVal x As Double)` has the same signature as `MyMethod(ByVal y As Double)`.

To demonstrate method overloading, Figure 4.7 presents an interface for a `Quadrilateral` application that determines the shape and perimeter of a quadrilateral. In this application, the user enters integer values for the length of the sides of a quadrilateral and presses the Process button to display the specific shape of the quadrilateral and its perimeter. When the user enters an integer only in the Side 1 text box, "Square" is displayed in the Shape box, along with the perimeter of the square in the Perimeter box. However, if the user enters integers for Side 1 and Side 2 (but not for Side 3 or Side 4), "Square" is displayed in the Shape box only if the two values are equal. If the values for Side 1 and Side 2 are not equal, "Rectangle" is displayed. If the user enters integers for all four sides, then "Quadrilateral" is displayed. If none of the above conditions are satisfied (that is, if certain key data are missing), the shape is "Undetermined" and the perimeter is 0.

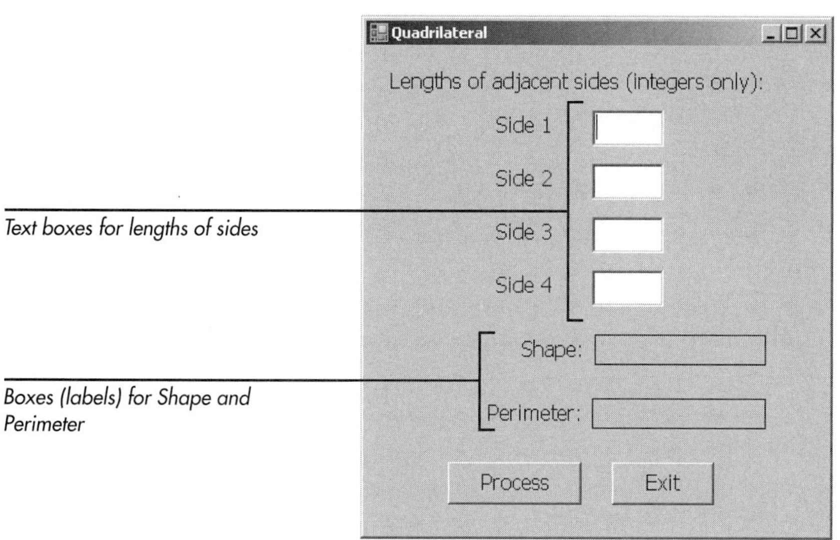

FIGURE 4.7 User interface for the Quadrilateral application

The code for Quadrilateral.vb is shown in Figure 4.8. The code for MainForm.vb can be found in Figure 4.9. The `Quadrilateral` class (Figure 4.8) declares and initializes the instance variables. Note that there are then four overloaded constructors, a default constructor `New()` followed by constructors with one, two, and three parameters. Each of these four constructors calls one of four overloaded methods, each named `ProcessQuadrilateral`, which are defined after the `Property` procedures.

The parameter lists of the four overloaded `ProcessQuadrilateral` methods differ only in the number of parameters. The no-parameter `ProcessQuadrilateral` method sets the `Perimeter` property to `0` and the `Shape` property to `"Undetermined"`. The one-parameter `ProcessQuadrilateral` method is for a square, the two-parameter for a rectangle, and the four-parameter for a general quadrilateral. Keep in mind that methods can be overloaded in terms of the number of parameters (as in this case) or the data types of the parameters, or both.

```
' Project name:       Quadrilateral Project
' Project purpose:    Displays the perimeter of a quadrilateral.
' Created/revised by: <your name> on <current date>

Option Explicit On
Option Strict On

Public Class Quadrilateral
    ' instance variables
    Private _side1 As Integer = 0
    Private _side2 As Integer = 0
    Private _side3 As Integer = 0
    Private _side4 As Integer = 0
    Private _perimeter As Integer = 0
    Private _shape As String = Nothing

```

(Figure is continued on next page)

```
    ' overloaded constructors
    Public Sub New()
        ProcessQuadrilateral()
    End Sub

    Public Sub New(ByVal sideA As Integer)
        Side1 = sideA
        ProcessQuadrilateral(Side1)
    End Sub

    Public Sub New(ByVal sideA As Integer, _
                   ByVal sideB As Integer)
        Side1 = sideA
        Side2 = sideB
        ProcessQuadrilateral(Side1, Side2)
    End Sub

    Public Sub New(ByVal sideA As Integer, _
                   ByVal sideB As Integer, _
                   ByVal sideC As Integer, _
                   ByVal sideD As Integer)
        Side1 = sideA
        Side2 = sideB
        Side3 = sideC
        Side4 = sideD
        ProcessQuadrilateral(Side1, Side2, Side3, Side4)
    End Sub

    ' Property procedures
    Public Property Side1() As Integer
        Get
            Return _side1
        End Get
        Set(ByVal Value As Integer)
            _side1 = Value
        End Set
    End Property

    Public Property Side2() As Integer
        Get
            Return _side2
        End Get
        Set(ByVal Value As Integer)
            _side2 = Value
        End Set
    End Property

    Public Property Side3() As Integer
        Get
            Return _side3
        End Get
        Set(ByVal Value As Integer)
            _side3 = Value
        End Set
    End Property

    Public Property Side4() As Integer
        Get
            Return _side4
        End Get
```

(Figure is continued on next page)

```
        Set(ByVal Value As Integer)
            _side4 = Value
        End Set
    End Property

    Public Property Perimeter() As Integer
        Get
            Return _perimeter
        End Get
        Set(ByVal Value As Integer)
            _perimeter = Value
        End Set
    End Property

    Public Property Shape() As String
        Get
            Return _shape
        End Get
        Set(ByVal Value As String)
            _shape = Value
        End Set
    End Property

    ' overloaded methods
```

No-parameters method

```
    Public Sub ProcessQuadrilateral()
        Perimeter = 0
        Shape = "Undetermined"
    End Sub

```

One-parameter method

```
    Public Sub ProcessQuadrilateral(ByVal side As Integer)
        Perimeter = 4 * side
        Shape = "Square"
    End Sub

```

Two-parameter method

```
    Public Sub ProcessQuadrilateral(ByVal sideA As Integer, _
                                    ByVal sideB As Integer)
        Perimeter = 2 * sideA + 2 * sideB
        Shape = "Rectangle"
    End Sub

```

Four-parameter method

```
    Public Sub ProcessQuadrilateral(ByVal sideA As Integer, _
                                    ByVal sideB As Integer, _
                                    ByVal sideC As Integer, _
                                    ByVal sideD As Integer)
        Perimeter = sideA + sideB + sideC + sideD
        Shape = "Quadrilateral"
    End Sub

End Class
```

FIGURE 4.8 Program code for the class `Quadrilateral` in the Quadrilateral application

The `MainForm` class (Figure 4.9) contains the `processButton_Click` event procedure. Within this procedure, nested `If...Else` logic determines which `TextBox` controls have data and calls the appropriate overloaded constructor. After the object `aQuadrilateral` is instantiated, its `Shape` and `Perimeter` properties are displayed in the interface. Figure 4.10 demonstrates how the application works with several sample runs.

Only `side1TextBox` *has a value*

Only `side1TextBox` *and* `side2TextBox` *have values*

All text boxes have values

```
' Project name:         Quadrilateral Project
' Project purpose:      Displays the perimeter of a quadrilateral.
' Created/revised by:   <your name> on <current date>

Option Explicit On
Option Strict On

Public Class MainForm

    Private aQuadrilateral As Quadrilateral

    Private Sub exitButton_Click(ByVal sender As Object, _
        ByVal e As System.EventArgs) Handles exitButton.Click
        Me.Close()
    End Sub

    Private Sub processButton_Click(ByVal sender As Object, _
        ByVal e As System.EventArgs) Handles processButton.Click
        ' nested If...Else logic
        If side1TextBox.Text <> Nothing AndAlso _
           side2TextBox.Text = Nothing AndAlso _
           side3TextBox.Text = Nothing AndAlso _
           side4TextBox.Text = Nothing Then
               aQuadrilateral = New Quadrilateral( _
                    Convert.ToInt16(side1TextBox.Text)) ' a square
        ElseIf side1TextBox.Text <> Nothing AndAlso _
               side2TextBox.Text <> Nothing AndAlso _
               side3TextBox.Text = Nothing AndAlso _
               side4TextBox.Text = Nothing Then
            If side1TextBox.Text = side2TextBox.Text Then
                aQuadrilateral = New Quadrilateral( _
                    Convert.ToInt16(side1TextBox.Text)) ' a square
            Else
                aQuadrilateral = New Quadrilateral( _
                    Convert.ToInt16(side1TextBox.Text), _
                    Convert.ToInt16(side2TextBox.Text)) ' a rectangle
            End If
        ElseIf side1TextBox.Text <> Nothing AndAlso _
               side2TextBox.Text <> Nothing AndAlso _
               side3TextBox.Text <> Nothing AndAlso _
               side4TextBox.Text <> Nothing Then
            aQuadrilateral = New Quadrilateral( _
                Convert.ToInt16(side1TextBox.Text), _
                Convert.ToInt16(side2TextBox.Text), _
                Convert.ToInt16(side3TextBox.Text), _
                Convert.ToInt16(side4TextBox.Text)) ' a quadrilateral
        Else
            aQuadrilateral = New Quadrilateral ' undetermined
        End If

        ' display results
        shapeLabel.Text = aQuadrilateral.Shape
        perimeterLabel.Text = _
            Convert.ToString(aQuadrilateral.Perimeter)

    End Sub
End Class
```

FIGURE 4.9 Program code for the class `MainForm` in the Quadrilateral application

FIGURE 4.10 Sample runs of the Quadrilateral application

Overloaded Methods in a Derived Class

If overloading is used within an inheritance hierarchy of classes, an overloaded method in a derived class must use the keyword `Overloads` in its declaration. This is the case even if the overloaded methods in the base class and the derived class have the same signature. Overloaded methods are demonstrated in the Overloaded Quadrilateral application, shown in Figures 4.11 and 4.12 (the `MainForm` class for this application is identical to the one shown in Figure 4.9).

Figure 4.11 contains the program code for the class `UndeterminedShape`, which has instance variables `_shape` and `_perimeter`, `Property` procedures `Shape` and `Perimeter`, and a general no-argument method `ProcessQuadrilateral`. Figure 4.12 contains the code for the class `Quadrilateral`, which inherits from `UndeterminedShape` and contains the remainder of the instance variables and `Property` procedures, as well as several overloaded methods. Because `Quadrilateral` inherits from `UndeterminedShape`, the keyword `Overloads` must be used in the method declarations. The output for this application will be identical to that for the Quadrilateral application (see Figure 4.10).

`_shape` *and* `_perimeter` *instance variables*

`Perimeter Property` *procedure*

```
Public Class UndeterminedShape

    Private _perimeter As Integer = 0
    Private _shape As String = Nothing

    Public Property Perimeter() As Integer
        Get
            Return _perimeter
        End Get
```

(Figure is continued on next page)

```
        Set(ByVal Value As Integer)
            _perimeter = Value
        End Set
    End Property

    Public Property Shape() As String
        Get
            Return _shape
        End Get
        Set(ByVal Value As String)
            _shape = Value
        End Set
    End Property

    Public Sub ProcessQuadrilateral()
        Perimeter = 0
        Shape = "Undetermined"
    End Sub
End Class
```

`Shape Property` *procedure*

No-argument method located here

FIGURE 4.11 Program code for the class `UndeterminedShape` in the Overloaded Quadrilateral application

```
' Project name:         Overloaded Quadrilateral Project
' Project purpose:      Displays the perimeter of a quadrilateral.
' Created/revised by:   <your name> on <current date>

Option Explicit On
Option Strict On

Public Class Quadrilateral
    Inherits UndeterminedShape

    Private _side1 As Integer = 0
    Private _side2 As Integer = 0
    Private _side3 As Integer = 0
    Private _side4 As Integer = 0

    ' overloaded constructors
    Public Sub New()
        ProcessQuadrilateral()
    End Sub

    Public Sub New(ByVal sideA As Integer)
        Side1 = sideA
        ProcessQuadrilateral(Side1)
    End Sub

    Public Sub New(ByVal sideA As Integer, _
                   ByVal sideB As Integer)
        Side1 = sideA
        Side2 = sideB
        ProcessQuadrilateral(Side1, Side2)
    End Sub

    Public Sub New(ByVal sideA As Integer, _
                   ByVal sideB As Integer, _
                   ByVal sideC As Integer, _
                   ByVal sideD As Integer)
```

`_shape` *and* `_perimeter` *instance variables omitted*

Overloaded constructors

(Figure is continued on next page)

`Shape` *and* `Perimeter` `Property` *procedures omitted*

Overloaded methods in derived class must use `Overloads` *keyword*

```
        Side1 = sideA
        Side2 = sideB
        Side3 = sideC
        Side4 = sideD
        ProcessQuadrilateral(Side1, Side2, Side3, Side4)
    End Sub

    ' Property procedures
    Public Property Side1() As Integer
        Get
            Return _side1
        End Get
        Set(ByVal Value As Integer)
            _side1 = Value
        End Set
    End Property

    Public Property Side2() As Integer
        Get
            Return _side2
        End Get
        Set(ByVal Value As Integer)
            _side2 = Value
        End Set
    End Property

    Public Property Side3() As Integer
        Get
            Return _side3
        End Get
        Set(ByVal Value As Integer)
            _side3 = Value
        End Set
    End Property

    Public Property Side4() As Integer
        Get
            Return _side4
        End Get
        Set(ByVal Value As Integer)
            _side4 = Value
        End Set
    End Property

    ' overloaded methods
    Public Overloads Sub ProcessQuadrilateral()
        Perimeter = 0
        Shape = "Undetermined"
    End Sub

    Public Overloads Sub ProcessQuadrilateral(ByVal side As Integer)
        Perimeter = 4 * side
        Shape = "Square"
    End Sub

    Public Overloads Sub ProcessQuadrilateral(ByVal sideA As Integer, _
                                              ByVal sideB As Integer)
        Perimeter = 2 * sideA + 2 * sideB
        Shape = "Rectangle"
    End Sub
```

(Figure is continued on next page)

Overloaded methods in derived class must use `Overloads` *keyword*

```
    Public Overloads Sub ProcessQuadrilateral(ByVal sideA As Integer, _
                                              ByVal sideB As Integer, _
                                              ByVal sideC As Integer, _
                                              ByVal sideD As Integer)
        Perimeter = sideA + sideB + sideC + sideD
        Shape = "Quadrilateral"
    End Sub

End Class
```

FIGURE 4.12 Program code for the class `Quadrilateral` in the Overloaded Quadrilateral application

Overriding Methods

Overloaded methods are methods in the same class or in an inheritance hierarchy with the same name but different parameter lists. Visual Basic knows which method to use based on the number and data types of the arguments in the method call. If the method with the right signature isn't found in a base class, then Visual Basic will move up the inheritance hierarchy to find the appropriate method. When calling an overloaded method, the number and data types of the arguments in the method call must exactly match the number and data types of the parameters in the method declaration.

Overriding methods is a different process. An **overridden method** is a method in a base class with exactly the same signature (same name and parameter list) as a method in a derived class. The method in the derived class that overrides the method in the base class has precedence and will be used by objects instantiated from the derived class. Objects instantiated from the base class will use the method in the base class even though it is overridden by a derived class.

A good example of overriding methods is found with the `ToString` method, which is often used to create a string that contains the basic information about objects instantiated from a class. Suppose a class called `TheBaseClass` has a `ToString` method and that it has a derived class called `TheDerivedClass`, which also has a `ToString` method. All classes automatically inherit from Visual Basic's `Object` class, which also contains a `ToString` method. But if an object instantiated from `TheBaseClass` calls the `ToString` method (as with `aBaseClassObject.ToString()`), it will use the `ToString` method in `TheBaseClass`, not the `ToString` method in `Object`. Likewise, an object instantiated from `TheDerivedClass` will use its `ToString` method, not the one in `TheBaseClass` or the `Object` class. Such overriding is illustrated in Figure 4.13.

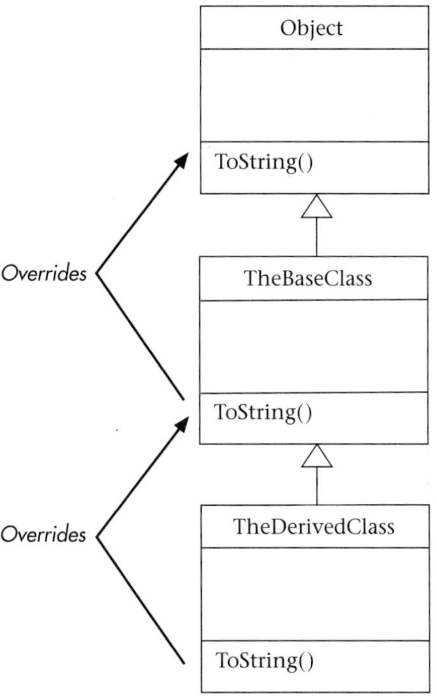

FIGURE 4.13 Overriding the `ToString` method

You can use the Overloaded Quadrilateral application in Figures 4.11 and 4.12 to create an example of overriding. Note that Figure 4.11 contains the method `ProcessQuadrilateral()` with no parameters. This method is not found in Figure 4.12, so when the application is run and the Process button is clicked (without entering any data in the interface), the `ProcessQuadrilateral()` method in Figure 4.11 is used. However, if the following code is added to Figure 4.12 and the declaration `Public Overridable Sub ProcessQuadrilateral()` is used in Figure 4.11, the output resulting from clicking the Process button demonstrates that overriding occurs, as shown in Figure 4.14.

```
Public Overrides Sub ProcessQuadrilateral()
    Perimeter = 0
    Shape = "Undetermined in derived"
End Sub
```

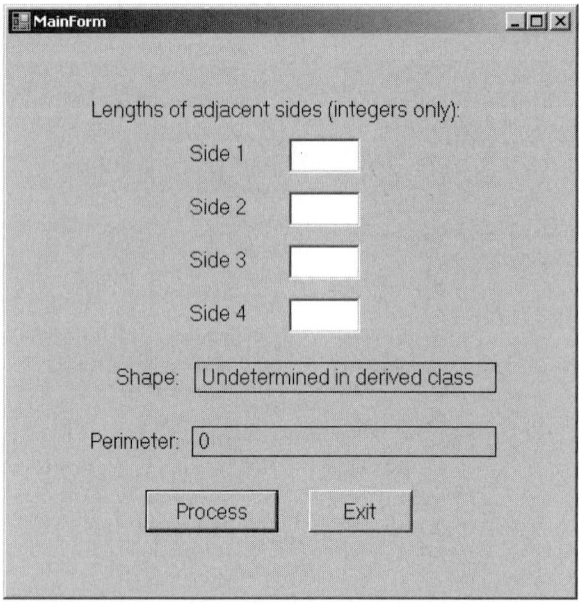

MainForm

Lengths of adjacent sides (integers only):

Side 1

Side 2

Side 3

Side 4

Shape: Undetermined in derived class

Perimeter: 0

Process Exit

FIGURE 4.14 Sample run of the Overridden Quadrilateral application

Note that the method declaration in the base class must use the `Overridable` keyword and the method declaration in the derived class must use the `Overrides` keyword. Otherwise, a syntax error will result.

USING INHERITANCE IN APPLICATIONS

Now that you understand the concepts behind class inheritance, you will investigate how to implement inheritance in an application. You will create a simple College Personnel application that uses inheritance as well as composition (another important class relationship covered in Chapter 3).

Planning the College Personnel Application Using UML

Suppose that you want to track information about students and faculty at a university. You could create `Student` and `Instructor` classes, but you realize that they have certain characteristics in common: both students and instructors are people who have ID numbers, names, and addresses. However, they also have some unique characteristics: students have a class level (freshman through graduate student) and a GPA, while instructors have a title (such as Ms., Mr., or Dr.) and a rank (assistant professor through professor). To take advantage of the similarities between these two groups, you could create a `Person` class that serves as a base class for both the `Student` and `Instructor` classes. A person's address could also be stored in a separate `Address` class that has a composition relationship with `Person.` The `Person` class has an `Address` object as one of its instance variables (as demonstrated in Chapter 3). A class diagram that reflects this design (using inheritance and composition) is shown in Figure 4.15. Note that each class in the diagram contains only its unique attributes. In addition, each class has its own `ToString` method to display just the unique data members within that class. You can use this design to implement the application.

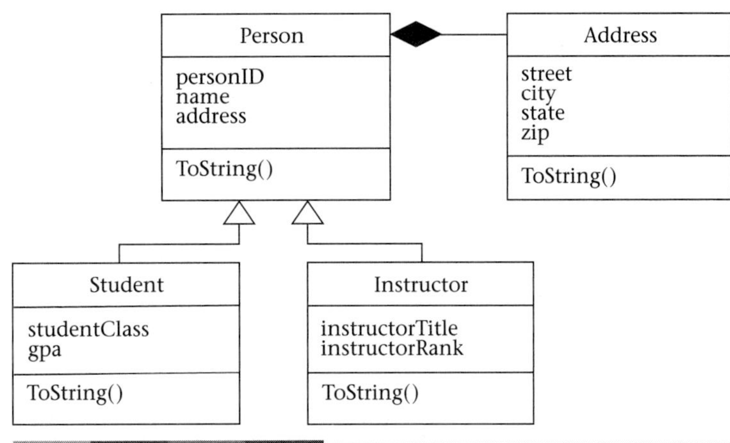

FIGURE 4.15 Class diagram for `Person`, `Address`, `Student`, and `Instructor` classes

Implementing the College Personnel Application

A user interface designed to collect `Student` data is shown in Figure 4.16. Note that many of the controls in Figure 4.16 are also used in the Human Resources interface in Figure 3.25. You can save application development time by reusing the controls in an existing application. Simply copy the controls from one form and paste them into another form, but make sure that you reset the control properties, such as `Name` and `TabIndex` (that is, tab order), to the appropriate values in the new application.

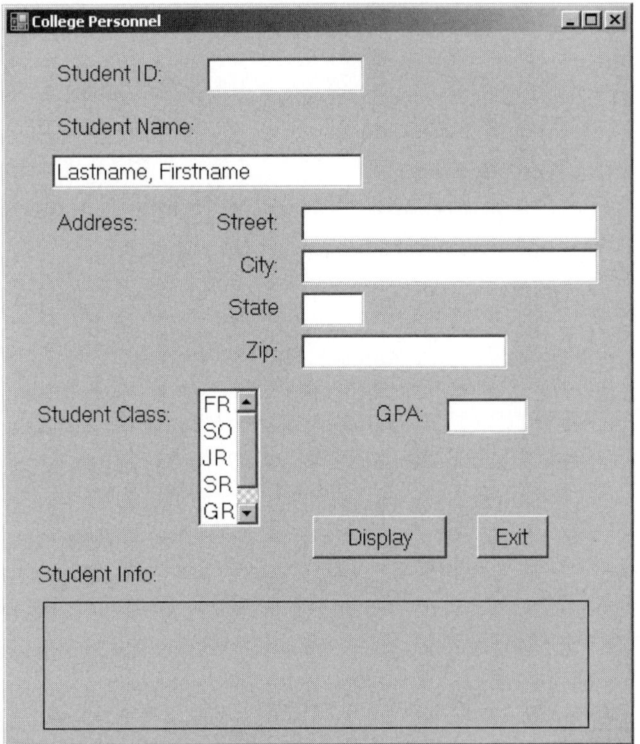

FIGURE 4.16 User interface for the College Personnel application

The `Person` class for the College Personnel application (Figure 4.17) serves as the base class for both the `Student` class and the `Instructor` class. It is very similar to the `Person` class used in the Human Resources application (Figure 3.22). The only major difference is due to the addition of the instance variable `_personId`. This addition necessitates the coding of a `PersonId Property` procedure and the inclusion of the `PersonId` property in the `ToString` method.

New instance variable `_personId` *added*

New `Property` *procedure added for* `_personId`

```
' Class name:           Person
' Class purpose:        Defines Person objects.
' Created/revised by:   <your name> on <current date>

Option Explicit On
Option Strict On

Public Class Person
    ' instance variables
    Private _personId As String
    Private _personName As String
    Private _address As Address

    ' constructor
    Public Sub New(Optional ByVal thePersonId As String = "", _
                   Optional ByVal thePersonName As String = "", _
                   Optional ByRef theAddress As Address = Nothing)
        _personId = thePersonId
        _personName = thePersonName
        _address = theAddress
    End Sub

    ' Property procedures
    Public Property PersonId() As String
        Get
            Return _personId
        End Get
        Set(ByVal Value As String)
            _personId = Value
        End Set
    End Property

    Public Property PersonName() As String
        Get
            Return _personName
        End Get
        Set(ByVal Value As String)
            _personName = Value
        End Set
    End Property

    Public Property Address() As Address
        Get
            Return _address
        End Get
        Set(ByVal Value As Address)
            _address = Value
        End Set
    End Property

```

(Figure is continued on next page)

```
    ' ToString function
    Public Overrides Function ToString() As String
        Return PersonId & ControlChars.CrLf & PersonName & _
               ControlChars.CrLf & Address.ToString()
    End Function

End Class
```

`PersonId` *property added to the* `ToString` *method*

FIGURE 4.17 Program code for the class **Person** in the College Personnel application

The `Student` class used in the College Personnel application (Figure 4.18) is also similar to the `Student` class in the College Course application (Figure 3.32). The first major difference is that the `Student` class is made to inherit from the `Person` class by adding an `Inherits` clause in the class declaration. Also note that the instance variables `_studentId`, `_studentName`, and `_studentAddress` are not needed in Figure 4.18 because these characteristics are provided by the instance variables in the base class `Person`. Next, there is a major change in the `Student` constructor. When the student ID, the student name, and the student address are provided to the `Student` constructor, a `Person` object first must be instantiated with its instance variables (`_personId`, `_personName`, and `_address` in Figure 4.17) set with the appropriate values for this student. You do this by using a special reference called **`MyBase`** (a Visual Basic keyword that refers to the base class of the current object). The statement `MyBase.New(theStudentId, theStudentName, theAddress)` (Line 19 in Figure 4.18) can therefore be interpreted as `Person.New(theStudentId, theStudentName, theAddress)` because `Person` is the base class of `Student.` Thus, `MyBase.New` in this case creates a `Person` object. Finally, notice that the `ToString` method in Figure 4.18 also uses the `MyBase` reference (Line 45). When a `Student` object is represented by a string using the `ToString` method in the `Student` class, the code `MyBase.ToString()` will cause the `ToString` method in the `Person` class to be executed, resulting in the creation of a string containing the student's ID, name, and address (stored in the instance variables of a `Person` object).

```
1  ' Class name:           Student
2  ' Class purpose:        Defines Student objects.
3  ' Created/revised by:   <your name> on <current date>
4
5  Public Class Student
6      Inherits Person
7
8      ' unique instance variables
9      Private _studentClass As String
10     Private _gpa As Decimal
11
12     ' constructor
13     Public Sub New(Optional ByVal theStudentId As String = "", _
14                    Optional ByVal theStudentName As String = "", _
15                    Optional ByVal theAddress As Address = Nothing, _
16                    Optional ByVal theStudentClass As String = "", _
17                    Optional ByVal theGpa As Decimal = 0)
```

`Inherits` *clause*

`_studentId`, `_studentName`, *and* `_studentAddress` *instance variables not needed*

(Figure is continued on next page)

Person *object instantiated using the* MyBase *reference*

The Person ToString *method called using the* MyBase *reference*

```
        'call Person constructor with the MyBase reference
        MyBase.New(theStudentId, theStudentName, theAddress)
        _studentClass = theStudentClass
        _gpa = theGpa
    End Sub

    ' Property procedures
    Public Property StudentClass() As String
        Get
            Return _studentClass
        End Get
        Set(ByVal Value As String)
            _studentClass = Value
        End Set
    End Property

    Public Property Gpa() As Decimal
        Get
            Return _gpa
        End Get
        Set(ByVal Value As Decimal)
            _gpa = Value
        End Set
    End Property

    ' ToString function
    Public Overrides Function ToString() As String
        Return MyBase.ToString() & ControlChars.CrLf _
            & "Class: " & StudentClass & " GPA: " & Gpa
    End Function

End Class
```

FIGURE 4.18 Code for the class **Student** in the College Personnel application

The Address class in the College Personnel application (not shown here) is identical to the one used in the Human Resources application (Figure 3.23). This is a prime example of code reuse—a well-designed class in one application can simply be reused in another application, thus saving programming effort, providing consistency, and avoiding costly errors. Also note that the Person class and the Student class are largely reused, both requiring only minor modifications.

When you need to reuse an existing class in a new application (as in the case of adding the Address class to the College Personnel application from the Human Resources application), you can simply add it as Figure 4.19 explains.

HOW TO...

Add an Existing Class to an Application

1. In the new application, click Project in the menu and then click Add Existing Item...
2. Click the arrow in the Look in: drop-down list and navigate to the desired class file(s) in an existing application.
3. Select the item(s) to add to the new application and click Add in the Add Existing Item dialog.

FIGURE 4.19 How to add an existing class to an application

Finally, the `MainForm` class in the College Personnel application (Figure 4.20) is coded to declare and instantiate objects `aStudent` and `anAddress`, set the values of their instance variables, and display student information in the interface. A sample run of this application is shown in Figure 4.21. You should study all aspects of the College Personnel application carefully to ensure that you understand the implementation of the object-oriented concepts of inheritance and composition.

```
Public Class MainForm
    ' declare objects
    Private aStudent As Student
    Private anAddress As Address

    Private Sub MainForm_Load(ByVal sender As System.Object, _
        ByVal e As System.EventArgs) Handles MyBase.Load
        ' instantiate objects
        aStudent = New Student
        anAddress = New Address
        Dim address1 As New Address
        Dim address2 As New Address( _
            "123 Main St.", "Anytown", "CA", "90001")

    End Sub

    Private Sub displayButton_Click(ByVal sender As System.Object, _
        ByVal e As System.EventArgs) Handles displayButton.Click

        ' get data from form, load into objects
        anAddress.Street = streetTextBox.Text
        anAddress.City = cityTextBox.Text
        anAddress.State = stateTextBox.Text
        anAddress.Zip = zipTextBox.Text

        aStudent.PersonId = studentIdTextBox.Text
        aStudent.PersonName = nameTextBox.Text
        aStudent.Address = anAddress
        aStudent.StudentClass = studentClassListBox.Text
        aStudent.Gpa = Convert.ToDecimal(gpaTextBox.Text)

        ' display student info
        studentInfoLabel.Text = aStudent.ToString()
    End Sub

    Private Sub exitButton_Click(ByVal sender As System.Object, _
        ByVal e As System.EventArgs) Handles exitButton.Click
        Me.Close()
    End Sub
End Class
```

FIGURE 4.20 Code for the class `MainForm` in the College Personnel application

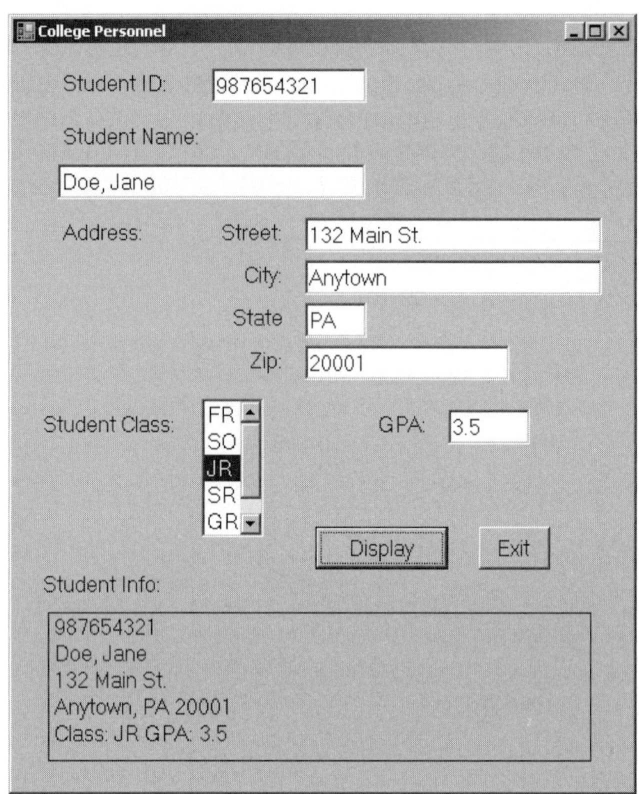

FIGURE 4.21 Sample run of the College Personnel application

ABSTRACT CLASSES AND METHODS

Object-oriented programmers use abstract classes and methods to make program code more organized and secure. In this section, you will first learn about abstract classes, then about abstract methods.

Abstract Classes

Thus far in this text, classes have been used almost exclusively as blueprints for instantiating objects. However, not all classes are used for that purpose. Often classes are created solely as convenient containers for common sets of data members and method members that other object-defining classes can inherit and implement. The application developer never intends to create objects of such a container class. To implement this intention, the programmer can create an abstract class. An **abstract class** is a class with data members and/or method members from which objects cannot be instantiated. Objects may be instantiated from classes that inherit the members of the abstract class. A class from which objects can be instantiated is called a **concrete class**.

As an example, take another look at the College Personnel application in Figures 4.17, 4.18, and 4.20. The `Person` class is a base class and the `Student` class is a derived class. The `MainForm` class provides the interface and much of the processing. Notice that a `Student` object and an `Address` object are instantiated in `MainForm`, but no `Person` objects are instantiated. This is because `Person` objects are not needed in this application. Therefore, to ensure that code written in the future will not create unnecessary or unwanted `Person` objects, the programmer could make a design decision and declare the `Person` class as abstract. To accomplish this, the `Person` class (Figure 4.17) must be declared using the keyword `MustInherit` as follows:

```
Public MustInherit Class Person
```

Thus, if the `MainForm` class attempts to instantiate a `Person` object with code such as `aPerson = New Person`, a compile-time error will result. Note that in a UML diagram, the name of an abstract class is italicized.

Abstract Methods

Additionally, an **abstract method** is a method that is *declared* in a base class but has no body or implementation in that base class. However, such an abstract method *must* be implemented in all derived classes. As with abstract classes, the reason for making a method abstract is to enforce a design decision. A method is declared in a base class where it logically belongs, but it must be implemented in a derived class where it physically belongs. Thus, an abstract class with abstract methods is created as a kind of contract, requiring all derived classes to fulfill their parts of the bargain (that is, to implement the abstract methods). The methods thus defined in the derived classes may have completely different implementations depending on the context within those classes, which is one of the primary reasons the method is made abstract in the base class. (If all the implementations are the same, just one nonabstract method should be coded in the base class.)

All this discussion about abstract classes and methods may sound a little confusing at first. To clarify, take a look at an example. Suppose you have a Geometric Shapes application involving a wide variety of shapes (circles, squares, triangles, etc.) and you would like the application to be able to calculate the areas of all these shapes. To accomplish this, you could declare an abstract method called `CalculateArea` in an abstract base class called `GeometricShape`. In that case, the abstract class must be declared using the keyword `MustInherit`, and the abstract method `CalculateArea` must be declared using the keyword `MustOverride`, as in the following example:

```
MustOverride Function CalculateArea() As Decimal ' in base class
```

Then, all classes that inherit from the abstract base class `GeometricShape` must provide an implementation of (that is, must override) the method `CalculateArea`.

The method `CalculateArea` that is implemented in a derived class must in turn be declared with the keyword `Overrides`, as follows, because it overrides the method `CalculateArea` in the abstract base class:

```
Overrides Function CalculateArea() As Decimal ' in derived class
```

To further explore the use of abstract classes and methods, suppose the abstract base class `GeometricShape` has two derived classes, `Circle` (with instance variable `_radius`) and `Square` (with instance variable `_side`). The `GeometricShape` class should have an instance variable `_area` and a `Property` procedure `Area` because area is a basic characteristic of any geometric shape. However, calculating the area of a circle and a square requires two very different formulas: `Math.PI * _radius * _radius` for the `Circle` and `_side * _side` for the `Square`. Therefore, a method called `CalculateArea`, made abstract in the

GeometricShape class, must be implemented in both the Circle and Square classes. Figures 4.22 through 4.26 show the classes and the output of this very simple but instructive application.

```
' Project name:          Geometric Shapes Project
' Project purpose:       Displays areas of circles and squares.
' Created/revised by:    <your name> on <current date>

Option Explicit On
Option Strict On

Public Class MainForm
    Private Sub exitButton_Click(ByVal sender As Object, _
    ByVal e As System.EventArgs) Handles exitButton.Click
        Me.Close()
    End Sub

    Private Sub processButton_Click(ByVal sender As Object, _
        ByVal e As System.EventArgs) Handles processButton.Click

        ' instantiate objects
        Dim aCircle As New Circle _
            (Convert.ToDecimal(dimensionTextBox.Text))
        Dim aSquare As New Square _
            (Convert.ToDecimal(dimensionTextBox.Text))

        ' output areas
        MessageBox.Show _
            (Convert.ToString(aCircle), _
                Convert.ToString(aCircle.GetType()))
        MessageBox.Show _
            (Convert.ToString(aSquare), _
                Convert.ToString(aSquare.GetType()))

    End Sub
End Class
```

FIGURE 4.22 Program code for the MainForm class in the Geometric Shapes application

```
' Class name: GeometricShape

Option Explicit On
Option Strict On

Public MustInherit Class GeometricShape ' abstract class
    ' instance variable
    Private _area As Decimal

    ' property procedure
    Property Area() As Decimal
        Get
            Return _area
        End Get
```

(Figure is continued on next page)

```
        Set(ByVal Value As Decimal)
            _area = Value
        End Set
    End Property

    ' abstract method
    MustOverride Function CalculateArea() As Decimal

    ' ToString function
    Public Overrides Function ToString() As String
        Return "Area: " & Area & ControlChars.CrLf
    End Function

End Class
```

FIGURE 4.23 Program code for the `GeometricShape` class in the Geometric Shapes application

```
' Class name: Circle

Option Explicit On
Option Strict On

Public Class Circle ' derived class
    Inherits GeometricShape

    'instance variable
    Private _radius As Decimal

    'constructor
    Sub New(ByVal theRadius As Decimal)
        Radius = theRadius
        MyBase.Area = CalculateArea()
    End Sub

    ' property procedure
    Public Property Radius() As Decimal
        Get
            Return _radius
        End Get
        Set(ByVal Value As Decimal)
            _radius = Value
        End Set
    End Property

    ' implements the abstract method
    Overrides Function CalculateArea() As Decimal
        Return Convert.ToDecimal(Math.PI * Radius * Radius)
    End Function

    ' ToString function
    Public Overrides Function ToString() As String
        Return "Radius of circle: " & Radius & ControlChars.CrLf _
             & MyBase.ToString()
    End Function

End Class
```

FIGURE 4.24 Program code for the `Circle` class in the Geometric Shapes application

```
' Class name: Square

Option Explicit On
Option Strict On

Public Class Square ' derived class
    Inherits GeometricShape

    ' instance variable
    Private _side As Decimal

    ' constructor
    Sub New(ByVal theSide As Decimal)
        Side = theSide
        MyBase.Area = CalculateArea()
    End Sub

    ' property
    Public Property Side() As Decimal
        Get
            Return _side
        End Get
        Set(ByVal Value As Decimal)
            _side = Value
        End Set
    End Property

    ' implementes the abstract method
    Overrides Function CalculateArea() As Decimal
        Return Side * Side
    End Function

    ' ToString function
    Public Overrides Function ToString() As String
        Return "Side of square: " & Side & ControlChars.CrLf _
             & MyBase.ToString()
    End Function

End Class
```

FIGURE 4.25 Code for the `Square` class in the Geometric Shapes application

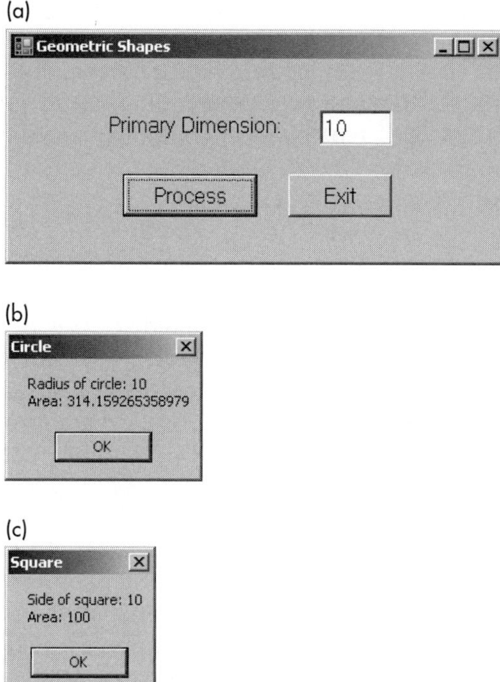

FIGURE 4.26 Sample run of the Geometric Shapes application

Note in Figure 4.22 that two objects are instantiated, `aCircle` and `aSquare`, based on the value stored in `dimensionTextBox.Text`. Then, a `MessageBox` is used to display the objects `aCircle` and `aSquare` (using the `ToString` methods in the `Circle` and `Square` classes). In Figure 4.23, the class `GeometricShape` is declared with the `MustInherit` keyword, making it an abstract class. The class `GeometricShape` has an instance variable `_area` and a `Property` procedure `Area` because all kinds of shapes that inherit from `GeometricShape` should have areas. Finally, `GeometricShape` declares an abstract method (with no implementation or body) called `CalculateArea` using the keyword `MustOverride` (because all derived classes must implement or override this method).

The `Circle` and `Square` classes in Figures 4.24 and 4.25, respectively, are very similar. Each has its own unique instance variable (`_radius` and `_side`, respectively) and a constructor that calls the `CalculateArea` function within its respective class in order to set the inherited `Area` property in `GeometricShape`. The `CalculateArea` method in these classes is made to override the `CalculateArea` method in `GeometricShapes` using the keyword `Overrides`. Each of the classes `GeometricShape`, `Circle`, and `Square` has its own `ToString` method that overrides the `ToString` method in the `Object` class. The output in Figure 4.26 shows the areas of a circle and a square with a radius and side of 10.

POLYMORPHISM AND OVERTYPING

The support of inheritance is a basic requirement of true object-oriented programming languages. Another important feature of object orientation is polymorphism. The term polymorphism literally means "many forms." In a biological context, polymorphism is used to describe a gene, trait, or mutation that occurs in several different versions. But in an OO context, polymorphism refers to other kinds of things that occur in several different versions, such as methods and objects.

You have already studied the OO topics of overloading and overriding methods. As you recall, an overloaded method in a class is a method with the same name but a different parameter list than another method in the same class or an inherited class. You would say that overloading is a type of polymorphism where several versions of the same method occur within a single class.

An overridden method is a method in a base class that has the same name and parameter list (that is, the same signature) as a method in one of its derived classes. Again, overriding is a type of polymorphism where several versions of the same method occur in different classes of an inheritance hierarchy. Thus, overloading and overriding are both examples of polymorphism.

However, when most OO programmers speak of polymorphism, they are usually referring to another interesting capability of an OO language. In this case, **polymorphism** is the ability of a variable with the data type of a base class to refer to a variable with the data type of a derived class. In other words, a variable that is declared as a data type of a base class has the ability to "store" (refer to) an object from any one of its derived classes. This more general type of variable is always aware of the more specific kind of object to which it refers. Therefore, this kind of general "polymorphic" variable can be used in programs to refer to objects of many different (derived) types, making such programs much more flexible and extensible (and requiring less code and fewer modifications). This kind of polymorphism could be called "overtyping" because one data type (of a base class) can refer to objects of many other data types (that is, of the derived classes).

As is usually the case with somewhat complex OO topics, examples are the best way to explore polymorphism. To illustrate polymorphic overtyping, consider the Geometric Shapes application in Figures 4.22 through 4.25. You can create a new application called Polymorphic Geometric Shapes that is completely identical except for the class `MainForm`. The `MainForm` class in Polymorphic Geometric Shapes is shown in Figure 4.27.

```
' Project name:         Polymorphic Geometric Shapes Project
' Project purpose:      Displays areas of circles and squares.
' Created/revised by:   <your name> on <current date>

Option Explicit On
Option Strict On

Public Class MainForm
    Private Sub exitButton_Click(ByVal sender As Object, _
    ByVal e As System.EventArgs) Handles exitButton.Click
        Me.Close()
    End Sub

    Private Sub processButton_Click(ByVal sender As Object, _
        ByVal e As System.EventArgs) Handles processButton.Click
        ' declare variables
        Dim shapeElement As GeometricShape

        ' instantiate objects
        Dim aSquare As New Square _
            (Convert.ToDecimal(dimensionTextBox.Text))
```

(Figure is continued on next page)

```
22          Dim aCircle As New Circle _
23              (Convert.ToDecimal(dimensionTextBox.Text))
24
25          ' array for three GeometricShape objects
26          Dim shapes(1) As GeometricShape
27
28          ' populate array with objects
29          shapes(0) = aCircle
30          shapes(1) = aSquare
31
32          ' output areas using For Each…Next loop
33          For Each shapeElement In shapes
34              MessageBox.Show _
35                  (Convert.ToString(shapeElement), _
36                   Convert.ToString( _
37                       shapeElement.GetType()).Substring(25))
38          Next
39      End Sub
40  End Class
```

FIGURE 4.27 Program code for the `MainForm` class in the Polymorphic Geometric Shapes application

The differences between the two `MainForm` classes in Figures 4.22 and 4.27 begin in Figure 4.27 where the variable `shapesElement` is declared to be of data type `GeometricShape` (Line 17). This variable is used to loop through an array called `shapes` that is declared with index 1 indicating a size of 2 (Line 26). Recall that array indexes begin with 0. Note that the code `Dim shapes(1) As GeometricShape` (Line 26) indicates that the elements of the `shapes` array are of the more general data type `GeometricShape` (not the specific data types `Circle` or `Square`). Thus, the `shapes` array can hold elements of many different derived types, making the application more flexible. If you add a new class called `Triangle` to this application (which would be very easy to do), very few other changes will be required in the `MainForm` class, making the application more extensible (that is, the application could be easily extended to include other shapes).

After `shapes` is declared, it is populated with the objects `aCircle` and `aSquare` (Lines 29–30). Then a `For Each...Next` statement (Line 33) is used to loop through the array and display each `shapeElement` in a `MessageBox`. Of great importance here is that when each `shapesElement` is displayed, the application knows which `ToString` method to use (the one in either the `Circle` class or the `Square` class) based on the specific data type referred to by `shapesElement`. This is the essence and beauty of polymorphism: the ease of referring to many specific forms (`Circle` and `Square`) of a more general type (`GeometricShape`).

Finally, the output for this application will be identical to that shown in Figure 4.26. Of course, the user doesn't know that the application employs advanced polymorphic techniques to accomplish its purpose. Note that the `GetType` and the `Substring` methods are used (Line 37) to display the appropriate caption in the `MessageBox`. The `GetType` method returns a string such as `Geometric_Shapes_Project.Circle`. The `Substring` method extracts the part of that string beginning with the character at position 25, which is the name of the class in this case.

VISUAL STUDIO 2005 CLASS DESIGNER

TIP

Visual Studio 2005 Express Edition does not include the Class Designer.

In order to develop OO applications in Chapters 3 and 4, you have used the Visual Studio IDE (integrated development environment) by creating a project, designing a user interface, adding classes, and coding procedures to model a real-world system. As you create a user interface, you use the Toolbox and drag-and-drop techniques to add components to a form. Then double-clicking a component in a form creates an event procedure to which you add your own custom code. You continue to add classes, writing code for instance variables, `Property` procedures, and methods. This is a good process for developing simple applications, but as applications grow more complex, additional tools can aid the process.

Visual Studio 2005 provides a new feature called the **Class Designer**, which is a visual design environment for the Common Language Runtime. It allows you to design a complete OO application in much the same way that you currently design a user interface, using the mouse and drag-and-drop techniques. The Class Designer also provides a visual representation of an OO application by creating a class diagram that makes it easier for you to edit existing code and communicate your application design to others. The following example begins with the Polymorphic Geometric Shapes application in Figure 4.27 (which also uses the classes in Figures 4.23 through 4.25) and demonstrates how to use the Class Designer to explore and modify the application.

Adding a Class Diagram to an Existing Application

Figure 4.28 explains how to add a class diagram to an existing application. Adding a class diagram opens the Class Designer.

HOW TO...

Add a Class Diagram to an Existing Application

1. Open an existing Visual Basic application (see Figure 4.29).
2. In the Visual Studio menu, click Project, click Add New Item..., click the Class Diagram icon (Figure 4.30), change the name of the class diagram (if desired), and click Add. The Class Designer appears (Figure 4.31).
3. Select all the files in the Solution Explorer that you want to display in the class diagram and drag them to the Class Designer window. Then display the Toolbox and expand the Class Designer category of tools (Figure 4.32).

FIGURE 4.28 How to add a class diagram to an existing application

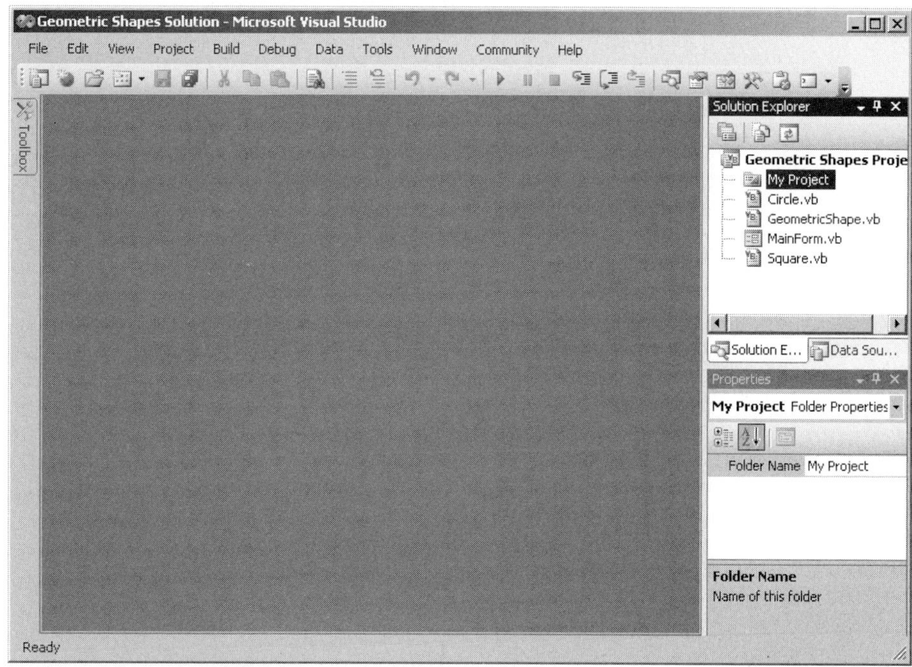

FIGURE 4.29 The Polymorphic Geometric Shapes application

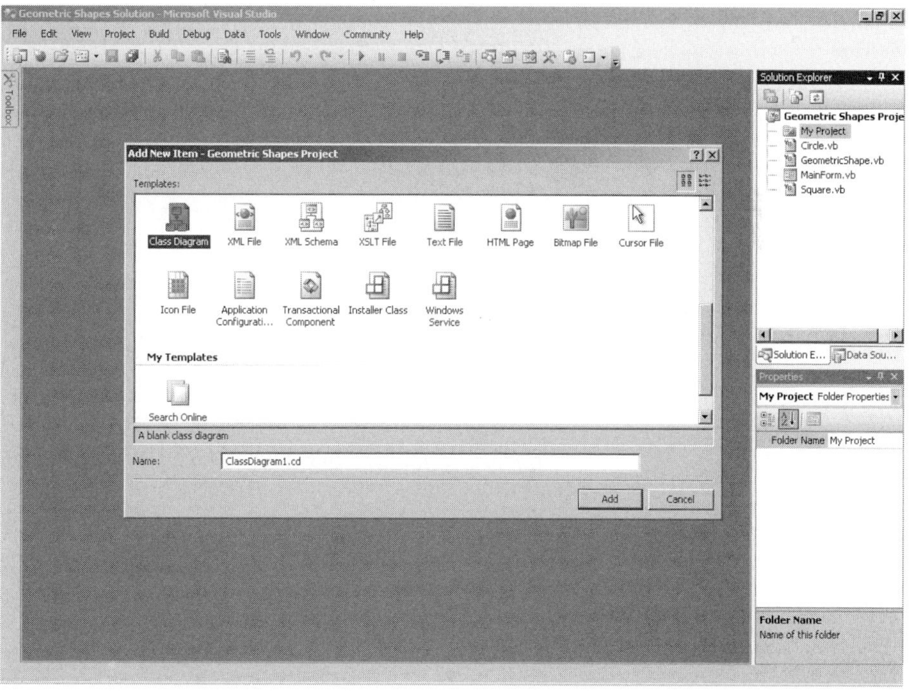

FIGURE 4.30 Adding a Class Diagram to an application

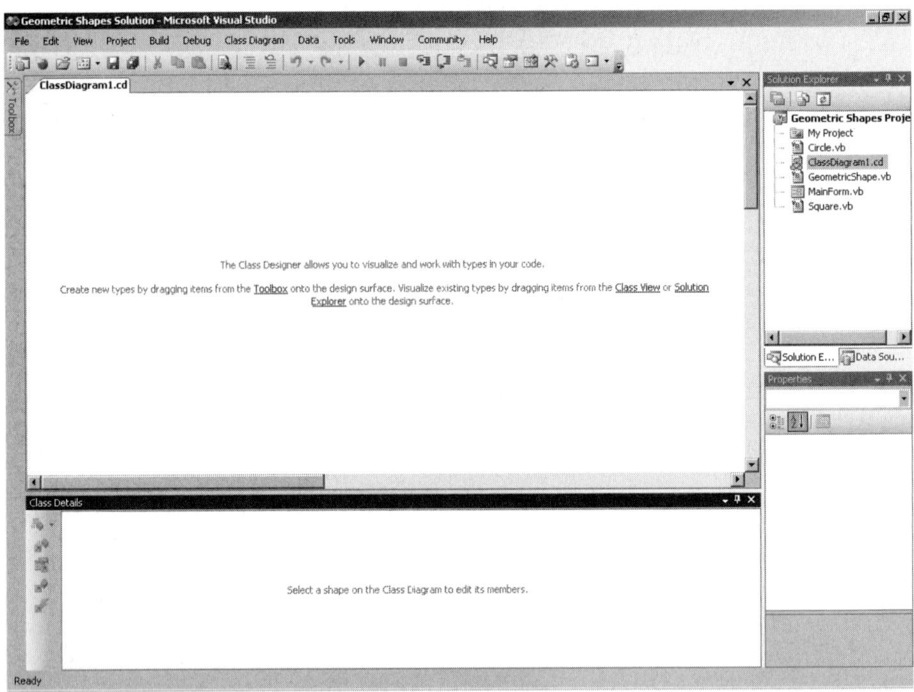

FIGURE 4.31 The Class Designer window

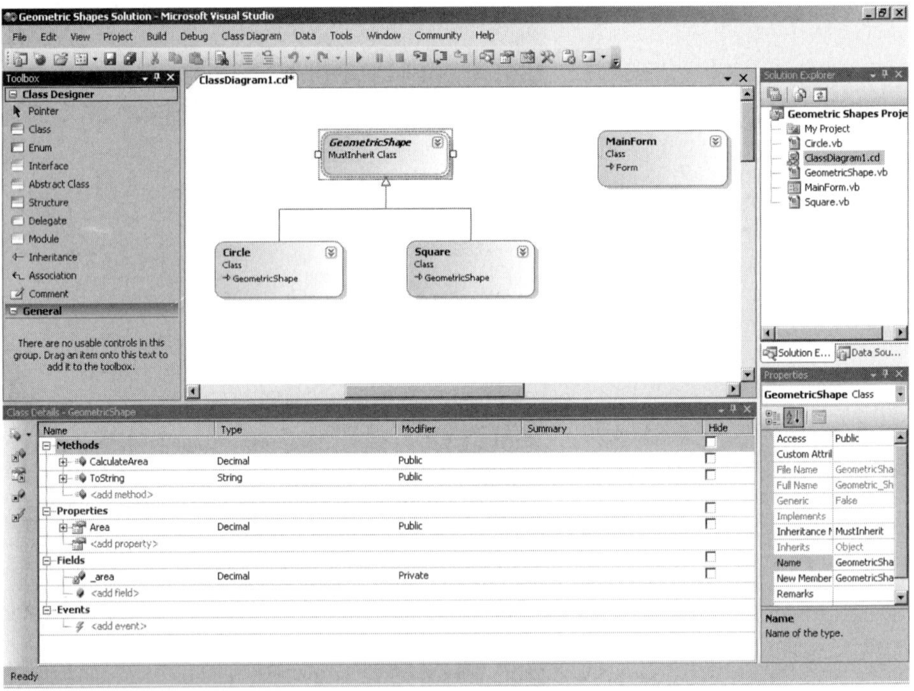

FIGURE 4.32 The class diagram for the Polymorphic Geometric Shapes application

The Class Designer in Figure 4.33 has many interesting features. First, the class diagram (contained in the file ClassDiagram1.vb) shows the four classes in this application. The class diagram illustrates that `GeometricShape` is an abstract class (its name is italicized with the text `MustInherit Class` below) and that `Circle` and `Square` inherit from `GeometricShape`. The `MainForm` class is also displayed, but it is not part of the inheritance hierarchy. By clicking the arrows in the upper right corner of a class in the class diagram, you can expand the class to reveal its members (see Figure 4.33). The expanded classes show their Fields (another term for variables), Properties, and Methods. Double-clicking any item in any of these classes in the class diagram opens the corresponding file and takes you to the location of that element within the file.

There are other interesting features of the class diagram. For example, you can select a class (or several classes using Shift+Click or dragging a box with the mouse) and adjust its width using its handles. You can also create a graphics file of the class diagram (for use in a Word or PowerPoint document) by right-clicking the class diagram and clicking Export Diagram as Image...

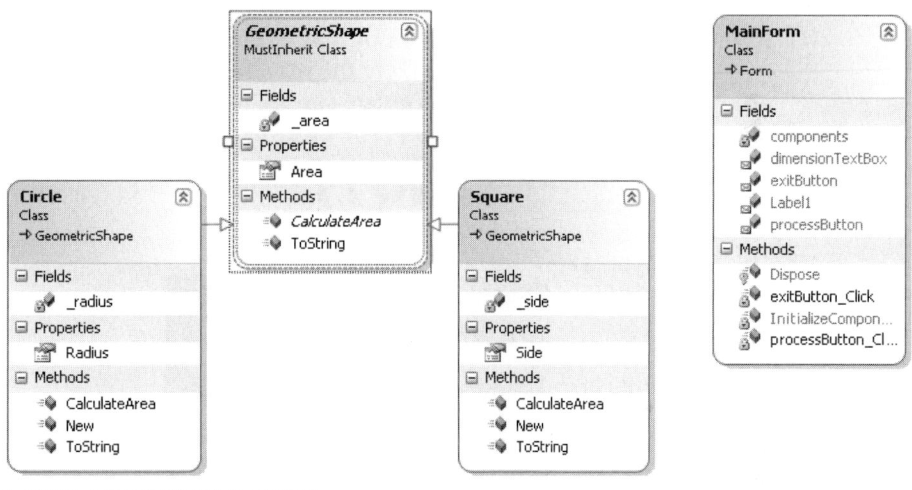

FIGURE 4.33 Class diagram with expanded classes

Note that the `GeometricShape` class is selected in the class diagram of Figures 4.32 and 4.33. The Class Details window (at the bottom of the Class Designer) therefore displays the details of the class `GeometricShape`. These details are in sections Methods, Properties, Fields, and Events. The Class Details window allows you to open the file by double-clicking an element in the window, to change the Type or Modifier for an element, to add a comment to the file (in the Summary column), to hide elements in the class diagram, and to add elements (methods, properties, fields, and events) to a class.

Adding a Class with the Class Designer

The previous section explained how to create a class diagram and how to use the Class Designer to navigate through an existing application. Now you will use the Class Designer to add a new class to the Polymorphic Geometric Shapes application. Figure 4.34 explains how to add a class with the Class Designer.

HOW TO...

Add a Class with the Class Designer

1. With the Class Designer open, open the Toolbox (see Figure 4.32).
2. Drag a class from the Toolbox to the class diagram and enter the name of the class in the New Class dialog box (for example, the `Triangle` class in Figure 4.35) and click OK. The new class appears in the class diagram.
3. To create an inheritance relationship between two classes, click the Inheritance tool in the Toolbox, then drag a line from the derived class to the base class in the class diagram (for example, the `Triangle` class in Figure 4.36).
4. To create an association relationship between two classes, click the Association tool in the Toolbox, then drag a line from one class (`ClassA`) to another class (`ClassB`), creating a `Property` procedure in `ClassA` of type `ClassB`.
5. Complete the modification of the application by adding code to the appropriate classes, including the user interface.

FIGURE 4.34 How to add a class diagram with the Class Designer

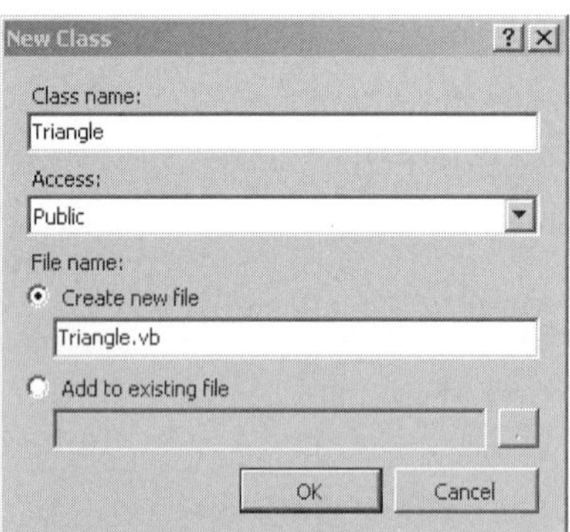

FIGURE 4.35 The New Class dialog box

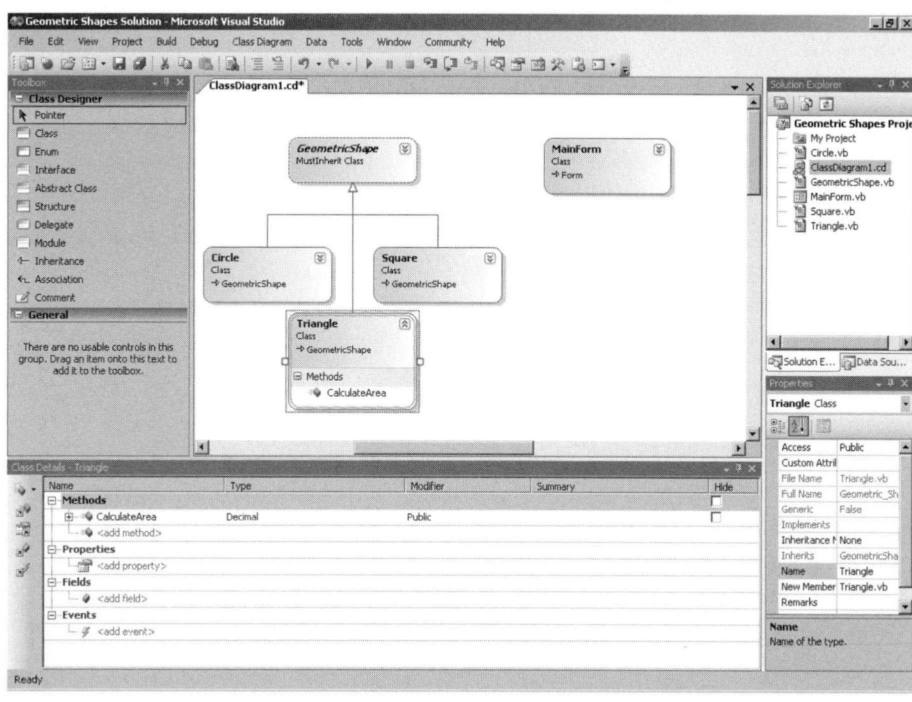

FIGURE 4.36 The `Triangle` class inherits the `GeometricShape` class

After completing Steps 1 and 2 in Figure 4.34 to add the `Triangle` class to the Polymorphic Geometric Shapes solution, double-click the `Triangle` class in the class diagram to reveal the following code:

```
Public Class Triangle
    Inherits GeometricShape



    Public Overrides Function CalculateArea() As Decimal

    End Function
End Class
```

This code is just a skeleton of a class. By simply dragging the Class component to the class diagram, giving it the name `Triangle`, and causing it to inherit from `GeometricShape`, the Class Designer generates the appropriate code. Next, you will see how to add the required code to complete the modification to the Polymorphic Geometric Shapes application.

Making Final Modifications to the Application

The value of the Class Designer is in giving the developer a bird's-eye view of the project and making some aspects of OO development easier. However, the programmer will still need to get down to the details of writing the code necessary to make the application work as planned.

For the modified Polymorphic Geometric Shapes application, the programmer must now complete the code for the `Triangle` class that was added to the class diagram (Figure 4.36). The next step is to copy and paste code from a similar class (such as `Square` in Figure 4.25) into the `Triangle` class and then modify the code to meet the special requirements of the `Triangle` class. After doing so, the `Triangle` class appears as in Figure 4.37, where new code is shaded.

```
1  ' Class name:          Triangle
2
3  Option Explicit On
4  Option Strict On
5
6  Public Class Triangle ' derived class
7      Inherits GeometricShape
8
9      ' instance variable
10     Private _side As Decimal
11
12     ' constructor
13     Sub New(ByVal theSide As Decimal)
14         Side = theSide
15         MyBase.Area = CalculateArea()
16     End Sub
17
18     ' property
19     Public Property Side() As Decimal
20         Get
21             Return _side
22         End Get
23         Set(ByVal Value As Decimal)
24             _side = Value
25         End Set
26     End Property
27
28     ' implements the abstract method
29     Overrides Function CalculateArea() As Decimal
30         Return Convert.ToDecimal(Side * Side * Math.Sqrt(3) / 4)
31     End Function
32
33     ' ToString function
34     Public Overrides Function ToString() As String
35         Return "Side of triangle: " & Side & ControlChars.CrLf _
36             & MyBase.ToString()
37     End Function
38
39 End Class
```

FIGURE 4.37 Program code for the modified `Triangle` class

Using the code in the `Square` class, only a few slight modifications are needed to finish the `Triangle` class. The formula for the area of a square in the `Square` class (Figure 4.25, Line 30) is `Side * Side`. In the `Triangle` class (Figure 4.37, Line 30), the formula for the area of an equilateral triangle (all three sides having the same length) becomes `Side * Side * Math.Sqrt(3) / 4`. You also need to convert the `Double` data type generated by `Math.Sqrt(3)` to a `Decimal` (the data type of `_area` in `GeometricShape`) using the `Convert.ToDecimal` method. The only other changes needed in `Triangle` are in a comment (Line 1) and in the `ToString` method (Line 35) to reflect the fact that this class deals with a triangle rather than a square.

Of course, the `MainForm` class will require some very minor modification. In the class diagram, double-click the `MainForm` class to display it in the Code View. First, instantiate a `Triangle` object by clicking the Process button. Then, increase the shapes array in size to 3 (using an index value of 2) and load the Triangle object into the shapes array. Also change the initial comments in the file. The completed code of the MainForm class is shown in Figure 4.38 with new code shaded, and a sample run is displayed in Figure 4.39. The fact that the Triangle class was added to the application so easily is evidence of the superior extensibility of the object-oriented approach.

```
' Project name:          Polymorphic Geometric Shapes Project
'                        with Class Diagram
' Project purpose:       Displays areas of circles, squares,
'                        and triangles.
' Created/revised by:    <your name> on <current date>

Option Explicit On
Option Strict On

Public Class MainForm
    Private Sub exitButton_Click(ByVal sender As Object, _
    ByVal e As System.EventArgs) Handles exitButton.Click
        Me.Close()
    End Sub

    Private Sub processButton_Click(ByVal sender As Object, _
        ByVal e As System.EventArgs) Handles processButton.Click
        ' declare variables
        Dim shapeElement As GeometricShape

        ' instantiate objects
        Dim aSquare As New Square _
            (Convert.ToDecimal(dimensionTextBox.Text))
        Dim aCircle As New Circle _
            (Convert.ToDecimal(dimensionTextBox.Text))
        Dim aTriangle As New Triangle _
            (Convert.ToDecimal(dimensionTextBox.Text))

        ' array for three GeometricShape objects
        Dim shapes(2) As GeometricShape

        ' populate array with objects
        shapes(0) = aCircle
        shapes(1) = aSquare
        shapes(2) = aTriangle

        ' output areas using For Each loop
        For Each shapeElement In shapes
            MessageBox.Show _
                (Convert.ToString(shapeElement), _
            Convert.ToString( _
                shapeElement.GetType()).Substring(25))
        Next
    End Sub
End Class
```

FIGURE 4.38 Program code for the modified MainForm class

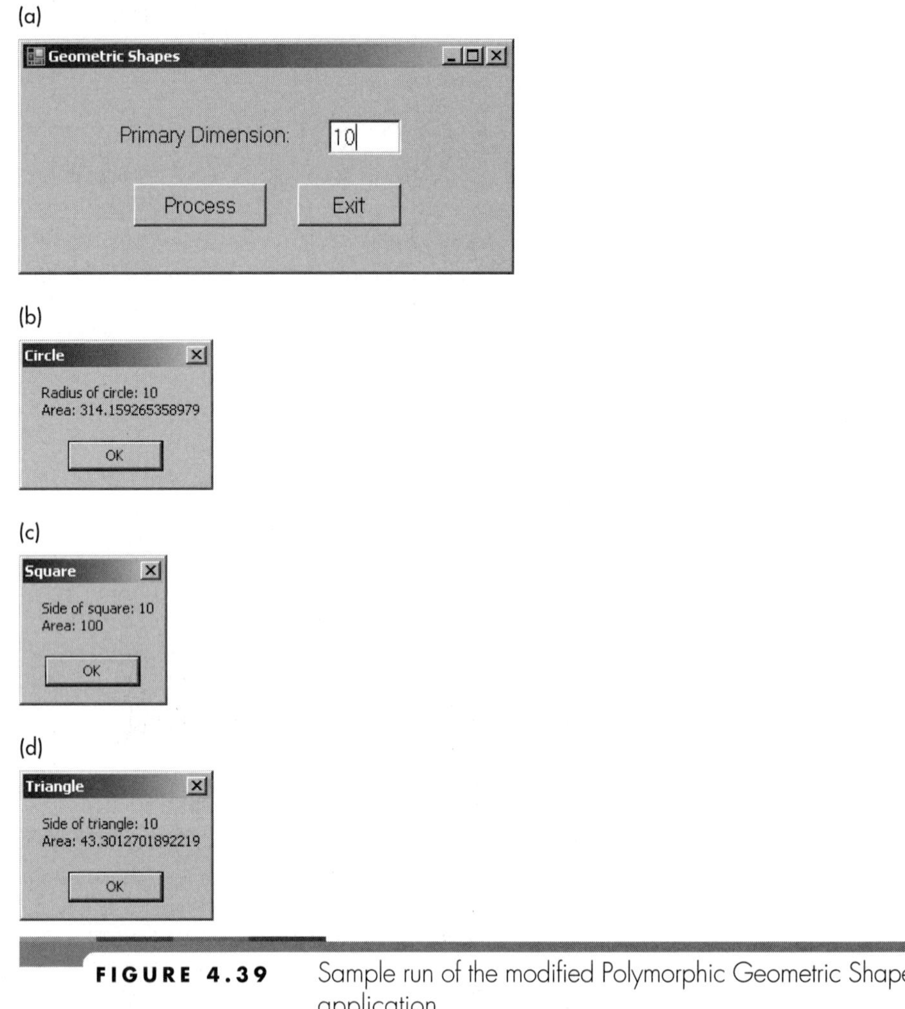

FIGURE 4.39 Sample run of the modified Polymorphic Geometric Shapes application

PROGRAMMING EXAMPLE

Employee Application

In this section we will create a Visual Basic application that allows the user to enter information about employees. The application will collect information about different kinds of employees (hourly and salaried) and calculate their gross pay. Name the project and the solution Employees. Name the form file MainForm.vb. Name the class files Employee.vb, HourlyEmployee.vb, and SalariedEmployee.vb. Create a class diagram called ClassDiagram1.cd in the Class Designer. Save the application in the \VbReloadedAdv\Chap04 folder.

Class Diagram

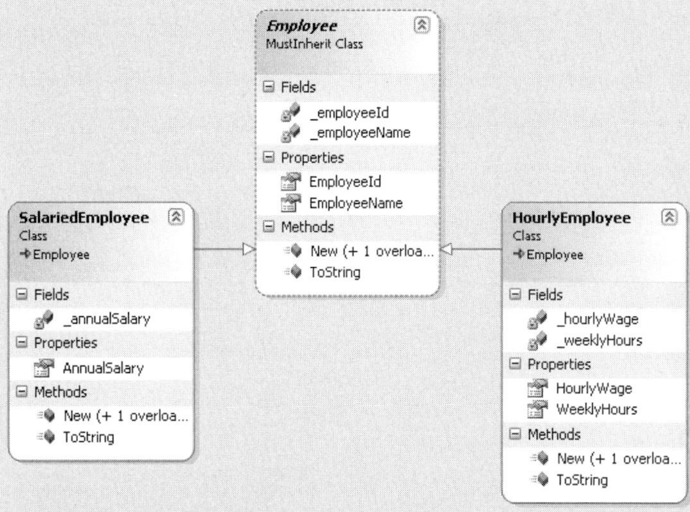

FIGURE 4.40 Class diagram for the Employee application

TOE Chart

Task	Object	Event
1. instantiate HourlyEmployee object or SalariedEmployee object 2. display employee info	calculateButton	Click
End the application	exitButton	Click
Make salaried text box visible, hourly text boxes not visible	salariedRadioButton	CheckedChanged
Make hourly text boxes visible, salaried text box not visible	hourlyRadioButton	CheckedChanged
Reset/clear text boxes	empIdTextBox	TextChanged
Get the employee ID	empIdTextBox	None
Get the employee name	nameTextBox	None
Get the annual salary	salaryTextBox	None
Get the hourly wage	wageTextBox	None
Get the weekly hours	hoursTextBox	None
Display employee information	empInfoLabel	None

FIGURE 4.41 TOE chart for the Employee application

User Interface

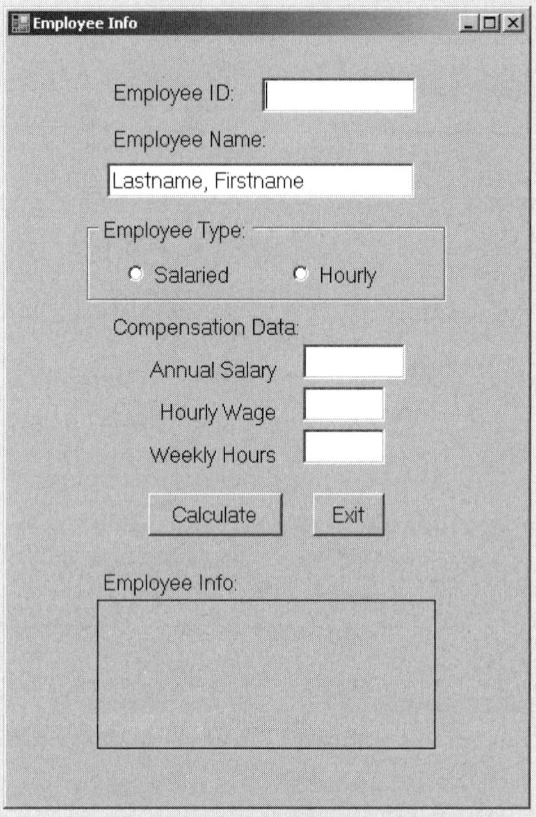

FIGURE 4.42 User interface for the Employee application

Pseudocode

`calculateButton Click` event procedure

1. if the salariedRadioButton is checked
   create a salaried employee object getting ID, name, and annual salary
   from text boxes
   calculate weekly pay by dividing annual salary by 52
   else
   create an hourly employee object getting ID, name, hourly wage, and
   weekly hours from text boxes
   calculate weekly pay by multiplying hourly wage by weekly hours
   end if
2. display employee info (ID, name, wage/salary information, and weekly pay) in the empInfoLabel
3. select all in empIdTextBox
4. set focus in empIdTextBox

`salariedRadioButton CheckedChanged` event procedure

1. make wageLabel, wageTextBox, hoursLabel, and hoursTextBox not visible
2. make salaryLabel and salaryTextBox visible

`hourlyRadioButton CheckedChanged` event procedure

1. make salaryLabel and salaryTextBox not visible
2. make wageLabel, wageTextBox, hoursLabel, and hoursTextBox visible

`empIdTextBox TextChanged` event procedure

1. set empIdTextBox to “Lastname, Firstname”
2. set salaryTextBox, hoursTextBox, wageTextBox, and empIdLabel to empty strings

`exitButton Click` event procedure

1. close application

Code

```
' Class name:          Employee
' Class purpose:       Defines Employee objects.
' Created/revised by:  <your name> on <current date>

Option Explicit On
Option Strict On

Public MustInherit Class Employee ' abstract class
    ' instance variables
    Private _employeeId As String
    Private _employeeName As String

    ' constructors
    Public Sub New()
        _employeeId = Nothing
        _employeeName = Nothing
    End Sub

    Public Sub New(ByVal employeeId As String, _
                   ByVal employeeName As String)
        _employeeId = employeeId
        _employeeName = employeeName
    End Sub

    ' Property procedures
    Public Property EmployeeId() As String
        Get
            Return _employeeId
        End Get
        Set(ByVal Value As String)
            _employeeId = Value
        End Set
    End Property

    Public Property EmployeeName() As String
        Get
            Return _employeeName
        End Get
        Set(ByVal Value As String)
            _employeeName = Value
        End Set
    End Property

    ' ToString function
    Public Overrides Function ToString() As String
        Return EmployeeId _
             & ControlChars.CrLf & EmployeeName _
             & ControlChars.CrLf
    End Function

End Class
```

FIGURE 4.43 Program code for the Employee.vb file

```
' Class name:           HourlyEmployee
' Class purpose:        Defines hourly employee objects.
' Created/revised by:   <your name> on <current date>

Public Class HourlyEmployee
    Inherits Employee

    ' instance variables
    Private _hourlyWage As Decimal
    Private _weeklyHours As Decimal

    ' constructors
    Public Sub New()
        _hourlyWage = 0
        _weeklyHours = 0
    End Sub

    Public Sub New(ByVal employeeId As String, _
                   ByVal employeeName As String, _
                   ByVal hourlyWage As Decimal, _
                   ByVal weeklyHours As Decimal)
        MyBase.New(employeeId, employeeName)
        _hourlyWage = hourlyWage
        _weeklyHours = weeklyHours
    End Sub

    ' Property procedures
    Public Property HourlyWage() As Decimal
        Get
            Return _hourlyWage
        End Get
        Set(ByVal Value As Decimal)
            _hourlyWage = Value
        End Set
    End Property

    Public Property WeeklyHours() As Decimal
        Get
            Return _weeklyHours
        End Get
        Set(ByVal Value As Decimal)
            _weeklyHours = Value
        End Set
    End Property

    ' ToString function
    Public Overrides Function ToString() As String
        Return "Hourly wage:  " & FormatCurrency(HourlyWage) _
             & ControlChars.CrLf _
             & "Weekly hours: " & WeeklyHours
    End Function

End Class
```

FIGURE 4.44 Program code for the HourlyEmployee.vb file

```
' Class name:           SalariedEmployee
' Class purpose:        Defines salaried employee objects.
' Created/revised by:   <your name> on <current date>

Public Class SalariedEmployee
    Inherits Employee

    ' instance variables
    Private _annualSalary As Decimal

    ' constructors
    Public Sub New()
        _annualSalary = 0
    End Sub

    Public Sub New(ByVal employeeId As String, _
                   ByVal employeeName As String, _
                   ByVal annualSalary As Decimal)
        MyBase.New(employeeId, employeeName)
        _annualSalary = AnnualSalary
    End Sub

    ' Property procedures
    Public Property AnnualSalary() As Decimal
        Get
            Return _annualSalary
        End Get
        Set(ByVal Value As Decimal)
            _annualSalary = Value
        End Set
    End Property

    ' ToString function
    Public Overrides Function ToString() As String
        Return "Annual salary: " & FormatCurrency(AnnualSalary)
    End Function

End Class
```

FIGURE 4.45 Program code for the SalariedEmployee.vb file

```
Public Class MainForm
    Inherits System.Windows.Forms.Form
    ' declare variables
    Private anHourlyEmployee As hourlyEmployee
    Private aSalariedEmployee As SalariedEmployee
    Private anEmployee As Employee
    Private weeklyPay As Decimal = 0

    Private Sub calculateButton_Click(ByVal sender As System.Object, _
        ByVal e As System.EventArgs) Handles calculateButton.Click
        ' instantiate objects
        If salariedRadioButton.Checked Then
            aSalariedEmployee = New SalariedEmployee( _
                empIdTextBox.Text, nameTextBox.Text, _
                Convert.ToDecimal(salaryTextBox.Text))
            weeklyPay = aSalariedEmployee.AnnualSalary / 52
            ' cast aSalariedEmployee as Employee
            anEmployee = aSalariedEmployee
```

(Figure is continued on next page)

```
        Else
            anHourlyEmployee = New hourlyEmployee( _
                empIdTextBox.Text, nameTextBox.Text, _
                Convert.ToDecimal(wageTextBox.Text), _
                Convert.ToDecimal(hoursTextBox.Text))
            weeklyPay = anHourlyEmployee.HourlyWage * _
                        anHourlyEmployee.WeeklyHours
            ' cast anHourlyEmployee as Employee
            anEmployee = anHourlyEmployee
        End If

        ' display employee info
        empInfoLabel.Text = anEmployee.EmployeeId _
                          & ControlChars.CrLf _
                          & anEmployee.EmployeeName _
                          & ControlChars.CrLf _
                          & anEmployee.ToString() _
                          & ControlChars.CrLf _
                          & "Weekly Pay: " & FormatCurrency(weeklyPay)

        empIdTextBox.SelectAll()
        empIdTextBox.Focus()
    End Sub

    Private Sub salariedRadioButton_CheckedChanged( _
        ByVal sender As Object, _
        ByVal e As System.EventArgs) Handles
        salariedRadioButton.CheckedChanged

        wageLabel.Visible() = False
        wageTextBox.Visible() = False
        hoursLabel.Visible() = False
        hoursTextBox.Visible() = False
        salaryLabel.Visible() = True
        salaryTextBox.Visible() = True
    End Sub

    Private Sub hourlyRadioButton_CheckedChanged( _
        ByVal sender As Object, _
        ByVal e As System.EventArgs) Handles _
        hourlyRadioButton.CheckedChanged

        wageLabel.Visible() = True
        wageTextBox.Visible() = True
        hoursLabel.Visible() = True
        hoursTextBox.Visible() = True
        salaryLabel.Visible() = False
        salaryTextBox.Visible() = False
    End Sub

    Private Sub empIdTextBox_TextChanged(ByVal sender As Object, _
        ByVal e As System.EventArgs) Handles empIdTextBox.TextChanged

        nameTextBox.Text = "Lastname, Firstname"
        salaryTextBox.Text = String.Empty
        wageTextBox.Text = String.Empty
        hoursTextBox.Text = String.Empty
        empInfoLabel.Text = String.Empty
    End Sub
```

(Figure is continued on next page)

```

    Private Sub exitButton_Click(ByVal sender As System.Object, _
    ByVal e As System.EventArgs) Handles exitButton.Click
        Me.Close()
    End Sub

End Class
```

FIGURE 4.46 Program code for the MainForm.vb file

Input/Output

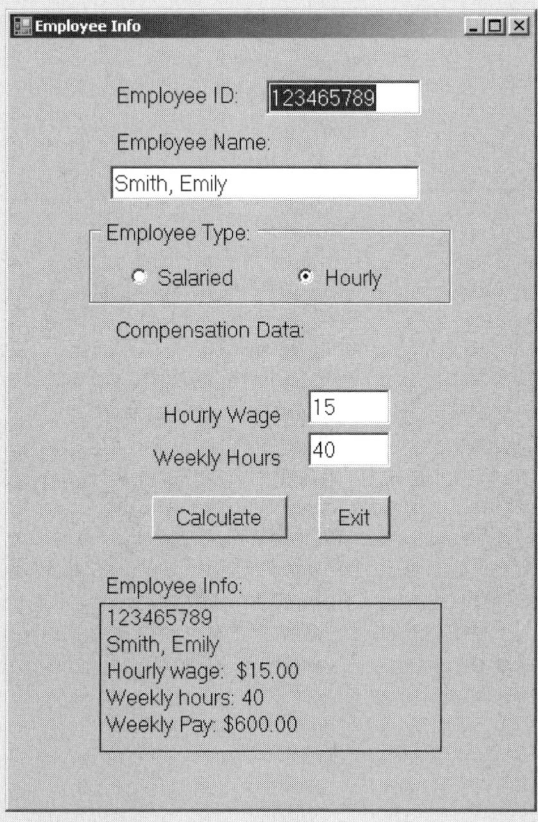

FIGURE 4.47 Sample run of the Employee application

Quick Review

- Inheritance is a special relationship between two classes in which one class (called the base class) gives to another class (called the derived class) direct access to all of its `Public` (not `Private`) data members and method members.
- Visual Basic has hundreds of predefined classes that inherit attributes and behaviors from other predefined classes. Additionally, you can create your own classes that inherit from predefined Visual Basic classes or other programmer-defined classes.

- An inheritance hierarchy is a treelike structure showing how classes inherit the members of other classes. The inheritance hierarchy of the .NET Framework classes can be found at *http://msdn.microsoft.com/library/*.
- `System.Object` (namespace `System`, class name `Object`) is the ultimate base class of all classes in the .NET Framework, the root of Visual Basic's abstract data type (ADT) hierarchy. All predefined .NET classes and classes that you create in applications derive from `Object`.
- Inheritance is called an is-a relationship between classes because an object created from a derived class "is an" instance of any of its base classes. Another term for an inheritance relationship is a generalization relationship because the base class is more general than the derived class (and the derived class is more specific than the base class).
- When you create an inheritance relationship using the keyword `Inherits`, the base class must be within the current namespace, must be within a namespace imported by the program, or must be a fully qualified class name (such as `System.Windows.Forms.Form`).
- The access modifier `Public` means that there are no restrictions on access to a class member. `Private` means that class members can be directly accessed only within the class in which the members are declared. `Friend` access means that a class member can be directly accessed from anywhere within the application in which it is defined. A `Protected` class member is directly accessible within the declaring class and classes that inherit from the declaring class. Finally, you can use the combination of access modifiers `Protected Friend`, which is the union of `Protected` and `Friend`.
- Using access modifiers (`Private`, `Public`, `Friend`, and `Protected`) appropriately is a demonstration of the principle of least privilege, which states that elements in a computing environment should be granted only information and resources that are immediately necessary. The purpose of access modifiers is to enhance protection of data and functionality from mistakes and malicious behavior.
- Any method in a class can be overloaded. An overloaded method in a class is one of two or more methods in the same class or inheritance hierarchy with the same name but different signatures. (A method signature is the combination of the method name and its parameter list.) A parameter list can differ by the number of parameters, the types of parameters, and/or the order of the parameters.
- If method overloading is used within an inheritance hierarchy of classes, an overloaded method in a derived class must use the keyword `Overloads` in its declaration.
- An overridden method is a method in a base class with exactly the same signature (same name and parameter list) as a method in a derived class. For method overriding, the method declaration in the base class must use the `Overridable` keyword and the method declaration in the derived class must use the `Overrides` keyword.
- In Visual Basic, to add classes from an existing application to a new application, click File, then click Add Existing Item. Components such as labels, text boxes, and buttons can be copied from one form and pasted into another form.
- An abstract class is a class from which objects cannot be instantiated. Instead, objects are instantiated from classes that inherit the members of the abstract class. A class from which objects can be instantiated is called a concrete class. Abstract classes must be declared using the keyword `MustInherit`.
- An abstract method is a method that is declared in a base class but that has no body or implementation in that base class. However, an abstract method must be implemented in all classes that are derived from the class containing

the abstract method. An abstract method must be declared in the base class with the keyword `MustOverride` and the overridden method in the derived class must be declared with the keyword `Overrides`.

- Polymorphism literally means "many forms." Both method overloading and method overriding are types of polymorphism. But polymorphism usually implies the ability of a variable with the data type of a base class to refer to a variable with the data type of a derived class. In other words, a variable that is declared as a data type of a base class has the ability to "store" (refer to) an object from any one of its derived classes. This kind of polymorphism could be called "overtyping."
- The Visual Studio 2005 Class Designer allows you to create a visual representation of an object-oriented application. The Class Designer contains a class diagram of the application and a Class Details window to work with the detailed members of a class. The value of the Class Designer is as a communication tool and an aid in application development.

Key Terms

abstract class—A class with data members and/or method members from which objects cannot be instantiated.

Abstract method—A method that is declared in a base class but has no body or implementation in that base class.

base class—A class from which another class (called the derived class) inherits `Public` members.

Class Designer—A visual design environment for the Common Language Runtime.

concrete class—A class from which objects can be instantiated.

inheritance—A special relationship between two classes in which one class (called the base class) gives to another class (called the derived class) direct access to all of its `Public` members.

inheritance hierarchy—A treelike structure showing inheritance relationships among classes.

is-a relationship—See **inheritance**.

method signature—The combination of the method name and its parameter list.

MyBase—A Visual Basic keyword that refers to the base class of the current object.

overloaded method—One of two or more methods in the same class or an inheritance hierarchy with the same name but different parameter lists.

overridden method—A method in a base class with exactly the same signature as a method in a derived class.

polymorphism—The ability of a variable with the data type of a base class to refer to a variable with the data type of a derived class.

principle of least privilege—A principle stating that elements in a computing environment should be granted only information and resources that are immediately necessary in order to enhance protection of data and functionality from faults and malicious behavior.

Review Questions

1. In a UML class diagram, an inheritance arrow points from the derived class to the base class.
   a. True
   b. False
2. The `SelectAll` method in the `ComboBox` class is inherited from the `TextBoxBase` class.
   a. True
   b. False
3. Composition is also known as an is-a relationship between classes.
   a. True
   b. False
4. A base class that a derived class inherits must be imported within the base class.
   a. True
   b. False
5. A method signature is the combination of the method name and its parameter list.
   a. True
   b. False
6. An overloaded method in a base class must be declared using the keyword `Overloads`.
   a. True
   b. False
7. An overridden method in a derived class must be declared using the keyword `Overridden`.
   a. True
   b. False
8. An abstract class must be declared using the keyword `Abstract`.
   a. True
   b. False
9. The implementation of an abstract method must be declared using the keyword `MustOverride`.
   a. True
   b. False
10. Overloading and overriding are both examples of polymorphism.
    a. True
    b. False
11. A derived class inherits all the ____ members of its base class.
    a. `Private`
    b. `Public`
    c. `Protected`
    d. all the above
12. The ultimate base class of all classes in the .NET Framework is ____.
    a. `Container`
    b. `MarshalByRefObject`
    c. `Object`
    d. `Control`

13. The Visual Basic keyword used to implement inheritance is ____.
    a. `Inherits`
    b. `IsA`
    c. `Overrides`
    d. `Overloads`

14. Which access modifier grants access within the declaring class and within any derived classes?
    a. `Private`
    b. `Public`
    c. `Protected`
    d. `Friend`

15. Which access modifier is best for an instance method?
    a. `Public`
    b. `Private`
    c. `Protected`
    d. `Friend`

16. The method `MyMethod(ByVal x As Double)` has the same signature as ____.
    a. `MyMethod(ByVal x As String)`
    b. `MyMethod(ByVal y As Double)`
    c. `MyMethod(ByVal x As Double, ByVal y As String)`
    d. none of the above

17. A method in a base class with the same signature as a method in a derived class is said to be ____.
    a. overloaded
    b. inherited
    c. overridden
    d. none of the above

18. The `ToString` method is an example of ____.
    a. method overloading
    b. method overriding
    c. an abstract method
    d. method inheritance

19. Polymorphism is most commonly regarded as ____.
    a. overtyping
    b. overloading
    c. overriding
    d. none of the above

20. Which of the following is least like the other three?
    a. polymorphism
    b. overloading
    c. overriding
    d. inheritance

Computer Exercises

When creating user interfaces in the following exercises, follow all conventions for an attractive, organized form with meaningful names for controls. When creating event procedures, use the `TryParse` method to ensure valid data are entered, use named constants when appropriate, and use format specifiers for output requiring special formatting. Your instructor may also request that you use TOE charts, pseudocode, flowcharts, and/or the Class Designer as planning aids. Follow all principles of good object-oriented design.

1. In this exercise, you modify the Quadrilateral application you viewed in this chapter. The modified application will allow the user to click radio buttons to select the type of quadrilateral.
   a. Use Windows to make a copy of the Quadrilateral Solution folder. Rename the folder **Quadrilateral Solution-RadioButton**.
   b. Open the Quadrilateral Solution file (Quadrilateral Solution.sln) contained in the \VbReloadedAdvanced\Chap04\Quadrilateral Solution-RadioButton folder.
   c. Modify the application's interface so that it uses radio buttons to select a square, rectangle, and general quadrilateral.
   d. Modify the application's code so that the appropriate constructors are called based on the radio button selection.
   e. Save the solution, test the application, and modify as necessary.

2. In this exercise you modify the College Personnel application you viewed in this chapter. The modified application will add a `Staff` class for college personnel who are not students or instructors.
   a. Use Windows to make a copy of the College Personnel Solution folder. Rename the folder **College Personnel Solution-Staff**.
   b. Open the College Personnel Solution file (College Personnel Solution.sln) contained in the \VbReloadedAdvanced\Chap04\College Personnel Solution-Staff folder.
   c. Create a `Staff` class with instance variables `_jobGrade` (values 1 through 5) and `_annualSalary`.
   d. Modify the application's interface so that it refers to "Personnel" instead of "Student".
   e. Provide radio buttons that allow the user to select Student, Instructor, or Staff.
   f. When a radio button is selected, use the InputBox function to collect the appropriate information about a student, instructor, or staff member.
   g. In the Personnel Info label, display the type of employee (student, instructor, or staff) and the appropriate information.
   h. Save the solution, test the application, and modify as necessary.

3. In this exercise you modify the original Geometric Shapes application (Figures 4.22 through 4.26) you viewed in this chapter. The modified application will include a `Triangle` class.
   a. Use Windows to make a copy of the Geometric Shapes Solution folder. Rename the folder **Circles Squares Triangles Solution**.
   b. Open the Geometric Shapes Solution file (Geometric Shapes Solution.sln) contained in the \VbReloadedAdvanced\Chap04\ Circles Squares Triangles Solution folder.
   c. Create a `Triangle` class for an equilateral triangle (all three sides are equal in length).
   d. Modify the application so that it displays the side and area information for the triangle in a `MessageBox`.
   e. Save the solution, test the application, and modify as necessary.

4. In this exercise you modify the Employee application you viewed in this chapter. The modified application will add a `CommissionEmployee` class.
   a. Use Windows to make a copy of the Employee Solution folder. Rename the folder **Employee Solution-Commission**.
   b. Open the Employee Solution file (Employee Solution.sln) contained in the \VbReloadedAdvanced\Chap04\Employee Solution-Commission folder.
   c. Create a `CommissionEmployee` class for an employee who receives a base annual salary plus a 10% commission on his or her annual sales.
   d. Modify the interface so that it contains a radio button for a commissioned employee and displays only the relevant text boxes for this type of employee when the radio button is clicked.
   e. The output label in the interface should display all employee information including salary, commission, and total earnings.
   f. Save the solution, test the application, and modify as necessary.

5. In this exercise you create an application that provides information about library items.
   a. Create a project called **Library**. Save the application in the \VBReloadedAdvanced\Chap04 folder.
   b. Design and create a user interface that allows the user to select between a book, a periodical, or a DVD, as well as provides information common to all three items.
   c. Create the `LibraryItem` class with an instance variable for item ID, item type, item title, publisher, and publication date.
   d. Create separate classes for `Book`, `Periodical`, and `Dvd`, all of which inherit `LibraryItem`. The instance variables for `Book` are authors (an array of individual `Person` objects, each having a name) and number of pages. The instance variables for `Periodical` are volume and number. The instance variables for `Dvd` are cast (an array of individual `Person` objects, each having a name) and running time (in minutes).
   e. Create a user interface that allows the user to select one of these types of items, enter the essential data using the `InputBox` function, and display the item data in a `MessageBox`. The application stores all `LibraryItem` objects in an array of type `LibraryItem` and keeps a count of all items created.
   f. The user interface has a Display All button that displays all the items stored in the array in a `MessageBox`.
   g. Save the solution, test the application, and modify as necessary.

6. In this exercise you create an application that displays information about three-dimensional geometric shapes.
   a. Create a project called **Three Dimensional Shapes**. Save the application in the \VBReloadedAdvanced\Chap04 folder.
   b. Design and create a user interface that allows the user to select between a sphere, a cube, or a tetrahedron (a pyramid with four identical triangular sides).
   c. Create an abstract `ThreeDimShapes` class with instance variables for surface area and volume. This class should have a `ToString` method. This class should also have a `CalculateArea` method and a `CalculateVolume` method
   d. Create separate classes for `Sphere`, `Cube`, and `Tetrahedron`, all of which inherit `ThreeDimShapes`. The instance variables for these classes should be for radius, side, and side, respectively. Each class should have a `ToString` method.

e. Create a user interface that allows the user to select one of these shapes, enter the essential data, and display the surface area and volume in a `MessageBox`.
f. Save the solution, test the application, and modify as necessary.

7. In this exercise you create an application that displays information about bank accounts.
   a. Create a project called **Banking**. Save the application in the \VBReloadedAdvanced\Chap04 folder.
   b. Design and create a user interface that allows the user to select between checking and savings accounts at a bank by using a `ListBox`.
   c. Create an abstract `BankAccount` class with instance variables for account number and balance and a `ToString` method.
   d. Create separate classes for `CheckingAccount` and `SavingsAccount`, both of which inherit `BankAccount`. The instance variable for `CheckingAccount` is monthly service charge, and for `SavingsAccount` is annual interest rate. Each class should have a `ToString` method.
   e. The user interface should allow the customer to make a deposit or withdrawal for either account. The `BankAccount` class has methods `Deposit` and `Withdraw`.
   f. Add a button to calculate month-end balance for both accounts by processing service charge and interest earned.
   g. Save the solution, test the application, and modify as necessary.

Case Projects

Transportation

Create an application called **Vehicles** that simulates trips taken by different kinds of vehicles. The application should have a class called `Vehicle` as well as a class for `Plane`, `Train`, and `Automobile`. Add some common attributes to the `Vehicle` class and some unique attributes to the other classes. The `Vehicle` class should have an overloaded method called `Transport` that models a trip of a given distance for each type of vehicle. The application should inform the user of the time required for each type of vehicle to make the trip.

ATM Simulator

Create an application called **ATM Simulator** that functions like an ATM and uses inheritance, overloading, overriding, and overtyping. The simulator should handle both checking and savings accounts and process deposits, withdrawals, and balance inquiries. Make the interface as realistic as possible. Assume the number pad on your computer is the number pad for the ATM.

The Universe

Create an application called **My Universe** that builds or destroys your own special universe at will. Use an abstract base class called `UniverseObject` with derived classes `Galaxy`, `Star`, and `Planet`. The `UniverseObject` class should contain at least one common attribute and the derived classes should contain at least one unique attribute. Create an application that creates galaxies, stars, and planets, and assigns stars to galaxies as well as planets to stars. The application should also destroy galaxies, stars, and planets. Note that a galaxy should contain stars, and stars should contain planets.. Include three buttons on the user interface, `Add`, `Remove`, and `Display`. The `Add`, `Remove`, and `Display` methods are located in the `UniverseObject` class. Users should be able to add or remove galaxies by making selections in combo boxes and clicking the appropriate buttons. Likewise, the user should be able to add or remove stars from galaxies, and add or remove planets from stars. The Display button should display the current structure of the universe. Use principles of object-oriented design in the solution.

CHAPTER

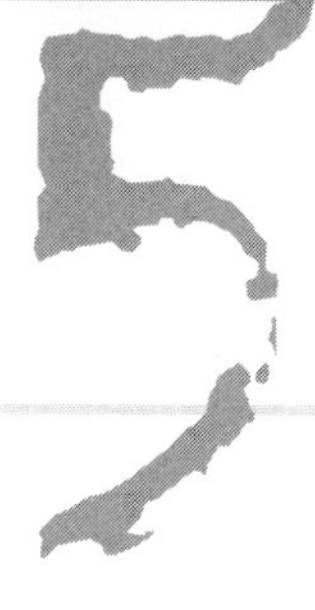

Input Validation, Error Handling, and Exception Handling

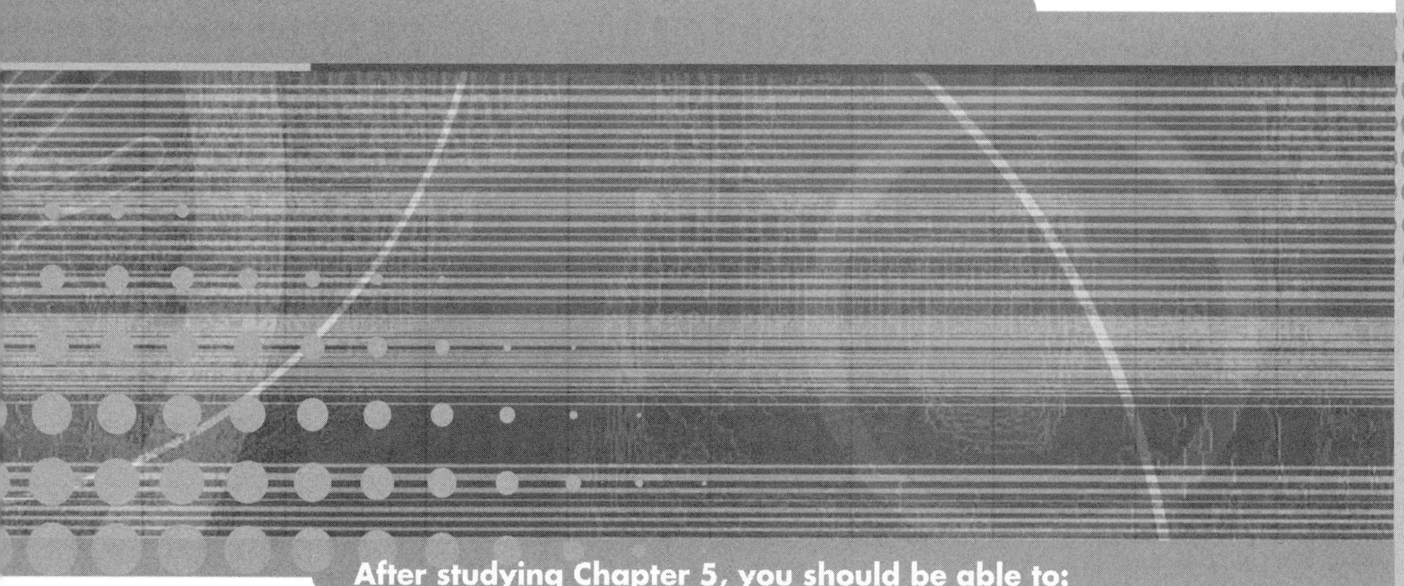

After studying Chapter 5, you should be able to:

- Perform input validation using a variety of techniques
- Describe the differences between runtime errors and exceptions
- Resolve runtime errors in a simple application
- Interpret error messages created by the Common Language Runtime
- Perform classic error handling in an application
- Discuss the inheritance hierarchy of Visual Basic exception classes
- Perform structured error handling in an application
- Create programmer-defined exceptions

After reviewing the basics of Visual Basic 2005 (in Chapters 1 and 2) and exploring the power of object-oriented programming (in Chapters 3 and 4), you are now well on your way to creating more advanced Visual Basic applications. As you create these more advanced applications, you'll find that they may be more prone to errors or glitches. So this is a good point to learn some techniques for dealing with problems in your code.

Your goal as a developer is to create software that meets users' requirements, is error free, and runs reliably. Users of your applications will often be very sophisticated, having experience with many different kinds of professional software. Such users will have high expectations for the software you create. You might spend weeks or months developing an application, but it will be useless for most users unless it runs accurately and smoothly. Applications that provide accurate information but occasionally **crash** (that is, terminate unexpectedly) will only frustrate your users.

An application may crash because of an error in the logic of a program (such as an array index out of bounds), or because a user enters the "wrong" kind of data (such as entering letters when numbers are expected). An application that keeps on running (instead of crashing) while giving the user a chance to correct mistakes is said to be **robust** (well constructed or reliable) and **fault tolerant** (tolerant of mistakes made by the user). Your goal as a programmer is to create robust, fault-tolerant applications. To accomplish this, you need to understand the types of errors that can occur in your applications.

You already have experience with techniques that help you avoid and correct compile-time errors. In this chapter you will focus on error-handling techniques, which help you detect and manage both data entry errors and runtime errors. You will also learn some other techniques, called exception-handling techniques, that will help you deal with other unusual conditions that can arise in your applications. But first, you'll learn some ways to prevent errors from arising in the first place.

INPUT VALIDATION

As the old saying goes, "An ounce of prevention is worth a pound of cure." This saying applies extremely well to the field of programming. In an ideal world, you would design applications that prevent errors from occurring at all. Many problems can originate when users enter data within an application's interface. In most applications presented thus far in this text, you merely hoped that users would enter the right kind of data when requested (for example, a valid state abbreviation or exactly five numeric characters for a ZIP code). However, as a programmer, you can arm the application with more than hope to ensure it captures valid data from the user.

Visual Basic provides many features for **input validation**, which is the process of validating data entered by the user before the data are used by the program. This section discusses the following ways that applications perform input validation:

- proper interface design
- trapping keystrokes
- the `Validating` event handler
- the `MaskedTextBox` control
- the `ErrorProvider` component

The following sections now briefly discuss each of these techniques.

Error Prevention Through Proper Interface Design

One way to ensure that errors are minimized is through the proper design of the user interface. For example, you could provide a text box in a form and prompt the user to enter a valid two-character, uppercase state abbreviation, hoping for the best, or you could use a `ListBox` control that contains all the valid state abbreviations. This requires the user to select from the list, thus ensuring that the state abbreviation is valid (although it still might not be the state that the user intended). Also, instead of providing a text box for a person to enter gender (perhaps M for male and F for female), the form could use two radio buttons, one for male and one for female.

As an example of error prevention through user interface design, the Skate-Away Sales application from Chapter 1 (Figure 1.26) has been modified in Figure 5.1 to use a `ListBox` for the state.

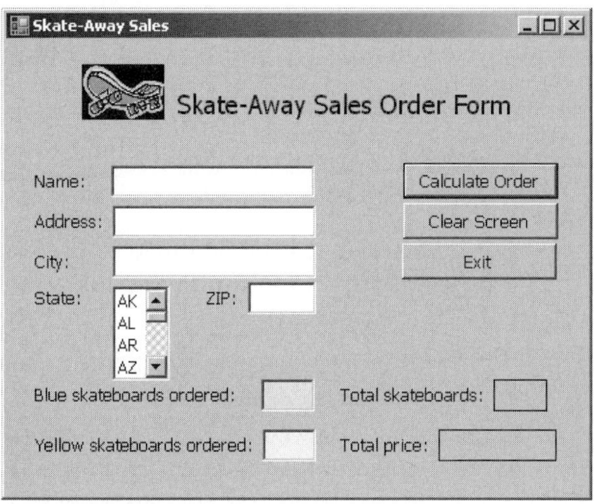

FIGURE 5.1 User interface for the Skate-Away Sales ListBox application

Input Validation by Trapping Keystrokes

For certain critical controls within a form (such as a text box that holds a credit card number), it is advisable to check each individual keystroke made by the user within that control to determine immediately if the character is valid. If the application determines that the character is invalid, your application can reject the keystroke and refrain from displaying it. For example, because credit card numbers contain only numeric digits, you could design your application to ignore any other kinds of characters (assuming hyphens are not allowed).

The .NET Framework `KeyPress` event can be used to check each keystroke made by the user within a specific control. This event fires whenever a character key is pressed while the control has focus. When the `KeyPress` event occurs, a `KeyPressEventArgs` object is created. The event procedure for the `KeyPress` event (coded by the programmer) receives the `KeyPressEventArgs` object, which has two properties:

- `Handled` gets or sets a `Boolean` value indicating whether the `KeyPress` event was handled. If `True`, the keystroke is rejected.
- `KeyChar` gets the character corresponding to the pressed key.

If you place a KeyPress event procedure in an application for a particular control, each keystroke within that control will generate a KeyPressEventArgs object that is received by the KeyPress event handler as e. Then the event procedure can check e.KeyChar for acceptability. If it is not acceptable, then e.Handled is set to True and the keystroke is totally ignored and not displayed in the control; otherwise, the keystroke is accepted and displayed within the control.

The Char class has several methods you can use to check for keystroke acceptability, such as IsDigit, IsLetter, and IsWhiteSpace. See *http://msdn.microsoft.com/library/* and search for "Char Members" for a complete list of methods in the Char class. For example, the following statement tells the current control to reject an input character if it is not a digit:

```
If Not Char.IsDigit(e.KeyChar) Then e.Handled = True
```

As an example of using the KeyPress event, consider again the Skate-Away Sales application. In this application, input validation for the number of blue or yellow skateboards ordered is performed using the Integer.TryParse method. This method, found within the calcButton_Click procedure, tries to convert the data entered into a text box to an integer. If the user clicks the Calculate button and the conversion fails (for example, the user enters nothing or something other than an integer for the number of skateboards), Integer.TryParse returns a 0.

This application can be modified to use the KeyPress event to ensure that the user enters valid input for the number of skateboards (either blue or yellow skateboards) immediately as each keystroke is made with either the blueTextBox or the yellowTextBox. The modification simply requires adding the following code to the MainForm class :

```
Private Sub skateBoards_KeyPress(ByVal sender As Object, _
    ByVal e As System.Windows.Forms.KeyPressEventArgs) _
    Handles blueTextBox.KeyPress, yellowTextBox.KeyPress

    If Not Char.IsDigit(e.KeyChar) Then
        e.Handled = True
        MessageBox.Show("Enter only numbers", "Error")
    End If

End Sub
```

Note that the complete code for the MainForm class can be found in the Skate-Away Sales Keypress application that accompanies this text. This code ensures that, while either the blueTextBox or yellowTextBox has focus, pressing any key other than a number is ignored and an error message is displayed. A sample run of the modified application, when the user attempts to enter a letter in the blueTextBox, is shown in Figure 5.2.

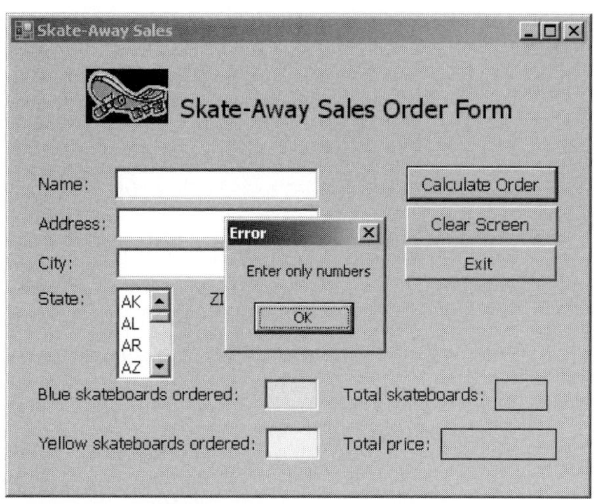

FIGURE 5.2 Sample run of the Skate-Away Sales KeyPress application

Input Validation with the `Validating` Event Handler

As you have probably already gathered, any form control that can receive free-form input (such as a text box or combo box) is prone to receiving invalid input from users. The previous section explored a way of validating user input within a text box one keystroke at a time, without leaving the control. Another useful technique is to validate the entire contents of a text box when the `Leave` event occurs.

The `Leave` event fires when the user Tabs away from the control or clicks on another control. The `Leave` event also fires when a program calls the `Select`, `SelectNextControl`, or `Focus` methods. Immediately after the `Leave` event fires for a control, a `Validating` event also fires if the `CausesValidation` property of the control is `True`, which is the default value. The `Validating` event enables you to write an event procedure to validate the entire contents of a control. The `Validating` event creates a `CancelEventArgs` object that has a `Cancel` property. If program logic determines that the input for the control is not valid, the `Cancel` property is set to `True` and the entire input for the control is ignored. If the value of `Cancel` is `False` (that is, if the input is deemed valid), the `Validated` event fires and program execution can proceed normally.

As an example of using the `Validating` event, the Skate-Away Sales Keypress application of Figure 5.2 is now modified to include an `emailTextBox` control to capture the customer's e-mail address. A `Validating` event handler is also added to help ensure that (1) an e-mail address has been entered and (2) the e-mail address has the correct format (that is, contains an "@" symbol followed by at least one "`.`". Following is the code for the `emailTextBox_Validating` event procedure that would be added to the `MainForm` class:

```
Private Sub emailTextBox_Validating(ByVal sender As Object, _
    ByVal e As System.ComponentModel.CancelEventArgs) _
    Handles emailTextBox.Validating
    Dim email As String = emailTextBox.Text

    If email.Length = 0 Then
        MessageBox.Show("E-mail required", "Error")
        emailTextBox.Focus()
```

```
        ElseIf _
            email.IndexOf("@").Equals(-1) OrElse _
            email.IndexOf(".").Equals(-1) OrElse _
            email.IndexOf("@") > email.IndexOf(".") Then
            MessageBox.Show("E-mail format is incorrect", "Error")
            emailTextBox.Focus()
            emailTextBox.SelectAll()
        End If
    End Sub
```

Recall that this procedure will be invoked automatically whenever the user leaves the `emailTextBox`. When this `Validating` event handler exectutes, the If clause checks whether text has been entered in `emailTextBox`. If so, the `ElseIf` clause checks whether the text entered by the user contains an "`@`", whether it contains a "`.`", and whether a "`.`" follows the "`@`". If any one of these conditions fails, an error message displays and focus returns to `emailTextBox`. Figure 5.3 shows a sample run of the Skate-Away Sales Validating application.

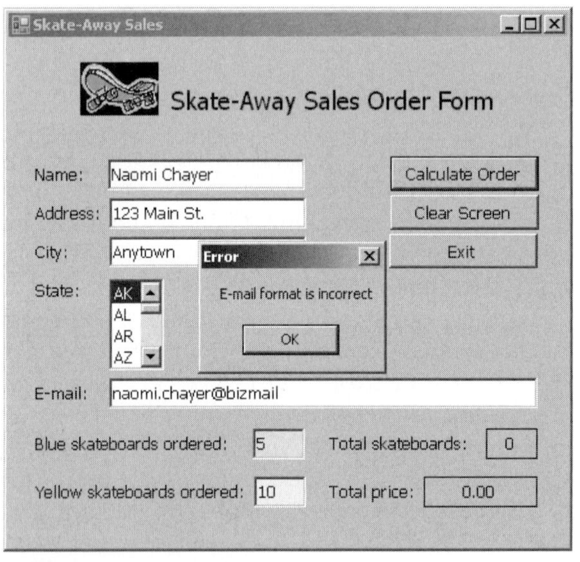

FIGURE 5.3 Sample run of the Skate-Away Sales Validating application

You might have noticed that the code in the `emailTextBox_Validating` procedure doesn't exactly guarantee that the e-mail address entered by the user is perfectly valid. It simply guarantees that there is an "`@`" followed by a "`.`". Thus the e-mail address "`@.`" would be considered valid. The next section provides another way to validate user input when a definite pattern of characters must be matched.

Using the `MaskedTextBox` Control for Input Validation

The `MaskedTextBox` control is a new feature of the .NET Framework 2.0 (similar to the `MaskedEdit` control of VB 6) that provides a wide variety of techniques for validating user input. The `MaskedTextBox` control is an enhanced `TextBox` that uses the `Mask` property to specify valid user input. Using the `MaskedTextBox`, you can create a character mask that specifies required and optional characters, the positions of such characters, the types of required characters (such as numeric or alphabetic), and the values and positions of literal characters (such as hyphens in a phone number or parentheses around an area code). You can even perform special processing with this control, such as converting alphabetic characters to uppercase or lowercase. Figure 5.4 explains how to use this new `MaskedTextBox` control.

HOW TO...

Use a `MaskedTextBox` Control

1. As with a `TextBox` control, drag a `MaskedTextBox` control to a form. Provide the control with a descriptive name, such as `phoneMaskedTextBox` for a telephone number.
2. If the Properties window for the `MaskedTextBox` control is not displayed, right-click on the control and click Properties.
3. Click the value field for the `Mask` property in the Properties window and click the ellipsis to display the Input Mask dialog box (see Figure 5.5). You can select one of the available predefined masks or create a custom mask using the available masking elements (see Table 5.1)
4. Add a `MaskInputRejected` event procedure for the `MaskedTextBox` control to handle invalid keystrokes within the `MaskedTextBox` (optional).
5. Add a `Validating` event procedure for the `MaskedTextBox` control to check the completed string against the `Mask` (optional).

FIGURE 5.4 How to use a `MaskedTextBox` control

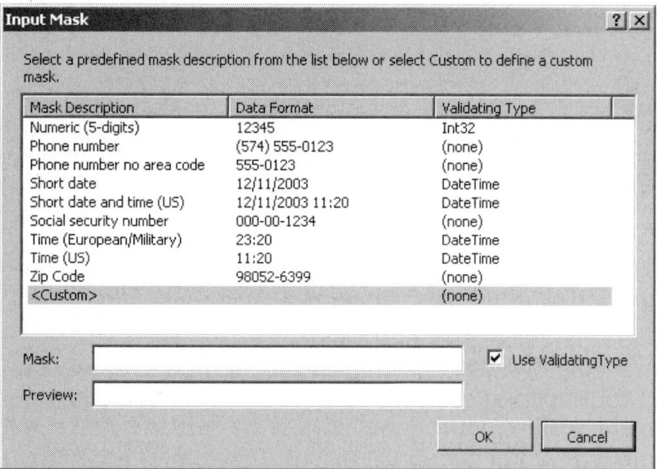

FIGURE 5.5 Input Mask dialog for the `MaskedTextBox` control

<table>
<tr><th>Masking Element</th><th>Description</th></tr>
<tr><td>0</td><td>Digit, required. This element will accept any single digit between 0 and 9.</td></tr>
<tr><td>9</td><td>Digit or space, optional.</td></tr>
<tr><td>#</td><td>Digit or space, optional. If this position is blank in the mask, it will be rendered as a space in the <code>Text</code> property. Plus (+) and minus (–) signs are allowed.</td></tr>
<tr><td>L</td><td>Letter, required. Restricts input to the ASCII letters a–z and A–Z. This mask element is equivalent to [a–zA–Z] in regular expressions.</td></tr>
<tr><td>?</td><td>Letter, optional. Restricts input to the ASCII letters a–z and A–Z. This mask element is equivalent to [a–zA–Z]? in regular expressions.</td></tr>
<tr><td>&</td><td>Character, required. If the <code>AsciiOnly</code> property is set to true, this element behaves like the "L" element.</td></tr>
<tr><td>C</td><td>Character, optional. Any non-control character. If the <code>AsciiOnly</code> property is set to <code>True</code>, this element behaves like the "?" element.</td></tr>
<tr><td>A</td><td>Alphanumeric, optional. If the <code>AsciiOnly</code> property is set to <code>True</code>, the only characters it will accept are the ASCII letters a–z and A–Z.</td></tr>
<tr><td>a</td><td>Alphanumeric, optional. If the <code>AsciiOnly</code> property is set to <code>True</code>, the only characters it will accept are the ASCII letters a–z and A–Z.</td></tr>
<tr><td>.</td><td>Decimal placeholder. The actual display character used will be the decimal symbol appropriate to the format provider, as determined by the control's <code>FormatProvider</code> property.</td></tr>
<tr><td>,</td><td>Thousands placeholder. The actual display character used will be the thousands placeholder appropriate to the format provider, as determined by the control's <code>FormatProvider</code> property.</td></tr>
<tr><td>:</td><td>Time separator. The actual display character used will be the time symbol appropriate to the format provider, as determined by the control's <code>FormatProvider</code> property.</td></tr>
<tr><td>/</td><td>Date separator. The actual display character used will be the date symbol appropriate to the format provider, as determined by the control's <code>FormatProvider</code> property.</td></tr>
<tr><td>$</td><td>Currency symbol. The actual character displayed will be the currency symbol appropriate to the format provider, as determined by the control's <code>FormatProvider</code> property.</td></tr>
<tr><td><</td><td>Shift down. Converts all characters that follow to lowercase.</td></tr>
<tr><td>></td><td>Shift up. Converts all characters that follow to uppercase.</td></tr>
<tr><td>|</td><td>Disable a previous shift up or shift down.</td></tr>
<tr><td>\</td><td>Escape. Escapes a mask character, turning it into a literal. "\\" is the escape sequence for a backslash.</td></tr>
<tr><td>All other characters</td><td>Literals. All non-mask elements will appear as themselves within <code>MaskedTextBox</code>. Literals always occupy a static position in the mask at run time, and cannot be moved or deleted by the user.</td></tr>
</table>

TABLE 5.1 Select Masking Elements for the `MaskedTextBox` Control

If you don't provide the event procedures in steps 4 and 5 of Figure 5.4, the input mask can guide users to enter the right kind of data, but the data they enter will not be validated. As an example of using the `MaskedTextBox` control, begin with the Skate-Away Sales Validating application (Figure 5.3) and perform the following steps:

1. Add a `phoneMaskedTextBox` control and an accompanying label to the user interface.
2. Click the ellipsis for the `Mask` property of `phoneMaskedTextBox` and select the Phone Number mask description in the Input Mask dialog box. The user interface should now appear as shown in Figure 5.6.
3. Add the following two event procedures to the `MainForm` class:

```
Private Sub phoneMaskedTextBox_MaskInputRejected( _
    ByVal sender As Object, _
    ByVal e As System.Windows.Forms.MaskInputRejectedEventArgs) _
    Handles phoneMaskedTextBox.MaskInputRejected
    ' checks each keystroke for validity
    MessageBox.Show("Invalid entry", "Error")
End Sub

Private Sub phoneMaskedTextBox_Validating(ByVal sender As Object, _
    ByVal e As System.ComponentModel.CancelEventArgs) _
    Handles phoneMaskedTextBox.Validating
    ' check if entire mask has been completed correctly
    If Not phoneMaskedTextBox.MaskCompleted Then
        MessageBox.Show("Invalid phone number", "Error")
    End If

End Sub
```

`MaskedTextBox` *control added*

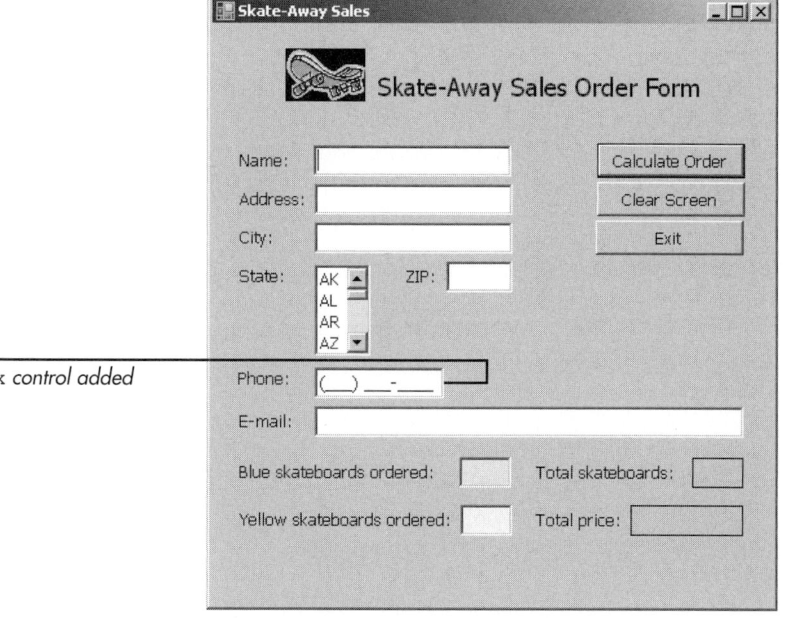

FIGURE 5.6 User interface for the Skate-Away Sales MaskedTextBox application

Figure 5.7 shows a sample run of the Skate-Away Sales MaskedTextBox application when the user fails to enter a complete phone number and tabs to the next control.

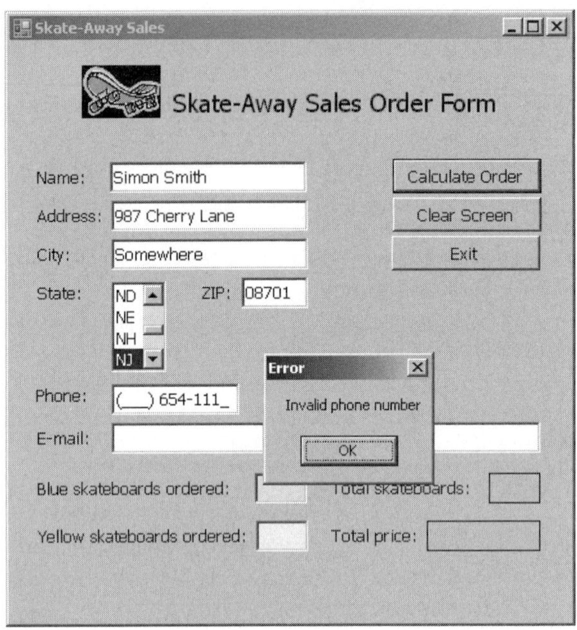

FIGURE 5.7 Sample run of the Skate-Away Sales MaskedTextBox application

Using the `ErrorProvider` Component for Input Validation

Yet another technique for validating user input involves the `ErrorProvider` component. The `ErrorProvider` component notifies the user that a data entry error has occurred in a particular control (such as a text box) without using a `MessageBox`. The `ErrorProvider` component displays a default error icon (which can be customized if desired) next to the control where the error occurred. When the user positions the mouse over the error icon, a ToolTip error message (provided by the program) displays, informing the user of the problem. Figure 5.8 explains how to use the `ErrorProvider` component.

HOW TO...

Use the ErrorProvider Component

1. In the Visual Studio Toolbox, expand the Components section and drag an `ErrorProvider` component to the form. A component name `ErrorProvider1` (which can be renamed) will be added to the component tray of the IDE.
2. Create a `TextChanged` event procedure to validate individual keystrokes within a control and/or a `Leave` event procedure to validate the entire text when the user leaves the control.
3. Within each validation event procedure, code the `SetError` method of the `ErrorProvider` component to display a ToolTip error message when the user positions the mouse over the error icon.

FIGURE 5.8 How to use an `ErrorProvider` component

As an example of using the `ErrorProvider` component, begin with the Skate-Away Sales MaskedTextBox application (Figure 5.6) and add an `ErrorProvider` component to validate the ZIP code in the user interface, using the following steps:

1. Add an `ErrorProvider` component to `MainForm`.
2. Add the following event procedure to validate individual keystrokes and the final entry in `zipTextBox`:

```
Private Sub zipTextBox_Validate(ByVal sender As Object, _
    ByVal e As System.EventArgs) _
    Handles zipTextBox.TextChanged, zipTextBox.Leave

    ' if not a numeric character, display error;
    ' else, don't display error
    If Not IsNumeric(zipTextBox.Text) Then
        ErrorProvider1.SetError(CType(sender, Control), _
            "Invalid character")
    Else
        ErrorProvider1.SetError(CType(sender, Control), "")
    End If

    ' if more than 5 digits in ZIP code, display error
    If zipTextBox.Text.Length > 5 Then
        ErrorProvider1.SetError(CType(sender, Control), _
            "Only 5 digits allowed")
    End If

    ' if no ZIP code entered, display error, reset focus
    If zipTextBox.Text.Length = 0 Then
        ErrorProvider1.SetError(CType(sender, Control), _
            "ZIP code required")
        zipTextBox.Focus()
    End If

End Sub
```

Note in the preceding sample code that there are three different `if` statements. The first two operate on the `TextChanged` event while the last one operates on the `Leave` event. A sample run of the Skate-Away Sales ErrorProvider application is shown in Figure 5.9.

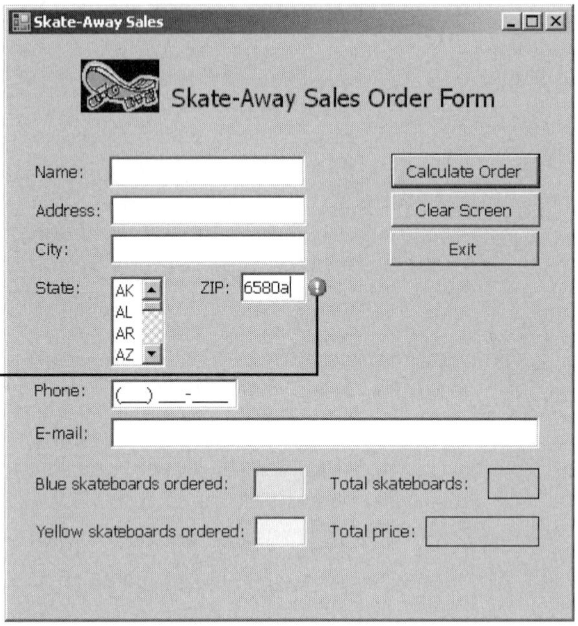

Error icon appears when "a" is entered

FIGURE 5.9 Sample run of the Skate-Away Sales ErrorProvider application

This section has presented several different techniques for validating user input. When you create an application, you (or your users) may prefer one technique over another, or you may find yourself using different techniques for different purposes within the same application. The remainder of this chapter will focus on additional methods for dealing with input errors as well as other kinds of problems that applications may encounter.

RUNTIME ERRORS AND EXCEPTIONS

Of course, as a programmer your goal is to develop software that is error free, robust, and fault tolerant. In the previous section, you learned how to handle errors made by users as they enter data within a user interface. Those errors are not in the program you created, but in the data entered by the user. However, part of your job is to write program code to deal with such data entry errors. In this section, you will learn about other kinds of errors that can occur within programs themselves and different ways that you can deal with such errors.

Types of Errors

In this text, you have already learned about many types of errors, including compile-time errors, runtime errors, and logic errors. So far, you have focused primarily on **compile-time errors** (errors that occur while the program is being compiled, usually due to violating a programming language's syntax) because they must be corrected before a program is able to run. **Runtime errors** (errors generated by the program during execution) are also important because they can cause a program to crash, thus frustrating the user. **Logic errors** (errors made by the programmer in designing or implementing the logic of a program) are perhaps the most insidious because they can often go undetected. A program containing a logic error may compile and run, but produce incorrect results, often without the user's knowledge.

Prior to the release of Visual Basic .NET, Visual Basic programmers relied on classic error handling to deal with runtime errors. **Classic error handling** refers to the way Visual Basic internally handles an error object called `Err`. This error object is automatically generated by a Visual Basic program when a runtime error occurs, such as when an array index is out of bounds. `Err` has certain properties, such as a specific error `Number`, the standard error `Description`, and the object that is the `Source` of the error. A Visual Basic program can use the `Err` object to handle runtime errors in an application, as you will soon see.

Runtime errors not only generate `Err` objects, but also generate specific kinds of `Exception` objects that the program can use to recover from problems. An **exception** is any exceptional, unusual, or abnormal condition that occurs during program execution (including runtime errors). `Exception` objects are created by your application when the program code attempts to do something it was not designed to do, such as convert an alphabetic character into a number, divide by zero, or read from a data file that doesn't exist. Your job as the programmer is to equip the application to handle these exceptions in a logical way that explains to the user what went wrong and how to remedy the problem (if possible), without, you hope, terminating (crashing) the application.

All Visual Basic runtime errors are exceptions, but not all exceptions are Visual Basic runtime errors. To be more specific, an exception is an object that contains information about any kind of abnormal condition. For example, an `Exception` object is created when an array index is out of bounds (a runtime error). An `Exception` object can also be created by the program when a user enters a negative number for her age. The latter is not a runtime error, but it is nevertheless an unusual condition that the program needs to handle. Figure 5.10 illustrates the relationship between runtime errors and exceptions.

Classic error handling can deal only with specific, standard Visual Basic runtime errors. In order to handle a wider variety of errors and exceptions in a more organized fashion, Visual Basic .NET introduced **structured exception handling**, a very different process for managing `Exception` objects that uses special program elements. Structured exception handling is usually preferred over classic error handling because of its enhanced power, flexibility, and organization. However, you will first learn about classic error handling for two reasons. First, classic error handling is still supported in Visual Basic .NET and you may encounter programs that use it. Second, understanding classic error handling will help you better understand and appreciate the improvements offered by structured exception handling.

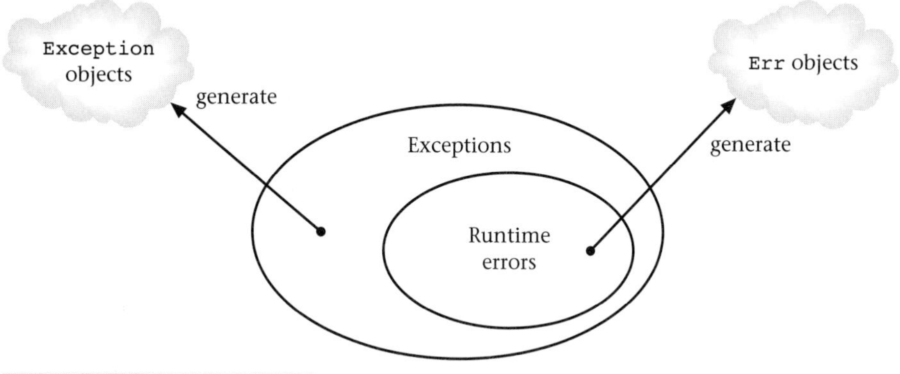

FIGURE 5.10 Relationship between runtime errors and exceptions

RUNTIME ERRORS IN A SIMPLE APPLICATION

To begin an exploration of both classic error handling and structured exception handling, consider the simple Division application in Figures 5.11 and 5.12. The interface in Figure 5.11 allows the user to divide one number (the dividend) by another (the divisor), resulting in the answer (the quotient). The program in Figure 5.12 does not contain any code to detect or handle any runtime errors. It simply assumes that the user will always enter numeric data in both text boxes and will not enter zero in the `divisorTextBox`. Under these conditions, the program will always work correctly. Figure 5.13 shows a sample run of the Division application.

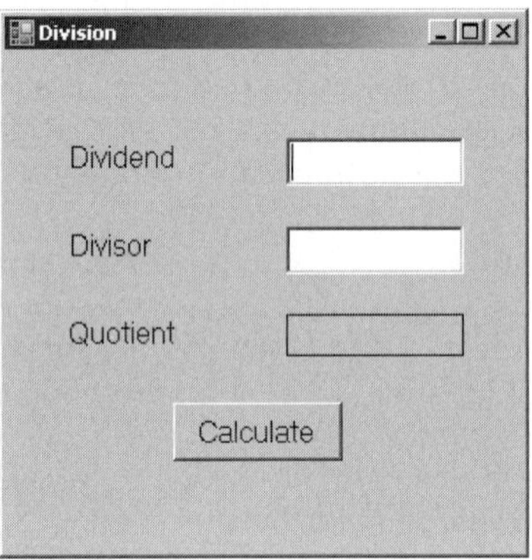

FIGURE 5.11 User interface for the Division application

```
Public Class MainForm
    Private Sub calculateButton_Click(ByVal sender As Object, _
        ByVal e As System.EventArgs) Handles calculateButton.Click

        ' declare variables
        Dim quotient As Decimal
        Dim dividend As Decimal
        Dim divisor As Decimal

        ' input
        dividend = Convert.ToDecimal(dividendTextBox.Text())
        divisor = Convert.ToDecimal(divisorTextBox.Text())

        ' processing
        quotient = dividend / divisor

        ' output
        quotientLabel.Text = Convert.ToString(quotient)

    End Sub
End Class
```

FIGURE 5.12 Program code for the `MainForm` class in the Division application

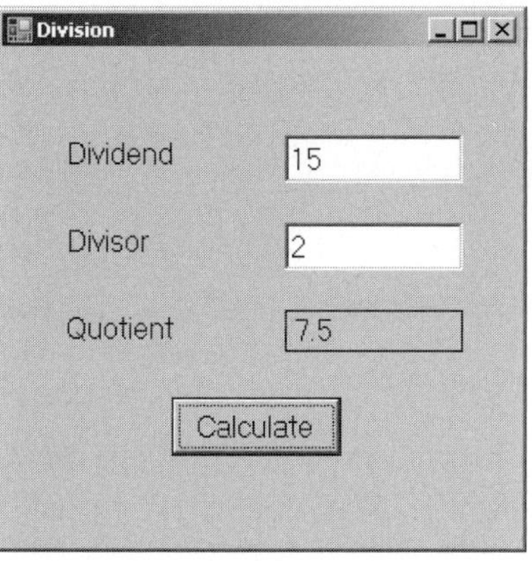

FIGURE 5.13 Sample run of the Division application

The Division application will run without fail as long as the user enters the right kind of data in the text boxes. However, users sometimes make mistakes and you, the programmer, must anticipate that possibility. For example, suppose the user enters nothing at all in the `dividendTextBox`. Figure 5.14 shows how the Visual Basic IDE responds in debug mode (that is, while you are testing the application within the IDE). Figure 5.15 shows the error message that a user would see if he or she makes the same kind of mistake when running the application in standard execution mode (that is, while running the Division Project.exe file).

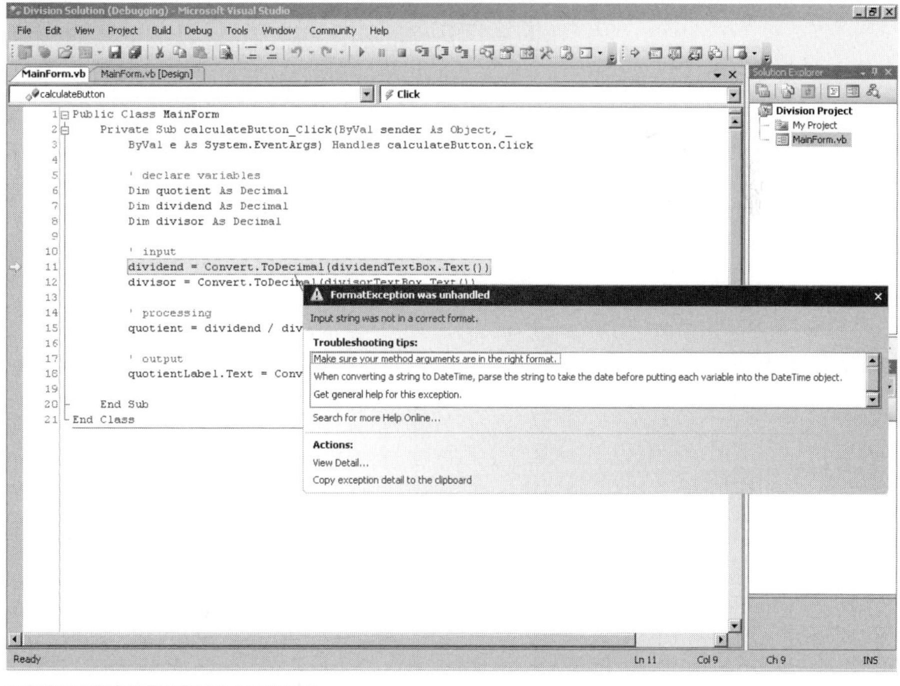

FIGURE 5.14 Error message displayed in debug mode

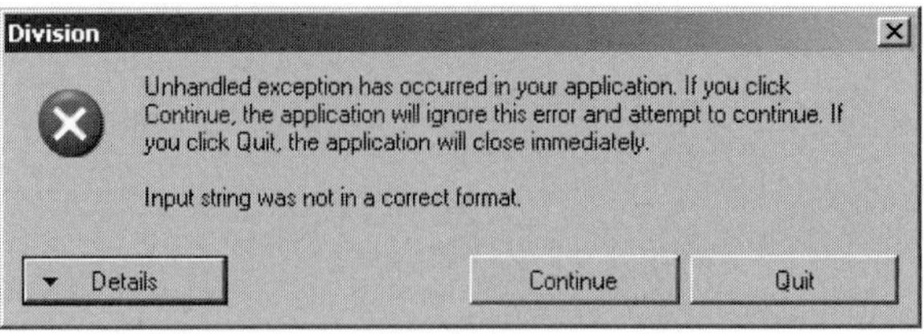

FIGURE 5.15 Error message displayed in standard execution mode

Figure 5.14 indicates that a runtime error (an error that occurs when the program is running) occurred. To be more precise, the warning window states that a `FormatException` occurred. (Recall that an exception is something unusual.) Specifically, the warning states that an object from the class `FormatException` was created and was unhandled, which means that the program did not handle or process this exception. Furthermore, the warning window provides additional useful information. It explains what caused the `FormatException`—an input string was not in the correct format. Also note that the Visual Basic IDE highlights Line 12 in the application (also shown in Figure 5.12) because the `Convert.ToDecimal` method cannot convert the empty string `""` to a `Decimal`. (The empty string is a result of nothing being entered in the `dividendTextBox`.) The error message presented to the user in Figure 5.15 conveys similar information. However, the dialog box in Figure 5.15 allows the user to click Continue and attempt to correct the problem.

You should realize that many different kinds of errors can occur in a single application. For example, Figure 5.16 shows what happens if you (the programmer) test the Division application by entering a zero in the `divisorTextBox`. (Remember that division by zero is mathematically undefined.) Figure 5.17 shows the error message that displays when a user makes the same mistake while running the executable application.

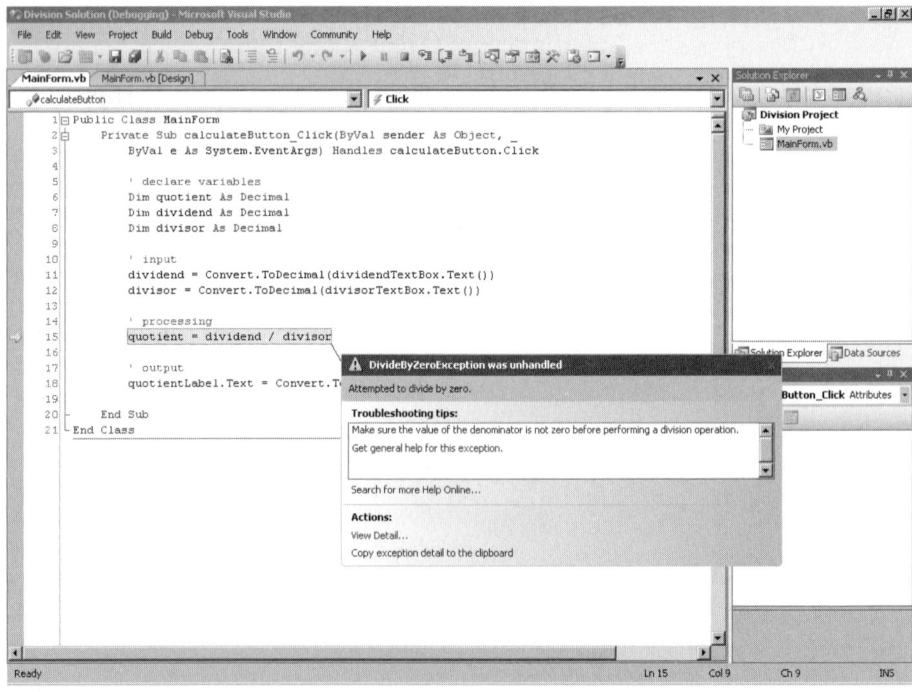

FIGURE 5.16 Error message displayed when dividing by 0 (debug mode)

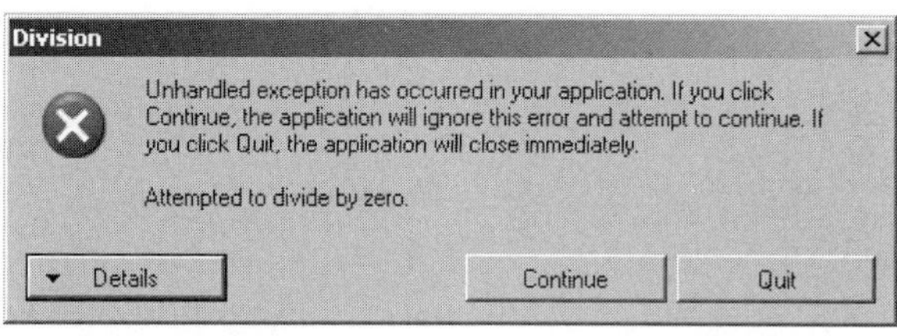

FIGURE 5.17 Error message displayed when dividing by 0 (standard execution mode)

In the next section you will apply classic error handling techniques to the Division application. You may find that classic error handling in Visual Basic is a little confusing, which is one of the reasons why the more recently developed structured exception handling process is preferred. You will learn about structured exception handling later in this chapter.

CLASSIC ERROR HANDLING IN VISUAL BASIC

Classic error handling in Visual Basic is accomplished using the `On Error` statement, of which there are several variations. The following sections discuss these variations in detail.

`On Error GoTo` <line>

The `On Error GoTo` *<line>* statement is used to place Visual Basic in **error-handling mode** (a state of a Visual Basic application that enables the features of classic error handling) and then jump to an indicated *<line>* in the program, which begins the error-handling code. You place the `On Error GoTo` *<line>* statement in the program before an anticipated error (such as number format error or division by zero) can occur. Then you add error-handling code following the labeled *<line>* in the program. The error-handling code (known as the **error handler**) will usually display a message to the user and exit the `Sub` procedure.

In the Division application, two different kinds of errors can occur, so two `On Error GoTo` *<line>* statements are necessary. As shown in Figure 5.18, the first `Error GoTo` *<line>* statement belongs in the input section (Line 10) and the second in the processing section (Line 15) of the class `MainForm`. You then create the two named lines (Lines 22 and 26) at the end of the `Sub` procedure. After each named line, error handling code is added (message boxes). Note that `Exit Sub` is used to exit the `Sub` procedure in three different places: if everything works without error (Line 20), if a `NumberFormatError` occurs (Line 24), and if a `DivisionByZeroError` occurs (Line 28).

```
1  Public Class MainForm
2      Private Sub calculateButton_Click(ByVal sender As Object, _
3          ByVal e As System.EventArgs) Handles calculateButton.Click
4          ' declare variables
5          Dim quotient As Decimal
6          Dim dividend As Decimal
7          Dim divisor As Decimal
8
```

(Figure is continued on next page)

Enter error handling mode

```
        ' input
        On Error GoTo NumberFormatError
        dividend = Convert.ToDecimal(dividendTextBox.Text())
        divisor = Convert.ToDecimal(divisorTextBox.Text())

        ' processing
        On Error GoTo DivisionByZeroError
        quotient = dividend / divisor

        ' output
        quotientLabel.Text = Convert.ToString(quotient)
        Exit Sub

NumberFormatError:  ' error-handler
        MessageBox.Show("Enter numbers and numbers only")
        Exit Sub

DivisionByZeroError:  ' error-handler
        MessageBox.Show("Cannot divide by zero")
        Exit Sub

    End Sub
End Class
```

FIGURE 5.18 Program code for the class `MainForm` in the Division application with `On Error GoTo` *<line>*

Examine the code in Figure 5.18 carefully to see how this error handling works. In the input section of Figure 5.18, the statement `On Error GoTo NumberFormatError` causes the application to enter error-handling mode. Then, any error that occurs after this statement (and before the next `On Error GoTo` *<line>* statement) causes the program to create an error object called `Err` and jump to the error handler labeled `NumberFormatError:`. When this error handler executes, a `MessageBox` is displayed. The code `Exit Sub` then causes the program to exit error-handling mode and immediately leave the `Sub` procedure. The user can then reenter acceptable data in the interface and click the Calculate button again. The result of entering nothing in the `dividendTextBox` is shown in Figure 5.19.

(a) Interface with incomplete data

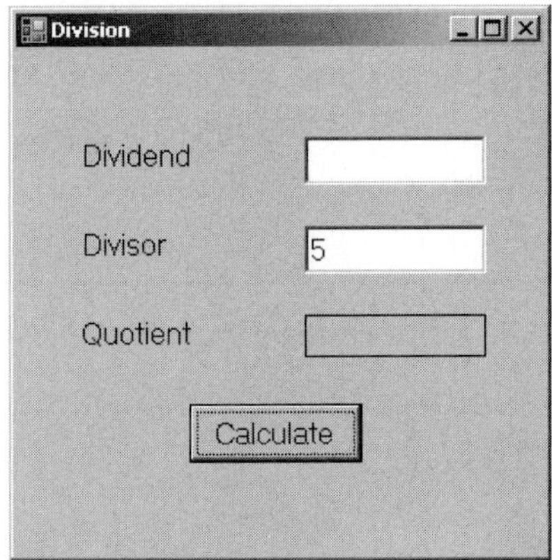

(b) Error message

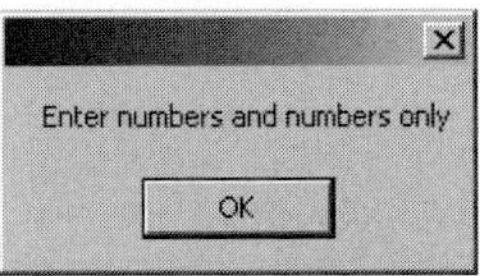

FIGURE 5.19 Sample run of Division application with classic error handling

Alternatively, the user may try to divide by zero by entering a non-zero number in the `dividendTextBox` and 0 in the `divisorTextBox`. If so, the statement `On Error Goto DivisionByZeroError` in the processing section causes the program to enter error-handling mode, and the expression `dividend / divisor` will generate an error object called `Err`. The program jumps to the line labeled `DivisionByZeroError:`, and the message box shown in Figure 5.20 is displayed. After the user clicks OK to close this dialog box, the statement `Exit Sub` causes the application to exit both error-handling mode and the `Sub` procedure. The user is then able to reenter acceptable data.

(a) Interface with division by 0

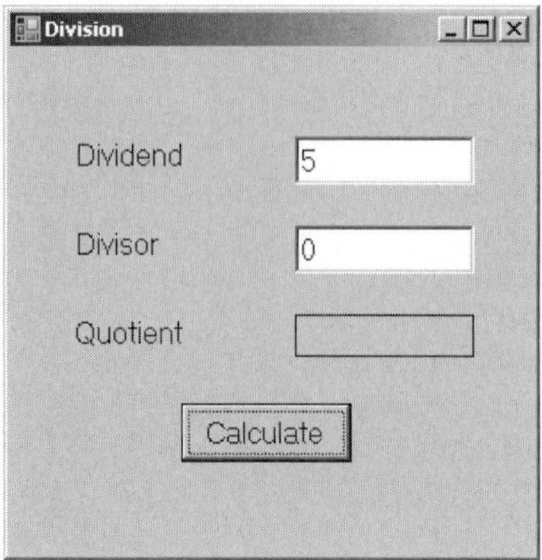

(b) Error message

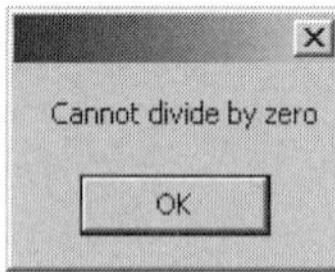

FIGURE 5.20 Sample run of Division application with classic error handling

Alternatives to `Exit Sub`

The example in Figure 5.18 uses `Exit Sub` to exit error-handling mode and immediately leave the `Sub` procedure. If you want to perform error handling within a `Function`, you would use the code `Exit Function` instead. You can also use the keyword `Resume` (instead of `Exit Sub`) in Figure 5.18 to repeat execution of the same statement that caused the error. This assumes that the user is given the opportunity to fix the problem that caused the error. Otherwise, the program may enter an infinite loop. For example, simply replacing `Exit Sub` in Figure 5.18 with `Resume` would create an infinite loop because the statement `quotient = dividend / divisor` (Line 16 in Figure 5.18) would be repeated with the same errant values. However, you can use the following code to replace the `DivisionByZeroError` error handler in Figure 5.18, allowing the user to enter a non-zero `divisor` within an input box:

```
DivisionByZeroError:   ' error-handler
        MessageBox.Show("Cannot divide by zero")
        divisor = InputBox("Reenter divisor", "Division Project")
        divisorTextBox.Text = divisor
        Resume
```

When the `Resume` statement executes, the statement `quotient = dividend / divisor` is repeated with a valid value for `divisor` and the program procedes normally. Additionally, you can use `Resume Next` to resume execution with the statement after the one that caused the error. For example, one statement in the program may try to read a file that doesn't exist, causing an error. Using the keyword `Resume` alone would simply repeat that same statement, causing an infinite loop. Using `Resume Next` would cause execution to skip to the next line of the program, which may be code that closes the open file.

On Error Resume Next

Classic error handling can also be performed using the On Error Resume Next statement. On Error Resume Next allows a program to simply skip a statement that causes an error and resume normal flow with the next statement. Errors can then be handled using traditional If...Then logic. For example, Figure 5.21 presents another version of the Division application that uses On Error Resume Next, the object Err, and Select Case to handle errors.

```
1  Public Class MainForm
2      Private Sub calculateButton_Click(ByVal sender As Object, _
3           ByVal e As System.EventArgs) Handles calculateButton.Click
4          ' declare variables
5          Dim quotient As Decimal
6          Dim dividend As Decimal
7          Dim divisor As Decimal
8
9          ' input
10         On Error Resume Next
11         dividend = Convert.ToDecimal(dividendTextBox.Text())
12         divisor = Convert.ToDecimal(divisorTextBox.Text())
13
14         ' processing
15         quotient = dividend / divisor
16
17         Select Case Err.Number
18             Case 0 ' no error
19             Case 13 ' number format
20                 MessageBox.Show("Default to quotient = 0")
21                 dividendTextBox.Text = ""
22                 divisorTextBox.Text = ""
23                 quotient = 0
24             Case 11 ' divide by 0
25                 MessageBox.Show("Default to divisor = 1")
26                 divisor = 1
27                 divisorTextBox.Text = Convert.ToString(divisor)
28                 quotient = dividend / divisor
29             Case Else
30                 ' display error code
31                 MessageBox.Show(Convert.ToString(Err.Number))
32                 Exit Sub
33         End Select
34
35         ' output
36         quotientLabel.Text = Convert.ToString(quotient)
37         Exit Sub
38     End Sub
39 End Class
```

FIGURE 5.21 Program code for the class MainForm in the Division application with On Error Resume Next

The program in Figure 5.21 uses the statement On Error Resume Next in the input section to establish how errors will be handled (that is, skipping any statement that creates an error object Err). For example, if the dividendTextBox does not contain a number, the object Err will be created by Visual Basic (Line 11) and the next statement in the program (Line 12) will be executed (getting the input from the divisorTextBox, followed by calculating the quotient). In this case, the number format for dividendTextBox is incorrect and the Number property of Err, which contains a numeric error code, will be 13. In this event, the Select Case statement will display a message box, empty the text boxes, and set the quotient to 0. If, on the other hand, the user tries to divide by 0, the object Err will be created by the quotient calculation in Line 15 (dividend / divisor) with a Number property (error code) of 11. The Select Case statement will then be executed next and Case 11 will be processed, setting the divisor to 1 and recalculating the quotient. You should try to run this program and make sure you understand how it works.

You can also use additional error-handling statements. For example, add the statement On Error GoTo 0 to a program to deactivate any previously installed error handler. The statement On Error GoTo -1 also deactivates any previously installed error handler and exits error-handling mode.

Disadvantages of Classic Error Handling

As you can see, classic error handling can be challenging. It is very difficult to understand how a program handles errors just by looking at the program code because of all the skipping and jumping that can occur. When you write basic program logic (such as quotient = dividend / divisor) and then interject special error-handling logic (such as the Select Case statement in Figure 5.21), a relatively simple program can become difficult to read and understand. The readability problem grows increasingly severe as the program becomes larger. To make matters worse, in classic error handling you cannot nest error-handling code. That is, you cannot place new error-handling code within previously existing error-handling code to process new errors that may be created.

Many of the errors discussed in this section can be addressed by using the input validation techniques presented earlier in this chapter. Input validation is often much less confusing than classic error handling, but input validation cannot handle many other kinds of potential errors, such as "array index out of bounds" or "file not found". Because of the confusion associated with classic error handling, Microsoft implemented structured exception handling in Visual Basic .NET. Structured exception handling is more intuitive and organized than classic error handling and utilizes true object-oriented capabilities. To learn more about structured exception handling, you will need to explore the exception classes in the .NET Framework.

EXCEPTION CLASSES IN THE .NET FRAMEWORK

The previous section took a brief look at the somewhat confusing classic error handling in Visual Basic, which was the norm before object-oriented Visual Basic .NET was released. These days, structured exception handling is the preferred way of dealing with runtime errors and other exceptions in a Visual Basic application. Before learning how to perform structured exception handling, you will learn about exception classes and their relationships.

Runtime Errors and Exceptions

As discussed previously, an exception is not exactly the same as a runtime error, although they are very similar. (Many programmers refer to exceptions and errors interchangeably.) In Visual Basic, a runtime error creates an object called Err, which has certain properties, such as an error Number and Description. Every runtime error in a Visual Basic program also generates a specific kind of exception object using predefined exception classes (such as `FormatException` or `DivideByZeroException`).

You can write special code that equips your application to handle these special exception objects. This exception-handling code can provide important custom error messages to the user and keep the application running. If you don't write code to handle the exceptions, Visual Basic's runtime environment (the Common Language Runtime or CLR) will automatically handle them for you by displaying standard error messages and subsequently shutting down the program. It is important to understand that the hundreds of exception classes in the .NET Framework are arranged in an inheritance hierarchy. A few of these classes are shown in Figure 5.22.

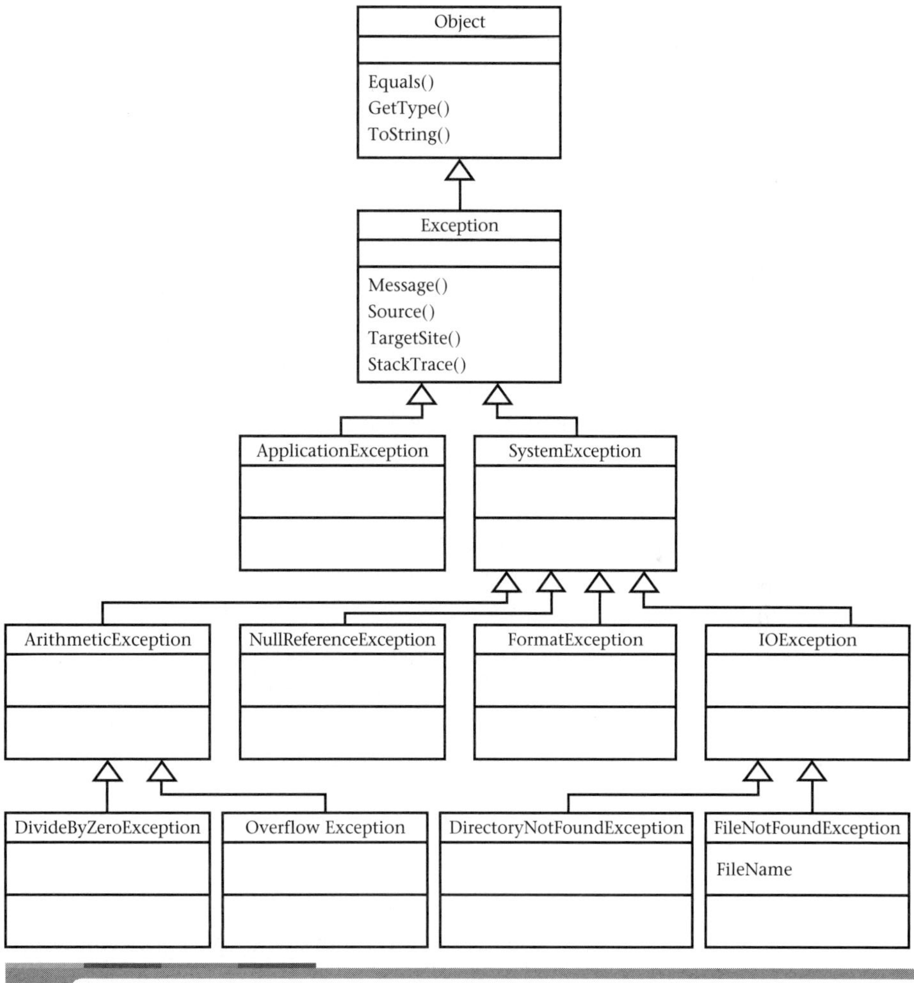

FIGURE 5.22 Inheritance hierarchy for selected exception classes

The Inheritance Hierarchy of Exception Classes

The inheritance hierarchy in Figure 5.22 begins with the `Object` class, the ultimate base class in the .NET Framework, which means that all other Visual Basic classes inherit ultimately from `Object`. (You first learned about this class in Chapter 4.) Some of the methods of the `Object` class are `Equals`, `GetType`, and `ToString`. At the next level in the inheritance hierarchy is the `Exception` class, which is used as the base class for all application exceptions. Note that `Exception` has several unique properties: `Message` (a description of the current exception), `Source` (the application or object causing the error), `TargetSite` (the method in the application where the exception originated), and `StackTrace` (a history of all method calls leading to the creation of the exception).

You saw the `Exception` class at work earlier in this chapter in the Division application (Figure 5.12). If the user attempts to divide by zero, the detailed error dialog box shown in Figure 5.23 displays the message "Attempted to divide by zero." This message is actually the content of the `Message` property. The list box contained in this dialog box displays the type of exception (`System.DivideByZeroException`). There are many other somewhat cryptic messages contained within the list box of Figure 5.23. For example, the `TargetSite` of the error can be seen from the statement, "at System.Decimal.Divide(Decimal d1, Decimal d2)", which refers to the `Divide` method in the `Decimal` structure in the `System` namespace. Finally, the `StackTrace` property contains the **method-call stack**, the sequence of method calls within an application that leads to the creation of an exception object. Figure 5.23 shows the `StackTrace` for the `DivideByZeroException`, including the `Sub` procedure `calculateButton_Click` in the `MainForm` class of the Division project. (At this point you don't have to worry about understanding all the details included within the stack trace.)

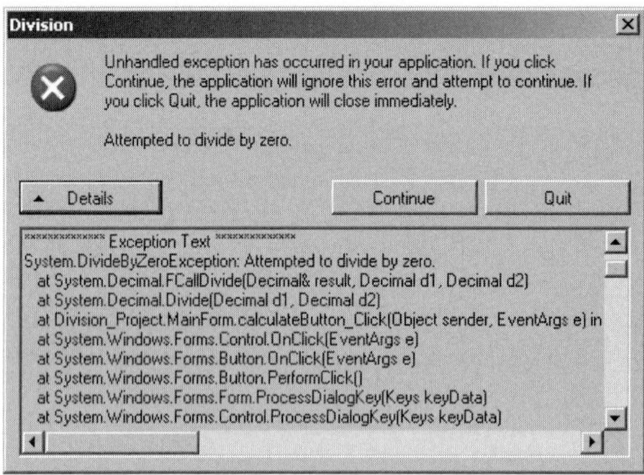

FIGURE 5.23 Detailed error message for Division application dividing by zero

Continuing down the inheritance hierarchy of Figure 5.22, note that the `ApplicationException` and `SystemException` classes inherit from `Exception`. The class `ApplicationException` is the class you use to generate custom programmer-defined exceptions in your applications (as you will see later in this chapter), while `SystemException` is the base class for all predefined exceptions in the `System` namespace. Several specific kinds of exceptions shown in Figure 5.22 inherit from `SystemException`, such as `ArithmeticException` (from which `DivideByZeroException` derives), `FormatException` (previously discussed in this chapter), and `IOException` (from which `FileNotFoundException` derives).You'll learn more about these exceptions later in this book. Detailed information about these classes (and all other exception classes) can be found at *http://msdn.microsoft.com/*. To look up information at this site, simply type the name of the class in the search box.

Note that most of the more specific exception classes in Figure 5.22 do not provide functionality that is not already contained in the `Exception` class. These derived classes are designed primarily to identify the type of exception occurring in an application and then utilize the properties and methods in the `Exception` class. However, some specific exception classes do provide unique capabilities. For example, the `FileNotFoundException` class has a property called `FileName`, which holds the name of the file referenced by the application but not found at the expected location. Next, you will learn how to work with the objects created from these exception classes whenever your applications encounter unexpected problems.

STRUCTURED EXCEPTION HANDLING IN VISUAL BASIC .NET

Whenever a runtime error occurs in a Visual Basic program, the Common Language Runtime (CLR) creates an exception object. In this section, you will learn how to handle these exception objects in a precise way using structured exception handling, making your applications more robust and fault tolerant.

The `Try...Catch...Finally` Statement

A program performs structured exception handling using a **`Try...Catch...Finally` statement**, which is a special combination of a `Try` block with its associated `Catch` block(s) and `Finally` block. Figure 5.24 shows how to use a `Try...Catch...Finally` statement in an application.

HOW TO...

Use a `Try...Catch...Finally` Statement

Syntax

```
Try
      Try block
Catch [exceptionObjectName As ExceptionClassName]
      Catch block
[additional Catch blocks]
[Finally]
      [Finally block]
End Try
```

Example

```
Public Class MainForm
    Private Sub calculateButton_Click(ByVal sender As Object, _
        ByVal e As System.EventArgs) Handles calculateButton.Click
        ' declare variables
        Dim quotient As Decimal
        Dim dividend As Decimal
        Dim divisor As Decimal
        Try
            ' input
            dividend = Convert.ToDecimal(dividendTextBox.Text())
            divisor = Convert.ToDecimal(divisorTextBox.Text())
```

(Figure is continued on next page)

```
            ' processing
            quotient = dividend / divisor

            ' output
            quotientLabel.Text = Convert.ToString(quotient)
            errorLabel.Text = ""
        Catch
            errorLabel.Text = "Please enter legal values"
        Finally
            MessageBox.Show(Me, "Ready for more input", "Ready")
        End Try
    End Sub
End Class
```

FIGURE 5.24 How to use a `Try...Catch...Finally` statement

Definitions of `Try`, `Catch`, and `Finally` Blocks

As you can see in Figure 5.24, the keyword `Try` is placed within the program code at a point just before the intended `Try` block. The **`Try` block** is a continuous section of program code that could possibly **throw** (create or generate) an exception object, including code that should not execute if an exception is thrown. The method that contains the `Try` block is called an **exception thrower** or **exception propagator**. In the example of Figure 5.24, a runtime error could occur because of any of the statements in either the input section or the processing section of the program, so these statements should be in the `Try` block. If an exception is thrown there, the output section should not be executed, so it should also be included in the `Try` block.

Following the `Try` block is the keyword `Catch`, which can be followed by an optional filter to specify the type of exception designed to be caught by this `Catch` block. The term *exceptionObjectName* is an identifier (provided by the programmer) for the object of type *ExceptionClassName* to be caught. The *ExceptionClassName* is usually a predefined .NET Framework exception class, but it can also be a programmer-defined exception class. After the keyword `Catch` is the **`Catch` block,** code in a `Try...Catch...Finally` statement designed to **catch** (handle or process) an exception object (for example, by displaying an error message to the user). The method that contains a `Catch` block is called an **exception catcher** or **exception handler**.

In the example of Figure 5.24, the optional filter is not used. Therefore this `Catch` block will catch all kinds of exception objects (that is, any that derive from the `Exception` class). If the optional filter is used, the `Catch` block can catch only an exception of type *ExceptionClassName*.

After the `Catch` block is the optional keyword `Finally`, which identifies the `Finally` block. The **`Finally` block** contains program code that performs final actions after a `Try` block or `Catch` block fully executes. Thus, a `Finally` block will always execute whether or not an exception is thrown within the `Try` block. The `Finally` block is often used to release any resources created in the `Try` block (such as closing data files that were opened in the `Try` block or performing any other type of required cleanup operations). For illustration purposes, the example in Figure 5.24 contains a `Finally` block that simply displays a message to the user.

How `Try`, `Catch`, and `Finally` Blocks Work

It is important to understand how the Common Language Runtime (CLR) handles exceptions within a given `Try...Catch...Finally` statement. If the CLR generates an exception object in a `Try` block because of an "exceptional" situation (such as trying to convert an empty string to a number), the CLR will immediately throw the exception to an appropriate `Catch` block. An appropriate `Catch` block is one with no optional filter or one with an *ExceptionClassName* that matches the type of exception thrown. Note that if an exception is thrown in a `Try` block, the `Try` block is immediately terminated and all variables local to the `Try` block are destroyed.

When an exception is caught by an appropriate `Catch` block, the `Catch` block is executed. However, if there is no appropriate `Catch` block present in the `Try...Catch...Finally` statement, the exception is thrown to the previous method in the stack trace (if one exists). The previous calling method may contain a `Catch` block designed to handle the exception. This process continues until the **uncaught exception** is either caught by an appropriate `Catch` block or eventually thrown to the CLR for processing. In the case of an uncaught exception, the CLR will display the predetermined error message for that type of exception and immediately terminate the application. The goal of the programmer is to catch and handle the exception before it is thrown to the CLR.

After a `Catch` block executes in a `Try...Catch...Finally` statement, the `Finally` block (if one exists) will always execute. If no exception is generated in a `Try` block, all the code in the `Try` block will be executed, all `Catch` blocks will be skipped, and the `Finally` block (if one exists) will always execute.

Figure 5.25 illustrates how `Try`, `Catch`, and `Finally` blocks interact with exceptions. According to the figure, Method A calls Method B. An exception of type Y is generated in the `Try` block of Method B. Since no matching `Catch` block is found in Method B, the `Finally` block of Method B executes and the exception object of type Y is thrown to the calling method, Method A. Method A does contain a `Catch` block of type Y, so that `Catch` block is executed and the `Finally` block of Method A executes.

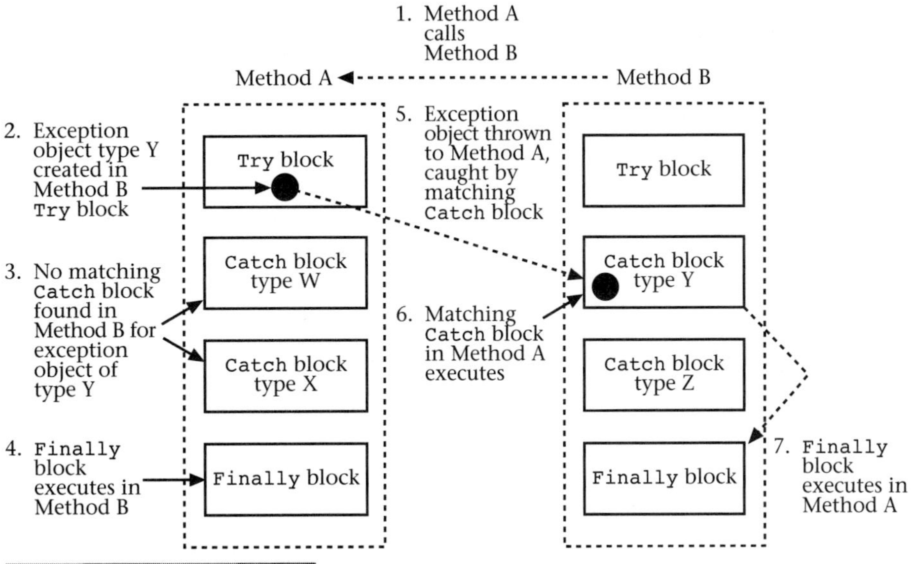

FIGURE 5.25 How `Try`, `Catch` and `Finally` blocks interact

A Simple `Try...Catch...Finally` Example

Note that the example in Figure 5.24 is based on the Division application in Figure 5.12. There are, however, four important modifications of this application. First, an `errorLabel` has been added near the bottom of the user interface. This label is used to display a custom error message to the user in the event an exception object is created. Second, a `Try` block is introduced after the variables are declared, but before input begins. The `Try` block includes the input, processing, and output sections of the `Sub` procedure `calculateButton_Click` because the input and processing sections can generate exceptions, and the output section should not execute if an exception is thrown. Third, a `Catch` block is added to display an error message in the `errorLabel` and remove any previous result displayed in the `quotientLabel`. Fourth, a `Finally` block is added to remind the user that the application is ready for another calculation. (This is not really required, but it is added for demonstration purposes.) Figure 5.26 shows a sample run of this modified Division application when the `dividendTextField` is empty, the `divisorTextField` contains a valid number, and the Calculate button is clicked.

(a) Using interface with error message

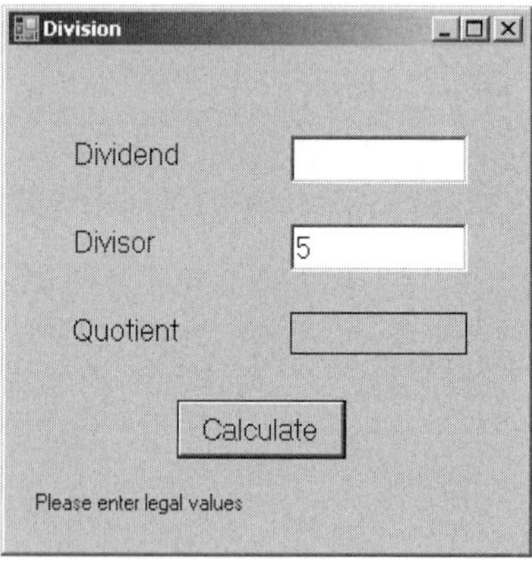

(b) Message box from `Finally` block

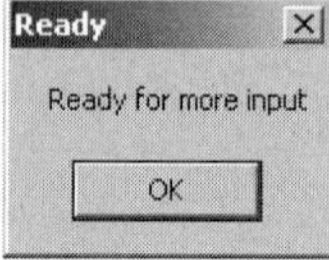

FIGURE 5.26 Sample run of Division application with `Try...Catch`

Multiple `Catch` Blocks

The sample run represented by Figure 5.26 caused an error message to be displayed because an exception of type `FormatException` was created. The example code in Figure 5.24 uses only one `Catch` block. Because this `Catch` block does not use an optional filter, it will catch any kind of exception thrown in the `Try` block. Note that the code in the `Try` block of Figure 5.24 could also throw a `DivisionByZeroException` (if the user enters a 0 in the `divisorTextBox` and clicks the Calculate button). You can use multiple `Catch` blocks in an application to catch specific kinds of exceptions using the optional filter. The code in

Figure 5.27 uses the Division application and three `Catch` blocks, one to catch a `FormatException` object, one to catch a `DivisionByZeroException` object, and one to catch any general `Exception` object.

```
Public Class MainForm
    Private Sub calculateButton_Click(ByVal sender As Object, _
        ByVal e As System.EventArgs) Handles calculateButton.Click
        ' declare variables
        Dim quotient As Decimal
        Dim dividend As Decimal
        Dim divisor As Decimal
        Try
            ' input
            dividend = Convert.ToDecimal(dividendTextBox.Text())
            divisor = Convert.ToDecimal(divisorTextBox.Text())

            ' processing
            quotient = dividend / divisor

            ' output
            quotientLabel.Text = Convert.ToString(quotient)
            errorLabel.Text = ""
        Catch formatExcep As FormatException
            errorLabel.Text = "Dividend or divisor not a number"
            quotientLabel.Text = ""
        Catch divideByZeroExcep As DivideByZeroException
            errorLabel.Text = "Division by zero not allowed"
            quotientLabel.Text = ""
        Catch excep As Exception
            errorLabel.Text = excep.GetType.ToString() & _
                ControlChars.CrLf & excep.Message
            quotientLabel.Text = ""
        End Try
    End Sub
End Class
```

FIGURE 5.27 Program code for the class `MainForm` in the Division application with multiple `Catch` blocks

It is important to realize that the ordering of `Catch` blocks in a given `Try...Catch...Finally` statement is critical for proper execution. Because exception classes are organized in an inheritance hierarchy, more specific `Catch` blocks should be listed in a program before more general `Catch` blocks. Otherwise, the more general `Catch` block will catch all the specific exceptions and the specific `Catch` blocks become useless. For example, in Figure 5.27 the `Catch` block for exception type `Exception` should be last because `Exception` is the most general kind of exception class. If it is placed first in the program, all types of exceptions would be caught by that `Catch` block and the program would lose the ability to handle different kinds of exceptions in different ways. Because the exception classes `FormatException` and `DivideByZeroException` are not in the same inheritance chain, the order of their respective `Catch` blocks does not matter.

Note that the `Exception Catch` block in Figure 5.27 will catch any kind of exception object because of the exception class hierarchy. This `Catch` block uses the exception object identifier `excep` to access the method `GetType` and the property `Message` to display the type of exception caught and the built-in error message for that type of exception. For example, Figure 5.28 shows the result of entering the value 1000000000000000000000000000000 (1 followed by 30 zeros, also known as one nonillion) as the dividend, entering 1 as the divisor, and clicking the Calculate button.

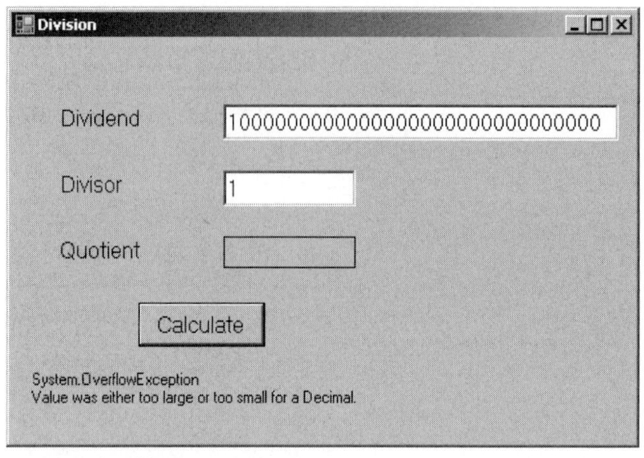

FIGURE 5.28 Sample run of Division application with multiple `Catch` blocks

Figure 5.28 shows the error message near the bottom of the interface. The name of the exception class is `OverflowException` and the standard message for that exception is "Value was either too large or too small for a Decimal." Of course, a separate `Catch` block could be added to the Division application just for this type of exception if desired.

More About the `Finally` Block

As discussed earlier, the `Finally` block is always executed, regardless of what happens in the `Try` or `Catch` blocks. Therefore, the `Finally` block is well suited for closing any application resources that had been previously opened or performing any other kind of program cleanup tasks. For example, consider the Friends application in Chapter 2 (Figure 2.70). When the form for this application loads, the application reads the contents of the text file `friends.txt` which contains the names of friends, and then displays the names in a list box. The user can then add new friends' names or remove existing friends' names. When the form closes, the contents of the list box are written to the text file. But what happens if the text file does not exist in the expected location? The application in Figure 2.70 handles this possibility by using an `If...Then` statement in the `MainForm_Load` procedure. However, this potential problem can also be handled using a `Try...Catch...Finally` statement, as shown in Figure 5.29.

```
Private Sub MainForm_Load(ByVal sender As Object, _
    ByVal e As System.EventArgs) Handles Me.Load
    ' reads names from a sequential access file and displays
    ' the names in a list box
    Dim text As String
    Dim name As String
    Dim newLineIndex As Integer
    Dim nameIndex As Integer

    ' clear the contents of the list box
    friendListBox.Items.Clear()
    Try
        text = My.Computer.FileSystem.ReadAllText("friends.txt")

        ' search for the newline character that separates
        ' each name; continue the search until there are
        ' no more newline characters
        newLineIndex = _
             text.IndexOf(ControlChars.NewLine, nameIndex)
        Do Until newLineIndex = -1
            ' the name begins with the character located in the
            ' nameIndex position; its length is the difference
            ' between the location of the newline
            ' character (newLineIndex) and the location of the
            ' first character in the name (nameIndex)
            name = text.Substring(nameIndex, _
                newLineIndex - nameIndex)

            ' add the name to the list box
            friendListBox.Items.Add(name)

            ' start the next search after the newline
            ' character, which has a length of 2
            nameIndex = newLineIndex + 2
            newLineIndex = text.IndexOf(ControlChars.NewLine, _
                nameIndex)
        Loop
    Catch fileNotFoundExcep As IO.FileNotFoundException
        MessageBox.Show("Could not find existing Friends file", _
             "Warning")
    Finally
        MessageBox.Show("Ready for Friends input", "Information")
    End Try
End Sub
```

FIGURE 5.29 `MainForm_Load` procedure in Friends application with `Try...Catch...Finally`

The `Try` block in Figure 5.29 contains code that tries to read the file `friends.txt` and then load the data from that file into the interface's list box. If this file is not found, a `FileNotFoundException` will be thrown and caught by the `Catch` block, informing the user that the file does not exist. This could prove to be important to the user if he or she is expecting to see many of his or her friends' names in the list box. Figure 5.30 shows the `MessageBox` that appears if the file `friends.txt` is not located in the same folder as the application.

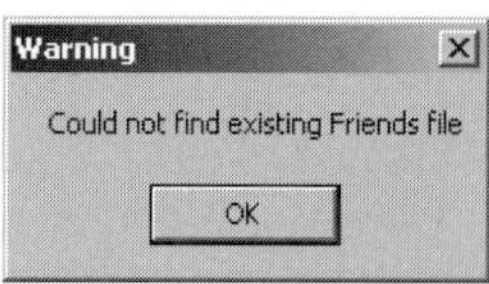

FIGURE 5.30 `MessageBox` displayed if file is not found

The `Finally` block in Figure 5.29 is simply used to reassure the user that the application is ready for operation, resulting in the `MessageBox` shown in Figure 5.31. Note that if the `friends.txt` file is present, all of the code in the `Try` block of Figure 5.29 will execute, the `Catch` block will be skipped, and then the `Finally` block will execute, producing the dialog box in Figure 5.31. If the `friends.txt` file is missing, a `FileNotFoundException` will be thrown because of the first statement in the `Try` block. Then the `Catch` block will execute, producing the dialog box in Figure 5.30. When this dialog box is closed, the `Finally` block will execute and the dialog box in Figure 5.31 will appear. The user can then decide whether to continue with the application or attempt to find the missing `friends.txt` file. (Note that if the friends.txt file is missing when the application starts, a new, but empty, `friends.txt` file will be created by Visual Basic, allowing the application to continue.)

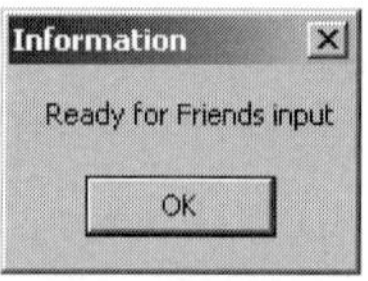

FIGURE 5.31 `MessageBox` displayed when `Finally` block executes

PROGRAMMER-DEFINED EXCEPTIONS

As stated previously, runtime errors and exceptions are not always the same. All Visual Basic runtime errors generate exception objects (as well as the object `Err`). Your program can also define its own custom exceptions, called **programmer-defined exceptions**, that are not associated with standard Visual Basic runtime errors. Doing so allows your application to handle many additional unusual situations (exceptions) that are not automatically created and processed by the Visual Basic Common Language Runtime (CLR).

For example, consider the Pet Information application in Chapter 2 (Figure 2.39). This application allows the user to enter a pet's name and age in input boxes and then displays this information in the user interface. However, the application doesn't verify that only valid pet ages are entered. For example, if the user mistakenly enters an age of –2 or enters no age at all, the application will simply display exactly what is entered because the variable `years` is of type `String`.

Creating a Programmer-Defined Exception Class

This Pet Information application is now modified to use exception handling. In particular, it will use the programmer-defined exception class called `IncorrectAgeException`. Figure 5.32 contains the code for the new

`IncorrectAgeException` class added to the Pet Information application and Figure 5.33 contains the code for the modified `MainForm` class.

```
Public Class IncorrectAgeException
    Inherits ApplicationException

    Public Sub New()
    End Sub

    Public Sub New(ByVal message As String)
        MyBase.New(message)
    End Sub

    Public Sub New(ByVal message As String, ByVal inner As Exception)
        MyBase.New(message, inner)
    End Sub
End Class
```

FIGURE 5.32 Program code for the `IncorrectAgeException` class in the modified Pet Information application

```
' Project name:          Pet Information Project
' Project purpose:       The project displays a message
'                        that contains a pet's name and age.
' Created/revised by:    <your name> on <current date>

Option Explicit On
Option Strict On

Public Class MainForm

    Private Sub DisplayMessage(ByVal pet As String, _
        ByVal years As String)
        ' displays the pet information passed to it

        Dim ageOfPet As Integer
        Try
            ageOfPet = Convert.ToInt16(years)
            If ageOfPet < 0 Then
                Throw New IncorrectAgeException( _
                     "Negative age not allowed")
            End If

            messageLabel.Text = "Your pet " & pet & " is " _
                & ageOfPet & " years old."
        Catch formatExcep As FormatException
            Throw New IncorrectAgeException( _
                 "Enter numbers only for age", formatExcep)
        End Try

    End Sub

    Private Sub getInfoButton_Click( _
         ByVal sender As Object, ByVal e As System.EventArgs) _
         Handles getInfoButton.Click
```

(Figure is continued on next page)

```
35          ' gets the pet information, then displays the
36          ' information in a message
37
38          Dim petName As String
39          Dim petAge As String
40          Try
41              petName = InputBox("Pet's name:", "Name Entry")
42              petAge = InputBox("Pet's age (years):", "Age Entry")
43
44              Call DisplayMessage(petName, petAge)
45          Catch incorrectAgeExcep As IncorrectAgeException
46              MessageBox.Show(incorrectAgeExcep.Message, "Warning")
47          End Try
48
49      End Sub
50
51      Private Sub exitButton_Click(ByVal sender As Object, _
52          ByVal e As System.EventArgs) Handles exitButton.Click
53          Me.Close()
54      End Sub
55  End Class
```

FIGURE 5.33 Program code for the `MainForm` class in the modified Pet Information application

TIP

Search for "user-defined exception" (another term for programmer-defined exception) at *http://msdn.microsoft.com/* for more information on creating exception classes.

The code in Figure 5.32 follows the Microsoft recommendations for creating your own exception classes. The recommendation suggests that you should give a programmer-defined exception class a meaningful name that ends with `Exception` (`IncorrectAgeException` in this case). This programmer-defined exception class should also derive from the `ApplicationException` class (the recommended base class for programmer-defined exceptions) to provide the application with the required exception-handling functionality.

Next, note in Figure 5.32 that there are three different constructors for this custom exception. First is a no-parameter constructor, second is a one-parameter constructor that receives only a custom message, and third is a two-parameter constructor that receives a custom `message` and an `Exception` object (called `inner`) as parameters. Note that the exception object is created with the keyword `MyBase`, which refers to the base class for the programmer-defined exception, `ApplicationException`. You will see how these constructors are utilized shortly.

Throwing Programmer-Defined Exceptions

Now turn your attention to the `MainForm` class in Figure 5.33. This class is very similar to `MainForm` in the original Pet Information application of Figure 2.39. However, the `String` variable `years` is now replaced by an `Integer` variable `ageOfPet` for output. Doing this allows the program to validate the numeric age of the pet. Another important change is, of course, the addition of `Try` and `Catch` blocks for exception handling.

First, focus on the `DisplayMessage` procedure (Line 11). The statement `ageOfPet = Convert.ToInt16(years)` attempts to convert the string contents of `years` to an integer, to be stored in `ageOfPet`. Suppose the user mistakenly enters –2 for the age of the pet. The `If...Then` statement in `DisplayMessage` will then create and throw a custom `IncorrectAgeException` object using the one-parameter constructor in the class `IncorrectAgeException`. (The argument sent by this constructor is the string "Negative age not allowed.") Note that there is no Catch block for an IncorrectAgeException in the DisplayMessage procedure, so the exception is thrown back to the method that called DisplayMessage, which is the getInfoButton_Click procedure. This procedure does have an IncorrectAgeException handler (that is, a Catch block) that creates a MessageBox, which in turn displays the Message property of the exception (in this case, the message is "Negative age not allowed"). This MessageBox is displayed in Figure 5.34. After this dialog box is closed, the user can reenter correct data for the pet's age.

FIGURE 5.34 MessageBox resulting from entering a negative pet age

Using the InnerException Property

Another unusual situation can occur when the user enters something other than a number for the pet's age (such as the word "two" or perhaps an empty string). In that case, the statement ageOfPet = Convert.ToInt16(years) in the DisplayMessage procedure will create a FormatException object. This procedure does have a Catch block for a FormatException, so this exception object is handled in DisplayMessage. However, suppose the programmer wants to treat this exception in a customized way. In that case, he or she can use the FormatException Catch block to create a new IncorrectAgeException object using the two-parameter constructor in the class IncorrectAgeException. Note that the message is now "Enter numbers only for age" and the constructor receives the FormatException object called formatExcep in its Exception parameter called inner. Because formatExcep was used to create a custom IncorrectAgeException object, incorrectAgeExcep has a property called InnerException, which contains the value FormatException. The programmer could make the program use this property to display additional information about this particular IncorrectAgeException object, using code such as incorrectAgeExcep.InnerException.Message. (In this case "Input string was not in a correct format" would be returned.)

Finally, since the DisplayMessage procedure does not have a Catch block for an IncorrectAgeException exception, the exception object created in the FormatException Catch block is thrown to the calling procedure, getInfoButton_Click. This procedure does have a Catch block for IncorrectAgeException, so the exception is handled there. Now the object incorrectAgeExcep has the property Message that holds the string "Enter numbers only for age", so the MessageBox shown in Figure 5.35 will be displayed. As you can see, structured exception handling may at times seem a little complex, but doing the same kinds of things with classic error handling would be much more complex (or impossible).

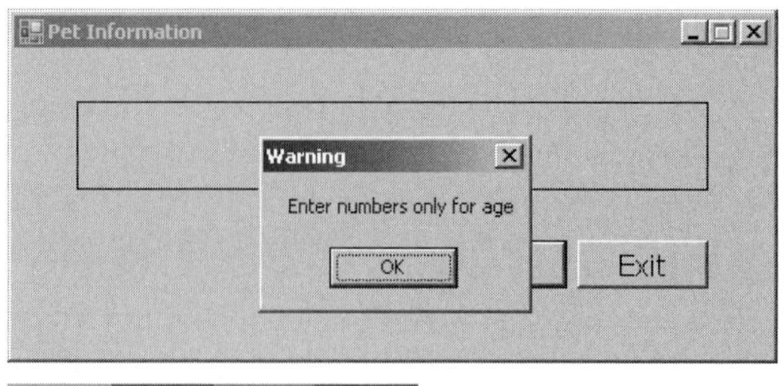

FIGURE 5.35 `MessageBox` resulting from entering a nonnumeric pet age

PROGRAMMING EXAMPLE

Employee Application with Structured Exception Handling

In this section we will modify the Employee application presented earlier in the Programming Example at the end of Chapter 4. The goal is to equip the application with structured exception handling. The TOE chart and user interface will remain the same, but the class diagram, pseudocode, and program code will be modified as shown in the following figures.

Class Diagram

The class diagram in Figure 5.36 shows that the class `MainForm` uses the classes `Employee`, `HourlyEmployee`, `SalariedEmployee`, and `MissingDataException`. Also, `HourlyEmployee` and `SalariedEmployee` inherit from `Employee`.

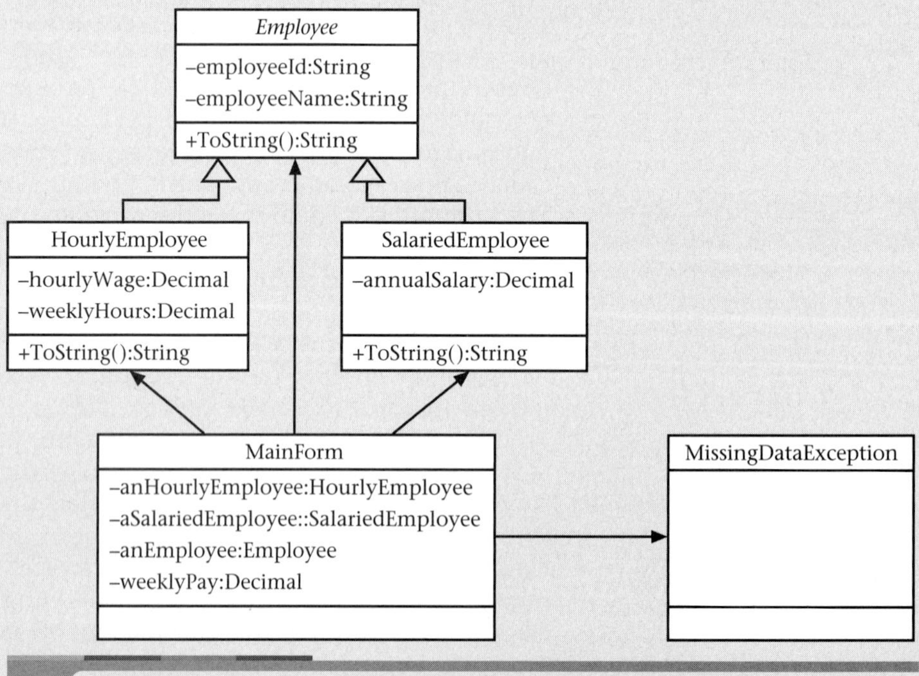

FIGURE 5.36 Class diagram for the Employee application

Pseudocode

The new pseudocode is shown in Step 2 (shaded).

`calculateButton Click` event procedure

1. if the salariedRadioButton is checked
   create a salaried employee object getting ID, name, and annual salary from text boxes
   calculate weekly pay by dividing annual salary by 52
   else
   create an hourly employee object getting ID, name, hourly wage, and weekly hours from text boxes
   calculate weekly pay by multiplying hourly wage by weekly hours
   end if
2. if employee ID is missing
   create a MissingDataException object
   end if
3. display employee info (ID, name, wage/salary information, and weekly pay) in the empInfoLabel
4. select all in empIdTextBox
5. set focus in empIdTextBox

Code

```
Public Class MainForm
    Inherits System.Windows.Forms.Form

    ' declare variables
    Private anHourlyEmployee As hourlyEmployee
    Private aSalariedEmployee As SalariedEmployee
    Private anEmployee As Employee
    Private weeklyPay As Decimal = 0

    Private Sub calculateButton_Click(ByVal sender As System.Object, _
        ByVal e As System.EventArgs) Handles calculateButton.Click

        Try
            ' instantiate objects
            If salariedRadioButton.Checked Then
                aSalariedEmployee = New SalariedEmployee( _
                    empIdTextBox.Text, nameTextBox.Text, _
                    Convert.ToDecimal(salaryTextBox.Text))
                weeklyPay = aSalariedEmployee.AnnualSalary / 52
                ' cast aSalariedEmployee as Employee
                anEmployee = aSalariedEmployee
            Else
                anHourlyEmployee = New HourlyEmployee( _
                    empIdTextBox.Text, nameTextBox.Text, _
                    Convert.ToDecimal(wageTextBox.Text), _
                    Convert.ToDecimal(hoursTextBox.Text))
                weeklyPay = anHourlyEmployee.HourlyWage * _
                            anHourlyEmployee.WeeklyHours
                ' cast anHourlyEmployee as Employee
                anEmployee = anHourlyEmployee
            End If

```

(Figure is continued on next page)

```
            ' throw programmer-defined exception
            If anEmployee.EmployeeId = String.Empty Then
                Throw New MissingDataException("Missing employee ID")
            End If

            ' display employee info
            empInfoLabel.Text = anEmployee.EmployeeId _
                              & ControlChars.CrLf _
                              & anEmployee.EmployeeName _
                              & ControlChars.CrLf _
                              & anEmployee.ToString() _
                              & ControlChars.CrLf _
                              & "Weekly Pay: " _
                              & FormatCurrency(weeklyPay)

            empIdTextBox.SelectAll()
            empIdTextBox.Focus()

        Catch formatExcep As FormatException
            MessageBox.Show( _
                "Enter numbers for Salary, Wage, and Hours", "Error")
        Catch missingDataExcep As MissingDataException
            MessageBox.Show(missingDataExcep.Message, "Error")
        End Try
    End Sub

    Private Sub salariedRadioButton_CheckedChanged( _
        ByVal sender As Object, _
        ByVal e As System.EventArgs) Handles _
        salariedRadioButton.CheckedChanged

        wageLabel.Visible() = False
        wageTextBox.Visible() = False
        hoursLabel.Visible() = False
        hoursTextBox.Visible() = False
        salaryLabel.Visible() = True
        salaryTextBox.Visible() = True
    End Sub


    Private Sub hourlyRadioButton_CheckedChanged( _
        ByVal sender As Object, _
        ByVal e As System.EventArgs) Handles _
        hourlyRadioButton.CheckedChanged

        wageLabel.Visible() = True
        wageTextBox.Visible() = True
        hoursLabel.Visible() = True
        hoursTextBox.Visible() = True
        salaryLabel.Visible() = False
        salaryTextBox.Visible() = False
    End Sub

    Private Sub empIdTextBox_TextChanged(ByVal sender As Object, _
        ByVal e As System.EventArgs) Handles empIdTextBox.TextChanged

        nameTextBox.Text = "Lastname, Firstname"
        salaryTextBox.Text = String.Empty
        wageTextBox.Text = String.Empty
        hoursTextBox.Text = String.Empty
        empInfoLabel.Text = String.Empty
    End Sub

```

(Figure is continued on next page)

```
    Private Sub exitButton_Click(ByVal sender As System.Object, _
    ByVal e As System.EventArgs) Handles exitButton.Click
        Me.Close()
    End Sub

End Class
```

FIGURE 5.37 Program code for the MainForm.vb file (new code shaded)

```
Public Class MissingDataException
    Inherits ApplicationException

    Public Sub New()
    End Sub

    Public Sub New(ByVal message As String)
        MyBase.New(message)
    End Sub

    Public Sub New(ByVal message As String, ByVal inner As Exception)
        MyBase.New(message, inner)
    End Sub
End Class
```

FIGURE 5.38 Program code for the MissingDataException.vb file

Input/Output

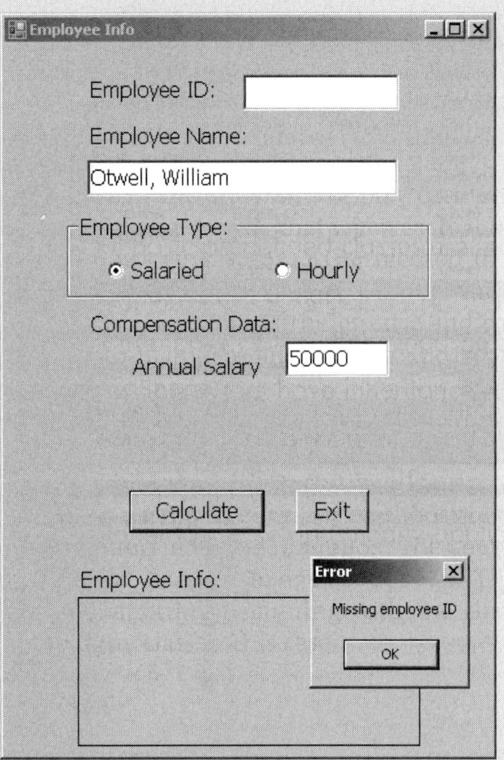

FIGURE 5.39 Sample run for the Employee application with structured exception handling

Quick Review

- One way to ensure that errors are minimized is through the proper design of the user interface in the first place, using controls such as `ListBox` and `RadioButton` instead of `TextBox`.
- The .NET Framework `KeyPress` event can be used to check each keystroke made by the user within a specific control. Another useful technique is to validate the entire contents of a text box when the `Leave` event occurs, thus making use of the `Validating` event.
- The `MaskedTextBox` control is a new feature of the .NET Framework 2.0 (similar to the `MaskedEdit` control of VB 6) that provides a wide variety of techniques for validating user input. The `MaskedTextBox` control is an enhanced `TextBox` that uses the `Mask` property to specify valid user input.
- Yet another technique for validating user input involves the `ErrorProvider` component. The `ErrorProvider` component notifies the user that a data entry error has occurred in a particular control (such as a text box) without using a message box.
- While you must always concentrate on developing applications that provide accurate results, you must also avoid delivering applications that may occasionally crash (that is, terminate unexpectedly).
- An application that keeps on running (instead of crashing) while giving the user a chance to correct mistakes is said to be robust (sturdy or well constructed) and fault tolerant (forgiving of user mistakes).
- Compile-time errors are violations of a programming language's syntax. Runtime errors are errors that occur during program execution. Logic errors are errors made by the programmer in designing or implementing the logic of a program.
- In Visual Basic, a runtime error creates an object called `Err`, which has certain properties, such as an error `Number` and `Description`. Every runtime error in a Visual Basic program also generates a specific kind of exception object using predefined exception classes.
- An exception is any kind of unusual or infrequent problem that occurs during program execution, including runtime errors. Structured exception handling is a process for managing program problems using exception objects.
- Classic error handling is the Visual Basic process for managing error objects generated by the program when standard runtime errors occur. Classic error handling in Visual Basic is accomplished using the `On Error` statement, of which there are several variations.
- The `On Error GoTo` *<line>* statement is used to place Visual Basic in error-handling mode (a state of a Visual Basic application that enables the features of classic error handling) and then jump to an indicated *<line>* in the program, which begins the error-handling code.
- The primary disadvantage of using classic error handling in Visual Basic is that the error-handling logic is intermixed with the basic program logic, making the program difficult to read and understand. It is also difficult to understand how the error-handling logic executes by inspecting the program.
- Visual Basic structured exception handling uses the `Try...Catch...Finally` statement to identify and handle exception objects thrown by an application. The `Try...Catch...Finally` statement contains a `Try` block, one or more `Catch` blocks designed to catch specific types of exception objects, and an optional `Finally` block.

- The inheritance hierarchy for .NET Framework exception classes begins with the `Object` class and continues at the next lower level with the `Exception` class, which is used as the base class for all application exceptions. Below the level of the `Exception` class are other levels with more specific exception classes, such as `ApplicationException`, `SystemException`, `ArithmeticException`, `IOException`, and so on.
- An exception thrown in a `Try` block will be handled by a matching `Catch` block, if it exists. If a matching `Catch` block does not exist in the `Try...Catch...Finally` statement, the exception is thrown to the calling method in search of a matching `Catch` block. This process continues until a matching `Catch` block is found. If no matching `Catch` block is found in the application, the Common Language Runtime (CLR) will display an error message and terminate the application.
- Multiple `Catch` blocks in a `Try...Catch...Finally` statement should be arranged from most specific to least specific. This arrangement enables different kinds of `Catch` blocks to handle exceptions of their respective types. For each `Try...Catch...Finally` statement used by an exception, the `Finally` block will always be executed (if it exists).
- You can define your own custom exception classes, called programmer-defined exceptions, in an application, which can contain code to throw and catch such exceptions under certain desired conditions.

Key Terms

catch—To utilize a `Catch` block to handle or process an exception.

`Catch` **block**—Code in a `Try...Catch...Finally` statement designed to catch and handle an exception object.

classic error handling—The Visual Basic process for managing the error object `Err` generated by the program when standard runtime errors occur.

compile-time error—An error that occurs while the program is being compiled, usually due to a syntax error.

crash—In the context of program execution, an unexpected termination.

error handler—Error-handling code that processes errors using classic error handling.

error-handling mode—A state of a Visual Basic application that enables the features of classic error handling.

exception—An exceptional, unusual, or abnormal condition that occurs during program execution; more specifically, an object that contains information about such a condition.

exception catcher—See **exception handler**.

exception handler—A method in a program that handles a thrown exception.

exception propagator—See **exception thrower**.

exception thrower—A method in a program that throws an exception.

fault tolerant—Term used to describe a program that can tolerate user errors without crashing.

`Finally` **block**—A section of code that performs final actions after a `Try` block or `Catch` block fully executes.

input validation—The process of validating data entered by the user before the data are used by the program.

logic error—A mistake made in the design and/or implementation of program logic that can result in incorrect output, which may not be apparent to the user.

method-call stack—The sequence of method calls (or call chain), displayed in the exception's stack trace, that leads to the creation of an exception object.

programmer-defined exception—A custom class created by the programmer to define an exception not already associated with a Visual Basic runtime error.

robust—A characteristic of a program that implies it is well constructed and performs reliably.

runtime error—An error that occurs while a program is running, usually causing the program to terminate unexpectedly if not handled.

structured exception handling—A process for managing program exceptions that uses a special `Try...Catch...Finally` statement to handle specific exception objects.

throw—To create or generate an exception.

`Try` block—A continuous section of program code, beginning with the keyword `Try`, that could possibly create an exception including code that should not execute if an exception is thrown.

`Try...Catch...Finally` statement—The combination of a `Try` block plus its associated `Catch` block(s) and `Finally` block.

uncaught exception—An exception that is not caught by any `Catch` block in the application and is therefore processed by the Common Language Runtime, resulting in program termination.

user-defined exception—see **programmer-defined exception**.

Review Questions

1. The object `Err` is critical to the exception-handling process in Visual Basic.
   a. True
   b. False

2. Structured exception handling is preferred to classic error handling.
   a. True
   b. False

3. All exceptions are runtime errors.
   a. True
   b. False

4. Standard Visual Basic error messages will allow the user to continue running the program.
   a. True
   b. False

5. A `FormatException` object is an `ArithmeticException` object.
   a. True
   b. False

6. An uncaught exception is handled by the CLR.
   a. True
   b. False
7. If an exception is not thrown in a `Try` block, the `Finally` block will execute anyway.
   a. True
   b. False
8. `Try...Catch...Finally` statements can be nested.
   a. True
   b. False
9. The more general `Catch` blocks should be listed first in a `Try...Catch...Finally` statement.
   a. True
   b. False
10. All logic errors generate exception objects.
    a. True
    b. False
11. Exception handling is designed to address which type of error?
    a. compile-time
    b. runtime
    c. logic
    d. all the above
12. Which of the following keywords is not a part of Visual Basic exception handling?
    a. `GoTo`
    b. `Finally`
    c. `Try`
    d. `Catch`
13. Which property is common to both the `Err` object and an `Exception` object?
    a. `InnerException`
    b. `Message`
    c. `Source`
    d. `StackTrace`
14. Which of the following classes should be used to create programmer-defined exception classes?
    a. `Exception`
    b. `ApplicationException`
    c. `ArithmeticException`
    d. `SystemException`
15. Which of the following is optional in a `Try...Catch...Finally` statement?
    a. `Try`
    b. `Catch`
    c. `Finally`
    d. none of the above

16. Which keyword is used to create a programmer-defined exception?
    a. `Try`
    b. `Throws`
    c. `Resume`
    d. `Catch`
17. Which property is often unique to a programmer-defined exception?
    a. `InnerException`
    b. `Source`
    c. `Message`
    d. `StackTrace`
18. Which of the following exception classes is usually involved with file processing?
    a. `NullReferenceException`
    b. `OverflowException`
    c. `ApplicationException`
    d. `IOException`
19. Which of the following `Exception` class properties contains the method where an exception originates?
    a. `TargetSite`
    b. `Source`
    c. `Message`
    d. `StackTrace`
20. Which of the following is not a property of the `Exception` class?
    a. `Message`
    b. `Source`
    c. `Number`
    d. `TargetSite`

Computer Exercises

When creating user interfaces, follow all conventions for an attractive, organized form with meaningful names for controls. Use named constants when appropriate, and use format specifiers for output requiring special formatting. Your instructor may also request that you use TOE charts, pseudocode, flowcharts, and/or UML diagrams as planning aids. Follow all principles of good object-oriented design.

1. In this exercise, you modify the Division application you viewed in this chapter. The modified application will use the `Validating` event and the ErrorProvider component to validate data entered by the user.
    a. Use Windows to make a copy of the folder Figure 05.12 Division Solution in the \VbReloadedAdvanced\Chap05\ folder. Rename the folder Division Solution With Validating.
    b. Open the Division Solution (Division Solution.sln) file contained in the \VbReloadedAdvanced\Chap05\ Figure 05.12 Division Solution\ folder.
    c. Modify the program code so that it uses the `Validating` event to ensure that only numeric data are entered in `divisorTextBox`.
    d. Modify the program code so that it uses the `ErrorProvider` component to ensure that only numeric data are entered in `dividendTextBox`.
    e. Save the solution, test the application, and modify as necessary.

2. In this exercise, you modify the Division application you viewed in this chapter. The modified application will handle a numeric overflow error using `On Error Resume Next`.
   a. Use Windows to make a copy of the folder Figure 05.12 Division Solution With Resume Next in the \VbReloadedAdvanced\Chap05\ folder. Rename the folder Division Solution With Resume Next Overflow.
   b. Open the Division Solution (Division Solution.sln) file contained in the \VbReloadedAdvanced\Chap05\ Division Solution With Resume Next folder.
   c. Modify the program code so that it handles a number overflow error (the result of entering a number that is too large or too small for the divisor or dividend) within the `Select Case` statement.
   d. Save the solution, test the application, and modify as necessary.

3. In this exercise, you modify the Skate-Away Sales application you viewed in Chapter 1. The modified application will utilize structured exception handling.
   a. Use Windows to make a copy of the Figure 01.25 Skate-Away Sales Solution folder in the \VbReloadedAdvanced\Chap01\ folder. Paste the copy in the \VbReloadedAdvanced\Chap05\ folder and rename it Skate-Away Sales Solution With Exception Handling.
   b. Open the Skate-Away Solution (Skate-Away Solution.sln) file contained in the \VbReloadedAdvanced\Chap05\Skate-Away Sales Solution With Exception Handling folder.
   c. Modify the program code so that it uses structured exception handling instead of the `TryParse` method to handle `FormatException` objects and `OverflowException` objects.
   d. Save the solution, test the application, and modify as necessary.

4. In this exercise, you modify the Glovers application you viewed in Chapter 2. The modified application will utilize structured exception handling.
   a. Use Windows to make a copy of the Figure 02.74 Glovers Solution folder in the \VbReloadedAdvanced\Chap02\ folder. Paste the copy in the \VbReloadedAdvanced\Chap05\ folder and rename it Glovers Solution With Exception Handling.
   b. Open the Glovers Solution (Glovers Solution.sln) file contained in the \VbReloadedAdvanced\Chap05\Glovers Solution With Exception Handling folder.
   c. Modify the program code so that it uses structured exception handling instead of the `FileExists` method to handle `FileNotFoundException` objects.
   d. Thoroughly test the application to determine if any other exceptions can be thrown. If so, modify the application to handle all possible exceptions.
   e. Save the solution, test the application, and modify as necessary.

5. In this exercise, you modify the College Course application you viewed in Chapter 3. The modified application will utilize classic error handling.
   a. Use Windows to make a copy of the Figure 03.29-33 College Course Solution folder in the \VbReloadedAdvanced\Chap03\ folder. Paste the copy in the \VbReloadedAdvanced\Chap05\ folder and rename it College Course Solution With Error Handling.
   b. Open the College Course Solution (College Course Solution.sln) file contained in the \VbReloadedAdvanced\Chap05\College Course Solution With Error Handling folder.
   c. Modify the program code so that it uses classic error handling to handle all types of runtime errors that can be created.
   d. Save the solution, test the application, and modify as necessary.

6. In this exercise, you modify the College Course application you viewed in Chapter 3. The modified application will utilize structured exception handling.
   a. Use Windows to make a copy of the Figure 03.29-33 College Course Solution folder in the \VbReloadedAdvanced\Chap03\ folder. Paste the copy in the \VbReloadedAdvanced\Chap05\ folder and rename it College Course Solution With Exception Handling.
   b. Open the College Course Solution (College Course Solution.sln) file contained in the \VbReloadedAdvanced\Chap05\ College Course Solution With Exception Handling folder.
   c. Modify the program code so that it uses structured exception handling to handle all types of exception objects that can be created.
   d. Save the solution, test the application, and modify as necessary.
7. In this exercise, you modify the Quadrilateral application you viewed in Chapter 4. The modified application will utilize structured exception handling.
   a. Use Windows to make a copy of the Figure 04.09-10 Quadrilateral Solution folder in the \VbReloadedAdvanced\Chap04\ folder. Paste the copy in the \VbReloadedAdvanced\Chap05\ folder and rename it Quadrilateral Solution With Exception Handling.
   b. Open the Quadrilateral Solution (Quadrilateral Solution.sln) file contained in the \VbReloadedAdvanced\Chap05\Quadrilateral Solution With Exception Handling folder.
   c. Create an exception class called `NegativeNumberException` that can be used to create an exception if the user enters negative dimensions for a quadrilateral.
   d. Modify the program code so that it uses structured exception handling to handle all types of exception objects that can be created.
   e. Save the solution, test the application, and modify as necessary.

Case Projects

Net Present Value with Exception Handling

Refer to the Net Present Value case project at the end of Chapter 1. If you already created this project, modify it by adding structured exception handling for all types of possible exceptions. If you did not already create this project, do so now and add structured exception handling for all types of possible exceptions.

Retail Sales with Exception Handling

Refer to the Retail Sales case project at the end of Chapter 3. If you already created this project, modify it by adding structured exception handling for all types of possible exceptions. If you did not already create this project, do so now and add structured exception handling for all types of possible exceptions.

DVD Collection

Create an application called **DVD Collection**. Design an interface that allows the user to enter the ID for a DVD, the title of a DVD, and the total running time (in minutes) of the DVD. When the Add DVD button is clicked on the interface, the data are added to a sequential file. When the Display button is clicked, the DVDs in the file are displayed in a `MessageBox`. Use structured exception handling to handle all types of possible exceptions including at least one type of programmer-defined exception.

CHAPTER

6 More about Windows Forms

After studying Chapter 6, you should be able to:

- Understand program code generated by Visual Basic for user interfaces
- Create a user interface with a flow layout and a table layout
- Create a user interface with tabbed pages and dialog forms
- Create a user interface with a menu and shortcut keys
- Create an application with a multiple document interface (MDI)

Earlier in this text you reviewed how to design and implement a basic graphical user interface, or GUI, using components such as `Label`, `Textbox`, `CheckBox`, and `Button`. GUIs are very important, as they are the sole means by which a user interacts with an application. Users have come to expect a wide variety of helpful GUI features in applications. Typical GUI features include tabbed windows, scroll bars, menus, and multiple documents. In this chapter, you will learn how to add such advanced features to your GUIs.

A CLOSER LOOK AT GUIs

Before discussing the details of creating more advanced GUIs, this section takes a closer look at what happens behind the scenes as you build a user interface. Understanding the code generated by Visual Basic as you build a GUI will help you enhance your interface's capabilities.

Forms and Components

Recall that in Visual Basic, a **form** is a window or dialog box that makes up an application's graphical user interface. In fact, a form is an instance of the class `Form`, which is in the namespace `System.Windows.Forms`. Thus, the fully qualified class name for `Form` is `System.Windows.Forms.Form`.

A form contains various components, which are usually added by dragging and dropping component icons from the Visual Basic Toolbox. A **component** is an object (that is, an instance of a class) that is added to a form to provide the form with functionality. Components derive much of their functionality from the `Component` class. Furthermore, a **control** is a visible component (such as `Label` or `Button`) that derives from the `Control` class, fully qualified as `System.Windows.Forms.Control`. For example, a component such as a button is an object from the class `Button` (`System.Windows.Forms.Button`). On the other hand, some form components, such as a `Timer` (`System.Windows.Forms.Timer`), do not have a graphical representation but simply provide functionality. In either case, when you drag a component to a form, Visual Basic adds to your application the code required to define and create an instance of that component's class. As you continue to change the properties of the component in the Properties window, Visual Basic continues to add the necessary code.

The Event-Handling Model

When a GUI application is executed and the user interacts with a control via the mouse or the keyboard (for example, by clicking a button), the control generates an **event** (a message indicating that a user action has occurred) within the application. GUI applications are said to be **event driven**, meaning that the GUIs generate events (via user actions) that drive the application's functionality. The event is passed to one or more **event handlers**, methods written by the programmer to provide the application with the desired responses.

Visual Basic uses an object from the `MulticastDelegate` class to implement event handling. In Visual Basic, a **delegate** is an instance of the `Delegate` class, which is a data structure that refers to either (1) a static method or (2) a class instance and an instance method of that class. Therefore, a **`MulticastDelegate`** is a data structure that can contain references to several different methods. An event generated by a GUI (such as a button click) calls a delegate that is registered for that event. The delegate in turn calls all methods (static methods or instance methods) that it references.

Visual Basic Generated Code for GUIs

Recall that when you create a GUI using the Visual Basic Form Designer, Visual Basic generates the required program code in the Code window. This section explores some of the details behind the code generated by Visual Basic as you build a GUI. Understanding such details should prove helpful as you add more advanced features to forms.

For starters, you can learn much by studying the simple case of creating an Exit button in a GUI. Figure 6.1 shows a project with a form named `MainForm` and a `Text` property value of "GUI Test". The Exit button in the GUI is named `exitButton` and has a `Text` property value of "Exit".

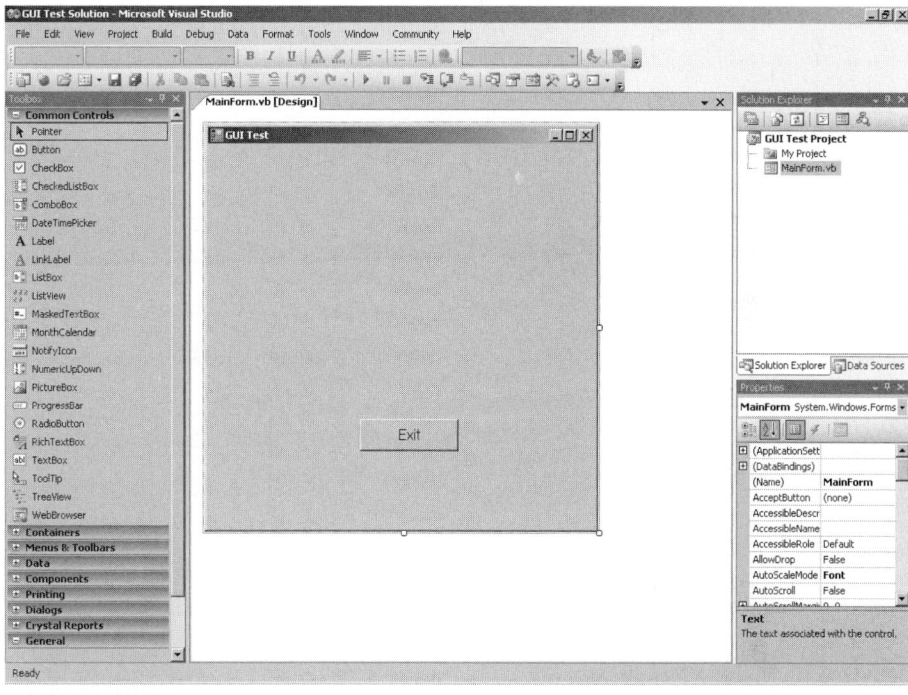

FIGURE 6.1 Form with a button in the GUI Test application

You can view the code for this application by right-clicking the open space in the Windows Form Designer, outside the form, and then clicking View Code. This displays the following code in the code window:

```
Public Class MainForm

End Class
```

This code is generated by Visual Basic. Here, you can see only the basic structure of the `MainForm` class. The details of the code for the GUI itself are hidden from view because you don't need to directly access or change the code that generates the GUI. Instead, you make changes in the GUI by dragging components to the form. However, to view the code generated by Windows Form Designer, you can follow the steps in Figure 6.2.

HOW TO...

View the Windows Form Designer Generated Code

1. With the Solution Explorer window open for an application, click the Show All Files button at the top of the Solution Explorer.
2. Click the plus sign next to the form file (such as Form1.vb or MainForm.vb) in the Solution Explorer.
3. Double-click the Designer file for the form (such as Form1.Designer.vb or MainForm.Designer.vb).

FIGURE 6.2 How to view the Windows Form Designer generated code

For the GUI Test application of Figure 6.1, the Windows Form Designer generated code is shown in Figure 6.3.

```
<Global.Microsoft.VisualBasic.CompilerServices.DesignerGenerated()> _
Partial Class MainForm
    Inherits System.Windows.Forms.Form

    'Form overrides dispose to clean up the component list.
    <System.Diagnostics.DebuggerNonUserCode()> _
    Protected Overrides Sub Dispose(ByVal disposing As Boolean)
        If disposing AndAlso components IsNot Nothing Then
            components.Dispose()
        End If
        MyBase.Dispose(disposing)
    End Sub

    'Required by the Windows Form Designer
    Private components As System.ComponentModel.IContainer

    'NOTE: The following procedure is required by the Windows Form
    'Designer
    'It can be modified using the Windows Form Designer.
    'Do not modify it using the code editor.
    <System.Diagnostics.DebuggerStepThrough()> _
    Private Sub InitializeComponent()
        Me.exitButton = New System.Windows.Forms.Button
        Me.SuspendLayout()
        '
        'exitButton
        '
        Me.exitButton.Location = New System.Drawing.Point(170, 301)
        Me.exitButton.Margin = New System.Windows.Forms.Padding( _
            4, 5, 4, 5)
        Me.exitButton.Name = "exitButton"
        Me.exitButton.Size = New System.Drawing.Size(112, 35)
        Me.exitButton.TabIndex = 0
        Me.exitButton.Text = "Exit"
        Me.exitButton.UseVisualStyleBackColor = True
        '
        'MainForm
        '
        Me.AutoScaleDimensions = New System.Drawing.SizeF(9.0!, 20.0!)
        Me.AutoScaleMode = System.Windows.Forms.AutoScaleMode.Font
        Me.ClientSize = New System.Drawing.Size(438, 420)
```

(Figure is continued on next page)

```
42         Me.Controls.Add(Me.Button1)
43         Me.Font = New System.Drawing.Font("Microsoft Sans Serif", _
44             12.0!, System.Drawing.FontStyle.Regular, _
45             System.Drawing.GraphicsUnit.Point, CType(0, Byte))
46         Me.Margin = New System.Windows.Forms.Padding(4, 5, 4, 5)
47         Me.Name = "Form1"
48         Me.Text = "GUI Test"
49         Me.ResumeLayout(False)
50
51     End Sub
52     Friend WithEvents exitButton As System.Windows.Forms.Button
53
54 End Class
```

FIGURE 6.3 Windows Form Designer generated code for GUI in the GUI Test application

First, note in Figure 6.3 that the class declaration for `MainForm` includes the `DesignerGenerated` attribute (Line 1), which signifies that Visual Basic will automatically generate the form. Then the keyword `Partial` (Line 2) indicates that this code for the `MainForm` class is only part of the class definition. (This part is for the GUI, while the rest will be supplied by the programmer with `Sub` procedures.) The `MainForm` class uses the code `Inherits System.Windows.Forms.Form` (that is, the `Form` class in namespace `System.Windows.Forms`) in Line 3 to inherit the properties and methods of the `Form` class.

There are several other important lines of code in Figure 6.3 that you should be able to recognize. First, observe the `Sub` procedure `Dispose` (Lines 6–12). This procedure is called automatically when the user closes the form, which then triggers the `Disposed` event. When this event occurs, the form and its components are removed by Visual Basic, releasing all resources (such as memory) used by the form and its components.

The variable `components` is then declared (Line 15). This variable represents the list of all components within the form and implements the interface `IContainer`, thus providing key functionality of form components (such as enabling the `Disposed` event).

Next, notice the `Sub` procedure called `InitializeComponent` (Lines 21–51). This procedure defines the component `exitButton` and the form `MainForm` for the GUI. Note that the attribute `System.Diagnostics.DebuggerStepThrough` is added to the `InitializeComponent` procedure. Doing so causes the IDE to skip `InitializeComponent` when the programmer is stepping through executed code in the IDE's debug mode. This saves debugging time. Within this method, the component `exitButton` is created (instantiated) with the keyword `New`. The `SuspendLayout` method is then called, which suppresses the raising of any `Layout` events that normally occur when controls are added to a container. (Such events could potentially interfere with displaying the form.) The `ResumeLayout` method is called at the end of this procedure (Line 49) to reinstate normal GUI functionality. Between the calls to `SuspendLayout` and `ResumeLayout`, the `exitButton` properties are set, the `exitButton` is added to the `MainForm`, and the `MainForm` properties are set.

Adding the `exitButton` control to the form is the first step toward providing the form with functionality. Before the button can be used, the programmer must add an event handler for this component. Recall that to create an event handler in Visual Basic you first view the code for the GUI. (If you are in Designer mode, right-click anywhere in the open area and click View Code.) Next, select the control `exitButton` from the Class Name drop-down list and then select the event `Click` from the Method Name drop-down list. For example, the event handler code created by Visual Basic for the exitButton control is as follows:

```
Private Sub exitButton_Click(ByVal sender As System.Object, _
    ByVal e As System.EventArgs) Handles exitButton.Click

End Sub
```

Because the programmer selected the component called exitButton and the event Click, Visual Basic names the Sub procedure exitButton_Click. Note that two objects are passed to this event handler. The first is sender, an Object reference to the component that generated the event (exitButton in this case). The second is the EventArgs object called e, which contains additional information about the event. The Handles keyword is used to specify the kinds of events the method will handle. In this case, the handler will execute only in the case of a Click of the exitButton. The programmer can add the code Me.Close() within this event procedure to provide the desired functionality (that is, closing this form).

Following the InitializeComponent procedure is the declaration of the Button object called exitButton (Line 52). The access modifier Friend makes this component accessible from anywhere in the application and the keyword WithEvents enables this component to trigger events, such as Click.

ENHANCING A GUI'S APPEARANCE AND FUNCTIONALITY

The previous section discussed some of the basic operations behind GUIs. While you have already created many forms in your Visual Basic applications, there are additional techniques you can learn to improve a form's appearance and functionality, thus making it more useful and easier to use. This section provides many tips for enhancing Windows application forms.

Form Startup Location

One thing to consider when designing a GUI is where on the screen the form will appear when the application is launched. By default, a form will appear at the Windows default location, which is near the upper-left corner of the screen. However, users may prefer that the form appear in some other location, such as the center of the screen. You can set the startup location by following the steps in Figure 6.4.

HOW TO...

Set the Startup Location of a Form

1. With the form displayed in the Designer, right-click the form to display the Properties Window.
2. Scroll the Properties Window to the StartPosition property.
3. Click the value box for the StartPosition property, then click the down arrow to display choices.
4. Select the desired value for the StartPosition property.

FIGURE 6.4 How to set the startup location of a form

If the `StartPosition` property value is `CenterScreen`, the form will be centered on the user's screen. If you choose `Manual`, set the (x, y) coordinates (in pixels) for the upper-left corner of the form (relative to the upper-left corner of the screen) in the `Location` property of the form. For example, a `Location` value of (150, 100) will place the upper-left corner of the form 150 pixels to the right (positive x direction) and 100 pixels down (positive y direction) from the upper-left corner of the screen.

Making a Form Scrollable

A form may contain more controls than will fit within the boundaries of the form. In that case, you can make your form scrollable with scroll bars that appear only when necessary. (This will resemble scroll bars that may appear on a Web page if the browser window is resized.) To make a form scrollable, select the form; then, in the Properties Window, select `True` for the `Autoscroll` property value. You can test this effect by running the application and resizing the form. Scroll bars should appear.

As an example, consider the GUI for the Birthday application shown in Figure 6.5. The form uses a `DateTimePicker` control (named `birthdayDateTimePicker`) for selecting a birth date and displays a `MessageBox` that tells the user the number of days until the next birth date. Figure 6.6 shows the Visual Basic code for the application and Figure 6.7 shows the result of a sample run.

Note in Figure 6.6 that the application uses the `DateTime` structure to declare the variables `birthDate` and `todaysDate` (Lines 18–19). It also uses `birthdateDateTimePicker.Value` to get the value selected from the `DateTimePicker` control and the `Today` property of the `DateTime` structure to provide the current date. Finally, the `DateDiff Function` is used to determine the number of days between `todaysDate` and the future `birthDate`. You should study the code in Figure 6.6 carefully.

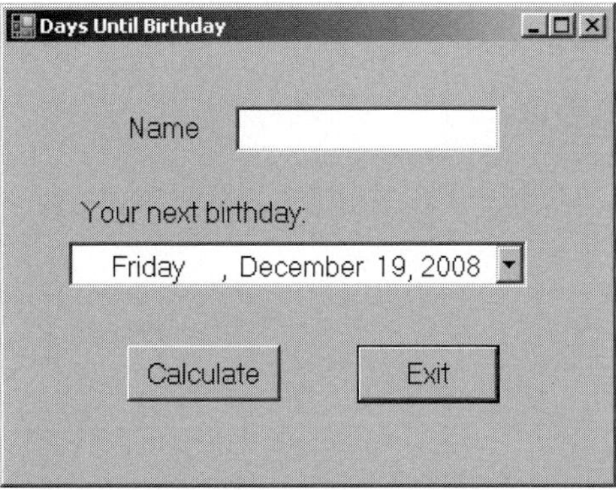

FIGURE 6.5 GUI for the Birthday application

```
1  ' Project name:          Birthday Project
2  ' Project purpose:       The project finds the number
3  '                        of days until a birthday.
4  ' Created/revised by:    <your name> on <current date>
5
6  Option Explicit On
7  Option Strict On
```

(Figure is continued on next page)

```
Public Class MainForm
    Private Sub exitButton_Click(ByVal sender As Object, _
        ByVal e As System.EventArgs) Handles exitButton.Click
        Me.Close()
    End Sub

    Private Sub calculateButton_Click(ByVal sender As Object, _
        ByVal e As System.EventArgs) Handles calculateButton.Click

        Dim birthDate As DateTime = birthdayDateTimePicker.Value
        Dim todaysDate As DateTime = #4/1/2008#
        Dim differenceInDays As Long = _
            DateDiff(DateInterval.Day, todaysDate, birthDate)
        Dim caption As String = "Your Birthday"
        Dim message As String = "Dear " & nameTextBox.Text & "," & _
            ControlChars.CrLf & "you have " & _
            differenceInDays.ToString & _
            " day(s)" & ControlChars.CrLf & "until your birthday"
        MessageBox.Show(message, caption)
    End Sub
End Class
```

FIGURE 6.6 Program code for the Birthday application

(a) Input

Days Until Birthday

Name John

Your next birthday:

Friday , December 19, 2008

Calculate Exit

(b) Output

FIGURE 6.7 Sample run of the Birthday application

While the application itself may be of interest to you, the point of this section is making a form scrollable. If the form in Figure 6.5 is reduced in size by the user (by clicking and dragging an edge or corner of the form), it may appear as shown in Figure 6.8 and would not be usable. However, if the `AutoScroll` property of the form is set to `True`, scroll bars will appear as shown in Figure 6.9. The scroll bars allow the user to access all controls in the form even though they may not be visible. A good application for the use of scroll bars in a form would be a fairly lengthy survey form with more survey items than can fit in a normally sized window.

FIGURE 6.8 Resized GUI for the Birthday application with `AutoScroll` set to `False`

FIGURE 6.9 Resized GUI for the Birthday application with `AutoScroll` set to `True`

The `FlowLayoutPanel` Control

If you take another look at Figure 6.8, you will notice that if a form is resized (and the `AutoScroll` property is set to `False`), the controls in the form remain in fixed positions. Even if `AutoScroll` is set to `True` and scroll bars allow access to controls, the controls still remain in relatively fixed positions. At times, however, it may be desirable for controls to automatically adjust their positions (or flow) when a form is resized. You can accomplish this by adding a `FlowLayoutPanel` control to a form. Figure 6.10 details how to create a flow layout in a form.

HOW TO...

Create a Flow Layout in a Form

1. With an empty form displayed in the Designer, drag a `FlowLayoutPanel` control from the Toolbox (in the Containers section) onto the form.
2. Resize the form and the `FlowLayoutPanel` to the desired sizes (the panel should nearly fill the form).
3. Select the `FlowLayoutPanel` and set its `Anchor` property to `Top`, `Bottom`, `Left`, `Right` (this allows components in the panel to flow in any direction).

(Figure is continued on next page)

4. Place controls (labels, text boxes, buttons) in the `FlowLayoutPanel`.
5. Test the form by running the program and resizing the form.

FIGURE 6.10 How to create a flow layout in a form

Figure 6.11 shows the Birthday application with a `FlowLayoutPanel`. As the form is resized, the components in the panel will automatically move (flow) to remain visible as long as the form itself is large enough to display all components.

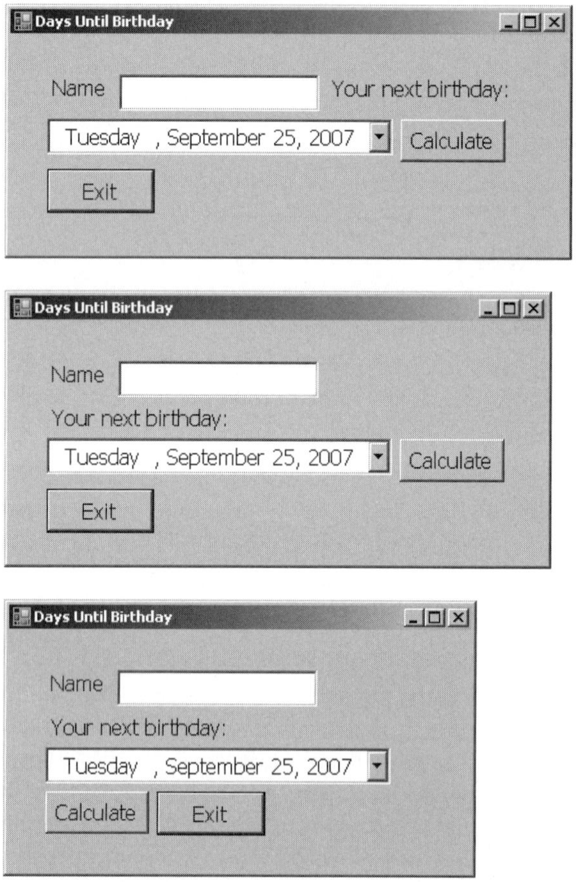

FIGURE 6.11 Sample run for the Birthday application with a `FlowLayoutPanel`

The `Margin` and `Padding` Properties

Another technique for improving the appearance of a form is using the `Margin` and `Padding` properties. The **`Margin` property** of a control determines the amount of space, in pixels, reserved around a control (`Left`, `Top`, `Right`, and `Bottom`) when calculating its automatic position in a `FlowLayoutPanel`. (The default is 3 pixels for each side.) The **`Padding` property** of a container control (a control that contains other controls) determines the amount of space, in pixels, reserved along the inside of containers (`Left`, `Top`, `Right`, and `Bottom`, with a default of 0 pixels for each side). Figure 6.12 shows the Birthday application with the `Margin` property of all controls set to 10, 10, 10, 10 and the `Padding` property of `flowLayoutPanel` set to 10, 10, 10, 10.

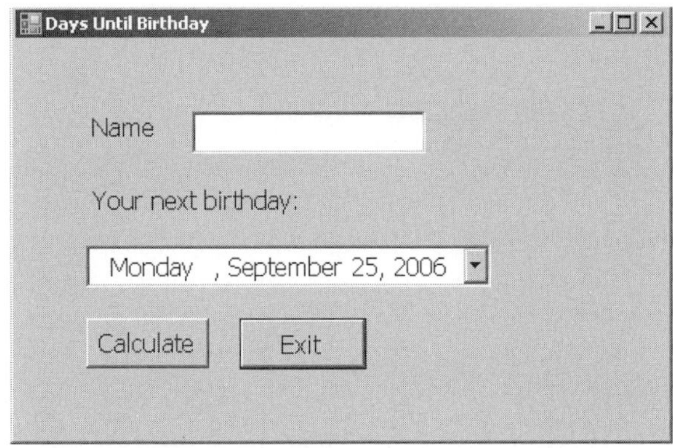

FIGURE 6.12 The Birthday application with a `FlowLayoutPanel`, `Margin`, and `Padding`

The `TableLayoutPanel` Control

The `TableLayoutPanel` control allows you to create a rectangular grid of rows and columns in which other controls can be placed. A table layout helps maintain an organized appearance for the form. You can place only one control in each cell of the table. Figure 6.13 explains how to create a table layout.

HOW TO...

Create a Table Layout in a Form

1. With an empty form displayed in the Designer, drag a `TableLayoutPanel` control from the Toolbox (in the Containers section) onto the form (see Figure 6.14).
2. Right-click the table and select Edit Rows and Columns, causing the Column and Row Styles dialog box to appear (see Figure 6.15).
3. Select either Rows or Columns in the Show: textbox to operate on the table rows and columns, respectively.
4. After selecting specific rows or columns in the Member list, select either Absolute, Percent, or AutoSize in the Size Type group. Alternatively, click the Add, Delete, or Insert buttons as necessary. Click OK when finished.
5. Place individual controls (labels, text boxes, buttons, etc.) in the table, one per cell.
6. To cause a control to span more than one column or row in the table, select the control and set the `RowSpan` or `ColumnSpan` properties for that control.
7. To adjust the alignment of a control within a cell, select the control and set the `Dock` or `Anchor` properties for that control.

FIGURE 6.13 How to create a table layout in a form

Figure 6.14 shows the result of placing a `TableLayoutPanel` control in an empty form. By default, a 2 × 2 table is created. Right-clicking the table and selecting Edit Rows and Columns causes the Column and Row Styles dialog box (shown in Figure 6.15) to appear.

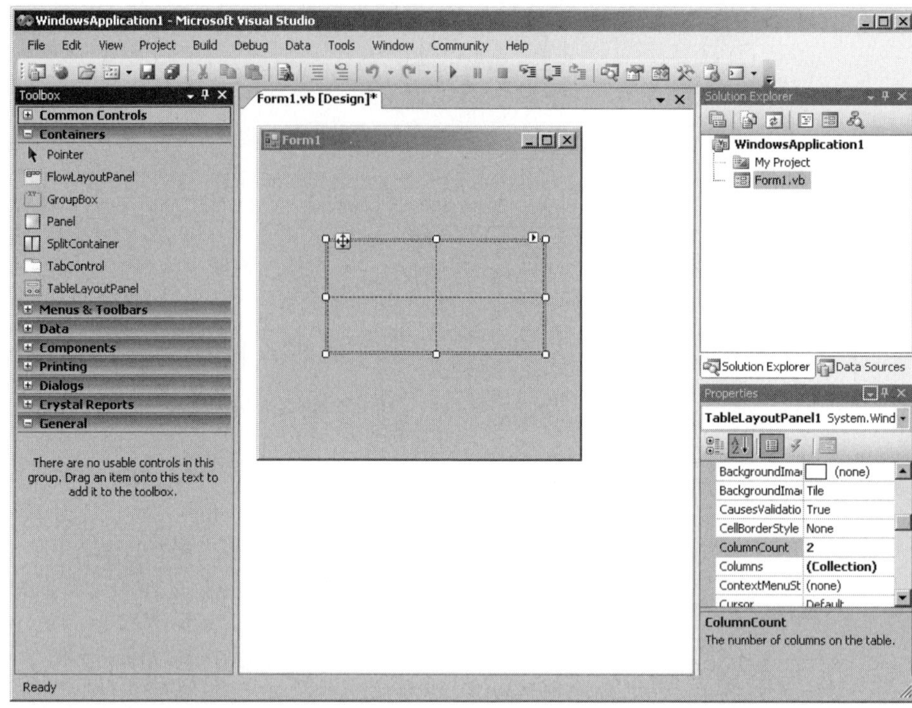

FIGURE 6.14 A `TableLayoutPanel` control added to a form

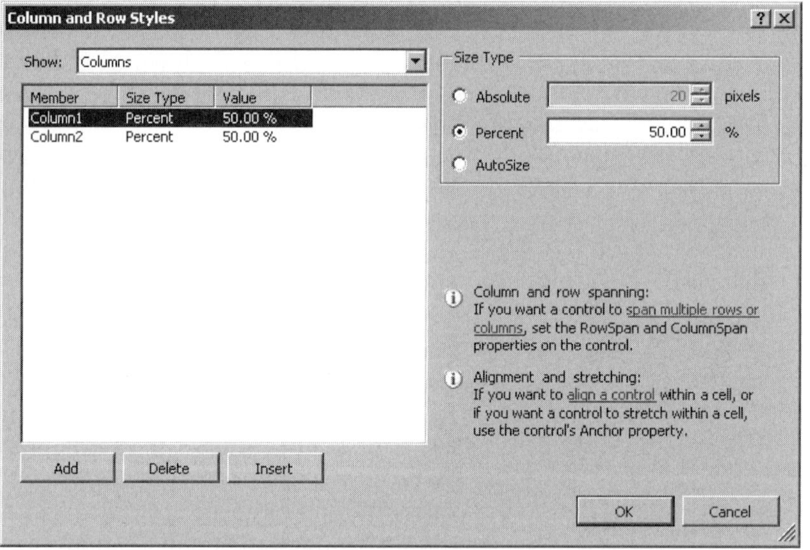

FIGURE 6.15 The Column and Row Styles dialog box for a table layout

In the case of the Birthday application, a table layout is employed to create the GUI shown in Figure 6.16. First, create a 3-row, 2-column table layout. Place the `nameLabel` and `nameTextBox` in the cells of the first row and the `birthdayLabel` and `birthdayDateTimePicker` in the cells of the second row. To achieve the alignment of these controls, set the `Anchor` property of the `nameLabel` to Top, Right and the `Anchor` property of the `nameTextBox` to Top, Left. Set the controls in the second row in the same way.

Achieving the arrangement of the buttons in Figure 6.16 is a little trickier. First, place a new `TableLayoutPanel` control (named `buttonTableLayoutPanel`) in the second column of the third row and delete one of the two rows of this table, leaving a 1 × 2 `TableLayoutPanel`. Then set the `ColumnSpan` property of this table to 2, meaning that this table will span two columns in the `birthdayTableLayoutPanel`. Next, place the `calculateButton` and the `exitButton` in the two columns of `buttonTableLayoutPanel`. To make the buttons fill these cells, set the `Anchor` property of each button to Left, Right. The result is the arrangement of all controls of the Birthday application in an orderly grid.

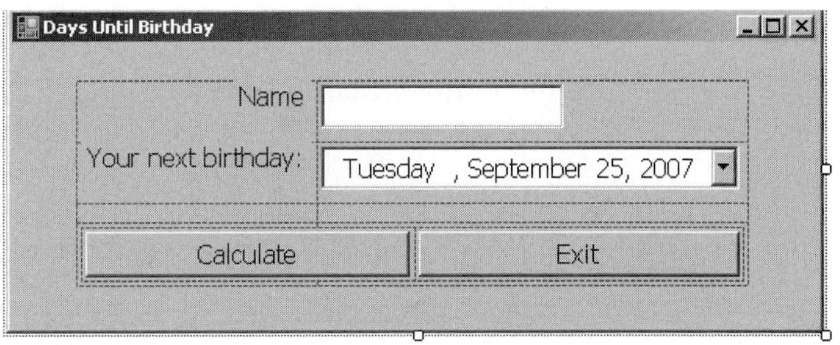

FIGURE 6.16 A table layout for the Birthday application

The `TabControl` Control

The `TabControl` control allows you to create a form with several related tabbed pages, such as the ones displayed in the Date and Time Properties dialog box in the Windows XP Control Panel (Figure 6.17). A `TabControl` can consist of two or more `TabPage` controls, each of which can contain various other controls. Using tabbed pages permits several different groups of related controls (each group on its own `TabPage`) to be displayed in a relatively small space within a single form. Figure 6.18 shows how to create a `TabControl` control with `TabPage` controls.

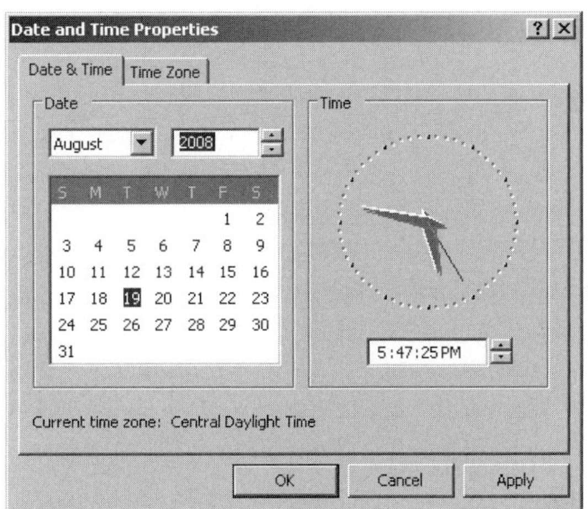

FIGURE 6.17 The Date and Time Properties dialog box for Windows XP Control Panel

HOW TO...

Create a TabControl in a Form

1. With an empty form displayed in the Designer, drag a TabControl control from the Toolbox (in the Containers section) onto the form.
2. Click on either tab to select the TabControl.
3. In the Properties window for the TabControl, scroll to the TabPages property and click the ellipsis icon to display the TabPage Collection Editor dialog box.
4. Within the TabPage Collection Editor dialog box, you can add or remove a TabPage and set the properties of each TabPage, such as the Name and the Text for each TabPage.
5. To select a particular TabPage, click the appropriate tab and then click the control area below the tab.
6. With a TabPage selected, add controls from the Toolbox to the TabPage as needed.

FIGURE 6.18 How to create a TabControl control in a form

As an example of using TabControl, reconsider the Birthday application in Figure 6.5. Instead of using a form with the calculateButton to make a MessageBox appear with the output, you can redesign the application to use a TabControl where one TabPage can receive the input and the other TabPage can display the output, as shown in Figure 6.19.

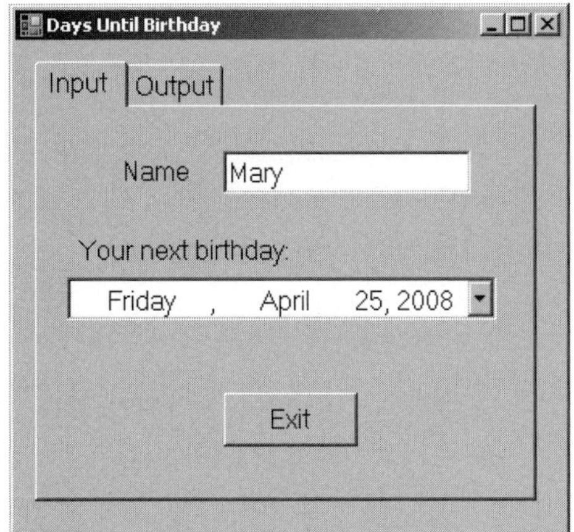

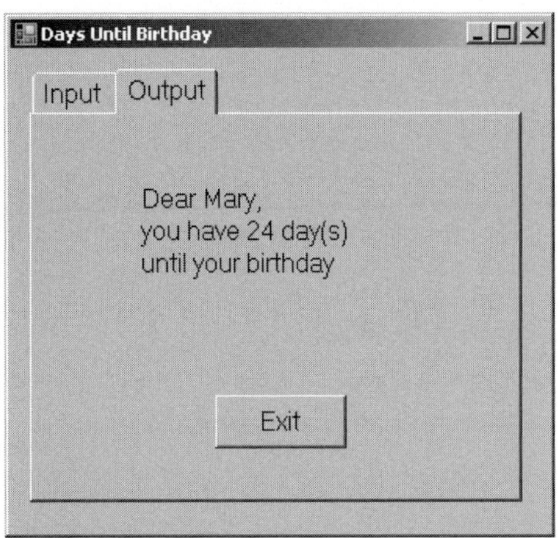

FIGURE 6.19 Sample run of the Birthday application with a `TabControl`

As Figure 6.19(a) indicates, the `birthdayTabControl` has two `TabPage` controls, `inputTabPage` and `outputTabPage`. The `nameTextBox` and `birthdayDateTimePicker` are placed in the `inputTabPage`. Figure 6.19(b) illustrates that an `outputLabel` is placed in the `outputTabPage`. An event procedure is added for the `Enter` event of the `outputTabPage` control as shown in Figure 6.20. Thus, if the user enters a name and a date in the `inputTabPage`, and then clicks the `outputTabPage` tab, the appropriate output is displayed in the `outputTabPage`.

```
' Project name:         Birthday Project
' Project purpose:      The project finds the number
'                       of days until a birthday and
'                       uses TabControl.
' Created/revised by:   <your name> on <current date>

Option Explicit On
Option Strict On

Public Class MainForm
    Private Sub outputTabPage_Enter(ByVal sender As Object, _
        ByVal e As System.EventArgs) Handles outputTabPage.Enter
```

(Figure is continued on next page)

```
        If nameTextBox.Text = String.Empty Then
            outputLabel.Text = "No name has been input"
        Else
            Dim birthDate As DateTime = birthdayDateTimePicker.Value
            Dim todaysDate As DateTime = #4/1/2008#
            Dim differenceInDays As Long = _
                DateDiff(DateInterval.Day, todaysDate, birthDate)
            Dim caption As String = "Your Birthday"
            Dim message As String = "Dear " & nameTextBox.Text & _
                "," & ControlChars.CrLf & "you have " & _
                differenceInDays.ToString & _
                " day(s)" & ControlChars.CrLf & "until your birthday"
            outputLabel.Text = message
        End If
    End Sub

    Private Sub inputExitButton_Click(ByVal sender As Object, _
        ByVal e As System.EventArgs) Handles inputExitButton.Click
        Me.Close()
    End Sub

    Private Sub outputExitButton_Click(ByVal sender As System.Object, _
        ByVal e As System.EventArgs) Handles outputExitButton.Click
        Me.Close()
    End Sub
End Class
```

FIGURE 6.20 Program code for the Birthday application with a `TabControl` control

Dialog Forms

Dialog forms provide a convenient way of getting quick standard responses (such as OK, Yes, No, Cancel, or Abort) from the user. A **dialog form** is a modal form that can return standard results using the `DialogResult` property. A **modal form** is one that requires the user to close the form before activating another window in the application. A **modeless form** does not have this requirement. Thus, the user can move from a modeless form to activate any other form in the application without exiting the modeless form.

A dialog box is created the same way as any other form. For example, if an application requires a Yes or No response from the user, the form could contain a `Label` control requesting the response along with a Yes button and a No button. A dialog form is special because it is displayed using the `ShowDialog` method. The `ShowDialog` method makes the dialog form a modal form, which must be exited before proceeding with the rest of the application. Also, the controls (usually buttons) on a dialog form can have their `DialogResult` properties set to standard values such as Yes, No, OK, or Cancel. These values of the `DialogResult` property can then be used to take appropriate action in the application.

As an example of a dialog form, consider a slight modification of the tab control Birthday application of Figure 6.19. If the user clicks the Exit button in either the Input or Output tabbed areas, the application simply closes. If closing an application is a critical action, you could add an extra confirmation step asking the user if she is sure she wants to exit. Figure 6.21 shows a dialog form used to get this response from the user.

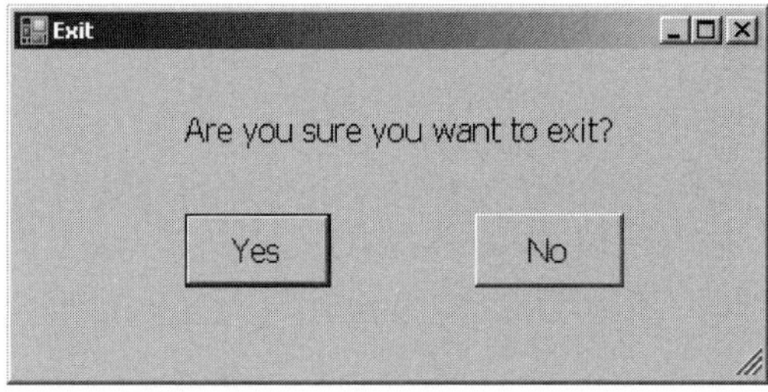

FIGURE 6.21 Dialog form for the Birthday application

The dialog form in Figure 6.21 is simply added to the Birthday application by clicking Project in the Visual Studio menu and then clicking Add Windows Form, followed by naming the file DialogForm.vb and clicking Add. Then add a `Label` ("Are you sure you want to exit?") and two buttons, `yesButton` and `noButton`. The key step is to set the `DialogResult` property of the `yesButton` to Yes and the `DialogResult` property of the `noButton` to No.

As the program code in Figure 6.22 demonstrates, the event procedures `inputExitButton_Click` and `outputExitButton_Click` are modified so that each calls (Lines 31 and 36) the new independent `Sub` procedure `exitApplication` (Lines 39–50). Within `exitApplication`, the application creates an instance of the new `DialogForm` called `exitDialogForm`. Then this `DialogForm` object calls the `ShowDialog` method. The `ShowDialog` method differs from the `Show` method in that using `ShowDialog` makes the form a modal form (one that must be exited to continue).

Next in the `exitApplication` procedure is a `Select Case` statement (Lines 34–48) that uses the value in `exitDialogForm.DisplayResult`. Recall that this enumeration (in the `System.Windows.Forms` namespace) contains "Yes" if the `yesButton` is clicked, and "No" if the `noButton` is clicked. Thus if `DisplayResult` is "Yes," the application exits, and if `DisplayResult` is "No," the `InitializeComponent` method is called. The GUI is then redrawn with its initial values.

```
1  ' Project name:        Birthday Project
2  ' Project purpose:     The project finds the number
3  '                      of days until a birthday and
4  '                      uses a dialog form.
5  ' Created/revised by:  <your name> on <current date>
6
7  Option Explicit On
8  Option Strict On
9
10 Public Class MainForm
11     Private Sub outputTabPage_Enter(ByVal sender As Object, _
12         ByVal e As System.EventArgs) Handles outputTabPage.Enter
13         If nameTextBox.Text = String.Empty Then
14             outputLabel.Text = "No name has been input"
15         Else
16             Dim birthDate As DateTime = birthdayDateTimePicker.Value
17             Dim todaysDate As DateTime = #4/1/2008#
18             Dim differenceInDays As Long = _
19                 DateDiff(DateInterval.Day, todaysDate, birthDate)
20             Dim caption As String = "Your Birthday"
```

(Figure is continued on next page)

```
            Dim message As String = "Dear " & nameTextBox.Text & _
                "," & ControlChars.CrLf & "you have " & _
                differenceInDays.ToString & _
                " day(s)" & ControlChars.CrLf & "until your birthday"
            outputLabel.Text = message
        End If
    End Sub

    Private Sub inputExitButton_Click(ByVal sender As Object, _
        ByVal e As System.EventArgs) Handles inputExitButton.Click
        exitApplication()
    End Sub

    Private Sub outputExitButton_Click(ByVal sender As System.Object, _
        ByVal e As System.EventArgs) Handles outputExitButton.Click
        exitApplication()
    End Sub

    Private Sub exitApplication()
        Dim exitDialogForm As New DialogForm
        exitDialogForm.ShowDialog()

        Select Case exitDialogForm.DialogResult
            Case Windows.Forms.DialogResult.Yes
                Application.Exit()
            Case Windows.Forms.DialogResult.No
                InitializeComponent()
        End Select

    End Sub
End Class
```

FIGURE 6.22 Program code for MainForm.vb in the Birthday application with a dialog form

MENUS

So far in this text, the functionality of a GUI has been triggered by simple events such as the user interacting with command buttons, text boxes, or other components. As GUIs grow more complex and versatile, a growing number of commands may need to be available to the user. One of the best ways of organizing a larger number of commands is with menus.

About Menus

As you know from your own experience with Windows applications, a **menu** is a list of items that specify options or groups of options for an application. Menus are vital to Visual Basic applications because they can hide a wide variety of commands from view until they are needed. This keeps a GUI free from unnecessary clutter, making it much easier to use.

From Visual Basic's perspective, a menu is actually a component (object) of the `MenuStrip` class that represents the container for the menu structure of a form. A menu contains **menu items** (objects of the class `MenuItem`) that represent the individual menu commands in a menu. The menu items that first appear in a menu are called top-level menu items. Each menu item can be a command for an application. Alternatively, a menu item can be a **parent menu** for other **submenu** items. For example, a `MenuStrip` in an application can have File as a top-level menu item that is a parent menu for a submenu that contains other menu items such as New..., Open..., Close, Save, and Exit. (Note the ... and the underlined letters. These have a significance that will be discussed shortly.) These submenu items can execute a method call when selected, which often involves opening a dialog box (window) that enables the user to perform many other useful tasks.

As another example, many Windows applications have a menu with a View menu item that expands into a submenu that contains a Toolbars menu item that also expands into a submenu that lists the various toolbars (Standard, Formatting, etc.) that can be selected by the user. Clicking any one of these individual toolbar menu items executes a command that causes the corresponding toolbar to display in the application.

Furthermore, all menu items can be associated with shortcut keys (or hot keys). A **shortcut key** is a single key or a combination of keys (often beginning with the Alt, Ctrl, or Shift keys) that the user can press to execute a menu item. In typical Windows applications, top-level menu items such as File can be executed by pressing Alt-F, as indicated by the underlined letter in File. Submenu items, such as the menu item Exit within the File submenu, can be executed by pressing a single key (x in the case of Exit).

Implementing Menus

This section demonstrates how to implement a main menu in an application and add individual menu items. You begin by adding a `MenuStrip` control to a form.

Adding a Menu

Adding a menu to a form is simple. With an empty form displayed in the Designer, drag a `MenuStrip` control from the Toolbox to any part in the form. Figure 6.23 shows the result of adding a menu (named `MenuStrip1` by default) to the form of the GUI Test application of Figure 6.1. Note the `MenuStrip1` icon displayed at the bottom of the IDE and the menu appearing in the form under the title bar. The IDE is now said to be in the Visual Studio .NET Menu Designer configuration.

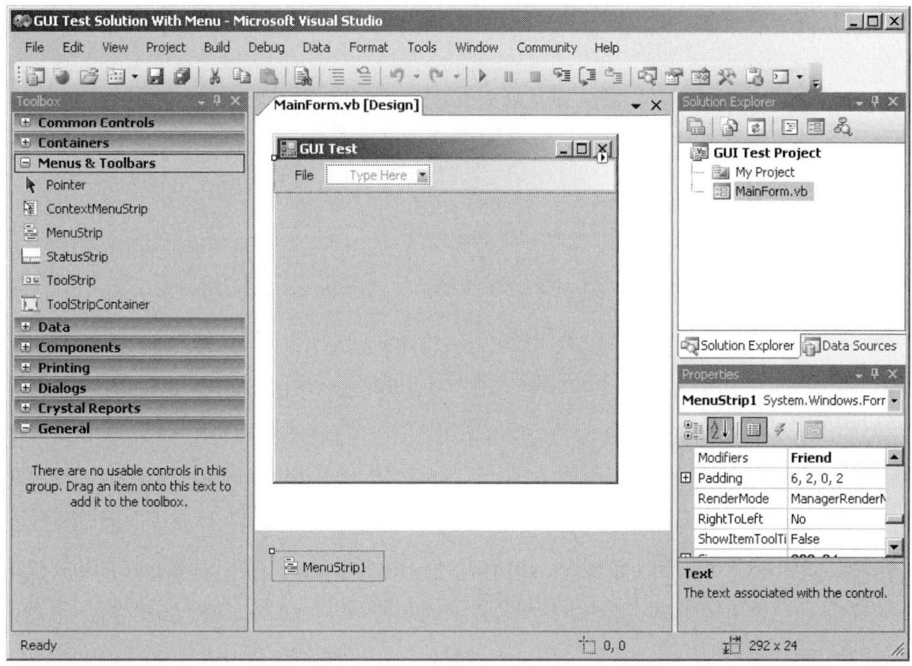

FIGURE 6.23 Form with a `MenuStrip` control added

Adding a Menu Item

The next step in implementing a complete menu structure is to add specific menu items to the menu, as described in Figure 6.24. You should carefully plan an application's menu structure before attempting to implement it.

HOW TO...

Add a Menu Item to a Menu

1. While in the Visual Studio .NET Menu Designer configuration, click the `MenuStrip` icon at the bottom of the IDE.
2. Click the Type Here text box below the title bar of the form.
3. Type the text for the menu item (such as File) and press Enter.
4. Click the Type Here text box next to an existing menu item to add a menu item at the same level or below a menu item to create a submenu item.
5. Repeat Steps 3 and 4 as necessary to complete the menu structure.
6. Click on the form when finished and click the Save icon in the toolbar.

FIGURE 6.24 How to add a menu item to a menu

The menu items shown in Figure 6.25 were created by following the steps in Figure 6.24. The menu has a top-level menu item File and a submenu item Close. Note that you can continue to add menu items by clicking the text box that is either to the right of or below an existing menu item. Clicking a text box to the right of an existing menu item adds a menu item at the same level, while clicking on a text box below an existing menu item adds a menu item at a submenu level.

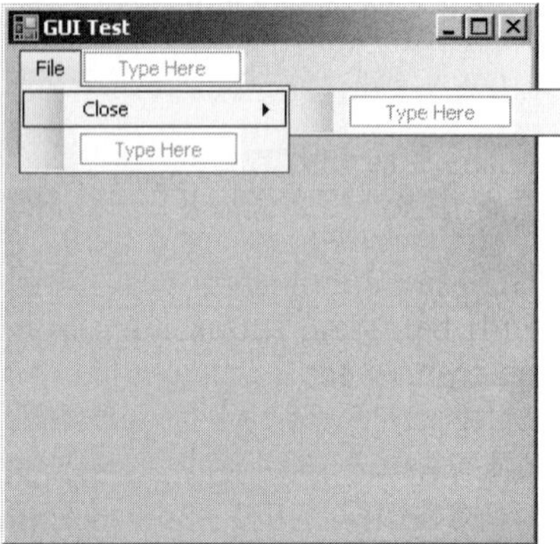

FIGURE 6.25 Form with top-level menu item File and submenu item Close

Adding Shortcut Keys

At this point in the development of the GUI Test application, the menu items can be executed only by clicking them. Figure 6.26 demonstrates how to add a shortcut key (or shortcut key combinations) to a menu item. The shortcut key will then provide an alternative means of selecting the menu item.

HOW TO...

Add a Letter Shortcut Key to a Menu Item

1. While in the Windows Form Designer, click the specific menu item.
2. In the Properties Window, scroll to the `Text` property.
3. In the value field of the `Text` property, type an ampersand (`&`) before the letter that corresponds to the letter shortcut key and press Enter.

FIGURE 6.26 How to add a letter shortcut key to a menu item

Note that if you designate a letter shortcut key for a submenu item using & in the `Text` property, the submenu item can be executed by simply pressing the letter without pressing the Alt key. In the GUI Test application, the Close menu item is selected and the letter C is preceded by the & symbol in the menu item's `Text` property, making the letter C a shortcut key for this menu item. Thus, pressing Alt-F will cause the submenu item Close to appear in the form, and then simply pressing C will select the Close menu item.

Shortcut keys can also be defined (with greater flexibility) using the `ShortcutKeys` property of a menu item. A very wide range of special shortcut keys (not including what can be provided using & and the `Text` property) can be defined, such as F1–F24, Ctrl-<letter>, Ctrl-Alt-<letter>, Shift-<number>, etc. Figure 6.27 explains the procedure.

HOW TO...

Use the `ShortcutKeys` Property of a Menu Item

1. While in the Windows Form Designer, click the specific menu item.
2. In the Properties Window, scroll to the `ShortcutKeys` property.
3. In the value field of the `ShortcutKeys` property, click none, one, two, or three of the check boxes for the Ctrl, Shift, or Alt prefix keys.
4. In the drop-down list of the `ShortcutKeys` property, select the desired key to be used in combination with the key(s) selected in Step 3.

FIGURE 6.27 How to use the `ShortcutKeys` property of a menu item

Note that selecting just C in the `ShortcutKeys` property for the Close menu item in Figure 6.28 is not allowed because that result can be achieved using the & symbol in the `Text` property of this menu item. However, clicking the Ctrl check box and clicking C in the drop-down list of the `ShortcutKeys` property is valid, making Ctrl-C the combination of keys that selects the Close menu item. As another example, clicking none of the check boxes of the `ShortcutKeys` property but selecting F1 from the drop-down list for the File menu item would be valid, making F1 the shortcut key for selecting File in the menu. This assumes that the & was not used for the File menu item in its `Text` property.

In the GUI Test application, the Close menu item is selected and the `ShortcutKeys` property is set to Ctrl-C. In fact, the `ShowShortcutKeys` property is `True` by default, so that the text Ctrl-C will also be displayed with the menu item Close, as seen in Figure 6.28. (Note that simply selecting the letter C as the shortcut key for the Close menu item would be a better choice, but Ctrl-C is chosen for the purpose of demonstration.)

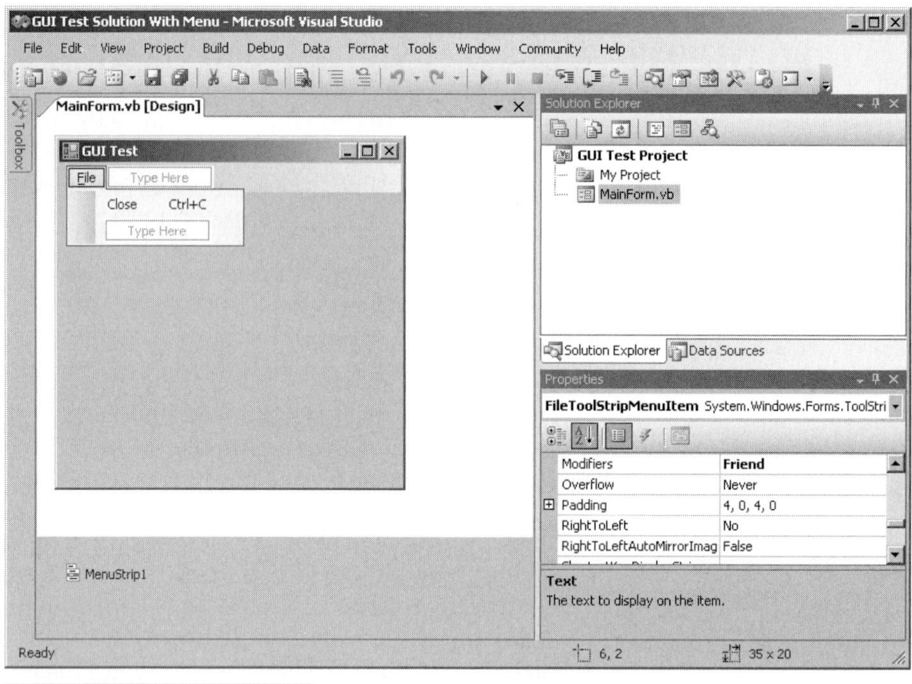

FIGURE 6.28 The shortcut keys for the Close menu item in the GUI Test application

Adding Functionality to Menu Items

Now that you have added a menu, menu items, and shortcut keys, it's time to provide some actual functionality to a menu item. Figure 6.29 shows how to add an event procedure to a menu item.

HOW TO...

Add an Event Procedure to a Menu Item

1. While in the Code View of the IDE, select the menu item from the Class Name drop-down list.
2. Select the Click event from the Method Name drop-down list.
3. Add the desired Visual Basic code within the event procedure.

FIGURE 6.29 How to add an event procedure to a menu item

For example, in the GUI Test application the menu item labeled Close should close the form. (Note that an event procedure is not needed for the File menu item because it serves as a parent menu item that displays the Close menu item.) Following the steps in Figure 6.29, an event procedure is added to the application and the code `Application.Exit()` is added within the procedure, as shown in Figure 6.30.

As a result of all the preceding changes made to the GUI Test application, selecting File, Close from the menu will produce the same result as clicking an Exit button or a Close button on the form.

```
Public Class MainForm

    Private Sub CloseToolStripMenuItem_Click( _
        ByVal sender As System.Object, _
        ByVal e As System.EventArgs)_
        Handles CloseToolStripMenuItem.Click

        Application.Exit()
    End Sub
End Class
```

FIGURE 6.30 Program code for the GUI Test application with a menu event

MULTIPLE-DOCUMENT-INTERFACE WINDOWS

Up to this point in this text, you have created only **single-document-interface (SDI) applications**—applications that support only one open window or document at a time. Simple applications, such as Windows Notepad or Paint, are examples of SDI applications. More complex applications, such as Microsoft Word or Adobe Photoshop, are often **multiple-document-interface (MDI) applications** that allow many documents to be open at once. MDI applications allow the user to easily move from document to document, performing required operations such as cut and paste.

The application window of an MDI program is called the **parent window** and each window within the application is called a **child window**. When the application is run, there is only one parent window, but there could be virtually any number of child windows, only one of which may be active at a time. Figure 6.31 explains how to create an MDI form.

HOW TO...

Create an MDI Form

1. Create a new Windows application with the default class `Form1` in the file Form1.vb.
2. Change the name of the file Form1.vb to MDI Parent Form.vb. (This filename is chosen for illustrative purposes. In fact, you can use any name.)
3. Change the `Name` property of the form to `MdiParentForm` and its `Text` property to MDI Parent Form (again, for illustrative purposes).
4. Make `MdiParentForm` the startup form for the project as follows: right-click the project in the Solution Explorer window, click Properties, select `MdiParentForm` from the Startup form: drop-down list, and click the Close button.
5. Set the `IsMdiContainer` property of the `MdiParentForm` to `True`.
6. Drag a `MenuStrip` control from the Toolbox to the `MdiParentForm` and add the menu item File. Add a submenu item called New to menu item File and a submenu item Window to menu item New.

(Figure is continued on next page)

7. In the Code View for `MdiParentForm`, create a `Click` event procedure for the Window submenu item. To do so, click the Class Name drop-down list, select `WindowToolStripMenuItem`, click the Method Name drop-down list, and select `Click`. Alternatively, double-click the Window submenu item.
8. Create a new empty form in the project as follows: click Project in the menu, click Add Windows Form, and click Add.
9. Change the name of the file Form1.vb to MDI Child Form.vb, change the `Name` property of the form to `MdiChildForm` (for illustrative purposes), and change the `Text` property of `MdiChildForm` to a meaningful, appropriate title for the form.
10. In the Code View for `MdiParentForm`, enter code similar to the following within the `WindowToolStripMenuItem_Click` event procedure. This code creates a new `MdiChildForm` object called `appMdiChildForm`, makes it a child of `MdiParentForm`, and then displays the child form in the parent form GUI.

```
Dim appMdiChildForm As New MdiChildForm
appMdiChildForm.MdiParent = Me
appMdiChildForm.Show()
```

FIGURE 6.31 How to create an MDI form

As an example of applying the procedure in Figure 6.31, modify the table layout Birthday application of Figure 6.16 to incorporate an MDI form. First, Steps 1–7 of Figure 6.31 are performed as part of a new solution called Birthday Solution with MDI. However, instead of Step 8, add the `MainForm` of the Birthday Solution with Table Layout (Figure 6.16) to the current MDI solution. (Click Project and click Add Existing Item... to add an existing form to a new project.) Adding an existing form to the Birthday Solution with MDI will save development time. Step 9 is then performed (substituting `MainForm` for `Form1`), followed by Step 10.

To further modify the MDI Birthday application, insert a new row in the table layout above the row of buttons and add a Label control to this row. This `Label` control will display the output (number of days until the birthday) instead of using a separate `MessageBox`, thus making the application more self-contained. Then, change the Exit button to a Reset button. Finally, add a File, Exit option to the `MenuStrip` to exit the application. Figure 6.32 displays the modifications of `MainForm` in the Birthday Solution with Table Layout resulting in `MdiChildForm` in Birthday Solution with MDI.

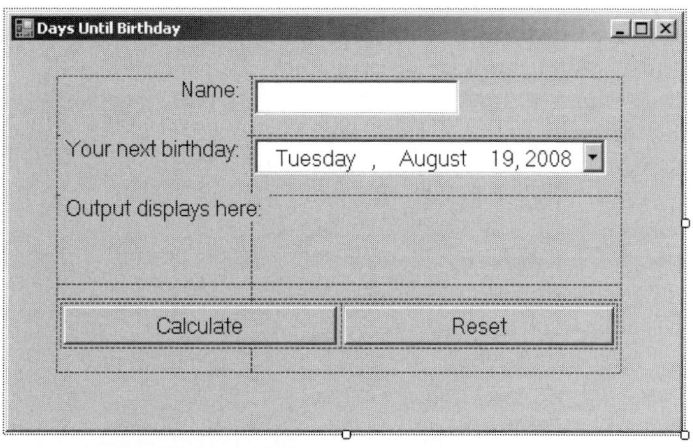

FIGURE 6.32 `MdiChildForm` in Birthday Solution with MDI

Figure 6.32 shows the table layout for the `MdiChildForm`. Figure 6.33 displays the program code for the file MdiChildForm.vb. Note that the control `outputLabel` has been added and placed in a new third row of the table (spanning both columns of that row). Also note that the `resetButton` control resets the `nameTextBox`, `birthdayDateTimePicker`, and the `outputLabel` when clicked.

```
Public Class MdiChildForm

    Private Sub resetButton_Click(ByVal sender As Object, _
        ByVal e As System.EventArgs) Handles resetButton.Click
        nameTextBox.Text = String.Empty
        birthdayDateTimePicker.Value = Today
        outputLabel.Text = "Output displays here"
    End Sub

    Private Sub calculateButton_Click(ByVal sender As Object, _
        ByVal e As System.EventArgs) Handles calculateButton.Click

        Dim birthDate As DateTime = birthdayDateTimePicker.Value
        Dim todaysDate As DateTime = #4/1/2008# 'Today
        Dim differenceInDays As Long = _
            DateDiff(DateInterval.Day, todaysDate, birthDate)
        Dim caption As String = "Your Birthday"
        Dim message As String = "Dear " & nameTextBox.Text & "," & _
            ControlChars.CrLf & "you have " & _
            differenceInDays.ToString & " day(s) until your birthday"
        outputLabel.Text = message
    End Sub

End Class
```

FIGURE 6.33 Program code for the MDI Birthday application's `MdiChildForm`

Figure 6.34 shows the `MdiParentForm` in the Designer. The submenu item Window is provided to create a new `MdiChildForm` and the submenu item Exit is added for exiting the application.

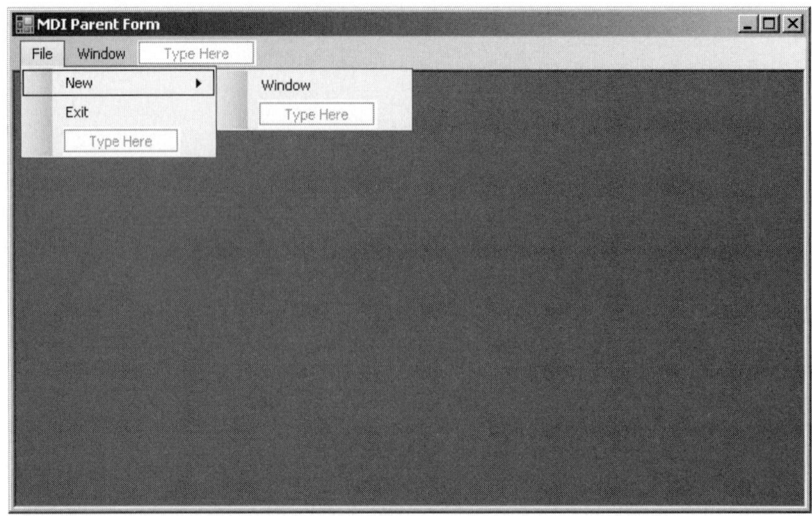

FIGURE 6.34 Modified MDI Birthday application's `MdiParentForm`

Figure 6.35 displays the program code for the `MdiParentForm`. Note first that the `MdiParentForm` class declares and initializes a `Private` instance variable `windowNumber` that will be used in the title bar of each new `MdiChildForm` created. The `WindowToolStripMenuItem_Click` event procedure in Figure 6.35 is responsible for creating and displaying an `MdiChildForm` object called `appMdiChildForm`. (The "app" refers to application.) This event procedure first increments `windowNumber` by 1. Then the `LayoutMdi` method is called using the enumeration `LayoutMdi` with the value Cascade, causing multiple windows to be arranged as cascaded windows in the parent form. The `LayoutMdi` method is called again using the value `ArrangeIcons`, causing minimized windows to be displayed neatly along the bottom of the parent form. The object `appMdiChildForm` is then created and calls the method `MdiParent`, making the `MdiParentForm` its parent. Finally, the `Text` property of `appMdiChildForm` is set and then the window is displayed.

The `ExitToolStripMenuItem_Click` event procedure calls the method `Application.Exit`. The `CloseToolStripMenuItem_Click` event procedure uses an `If...Then...Else` statement to close the active `MdiChildForm` object. The code `Convert.ToString(Me.ActiveMdiChild) = Nothing` refers to the property `ActiveMdiChild` of `Me` (the current `MdiParentForm`). The property `ActiveMdiChild` returns the active MDI child object (if one exists), `Nothing` otherwise. If the value of `Me.ActiveMdiChild` is not `Nothing`, then a child form is active and it will be closed.

Finally, the `MdiParentForm_MdiChildActivate` event procedure is called when the `MdiChildActivate` event is raised by `MdiParentForm` (whenever an `MdiChildForm` object is activated or closed), resulting in the display of a `MessageBox`. Figure 6.36 provides a sample run of the MDI Birthday application.

```
Public Class MdiParentForm
    Private windowNumber As Integer = 0 ' for display in title bar

    Private Sub WindowToolStripMenuItem_Click( _
        ByVal sender As Object, _
        ByVal e As System.EventArgs) _
        Handles WindowToolStripMenuItem.Click

        windowNumber += 1 ' increase by 1
        Me.LayoutMdi(MdiLayout.Cascade) ' windows are cascaded
        Me.LayoutMdi(MdiLayout.ArrangeIcons) ' icons arranged at bottom
        Dim appMdiChildForm As New MdiChildForm ' create window
        appMdiChildForm.MdiParent = Me ' make a child of MdiParentForm
        appMdiChildForm.Text = "Window " & windowNumber ' set title
        appMdiChildForm.Show() ' display
    End Sub

    Private Sub ExitToolStripMenuItem_Click( _
        ByVal sender As Object, _
        ByVal e As System.EventArgs) _
        Handles ExitToolStripMenuItem.Click

        Application.Exit()
    End Sub

    Private Sub CloseToolStripMenuItem_Click( _
        ByVal sender As Object, _
        ByVal e As System.EventArgs) _
        Handles CloseToolStripMenuItem.Click

        If Convert.ToString(Me.ActiveMdiChild) = Nothing Then
            MessageBox.Show("No window is active", "MDI Parent")
        Else
            Me.ActiveMdiChild.Close()
        End If

    End Sub

    Private Sub MdiParentForm_MdiChildActivate( _
        ByVal sender As Object, _
        ByVal e As System.EventArgs) Handles Me.MdiChildActivate
        MessageBox.Show("Happy Birthday!", "Days Until Birthday")
    End Sub
End Class
```

FIGURE 6.35 Program code for the MDI Birthday application's `MdiParentForm`

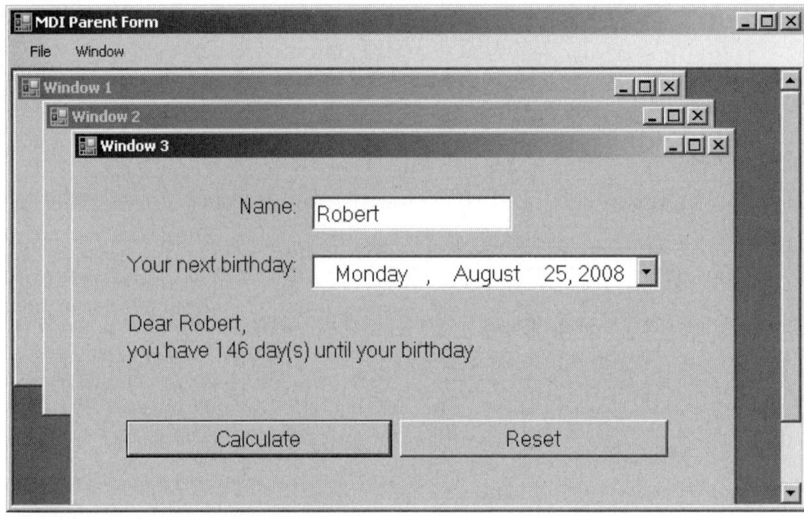

FIGURE 6.36 Sample run of the MDI Birthday application

As the Birthday application code in Figure 6.35 demonstrates, there are several useful properties, methods, and events associated with MDI forms. The more common ones are summarized in Table 6.1.

Property	Description
`IsMdiContainer`	For an MDI parent form, indicates if a `Form` is used as an MDI container (has value `True` or `False`, read-only)
`ActiveMdiChild`	Returns the `Form` that is the currently active MDI child (returns `Nothing` if there is no active MDI child)
`MdiChildren`	Returns an array of `Forms` that are currently MDI children
`IsMdiChild`	For an MDI child form, indicates if a `Form` is an MDI child (has value `True` or `False`, read-only)
`MdiParent`	Returns the MDI parent `Form` of the child
Method	**Description**
`LayoutMdi`	Determines how child forms are displayed on an MDI parent using one of the following `MdiLayout` enumeration values: • `MdiLayout.ArrangeIcons`—arranges minimized window icons along the bottom of the parent • `MdiLayout.Cascade`—open windows cascade (overlap) • `MdiLayout.TileHorizontal`—open windows fill the parent in a horizontal arrangement • `MdiLayout.TileVertical`—open windows fill the parent in a vertical arrangement

(Table is continued on next page)

Event	Description
`MdiChildActivate`	Raised when an MDI child is closed or activated

TABLE 6.1 Common properties, methods, and events for MDI forms

PROGRAMMING EXAMPLE

MDI Future Value Calculator

In this section you will create a Future Value Solution that uses an MDI form.

Pseudocode

`MainForm`

The `MainForm` is an MDI parent form with a top-level menu including the menu items File and Help. The File menu item has the following submenu items: New, Close, and Exit.

***`NewToolStripMenuItem_Click`* event procedure**

1. create new CalculatorForm document
2. make new document an MDI child of MainForm
3. increment documentNumber
4. set title for new document (Document n)
5. display new document

***`CloseToolStripMenuItem_Click`* event procedure**

1. close the active document

***`ExitToolStripMenuItem_Click`* event procedure**

1. exit the application

***`HelpToolStripMenuItem_Click`* event procedure**

1. display help text

`CalculatorForm`

The CalculatorForm is an MDI child form that calculates future value.

***`calculateButton_Click`* event procedure**

1. declare variables: payment, periods, apr, futureValue, futureValueStr
2. get payment, periods, and apr from text boxes
3. calculate futureValue using Visual Basic FV function
4. convert futureValue to currency format
5. display futureValueStr

***`resetButton_Click`* event procedure**

1. set all text boxes and output label to empty strings
2. set focus on paymentTextBox

Code

```
Public Class MainForm
    Private documentNumber As Integer = 0

    Private Sub NewToolStripMenuItem_Click( _
        ByVal sender As System.Object, _
        ByVal e As System.EventArgs) Handles NewToolStripMenuItem.Click

        Dim appMdiChildForm As New CalculatorForm ' create new document
        appMdiChildForm.MdiParent = Me ' make document an MDI child
        documentNumber += 1 ' increment document number
        appMdiChildForm.Text = "Document " & documentNumber ' set title
        appMdiChildForm.Show() ' display document
    End Sub

    Private Sub CloseToolStripMenuItem_Click( _
        ByVal sender As System.Object, _
        ByVal e As System.EventArgs) _
        Handles CloseToolStripMenuItem.Click
        ActiveMdiChild.Close() ' close active document
    End Sub

    Private Sub ExitToolStripMenuItem_Click( _
        ByVal sender As System.Object, _
        ByVal e As System.EventArgs) _
        Handles ExitToolStripMenuItem.Click
        Application.Exit() ' exit application
    End Sub

    Private Sub HelpToolStripMenuItem_Click( _
        ByVal sender As System.Object, _
        ByVal e As System.EventArgs) _
        Handles HelpToolStripMenuItem.Click

        Dim helpString As String
        helpString = _
            "Monthly Payment is amount invested each month." _
            & ControlChars.CrLf & _
            "Number of Months is number of months payment is made." _
            & ControlChars.CrLf & _
            "Annual Interest Rate is percent interest (5 means 5%)." _
            & ControlChars.CrLf & _
            "Future Value is final value of the investment."
        MessageBox.Show(helpString, "Future Value Help") ' display help
    End Sub
End Class
```

FIGURE 6.37 Program code for the MainForm.vb file

```
Public Class CalculatorForm

    Private Sub calculateButton_Click(ByVal sender As System.Object, _
        ByVal e As System.EventArgs) Handles calculateButton.Click
        ' declare variables
        Dim payment As Double
        Dim periods As Integer
        Dim apr As Double
        Dim futureValue As Double
        Dim futureValueStr As String
        ' input
        payment = Convert.ToDouble(paymentTextBox.Text)
        periods = Convert.ToInt16(periodsTextBox.Text)
        apr = Convert.ToDouble(aprTextBox.Text)
        ' process
        futureValue = _
            FV((apr / 100) / 12, periods, -payment)
        futureValueStr = FormatCurrency(futureValue)
        ' output
        outputLabel.Text = futureValueStr
    End Sub

    Private Sub resetButton_Click(ByVal sender As System.Object, _
        ByVal e As System.EventArgs) Handles resetButton.Click
        ' reset all text fields and output label
        paymentTextBox.Text = String.Empty
        periodsTextBox.Text = String.Empty
        aprTextBox.Text = String.Empty
        outputLabel.Text = String.Empty
        paymentTextBox.Focus()
    End Sub
End Class
```

FIGURE 6.38 Program code for the CalculatorForm.vb file

Input/Output

(a) Selecting File, New

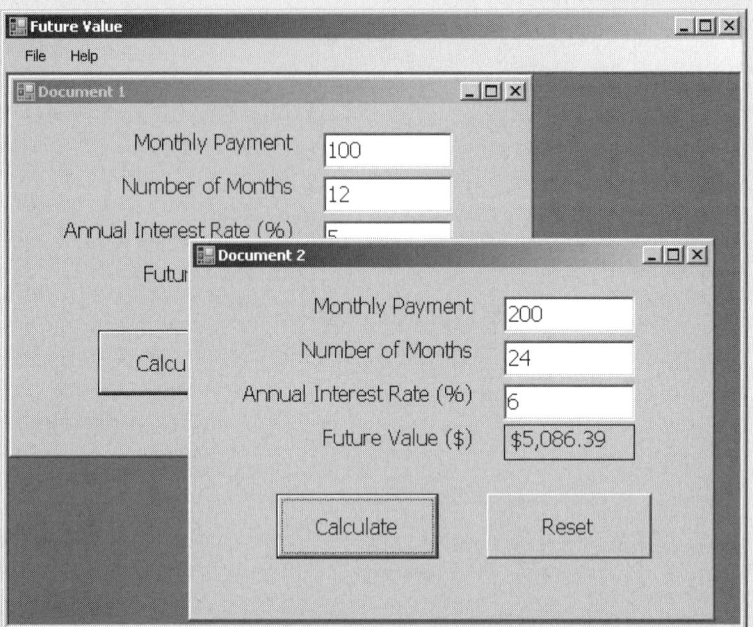

(b) Selecting Help

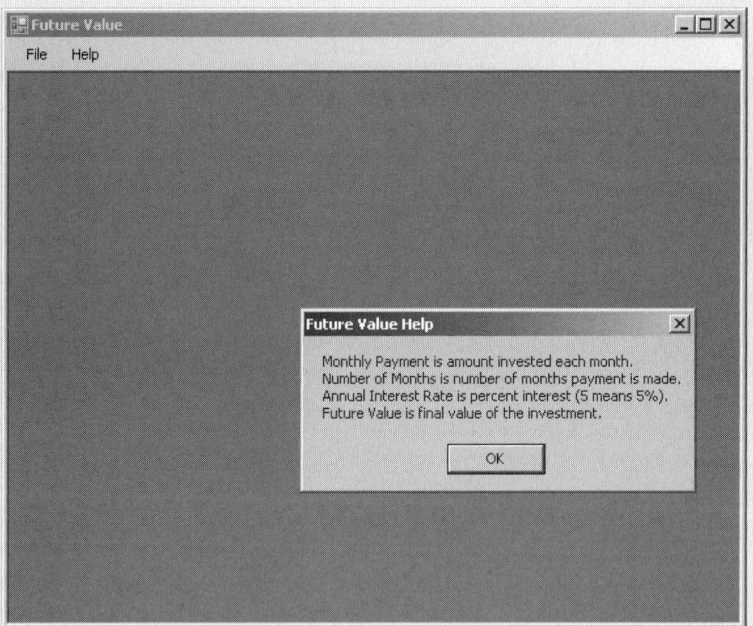

FIGURE 6.39 Sample run of the Future Value application

Quick Review

- Sophisticated users have come to expect a wide variety of helpful GUI features in a wide range of applications, such as Windows Internet Explorer and Microsoft Office. Such features include tabbed windows, scroll bars, menus, and multiple documents.
- A form is a graphical element that appears on the screen, such as a dialog box, window, or multiple-document-interface (MDI) window. A form contains various components, which are usually added by dragging and dropping component icons from the Visual Basic Toolbox.
- A component is an object that ultimately derives much of its functionality from the `Component` class. Furthermore, a control is a visible component (such as `Label` or `Button`) that derives from the `Control` class.
- Some components that are added to a form, such as a `Timer` (`System.Windows.Forms.Timer`), do not have a graphical representation, but simply provide functionality.
- When a user interacts with a control by using the mouse or the keyboard, the control raises an event within the application. GUI applications are said to be event driven, meaning that the GUIs generate events that drive the application's functionality. The event is passed to one or more event handlers, methods written by the programmer to provide the application with the desired responses.
- When you create a GUI using the Visual Basic Form Designer, Visual Basic generates the required program code in the Code window. Understanding this code helps you create advanced GUI features.
- The `StartPosition` property of a form gets or sets the start position of a form at run time.
- The `AutoScroll` property of a form allows scroll bars to appear in a form if controls are placed outside the form's visible boundaries.
- The `FlowLayoutPanel` control represents a panel that dynamically lays out its contents horizontally or vertically as the size of the panel changes.
- The `Margin` property of a control determines the amount of space, in pixels, reserved around a control when calculating its automatic position in a `FlowLayoutPanel`. The `Padding` property of a container control determines the amount of space, in pixels, reserved along the inside of containers.
- The `TableLayoutPanel` control allows you to create a rectangular grid of rows and columns in which other controls can be placed. A table layout helps maintain an organized appearance for the form.
- The `TabControl` control allows you to create a form with several tabbed pages. A `TabControl` can consist of two or more `TabPage` controls, each of which can contain various other controls. Using tabbed pages permits several different groups of related controls (each group on its own `TabPage`) to be displayed in a relatively small space within a single form.
- A dialog form is a modal form that can return standard results using the `DialogResult` property. A modal form is one that requires the user to close the form before activating another window in the application. A modeless form does not have this requirement.
- A menu is a component of the `MenuStrip` class that represents the container for the menu structure of a form. A menu contains menu items (objects of the class `MenuItem`) that represent the individual menu commands in the menu structure. Each menu item can be a command for an application. Alternatively, a menu item can be a parent menu for other submenu items.

- All menu items can have key shortcuts (or hot keys) that are accessed by pressing a single key or a combination of keys (often beginning with the Alt, Ctrl, or Shift keys) to execute a menu item.
- Complex applications, such as Microsoft Word or Adobe Photoshop, are often MDI applications that allow many documents to be opened at once. The application window of an MDI program is called the parent window and each window within the application is called a child window.

Key Terms

child window—The window within the parent window of an MDI program.

component—An object (that is, an instance of a class) that is added to a form to provide the form with functionality.

control—A visible component.

delegate—An instance of the `Delegate` class, which is a data structure that refers to either (1) a static method or (2) a class instance and an instance method of that class.

dialog form—A modal form that returns standard results using the `DialogResult` property.

event—A message announcing that a user action has occurred.

event driven—The characteristic of an application whereby events control the application's functionality.

form—A window or dialog box that makes up an application's graphical user interface.

`Margin` **property**—A property of a control that determines the amount of space, in pixels, reserved around a control when calculating its automatic position in a `FlowLayoutPanel`.

modal form—A form that must be closed or hidden before the user can continue working with the application.

modeless form—A form that is not modal.

`MultiCastDelegate`—A class that defines a data structure that can contain references to several different methods.

multiple-document-interface (MDI) application—An application that allows many documents to be opened at once.

`Padding` **property**—A property of a container control that determines the amount of space, in pixels, reserved along the inside of containers.

parent menu—A menu item that is a menu for other menu items.

parent window—The application window of an MDI program.

shortcut key—A key or combination of keys that execute a menu item.

single-document-interface (SDI) application—An application that supports only one open window or document at a time.

submenu—A menu contained within another menu item.

Review Questions

1. A control and a component are essentially the same thing.
   a. True
   b. False
2. A dialog form is a modal form.
   a. True
   b. False
3. The Ctrl key must be used as a shortcut key for a top-level menu item.
   a. True
   b. False
4. It is easier to use the `ShortcutKeys` property to set a shortcut key for a top-level menu item.
   a. True
   b. False
5. SDI stands for Secure Document Interface.
   a. True
   b. False
6. The `Dispose` method is called when a form is closed.
   a. True
   b. False
7. The Class Name list used for event handling is accessible in Form Designer.
   a. True
   b. False
8. The `CenterScreen` value of a form's `StartPosition` attribute requires an x and y value.
   a. True
   b. False
9. The `Padding` property controls the amount of space reserved around a control.
   a. True
   b. False
10. A `TableLayoutPanel` control can be nested within another `TableLayoutPanel` control.
    a. True
    b. False
11. Which .NET Framework namespace is used primarily for GUIs?
    a. `System.Web.UI`
    b. `System.IO`
    c. `System.Windows.Forms`
    d. `System.Data`
12. Which symbol is used with preprocessor directives?
    a. `@`
    b. `&`
    c. `#`
    d. `^`

13. Which method is called within the constructor of a form?
    a. `InitializeComponent`
    b. `SuspendLayout`
    c. `ResumeLayout`
    d. `Close`
14. Which is not a value of the `DialogResult` enumeration?
    a. Abort
    b. Cancel
    c. Continue
    d. Yes
15. Which of the following `MdiLayout` enumeration values causes open documents to overlap?
    a. `ArrangeIcons`
    b. `TileHorizontal`
    c. `TileVertical`
    d. `Cascade`
16. Which of the following is not an MDI form property?
    a. `ActiveMdiChild`
    b. `LayoutMdi`
    c. `MdiChildActivate`
    d. `MdiParent`
17. Which of the following is an MDI form method?
    a. `ActiveMdiChild`
    b. `LayoutMdi`
    c. `MdiChildActivate`
    d. `MdiParent`
18. Which of the following exception classes is usually involved with file processing?
    a. `NullReferenceException`
    b. `OverflowException`
    c. `ApplicationException`
    d. `IOException`
19. Which class is used primarily for event handling?
    a. `Attribute`
    b. `Array`
    c. `MulticastDelegate`
    d. `Object`
20. Which method is used to place controls within a container?
    a. `Add`
    b. `InitializeComponent`
    c. `ResumeLayout`
    d. `Dispose`

Computer Exercises

When creating user interfaces, follow all conventions for an attractive, organized form with meaningful names for controls. Use named constants when appropriate, and use format specifiers for output requiring special formatting.

Your instructor may also request that you use TOE charts, pseudocode, flow-charts, and/or UML diagrams as planning aids.

1. In this exercise, you create a user interface and carefully document the program code generated by the Visual Basic IDE. The modified application will add two numbers.
   a. Create a new Windows application called **Addition Solution** with a blank form named `MainForm`. Save the solution in the \VbReloadedAdvanced\Chap06\ folder.
   b. Before adding controls to the form, copy all the code in the file MainForm.Designer.vb and paste it in a text document using a text editor or word processor. Save the text document with the filename **Addition Solution Code**.
   c. Add two labels and two text boxes for numbers that are to be added. After each individual control is added and its properties are set, copy to the text document in sequence the new code generated by Visual Basic in MainForm.Designer.vb.
   d. Add an output label, a Calculate button, and an Exit button. As you add each control and set its properties, copy in sequence to the text document the new code generated by Visual Basic.
   e. Create the event procedures for the Calculate button and the Exit button. As you complete each procedure, copy in sequence the new code generated by Visual Basic to the text document.
   f. Finally, copy the complete program code to the text document.
   g. Save and test the application. Save and print the text document.

2. In this exercise, you modify the Addition Solution you created in Exercise 1. The modified application will use the `StartPosition` property and the `AutoScroll` property.
   a. Create a new project and save it as **Addition Solution Revised** in the \VbReloadedAdvanced\Chap06\ folder. Add the user interface that you created in Exercise 1 to this new project.
   b. Set the `StartPosition` property for the form to `Manual` and then set the `Location` property to a reasonable value.
   c. Set the `AutoScroll` property for the form to `True`.
   d. Save the solution, test the application, and modify as necessary.

3. In this exercise, you modify the Skate-Away Sales application you viewed in Chapter 1. The modified application will utilize a table layout.
   a. Use Windows to make a copy of the Figure 01.27 Skate-Away Sales Solution folder in the \VbReloadedAdvanced\Chap01\ folder. Paste the copy in the \VbReloadedAdvanced\Chap06\ folder and rename it **Skate-Away Solution with Table Layout**.
   b. Open the Skate-Away Solution (Skate-Away Solution.sln) file contained in the \VbReloadedAdvanced\Chap05\Skate-Away Solution With Table Layout folder.
   c. Modify the form so that all controls are located in a `TableLayoutPanel` control. Use the `RowSpan` and `ColumnSpan` properties of the `TableLayoutPanel` control when necessary to improve the form's appearance.
   d. Save the solution, test the application, and modify as necessary.

4. In this exercise, you modify the Item Prices application you viewed in Chapter 2. The modified application will allow it to employ structured exception handling.
   a. Use Windows to make a copy of the Figure 02.15 Item Prices Solution folder in the \VbReloadedAdvanced\Chap02\ folder. Paste the copy in

the \VbReloadedAdvanced\Chap06\ folder and rename it **Item Prices Solution with Flow Layout**.

b. Open the Item Prices Solution (Item Prices Solution.sln) file contained in the \VbReloadedAdvanced\Chap06\ Item Prices Solution with Flow Layout folder.
c. Modify the user interface to include a `FlowPanelLayout` control.
d. Thoroughly test the application using different form sizes. Use the `Margin` and `Padding` properties to improve the form's appearance.
e. Save the solution, test the application, and modify as necessary.

5. In this exercise, you modify the Shapes application you viewed in Chapter 3. The modified application will utilize the `TabControl` control.
   a. Use Windows to make a copy of the Figure 03.12-14 Shapes Solution folder in the \VbReloadedAdvanced\Chap03\ folder. Paste the copy in the \VbReloadedAdvanced\Chap06\ folder and rename it **Shapes Solution with Tabbed Pages**.
   b. Open the Shapes Solution (Shapes Solution.sln) file contained in the \VbReloadedAdvanced\Chap06\ Shapes Solution with Tabbed Pages folder.
   c. Modify the program code so that the first tabbed page collects the side measurement of the square. The second tabbed page should display the area of the square, and the third tabbed page should display the perimeter of the square.
   d. Each tabbed page should have an Exit button. However, no Display buttons are needed. The output tabbed pages should display the result when selected.
   e. The input tabbed page should have a Reset button that clears the measurement text field and places the cursor in that text field.
   f. Save the solution, test the application, and modify as necessary.

6. In this exercise, you modify the Friends application you viewed in Chapter 2. The modified application will include a menu.
   a. Use Windows to make a copy of the Figure 02.71 Friends Solution folder in the \VbReloadedAdvanced\Chap02\ folder. Paste the copy in the \VbReloadedAdvanced\Chap06\ folder and rename it **Friends Solution with Menu**.
   b. Open the Friends Solution (Friends Solution.sln) file contained in the \VbReloadedAdvanced\Chap06\ Friends Solution with Menu folder.
   c. Add a menu to the user interface. The top-level menu should have the following menu items: File and Edit.
   d. The File menu item should have the following submenu items: New and Exit. The selection File, New should display the Name text box and Friends text area. The selection File, Exit should exit the application.
   e. The Edit menu item should have the following submenu items: Add and Remove. The selection Edit, Add should add a name to the friends list and the selection Edit, Remove should remove a name from the friends list.
   f. Save the solution, test the application, and modify as necessary.

7. In this exercise, you modify the Human Resources application you viewed in Chapter 3. The modified application will include an MDI form.
   a. Use Windows to make a copy of the Figure 03.22-24 Human Resources Solution folder in the \VbReloadedAdvanced\Chap03\ folder. Paste the copy in the \VbReloadedAdvanced\Chap06\ folder and rename it **Human Resources Solution with MDI**.
   b. Open the Human Resources Solution (Human Resources Solution.sln) file contained in the \VbReloadedAdvanced\Chap05\Human Resources Solution with MDI folder.

c. Create an MDI form that uses a File, New menu selection to produce an MDI child form identical to the one in Figure 3.28. This MDI child form should have a title bar that displays “Person n” where “n” is the total number of child forms opened.
d. Add a Close menu item to the File menu item that closes the active child form. Add an Exit menu item that exits the application.
e. Save the solution, test the application, and modify as necessary.

Case Projects

Type-It Text Editor

Create a simple text editor application called Type-It. Refer to the Notepad (or similar) text editor and create much of the same functionality, including the following menu selections: (1) File, Save As; (2) Edit, Select All; and (3) Format, Font.

Tic-Tac-Toe

Create an application that allows the user to play Tic-Tac-Toe. Use an interface with a 3 × 3 `TableLayoutPanel` control. Clicking on a text box in each cell should alternatively create an X or an O in that text box. The game should automatically determine when there is a winner. Make the `TableLayoutPanel` and text boxes resize automatically to fit within the form whenever it is resized.

OO Media Collection

Create an object-oriented application that creates objects of type Book, DVD, and Periodical. The user interface should include a `TabControl` control, with one tabbed page for each media type. Each tabbed page should collect the vital information about each type. A button on each tabbed page should take the information, create the object, and write the object data to a sequential file.

CHAPTER

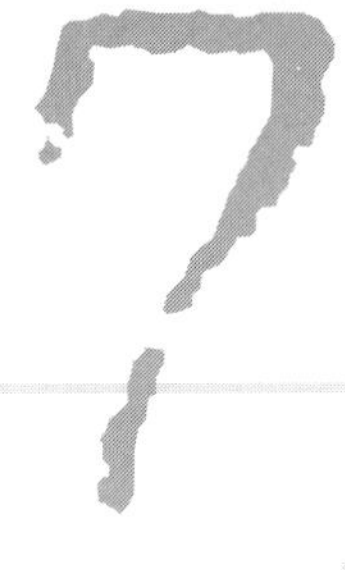

Relational Databases and SQL

After studying Chapter 7, you should be able to:

- Discuss the structure of a client/server system
- Explain how data are stored in a relational database
- Create queries using the structured query language (SQL)
- Execute queries on a database using Microsoft Access and Microsoft SQL Server
- Create a database using Microsoft SQL Server

The first six chapters of this text have focused on two major aspects of application development: (1) the user interface and (2) application logic. The user interface (covered primarily in Chapters 1 and 6) consists of one or more forms containing objects such as labels, textboxes, buttons, and menus. The application logic (covered mostly in Chapters 2 through 5) involves the use of variables, arrays, programming structures (selection and repetition), object-oriented design, and exception handling to solve a particular problem. The third and arguably the most critical component of application development is data, which was briefly addressed at the end of Chapter 2 (concerning sequential files). You'll learn more about data in this chapter.

Specifically, this chapter provides the background you need to use a very important Microsoft technology known as ADO.NET. Perhaps you have already heard of ADO and ADO.NET and wondered what it's all about. Basically, it's all about data. So before you can begin working with ADO or ADO.NET, you must acquire a solid understanding of data and databases. Your study of the details of ADO.NET will begin in Chapter 8.

Note that to work with the examples and complete the exercises in this chapter and Chapter 8, you will need to use Microsoft Access and Microsoft SQL Server Express database software. Your institution or organization probably has Microsoft Access software already available, and Microsoft SQL Server Express can be downloaded for free, as explained later in this chapter.

OVERVIEW OF DATA, SYSTEMS, AND ADO.NET

Before you can create Visual Basic applications that make extensive use of data, you need a thorough understanding of how data are usually organized and how information systems interact with data. This section provides a brief overview of these important topics.

Data

The word "**data**" is actually the plural of the word "**datum**," which refers to a single item of factual knowledge obtained from measurement or observation. A datum may be the fact that a given employee in a certain company earns a certain wage for each hour worked. For example, Employee 101 may earn $15.00 per hour. This fact is a datum. Data, as the plural of datum, is thus an entire collection of factual knowledge. Thus, employee wage data could be the collection of all values of hourly wages for all employees in a company. (For example, Employee 101 makes $15.00 per hour, Employee 102 makes $20.00 per hour, and so on.) The Human Resources Department could therefore provide these data to the Payroll Department in list form, as shown in Table 7.1.

Employee number	Hourly wage
101	15.00
102	20.00
103	17.50
104	10.50
...	...

TABLE 7.1 An employee wage data table

You could describe the data in Table 7.1 as employee wage data because each datum provides the employee number and his/her hourly wage. Another kind of payroll data would be the hours worked by each employee during a given week and would look like the table in Table 7.2. These data could be described as employee hours data, and the Production Department could provide this table of values to the Payroll Department at the end of each week.

Employee number	Weekly hours (w/e 4/5/2008)
101	40.0
102	35.0
103	37.5
104	50.0
...	...

TABLE 7.2 An employee hours data table

Of course, data such as these are almost always stored in some kind of computer file for use by a computer-based payroll application. (Such an application might be developed by a programmer like you using Visual Basic 2005.) In the case of computer-based applications, the data tables previously mentioned would be given names more suitable for computer processing, such as employee_wage and employee_hours.

Information

Information is something different from data. Data represents knowledge obtained from measurement or observation, while **information** represents knowledge obtained by processing data. For example, a table of gross weekly pay for all employees represents information because gross weekly pay is determined by processing employee wage and employee hours data, as shown in Table 7.3. (Note that Employee 104 gets time and a half for hours over 40.) The Payroll Department could take written lists of employee wages and employee hours and calculate gross weekly pay by hand, or a computer application could use the computer files that contain employee_wage data and employee_hours data to produce information that could be called employee_gross_pay.

Employee number	Hourly wage	Weekly hours (w/e 4/5/2008)	Gross weekly pay
101	15.00	40.0	600.00
102	20.00	35.0	700.00
103	17.50	37.5	656.25
104	10.50	50.0	577.50
...	...	...	...

TABLE 7.3 An employee gross pay information table

Data Files

In Chapter 2, you reviewed how to read data from and write data to sequential data files using Visual Basic. In the example above, the employee wage and employee hours data could be stored in two separate sequential data files named employee_wage.txt and employee_hours.txt. A Payroll application could read the data from these files and produce a sequential file called employee_gross_pay.txt. Figure 7.1 shows the contents of these files in Notepad.

(a) Employee wage data

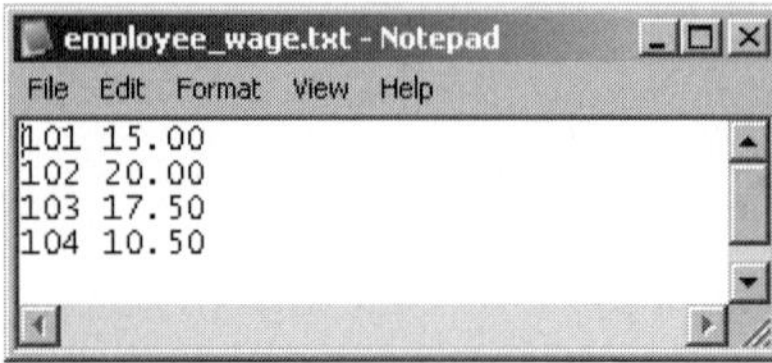

(b) Employee hours data

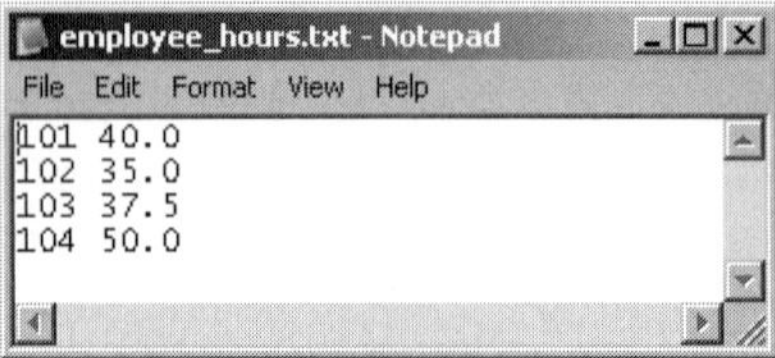

(c) Employee gross pay data

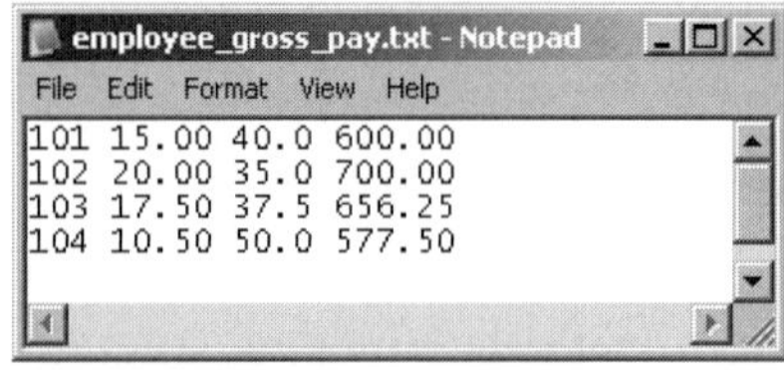

FIGURE 7.1 Files used by a Payroll application

You also learned in Chapter 2 that files such as these contain **records** (a complete set of data, such as an employee_wage record for Employee 101) and each record contains **fields** (a space reserved for a datum, such as a wage field for the employee_wage table). The data in files such as employee_wage.txt are usually delimited (separated) by special characters such as a space or a comma. Individual files such as employee_wage.txt and employee_gross_pay.txt are sometimes called **flat files** because they contain no other structure than simple records and fields that could be written on a flat (two-dimensional) piece of paper.

Databases and Database Management Systems

A collection of files that store data, such as those in Figure 7.1, can be called a data store. In general, a **data store** is any organized collection of data. On the other hand, a data store that has a special structure for facilitating computerized storage, retrieval, and manipulation of the data is called a **database**. Most data in modern, large-scale computer applications are stored not in simple flat file data stores, but in databases. The software used to create and access a database is called a **database management system** (DBMS).

The most popular type of database in use today is the **relational database**, which is a database that follows the relational model. The **relational model** is simply a way of organizing data in related tables based on strict mathematical principles. A relational database is created and managed by a **relational database management system** (RDBMS). More information about relational databases and RDBMSs will be provided later in this chapter. Now that you have a very brief background in data and databases, you are ready to get an overview of client/server systems and ADO.NET.

Client/Server Systems

In Chapter 2, you created Visual Basic applications that accessed sequential data files using the methods `My.Computer.FileSystem.WriteAllText` and `My.Computer.FileSystem.ReadAllText`. This approach is very simple because the data are stored in flat files that reside on the same computer as the Visual Basic application file. In the real world, the application and the database may be logically (and physically) separated in what is called a client/server system. A **client/server system** is a system in which software is distributed across networked hardware components consisting of clients that send requests for services, and a server that provides responses to the requests.

In the simplest form of a client/server system there are three hardware components: (1) one or more clients, (2) a network, and (3) a server, as shown in Figure 7.2. The clients store the application and the server stores the database, while the network provides communication capabilities between clients and server. (A server that stores the database and DBMS is called a **database server**.) The client is usually a PC or workstation operated by individual users while the server may be a more powerful PC (with extra memory, processing speed, and secondary storage), a midrange computer, or a mainframe that is managed by network and database administrators. Midrange computers and mainframes are capable of holding large databases and quickly processing data requests from many clients.

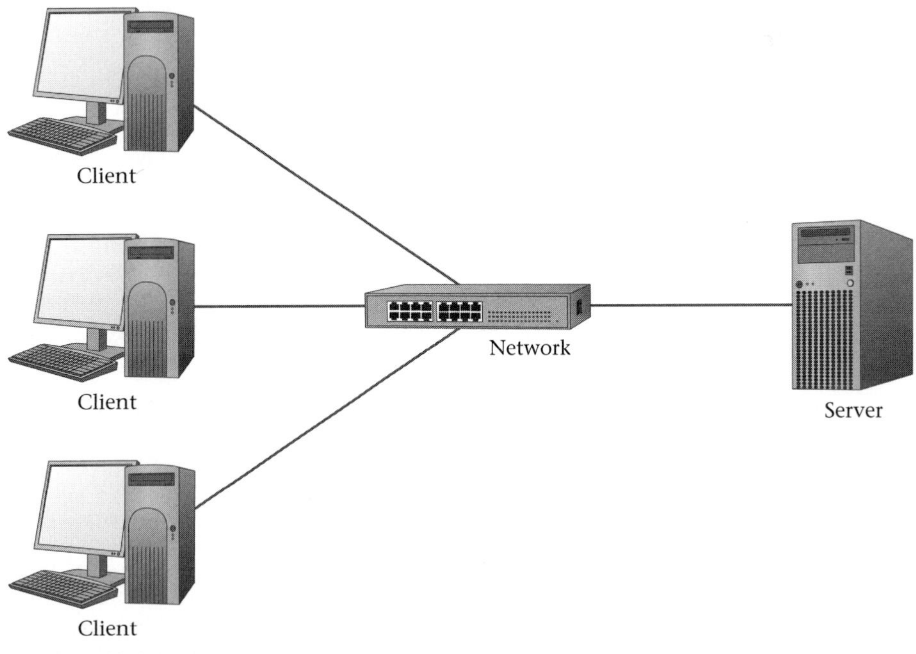

FIGURE 7.2 A simple client/server system

Of course, hardware without software is useless. A client/server system has software components as well. The server typically has two kinds of software components: (1) the network operating system (such as Windows Server 2003), which enables the transfer of data between client and server, and (2) the DBMS (such as Windows SQL Server, DB2, or Oracle), which processes requests from the clients for storage and retrieval of data to and from the database.

The client also has two basic kinds of software components: (1) application software, such as that provided by packaged software (such as Microsoft Office) or custom-built software (such as software you create using Visual Basic 2005), and (2) a data access application programming interface (API). A **data access application programming interface (API)** is software that provides an interface (that is, a means of interaction) between the application and the database. The interaction between these software components in a client/server system is shown in Figure 7.3. The cloud symbols in Figure 7.3 represent software elements of the system.

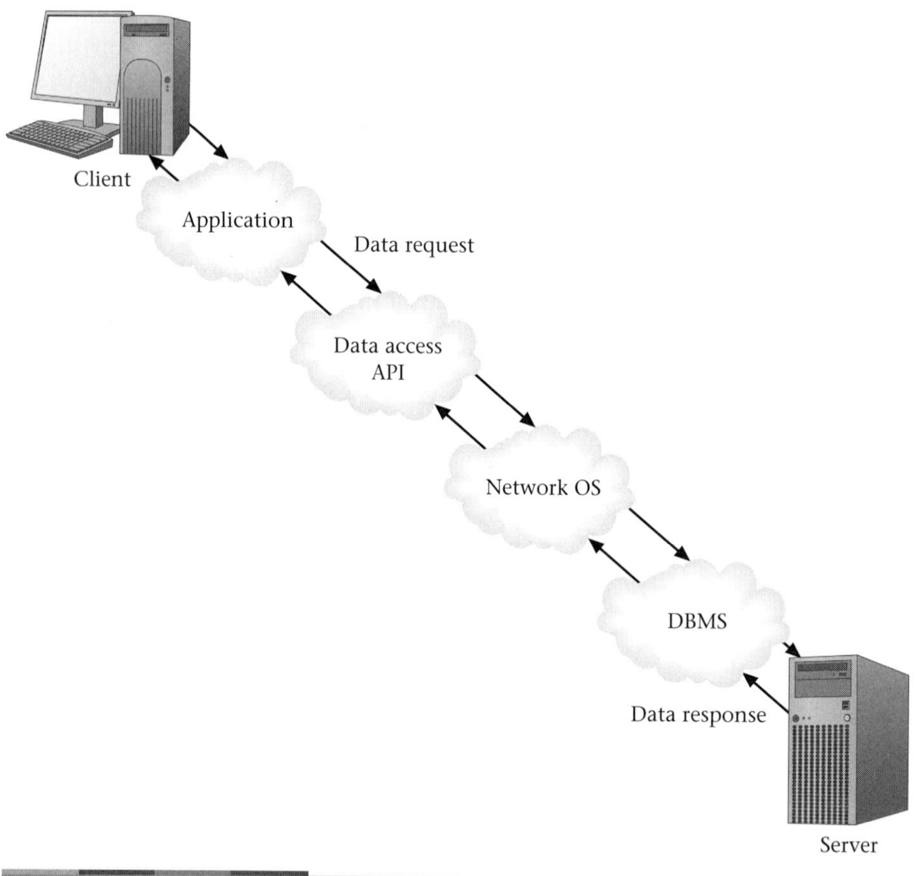

FIGURE 7.3 Software components in a client/server system

ADO and ADO.NET

As mentioned earlier, the focus of the next chapter (Chapter 8) is ADO.NET. But a brief overview of ADO.NET is helpful now. What is ADO.NET? Simply put, ADO.NET is the data access API illustrated in Figure 7.3. It provides a way of communicating with databases. Before ADO.NET (released in 2002) existed, there was ADO (released in 1996). ADO stands for **ActiveX Data Objects**, which is a Microsoft technology for accessing data from a wide variety of data stores in both Windows applications and Web applications.

ADO.NET, part of the .NET Framework, is an enhanced version of ADO designed specifically for Microsoft .NET applications. The advantages of ADO.NET over ADO include (1) the ability to work with data represented in XML (Extensible Markup Language, to be discussed later in this text), (2) integration with the rest of the Microsoft .NET Framework, and (3) greatly increased control and flexibility in working with all types of data sources.

Before you can use ADO.NET, you have to understand databases. The next several sections provide you with a basic understanding of how databases are created and organized. Keep in mind that entire books are written about database technology. The discussion in this chapter will be brief, but you can always learn more by consulting books specifically devoted to the topic.

THE RELATIONAL DATABASE MODEL

So far in this chapter, you have heard much about databases. However, this subject may be fairly new to you. Databases are by far the most popular way of storing data, and the relational database model is by far the most popular structure for databases. This section will discuss the basics of relational databases and use an example called the Northwind Traders database. The Northwind Traders database (filename northwind.mdb) is a standard example of a fairly complex relational database that is included with the Microsoft Access relational database management system (RDBMS). You may be familiar with Microsoft Access, which will be used in this section to discuss relational databases in general. Additionally, the more advanced Microsoft SQL Server 2005 Express Edition will be used later in this chapter. You will probably encounter Access and SQL Server (or similar products) in your future career. Figure 7.4 explains how to open an existing Microsoft Access database.

HOW TO...

Open a Microsoft Access Database

1. Verify that you have Microsoft Access installed on your computer.
2. Locate the file named northwind.mdb on your computer (click Start and then click Search if necessary), right-click the file icon for northwind.mdb and click Open (or double-click the northwind.mdb file icon). If you cannot locate the file named northwind.mdb on your computer, you will need to install it from Microsoft Access. To install the sample database feature, open Help menu, point to Sample Databases and then click Northwind Sample Database. Click Yes in the dialog box that asks if you would like to install the feature.
3. Click the Open button on the Security Warning dialog box.
4. Click OK on the Northwind Traders title screen.
5. Click the Display Database Window button on the Main Switchboard dialog box.

FIGURE 7.4 How to open a Microsoft Access database

Performing the steps in Figure 7.4 for the Northwind database produces the view shown in Figure 7.5. (You may see a table other than Employees highlighted.) Notice that the Tables object is highlighted in the Objects list in the database window. In the work area of the database window you will see three options listed for creating tables and a list of the existing tables in the Northwind database, beginning with Categories and ending with Suppliers.

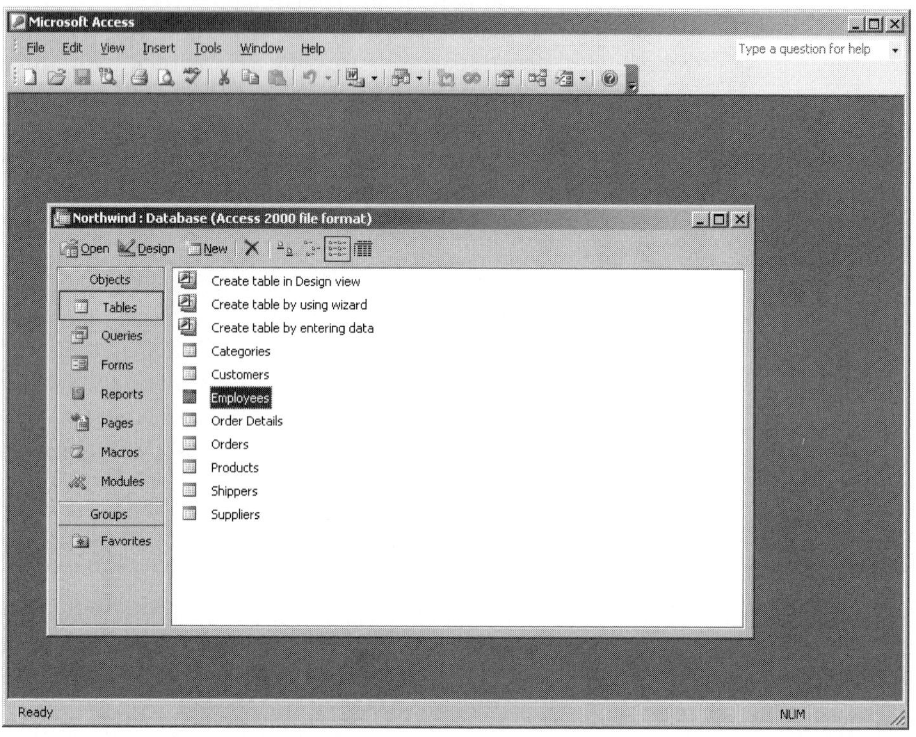

FIGURE 7.5 Microsoft Access database window for the Northwind database

Tables

Data in a relational database are stored in tables; a table is a structure consisting of rows and columns. Each individual data item (datum) is placed in one cell of the table (an intersection of a row and a column). Each row in a table represents a data record and each column in a table represents a data field. Furthermore, a record conceptually represents a real-world entity and each field conceptually represents an attribute or characteristic of that entity. Figure 7.6 shows the contents of the Employees table.

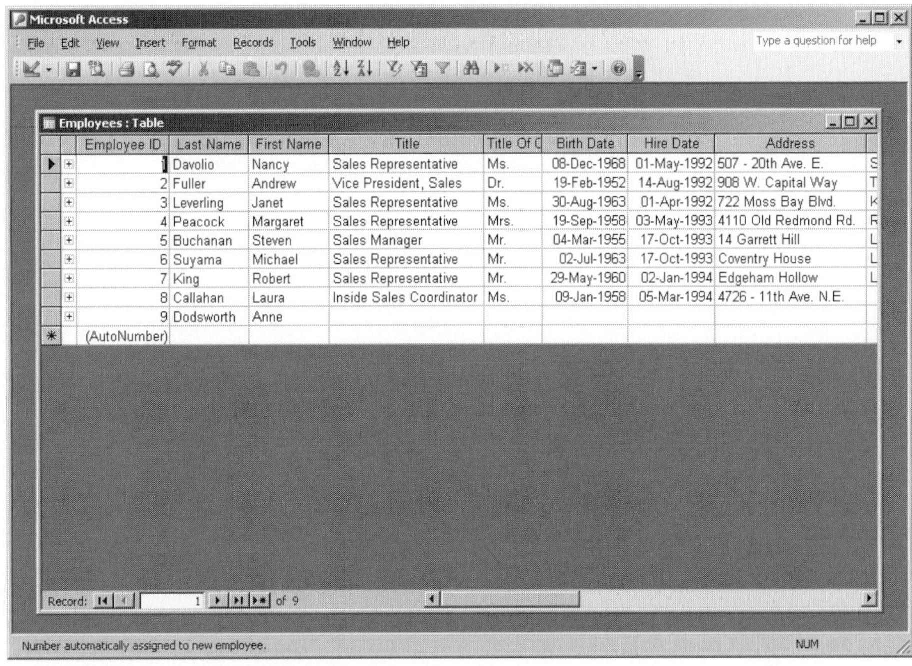

Employee ID	Last Name	First Name	Title	Title Of C	Birth Date	Hire Date	Address	
1	Davolio	Nancy	Sales Representative	Ms.	08-Dec-1968	01-May-1992	507 - 20th Ave. E.	S
2	Fuller	Andrew	Vice President, Sales	Dr.	19-Feb-1952	14-Aug-1992	908 W. Capital Way	T
3	Leverling	Janet	Sales Representative	Ms.	30-Aug-1963	01-Apr-1992	722 Moss Bay Blvd.	K
4	Peacock	Margaret	Sales Representative	Mrs.	19-Sep-1958	03-May-1993	4110 Old Redmond Rd.	R
5	Buchanan	Steven	Sales Manager	Mr.	04-Mar-1955	17-Oct-1993	14 Garrett Hill	L
6	Suyama	Michael	Sales Representative	Mr.	02-Jul-1963	17-Oct-1993	Coventry House	L
7	King	Robert	Sales Representative	Mr.	29-May-1960	02-Jan-1994	Edgeham Hollow	L
8	Callahan	Laura	Inside Sales Coordinator	Ms.	09-Jan-1958	05-Mar-1994	4726 - 11th Ave. N.E.	
9	Dodsworth	Anne						
(AutoNumber)								

FIGURE 7.6 Contents of the Employees table in the Northwind database

Notice in Figure 7.6 that eight columns (fields) in the Employees table are shown. (Several other columns are not shown.) There are also nine rows (records) in the Employees table. Thus, each record represents an individual employee of Northwind Traders and each field represents an attribute of an employee.

Primary Keys

It's important that each record in a table is uniquely identified. For example, if an employee is supposed to receive a raise, it's important that the right employee is selected in the database. If two employees in a table have the same name, confusion would arise about which is which. Therefore, the Employees table needs a field called Employee ID that contains a unique number for each record.

To ensure that each record is unique, each table in a database is usually assigned a primary key. A **primary key** is one or more fields in a database table that, taken in combination, form a unique value and thus uniquely identify a record. For example, in the Employees table, the Employee ID field is the primary key. No two employees can have the same ID. Since Employee ID is the primary key, another employee with Employee ID = 9 cannot be entered. (The RDBMS enforces this rule, preventing someone from entering an existing Employee ID.)

Relationships

The power of a relational database lies in the relationships between tables. Each table in a relational database should represent only one kind of entity. (For example, an employee is an entity, so there is an Employees table.) At the same time, each table should contain only the fields that are absolutely essential for describing that entity. For example, the Employees table in Figure 7.6 contains only the fields required to completely describe an employee. All the important entities at Northwind Traders require tables in which to store their data. Thus, the database needs a table that describes orders and another table that describes customers. However, these tables are related to each other in that employees are responsible for orders and customers place orders. In the Northwind database, there are many tables and relationships between these tables, as shown in the relationships window of Access in Figure 7.7. (You can open the Relationships window by clicking the Relationships icon in the Database toolbar.) Don't worry if Figure 7.7 looks a little imposing—you will be focusing on only a small number of the relationships at a time.

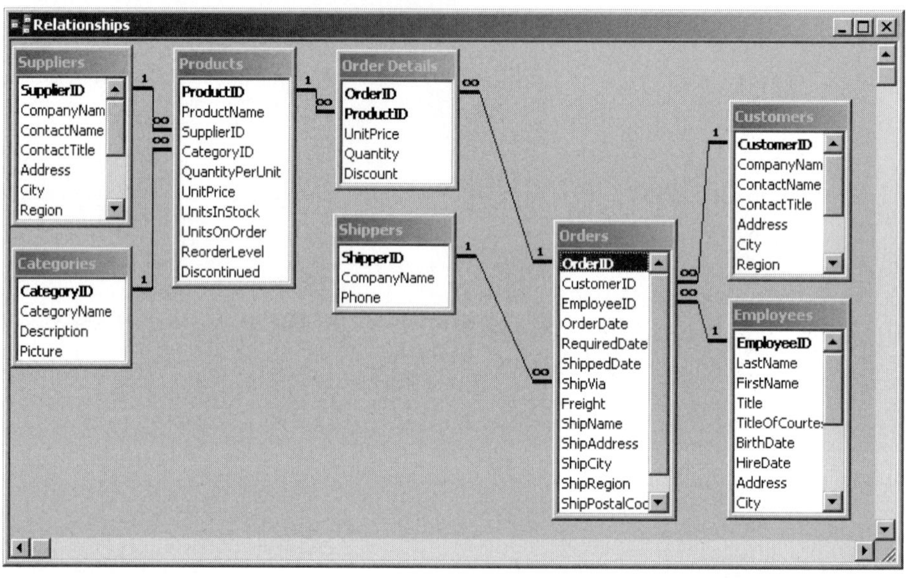

FIGURE 7.7 Relationships window of the Northwind database

The diagram in Figure 7.7, known as an **entity-relationship diagram (ERD)**, is a pictorial representation of the entities (tables), the entity attributes (fields), and the relationships between the entities in a relational database. To get a sense of how these relationships work, first focus only on the relationships among the Employees, Orders, and Customers tables in Figure 7.7. (These are on the right-hand side; you can ignore all other relationships for now.) Note the lines connecting these tables. These lines indicate that the tables are related. A relationship between two tables in an RDBMS is created by including a foreign key within a table. A **foreign key** is a primary key of one table included as a field of another table. For example, Figure 7.7 shows the Employees table with EmployeeID as its primary key (in bold). The Orders table also has a primary key called OrderID that uniquely identifies each order. However, in the real world of Northwind Traders, each employee is responsible for one or more orders, so the EmployeeID field is deliberately included in the Orders table as a foreign key. This ensures that each order is associated with a particular employee. Figure 7.8 shows some sample data from the Orders table to illustrate this very important point.

Orders : Table

Order ID	Customer	Employee	Order Date	Required Date	Shipped Date	Ship Via
10248	Wilman Kala	Buchanan, Steven	04-Jul-1996	01-Aug-1996	16-Jul-1996	Federal Shipping
10249	Tradição Hipermercados	Suyama, Michael	05-Jul-1996	16-Aug-1996	10-Jul-1996	Speedy Express
10250	Hanari Carnes	Peacock, Margaret	08-Jul-1996	05-Aug-1996	12-Jul-1996	United Package
10251	Victuailles en stock	Leverling, Janet	08-Jul-1996	05-Aug-1996	15-Jul-1996	Speedy Express
10252	Suprêmes délices	Peacock, Margaret	09-Jul-1996	06-Aug-1996	11-Jul-1996	United Package
10253	Hanari Carnes	Leverling, Janet	10-Jul-1996	24-Jul-1996	16-Jul-1996	United Package
10254	Chop-suey Chinese	Buchanan, Steven	11-Jul-1996	08-Aug-1996	23-Jul-1996	United Package
10255	Richter Supermarkt	Dodsworth, Anne	12-Jul-1996	09-Aug-1996	15-Jul-1996	Federal Shipping
10256	Wellington Importadora	Leverling, Janet	15-Jul-1996	12-Aug-1996	17-Jul-1996	United Package
10257	HILARIÓN-Abastos	Peacock, Margaret	16-Jul-1996	13-Aug-1996	22-Jul-1996	Federal Shipping
10258	Ernst Handel	Davolio, Nancy	17-Jul-1996	14-Aug-1996	23-Jul-1996	Speedy Express
10259	Centro comercial Moctezuma	Peacock, Margaret	18-Jul-1996	15-Aug-1996	25-Jul-1996	Federal Shipping
10260	Old World Delicatessen	Peacock, Margaret	19-Jul-1996	16-Aug-1996	29-Jul-1996	Speedy Express
10261	Que Delícia	Peacock, Margaret	19-Jul-1996	16-Aug-1996	30-Jul-1996	United Package
10262	Rattlesnake Canyon Grocery	Callahan, Laura	22-Jul-1996	19-Aug-1996	25-Jul-1996	Federal Shipping
10263	Ernst Handel	Dodsworth, Anne	23-Jul-1996	20-Aug-1996	31-Jul-1996	Federal Shipping
10264	Folk och fä HB	Suyama, Michael	24-Jul-1996	21-Aug-1996	23-Aug-1996	Federal Shipping
10265	Blondel père et fils	Fuller, Andrew	25-Jul-1996	22-Aug-1996	12-Aug-1996	Speedy Express
10266	Wartian Herkku	Leverling, Janet	26-Jul-1996	06-Sep-1996	31-Jul-1996	Federal Shipping
10267	Frankenversand	Peacock, Margaret	29-Jul-1996	26-Aug-1996	06-Aug-1996	Speedy Express
10268	GROSELLA-Restaurante	Callahan, Laura	30-Jul-1996	27-Aug-1996	02-Aug-1996	Federal Shipping
10269	White Clover Markets	Buchanan, Steven	31-Jul-1996	14-Aug-1996	09-Aug-1996	Speedy Express
10270	Wartian Herkku	Davolio, Nancy	01-Aug-1996	29-Aug-1996	02-Aug-1996	Speedy Express

Record: 1 of 830

FIGURE 7.8 Orders table with the foreign key EmployeeID

The Orders table in Figure 7.8 shows the Order ID, the Customer, and the Employee for each order record. Referring back to Figure 7.7, you will see that the Orders table contains both CustomerID and EmployeeID as foreign keys, thus establishing a relationship among those tables. However, in Figure 7.8 you don't see the fields CustomerID and EmployeeID in the Orders table. Instead, you see Customer and Employee. This is because Microsoft Access has the ability to display the names instead of the IDs of customers and employees associated with particular orders to make the table easier to read. However, the Customer and Employee fields are actually based on the unique customer and employee IDs. Thus, the primary key for the Orders table is Order ID; CustomerID and EmployeeID are foreign keys.

The line connecting the Customer and Employee tables to the Order table in Figure 7.7 has the number 1 at one end (next to the Customers table and the Employees table) and a symbol for "many" (∞) at the other end (next to the Orders table). These symbols refer to the cardinality of a relationship. Cardinality is a big word for a simple concept—the number of elements in a set or group of elements. Thus, the **cardinality** of a relationship between Tables A and B in a database is the number of rows in Table B that can be associated with each row in Table A. For the Employees-Orders relationship, one (1) employee can have many (∞) orders. Also note the cardinality of the Customers-Orders relationship. Just as with the Employees-Orders relationship, the Customers-Orders relationship is one-to-many (one customer can have many orders with Northwind Traders).

Now that you have a basic understanding of a relational database, with its tables, rows, columns, and relationships, you will learn how to extract useful information using structured query language.

STRUCTURED QUERY LANGUAGE

The previous section introduced you to some of the basic concepts of relational databases and the Microsoft Access RDBMS. In this section, you will learn how to use **structured query language (SQL)**, which is a standard language used to store, retrieve, and manipulate data within a relational database. This section provides some details about SQL (pronounced either "S-Q-L" or "sequel") with examples drawn from the Northwind Traders database. Later, you will learn how to use SQL with the more sophisticated and powerful Microsoft SQL Server RDBMS.

TIP

By convention, the keywords in an SQL statement are written in all uppercase.

The SELECT Statement

A basic SQL `SELECT` statement is used to retrieve all rows (records) from a single table for certain specified columns (fields). In a database context, a **query** is a set of instructions for extracting data from a database, so the `SELECT` statement can also be called a query. Figure 7.9 demonstrates how to use the `SELECT` statement.

HOW TO...

Use the SELECT Statement

Syntax

`SELECT` *field1, field2, ...* `FROM` *tableName*

Example 1

```
SELECT * FROM Employees
```

Example 2

```
SELECT LastName, FirstName FROM Employees
```

FIGURE 7.9 How to use the `SELECT` statement

In Example 1 of Figure 7.9, the asterisk (*) is used as a wildcard character to represent all fields in the table. In Example 2, only the specific fields requested are listed. For the Northwind Traders database, the query in Example 2 would yield the result shown in Figure 7.10.

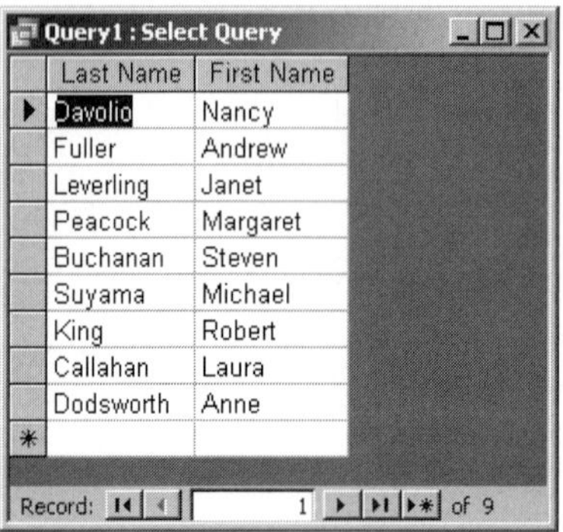

Query1 : Select Query

Last Name	First Name
Davolio	Nancy
Fuller	Andrew
Leverling	Janet
Peacock	Margaret
Buchanan	Steven
Suyama	Michael
King	Robert
Callahan	Laura
Dodsworth	Anne

Record: 1 of 9

FIGURE 7.10 Result of a `SELECT` statement

The WHERE Clause

Note that the `SELECT` statement returns all records in a table. In many cases, you want to retrieve only rows that meet certain selection criteria. This is accomplished using the optional `WHERE` clause in a `SELECT` statement, as shown in Figure 7.11.

HOW TO...

Use the WHERE Clause

Syntax

SELECT *field1*, *field2*, ... **FROM** *tableName* **WHERE** *criteria*

Example 1

```
SELECT OrderID, CustomerID, Freight FROM Orders WHERE Freight > 100
```

Example 2

```
SELECT * FROM Customers WHERE CompanyName LIKE 'B*'
```

FIGURE 7.11 How to use the **WHERE** clause

TIP

You can also use the wildcard character question mark (?) in pattern matching. The ? represents any single character, while the * represents any number of characters.

Example 1 in Figure 7.11 has a `WHERE` clause with the criteria `Freight > 100`, which uses the > operator. Example 2 has criteria that use the `LIKE` operator for pattern matching with the wildcard character `*`. Thus, the criteria `CompanyName LIKE 'B*'` will extract all company names that begin with the letter `B`. The result of applying the query in Example 2 of Figure 7.11 is shown in Figure 7.12.

Query2 : Select Query

Customer ID	Company Name	Contact Name	Contact Title	Address
BERGS	Berglunds snabbköp	Christina Berglund	Order Administrator	Berguvsvägen 8
BLAUS	Blauer See Delikatessen	Hanna Moos	Sales Representative	Forsterstr. 57
BLONP	Blondel père et fils	Frédérique Citeaux	Marketing Manager	24, place Kléber
BOLID	Bólido Comidas preparadas	Martín Sommer	Owner	C/ Araquil, 67
BONAP	Bon app'	Laurence Lebihan	Owner	12, rue des Bouchers
BOTTM	Bottom-Dollar Markets	Elizabeth Lincoln	Accounting Manager	23 Tsawassen Blvd.
BSBEV	B's Beverages	Victoria Ashworth	Sales Representative	Fauntleroy Circus

Record: 1 of 7

FIGURE 7.12 The result of a query with a **WHERE** clause

The ORDER BY Clause

Data extracted from a database often need to be sorted. Sorting is performed by using the optional `ORDER BY` clause in a query as shown in Figure 7.13.

HOW TO...

Use the ORDER BY Clause

Syntax

SELECT *field1*, *field2*, ...
FROM *tableName*
ORDER BY *fieldA*, *fieldB*,... [ASC | DESC]

Example 1

```
SELECT *
FROM Customers
WHERE CompanyName LIKE 'B*'
ORDER BY CompanyName
```

(Figure is continued on next page)

```
Example 2
SELECT OrderID, CustomerID, Freight
FROM Orders
WHERE Freight > 100
ORDER BY Freight DESC
```

FIGURE 7.13 How to use the `ORDER BY` clause

Note that the examples in Figure 7.13 have been formatted so that certain keywords begin a new line. This is done only for the sake of readability as SQL statements become longer. The sort order (ASC or DESC) is optional, with the default being ASC (ascending). The result of the query in Example 2 of Figure 7.13 is shown in Figure 7.14.

Query3 : Select Query

Order ID	Customer	Freight
10540	QUICK-Stop	$1,007.64
10372	Queen Cozinha	$890.78
11030	Save-a-lot Markets	$830.75
10691	QUICK-Stop	$810.05
10514	Ernst Handel	$789.95
11017	Ernst Handel	$754.26
10816	Great Lakes Food Market	$719.78
10479	Rattlesnake Canyon Grocery	$708.95
10983	Save-a-lot Markets	$657.54
11032	White Clover Markets	$606.19
10897	Hungry Owl All-Night Grocers	$603.54
10912	Hungry Owl All-Night Grocers	$580.91
10612	Save-a-lot Markets	$544.08
10847	Save-a-lot Markets	$487.57
10634	Folies gourmandes	$487.38
10633	Ernst Handel	$477.90
10430	Ernst Handel	$458.78
10841	Suprêmes délices	$424.30
10836	Ernst Handel	$411.88
10941	Save-a-lot Markets	$400.81

Record: 1 of 187

FIGURE 7.14 The result of a query with an `ORDER BY` clause

Merging Data with `INNER JOIN`

The previous examples of SQL statements involve only single tables. However, the real power of a relational database lies in the relationships among many data tables. Thus, it is often the case that information from a relational database must be derived from two or more tables. This is accomplished with the `INNER JOIN` operation in a `SELECT` statement, as shown in Figure 7.15.

HOW TO...

Use the INNER JOIN Operation

Syntax

```
SELECT field1, field2, ...
FROM table1
INNER JOIN table2
   ON table1.fieldA = table2.fieldB
```

Example 1

```
SELECT OrderID, CompanyName, OrderDate
FROM Customers
INNER JOIN Orders
   ON Customers.CustomerID = Orders.CustomerID
```

Example 2

```
SELECT CompanyName, ProductName, UnitPrice
FROM Products
INNER JOIN Suppliers
   ON Products.SupplierID = Suppliers.SupplierID
WHERE UnitPrice > 10
ORDER BY CompanyName, ProductName
```

FIGURE 7.15 How to use the INNER JOIN operation

The syntax of Figure 7.15 shows a SELECT statement beginning in the usual way where fields are selected. However, the fields *field1*, *field2*, ... can come from two different tables. The keyword FROM specifies one of the tables (called *table1*) and the keywords INNER JOIN specify a second table (called *table2*). These two tables must contain some of the same data in order for the query to work. It is the keyword ON that finds matching data within *fieldA* and *fieldB* of *table1* and *table2*, respectively. Note that to completely specify a field in a table, the notation *table1.fieldA* is used following the keyword ON. This way of specifying a field (using the table name and the field name) prevents confusion if fields in different tables have the same name. Therefore, if a data value in *table1.fieldA* (say in row x) matches a data value in *table2.fieldB* (say in row y), then the data values in *field1*, *field2*, ... from both *table1* (row x) or *table2* (row y) will be added as a single combined record to the query results.

The logic behind INNER JOIN can be a little confusing and is best explained with examples. In Example 1 of Figure 7.15, the fields OrderID, CompanyName, and OrderDate are selected from the tables Customers and Orders, but data will be displayed only from the rows where the CustomerID values in both tables match. Figure 7.16 shows some sample data from Customers, Orders, and the resulting query.

(a) Customers table

Customers : Table

Customer ID	Company Name	Contact Name	Contact Title	
ALFKI	Alfreds Futterkiste	Maria Anders	Sales Representative	Obe
ANATR	Ana Trujillo Emparedados y helados	Ana Trujillo	Owner	Avd
ANTON	Antonio Moreno Taquería	Antonio Moreno	Owner	Mat
AROUT	Around the Horn	Thomas Hardy	Sales Representative	120
BERGS	Berglunds snabbköp	Christina Berglund	Order Administrator	Berg
BLAUS	Blauer See Delikatessen	Hanna Moos	Sales Representative	Fors
BLONP	Blondel père et fils	Frédérique Citeaux	Marketing Manager	24,
BOLID	Bólido Comidas preparadas	Martín Sommer	Owner	C/ A
BONAP	Bon app'	Laurence Lebihan	Owner	12,
BOTTM	Bottom-Dollar Markets	Elizabeth Lincoln	Accounting Manager	23 T
BSBEV	B's Beverages	Victoria Ashworth	Sales Representative	Faul
CACTU	Cactus Comidas para llevar	Patricio Simpson	Sales Agent	Cerr
CENTC	Centro comercial Moctezuma	Francisco Chang	Marketing Manager	Sier
CHOPS	Chop-suey Chinese	Yang Wang	Owner	Hau
COMMI	Comércio Mineiro	Pedro Afonso	Sales Associate	Av.
CONSH	Consolidated Holdings	Elizabeth Brown	Sales Representative	Berk
DRACD	Drachenblut Delikatessen	Sven Ottlieb	Order Administrator	Wal
DUMON	Du monde entier	Janine Labrune	Owner	67,
EASTC	Eastern Connection	Ann Devon	Sales Agent	35 K
ERNSH	Ernst Handel	Roland Mendel	Sales Manager	Kirc
FAMIA	Familia Arquibaldo	Aria Cruz	Marketing Assistant	Rua

Record: 1 of 91

CustomerID = CHOPS in Customers table

(b) Orders table

Orders : Table

Order ID	Customer	Employee	Order Date	Required Date	Shipped Date	
10248	Wilman Kala	Buchanan, Steven	04-Jul-1996	01-Aug-1996	16-Jul-1996	Fe
10249	Tradição Hipermercados	Suyama, Michael	05-Jul-1996	16-Aug-1996	10-Jul-1996	Sp
10250	Hanari Carnes	Peacock, Margaret	08-Jul-1996	05-Aug-1996	12-Jul-1996	Un
10251	Victuailles en stock	Leverling, Janet	08-Jul-1996	05-Aug-1996	15-Jul-1996	Sp
10252	Suprêmes délices	Peacock, Margaret	09-Jul-1996	06-Aug-1996	11-Jul-1996	Un
10253	Hanari Carnes	Leverling, Janet	10-Jul-1996	24-Jul-1996	16-Jul-1996	Un
10254	Chop-suey Chinese	Buchanan, Steven	11-Jul-1996	08-Aug-1996	23-Jul-1996	Un
10255	Richter Supermarkt	Dodsworth, Anne	12-Jul-1996	09-Aug-1996	15-Jul-1996	Fe
10256	Wellington Importadora	Leverling, Janet	15-Jul-1996	12-Aug-1996	17-Jul-1996	Un
10257	HILARIÓN-Abastos	Peacock, Margaret	16-Jul-1996	13-Aug-1996	22-Jul-1996	Fe
10258	Ernst Handel	Davolio, Nancy	17-Jul-1996	14-Aug-1996	23-Jul-1996	Sp
10259	Centro comercial Moctezuma	Peacock, Margaret	18-Jul-1996	15-Aug-1996	25-Jul-1996	Fe
10260	Old World Delicatessen	Peacock, Margaret	19-Jul-1996	16-Aug-1996	29-Jul-1996	Sp
10261	Que Delícia	Peacock, Margaret	19-Jul-1996	16-Aug-1996	30-Jul-1996	Un
10262	Rattlesnake Canyon Grocery	Callahan, Laura	22-Jul-1996	19-Aug-1996	25-Jul-1996	Fe
10263	Ernst Handel	Dodsworth, Anne	23-Jul-1996	20-Aug-1996	31-Jul-1996	Fe
10264	Folk och fä HB	Suyama, Michael	24-Jul-1996	21-Aug-1996	23-Aug-1996	Fe
10265	Blondel père et fils	Fuller, Andrew	25-Jul-1996	22-Aug-1996	12-Aug-1996	Sp
10266	Wartian Herkku	Leverling, Janet	26-Jul-1996	06-Sep-1996	31-Jul-1996	Fe
10267	Frankenversand	Peacock, Margaret	29-Jul-1996	26-Aug-1996	06-Aug-1996	Sp
10268	GROSELLA-Restaurante	Callahan, Laura	30-Jul-1996	27-Aug-1996	02-Aug-1996	Fe

Record: 1 of 830

OrderID = 10254

CompanyID = CHOPS in Orders table

OrderDate = 11-Jul-1996

(c) Query joining Customers and Orders

Query4 : Select Query

Order ID	Company Name	Order Date
10259	Centro comercial Moctezuma	18-Jul-1996
10254	Chop-suey Chinese	11-Jul-1996
10370	Chop-suey Chinese	03-Dec-1996
10519	Chop-suey Chinese	28-Apr-1997
10731	Chop-suey Chinese	06-Nov-1997
10746	Chop-suey Chinese	19-Nov-1997
10966	Chop-suey Chinese	20-Mar-1998
11029	Chop-suey Chinese	16-Apr-1998
11041	Chop-suey Chinese	22-Apr-1998
10290	Comércio Mineiro	27-Aug-1996
10466	Comércio Mineiro	06-Mar-1997
10494	Comércio Mineiro	02-Apr-1997
10969	Comércio Mineiro	23-Mar-1998
11042	Comércio Mineiro	22-Apr-1998

Record: 1 of 830

OrderID 10254 displayed in `INNER JOIN`

FIGURE 7.16 Result of query from Example 1 in Figure 7.15

In Figure 7.16a you will find a record for CustomerID = CHOPS (in which company name is "Chop-suey Chinese"). Figure 7.16b also contains a record for CustomerID = CHOPS with an OrderDate of 11-Jul-1996. (Actually, the Northwind Traders database is configured to display the company name in the second column of the Orders table even though the table actually contains the CustomerID in that column.) Therefore, the query based on the `INNER JOIN` operation in Figure 7.16c displays the OrderID from Orders, the CompanyName from Customers, and the OrderDate from Orders for only the cases where the CustomerID matches in both Customers and Orders.

Example 2 in Figure 7.15 illustrates that after the `INNER JOIN` operations, you can also add a `WHERE` clause and an `ORDER BY` clause. The result of this query on the Northwind Traders database is shown in Figure 7.17. Only UnitPrice values greater than $10 are displayed and the results are sorted by ProductName within CompanyName.

UnitPrice > 10

Query5 : Select Query

Company Name	Product Name	Unit Price
Aux joyeux ecclésiastiques	Chartreuse verte	$18.00
Aux joyeux ecclésiastiques	Côte de Blaye	$263.50
Bigfoot Breweries	Laughing Lumberjack Lager	$14.00
Bigfoot Breweries	Sasquatch Ale	$14.00
Bigfoot Breweries	Steeleye Stout	$18.00
Cooperativa de Quesos 'Las Cabras'	Queso Cabrales	$21.00
Cooperativa de Quesos 'Las Cabras'	Queso Manchego La Pastora	$38.00
Escargots Nouveaux	Escargots de Bourgogne	$13.25
Exotic Liquids	Chai	$18.00
Exotic Liquids	Chang	$19.00
Forêts d'érables	Sirop d'érable	$28.50
Forêts d'érables	Tarte au sucre	$49.30
Formaggi Fortini s.r.l.	Gorgonzola Telino	$12.50
Formaggi Fortini s.r.l.	Mascarpone Fabioli	$32.00

Record: 1 of 63

FIGURE 7.17 Result of query from Example 2 in Figure 7.15

The `INSERT` Statement

Not only can you query a database using the `SELECT` statement, you can actually add (insert) new data into a database with the SQL `INSERT` statement, as shown in Figure 7.18.

HOW TO...

Use the `INSERT` Statement

Syntax

```
INSERT INTO tableName ( field1, field2, ... , fieldN )
   VALUES ( value1, value2, ... , valueN )
```

Example

```
INSERT INTO Shippers ( ShipperID, CompanyName, Phone )
   VALUES (4, 'Overnight Express', '(503) 555-1234')
```

FIGURE 7.18 How to use the `INSERT` statement

The syntax shown in Figure 7.18 specifies a *tableName* into which a record will be inserted. Following the *tableName* is a comma-separated list of field names (in parentheses) into which data values will be added. The keyword `VALUES` is followed by a comma-separated list of values (in parentheses) that will be placed in the corresponding fields. The value list must exactly match the field list in terms of the number of items in the lists and the data types of the values and fields. The example in Figure 7.18 places the integer 4, the string '(Overnight Express', and the string '(503) 555-9931' into a new record with fields ShipperID, CompanyName, and Phone. (Note that strings are enclosed in single quotes.) Figure 7.19 shows the contents of the Shippers table before and after the example query is executed.

(a) Shippers table before `INSERT`

Shippers : Table

Shipper ID	Company Name	Phone
1	Speedy Express	(503) 555-9831
2	United Package	(503) 555-3199
3	Federal Shipping	(503) 555-9931
utoNumber)		

Record: 1 of 3

(b) Shippers table after `INSERT`

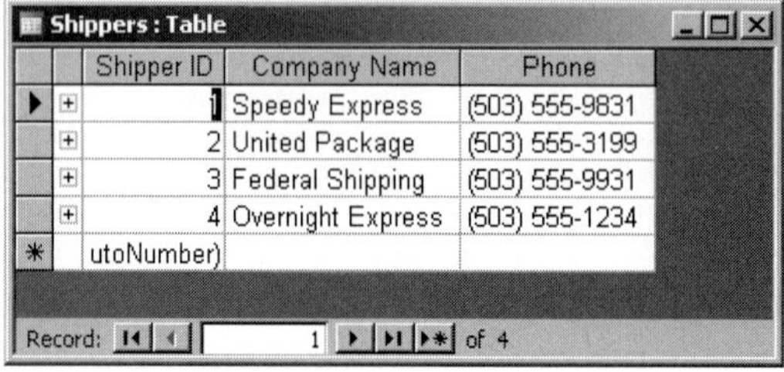

Shippers : Table

Shipper ID	Company Name	Phone
1	Speedy Express	(503) 555-9831
2	United Package	(503) 555-3199
3	Federal Shipping	(503) 555-9931
4	Overnight Express	(503) 555-1234
utoNumber)		

Record: 1 of 4

FIGURE 7.19 The Shippers table before and after an `INSERT` statement

The `UPDATE` Statement

As you've seen, the `INSERT` statement adds an entire record to a table. Another basic database operation is to change the contents of existing records. You can do this with the `UPDATE` statement as shown in Figure 7.20.

HOW TO...

Use the `UPDATE` Statement

Syntax

UPDATE *tableName*
  SET *fieldName1* = *value1*, *fieldName2* = *value2*, ... , *fieldNameN* = *valueN*
  WHERE *criteria*

Example 1

```
UPDATE Shippers
   SET Phone = '(501) 555-8720'
   WHERE CompanyName = 'Overnight Express'
```

Example 2

```
UPDATE Orders
   SET ShippedDate = #7/17/1996#
   WHERE ShippedDate = #7/16/1996# AND ShipVia = 3
```

FIGURE 7.20 How to use the `UPDATE` statement

The syntax for the `UPDATE` statement in Figure 7.20 first specifies a *tableName*. Then the `SET` keyword precedes a comma-separated list of fieldnames that are set equal to values. The all-important `WHERE` clause contains criteria to specify the rows in the table where values will be updated.

Example 1 in Figure 7.20 changes the value of the Phone field in the Shippers table where the CompanyName field contains the string 'Overnight Express'. Example 2 illustrates two new techniques: First, dates are specified in Access SQL statements with the format #mm/dd/yyyy#. Second, a `WHERE` clause can contain a compound statement using keywords `AND`, `OR`, and `NOT`. In the case of Example 2, all orders using Federal Shipping (ShipVia = 3) scheduled to be shipped on 7/16/1996 are delayed to 7/17/1996.

The DELETE Statement

Finally, the `DELETE` statement can be used to delete rows from a table, as Figure 7.21 shows.

HOW TO...

Use the DELETE Statement

Syntax

`DELETE FROM` *tableName* `WHERE` *criteria*

Example

```
DELETE FROM Shippers WHERE ShipperID = 4
```

FIGURE 7.21 How to use the `DELETE` statement

The syntax for the `DELETE` statement is very simple. It includes a *tableName* and *criteria*. The example in Figure 7.21 would delete the shipper Overnight Express that was inserted in Figure 7.18.

Executing SQL Statements in Microsoft Access

So far, this section has provided you with detailed information on how to formulate SQL statements that can be used in Microsoft Access to query a database. It has also shown you the results of executing many different kinds of SQL statements in Access. You should try to form your own SQL statements and experiment with the Northwind Traders database. Figure 7.22 details how to execute SQL statements in Access.

HOW TO...

Execute SQL Statements in Microsoft Access

1. Open the database and display the Database Window as explained in Figure 7.4.
2. To view the field names for a table, click Tables in the Objects list, click on a table in the work area, and click Design at the top of the Database Window.

(Figure is continued on next page)

3. To view the data in a table, click Tables in the Objects list, click on a table in the work area, and click Open at the top of the Database Window.
4. To create a new SQL query, click Queries in the Objects list, click New at the top of the Database Window, click Design View in the New Query dialog box, and click OK. Click Close in the Show Table dialog box, click View in the menu, and click SQL View.
5. Type the SQL code in the query text area and click the close button. Click Yes to save changes, type the name of the query in the Save As dialog box, and click OK.
6. To test the query, double-click the query in the Database Window.
7. To modify the query, click Queries in the Objects list and click the query in the Database Window. Click Design at the top of the Database Window.

FIGURE 7.22 How to execute SQL statements in Microsoft Access

Now that you understand the basics of relational databases and SQL, you are ready to explore how to use the more sophisticated and powerful Microsoft SQL Server 2005 relational database management system. This is the final step before embarking on an exploration of ADO.NET in Chapter 8.

USING MICROSOFT SQL SERVER 2005

In the previous section, you used Microsoft Access and SQL to perform operations on the Northwind Traders relational database (filename northwind.mdb). In this section, you will learn how to use Microsoft SQL Server 2005 to work with the same database. SQL Server, like Microsoft Access, is a relational database management system (RDBMS). Throughout the remainder of this text you will use the Microsoft SQL Server 2005 Express Edition, which is available for free download at *http://msdn.microsoft.com/vstudio/express/sql/* (see Figure 7.23). SQL Server is the type of RDBMS that you are more likely to encounter in large-scale, real-world systems. Figure 7.24 demonstrates how to download SQL Server Express and the sample database files used in this chapter.

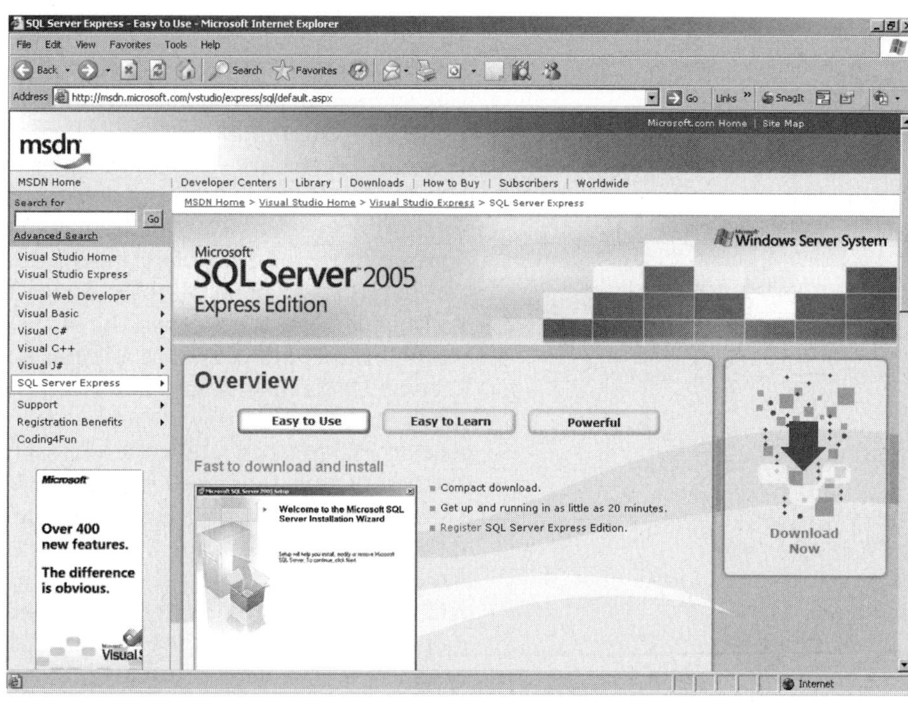

FIGURE 7.23 Microsoft SQL Server 2005 Express Edition Web page

HOW TO...

Download SQL Server Express and Sample Database Files

1. Using a Web browser, go to *http://msdn.microsoft.com/vstudio/express/sql/* (see Figure 7.23). Click the Download Now link to go to *http://msdn.microsoft.com/vstudio/express/sql/download/*.
2. The installation procedure assumes you have already installed Visual Studio 2005 with the .NET Framework 2.0, which you have been using throughout this text. It also assumes you have uninstalled any beta versions of SQL Server 2005, Visual Studio 2005, and the .NET Framework 2.0. If such is the case, click the Download link for Microsoft SQL Server 2005 Express Edition.
3. After downloading the SQLEXPR.EXE installation file, run the file to begin the installation process, completing the steps in the Installation Wizard.
4. Next, click the Download link for SQL Server Management Studio Express (the user interface for SQL Server Express). After downloading the file SQLServer2005_SSMSEE.msi, run it to begin the installation process, completing the steps in the Installation Wizard.
5. On the same download page (*http://msdn.microsoft.com/vstudio/express/sql/download/*), click the Download links for SQL Server 2005 Samples. On the new page that opens in the browser, click the link for AdventureWorksDB.msi to download the AdventureWorks sample database. After downloading the file, run it to begin the installation process, completing the steps in the Installation Wizard.

(Figure is continued on next page)

TIP

An SQL Server database consists of two files, such as MyData.mdf (which contains the data) and MyData_log.ldf (which contains a log of transactions or changes to the database). You can attach an existing database to SQL Server Express as follows: copy both files to your computer (server), right-click the Databases node in SQL Server Management Studio Express, click Attach, click Add in the Attach Databases dialog box, locate the .mdf file in the Locate Database Files dialog box, click OK, and then click OK again.

6. This chapter will work specifically with the Northwind Traders database, so there are some additional steps required to access this database. Beginning at *http://www.microsoft.com*, click the Downloads link on the left, then click All Downloads on the left. Then click the letter S near the top of the page and click the SQL Server link. Finally, click the Northwind and pubs Sample Databases link.
7. On the Northwind and pubs database download page, you can download scripts that will install these databases on your computer. Click the Download button and run the file SQL2000SampleDb.msi, following the instructions in the Installation Wizard.
8. To complete the installation of the sample databases (Northwind and pubs), run the scripts downloaded in Step 7 as follows: click Start, point to All Programs, and click Microsoft SQL Server 2000 Sample Database Scripts. Double-click the instnwnd.sql file in the window (launching SQL Server Management Studio Express) and click Connect in the Connect to Database Engine dialog box. Finally, click the Execute button in the SQL Editor toolbar. This loads the Northwind database in SQL Server Express. You should also repeat this step for the instpubs.sql file to install the pubs database, which will also be used in this and later chapters.
9. Close the SQL Server Management Studio Express window.

FIGURE 7.24 How to download SQL Server Express and sample database files

Viewing a Database in SQL Server Express

Now that you have downloaded SQL Server Express and the Northwind Traders and pubs databases, you are ready to learn how to use SQL Server Express. Figure 7.25 demonstrates how to use SQL Server Express to view the contents of the Northwind Traders database, which has the filename northwind.mdf.

HOW TO...

View a Database in SQL Server Express

1. To launch SQL Server Express, click Start in the taskbar. Point to All Programs, point to Microsoft SQL Server 2005, and click SQL Server Management Studio Express.
2. In the Connect to Server dialog box (Figure 7.26), click the Server name list arrow and select the computer where SQL Server is installed. (Select your own computer if you downloaded SQL Server Express.) Finally, click Connect. The SQL Server Management Studio Express window appears, as shown in Figure 7.27.
3. Expand the Databases folder in the Object Explorer window by clicking the plus sign (+) immediately to the left of Databases. This reveals the Northwind and pubs databases.

(Figure is continued on next page)

4. View the contents of the Northwind database within the Databases folder by clicking the plus sign to the left of the Northwind node. Continue expanding additional subnodes. For example, you could expand the Tables node under each database, then the individual table node under Tables, and the Columns node under the table name. (Note that table names are prefixed with dbo., which stands for "database object".)
5. Right-click a table in the Object Explorer (such as dbo.Customers in the Northwind database) and click Open Table to view the table contents.

Example

See Figure 7.28 for an example of opening the Shippers table in the Northwind database.

FIGURE 7.25 How to view a database in SQL Server Express

User's computer on which SQL Server Express is installed

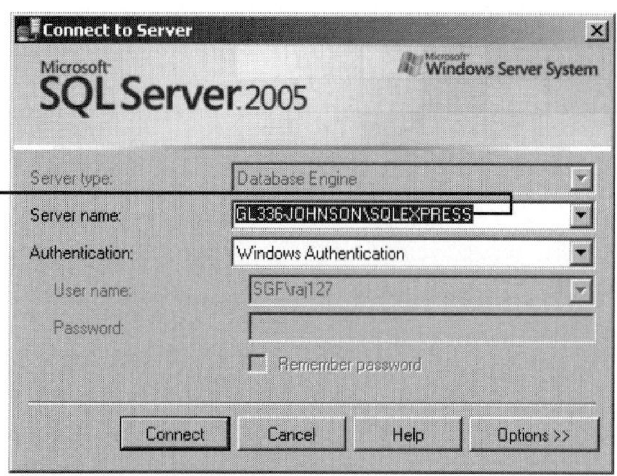

FIGURE 7.26 The Connect to Server dialog box

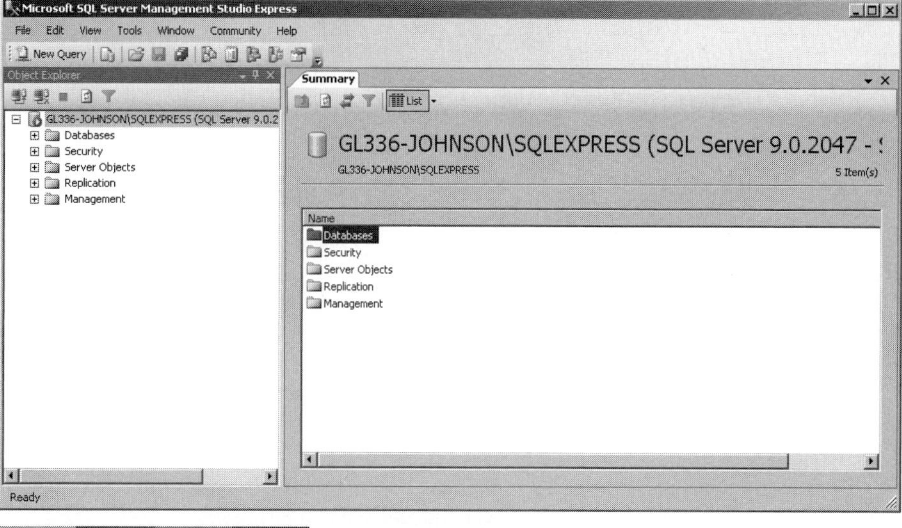

FIGURE 7.27 The SQL Server Management Studio Express window

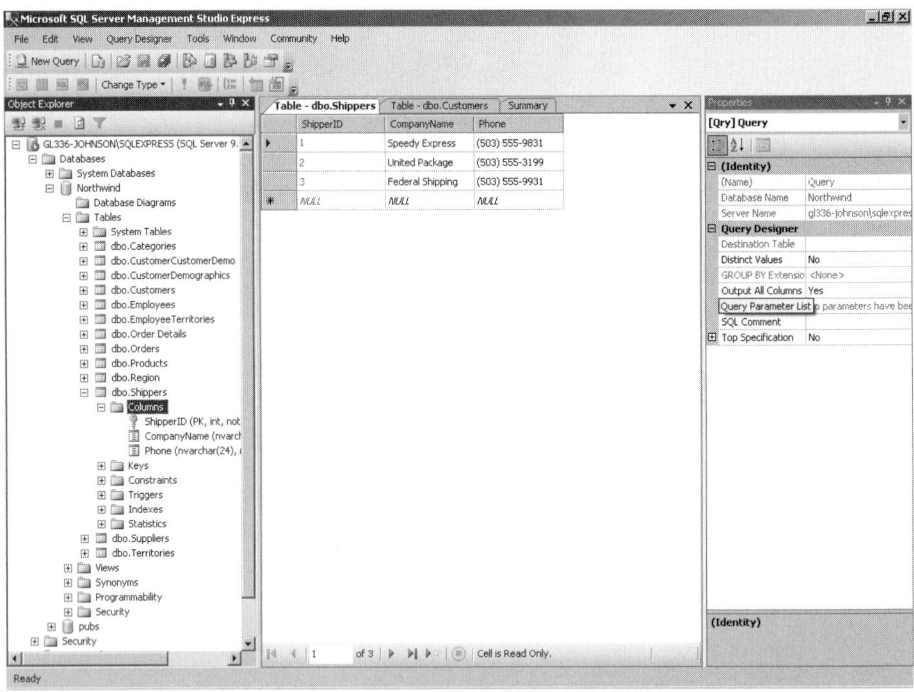

FIGURE 7.28 The Shippers table in the Northwind database

The work area of the SQL Server window in Figure 7.28 shows the contents of the Shippers table in the Northwind database file named northwind.mdf. Note that these are the same contents as shown in Figure 19(a) using Microsoft Access and the northwind.mdb file. The Object Explorer in Figure 7.28 shows the tables of the Northwind database, such as dbo.Categories, dbo.Employees, and dbo.Shippers. Finally, the dbo.Shippers table is expanded into its components with the columns node expanded, revealing ShipperID (the primary key), CompanyName, and Phone. As you can see, the Object Explorer contains a great deal of detailed information about installed databases.

Creating a Query in SQL Server Express

Earlier in this chapter, you created several queries using SQL and Microsoft Access. The process for creating a query in SQL Server is similar, as explained in Figure 7.29.

HOW TO...

Create a Query in SQL Server Express

1. In the Object Explorer, right-click the database node (such as Northwind) and select New Query. A blank SQL Editor appears.
2. In the SQL Editor, type the SQL code. You should observe the capitalization and indentation conventions for writing SQL code.
3. In the SQL Server Express menu, select File, Save SQLQuery1.sql As.... (An SQL Server query file has extension .sql.)

(Figure is continued on next page)

4. In the File name: textbox, type the file name (with extension .sql) and click Save. The default location of the file is the SQL Server Management Studio Express/Projects folder.

Example
See Figure 7.30 for an example of creating a query similar to the one shown in Figure 7.18.

FIGURE 7.29 How to create a query in SQL Server Express

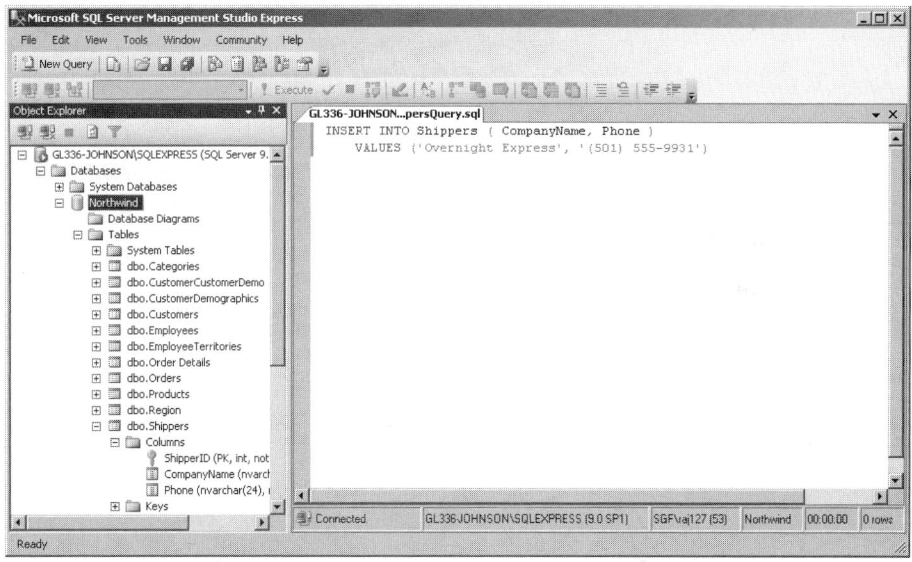

FIGURE 7.30 An `INSERT` query in SQL Server Express

Note in Figure 7.30 that SQL keywords are entered in uppercase by convention. Also note that the query in Figure 7.30 is not exactly the same as the one shown in Figure 7.18 (for Microsoft Access). In SQL Server Express, a default setting will not allow a query to explicitly set the value of an automatically generated primary key (the ShipperID column, in this case). Therefore, the `INSERT` statement in Figure 7.30 simply sets the values of the CompanyName and Phone columns. The ShipperID column value will be set automatically by SQL Server Express. Next you will learn how to execute a query in SQL Server Express (Figure 7.31).

HOW TO...

Execute a Query in SQL Server Express

1. In the SQL Server Express menu, click File, point to Open, and then click File. The Open File dialog box opens. Navigate to the folder where a query has been stored (normally the SQL Server Management Studio Express\Projects folder).

(Figure is continued on next page)

2. In the Open File dialog box, use the Look in: drop-down list to navigate to the desired SQL query. Click the query file (.sql extension) and click Open.
3. In the Connect to Database Engine dialog box, click the Server name list arrow, select the appropriate server, and click Connect.
4. In the SQL Editor toolbar, select the desired database (such as Northwind) from the Available Databases drop-down list.
5. In the SQL Editor toolbar, click the Execute button.

Example

See Figure 7.32 for an example of executing the query shown in Figure 7.15, Example 1.

FIGURE 7.31 How to execute a query in SQL Server Express

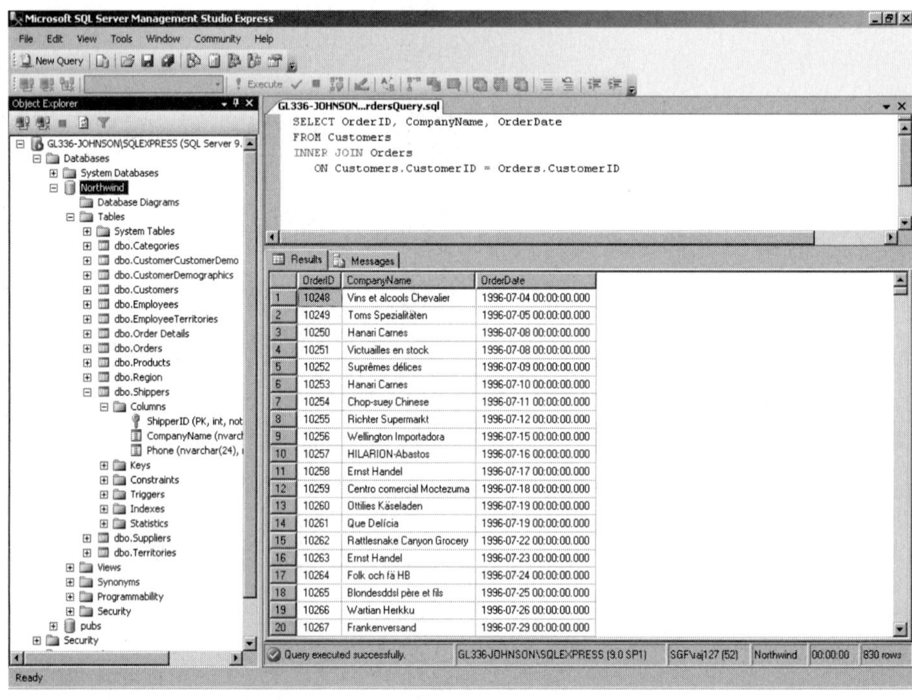

FIGURE 7.32 Result of executing the query in Figure 7.15, Example 1

Note that the query results displayed in Figure 7.32 using SQL Server Express are similar to those displayed in Figure 7.16(c) using Microsoft Access (with the exception of sorting and date formatting).

Creating a Database in SQL Server Express

So far in this chapter you have learned how to query a database using Microsoft Access and Microsoft SQL Server 2005 Express Edition. Doing so presupposes that you already have a database with which to work. However, you may at times need to create your own database. While there are entire courses on relational database design, this section will briefly explain the basics of creating a simple database using SQL Server Express. Figure 7.33 explains how to begin the process of creating a database.

HOW TO...

Create a Database in SQL Server Express

1. In SQL Server Express, right-click Databases and then click New Database. The New Database dialog box appears.
2. In the New Database dialog box, type the name of the database in the Database name textbox. Click OK. (You may need to maximize the dialog box to view the OK button.) The new database appears in the Object Explorer.
3. In the Object Explorer, expand the new database and right-click the Tables icon within the database. Click New Table. The Table Designer appears.
4. In the Table Designer, type the Column Name (no spaces), select an appropriate Data Type (from the drop-down list), and click the Allow Nulls check box only if null values should be permitted. Continue adding columns to the table as needed.
5. To make a column a primary key, right-click the column in the Table Designer and click Set Primary Key. A key icon appears to the left of the Column Name.
6. To save a newly created table, click the Save icon in the Standard toolbar, type the name of the table in the Choose Name dialog box, and click OK. Continue adding tables to the database as needed. Close the Table Designer for that table by clicking the Close button.
7. To add data to a table, right-click the table in the Object Explorer and click Open Table. Add data in the table cells as necessary.

Example
See Figures 7.34 through 7.36 for an example of creating the new database called Courses.

FIGURE 7.33 How to create a database in SQL Server Express

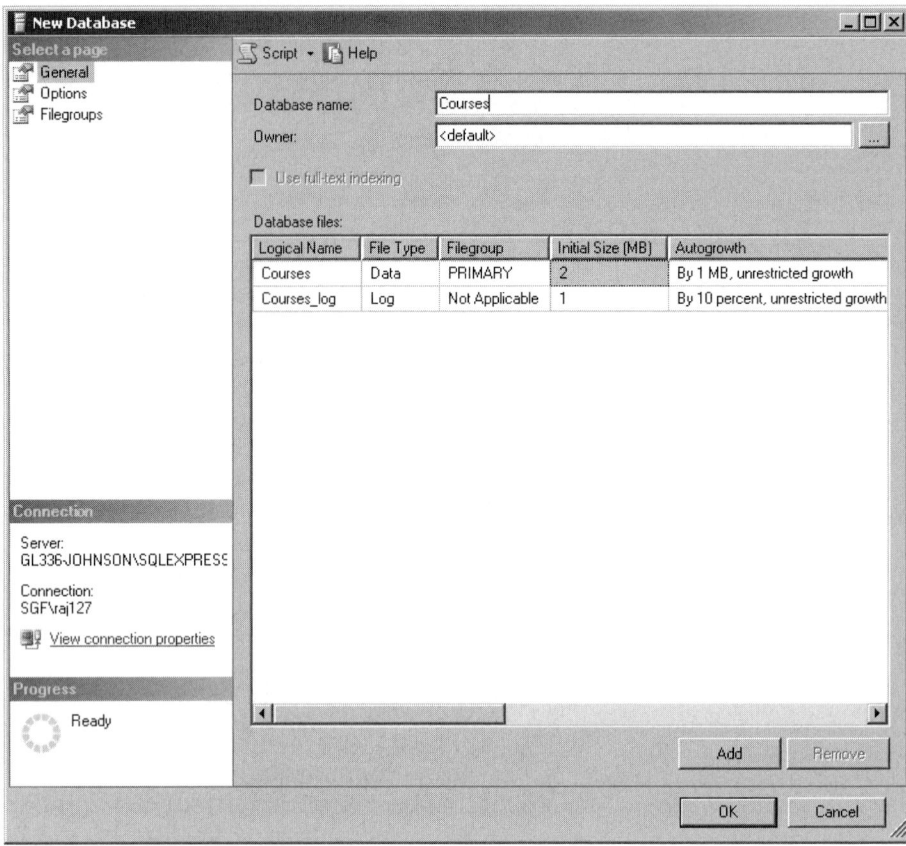

FIGURE 7.34 New Database dialog box in SQL Server Express

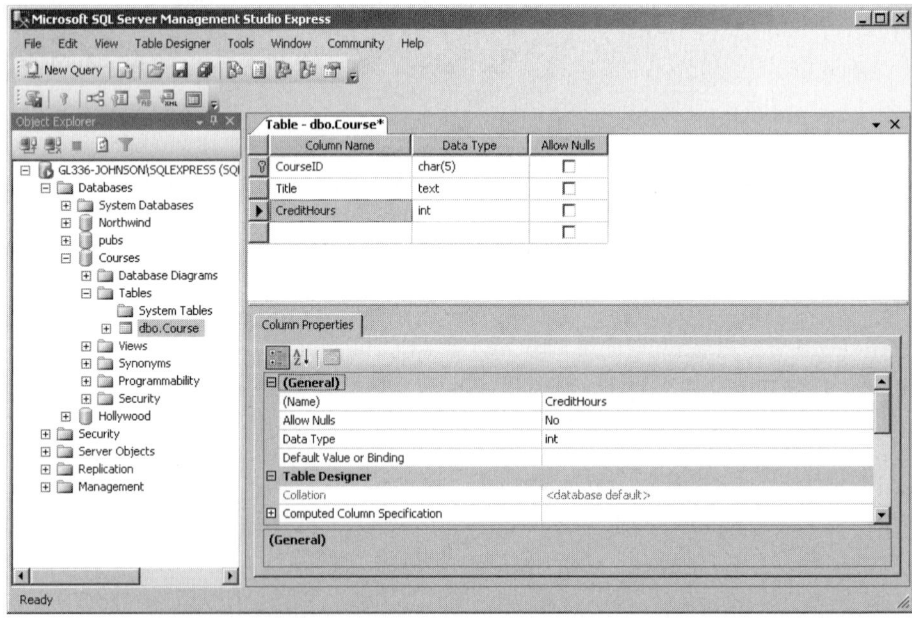

FIGURE 7.35 Table Designer in SQL Server Express

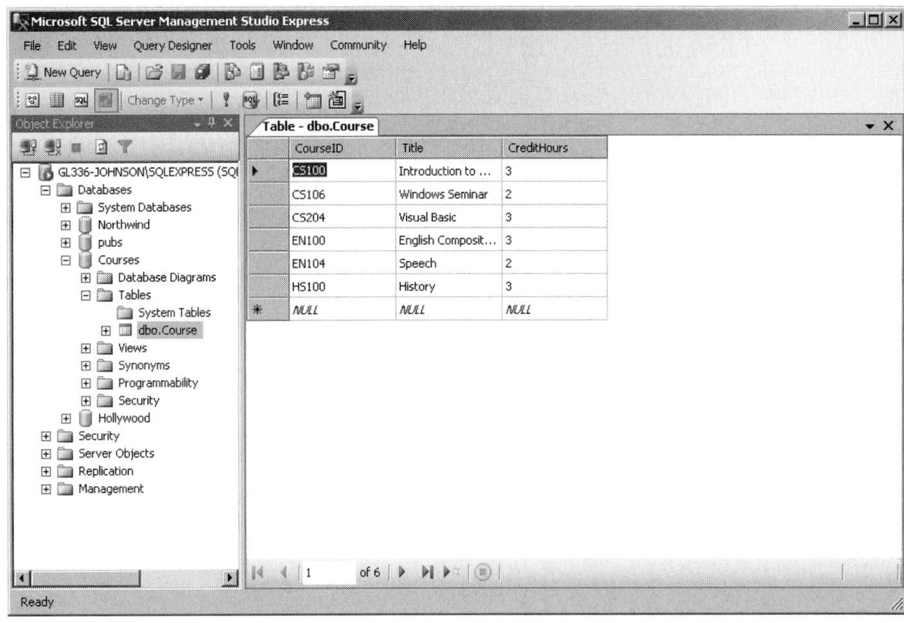

FIGURE 7.36 Data in the Course table

Search for "SqlDataType Enumeration" at *http://msdn.microsoft.com/library/* to learn more about the various data types supported by SQL Server Express.

Figure 7.34 shows the New Database window introduced in Steps 1 and 2 of Figure 7.33. The database name is Courses and its initial size is 2 MB. Figure 7.35 displays the addition of the Course table to the Courses database, as discussed in Steps 3–6 of Figure 7.33. Note that column CourseID has data type char(5), which means the field must be exactly 5 alphanumeric characters in length. The column CourseID is also a primary key, as indicated by the key icon on the left. Other columns in Course have data type text (variable length) and int (integer). Figure 7.36 shows the data added to the Course table. There are six courses in the Course table, each with a Title and CreditHours value.

PROGRAMMING EXAMPLE

Hollywood Database

In this example we will create a database using Microsoft SQL Server 2005 Express Edition. The database, called Hollywood, stores movies, actors, and the roles that actors have in movies. The database will contain a table called Movies, a table called Actors, and a table called Roles. Each movie can have several actors and each actor can be in several movies. The database will have a query that displays the movie title with the actors' names and movie release date. The query is sorted by movie title, actor last name, and actor first name. The tables are populated with many records of meaningful data.

Entity-Relationship Diagram

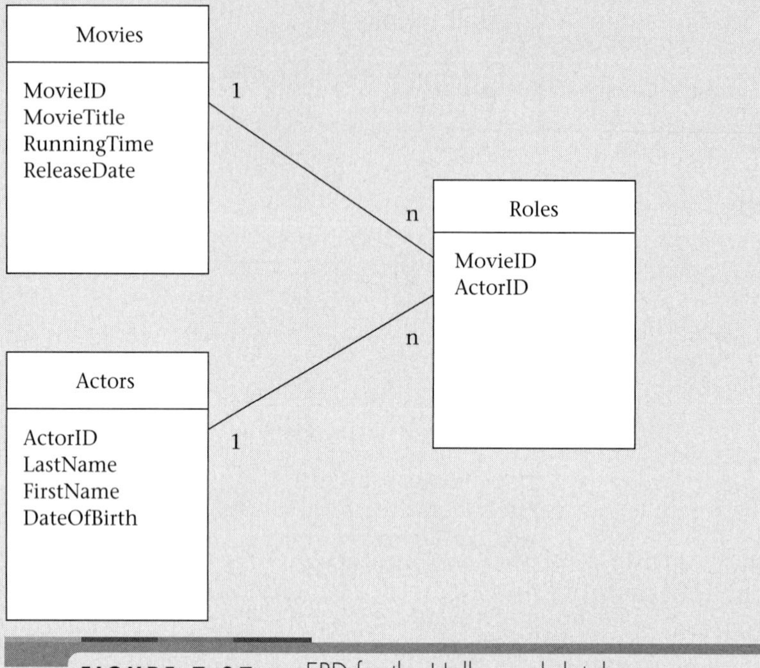

FIGURE 7.37 ERD for the Hollywood database

Table Structure

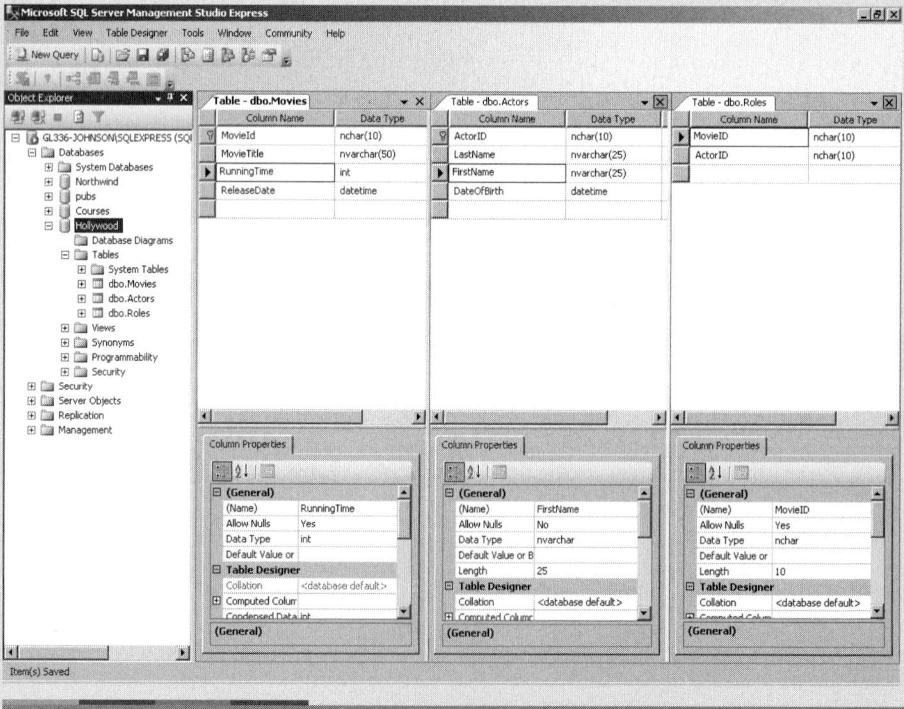

FIGURE 7.38 Table structure for the Hollywood database

Table Contents

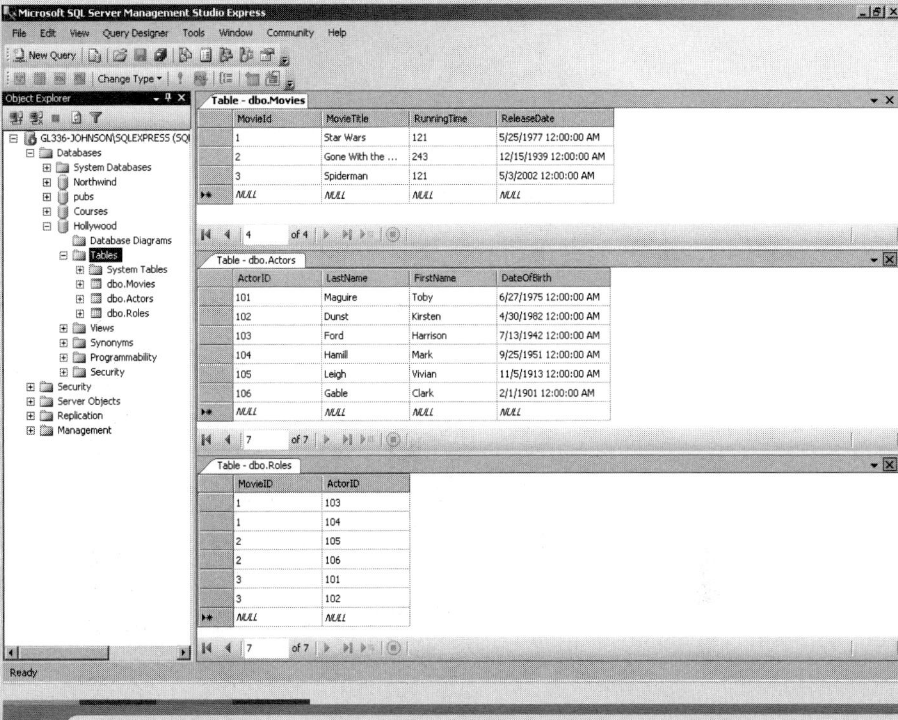

FIGURE 7.39 Table contents for the Hollywood database

SQL Query and Results

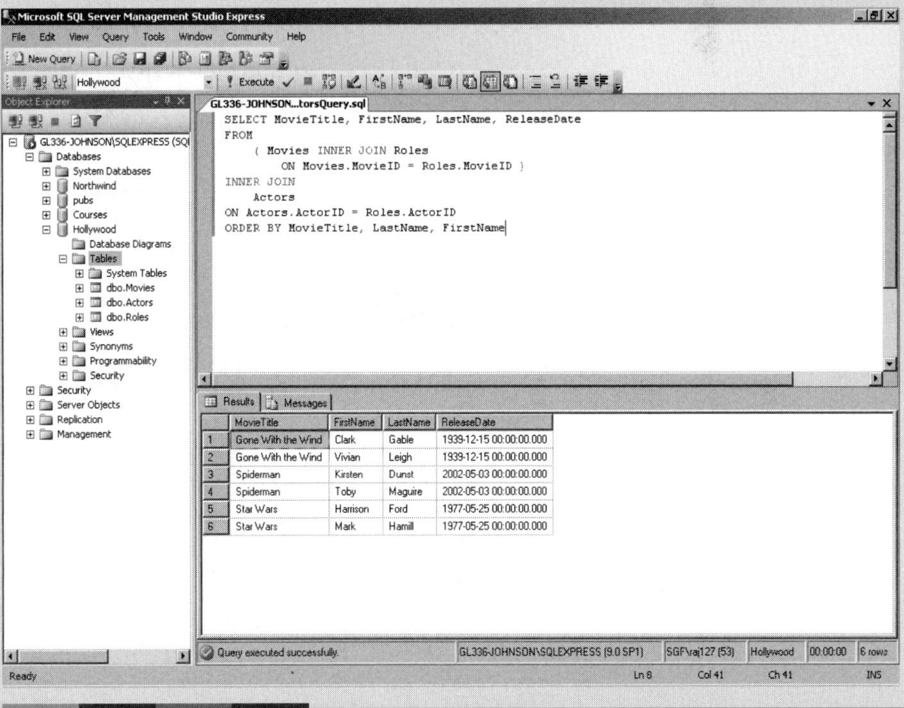

FIGURE 7.40 SQL query and results for Hollywood database

Quick Review

- The word "data" is actually the plural of the word "datum," which is a single item of factual knowledge obtained from measurement or observation. Data, as the plural of datum, is thus an entire collection of factual knowledge.
- Information is something that can be considered different from data. Data represents knowledge obtained from measurement or observation while information represents knowledge obtained by processing data.
- Data files have records (a complete set of data) and fields (a space reserved for a datum). Simple data files are called flat files because they contain no other structure than simple records and fields that could be written on a flat (two-dimensional) piece of paper.
- A data store is any organized collection of data. A data store that has a special structure for facilitating computerized storage, retrieval, and manipulation of the data is called a database. The software used to create and access a database is called a database management system (DBMS).
- The most popular type of database in use today is the relational database, which is a database that follows the relational model. The relational model is simply a way of organizing data in related tables based on strict mathematical principles. A relational database is created and managed by a relational database management system (RDBMS).
- An application and a database may be logically (and physically) separated in what is called a client/server system. In the simplest form of a client/server system there are three hardware components: (1) one or more clients, (2) a network, and (3) a server. The clients store the application and the server stores the database, while the network provides communication capabilities between clients and server.
- The client in a client/server system is usually a PC or workstation belonging to individual users, while the server may be a more powerful PC (with extra memory, processing speed, and secondary storage), a midrange computer, or a mainframe. Midrange computers and mainframes are capable of holding large databases and quickly processing data requests from many clients.
- The server in a client/server system typically has two kinds of software components: (1) the network operating system, which enables the transfer of data between client and server, and (2) the DBMS, which processes requests from the clients for storage and retrieval of data to and from the database.
- The client in a client/server system also has two basic kinds of software components: (1) application software, and (2) a data access application programming interface (API). A data access API is software that provides an interface between the application and the database.
- ADO stands for ActiveX Data Objects, which is a Microsoft technology for accessing data from a wide variety of data stores in both Windows applications and Web applications. ADO.NET, part of the Microsoft .NET Framework, is an enhanced version of ADO designed specifically for Microsoft .NET applications.
- The data in a relational database are stored in tables; a table is a structure consisting of rows and columns. Each individual data item (datum) is placed in one cell of the table (an intersection of a row and a column). Each row in a table represents a data record and each column in a table represents a data field. Furthermore, a record conceptually represents a real-world entity, and each field conceptually represents an attribute or characteristic of that entity.
- A primary key is one or more fields in a database table that, taken in combination, form a unique value and thus uniquely identify a record.

- Each table in a relational database should represent only one kind of entity, and the table should contain only the fields that are absolutely essential for describing that entity. A relationship between two tables in an RDBMS is created by including a foreign key in one of the tables. A foreign key is a primary key of one table included as a field of another table.
- Cardinality is the number of elements in a set or group of elements. Thus, the cardinality of a relationship between Tables A and B in a database is the number of rows in Table B that can be associated with each row in Table A.
- Structured query language (SQL) is a standard language used to store, retrieve, and manipulate data within a relational database. A query is a set of instructions for extracting data from a database.
- A basic SQL `SELECT` statement is used to retrieve all rows (records) from a single table for certain specified columns (fields). A `WHERE` clause in a `SELECT` statement is used to retrieve rows that meet certain selection criteria. Sorting is performed by using the optional `ORDER BY` clause in a `SELECT` statement. The `INNER JOIN` operation in a `SELECT` statement is used to extract related information from two or more tables.
- The `INSERT` statement is used to add (insert) new data into a database. The `UPDATE` statement is used to change the contents of existing records. The `DELETE` statement is used to delete rows from a table.

Key Terms

ActiveX Data Objects (ADO)—A Microsoft technology for accessing data from a wide variety of data stores in both Windows applications and Web applications.

ADO.NET—An enhanced version of ADO designed specifically for Microsoft .NET applications.

cardinality—When referring to a relationship between Tables A and B in a database, the number of rows in Table B that can be associated with each row in Table A.

client/server system—A system in which software is distributed across networked hardware components consisting of clients, which send requests for services, and a server, which provides responses to the requests.

data—The plural of datum; an entire collection of factual knowledge.

data access application programming interface (API)—Software that provides an interface between the application and the database.

data store—Any organized collection of data.

database—A data store that has a special structure for facilitating computerized storage, retrieval, and manipulation of data.

database management system (DBMS)—Software designed to create and access a database.

datum—A single item of factual knowledge obtained from measurement or observation. The singular of data

entity-relationship diagram (ERD)—A pictorial representation of the entities (tables), the entity attributes (fields), and the relationships between the entities in a relational database.

field—A space reserved for a datum.

flat file—A way of structuring data in simple records and fields that could be written on a flat (two-dimensional) piece of paper.

foreign key—A primary key of one table included as a field of another table.

information—Knowledge obtained by processing data.

primary key—One or more fields in a database table that, taken in combination, form a unique value and thus uniquely identify a record.

query—A set of instructions for extracting data from a database.

record—A complete set of data, usually consisting of several fields.

relational database—A database that follows the relational model.

relational model—A way of organizing data in related tables based on strict mathematical principles.

structured query language (SQL)—A standard language used to store, retrieve, and manipulate data within a relational database.

Review Questions

1. Data and information are essentially the same.
   a. True
   b. False
2. A flat file consists of simple records and fields.
   a. True
   b. False
3. A data store is more complicated than a database.
   a. True
   b. False
4. In a client/server system, there are usually many servers and one client.
   a. True
   b. False
5. In a relational table, rows represent entities and columns represent entity attributes.
   a. True
   b. False
6. A primary key in a relational table can consist of more than one column.
   a. True
   b. False
7. A foreign key in a relational table must contain unique values.
   a. True
   b. False
8. An SQL `SELECT` statement is used to select rows from a table.
   a. True
   b. False
9. In the Northwind database, one instance of Products can have many instances of Categories.
   a. True
   b. False

10. In the Northwind database, the Employees table is related to the Order Details table.
    a. True
    b. False
11. A relational database stores data in ____.
    a. files
    b. tables
    c. queries
    d. arrays
12. Which of the following is not usually considered part of a client/server system?
    a. network
    b. server
    c. user
    d. workstation
13. The ADO.NET is what type of software?
    a. DBMS
    b. network operating system
    c. application
    d. data access API
14. Which SQL statement is not valid for the Northwind database?
    a. `SELECT LastName, FirstName FROM Employees`
    b. `SELECT LastName, FirstName FROM Customers`
    c. `SELECT * FROM Customers`
    d. `SELECT * FROM Employees`
15. Which field is not a key field (primary or foreign) in the Products table of the Northwind database?
    a. CategoryID
    b. ShipperID
    c. ProductID
    d. SupplierID
16. What is the primary key for the Order Details table in the Northwind database?
    a. OrderID
    b. ProductID
    c. combination of OrderID and ProductID
    d. none of the above
17. How many records would be displayed if the query in Figure 7.36 used `'HIS'` instead of `'CIS'`?
    a. 0
    b. 1
    c. 2
    d. 3
18. Which SQL keyword is not used for sorting the results of a query?
    a. `ASC`
    b. `LIKE`
    c. `ORDER`
    d. `DESC`

19. Which SQL keyword is used specifically for pattern matching?
    a. `ORDER`
    b. `LIKE`
    c. `JOIN`
    d. `WHERE`

20. Which SQL keyword is used to change values in an existing record?
    a. `SET`
    b. `VALUES`
    c. `ON`
    d. `LIKE`

Computer Exercises

When creating solutions for the following exercises, follow all conventions for the structured query language. You will need to use a computer with Microsoft Access and/or Microsoft SQL Server Express Edition installed for these exercises.

1. In this exercise you create a query for the Northwind Traders database in Microsoft Access.
   a. Copy the Microsoft Access Northwind Traders database (northwind.mdb) included with the Microsoft Access installation to the \VbReloadedAdvanced\Chap07\ folder.
   b. Open the Northwind Traders database file (northwind.mdb) in the \VbReloadedAdvanced\Chap07\ folder.
   c. Formulate an SQL statement that creates a query called DisplayProductQuery. The query should display all fields in the Products table for beverages sorted by price (descending). Save the query, test the application, and modify as necessary.
   d. Formulate another SQL statement that creates a query called DisplayOrdersQuery. The query should display the order ID, customer ID, order date, product ID, product price, product quantity, and product discount for all orders bound for Germany. Save the query, test the application, and modify as necessary.
   e. Close the database window.

2. In this exercise you create an ERD for the Grocer-to-Go database (included with the installation of Microsoft Access) and create a query for the same database in Microsoft Access.
   a. Copy the Microsoft Access Grocer-to-Go database (grocertogo.mdb) included with the Microsoft Access installation to the \VbReloadedAdvanced\Chap07\ folder.
   b. Open the Grocer-to-Go database file (grocertogo.mdb) in the \VbReloadedAdvanced\Chap07\ folder.
   c. Study the tables in the database and create an entity-relationship diagram (ERD) for the database using Microsoft Word (or other drawing software). Save the ERD file as grocertogo.doc (or other appropriate extension). Use the symbol 1 for one and n for many to describe the cardinality of the relationships.
   d. Formulate an SQL statement that creates a query called DisplayProduct. The query should display the product ID, product name, product category, and product price sorted by product name. Save the query, test the application, and modify as necessary.

   e. Formulate another SQL statement that creates a query called DeleteProductsQuery. The query should delete all products manufactured by Sparkle Co. Save the query, test the application, and modify as necessary.
   f. Close the database window.

3. In this exercise you will repeat Exercise 1 using Microsoft SQL Server Express Edition.
   a. Locate the northwind.mdf file on your system and make a backup copy called northwind_backup.mdf that can be used to restore the database to its original condition if necessary.
   b. Run SQL Server Management Studio Express.
   c. Expand the Northwind database.
   d. Formulate an SQL statement that creates a query called **DisplayProductQuery.sql**. The query should display all fields in the Products table for beverages sorted by price (descending). Save the query, test the application, and modify as necessary.
   e. Formulate another SQL statement that creates a query called **DisplayOrdersQuery.sql**. The query should display the order ID, customer ID, order date, product ID, product price, product quantity, and product discount for all orders bound for Germany. Save the query, test the application, and modify as necessary.

4. In this exercise you create an ERD, create a new table, and create a query for the pubs database using Microsoft SQL Server Express Edition.
   a. Locate the pubs.mdf file on your system and make a backup copy called pubs_backup.mdf that can be used to restore the database to its original condition if necessary.
   b. Run SQL Server Management Studio Express.
   c. Expand the pubs database.
   d. Study the tables in the database and create an entity-relationship diagram (ERD) for the authors, titles, and publishers tables using Microsoft Word (or other drawing software). Save the ERD file as pubs.doc (or other appropriate extension). Use the symbol 1 for one and n for many to describe the cardinality of the relationships.
   e. Formulate an SQL statement that creates a query called **TitlesAuthorsPubsQuery.sql**. The query should display the titles, authors, and publishers for all books (sorted by title and by author last name) in the database. Save the query, test the application, and modify as necessary.

5. In this exercise you create an ERD, create a new table, and create a query for the Northwind database using Microsoft SQL Server Express Edition.
   a. Locate the northwind.mdf file on your system and make a backup copy called northwind_backup.mdf that can be used to restore the database to its original condition if necessary.
   b. Run SQL Server Management Studio Express.
   c. Expand the Northwind database.
   d. Study the tables in the database and create an entity-relationship diagram (ERD) for the Customers, Employees, and Orders tables (using Microsoft Word or other drawing software). Save the ERD file as northwind5.doc (or other appropriate extension). Use the symbol 1 for one and n for many to describe the cardinality of the relationships.

e. Remove the HomePhone column in Employees and add EmployeePhoneID. Add a table called EmployeePhones with fields EmployeeID, PhoneNumber (format xxx-xxx-xxxx), and PhoneType (values H, W, or C for home, work, or cell, respectively). Manually add phone data for all employees.
f. Formulate an SQL statement that creates a query. The query should display a phone directory for all employees, sorted by last name, including all types of phones. Save the query as **EmployeePhoneQuery.sql**, test the application, and modify as necessary.

6. In this exercise you create an ERD and a query using the Hollywood database created in this chapter's Programming Example.
   a. Locate the Hollywood.mdf file included in the \VbReloadedAdvanced\Chap07\ folder and make a backup copy called Hollywood _backup.mdf that can be used to restore the database to its original condition if necessary.
   b. Run SQL Server Management Studio Express.
   c. Attach the Hollywood database to the databases in SQL Server Management Studio Express.
   d. Add a table called BestPicture with columns BestPictureID, Year, and MovieID. Create an ERD to show the relationships among all tables in the database (using Microsoft Word or other drawing software). Save the ERD file as Hollywood.doc (or other appropriate extension). Use the symbol 1 for one and n for many to describe the cardinality of the relationships.
   e. Search the Internet to find the Academy Awards for Best Picture for several years and load appropriate data in all tables within the database.
   f. Create a query that contains movie year and title for the Best Picture award sorted by year. Save the query as **BestPictureQuery.sql**, test the application, and modify as necessary.

7. In this exercise you create an ERD and a query using the AdventureWorks database (available for download as explained in Figure 7.24).
   a. Locate the AdventureWorks_Data.mdf file on your system and make a backup copy called AdventureWorks_Data_backup.mdf that can be used to restore the database to its original condition if necessary.
   b. Run SQL Server Management Studio Express.
   c. Expand the AdventureWorks database.
   d. Add columns in the HumanResources.Employee table for FirstName, MiddleInitial, and LastName.
   e. Create an ERD for the tables HumanResources.Employee, HumanResources.EmployeeAddress, and Person.Address (using Microsoft Word or other drawing software). Save the ERD file as AdventureWorks.doc (or other appropriate extension). Use the symbol 1 for one and n for many to describe the cardinality of the relationships.
   f. Using the three tables in part (d), create a query that contains just the data required for employee mailing labels. The query should be sorted by employee last name and then by first name. Save the query as **EmployeeMailingLabelQuery.sql**, test the application, and modify as necessary.
   g. Create another query called UpdateEmployeeQuery.sql that updates all pertinent information for a specific employee who changes address; test the application, and modify as necessary.

Case Projects

CD Collection

Create an ERD for a database called CDCollection that includes a CDs table and a Tracks table. Create a database called **CDCollection using SQL Server Express**. Create a table for CDs and another table for music tracks on the CDs. Include several meaningful fields in both tables. Enter real data from at least three CDs. Create a query that lists the CDs with each CD's tracks in the order that they appear on the CD.

Friends

Create an ERD for a database called MyFriends that includes a Friends table, a Hobbies table, and a Movies table. A friend can have several hobbies and several favorite movies. Create the database called **MyFriends using SQL Server Express** and create the required tables. Enter data for several of your friends. Create a query that lists only the friends' names and hobbies sorted by last name. Create another query that lists only the friends' names and favorite movies sorted by movie, then by last name.

Courses

Enhance the Courses database presented in this chapter using SQL Server Express. Create an ERD that includes a Students table and a Schedule table. A student can take several courses and a course can have several students. Create a separate table in the ERD with fields StudentID and CourseID. Add the Students table and the StudentCourse table in the database and populate all tables with several records. Create three queries, each of which extracts data from two different tables.

CHAPTER

8

Accessing Data with ADO.NET

After studying Chapter 8, you should be able to:

- Discuss the important features of ADO.NET
- Add data connections and data sources to an application
- Add elements of a data source to a form
- Add and modify an SQL query for a data source
- Add an SQL query that uses a stored procedure
- Create an application that displays tables, views, and stored procedures

Business, scientific, and personal data are often stored in relational databases that can be accessed using SQL (structured query language). Chapter 7 provided you with a basic understanding of data, relational databases, and SQL. However, your use of SQL was strictly within the confines of a database management system (DBMS), such as Microsoft Access or Microsoft SQL Server.

TIP

The data access API for the .NET Framework is called ADO.NET. For the Java language it is called JDBC (Java Database Connectivity).

Chapter 7 also gave you a very brief introduction to ADO.NET, which is a data access API (application program interface). Recall that an API is a set of routines, protocols, and tools that define how a service is performed in an application. Thus, ADO.NET simply defines how an application (such as one written with Visual Basic 2005) accesses a database. Since data and databases are so extremely vital to real-world computer applications, it is important for you to learn how to use ADO.NET in conjunction with Visual Basic.

OVERVIEW OF ADO.NET

The previous chapter gave you a very broad overview of ADO.NET. Now this section explores the details of how ADO.NET works. You need to understand these details to work effectively with ADO.NET in your applications.

What Is ADO.NET?

In Chapter 7, a data store was defined as any organized collection of data and a database was defined as a data store whose contents can be systematically and easily accessed, managed, and updated. ADO.NET is a data access API capable of accessing Microsoft SQL Server databases as well as any other kind of data store that implements OLE DB. Such data stores include simple text files, electronic spreadsheets, Microsoft Access databases, or other types of databases. **OLE DB** (**Object Linking and Embedding for Databases**) is a Microsoft technology for interfacing with data stores. It comes under the umbrella of the **Component Object Model (COM)**, a Microsoft technology for intersoftware communication using objects. In addition to accessing data in data stores, ADO.NET is also capable of accessing data in **XML (eXtensible Markup Language)** format. XML is a simple, widely used, human-readable, text-based format for storing data using customized tags similar to those found in Web pages. XML will be further explored in Chapter 10.

ADO vs. ADO.NET

To better understand ADO.NET, it is helpful to compare it to an earlier Microsoft technology called ADO. **ADO (ActiveX Data Objects)** was the Microsoft data access API introduced in 1996. ADO was based on the OLE DB standard for interfacing with a data store, whereas ADO.NET, released in 2002, is based on the newer Microsoft .NET Framework. Therefore, ADO.NET represents a major improvement over ADO.

There are many practical differences between ADO and ADO.NET. Unlike ADO, ADO.NET does not require that the application be continuously connected to a database during program execution. Such a continuous connection prevents other applications from accessing the database. Instead, ADO.NET allows the application to quickly download the required data from a central database to the individual user's computer (or transfer data from the user's computer to a central database) and then close the data connection, thus allowing many other users to access the same database in a similar way. Also, ADO.NET provides more control than ADO over how modified data from different users are stored back to the central database, thus assuring the integrity in the database. Operating in this disconnected mode makes applications that use ADO.NET more **scalable** than applications that use ADO, meaning that the application is more capable of handling increasing (larger-scale) demands from more users over time.

Another advantage of ADO.NET over ADO is its support of XML, an increasingly important format for data storage. Additionally, ADO.NET represents data using **strongly typed objects** (objects whose type can be checked at compile time), making it easier to develop object-oriented applications that require database access. As you can see, ADO.NET delivers many advantages to .NET applications. To better understand how to work with ADO.NET, you need to break it down into its components, as the next section explains.

The Details of ADO.NET

For an application to interact with a database (or any other data store), a data access API (such as ADO.NET) must effectively bridge the gap between the two. Figure 8.1 illustrates how ADO.NET interacts with a database and an application. The simplified version in Figure 8.1(a) illustrates that ADO.NET enables data transfer between a database and an application. Figure 8.1(b) expands the simplified view into the detailed components of ADO.NET that will be explored throughout this chapter. Although Figure 8.1(b) may look complicated now, the good news is that Visual Basic makes much of the data access with ADO.NET automatic with simple drag-and-drop techniques.

(a) Simplified view of ADO.NET

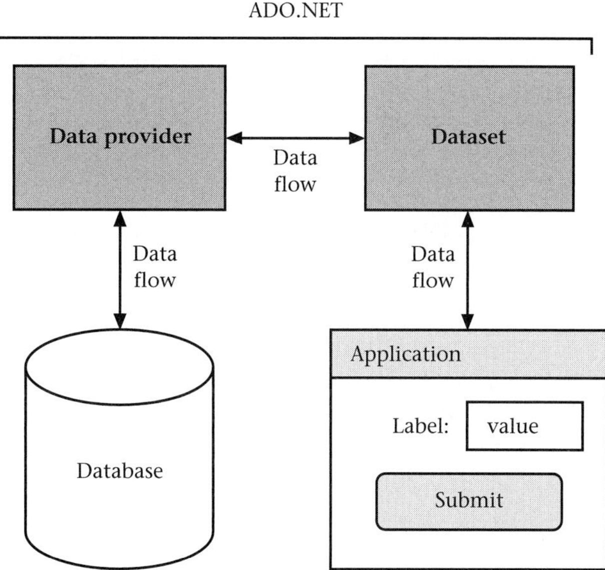

(b) Detailed view of ADO.NET using an SQL Server database

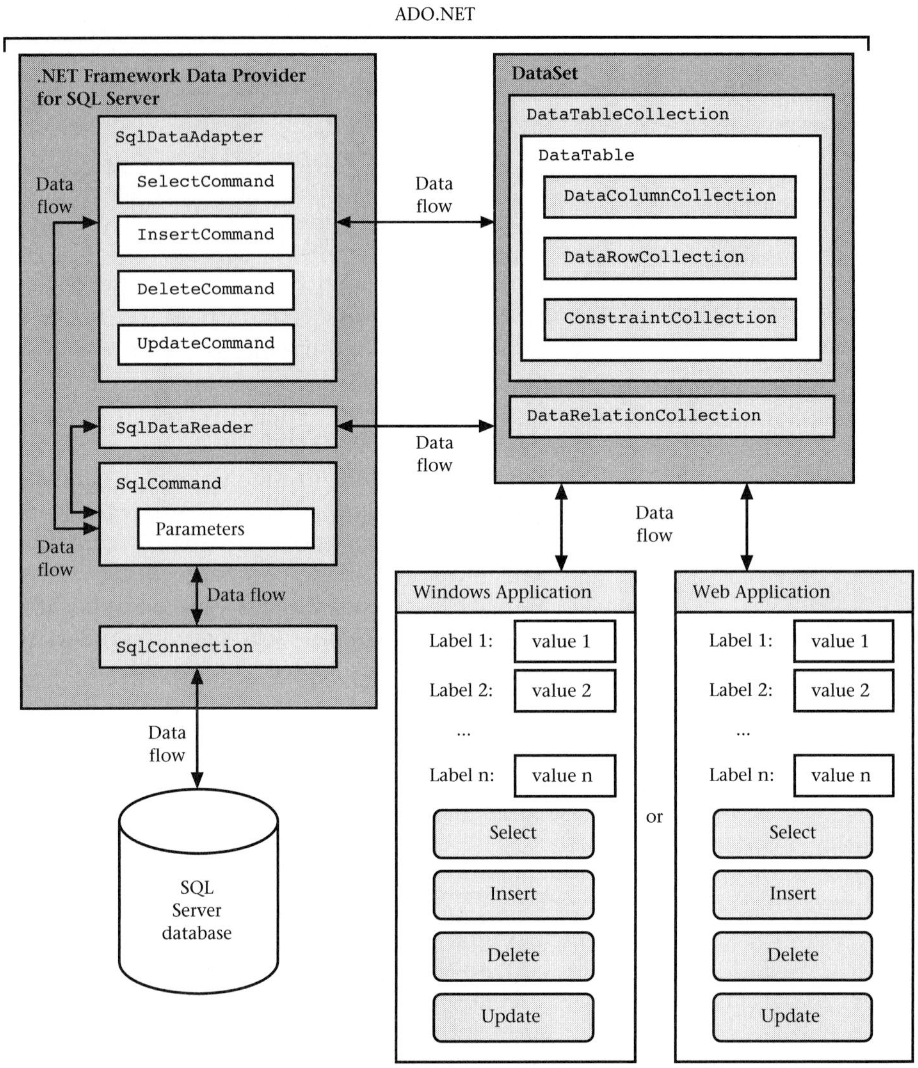

FIGURE 8.1 How ADO.NET links a database and an application

Database and Application

To begin your exploration of ADO.NET, focus on the database in Figure 8.1(a). A database is usually created using a relational database management system (RDBMS), such as SQL Server, Oracle, DB2, or Access. This database can reside on a separate computer (a database server) or on the user's computer (as is the case with the examples in this chapter). The usual situation in the real world is that many users, using many different computers, access one or more database servers via a network. In any case, the principles of database access remain the same.

Next, focus on the application in Figure 8.1(a). This application could be a Windows application written in a .NET language, such as Visual Basic or C#, or a Web application written using ASP.NET. (You'll learn about ASP.NET in the next chapter.) The objective is to get the data from the database to the application so the user can view the data and possibly make changes to the data. Then the application needs the ability to send the updated data back to the database. That's why the arrows in Figure 8.1(a) point in both directions.

ADO.NET Bridges the Gap

Finally, Figure 8.1(a) shows that ADO.NET is the software that bridges the gap between database and application. ADO.NET consists of two major parts, the data provider and the dataset. A **data provider** is a set of classes that provides the link between the dataset and the database. The data provider works directly with the database to extract data requested by the application for the dataset. A **dataset** is a separate memory resident representation of only that part of the database which an application needs. An application may need only a small part of a very large database (perhaps only one or just a few tables or queries) or it may need the entire database. If the application updates (changes) the data in the dataset, the data provider writes the dataset back to the database.

Disconnected Database Access

The data provider normally makes a connection with a database, quickly gets the required data for the dataset, and then disconnects from the database. Then the user can view the data and make any necessary changes. Finally, the user can save the updated data back to the database by connecting, immediately transferring the data, and then disconnecting. There are two major advantages of using a separate, disconnected dataset instead of remaining connected to the database for a longer period of time: (1) a smaller dataset stored on the user's computer provides the application with faster access to data, and (2) the database, when disconnected from the user's computer, is available to other users. If the application worked directly with the database instead of a dataset, all other users would be locked out of the database until the application finished its tasks.

ADO.NET Components

Figure 8.1(b) provides a more detailed view of the inner workings of ADO.NET. The two major parts of ADO.NET, the data provider and the dataset, are expanded to reveal their components. The dataset will be examined first.

Notice in Figure 8.1(b) that a `DataSet` object contains many other objects. First, a `DataSet` contains a `DataTableCollection` object. This represents a collection of all the individual `DataTable` objects that the application needs. (A `DataTable` object in the `DataSet` corresponds to a table in the database.) Each `DataTable` object has a `DataColumnCollection` object (the collection of all `DataColumn` objects in a `DataTable`), a `DataRowCollection` object (the collection of `DataRow` objects), and a `ConstraintCollection` object (the collection of all primary key and foreign key constraints for the `DataTable` objects). `DataColumn` objects define a column's data type, whether or not null values are allowed, whether the column is read-only or read-write, and so on. `DataRow` objects contain the data for `DataTable` rows and control how to retrieve, insert, delete, and update values in these rows. The `DataRelationCollection` object contains relationship information between two tables. (This occurs when two tables contain columns that hold identical data, such as primary key/foreign key relationships.)

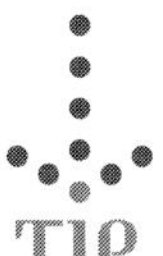

TIP

Note that the classes in the Oracle data provider in ADO.NET are called `OracleConnection`, `OracleDataReader`, and so on. Likewise, the OLE DB data provider classes are called `OleDbConnection`, `OleDbDataReader`, and so on.

The other major component of ADO.NET in Figure 8.1(b) is the data provider. ADO.NET includes data providers for SQL Server, Oracle, and any other database that implements the OLE DB or ODBC standards. Following is an alphabetical list of the specific classes in the SQL Server Data Provider shown in Figure 8.1(b):

- `SqlCommand`—represents an SQL statement or stored procedure to execute against a database; it may contain parameters or variables)
- `SqlConnection`—represents an open connection to the database, including database location and logon information

- `SqlDataAdapter`—uses `SqlCommand` and its properties (`SelectCommand`, `InsertCommand`, ...) to fill a dataset or update a SQL Server database
- `SqlDataReader`—uses `SqlCommand` for more rapid forward-only (read-only) retrieval of data from a database to the dataset

The data provider is used to fill the `DataSet` with data from the database and to update the database with new information from the application. The data provider in Figure 8.1(b) shows the four core objects most often used. Note that `SQLDataAdapter` has four properties that are used to execute the most common types of commands on a database (select, insert, delete, and update). The `SQLCommand` object is also used for any other kind of SQL command or stored procedure.

LINKING A DATABASE AND AN APPLICATION

The previous discussion has been very theoretical. Now it's time for practicalities. In this section you will learn how to use Visual Basic 2005 to link an SQL Server database to a Visual Basic application. (Appendix C provides examples using Microsoft Access.) Figure 8.2 shows the Visual Studio window for the Northwind application with an empty form. Note that the Solution Explorer, Properties, and Server Explorer windows are displayed. (If you are using Visual Basic Express Edition, the Server Explorer window is called the Database Explorer window.)

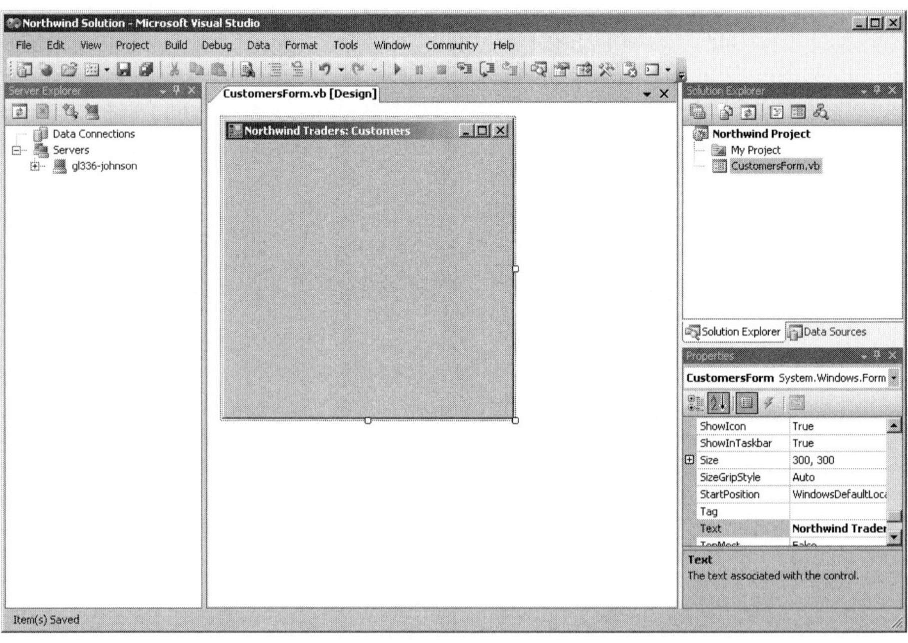

FIGURE 8.2 Visual Studio window for the Northwind application

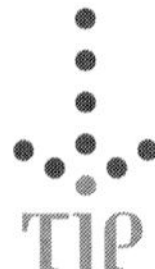

TIP

To view available servers, click View in the Visual Studio menu and then click Server Explorer. If you are using Visual Basic Express Edition, the Server Explorer window is called the Database Explorer window.

The form in Figure 8.2 (filename CustomersForm.vb) will be used to display records of the Customers table in the Northwind database created using SQL Server. Figure 8.3 shows the structure of the Customers table as viewed in SQL Server. (See Chapter 7 for a complete discussion of the Northwind database.)

The process of creating a Visual Basic application that utilizes a database involves four basic steps: (1) adding a data connection to the application, (2) adding a data source (dataset) to the application, (3) adding controls to a form to display the dataset, and (4) adding controls to a form to execute queries (select, add, delete, and update) on the dataset. This section covers the first two steps while the remainder of the chapter covers the last two steps.

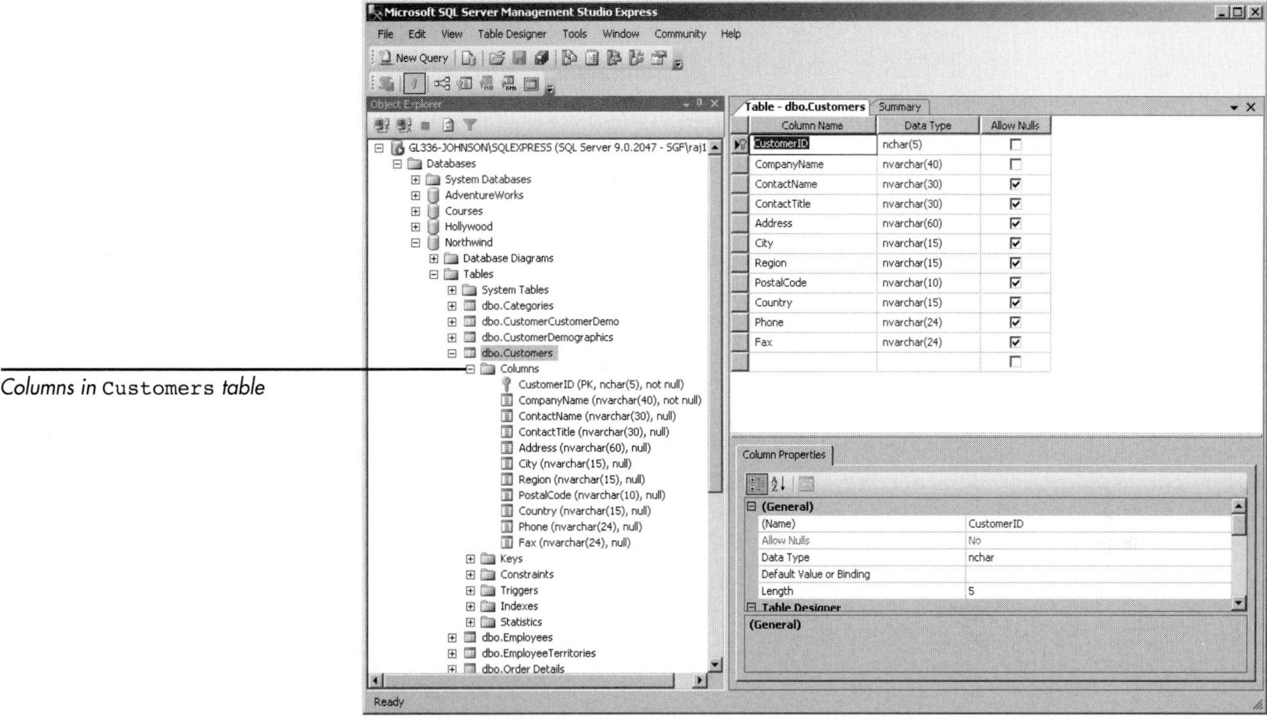

Columns in `Customers` *table*

FIGURE 8.3 Structure of the Customers table in the Northwind database

Adding a Data Connection to an Application

The first requirement for displaying database contents in an application form is adding a data connection to an application. Figure 8.4 details how to accomplish this.

HOW TO...

Add a Data Connection to an Application

1. Create a Visual Basic application with an empty form (as in Figure 8.2). To be safe, make sure that any other application using the data source is closed during this process. (Note that the figures illustrating these steps make use of the Northwind application.)
2. To display the Server Explorer window in Visual Studio, click View in the menu and then click Server Explorer.
3. Right-click the Data Connections icon in the Server Explorer and click Add Connection. The Choose Data Source dialog box appears, as shown in Figure 8.5. Click the appropriate data source in the list (in this case, the selection is for Microsoft SQL Server Database File). Click Continue.

(Figure is continued on next page)

4. The Add Connection dialog box appears, as shown in Figure 8.6. Click the Browse button, navigate to the desired database file, select the database file, and click Open.
5. In the Add Connection dialog box, click Test Connection. If all settings are correct, you will see the Microsoft Visual Studio dialog box shown in Figure 8.7; if not, an error message will be displayed and you will need to review Steps 3–4. (You may need to check with your instructor or your organization's database administrator.)
6. If the connection test is successful, click OK in the connection test result dialog box and click OK in the Add Connection dialog box. The Server Explorer window in Visual Studio will now show the NORTHWND.MDF file under Data Connections.

FIGURE 8.4 How to add a data connection to an application

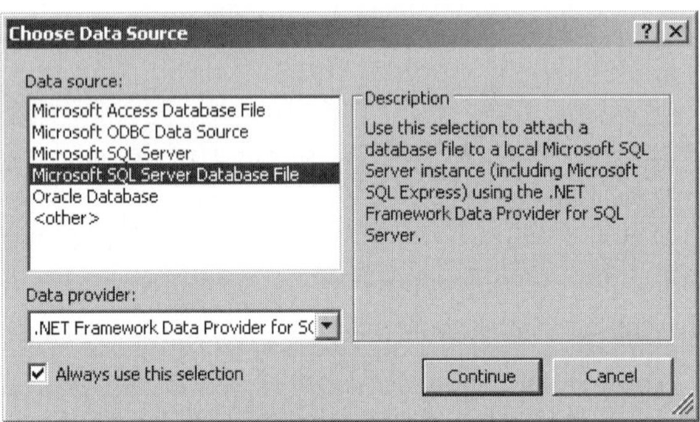

FIGURE 8.5 The Choose Data Source dialog box

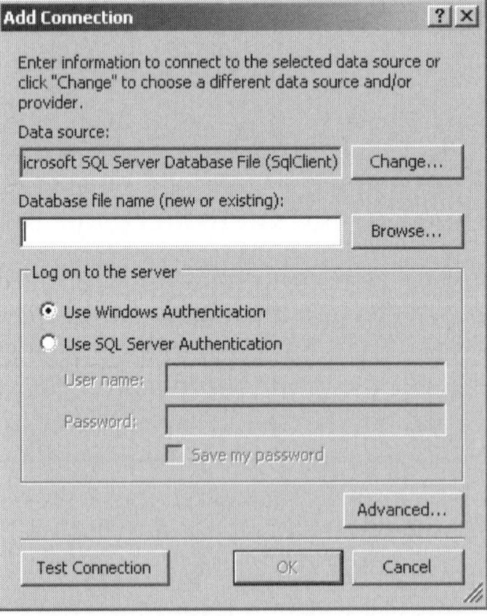

FIGURE 8.6 The Add Connection dialog box

TIP

The Use SQL Server Authentication option shown in Figure 8.6 is for establishing a separate additional logon for a particular database, in addition to the normal Windows Authentication logon.

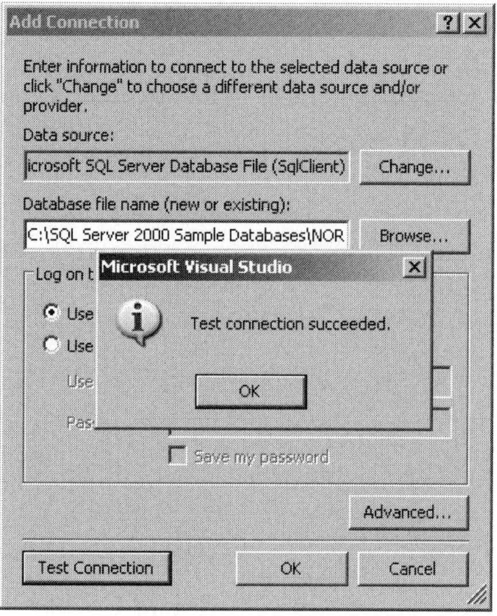

FIGURE 8.7 Dialog for a successful connection test

Figure 8.8 shows the results of performing the steps in Figure 8.4 for the Northwind application. In Step 3, the data source *Microsoft SQL Server Database File* option was used along with the default *Windows Authentication* logon option (Figure 8.6).

Data connection to NORTHWND.MDF

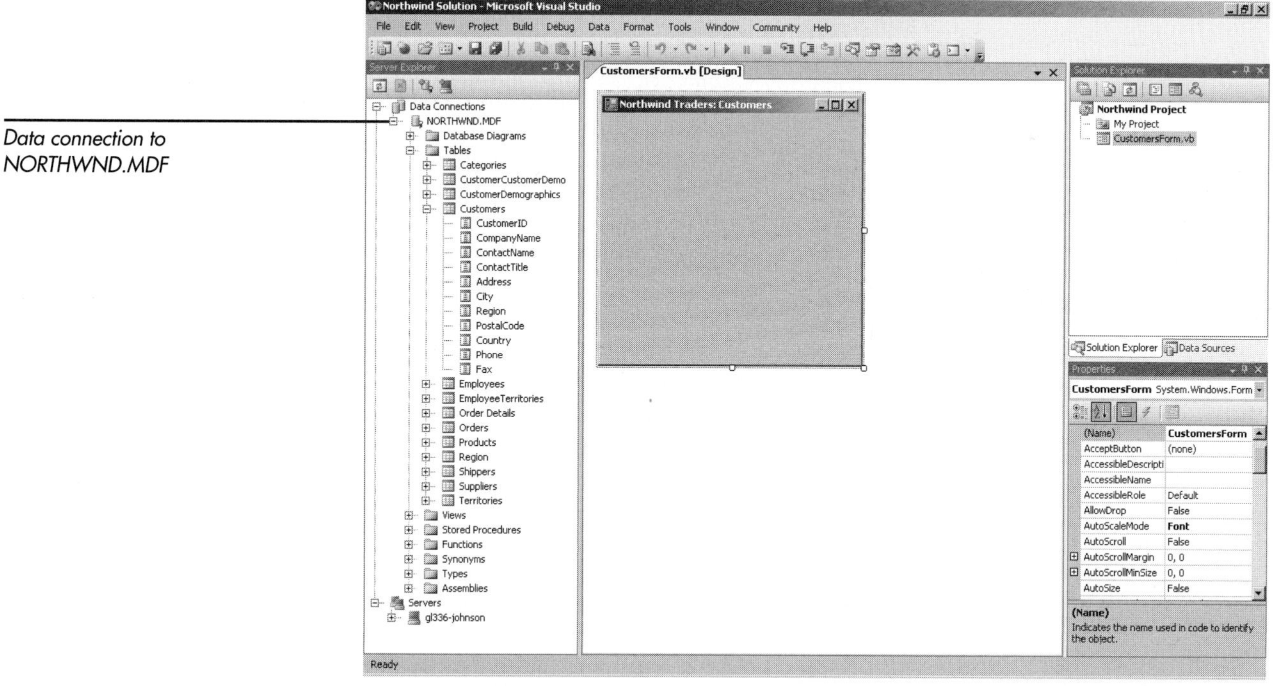

FIGURE 8.8 Northwind application with a data connection to NORTHWND.MDF

After successfully adding a data connection to the Northwind application, the application window should appear as in Figure 8.8. Note that the data connection in the Server Explorer has been expanded to display the columns in the

`Customers` table. All the database elements shown in the Server Explorer are exactly the same as those viewed with SQL Server in Chapter 7 (see Figure 7.32). In fact, you can make the same changes to the database from within Visual Studio that you can using SQL Server Management Studio Express. Next you will learn how to add a data source to an application.

Adding a Data Source to an Application

Figure 8.4 explains how to add a data connection to an application. A data connection simply tells the application where the database is located and allows the user to log on to the database. Next, you will need to add a data source to the application. A data source specifies exactly which parts of the database (which Tables, Columns, Views, Stored Procedures, and so on) are needed by the application. Figure 8.9 explains how to add a data source.

HOW TO...

Add a Data Source to an Application

1. Begin with an application that has a data connection (as described in Figure 8.4). In the Visual Studio menu, click Data and then click Show Data Sources. The Data Sources window appears.
2. In the Visual Studio menu, click Data and then click Add New Data Source. The Data Source Configuration Wizard opens. The first page of the wizard, the Choose a Data Source Type page, is shown in Figure 8.10.
3. In the Choose a Data Source Type page, click the Database option and then click Next. The Choose Your Data Connection page opens.
4. Select the desired data connection. (You may have only one, but your application could use connections to several databases.) Click Next.
5. If the data connection you selected in Step 4 is for a database located on the same computer as your application (a local data file), a dialog box will appear and ask if you want to copy the data file to your project. Click Yes to copy the original database to your project folder; click No to keep the connection with the original database. (You may want to click Yes to copy the database to your project if you need to give a copy of your project to someone else, such as your instructor.) In either case, the next page of the wizard will open.
6. In the Save the Connection String to the Application Configuration File page of the Data Source Configuration Wizard, use the default name for the connection string (a string containing data connection parameters) or type a new name and click Next. This connection string will appear in the app.config file in the Solution Explorer and can be modified if the database location is ever changed. The Choose Your Database Objects page opens, as shown in Figure 8.11.
7. In the Choose Your Database Objects page, a list of database objects with check boxes (Tables, Views, Stored Procedures, and Functions) is presented for possible inclusion in the newly created `DataSet` object (shown at the bottom of the wizard). Click the + next to each type of object to expand the list. Check only those objects required (such as a particular table or columns within a table) for your application. After you have made your selections, click Finish.

FIGURE 8.9 How to add a data source to an application

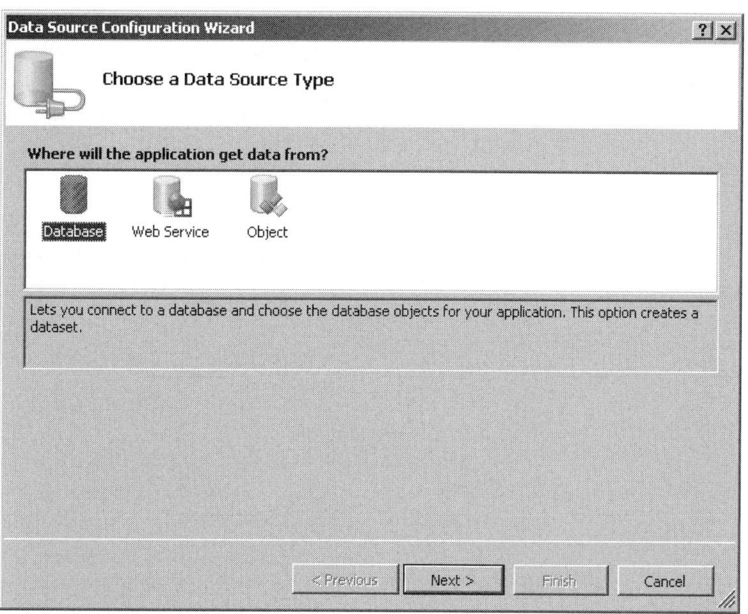

FIGURE 8.10 The *Data Source Configuration Wizard*

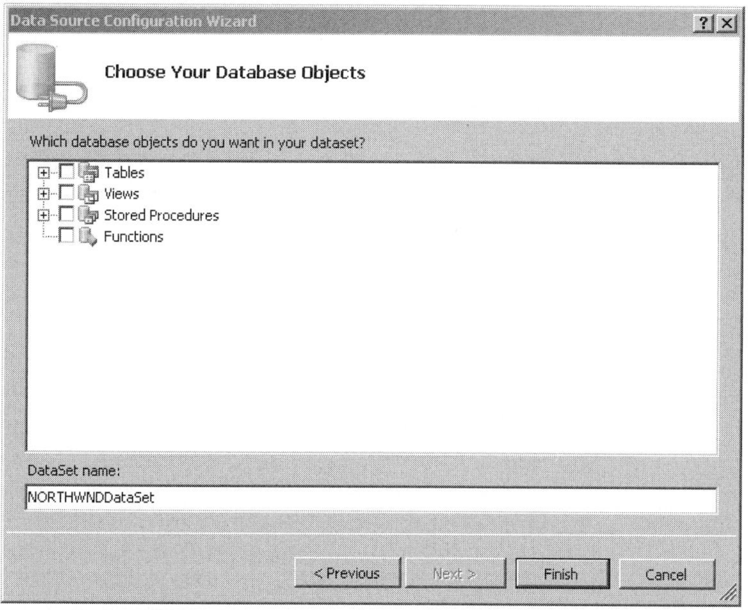

FIGURE 8.11 The final page of the *Data Source Configuration Wizard*

Figure 8.12 shows the results of the steps in Figure 8.9 as applied to the Northwind application. The NORTHWND.MDF database file was selected for the data connection in Step 4 and Yes was selected in Step 5 (to copy the database file to the project). In Step 7, only the Customers table was selected for inclusion in the `DataSet`.

The Server Explorer exposes the complete Northwind database, which is now copied to the application's project folder. The Data Sources window shows the `NORTHWNDDataSet`, which contains only the `Customers` table (all columns are

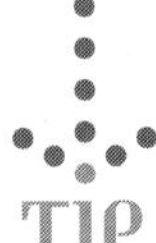

TIP

The database shown in the Server Explorer can be further expanded into components (individual tables, columns, etc.). You can modify the database (add tables, queries, data, etc.) just as if you were using SQL Server Management Studio Express.

included). The Solution Explorer shows three new files: app.config (the application configuration file, written in XML format, which contains the connection string), NORTHWND.MDF (the SQL Server database file), and NORTHWNDDataSet.xsd. (As the file extension implies, NORTHWNDDataSet.xsd is the XML schema definition, which simply defines the database objects contained in the `DataSet.`) You will learn more about XML in Chapter 10.

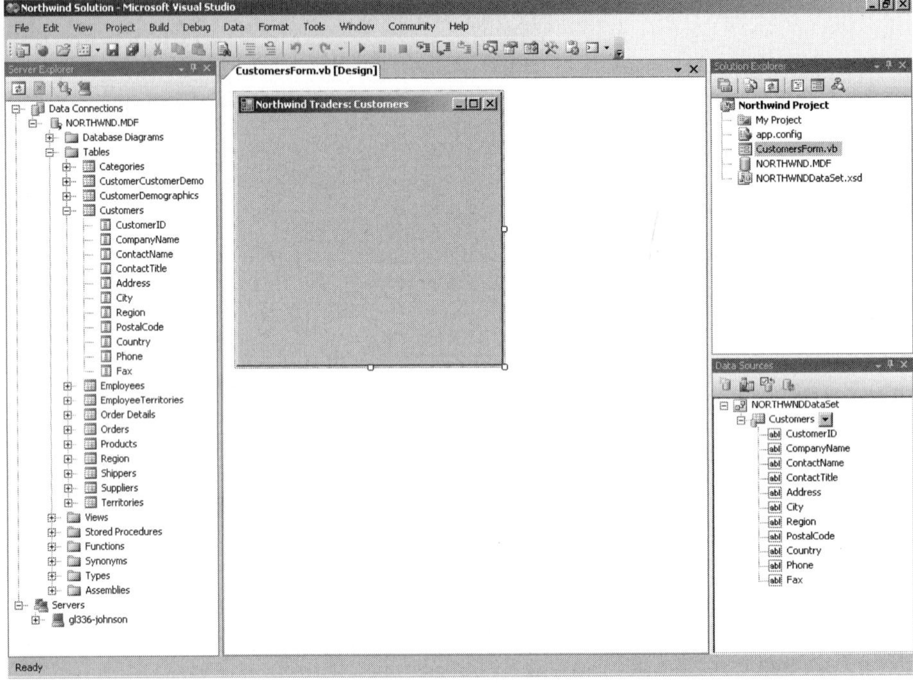

FIGURE 8.12 The Northwind application with database added

The Application's `DataSet`

A bit more should be said about the file NORTHWNDDataSet.xsd. This is an XML file that represents the Northwind application's `DataSet` object, called `NORTHWNDDataSet`. This `DataSet` was formed based on the database objects selected in Step 7 of Figure 8.9 (also see Figure 8.11). Double-clicking this file graphically displays the entire `DataSet` for this application (see Figure 8.13). Only one table (`Customers`) is currently part of the `DataSet`. The top section of the `DataSet` graphic (near the center of Figure 8.13) represents the `Customers` `DataTable` object. (Recall from Figure 8.1(b) that a `DataTable` object is contained within a `DataSet` object.) The bottom section of the `DataSet` graphic in Figure 8.13 represents the `CustomersTableAdapter` object. This is similar to the more general `DataAdapter` object illustrated in Figure 8.1(b). A `TableAdapter` object contains a `Connection` object and has the properties `DeleteCommand`, `InsertCommand`, `SelectCommand`, and `UpdateCommand`, as seen in the Properties window of Figure 8.13. Also note in the graphic for `CustomersTableAdapter` that two methods are shown, `Fill` and `GetData`. The `Fill` method is used by a `TableAdapter` to get data from a database to fill an existing `DataTable`, while the `GetData` method is used to get data and fill a new `DataTable` in the `DataSet`.

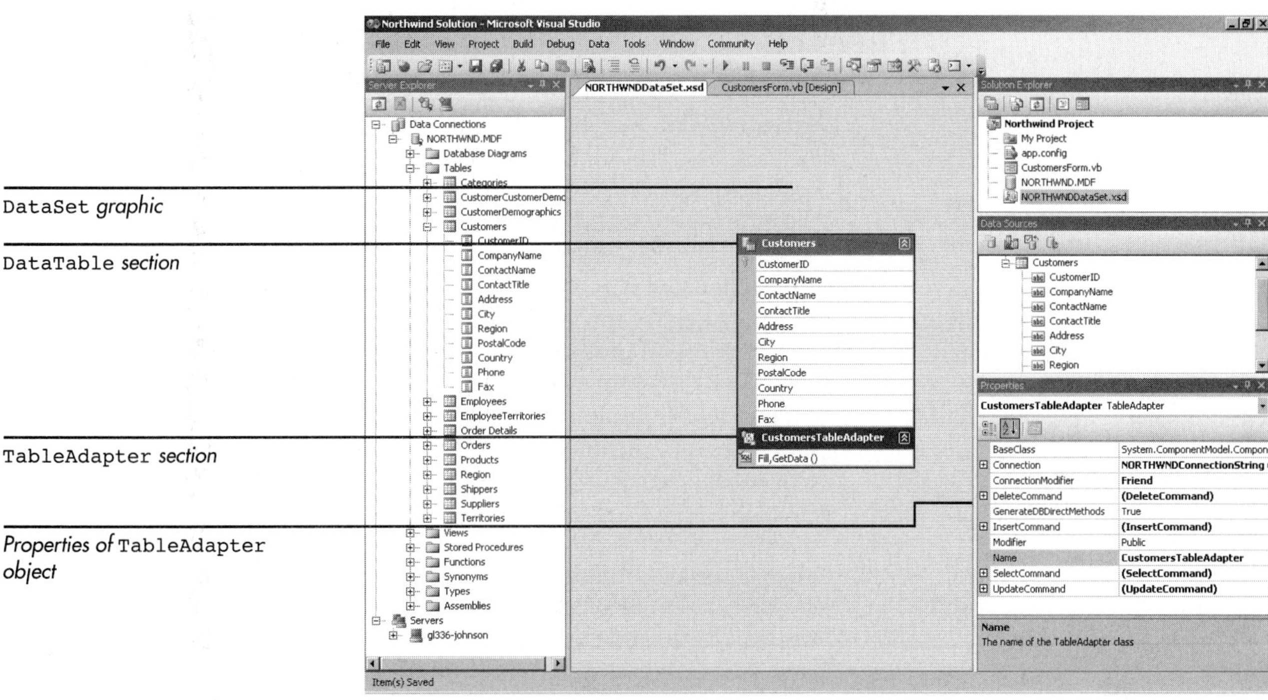

FIGURE 8.13 `DataSet` for the Northwind application with `DataTable` and `TableAdapter` objects

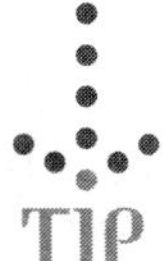

TIP

`TableAdapter` is new in ADO.NET 2.0. It is like `DataAdapter` except that it has a built-in connection object and is able to execute multiple queries.

Recall that the `DataSet` object pictured in Figure 8.13 is a memory resident cache (store) of data obtained from the underlying database just for this application (in this case, the `Customers` table of the Northwind database). When the application runs, it immediately makes a connection with the Northwind database (stored within the project), gets the data from the `Customers` table, and then quickly closes the connection so other applications can then connect to the database.

Now that your application has a data connection (NORTHWND.MDF) and a data source (NORTHWNDDataSet), you are ready to add components to the application form that will be able to access the database.

ADDING DATABASE FUNCTIONALITY TO AN APPLICATION

An application with only a data connection and a data source is far from complete. It needs controls, such as labels, text fields, and buttons, to perform operations using the database. The next section explores a very useful component for working with a database, the `DataGridView` control.

Creating a `DataGridView` in a Form

A `DataGridView` control in a form displays the rows and columns of a table or query in a familiar grid format, just as data would be displayed from within the database itself. Figure 8.14 explains how to add a `DataGridView` to a form.

HOW TO...

Add a `DataGridView` to a Form

1. With an empty form displayed in the Windows Form Designer, make sure that the Data Sources window is open. (Click Data and click Show Data Sources in the menu to open the Data Sources window, as shown in Figure 8.15.) Drag a table from the Data Sources window to the form. A `DataGridView` control appears on the form.
2. To make the `DataGridView` fill the form, click the `DataGridView` so that its properties appear in the Properties window. In the Properties window, scroll to the `Dock` property (which controls where a component "docks" itself in a container), click the value of the `Dock` property, and select the center section of the graphic to select the value `Fill`. (You may, however, prefer not to fill the form with the `DataGridView`.)
3. Adjust the size of the form as necessary.
4. To add or remove columns in the `DataGridView` and make changes to the properties of individual columns, such as `HeaderText`, `ReadOnly`, `Resizeable`, and `Width`, right-click on the `DataGridView` and click *Edit Columns...* Make the necessary changes in the Edit Columns dialog box and click OK.

FIGURE 8.14 How to add a `DataGridView` to a form

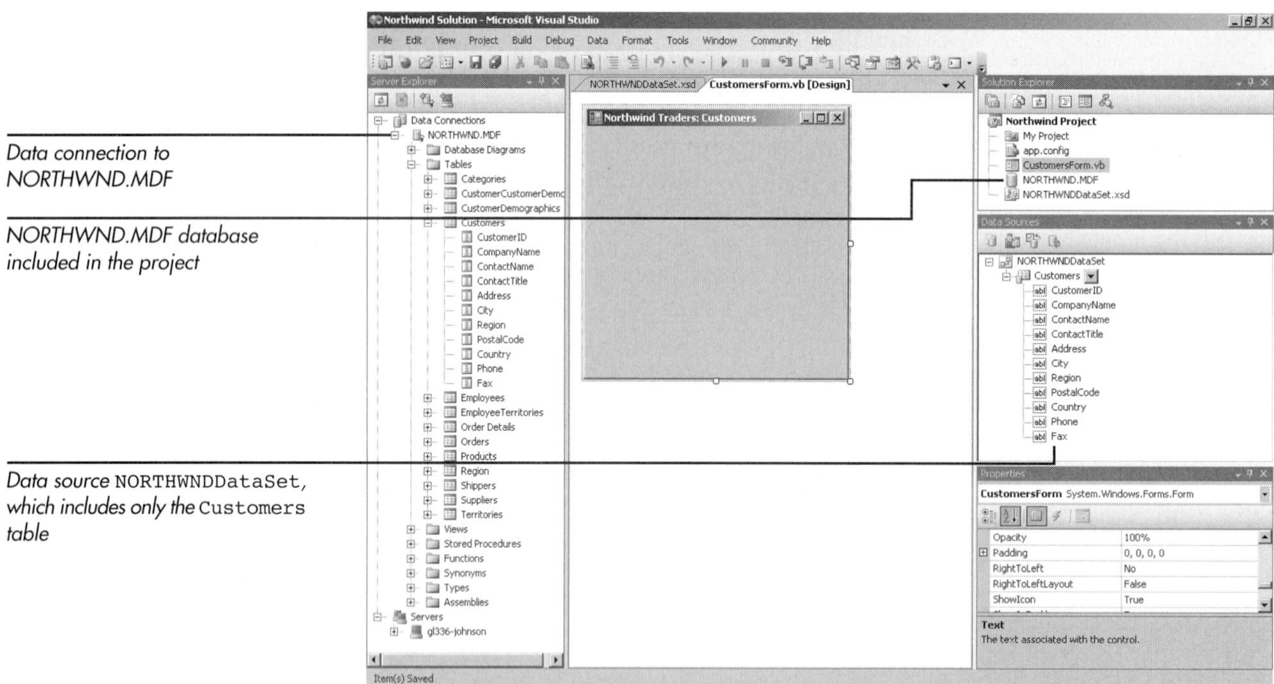

FIGURE 8.15 The Northwind application prior to adding a `DataGridView`

Certain features of a `DataGridView` can be accessed using the smart tag arrow (the small white square with an enclosed black arrow-head near the upper right corner of the `DataGridView`). The `DataGridView` Tasks window allows you to edit columns in the `DataGridView`, enable/disable database transactions, and dock the `DataGridView` to the form (among other things).

Applying the steps in Figure 8.14 to the Northwind application of Figure 8.15 results in the `DataGridView` object shown in Figure 8.16. (In the figure, the `DataGridView` has been made to fill the form and various windows of the IDE have been hidden.) The component tray (at the bottom of the Windows Form Designer) contains four kinds of components (objects). `NORTHWNDDataSet` is the `DataSet` object for the Northwind database, while `CustomersTableAdapter` is the link between the `DataSet` and the database. The other components are described next.

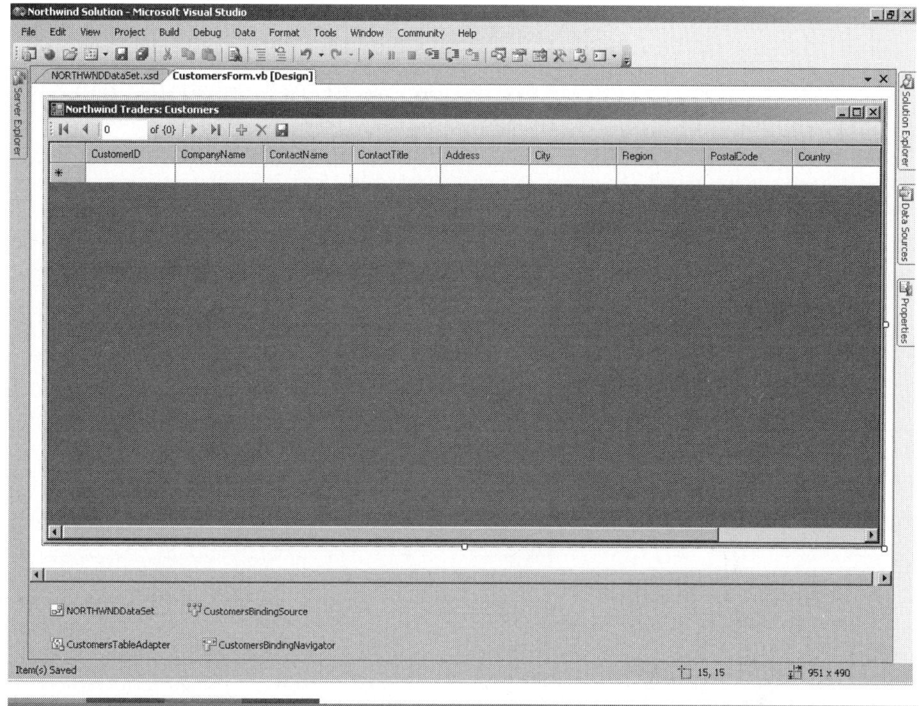

FIGURE 8.16 A `DataGridView` in the Northwind application

`BindingSource` and `BindingNavigator` Objects

Two other important objects are shown in the component tray of Figure 8.16: `CustomersBindingSource` and `CustomersBindingNavigator`. A `BindingSource` component binds or links a form component (`CustomersDataGridView`, in this case) to a `DataTable` (`Customers`) in a `DataSet` (`CustomersDataSet`), thus allowing the form component to display data. A `BindingSource` component also handles **concurrency management**, a database management process for maintaining data consistency when two or more users access the same data simultaneously. The default concurrency process for ADO.NET is called **optimistic concurrency**. In this form of concurrency, when multiple users are trying to update the same value in a database at the same time, the first update is processed and other users are simply notified of the concurrency violation so they may try again. In the other type of concurrency, **pessimistic concurrency**, when one user retrieves a row of data for possible updates, that row is locked and cannot be retrieved by other users until the first user releases it. Thus, pessimistic concurrency is safer, but it ties up database resources longer when many users are contending for database resources. Optimistic concurrency can force users to reprocess their transactions, but conflicts are unlikely to occur when few users are contending for database resources.

The `CustomersBindingNavigator` object, also shown in the component tray of Figure 8.16, is responsible for navigating and manipulating the data in a `DataGridView` object. A `BindingNavigator` component is associated with the `ToolStrip` buttons shown at the top of the `DataGridView` in Figure 8.16. Thus, a `BindingNavigator` allows you to move from row to row, add new rows, delete existing rows, and save changes in data to the database.

Summarizing the `DataGridView`

This section has focused on adding database functionality to an application using the `DataGridView` object. To see how data appear in a `DataGridView` object, a sample run of the Northwind application produces the window shown in Figure 8.17.

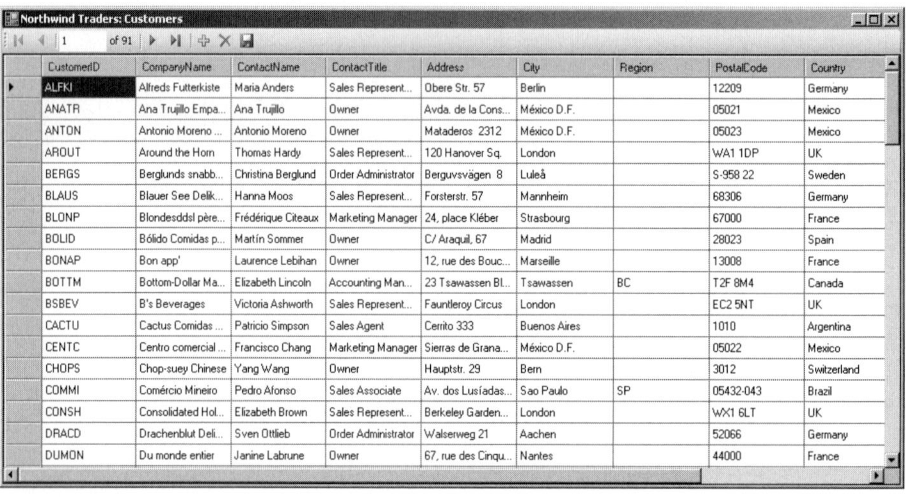

CustomerID	CompanyName	ContactName	ContactTitle	Address	City	Region	PostalCode	Country
ALFKI	Alfreds Futterkiste	Maria Anders	Sales Represent...	Obere Str. 57	Berlin		12209	Germany
ANATR	Ana Trujillo Empa...	Ana Trujillo	Owner	Avda. de la Cons...	México D.F.		05021	Mexico
ANTON	Antonio Moreno ...	Antonio Moreno	Owner	Mataderos 2312	México D.F.		05023	Mexico
AROUT	Around the Horn	Thomas Hardy	Sales Represent...	120 Hanover Sq.	London		WA1 1DP	UK
BERGS	Berglunds snabb...	Christina Berglund	Order Administrator	Berguvsvägen 8	Luleå		S-958 22	Sweden
BLAUS	Blauer See Delik...	Hanna Moos	Sales Represent...	Forsterstr. 57	Mannheim		68306	Germany
BLONP	Blondesddsl père...	Frédérique Citeaux	Marketing Manager	24, place Kléber	Strasbourg		67000	France
BOLID	Bólido Comidas p...	Martín Sommer	Owner	C/ Araquil, 67	Madrid		28023	Spain
BONAP	Bon app'	Laurence Lebihan	Owner	12, rue des Bouc...	Marseille		13008	France
BOTTM	Bottom-Dollar Ma...	Elizabeth Lincoln	Accounting Man...	23 Tsawassen Bl...	Tsawassen	BC	T2F 8M4	Canada
BSBEV	B's Beverages	Victoria Ashworth	Sales Represent...	Fauntleroy Circus	London		EC2 5NT	UK
CACTU	Cactus Comidas ...	Patricio Simpson	Sales Agent	Cerrito 333	Buenos Aires		1010	Argentina
CENTC	Centro comercial ...	Francisco Chang	Marketing Manager	Sierras de Grana...	México D.F.		05022	Mexico
CHOPS	Chop-suey Chinese	Yang Wang	Owner	Hauptstr. 29	Bern		3012	Switzerland
COMMI	Comércio Mineiro	Pedro Afonso	Sales Associate	Av. dos Lusíadas...	Sao Paulo	SP	05432-043	Brazil
CONSH	Consolidated Hol...	Elizabeth Brown	Sales Represent...	Berkeley Garden...	London		WX1 6LT	UK
DRACD	Drachenblut Deli...	Sven Ottlieb	Order Administrator	Walserweg 21	Aachen		52066	Germany
DUMON	Du monde entier	Janine Labrune	Owner	67, rue des Cinqu...	Nantes		44000	France

FIGURE 8.17 Sample run for the Northwind application

TIP

The data in a `DataGridView` can be sorted for any column by simply clicking the column header. Alternating clicks will sort in ascending or descending order.

This discussion of adding a `DataGridView` to a form introduced three new classes: `TableAdapter`, `BindingSource`, and `BindingNavigator`. These classes were not included in the more general diagram in Figure 8.1. To bring that figure up to date, Figure 8.18 shows how these classes are used to connect a database with an application. Note that the `TableAdapter` object contains a connection object and is also capable of executing multiple queries against a `DataSet`, and can thus interface with multiple `DataTable` objects. You will learn more about using SQL queries in an application later in this chapter.

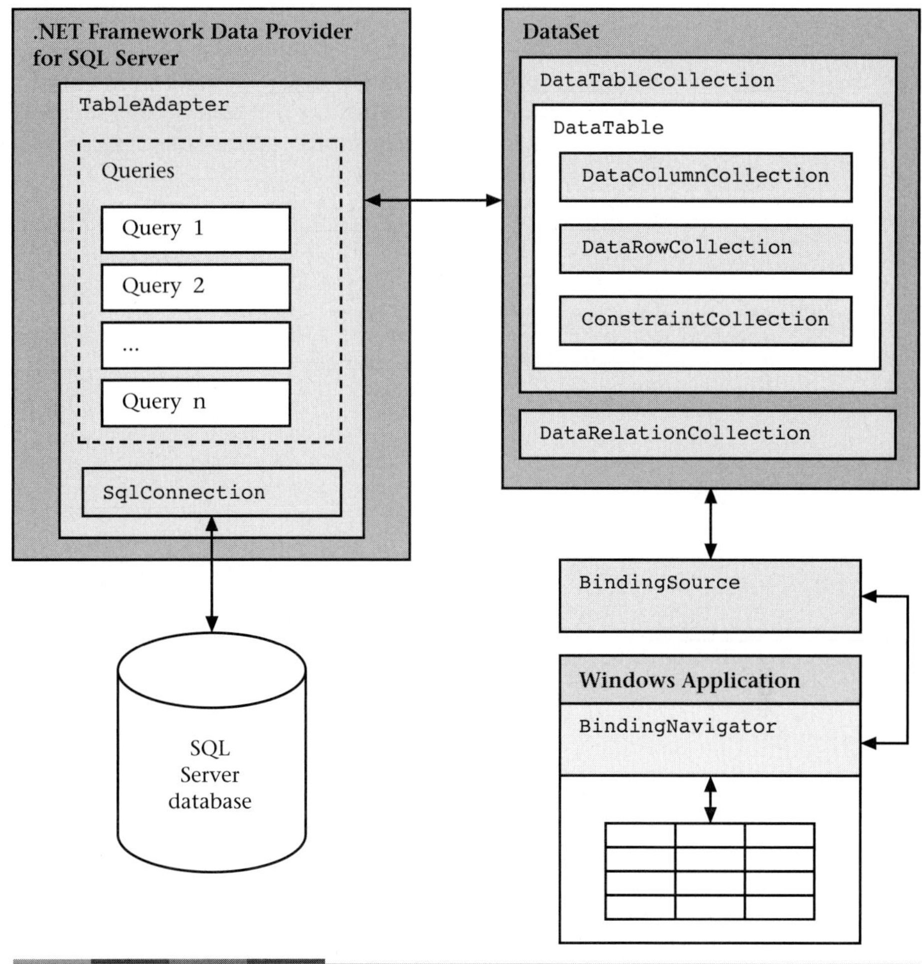

FIGURE 8.18 `TableAdapter`, `BindingSource`, and `BindingNavigator` in an application

Program Code for the Northwind Application

So far, the Northwind application has been created by using drag-and-drop techniques. However, it is instructive to view the code behind the form. Figure 8.19 provides a view of the automatically generated code for `CustomersForm`. Recall that the keyword `Me` refers to the current object, in this case `CustomersForm`. The `CustomersForm_Load` procedure (Lines 12–19) uses the `Fill` method of the `CustomersTableAdapter` object to populate the `Customers` table in the `NORTHWNDDataSet`. As a result, the `CustomersBindingSource` object automatically fills the `DataGridView` with the data from the `Customers` table.

Also, the `CustomersBindingNavigatorSaveItem_Click` procedure in Figure 8.19 (Lines 3–10) is called when the user clicks the Save icon in the `DataGridView`. First, within this procedure the `CustomersForm` (`Me`) calls the `Validate` method. This causes any controls in the form to be checked for valid data entry. (In this case, there is only one control, the `DataGridView`.) For example, if you delete a customer name in the `DataGridView` and click the Save icon, the `Validate` method will cause an error message to appear because, due to constraints added to the SQL Server database, the `CustomerName` field is not allowed to be null.

Next, within the `CustomersBindingNavigatorSaveItem_Click` procedure, the `CustomersBindingSource` object calls the `EndEdit` method. This method applies the changes in the `DataGridView` to the `NORTHWNDDataSet`. Finally, the `CustomersTableAdapter` object calls the `Update` method to write the current `DataSet` (`NORTHWNDDataSet.Customers`) to the Northwind database.

```
Public Class CustomersForm

    Private Sub CustomersBindingNavigatorSaveItem_Click( _
        ByVal sender As System.Object, ByVal e As System.EventArgs) _
        Handles CustomersBindingNavigatorSaveItem.Click
        Me.Validate()
        Me.CustomersBindingSource.EndEdit()
        Me.CustomersTableAdapter.Update(Me.NORTHWNDDataSet.Customers)

    End Sub

    Private Sub CustomersForm_Load(ByVal sender As System.Object, _
        ByVal e As System.EventArgs) Handles MyBase.Load
        'TODO: This line of code loads data into the
        ''NORTHWNDDataSet.Customers' table. You can move, or remove it,
        ' as needed.
        Me.CustomersTableAdapter.Fill(Me.NORTHWNDDataSet.Customers)

    End Sub
End Class
```

FIGURE 8.19 Program code for the `CustomersForm` class with a `DataGridView`

Creating a Details Form

As an alternative to a `DataGridView`, you can drag a data source to a form to automatically create controls that display one record at a time. You can even preselect the type of control used for displaying data. This procedure is detailed in Figure 8.20.

HOW TO...

Create a Details Form

1. With an empty form displayed in the Windows Form Designer (as seen previously in Figure 8.12), make sure that the Data Sources window is open. (Click Data in the Visual Studio menu and then click Show Data Sources to open the Data Sources window.)
2. Click the desired table in the Data Sources window. A drop-down arrow appears to the right of the table name.
3. Click the drop-down arrow and then click Details in the list.
4. Click the + sign to the left of the table to expand it into its fields. By default, a `TextField` icon is displayed to the left of each field.
5. Click on a specific field to display a drop-down arrow for that field. Click the drop-down arrow to display a list of alternative control types (`Label`, `ComboBox`, etc.). Click the desired control type for that field. (See Figure 8.21 for an example.)

(Figure is continued on next page)

6. When you are finished configuring all fields for the table in the Data Sources window, drag the table from the Data Sources window to the form. Labels and other controls are automatically added to the form, including `DataSet`, `BindingSource`, `TableAdapter`, and `BindingNavigator` controls in the component tray.
7. Modify the locations, sizes, and other properties of the individual controls on the form as necessary.

FIGURE 8.20 How to create a Details form

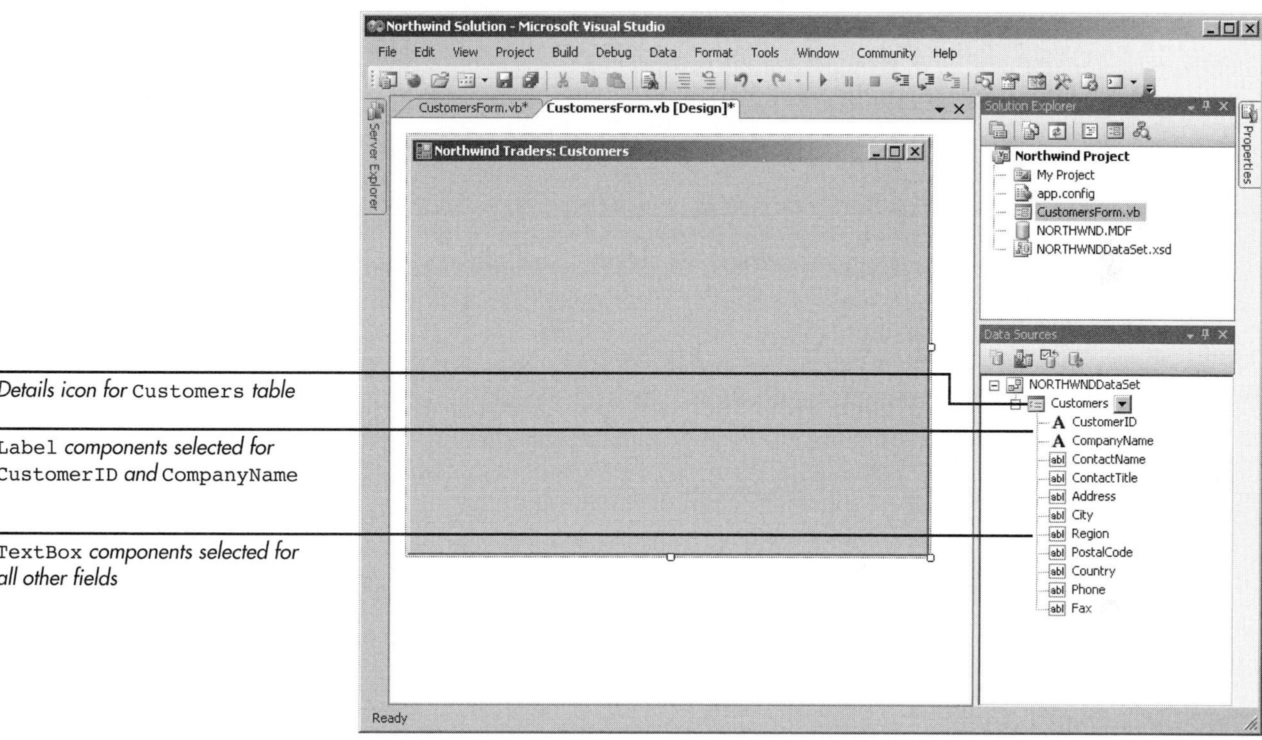

FIGURE 8.21 Northwind application prior to creating a Details form

Figure 8.22 shows the result of applying all the steps in Figure 8.20 to the Northwind application. Note that the first two fields in the Data Sources window have been changed to labels. This prevents the user from changing the `CustomerID` and the `CompanyName`. Note also that the `CustomersForm` has the same `BindingNavigation` toolbar as the Northwind application with a `DataGridView`, allowing the user to move from row to row, add a new row, delete a row, and update (save) a row. The only difference is that the Details view shows just one record at a time, while the `DataGridView` displays many records at once.

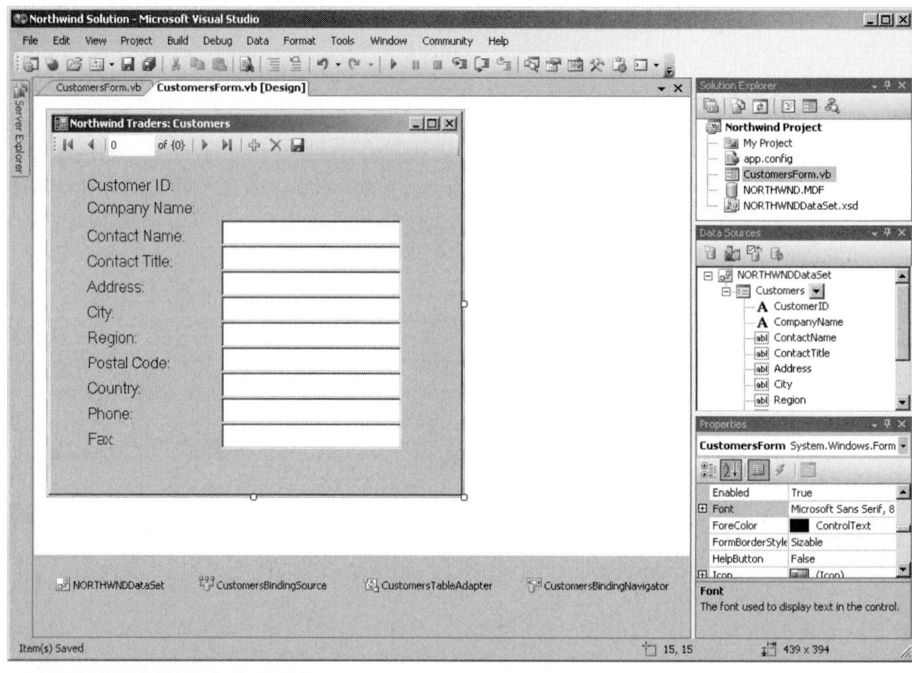

FIGURE 8.22 The Northwind application with a Details form

In case you were wondering, the program code for this new Northwind application with the Details form is exactly the same as the application with the `DataGridView` control (see Figure 8.19). The functionality of both applications is the same—only the controls used to display the data are different. Figure 8.23 shows a sample run of this application

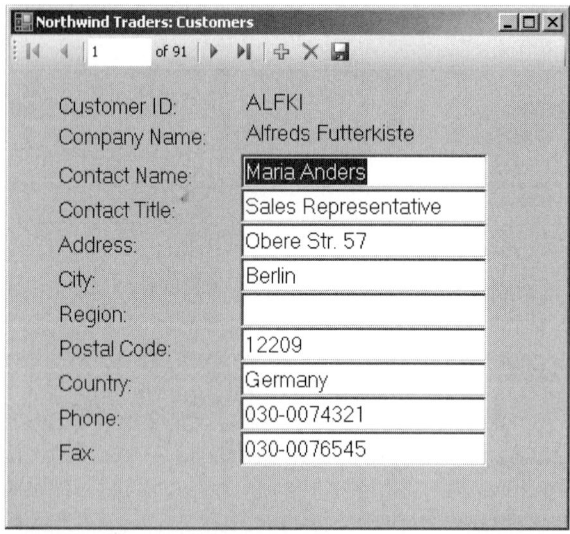

FIGURE 8.23 Sample run of the Northwind application with a Details form

USING SQL IN APPLICATIONS

In Chapter 7, you learned how to write a wide variety of SQL statements to manipulate data in a database. However, you used SQL only from within the database management system itself (either Microsoft Access or SQL Server). Now you will explore how to utilize SQL within a Visual Basic application.

Modify the Query in a Data Source

Recall that a **query** is a set of instructions written in SQL. For example, the following SQL statement is a very simple query that selects all the data in the `Customers` table in the Northwind database:

```
SELECT * FROM Customers
```

In the previous section, you learned how to add a data source to a form and display data from a table using either the `DataGridView` or the Details view. However, the examples shown simply displayed all data in a table by default. Many times you will want to be more selective regarding the data displayed in a form. Figure 8.24 demonstrates how you can modify the query that displays data from a data source.

HOW TO...

Modify the Query in a Data Source

1. In the application's Solution Explorer, double-click the data source's XML Schema Definition file (the file with the .xsd extension). The objects in the `DataSet` will be displayed. (You saw an example of this earlier in Figure 8.13.)
2. Right-click the `TableAdapter` object in the schema and then click Configure. The TableAdapter Configuration Wizard opens, as shown in Figure 8.25. The first page of this wizard, the Enter a SQL Statement page, presents a default SQL statement that selects all columns of the table. You can directly modify this default SQL statement by entering the code for an SQL statement in the white box or by clicking the Query Builder button to modify the query. If you choose to modify the default SQL statement directly, make the desired changes in the white box and go to Step 5; otherwise, click the Query Builder button, causing the Query Builder window to open.
3. In the Query Builder window (Figure 8.26), you can use the Diagram pane (the top pane containing a graphic of the table or tables involved), the Criteria pane (the second pane with the grid of rows and columns), and/or the SQL pane (the third pane containing an SQL statement) to modify the query. If you are unfamiliar with the Query Builder, experiment with these three panes to see how changes in one pane affect the others.
4. When the query is complete in the Query Builder, click the Execute Query button to view the results in the Results pane (the bottom pane). When the modified query is acceptable, click OK.
5. The modified query is now visible in the TableAdapter Configuration Wizard (Figure 8.27). Click Next.

(Figure is continued on next page)

6. In the Choose Methods to Generate page (Figure 8.28), check all three categories of methods to interact with the database and click Next. Click Finish to accept all changes to the configuration of the `TableAdapter`.
7. Save the `DataSet` schema file and close the file.

FIGURE 8.24 How to modify a query in a data source

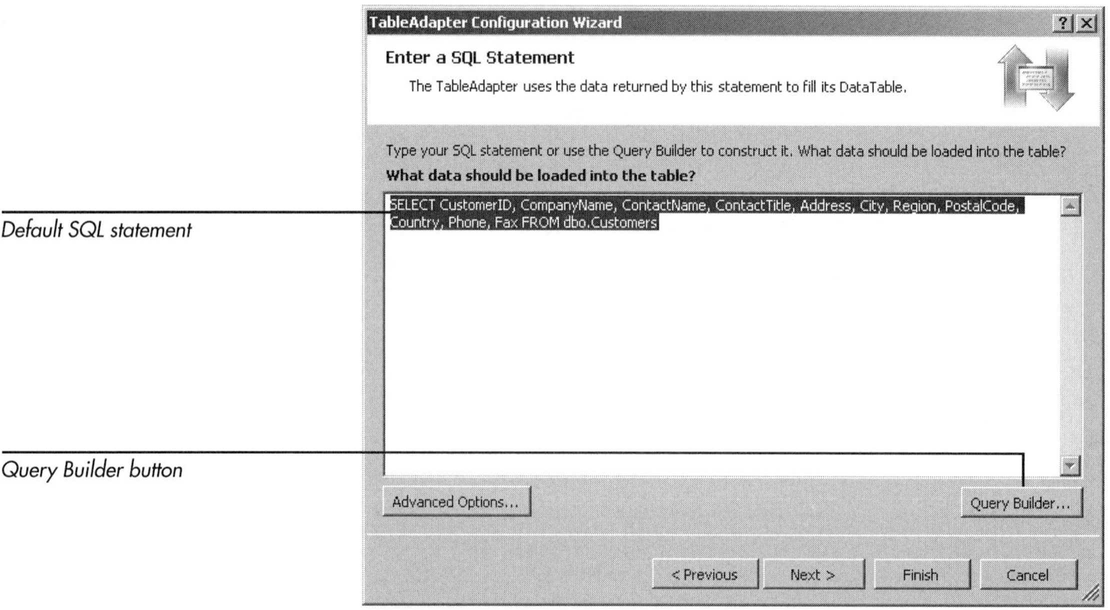

FIGURE 8.25 The TableAdapter Configuration Wizard

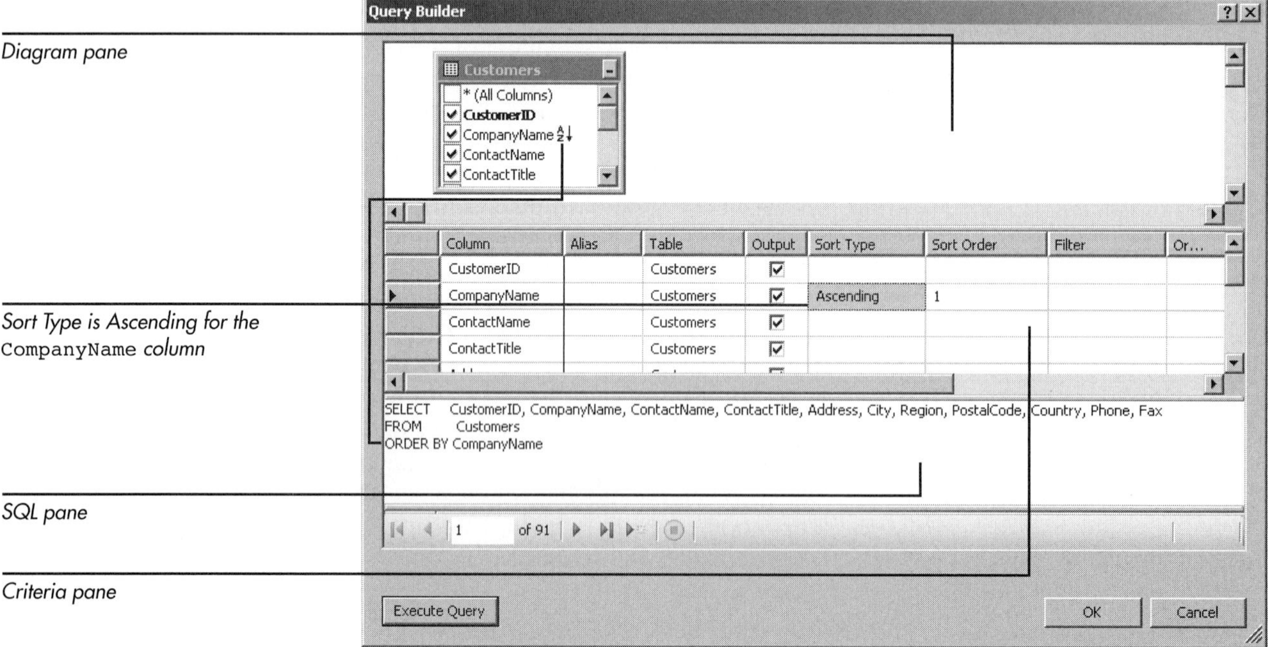

FIGURE 8.26 The Query Builder—modifying an existing query

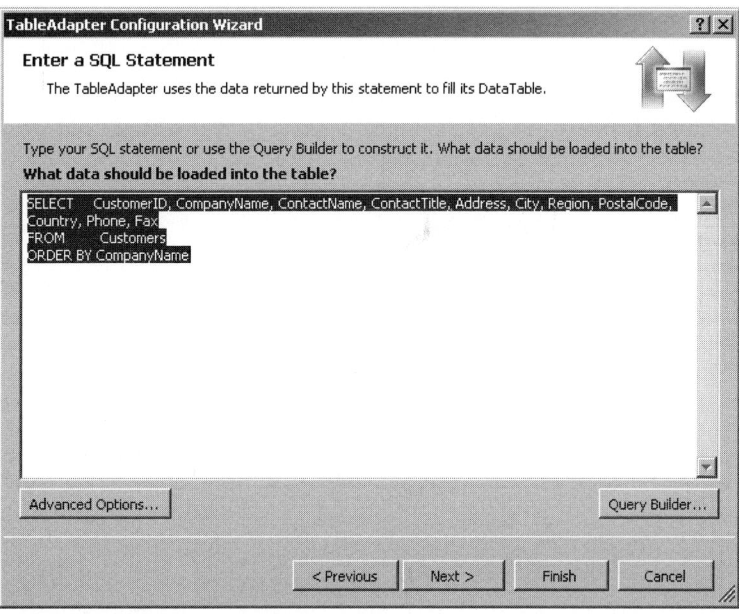

FIGURE 8.27 Modified query in the TableAdapter Configuration Wizard

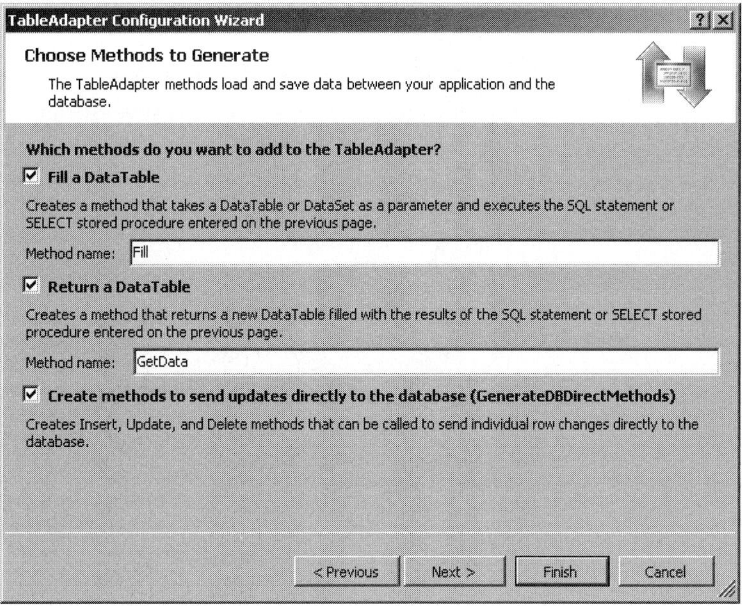

FIGURE 8.28 Choose Methods to Generate page of the TableAdapter Configuration Wizard

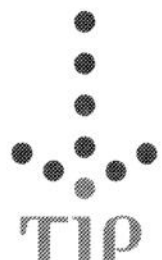

TIP

You can also modify a query for a **`TableAdapter`** by right-clicking the **`TableAdapter`** icon in the Windows Form Designer and clicking Add Query... or by selecting a form, clicking Data in the Visual Studio menu, and clicking Add Query...

The steps listed in Figure 8.24 were applied to the `NORTHWNDDataSet` (which consists of all columns in the `Customers` table), adding a sort criterion. Notice in the Criteria pane in Figure 8.26 that Ascending was selected in the Sort Type column for the `CompanyName` field, which caused the code `ORDER BY CompanyName` to be added to the SQL statement and an A → Z graphic to be added next to CompanyName in the Diagram pane (as shown in Figure 8.26). Now, when the form loads, the data will be sorted by company name rather than by customer ID, as shown in Figure 8.29.

`DataGridView` *sorted by CompanyName Ascending*

Northwind Traders: Customers

1 of 91

CustomerID	CompanyName	ContactName	ContactTitle	Address	City	Region	PostalCode	Country
ALFKI	Alfreds Futterkiste	Maria Anders	Sales Represent...	Obere Str. 57	Berlin		12209	Germany
ANATR	Ana Trujillo Empa...	Ana Trujillo	Owner	Avda. de la Cons...	México D.F.		05021	Mexico
ANTON	Antonio Moreno ...	Antonio Moreno	Owner	Mataderos 2312	México D.F.		05023	Mexico
AROUT	Around the Horn	Thomas Hardy	Sales Represent...	120 Hanover Sq.	London		WA1 1DP	UK
BERGS	Berglunds snabb...	Christina Berglund	Order Administrator	Berguvsvägen 8	Luleå		S-958 22	Sweden
BLAUS	Blauer See Delik...	Hanna Moos	Sales Represent...	Forsterstr. 57	Mannheim		68306	Germany
BLONP	Blondesddsl père...	Frédérique Citeaux	Marketing Manager	24, place Kléber	Strasbourg		67000	France
BOLID	Bólido Comidas p...	Martín Sommer	Owner	C/ Araquil, 67	Madrid		28023	Spain
BONAP	Bon app'	Laurence Lebihan	Owner	12, rue des Bouc...	Marseille		13008	France
BOTTM	Bottom-Dollar Ma...	Elizabeth Lincoln	Accounting Man...	23 Tsawassen Bl...	Tsawassen	BC	T2F 8M4	Canada
BSBEV	B's Beverages	Victoria Ashworth	Sales Represent...	Fauntleroy Circus	London		EC2 5NT	UK
CACTU	Cactus Comidas ...	Patricio Simpson	Sales Agent	Cerrito 333	Buenos Aires		1010	Argentina
CENTC	Centro comercial ...	Francisco Chang	Marketing Manager	Sierras de Grana...	México D.F.		05022	Mexico
CHOPS	Chop-suey Chinese	Yang Wang	Owner	Hauptstr. 29	Bern		3012	Switzerland
COMMI	Comércio Mineiro	Pedro Afonso	Sales Associate	Av. dos Lusíadas...	Sao Paulo	SP	05432-043	Brazil
CONSH	Consolidated Hol...	Elizabeth Brown	Sales Represent...	Berkeley Garden...	London		WX1 6LT	UK
WANDK	Die Wandernde ...	Rita Müller	Sales Represent...	Adenauerallee 900	Stuttgart		70563	Germany
DRACD	Drachenblut Deli...	Sven Ottlieb	Order Administrator	Walserweg 21	Aachen		52066	Germany

FIGURE 8.29 Sample run of the Northwind application with a modified query

Adding a New Query for a `DataGridView`

Quite often you will need to add several new queries to an application to allow the user different views of the data in a database. Figure 8.30 explains how to do this for a `DataGridView` control.

HOW TO...

Add a New Query for a `DataGridView`

1. Select the `DataGridView` control in the Windows Form Designer. In the Visual Studio menu, click Data and then click Add Query.
2. In the Search Criteria Builder window, click the New query name option button and type a query name in the text box (no spaces). See Figure 8.31.
3. Either create the new query in the Query Text: area or click the Query Builder... button. (See Figure 8.24, Steps 3 and 4, for details on using the Query Builder; see Figure 8.32 for an example of creating a new query in the Query Builder.)
4. If you created the query in the Query Builder, click the Execute Query button to view the results in the Result (bottom) pane (see Figure 8.33). When the query is acceptable, click OK in the Query Builder and then click OK in the Search Criteria Builder. A new `ToolStrip` object is created and appears in the Component tray at the bottom of the Visual Basic IDE. An accompanying `ToolStripButton` object is also created and appears just below the navigation bar near the top of the form (see Figure 8.34).

(Figure is continued on next page)

5. To change the properties of the `ToolStripButton`, click Properties, and change the properties (such as `Text`) as desired. For example, the text "BcCustomersQuery" that appears in a `ToolStripButton` can be changed to something more readable, such as "BC Customers".
6. To move the `ToolStripButton` object, click the `ToolStrip` object in the Component tray; a smart tag appears at the far right edge of the `ToolStripButton`. Click the smart tag arrow and then select None from the Dock drop-down list. Click the left edge of the `ToolStrip` again and drag the `Toolstrip` to the desired location in the form (such as next to the navigation bar).
7. Save all files and test the application.

FIGURE 8.30 How to add a new query to a data source

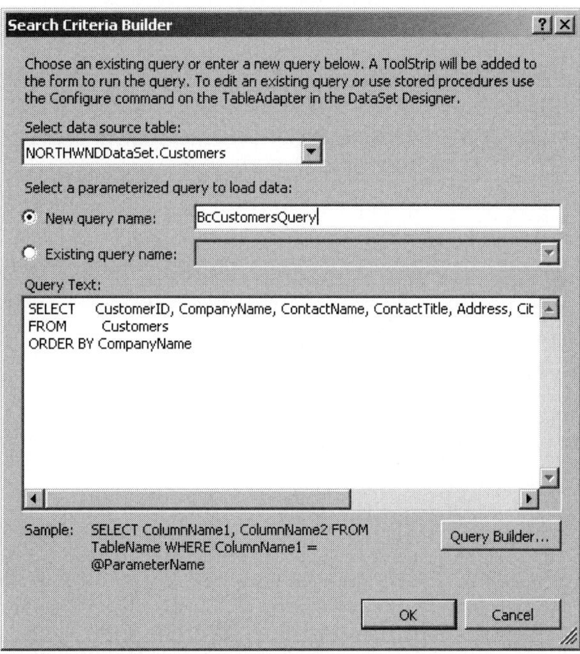

FIGURE 8.31 The Search Criteria Builder dialog box

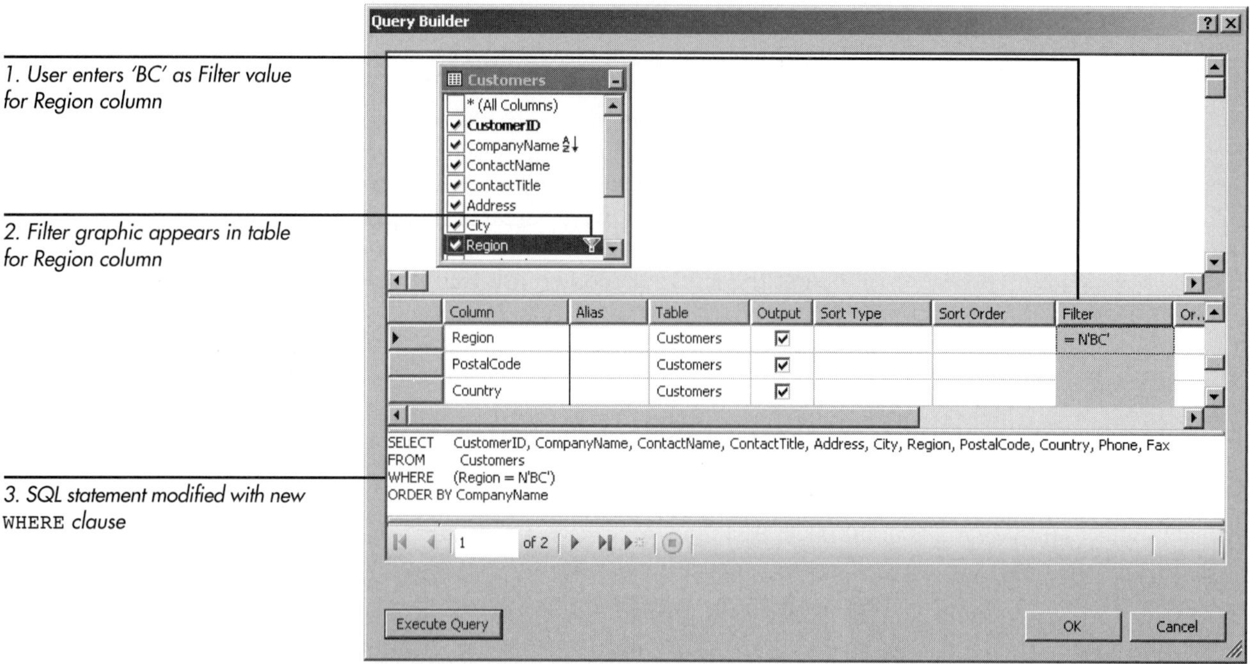

FIGURE 8.32 A new query in the Query Builder

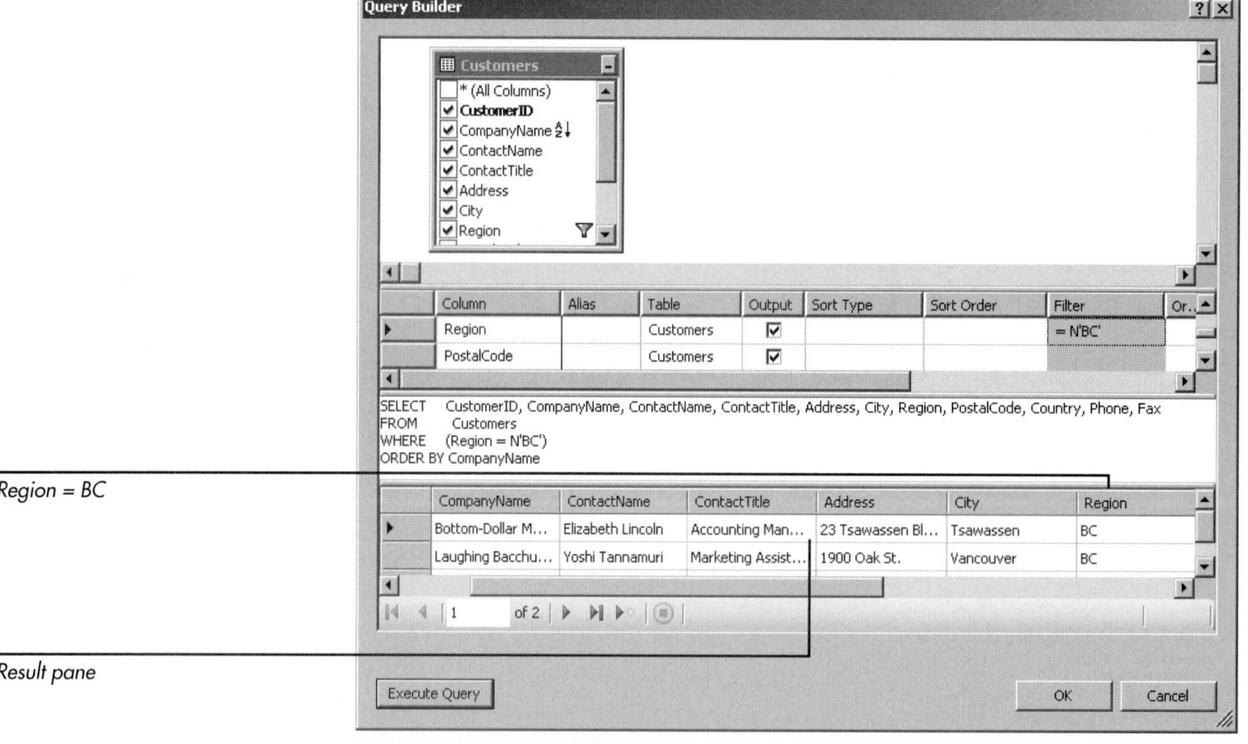

FIGURE 8.33 Result of clicking the Execute Query button

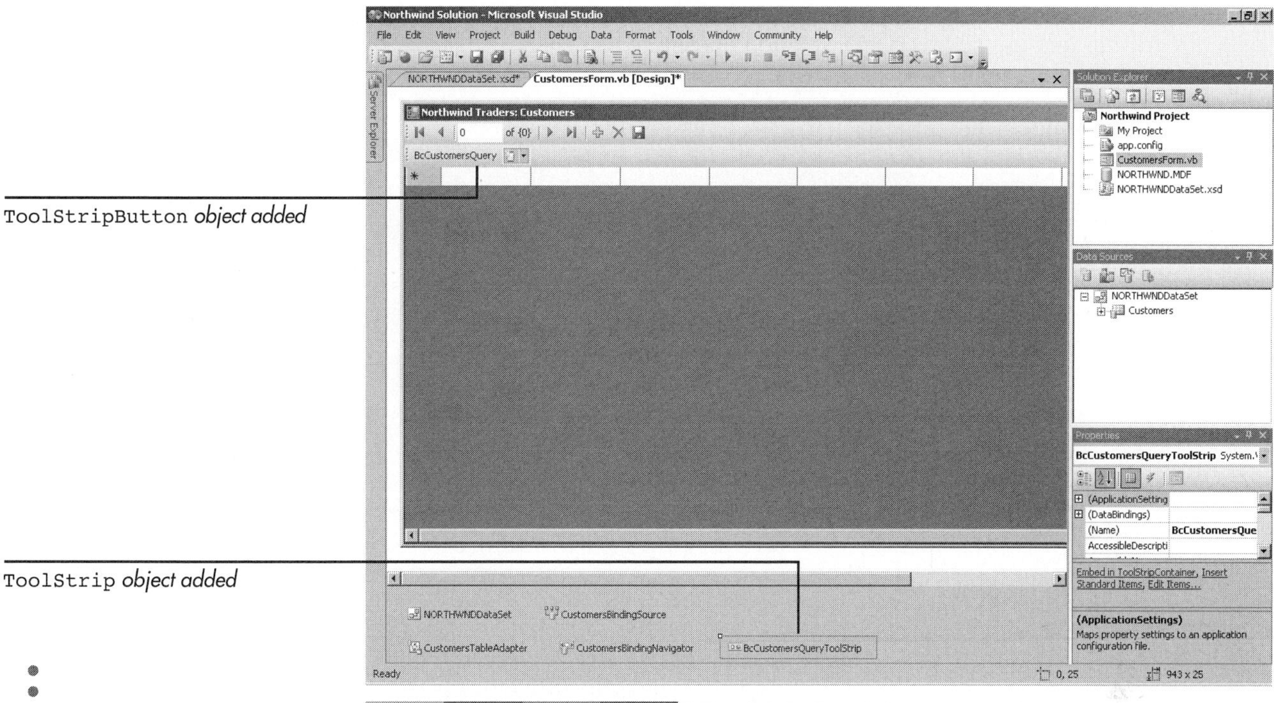

FIGURE 8.34 Northwind application with new query added

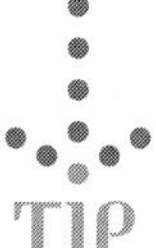

TIP

There are several different versions of SQL used by different database software vendors. All versions are very similar, with only a few slight differences. The version of SQL used by Microsoft SQL Server is called Transact-SQL. This version of SQL adds the character N to data types and data values. This denotes that Unicode characters are being used. The letter N stands for national language character set.

The steps in Figure 8.30 were applied to the Northwind application originally represented by Figure 8.29. A query, called `BcCustomersQuery`, was added to display only the customers where the value of the `Region` column is BC (British Columbia). The Query Builder for this query is shown in Figure 8.32. The value `BC` was simply typed in the cell in the Criteria pane (second pane from the top) for the Region row and the Filter column. (A filter is a criterion that a column value must meet.) You could also type `=BC` or `='BC'` in the Filter cell. The Query Builder changes the SQL statement, adding the code `WHERE Region = N'BC'`.

When the TableAdapter Configuration Wizard is completed, the Northwind application has a new component called `BcCustomersToolStrip`, which was moved to the `CustomersBindingNavigator` toolbar. The result of running this application and clicking the new BC Customers button is shown in Figure 8.35.

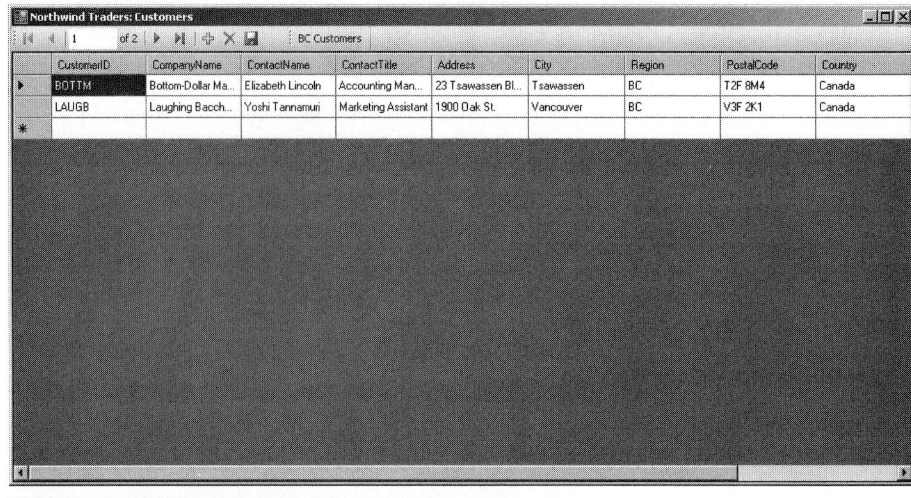

FIGURE 8.35 Sample run of the Northwind application with new query `BcCustomerQuery`

The program code for the Northwind application of Figure 8.35 is shown in Figure 8.36. Note that the only difference between this code and that in Figure 8.19 is the addition of the last `Sub` procedure, `BcCustomersToolStripButton_Click`. Visual Basic automatically generates this procedure, which includes a `Try` statement. Within the `Try` statement, the object `Me` (the `CustomersForm`), which contains the `CustomersTableAdapter` object, calls the `BcCustomersQuery` using the `Customers DataTable` in the `NORTHWNDDataSet` as its argument. The `Catch` statement will catch and display any error messages that result, such as when any of the required objects (a query, a `DataSet`, or a `DataTable`) are not present.

```
Public Class CustomersForm

    Private Sub CustomersBindingNavigatorSaveItem_Click( _
        ByVal sender As System.Object, ByVal e As System.EventArgs) _
        Handles CustomersBindingNavigatorSaveItem.Click
        Me.Validate()
        Me.CustomersBindingSource.EndEdit()
        Me.CustomersTableAdapter.Update(Me.NORTHWNDDataSet.Customers)

    End Sub

    Private Sub CustomersForm_Load(ByVal sender As System.Object, _
        ByVal e As System.EventArgs) Handles MyBase.Load
        'TODO: This line of code loads data into the
        ''NORTHWNDDataSet.Customers' table. You can move, or remove it,
        ' as needed.
        Me.CustomersTableAdapter.Fill(Me.NORTHWNDDataSet.Customers)

    End Sub

    Private Sub BcCustomersQueryToolStripButton_Click( _
        ByVal sender As System.Object, ByVal e As System.EventArgs) _
        Handles BcCustomersQueryToolStripButton.Click
```

(Figure is continued on next page)

```
        Try
            Me.CustomersTableAdapter.BcCustomersQuery( _
                Me.NORTHWNDDataSet.Customers)
        Catch ex As System.Exception
            System.Windows.Forms.MessageBox.Show(ex.Message)
        End Try

    End Sub
End Class
```

FIGURE 8.36 Program code for the Northwind application with new query `BcCustomersQuery`

Implementing a Query Using a Stored Procedure

A stored procedure is a query written in SQL Server's version of SQL called **Transact-SQL** (or T-SQL for short). T-SQL is very advanced, capable of creating a query that implements variables, conditional logic, loops, and flow control. (These advanced features of T-SQL will not be covered in this text.) Once a stored procedure is written in SQL Server, a query can be implemented in a Visual Basic application based on the stored procedure. Figure 8.37 explains how this is done.

HOW TO...

Implement a Query Using a Stored Procedure

1. Assuming that a stored procedure exists in an SQL Server database, open the `DataSet` Designer by double-clicking the XML schema definition file (the one with the .xsd extension) in the Solution Explorer.
2. In the `DataSet` Designer, right-click the `TableAdapter` object, point to Add, and then click Query (in the Visual Basic Express Edition, right-click the `TableAdapter` object and then click Add Query).
3. On the Choose a Command Type page of the TableAdapter Query Configuration Wizard, click the option for Use existing stored procedure (see Figure 8.38). Click Next.
4. On the Choose an existing stored procedure page, select a stored procedure from the drop-down list. The parameters (variables) and result columns are displayed (see Figure 8.39, which illustrates using the `FindRegion` stored procedure). Click Next.
5. On the Choose the shape of data page, click the appropriate option for the shape of data to be returned (tabular, single value, or no value) as shown in Figure 8.40. Click Next.
6. On the Choose Methods to Generate page, type the names of the methods associated for this query (see Figure 8.41, which uses the `FindRegion` stored procedure). The `FillBy` method fills an existing `DataTable,` while the `GetDataBy` method generates a new `DataTable`. Click Next.

(Figure is continued on next page)

7. If the results on the Wizard Results page are acceptable, click Finish; otherwise, click Previous to make necessary changes (see Figure 8.42).
8. Save the `DataSet` Designer file. See Figure 8.43 for an example of the Northwind application that includes the new `FillByFindRegion` query.
9. Add controls to the form (such as a `DataGridView`, as presented in Figure 8.14) and then add the new query to the control (such as a `ToolStripButton`, as explained in Figure 8.30) to implement the new query based on a stored procedure. However, in Step 2 of Figure 8.30, you would select Existing query name instead of New query name because you have already created the query using a stored procedure, as shown in Figure 8.44.

FIGURE 8.37 How to use a stored procedure in a query

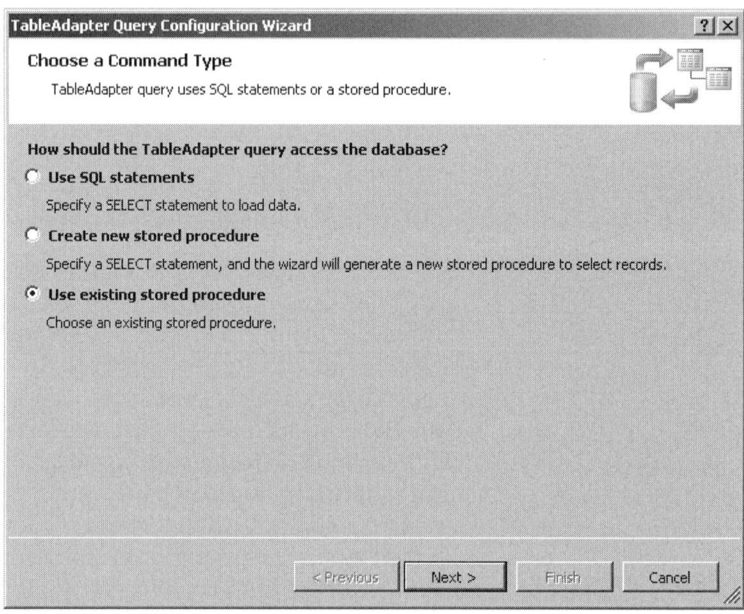

FIGURE 8.38 Choose a Command Type

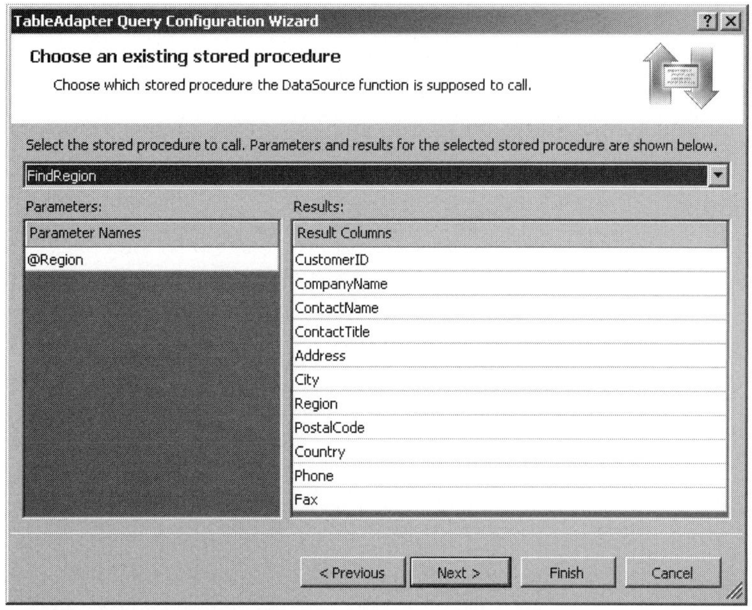

FIGURE 8.39 Choose an existing stored procedure

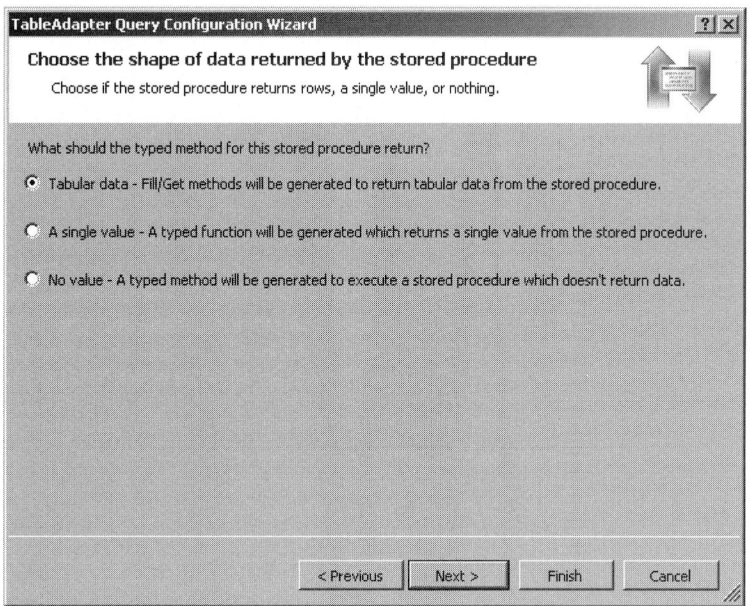

FIGURE 8.40 Choose the shape of data returned by the stored procedure

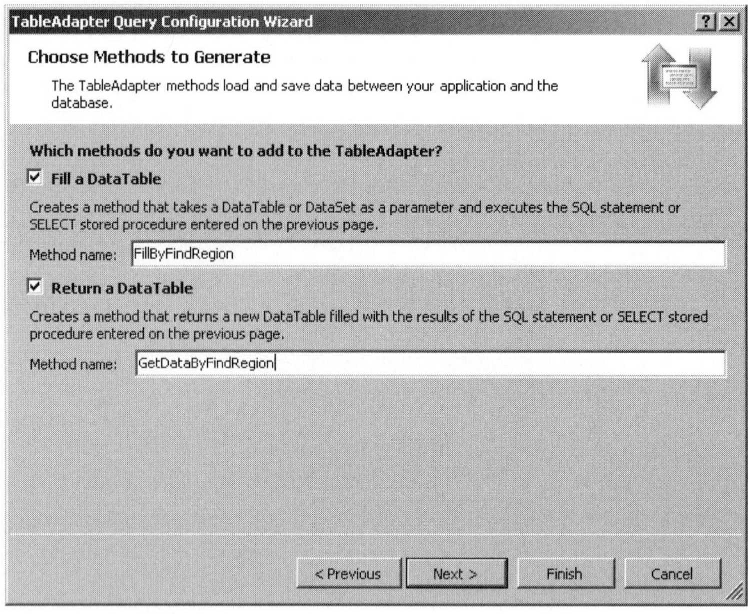

FIGURE 8.41 Choose Methods to Generate

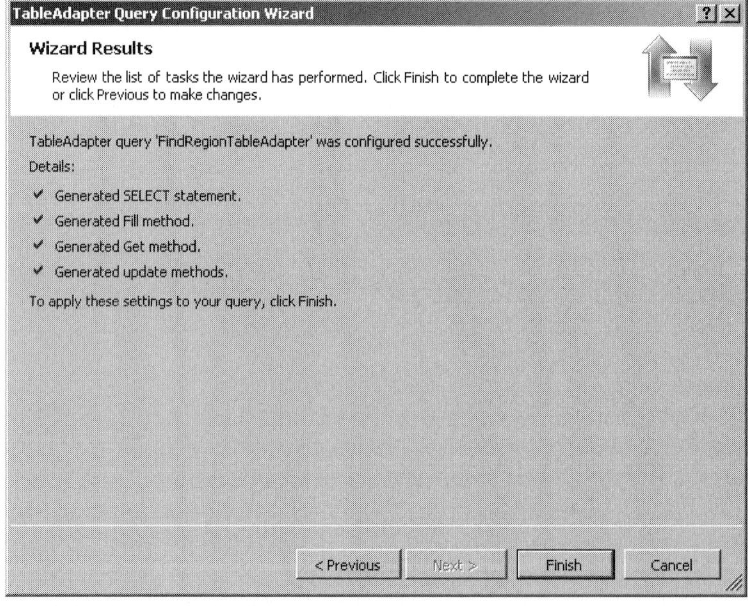

FIGURE 8.42 Wizard Results

`FindRegion` *stored procedure in Northwind database*

`FillByFindRegion` *query in* `NORTHWINDDataSet`

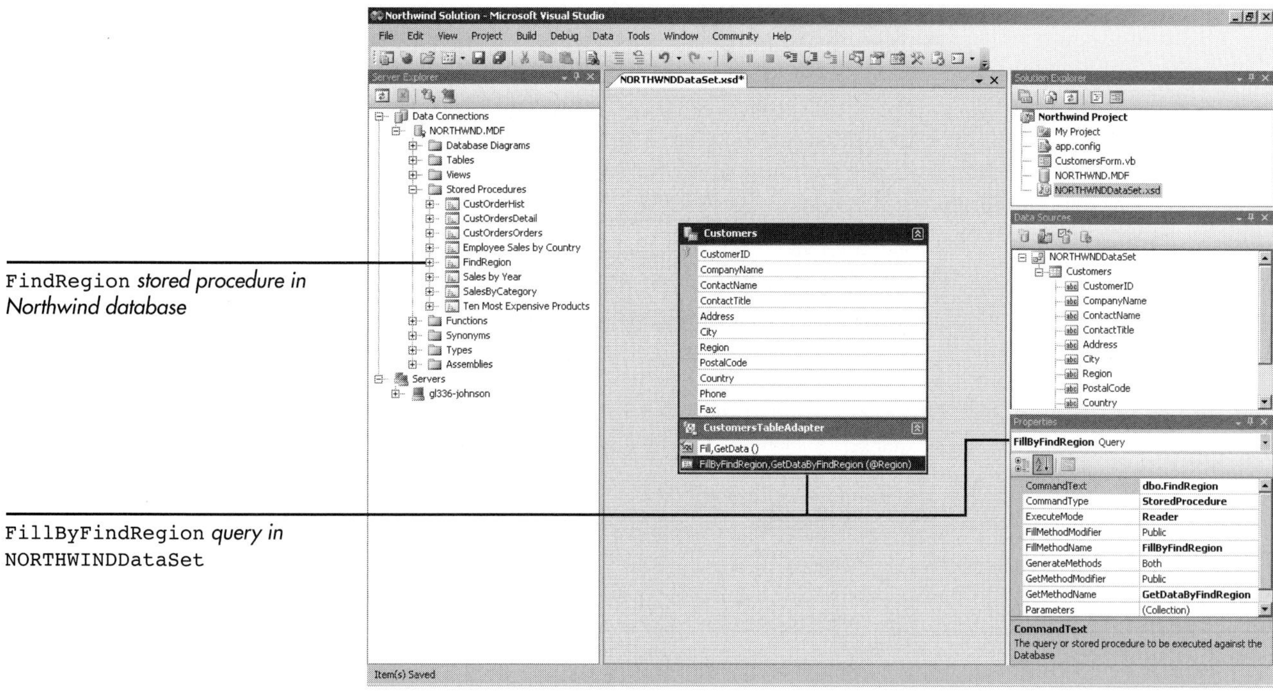

FIGURE 8.43 Northwind application with the `FillByFindRegion` query

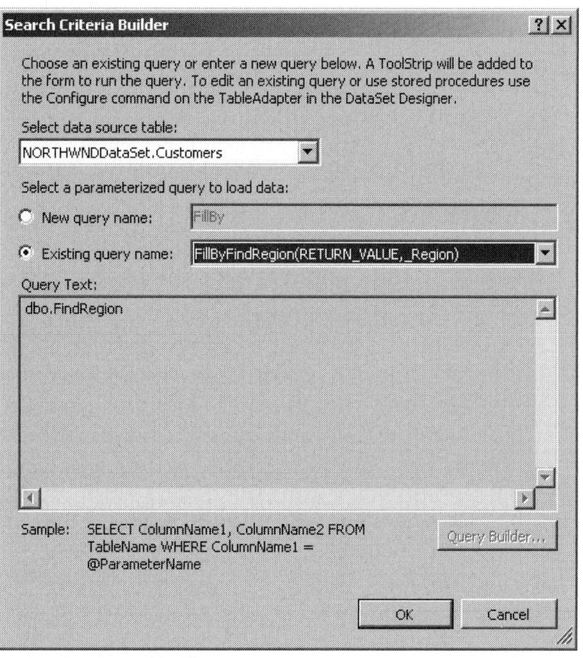

FIGURE 8.44 Adding the existing query `FillByFindRegion` to a `DataGridView`

The steps of Figure 8.37 are now applied to the Northwind application using a `DataGridView` and a query based on the `FindRegion` stored procedure (created in Chapter 7). Figure 8.45 shows the `FindRegion` stored procedure from within the Visual Basic IDE. (Recall that you can view a stored procedure in Visual Basic by opening the Server Explorer window, expanding the Stored Procedures node of the database, and double-clicking the desired stored procedure.)

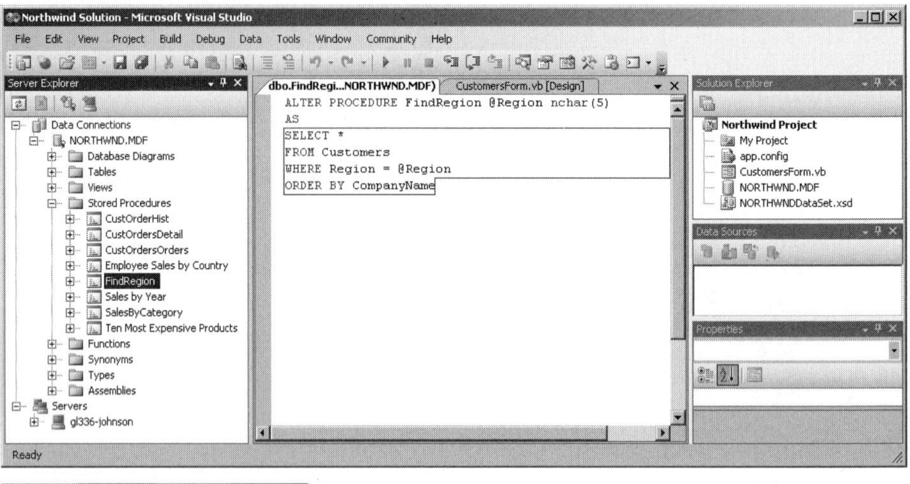

FIGURE 8.45 The `FindRegion` stored procedure in the Northwind database

The `FindRegion` stored procedure in Figure 8.45 includes the parameter `@Region`, which serves as a variable, the value of which the user supplies. For example, if `@Region` is BC (British Columbia), the query that uses this stored procedure would be as follows:

```
SELECT * FROM Customers WHERE Region = BC ORDER BY CompanyName
```

When the steps of Figure 8.37 are applied to the Northwind application using a `DataGridView` and a query based on the `FindRegion` stored procedure, the result is the application shown in Figure 8.46, which includes a `FillByFindRegionToolStrip`. Notice that the `ToolStrip` contains a label, a text box, and a button. The `Text` properties of the label and button have been altered to be more readable for the user. To use the application, the user would enter a region (such as BC for British Columbia) in the `ToolStrip` text box and click the Find Region button to execute the query. The results display in the `DataGridView`. A sample run of this application is shown in Figure 8.47.

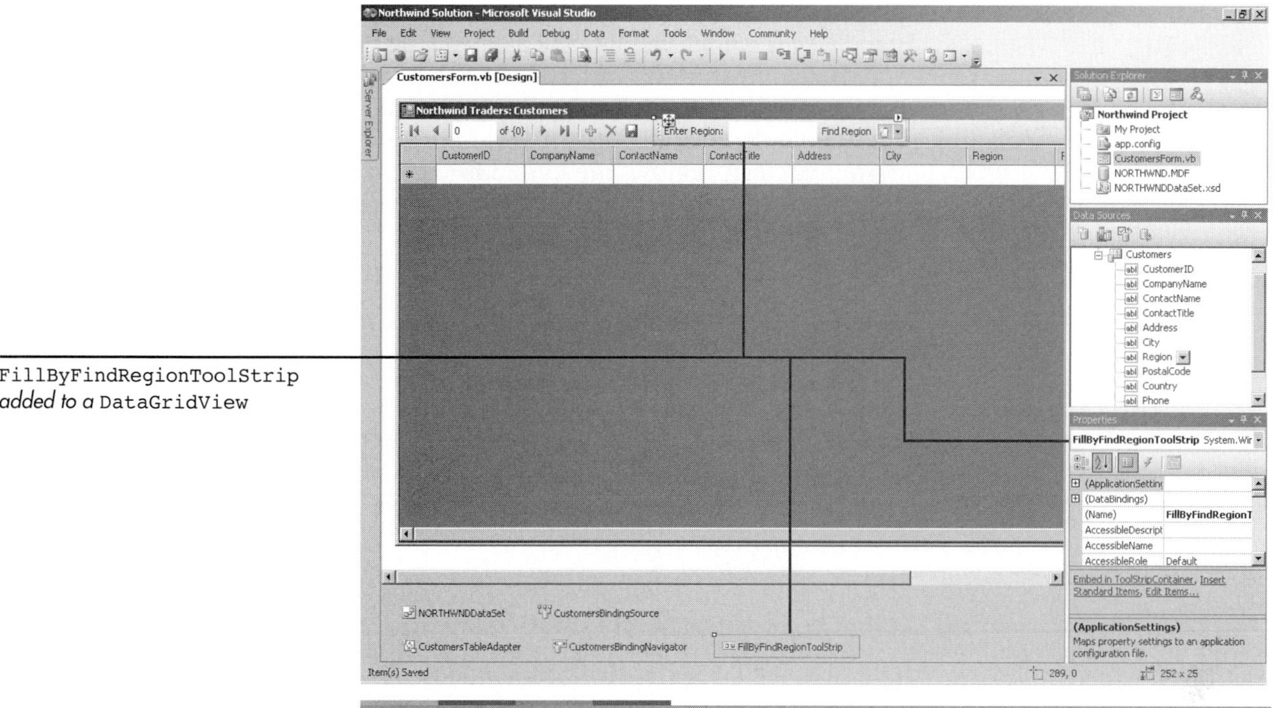

FIGURE 8.46 Northwind application that uses a stored procedure

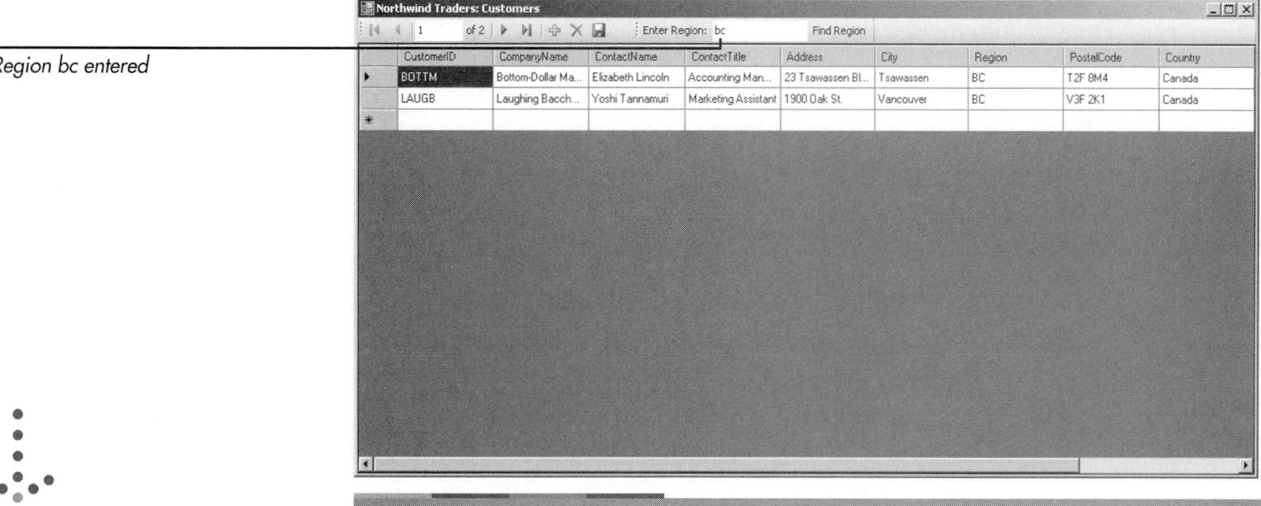

FIGURE 8.47 Sample run of the Northwind application using a stored procedure

TIP

You can also create a new stored procedure in an SQL Server database by opening the Server Explorer in Visual Studio, right-clicking the Stored Procedures folder for a data connection, and clicking Add New Stored Procedure.

The program code of the Northwind application in Figure 8.46 is shown in Figure 8.48. After applying the steps in Figure 8.37, Visual Basic added the procedure `FillByFindRegionToolStripButton_Click` (Lines 21–31). In this procedure, the `CustomersTableAdapter` calls the method (query) `FillByFindRegion` using the `Customers` table in the `NORTHWNDDataSet` based on the contents in the `Text`

TIP

You can view many of the existing stored procedures in the Northwind SQL Server database by double-clicking the stored procedure in the Server Explorer. As you can see, stored procedures can be very powerful and complex.

property of the `_RegionToolStripTextBox`. Observe this code carefully to understand how it is implementing the `FindRegion` stored procedure.

Finally, you should observe from the code in Figure 8.48 that when the `CustomersForm` loads (when the application is initially run), all data from the `Customers` table will fill the `DataGridView`. If this is not what you desire, you can remove the `CustomersForm_Load` procedure from the program code. You could then follow the steps of Figure 8.30 to add a new query to the `DataGridView`, such as `SELECT * FROM Customers ORDER BY CustomerName`, with a new `ToolStrip`, allowing the user to either display all customers in the application or to display only those customers in a certain specified region.

```
Public Class CustomersForm

    Private Sub CustomersBindingNavigatorSaveItem_Click( _
        ByVal sender As System.Object, ByVal e As System.EventArgs) _
        Handles CustomersBindingNavigatorSaveItem.Click
        Me.Validate()
        Me.CustomersBindingSource.EndEdit()
        Me.CustomersTableAdapter.Update(Me.NORTHWNDDataSet.Customers)

    End Sub

    Private Sub CustomersForm_Load(ByVal sender As System.Object, _
        ByVal e As System.EventArgs) Handles MyBase.Load
        'TODO: This line of code loads data into the
        ''NORTHWNDDataSet.Customers' table. You can move, or remove it,
        ' as needed.
        Me.CustomersTableAdapter.Fill(Me.NORTHWNDDataSet.Customers)

    End Sub

    Private Sub FillByFindRegionToolStripButton_Click( _
        ByVal sender As System.Object, ByVal e As System.EventArgs)
        Try
            Me.CustomersTableAdapter.FillByFindRegion( _
                Me.NORTHWNDDataSet.Customers, _
                _RegionToolStripTextBox.Text)
        Catch ex As System.Exception
            System.Windows.Forms.MessageBox.Show(ex.Message)
        End Try

    End Sub

End Class
```

FIGURE 8.48 Program code for Northwind application that uses a stored procedure

PROGRAMMING EXAMPLE

Northwind Menu Application

Throughout this chapter, you have been working with bits and pieces of the extensive Northwind database. In this example, you will create a broader application for Northwind Traders that uses a startup form with a menu. The menu allows the user to view and update customer and employee data. The menu also gives the user two views: an alphabetical listing of products and a list of all current products. Finally, the menu accesses two stored procedures: most expensive products and sales by year. Before creating forms and writing Visual Basic code, you will need to perform the following basic steps:

1. Create a new Visual Basic project called Northwind Menu.
2. Add a data connection to the SQL Server Northwind database file (NORTHWND.MDF).
3. Add a new data source (dataset) from the Northwind database consisting of the tables `Customers` and `Employees`, the views Alphabetical List of Products and Current Products List, and the stored procedures Sales By Year and Ten Most Expensive Products.

Pseudocode

`MainForm` ***startup form***

1. create event procedure for Customers table submenu item
2. create event procedure for Employees table submenu item
3. create event procedure for Alphabetical products view submenu item
4. create event procedure for Current products view submenu item
5. create event procedure for Sales By Year stored procedure submenu item
6. create event procedure for Ten Most Expensive Products stored procedure submenu item

`MainForm` is the startup form containing a 3D panel group and the label "Northwind Traders." More importantly, it contains a menu so the user can select Tables, Views, or Procedures. Views are objects in an SQL Server database that are created with a tool nearly identical to the Query Builder that you used in Section 8.4. Simply right-click the Views folder in the Server Explorer and click Add New View to use the tool. Procedures are stored procedures in the SQL Server database that were also discussed in Section 8.4. `MainForm` is shown in the Windows Form Designer in Figure 8.49.

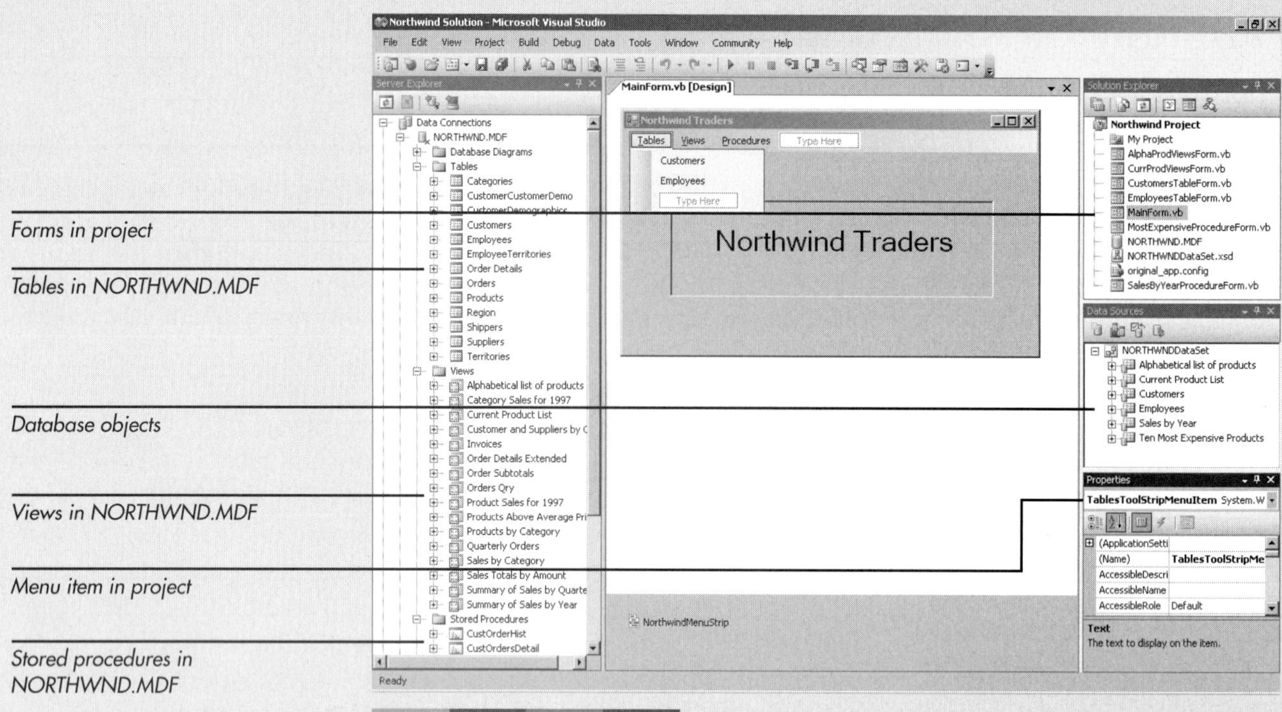

FIGURE 8.49 Visual Studio IDE for the Northwind Menu application

`CustomersToolStripMenuItem Click` ***event procedure***

1. create new `CustomersTableForm`
2. display new form

`EmployeesToolStripMenuItem Click` ***event procedure***

1. create new `EmployeesTableForm`
2. display new form

`AlphaProdToolStripMenuItem Click` ***event procedure***

1. create new `AlphaProdViewsForm`
2. display new form

`CurrProdToolStripMenuItem Click` ***event procedure***

1. create new `CurrProdViewsForm`
2. display new form

`SalesByYearToolStripMenuItem Click` ***event procedure***

1. create new `SalesByYearProcedureForm`
2. display new form

`MostExpensiveToolStripMenuItem Click` ***event procedure***

1. create new `MostExpensiveProcedureForm`
2. display new form

Code

The `MainForm` class contains the event procedures for each of the six submenu items as shown in Figure 8.50(a). Each of the individual forms referenced in Figure 8.50(a) was created by clicking Project and clicking Add Windows Form in the Visual Studio window. Pseudocode is not listed for these forms, as their functionality is created automatically by simply dragging the appropriate dataset object (table, view, or stored procedure) from the Data Sources window to the new form. The resulting code for three of these forms (automatically generated by Visual Basic) is listed in Figure 8.50(b), (c), and (d).

(a) Program code for the `MainForm` class

```
Public Class MainForm

    Private Sub CustomersToolStripMenuItem_Click( _
        ByVal sender As System.Object, ByVal e As System.EventArgs) _
        Handles CustomersToolStripMenuItem.Click
        Dim newForm As New CustomersTableForm
        newForm.ShowDialog()
    End Sub

    Private Sub EmployeesToolStripMenuItem_Click( _
        ByVal sender As System.Object, ByVal e As System.EventArgs) _
        Handles EmployeesToolStripMenuItem.Click
        Dim newForm As New EmployeesTableForm
        newForm.ShowDialog()
    End Sub

    Private Sub AlphaProdToolStripMenuItem_Click( _
        ByVal sender As System.Object, ByVal e As System.EventArgs) _
        Handles AlphaProdToolStripMenuItem.Click
        Dim newForm As New AlphaProdViewsForm
        newForm.ShowDialog()
    End Sub

    Private Sub CurrProdToolStripMenuItem_Click( _
        ByVal sender As System.Object, ByVal e As System.EventArgs) _
        Handles CurrProdToolStripMenuItem.Click
        Dim newForm As New CurrProdViewsForm
        newForm.ShowDialog()
    End Sub

    Private Sub SalesByYearToolStripMenuItem_Click( _
        ByVal sender As System.Object, ByVal e As System.EventArgs) _
        Handles SalesByYearToolStripMenuItem.Click
        Dim newForm As New SalesByYearProcedureForm
        newForm.ShowDialog()
    End Sub

    Private Sub MostExpensiveToolStripMenuItem_Click( _
        ByVal sender As System.Object, ByVal e As System.EventArgs) _
        Handles MostExpensiveToolStripMenuItem.Click
        Dim newForm As New MostExpensiveProcedureForm
        newForm.ShowDialog()
    End Sub

End Class
```

(Figure is continued on next page)

(b) Program code for the `CustomersTableForm` class

```
Public Class CustomersTableForm

    Private Sub CustomersBindingNavigatorSaveItem_Click( _
        ByVal sender As System.Object, ByVal e As System.EventArgs) _
        Handles CustomersBindingNavigatorSaveItem.Click
        Me.Validate()
        Me.CustomersBindingSource.EndEdit()
        Me.CustomersTableAdapter.Update(Me.NORTHWNDDataSet.Customers)

    End Sub

    Private Sub CustomersTableForm_Load( _
        ByVal sender As System.Object, ByVal e As System.EventArgs) _
        Handles MyBase.Load

        Me.CustomersTableAdapter.Fill(Me.NORTHWNDDataSet.Customers)

    End Sub
End Class
```

(c) Program code for the `AlphaProdViewsForm` class

```
Public Class AlphaProdViewsForm

    Private Sub AlphaProdViewsForm_Load( _
        ByVal sender As System.Object, ByVal e As System.EventArgs) _
        Handles MyBase.Load

        Me.Alphabetical_list_of_productsTableAdapter.Fill( _
            Me.NORTHWNDDataSet.Alphabetical_list_of_products)

    End Sub
End Class
```

(d) Program code for the `SalesByYearProcedureForm` class

```
Public Class SalesByYearProcedureForm

    Private Sub FillToolStripButton_Click( _
        ByVal sender As System.Object, ByVal e As System.EventArgs) _
        Handles FillToolStripButton.Click
        Try
            Me.Sales_by_YearTableAdapter.Fill( _
                Me.NORTHWNDDataSet.Sales_by_Year, _
                New System.Nullable(Of Date)( _
                CType(Beginning_DateToolStripTextBox.Text, Date)), _
                New System.Nullable(Of Date)( _
                CType(Ending_DateToolStripTextBox.Text, Date)))
        Catch ex As System.Exception
            System.Windows.Forms.MessageBox.Show(ex.Message)
        End Try

    End Sub
End Class
```

FIGURE 8.50 Program code for various forms in the Northwind Menu application

Note that the `CustomerTableForm` class in Figure 8.50(b) has a `CustomersBindingNavigatorSaveItem_Click` procedure that allows the user to save changes back to the database. The `AlphaProdViewsForm` class in Figure 8.50(c) is simply a View, so it does not have a `BindingNavigatorSaveItem`. A View is similar to a stored procedure, but it is read-only and cannot be updated. The `SalesByYearProcedureForm` class in Figure 8.50(d) has some complex code because the stored procedure contains two parameters (variables), `@Beginning_Date` and `@Ending_Date`. The information in this and preceding chapters should make all the code in these forms very understandable for you.

Input/Output

A sample run of the Northwind Menu application is presented in Figure 8.51, displaying each of the forms corresponding to the program code in Figure 8.50. Figure 8.51(a) shows the startup form (`MainForm`) for the application, which contains the menu. Subsequent forms in Figure 8.51 are the result of clicking each of the three menu items in Figure 8.51(a) and then selecting the first submenu item for each. Note that the user must supply a beginning and ending date for the Sales By Year query.

(a)

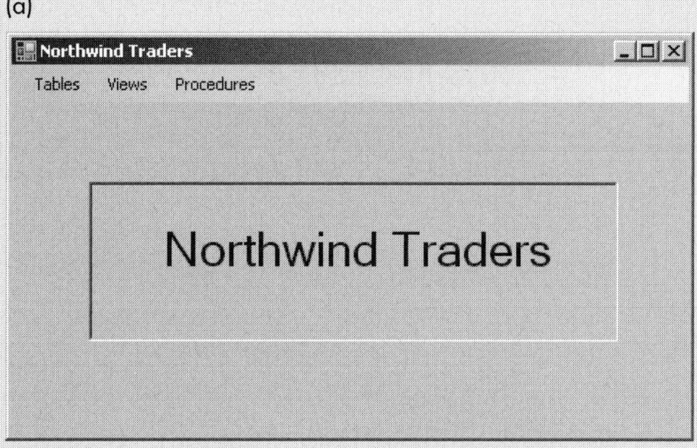

(b)

CustomerID	CompanyName	ContactName	ContactTitle	Address	City	Region
ALFKI	Alfreds Futterkiste	Maria Anders	Sales Represent...	Obere Str. 57	Berlin	
ANATR	Ana Trujillo Empa...	Ana Trujillo	Owner	Avda. de la Cons...	México D.F.	
ANTON	Antonio Moreno ...	Antonio Moreno	Owner	Mataderos 2312	México D.F.	
AROUT	Around the Horn	Thomas Hardy	Sales Represent...	120 Hanover Sq.	London	
BERGS	Berglunds snabb...	Christina Berglund	Order Administrator	Berguvsvägen 8	Luleå	
BLAUS	Blauer See Delik...	Hanna Moos	Sales Represent...	Forsterstr. 57	Mannheim	
BLONP	Blondesddsl père...	Frédérique Citeaux	Marketing Manager	24, place Kléber	Strasbourg	
BOLID	Bólido Comidas p...	Martín Sommer	Owner	C/ Araquil, 67	Madrid	
BONAP	Bon app'	Laurence Lebihan	Owner	12, rue des Bouc...	Marseille	
BOTTM	Bottom-Dollar Ma...	Elizabeth Lincoln	Accounting Man...	23 Tsawassen Bl...	Tsawassen	BC
BSBEV	B's Beverages	Victoria Ashworth	Sales Represent...	Fauntleroy Circus	London	
CACTU	Cactus Comidas ...	Patricio Simpson	Sales Agent	Cerrito 333	Buenos Aires	
CENTC	Centro comercial ...	Francisco Chang	Marketing Manager	Sierras de Grana...	México D.F.	
CHOPS	Chop-suey Chinese	Yang Wang	Owner	Hauptstr. 29	Bern	
COMMI	Comércio Mineiro	Pedro Afonso	Sales Associate	Av. dos Lusíadas...	Sao Paulo	SP
CONSH	Consolidated Hol...	Elizabeth Brown	Sales Represent...	Berkeley Garden...	London	
DRACD	Drachenblut Deli...	Sven Ottlieb	Order Administrator	Walserweg 21	Aachen	
DUMON	Du monde entier	Janine Labrune	Owner	67, rue des Cinqu...	Nantes	

(c)

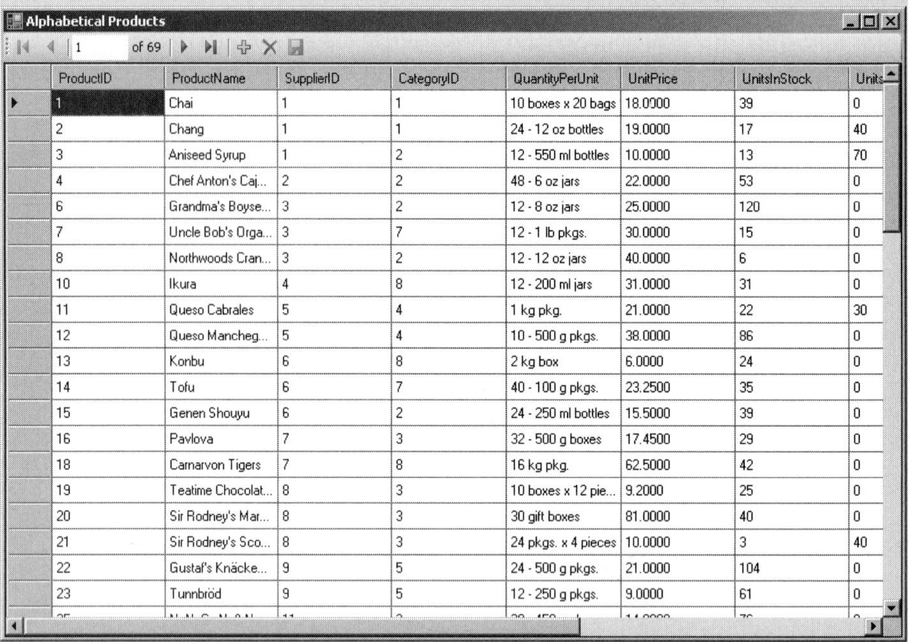

Alphabetical Products

1 of 69

	ProductID	ProductName	SupplierID	CategoryID	QuantityPerUnit	UnitPrice	UnitsInStock	Units
▶	1	Chai	1	1	10 boxes x 20 bags	18.0000	39	0
	2	Chang	1	1	24 - 12 oz bottles	19.0000	17	40
	3	Aniseed Syrup	1	2	12 - 550 ml bottles	10.0000	13	70
	4	Chef Anton's Caj...	2	2	48 - 6 oz jars	22.0000	53	0
	6	Grandma's Boyse...	3	2	12 - 8 oz jars	25.0000	120	0
	7	Uncle Bob's Orga...	3	7	12 - 1 lb pkgs.	30.0000	15	0
	8	Northwoods Cran...	3	2	12 - 12 oz jars	40.0000	6	0
	10	Ikura	4	8	12 - 200 ml jars	31.0000	31	0
	11	Queso Cabrales	5	4	1 kg pkg.	21.0000	22	30
	12	Queso Mancheg...	5	4	10 - 500 g pkgs.	38.0000	86	0
	13	Konbu	6	8	2 kg box	6.0000	24	0
	14	Tofu	6	7	40 - 100 g pkgs.	23.2500	35	0
	15	Genen Shouyu	6	2	24 - 250 ml bottles	15.5000	39	0
	16	Pavlova	7	3	32 - 500 g boxes	17.4500	29	0
	18	Carnarvon Tigers	7	8	16 kg pkg.	62.5000	42	0
	19	Teatime Chocolat...	8	3	10 boxes x 12 pie...	9.2000	25	0
	20	Sir Rodney's Mar...	8	3	30 gift boxes	81.0000	40	0
	21	Sir Rodney's Sco...	8	3	24 pkgs. x 4 pieces	10.0000	3	40
	22	Gustaf's Knäcke...	9	5	24 - 500 g pkgs.	21.0000	104	0
	23	Tunnbröd	9	5	12 - 250 g pkgs.	9.0000	61	0

(d)

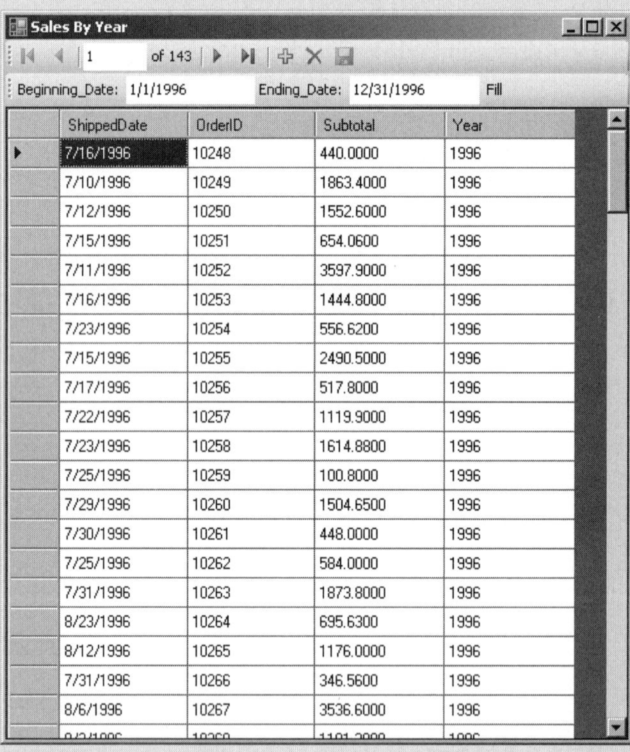

Sales By Year

1 of 143

Beginning_Date: 1/1/1996 Ending_Date: 12/31/1996 Fill

	ShippedDate	OrderID	Subtotal	Year
▶	7/16/1996	10248	440.0000	1996
	7/10/1996	10249	1863.4000	1996
	7/12/1996	10250	1552.6000	1996
	7/15/1996	10251	654.0600	1996
	7/11/1996	10252	3597.9000	1996
	7/16/1996	10253	1444.8000	1996
	7/23/1996	10254	556.6200	1996
	7/15/1996	10255	2490.5000	1996
	7/17/1996	10256	517.8000	1996
	7/22/1996	10257	1119.9000	1996
	7/23/1996	10258	1614.8800	1996
	7/25/1996	10259	100.8000	1996
	7/29/1996	10260	1504.6500	1996
	7/30/1996	10261	448.0000	1996
	7/25/1996	10262	584.0000	1996
	7/31/1996	10263	1873.8000	1996
	8/23/1996	10264	695.6300	1996
	8/12/1996	10265	1176.0000	1996
	7/31/1996	10266	346.5600	1996
	8/6/1996	10267	3536.6000	1996

FIGURE 8.51 Sample run for the Northwind Menu application

Quick Review

- ADO.NET is a data access API with capabilities of accessing Microsoft SQL Server databases as well as any other kind of data store (simple text files, electronic spreadsheets, Microsoft Access, or other database software) that implements OLE DB.
- OLE DB stands for Object Linking and Embedding for Databases, a Microsoft technology for interfacing with data stores. OLE DB comes under the umbrella of Microsoft's Component Object Model (COM), a standard technology for intersoftware communication using objects.
- ADO.NET is also capable of accessing data in XML (eXtensible Markup Language) format. XML is a simple, widely used, human-readable, text-based format for storing data using customized tags similar to the HTML code found in Web pages. XML will be further explored later in this text.
- ADO (ActiveX Data Objects) is the Microsoft data access API that preceded ADO.NET. The latest version of ADO.NET is 2.0, released in 2004. ADO is based on the OLE DB standard for interfacing with a data store, while ADO.NET is based on the newer Microsoft .NET Framework.
- ADO.NET does not require that the application be continuously connected to a database during program execution. Operating in this disconnected mode makes applications that use ADO.NET more scalable, meaning that the application is more capable of handling increasing demands from many users over time.
- Another advance associated with ADO.NET is its support of XML. Additionally, ADO.NET represents data using strongly typed objects (objects whose type can be checked at compile time), which makes it easier to develop object-oriented applications.
- In order for an application (Windows or Web) to access a database using ADO.NET, the database must first interface with a .NET Framework data provider for that specific type of database. The data provider provides the data in the form of a dataset stored in computer memory, which can then be accessed by the application.
- A .NET Framework `DataSet` object contains a `DataTableCollection` object, which contains one or more `DataTable` objects. A `DataTable` object contains a `DataColumnCollection` object, a `DataRowCollection` object, and a `ConstraintCollection` object. A `DataSet` object also contains a `DataRelationCollection` object.
- A data provider is the interface between the database and the dataset, and it contains classes such as `Connection` to connect to a database, `Command` to store SQL commands, `DataReader` to provide high-speed, read-only data for an application, and `DataAdapter` to fill a dataset.
- The process of creating a Visual Basic application that utilizes a database involves four basic steps: (1) adding a data connection to the application, (2) adding a data source (dataset) to the application, (3) adding controls to a form to display the dataset, and (4) adding controls to a form to execute queries (select, add, delete, and update) on the dataset.
- The Visual Studio window contains the Server Explorer (which displays the database), the Solution Explorer (which displays project files), the Data Sources window (which displays the dataset), and the Windows Form Designer (which displays the application form and its components).

- Important application files include app.config (which contains the database connection string), the database (optionally included within the project itself), the XML schema definition file (with extension .xsd, which contains the structure of the dataset), and the application file (which contains the Visual Basic code for interfacing with a database).
- A `DataGridView` control in a form displays the rows and columns of a table or query in a familiar grid format, just as data would be displayed from within the database itself. The `DataGridView` uses a `BindingSource` object to link to a `DataSet` object and a `BindingNavigator` object to manipulate the rows in a `DataGridView`.
- A `BindingSource` component also handles concurrency management, a database management process for maintaining data consistency when two or more users access the same data simultaneously.
- The default concurrency process for ADO.NET is called optimistic concurrency, which means that when multiple users are trying to update the same value in a database, the first update is processed and other users are notified of the concurrency violation.
- The other concurrency process is called pessimistic concurrency, which means that when one user retrieves a row of data for possible updates, that row is locked and cannot be retrieved by other users until the first user releases it.
- Instead of using a `DataGridView` in a form, you can create a Details view that operates in exactly the same manner but displays only one record at a time in individual form controls, such as text boxes.
- Queries (SQL statements) that are created automatically with a DataGridView or a Details view can be modified by the programmer. New queries (such as select, add, delete, or update) that are executed by new form components, such as buttons, can also be created by the programmer.
- New queries can also use stored procedures (SQL code that uses parameters) that are contained within a database. Application components, such as text boxes, provide for input from the user that is passed to stored procedure parameters. The stored procedure is then executed to provide the desired outcome (select, add, delete, or update).

Key Terms

ADO (ActiveX Data Objects)—The Microsoft data access API (released in 1996) that preceded ADO.NET (released in 2002).

Component Object Model (COM)—A Microsoft technology for inter-software communication using objects.

concurrency management—A database management process for maintaining data consistency when two or more users access the same data simultaneously.

data provider—A set of classes that provide the link between the dataset and the database.

dataset—A memory resident representation of only the part of a database that an application needs.

OLE DB (Object Linking and Embedding for Databases)—A Microsoft technology for interfacing with data stores that comes under the umbrella of the Component Object Model (COM).

optimistic concurrency—A policy of concurrency management in which the first update is processed and other users are notified of a concurrency violation when multiple users are trying to update the same value in a database.

pessimistic concurrency—A policy of concurrency management in which a row of data retrieved by a user for possible updates is locked and cannot be retrieved by other users until the first user releases it.

query—A set of instructions written in SQL (structured query language).

scalable—The characteristic of an application that makes it more capable of handling increasing demands from many users over time.

strongly typed objects—Objects whose type can be checked at compile time.

Transact-SQL—Microsoft SQL Server version of SQL.

XML (eXtensible Markup Language)—A simple, widely used, human-readable, text-based format for storing data using customized tags similar to the HTML code found in Web pages.

Review Questions

1. SQL Server is a data access API.
   a. True
   b. False
2. XML is a text-based format similar to HTML.
   a. True
   b. False
3. A data access API that operates in disconnected mode makes applications more scalable.
   a. True
   b. False
4. A `DataSet` object contains a `Command` object.
   a. True
   b. False
5. ADO.NET usually operates in disconnected mode.
   a. True
   b. False
6. The app.config file is in XML format.
   a. True
   b. False
7. Using optimistic concurrency makes an application more scalable.
   a. True
   b. False
8. SQL Server uses an SQL called PL/SQL.
   a. True
   b. False

9. A parameter in an SQL Server stored procedure is preceded by an `@`.
   a. True
   b. False

10. The Details view of a dataset in a form displays multiple rows of data.
    a. True
    b. False

11. COM stands for Component ____ Model.
    a. object
    b. online
    c. open
    d. output

12. Which of the following does not belong to a DataTable object?
    a. `DataColumnCollection`
    b. `DataRowCollection`
    c. `DataRelationCollection`
    d. `ConstraintCollection`

13. The file extension .xsd stands for XML schema ____.
    a. database
    b. definition
    c. data
    d. debugger

14. Which method sends values from a `DataSet` object to the database?
    a. `Validate`
    b. `Fill`
    c. `EndEdit`
    d. `Update`

15. Which Visual Studio window contains the `DataSet` object?
    a. Server Explorer
    b. Solution Explorer
    c. Data Sources
    d. Properties

16. A stored procedure is contained within a ____.
    a. `TableAdapter`
    b. `BindingNavigator`
    c. `DataSet`
    d. database

17. Which type of object is responsible for concurrency management?
    a. `TableAdapter`
    b. `BindingSource`
    c. `DataSet`
    d. `BindingNavigator`

18. A dataset is stored ____.
    a. in the project folder
    b. in memory
    c. on a database server
    d. in a data provider

19. Which type of object involves database logon procedures?
    a. `Command`
    b. `Connection`
    c. `DataReader`
    d. `DataAdapter`

20. A connection string is located in which type of file?
    a. .config
    b. .vb
    c. .xsd
    d. .mdf

Computer Exercises

The following exercises assume that you have installed Microsoft SQL Server 2005 Express Edition on your computer. When creating user interfaces, follow all conventions for an attractive, organized form with meaningful names for controls. Also follow all conventions for writing Visual Basic code and SQL statements. Your instructor may also request that you use TOE charts, pseudocode, flowcharts, ER diagrams, and/or UML diagrams as planning aids.

1. In this exercise you create an application that displays the contents of the `Categories` table in the Northwind database using a `DataGridView` object.
   a. Create a project called **Northwind Categories DataGridView**. Save the application in the \VBReloadedAdvanced\Chap08 folder.
   b. Design and create a user interface that uses a `DataGridView` object to display the contents of the `Categories` table in the Northwind database.
   c. Save the solution, test the application, and modify as necessary.

2. In this exercise you create an application that displays the contents of the Categories table in the Northwind database using a Details view.
   a. Create a project called **Northwind Categories Detail**. Save the application in the \VBReloadedAdvanced\Chap08 folder.
   b. Design and create a user interface that uses a Details view to display the contents of the Categories table in the Northwind database.
   c. Save the solution, test the application, and modify as necessary.

3. In this exercise you create an application that displays the contents of the `Employees` table in the pubs database (included in the installation of SQL Server 2005 Express) using a `DataGridView` object and allow for a search of hire dates.
   a. Create a project called **Pubs Employees Hiredate**. Save the application in the \VBReloadedAdvanced\Chap08 folder.
   b. Design and create a user interface that uses a `DataGridView` object to display the contents of the `Employees` table in the pubs database.
   c. Create a stored procedure that displays the contents of the Employees table and contains two parameters, `@BeginningDate` and `@EndingDate`. (Hint: See the Programming Example at the end of the chapter.)
   d. Add labels, text boxes, and a button to the form for inputting the dates and executing the stored procedure.
   e. Save the solution, test the application, and modify as necessary.

4. In this exercise you create an application that displays the contents of the `authors` table in the pubs database (included in the installation of SQL Server 2005 Express) using a `DataGridView` object and allow for a search of states where the authors live.
   a. Create a project called **Pubs Authors State**. Save the application in the \VBReloadedAdvanced\Chap08 folder.
   b. Design and create a user interface that uses a Details view to display the contents of the `authors` table in the pubs database.
   c. Modify the query in the `DataSet` to sort the results by author last name.
   d. Create a stored procedure that displays the contents of the `Authors` table and contains a parameter for the state of residence.
   e. Add a label, text box, and button to the navigation toolstrip for inputting the dates and executing the stored procedure.
   f. Save the solution, test the application, and modify as necessary.
5. In this exercise you create an application that displays the contents of an inner join of the `title` and `publishers` tables in the pubs database (included in the installation of SQL Server 2005 Express) using a `DataGridView` object.
   a. Create a project called **Pubs Title Publisher**. Save the application in the \VBReloadedAdvanced\Chap08 folder.
   b. Design and create a user interface that uses a `DataGridView` to display an inner join of the title and publishers tables in the pubs database. (Hint: Add a query to one of the table's `TableAdapter` objects.) The data should display when the form loads.
   c. Save the solution, test the application, and modify as necessary.
6. In this exercise you create an application with a menu to display information from the GrocerToGo database (included in the installation of SQL Server 2005 Express).
   a. Create a project called **GrocerToGo**. Save the application in the \VBReloadedAdvanced\Chap08 folder.
   b. Create a startup form with a menu that includes the items Tables (with submenu items for each table) and Views (with submenu items Product Price and Product Name/Category).
   c. The Product Price display should be a `DataGridView` showing the product ID, product name, and product price. The Product Name/Category display should be a Details view showing product ID, product name, category ID, and category name sorted by product name.
   d. Save the solution, test the application, and modify as necessary.
7. In this exercise you create an application with a menu to display information from the Store database.
   a. Create a project called **Store**. Save the application in the \VBReloadedAdvanced\Chap08 folder.
   b. Create a startup form with a menu that includes the items Tables (with submenu items for each table) and Views (with submenu items Products and Order Details).
   c. The Product display should be a `DataGridView` showing the product ID, product name, unit cost, and product description. The Order Details display should have a text box to receive an order ID and should also provide the product ID, product name, quantity, and unit cost.
   d. Save the solution, test the application, and modify as necessary.

Case Projects

CD Collection

This project is based on the corresponding project in Chapter 7. Create an ERD for a database called CDCollection that includes a CDs table and a Tracks table. Using SQL Server Express, create a database called **CDCollection**. Create a table for CDs and another table for music tracks on the CDs. Include several meaningful fields in both tables. Enter real data from at least three CDs. Create a query that lists the CDs, with each CD's tracks in the order that they appear on the CD. Create an application called **CD Collection** that displays the query in a `DataGridView` and includes text boxes for various searches.

Friends

This project is based on the Friends project in Chapter 7. Create an ERD for a database called MyFriends that includes a Friends table, a Hobbies table, and a Movies table. A friend can have several hobbies and several favorite movies. Using SQL Server Express, create the database called **MyFriends** and create the required tables. Enter data for several of your friends. Create a query that lists only the friends' names and hobbies sorted by last name. Create another query that lists only the friends' names and favorite movies sorted by movie, then by last name. Create an application called **My Friends** that uses a menu to access these queries. The displays should include text boxes for various searches.

Courses

This project is based on the Courses project in Chapter 7. Enhance the Courses database presented in Chapter 7 using SQL Server Express. Create an ERD that includes a Students table and a Schedule table. A student can take several courses and a course can have several students. Create a separate table in the ERD with fields `StudentID` and `CourseID`. Add the `Students` table and the `StudentCourse` table in the database and populate all tables with several records. Create three queries, each of which extracts data from two different tables. Create an application called **Courses** that uses a menu to access these queries. The displays should include text boxes for various searches.

CHAPTER

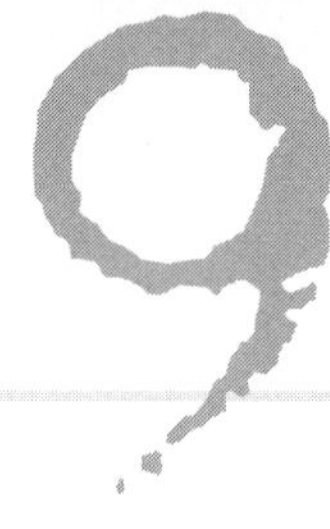

An Introduction to ASP.NET

After studying Chapter 9, you should be able to:

- Explain concepts related to Web pages, client/server architecture, and multi-tier architecture
- Explain the concepts of client-side scripting and server-side scripting
- Create a Web site using ASP.NET
- Use several kinds of Web controls in a Web form
- Create a layout for a Web form using a table

It's hard to overstate the impact of the Internet and the World Wide Web (WWW) on world culture. The Internet is a vast network of networks using a common communication standard (TCP/IP), linking millions of computers to one another. The WWW is just one of many services offered via the Internet (along with services such as electronic mail, Telnet, and FTP). However, the WWW is by far the largest and fastest-growing component of the Internet.

The Internet had its beginnings in the 1960s as a military project in the United States. International development of the Internet continued into the 1970s and 1980s, culminating in the introduction of the WWW in 1991. Since then, the WWW (or just "Web") has experienced phenomenal growth in areas of communication, education, entertainment, and e-commerce. Much of the present usefulness of the Web is due to improved technology for developing computer Web applications for business and science. This and the next chapter will focus on one such vital Web application development technology, ASP.NET.

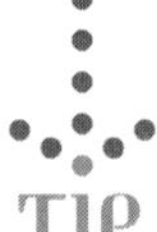

TIP

The Web applications presented in this chapter are included in this book's data files, available for download at *http://www.course.com*. To open the Visual Studio solution for a given project (for the purpose of viewing and/or modifying the code), open the .sln file, which is located in the Project folder for that solution. To run the application on a Web server, copy the Web application folder (located within the WebSites folder for the project) to a Web server that is capable of executing ASP.NET files.

In Chapter 8, you learned that ADO.NET is an important new Microsoft technology that provides an interface between Windows applications and data stores, replacing the earlier ADO technology. In this chapter, you will learn about ASP.NET, another recent Microsoft technology that enables the development of highly interactive Web sites, Web applications, and XML Web services, replacing Microsoft's earlier ASP technology.

Just like ADO.NET, ASP.NET is built on the Microsoft .NET Framework, thus utilizing the Common Language Runtime (CLR). This allows ASP.NET files to be written in a wide variety of .NET languages (including Visual Basic, J#, and C#), as well as in some open-source languages such as Perl and Python. One of the goals of ASP.NET is to make Web application development very similar to Windows application development, which you have studied in the first eight chapters of this book.

INTRODUCTION TO WEB APPLICATIONS

Before learning about ASP.NET, you first need to understand some basics about creating Web pages and about client/server architecture. If you are already well versed in HTML, scripting languages, and client/server concepts, you may be able to skip ahead to the discussion of ASP.NET at the end of this section (or you may enjoy the review).

Creating Web Pages

Developing simple Web pages is a fairly straightforward task. After all, a Web page is simply a text file written using **Hypertext Markup Language** (HTML) with a file extension of .htm or .html. You can create an HTML file using a simple text editor, such as Notepad. Figure 9.1 shows an HTML document called HelloWorld.htm opened in Notepad.

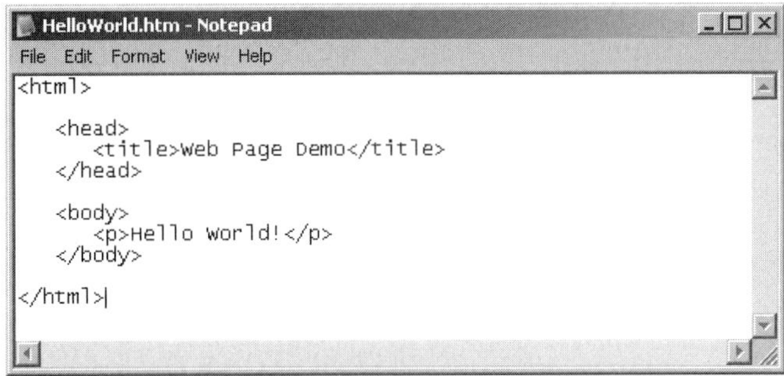

FIGURE 9.1 HelloWorld.htm written using Notepad

A simple Web page contains several **HTML elements**, which are sections within a Web page that define the page's structure, content, and functionality. An element usually consists of the following:

- **start tag**: a special code enclosed in angle brackets that begins the definition of an HTML element
- **element content**: some text or other HTML elements contained within an HTML element
- **end tag**: the same special code used in the start tag, preceded by a forward slash, enclosed in angle brackets, and placed at the end of an HTML element.

Table 9.1 lists information about the HTML elements found in Figure 9.1.

Element	Element Description	Start Tag	Element Content in Figure 9.1	End Tag
`html`	The root element that contains all other elements	`<html>`	`head` and `body` elements	`</html>`
`head`	Heading information about the Web page	`<head>`	`title` element	`</head>`
`title`	Text that appears in a browser's title bar	`<title>`	Web Page Demo	`</title>`
`body`	Body of the page that appears in the browser's window	`<body>`	`paragraph` element	`</body>`
`p`	Paragraph in a Web page	`<p>`	Hello World!	`</p>`

TABLE 9.1 Selected HTML Elements Found in Figure 9.1

There are dozens of different kinds of HTML tags, each designed to perform a specific task. Some examples include `<img>` for displaying images or graphics, `<a>` for creating hyperlinks (the letter `a` stands for anchor, another term for hyperlink), `<table>` for displaying tables, and `<form>` for displaying data-entry forms. This chapter does not go into the details of creating Web pages with HTML, but many good sources of information are available, such as the Course Technology text *HTML: Complete Concepts and Techniques* by Shelly, Cashman, Woods, and Dorin.

An Internet browser, such as Microsoft Internet Explorer, is used to open an HTML file located on the same computer, on an **intranet** (a private network that uses Internet technology), or on the Internet. The browser downloads the HTML file, reads it line by line, interpreting the HTML tags, and displays the page content accordingly. When the file HelloWorld.htm is run on the user's computer, it will open in a browser and appear as in Figure 9.2.

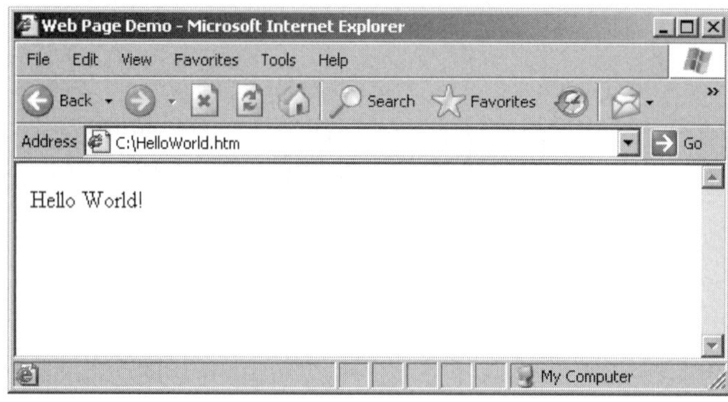

FIGURE 9.2 HelloWorld.htm opened on the user's computer

As you can see from Figure 9.2, a Web page can be located on a client's (user's) computer (for example, on the C drive) and opened using a browser. A Web page can also be located on a remote computer, known as a server. Servers, and the clients they serve, are discussed next.

Client/Server Architecture for Web Applications

You learned in Chapter 7 that a client/server system is one in which software is distributed across networked hardware components consisting of clients, which send requests for services, and a server, which provides responses to such requests. In the case of Web applications, the client is a Web browser on the user's computer and the server is a **Web server**, a computer with special software that stores Web pages and is connected to the Internet. If an HTML file is copied to a Web server, it can be downloaded and viewed on a client computer, as shown in Figure 9.3. Web server software (such as Microsoft Internet Information Services or IIS) knows how to receive requests for a Web page from clients and how to respond to those requests by sending pages to the client.

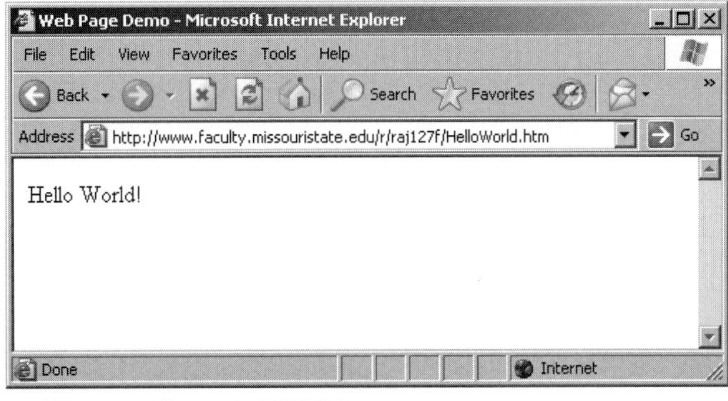

FIGURE 9.3 HelloWorld.htm downloaded from a Web server

Note that the only difference between Figures 9.2 and 9.3 is the content of the Address text boxes, which contain the file's URL (Uniform Resource Locator), the detailed location of the file. In Figure 9.2, the URL is C:\HelloWorld.htm. (This means that the file is in the root directory of drive C on the client.) In Figure 9.3, the URL is *http://www.faculty.missouristate.edu/r/raj127f/HelloWorld.htm.*

The URL in Figure 9.3 contains the protocol (communication rules) used for transferring Web pages from a Web server to a client. This protocol is http:// for Web pages. HTTP stands for **Hypertext Transfer Protocol**, the set of rules for exchanging files on the World Wide Web. Following the protocol is the service (www) and the **domain name** of the Web server (faculty.missouristate.edu), which is the text name corresponding to the unique numeric IP address of a computer on the Internet. Note that the last part of the domain name, called the top-level domain, is edu in this case, which represents educational institutions. (Other top-level domains are com, org, net, mil, and gov.)

Following the domain name in the URL of Figure 9.3 is the folder path where the file is located on the server (r/raj127f/). Last is the name of the file itself (HelloWorld.htm). Thus, r/raj127f/HelloWorld.htm is the complete path to the file on the faculty.missouristate.edu server. The **HTTP transaction** (the Web client requesting a file and the Web server responding to the request using HTTP) is shown in Figure 9.4. (The cloud symbol in Figure 9.4 represents the somewhat nebulous or ill-defined Internet.)

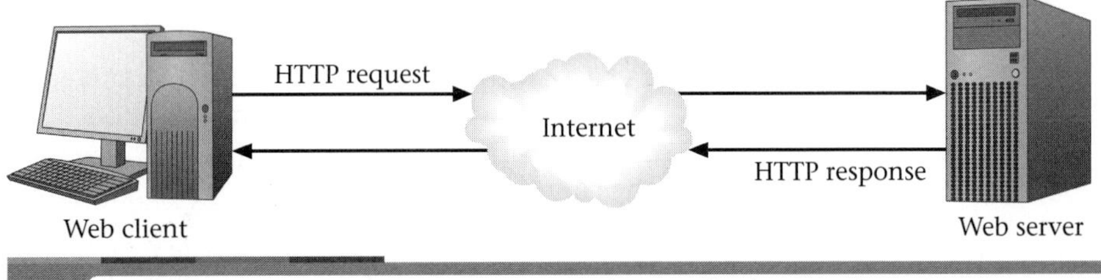

FIGURE 9.4 HTTP transaction with a Web client and Web server

When the client receives the file from the server, the browser software attempts to interpret the HTML code (things like `<title>Web Page Demo</title>`) and render (display) the page properly. In the case of HelloWorld.htm, the result of such rendering is Figure 9.3.

Multi-tier Architecture for Web Applications

A **Web application** (a computer application that uses a Web browser as the user interface) can use a simple client/server architecture or a **multi-tier architecture** (also called *n*-tier architecture). An *n*-tier architecture places different basic components of the application on *n* distinct software layers or tiers. A common three-tier architecture has a **presentation tier** (the user interface), the **logic tier** (programs that execute the logic of the application and communicate with the other tiers), and the **data tier** (data, which is often stored in a relational database). For a Web application, the presentation tier is a Web browser, the logic tier is HTML files and others (such as ASP.NET files, as you will soon learn) on a Web server, and the data tier is a database server. Figure 9.5 shows these three tiers as well as the people and technologies that interact with them.

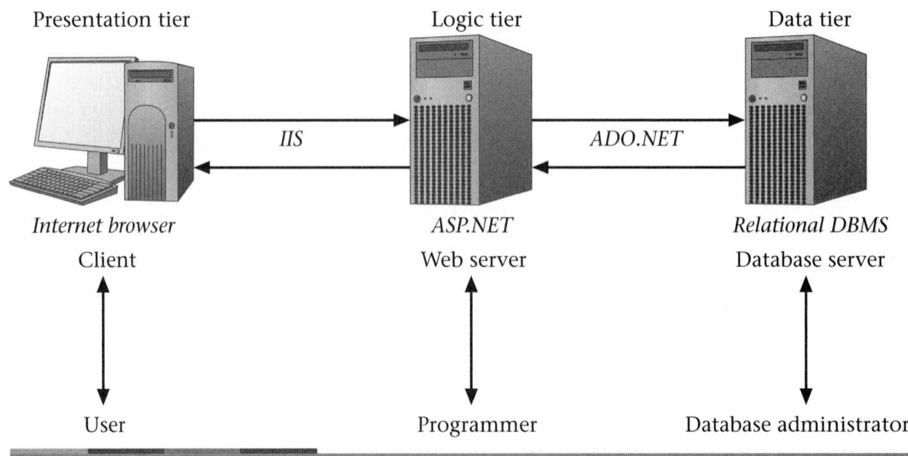

FIGURE 9.5 Three-tier system architecture for a Web application

You are undoubtedly familiar with the presentation tier (a Web browser), and the previous two chapters have discussed the data tier (relational databases). This chapter will focus on creating ASP.NET files in the logic tier, while the next chapter will incorporate the data tier using ASP.NET.

SCRIPTING AND ASP.NET

A programmer creates computer programs for the presentation and logic tiers of a multi-tier application. The presentation tier involves creating forms that contain components such as labels, text boxes, lists, and buttons (the user interface). The logic tier involves writing program code to process the information obtained from the presentation tier and the data tier. When you create Windows applications, the program code involves creating Windows forms, classes, and event procedures using a programming language such as Visual Basic. Web applications, on the other hand, are different because they use a Web browser as the user interface. There are many other important differences (and many similarities) when working with Web applications. This section focuses on writing program code within the logic tier of a Web application.

Client-Side Scripting

Web pages consisting only of HTML code are very static—they don't do much except display information (text and graphics) to the user. In order to create real Web applications (programs that actually process data and produce useful information), Web pages need processing capability. They need to utilize a programming language that can perform calculations and make decisions.

Static Web pages were greatly improved with the introduction of JavaScript in late 1995 by Netscape. JavaScript is a **scripting language**, a programming language that can be used within a Web page. Microsoft soon followed with its own scripting language, VBScript. Using a scripting language, a **script** (a set of instructions interpreted by another program rather than the computer processor) is embedded within a Web page using a special `<script>` tag. The Web browser is capable of interpreting the JavaScript code to define variables, execute if...then logic, create arrays, and perform loops. These are all the basic things that a programming language needs to do.

In programming with a scripting language, the scripting code itself is either embedded in the Web page or placed in a separate script file that is referenced by the Web page. Downloading these scripts to the browser (the client) for execution is known as **client-side scripting**. Client-side scripting makes Web pages dynamic and interactive. It comes with some disadvantages, however, including longer download times. Also, using scripting codes is insecure, because anyone can download, view, and possibly steal your JavaScript applications.

Figure 9.6 shows a relatively simple HTML file with JavaScript code and the result of viewing the file in a browser. (You aren't expected to completely understand all the JavaScript and HTML code in Figure 9.6.) Figure 9.6(a) shows the file with an html element, a `head` element, and a `body` element.

(a) Program code for HelloWorldJavaScript.htm

HelloWorldJavaScript.htm - Notepad

File Edit Format View Help

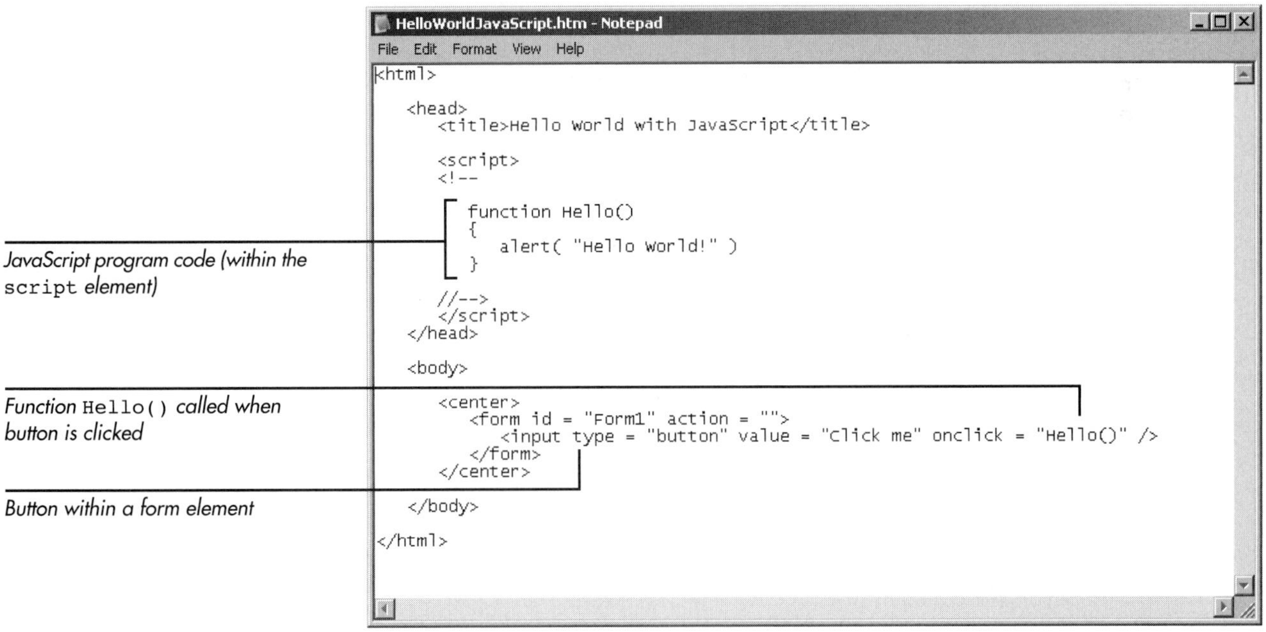

```
<html>

   <head>
      <title>Hello World with JavaScript</title>

      <script>
      <!--

         function Hello()
         {
            alert( "Hello World!" )
         }

      //-->
      </script>
   </head>

   <body>

      <center>
         <form id = "Form1" action = "">
            <input type = "button" value = "Click me" onclick = "Hello()" />
         </form>
      </center>

   </body>

</html>
```

JavaScript program code (within the `script` element)

Function `Hello()` called when button is clicked

Button within a form element

(b) Sample run of HelloWorldJavaScript.htm

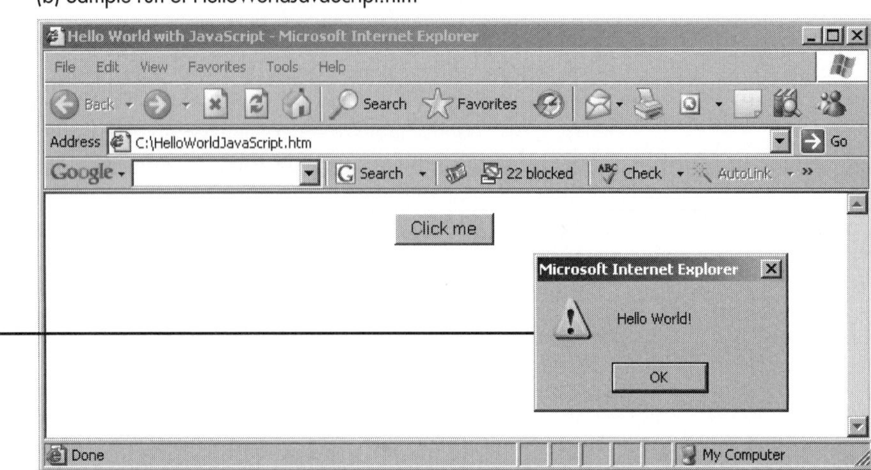

JavaScript alert box appears when button is clicked

FIGURE 9.6 Program code and sample run for HelloWorldJavaScript.htm

First, focus on the `body` element. It contains a form element (centered because it is contained within a `center` element) with a button containing the text `"Click Me"`. When the button is clicked, the JavaScript `function` named `Hello()` is called. Next, take a look at the `head` element. Within this is the `script` element that contains the JavaScript code that defines the `function`. When `Hello()` is called, it creates an `alert` box that displays the message `"Hello World"`. Figure 9.6(b) shows the result of viewing HelloWorldJavaScript.htm in a browser and clicking the button.

This is just a very small example of how a user can interact with a Web page (click a `button`) and get a response (an `alert` box). Real-world Web applications would contain hundreds of lines of very complex JavaScript code. Much of the dynamic nature and functionality that you see in Web sites are made possible with JavaScript client-side scripting. However, there is a faster and more secure way of providing interactivity and processing capability: server-side scripting.

Server-Side Scripting

Creating dynamic Web pages with client-side scripting is fine for many kinds of applications. However, for other applications, particularly those involving databases, server-side scripting is better. In **server-side scripting**, program code is still embedded in a Web page (or stored in a file referenced by the Web page), but the program code is executed on the server instead of on the client. The most common server-side scripting technologies (all released in the mid-1990s) are PHP (the open-source Personal Home Page Tools), ASP (Microsoft's Active Server Pages), and JSP (Sun Microsystems' JavaServer Pages).

When the client (that is, the browser) requests a Web page file containing server-side scripts, it does not receive the file immediately, as is the case with client-side scripting. Instead, the Web server first executes the server-side scripts in the requested file, creating a pure HTML file that is then delivered to the client. This way, processing is faster, downloading is quicker, and the user is allowed to see only the resulting HTML code, not the original server-side scripts. Figure 9.7 shows an example of a simple ASP file before and after it is processed by the server.

(a) HelloWorldASP.asp on the server

Server-side script between <% and %>

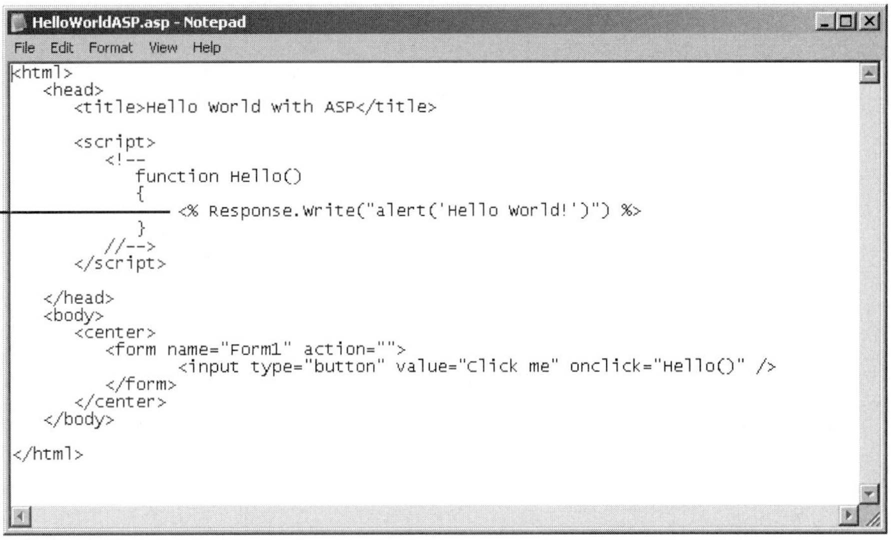

```
HelloWorldASP.asp - Notepad
File Edit Format View Help
<html>
   <head>
      <title>Hello World with ASP</title>

      <script>
         <!--
            function Hello()
            {
               <% Response.Write("alert('Hello World!')") %>
            }
         //-->
      </script>

   </head>
   <body>
      <center>
         <form name="Form1" action="">
               <input type="button" value="Click me" onclick="Hello()" />
         </form>
      </center>
   </body>

</html>
```

(b) HelloWorldASP.asp on the client

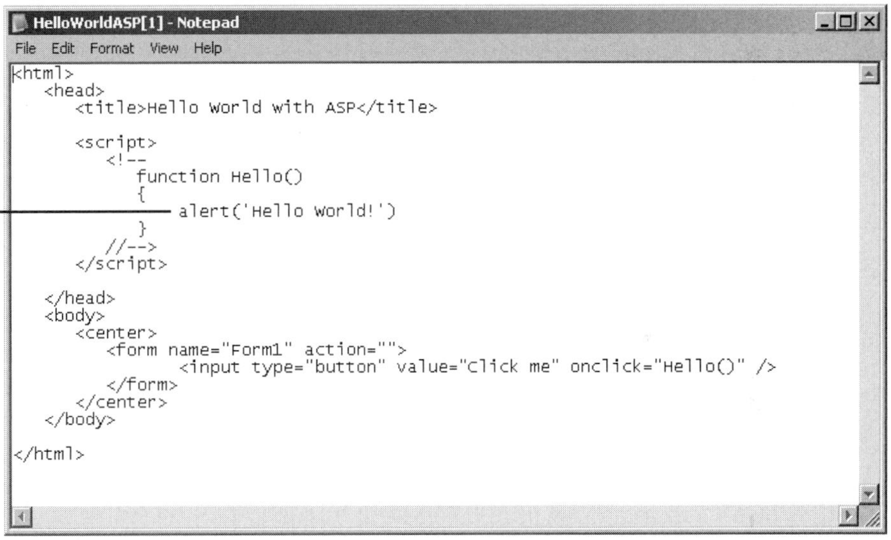

Server-side script replaced with contents of `Response.write`

```
HelloWorldASP[1] - Notepad
File Edit Format View Help
<html>
   <head>
      <title>Hello World with ASP</title>

      <script>
         <!--
            function Hello()
            {
               alert('Hello World!')
            }
         //-->
      </script>

   </head>
   <body>
      <center>
         <form name="Form1" action="">
               <input type="button" value="Click me" onclick="Hello()" />
         </form>
      </center>
   </body>

</html>
```

FIGURE 9.7 HelloWorldASP.asp on the server and on the client

The files shown in Figure 9.7 are both named HelloWorldASP.asp. The file in Figure 9.7(a) resides on the server. The only difference between this file and the one in Figure 9.6(a) is the line of code between the delimiters `<%` and `%>`, which is called a **render block**. Any file that contains these delimiters must be named with the .asp extension; these delimiters make the file an ASP file, not an HTML file. When the client requests the file HelloWorldASP.asp, the file extension .asp tells the server to check for render blocks. The server then executes the server-side scripts and delivers the resulting HTML code to the browser. In Figure 9.7(a), the code in the render block is the following:

```
Response.Write("alert('Hello World!')")
```

`Response` is an ASP object that manages output from the server to the client. It calls the `Write` method, which writes the code `alert('Hello World!')` to the page that will be delivered to the client. Figure 9.7(b) shows the file received by the browser, which is now identical to the file in Figure 9.6(a). The output in the browser resulting from downloading HelloWorldASP.asp is exactly the same as that shown in Figure 9.6(b). The user can see no difference in the output. When the user right-clicks the browser window and clicks View Code, he or she will see Figure 9.7(b) and will not be able to see the render block shown in Figure 9.7(a). The server-side scripts within the <% %> delimiters cannot be seen by the user. These render blocks will almost always contain much more complex code than that shown in Figure 9.7(a).

Using ASP is a definite improvement over using JavaScript. However, the new Microsoft ASP.NET technology for creating Web applications is much better than ASP.

What Is ASP.NET?

ASP.NET is the latest Microsoft technology for developing highly interactive Web applications. ASP.NET serves basically the same purpose as classic ASP (that is, server-side scripting), but in a drastically improved way. An ASP.NET file has a .aspx file extension (instead of .asp or .htm) and is called a Web form instead of a Web page. Web forms can contain ordinary HTML controls (such as text boxes and buttons), and special ASP.NET server controls (also called Web server controls). **Web server controls** are similar to HTML controls, but they are objects that have many properties and can call complex event procedures. In this regard, Web server controls are very similar to the Windows application controls that you have used throughout this text.

The advantages of ASP.NET over classic ASP include the following:

- ASP.NET is part of the .NET Framework, which means that it is totally object-oriented and is supported by the CLR. This means you can develop Web applications using a variety of languages such as Visual Basic, JScript, C#, and Visual J#.
- ASP.NET supports a more structured approach to server-side scripting compared to the often piecemeal process of mixing ASP code with HTML code, which often results in confusing, unstructured code that is difficult to maintain.
- ASP.NET allows the programmer to create controls (such as forms, text boxes, and buttons) using the simpler and more organized .NET event-driven model. You can even separate the user interface (the Web page) from its application logic in a separate Visual Basic file (called the code-behind file).
- ASP.NET code is compiled rather than interpreted, which improves performance and helps the programmer catch design-time errors.
- ASP.NET supports ADO.NET, an improved way of interfacing with databases.

In the next section, you will begin to learn how to create ASP.NET Web applications.

CREATING A WEB SITE WITH ASP.NET

Now that you have some background in Web pages, Web servers, and scripting languages, it's time to begin creating a simple Web site using ASP.NET. In this section you will create an ASP.NET Web site and add some simple content to a Web form.

Creating an ASP.NET Web Site

Figure 9.8 explains how to create an ASP.NET Web site using Visual Studio.

HOW TO...

Create an ASP.NET Web Site

1. Launch Microsoft Visual Studio 2005. In the Visual Studio menu, click File and click New Web Site. The New Web Site dialog box opens, as shown in Figure 9.9.
2. Click the ASP.NET Web Site icon. In the Location drop-down list, click File System to save the Web site on your local computer. In the Language drop-down list, click Visual Basic. (Visual C# and Visual J# are also available if you prefer.) These selections may already be the default settings as you see in Figure 9.9.
3. Click the Browse button in the New Web Site dialog box. The Choose Location dialog box appears with File System selected by default. To create a Web site on your local file system, navigate to the desired location. (By default, Visual Studio will create a Web site called WebSite1 as shown in Figure 9.10, but you can select any location for the Web site.)
4. Complete the location for the Web site by typing the name of the folder in which the Web site will be located (such as MyFirstSite instead of WebSite1) in the Folder text box of the Choose Location dialog box. Click OK. If the folder you selected for the Web site does not exist, a dialog box will appear and will ask if you want to create the folder. Click Yes. Then click OK in the New Web Site dialog box.
5. In Visual Studio, a new blank Web page named Default.aspx appears in the Designer. (Note that the Design tab is selected at the bottom of the Designer.)
6. Click the Source tab at the bottom of the Designer to view the source code for Default.aspx. Then click View and click Solution Explorer to open the Solution Explorer. Finally, click the plus sign (+) next to Default.aspx to reveal the file Default.aspx.vb. See Figure 9.11.

FIGURE 9.8 How to create an ASP.NET Web site

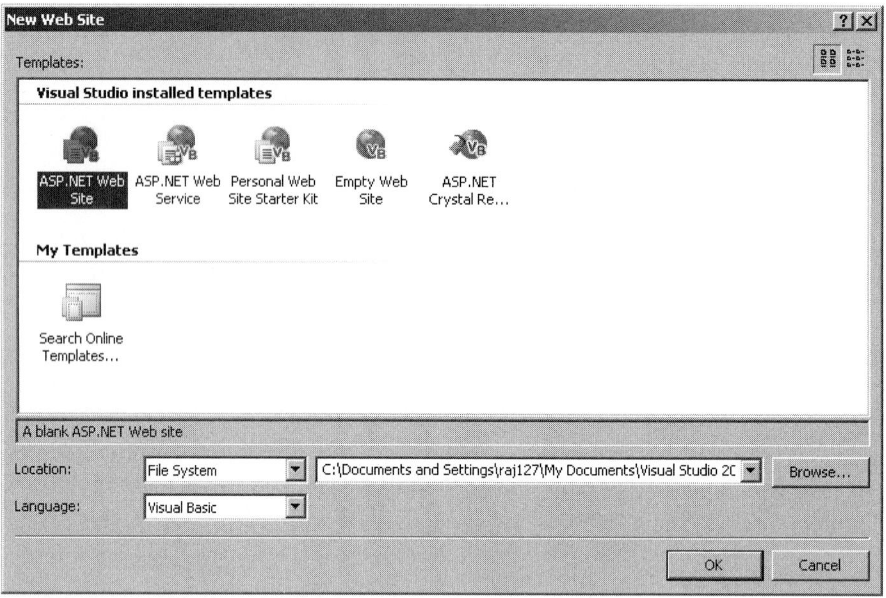

FIGURE 9.9 The New Web Site dialog box

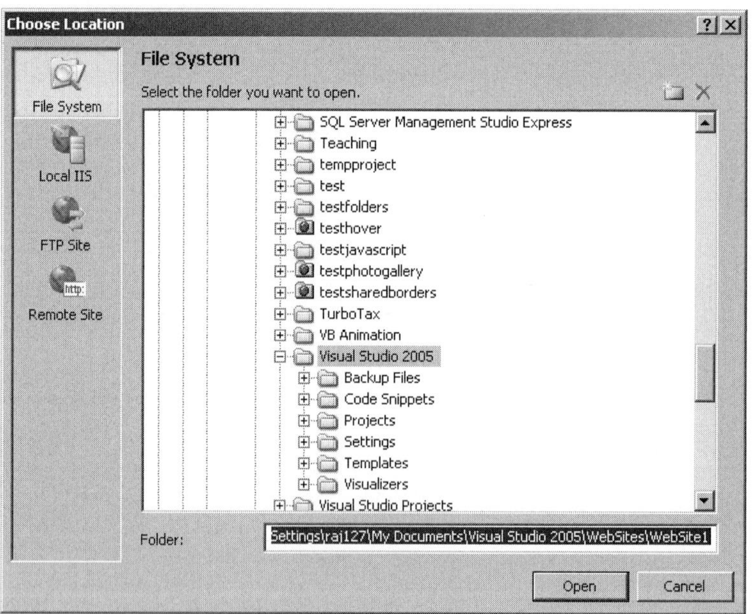

FIGURE 9.10 The Choose Location dialog box

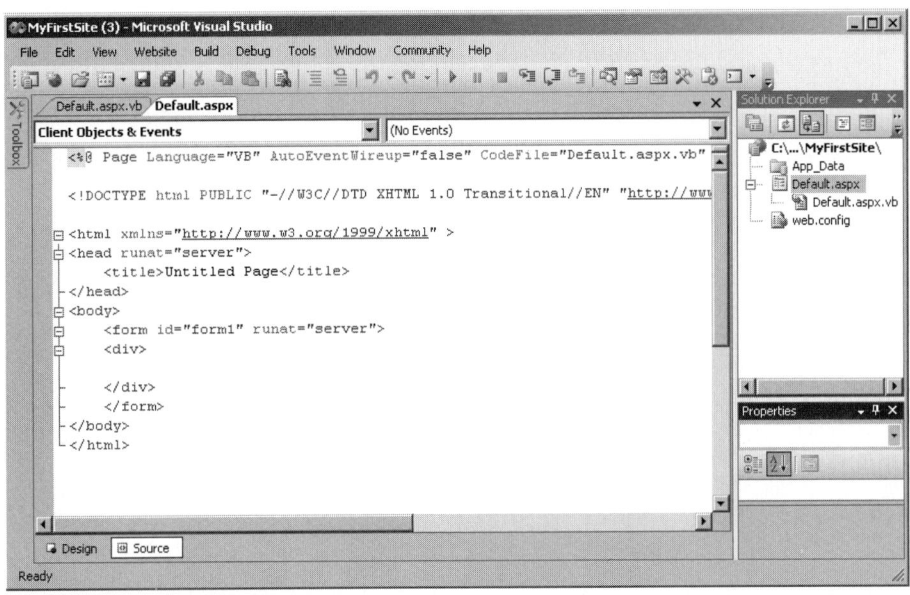

FIGURE 9.11 The Visual Studio IDE displaying code for Default.aspx

Exploring an ASP.NET Web Form

As always, the Server Explorer in Figure 9.11 displays the files in the solution. Of importance right now is, of course, the Default.aspx file (the Web form). However, you will also see a file called Default.aspx.vb. This is a Visual Basic code-behind file. A **code-behind file** is a Visual Basic class containing the event procedures that accompany controls (such as text boxes, lists, and buttons) placed on an ASP.NET Web form.

The code window in Figure 9.11 displays the code automatically generated for a blank Web form. The very first line of code begins and ends with the special delimiters `<%` and `%>`. As with classic ASP, these delimiters designate code that is run at the server, not at the client. This particular code at the beginning of the file performs setup tasks, such as identifying the programming language to be used (`VB` in this case) and the code-behind file (`Default.aspx.vb`).

The second line of code in Figure 9.11 (beginning with `<!DOCTYPE`) is a special document type declaration. A **document type declaration** is a formal declaration that begins with the keyword `DOCTYPE`, followed by the name of the base element of the document, followed by the specification of the markup language to be used. In the case of Default.aspx, the base element is `html` and the specification is `XHTML 1.0 Transitional` (which is a standard to which the HTML document must comply to be considered valid).

The remainder of the code in Figure 9.11 consists simply of HTML tags that you find in any Web page. The `html` tag has an attribute `xmlns="http://www.w3.org/1999/xhtml"`, which identifies the XML namespace for this document. An **XML namespace** is a collection of names, identified by a URI (Uniform Resource Identifier) reference, which is used in XML documents as element types and attribute names. An XML namespace provides a simple method for establishing unique element types and attribute names in an XML document, such as in the Default.aspx document. The URI in Figure 9.11 is *http://www.w3.org/1999/xhtml*. Therefore, all the element types and attribute names used in Default.aspx are considered part of this namespace.

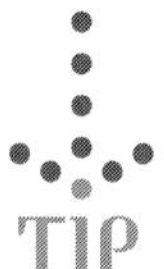

TIP

An XML namespace is very different from a Microsoft .NET Framework namespace. In the .NET Framework, a namespace is a hierarchical scheme for categorizing classes, structures, and enumerations. For example, the System namespace contains the Windows.Forms namespace, which contains the class Button, making the fully qualified name for the Button class System.Windows.Forms.Button.

The same element types and attribute names used in a different namespace would be considered different from those used in the *http://www.w3.org/1999/xhtml* namespace. For example, the element type `form` in Default.aspx would be considered different from the element type `form` used in a document that uses a different namespace. In large Web applications, many Web pages may interact, and naming conflicts can arise among elements and attributes if appropriate namespaces are not used.

As you know, ASP.NET is similar to ASP. However, what distinguishes the ASP.NET file Default.aspx in Figure 9.11 from other classic ASP files can be found in the following code:

```
<form id="form1" runat="server">
```

Note the `form` attribute `runat` with the value `"server"`. This is a unique ASP.NET technique for directing this HTML element (`form`, in this case) to be executed on the server, not on the client. Thus, Web form elements can be more comprehensively and carefully controlled by the server, as you will see in following examples.

Adding Content to a Web Form

Now that you have created a Web site with a Default.aspx file, you are ready to add content to make the Web form functional. You have two choices: First, you can make Default.aspx behave like an ordinary HTML file (that is, a Web page) by typing text on the page and dragging HTML controls onto the page from the Visual Studio Toolbox (in the HTML section). Alternatively, you can make Default.aspx a more fully functional ASP.NET Web form by adding special Web server controls from the Standard section of the Toolbox. Since this chapter is about creating ASP.NET Web sites with Web forms (not ordinary HTML Web pages), the second approach is taken here. Figure 9.12 shows how to add content to a Web form including Web server controls.

HOW TO...

Add Content to a Web Form

1. After creating a new ASP.NET Web site (see Figure 9.8), click the Design tab at the bottom of the Designer to enter Design mode.
2. To display the familiar Formatting toolbar, click View in the Visual Studio menu, point to Toolbars, and then click Formatting.
3. To view the Toolbox, click View in the Visual Studio menu and then click Toolbox.
4. To change the Properties of the Web form, click View in the Visual Studio menu and then click Properties Window. Click the drop-down list at the top of the Properties window and click DOCUMENT. Change the Title properties from "Untitled Page" to a more meaningful title.
5. To change the name of the Web form, right-click the .aspx file in the Solution Explorer, click Rename, type the new file name (including the .aspx extension), and press Enter.

(Figure is continued on next page)

6. To add text to the Web form, simply click on the page, press the Enter key as necessary, and type. You can also select text and format it using buttons in the Formatting toolbar, as with most other Windows applications.
7. To move to a new line on the Web form, press Enter. (Or press Shift+Enter to move to a new line without adding an intervening blank line.)
8. To add a control to the Web form, drag the control (such as a `Button` or a `Label`) from the Standard section of the Toolbox to the page.
9. To view and change the properties of an element on the Web form, click the element (such as text or a control) and use the Properties window.
10. Click the Save All button in the toolbar to save changes.
11. To test the Web form, click the Start Debugging button in the toolbar (or press F5). If the Debugging Not Enabled dialog box appears, click the Modify option and click OK to enable debugging.

FIGURE 9.12 How to add content to a Web form

Starting with the blank Web page Default.aspx, the steps in Figure 9.12 were applied. In Step 4, the title of the page was changed to "First Web Form". In Step 5, the text "My First Web Form" was added and the font size was changed to 48pt. Applying Step 8, two controls were added to the Web form: a `Button` with the `ID` property set to `displayButton` and the `Text` property set to "Click Me"; a `Label` with the ID property set to `displayLabel` and the `Text` property set to `""`. The Web form was renamed FirstWebForm.aspx. These actions resulted in the Web form shown in Figure 9.13. (Note the Property window for the DOCUMENT.)

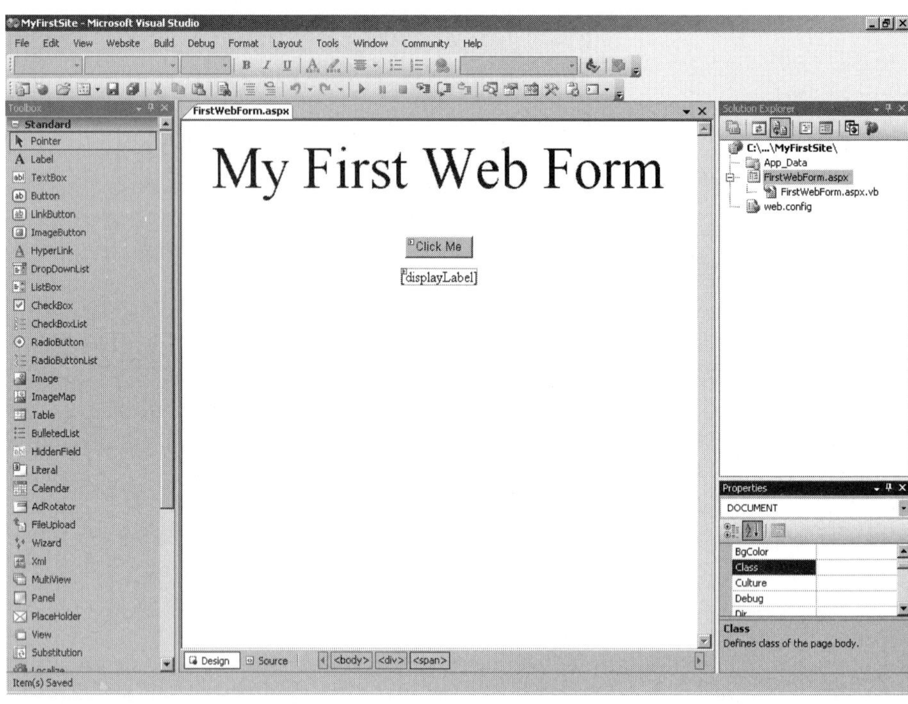

FIGURE 9.13 Design view of FirstWebForm.aspx

Figure 9.14 shows the ASP.NET code for FirstWebForm.aspx, obtained by clicking the Source tab at the bottom of the Designer in Visual Studio. You have already learned about the first few lines of code in Figure 9.14. Note that the `head` element has the attribute `runat="server"`, which indicates that this HTML element will be executed on the server, not the client.

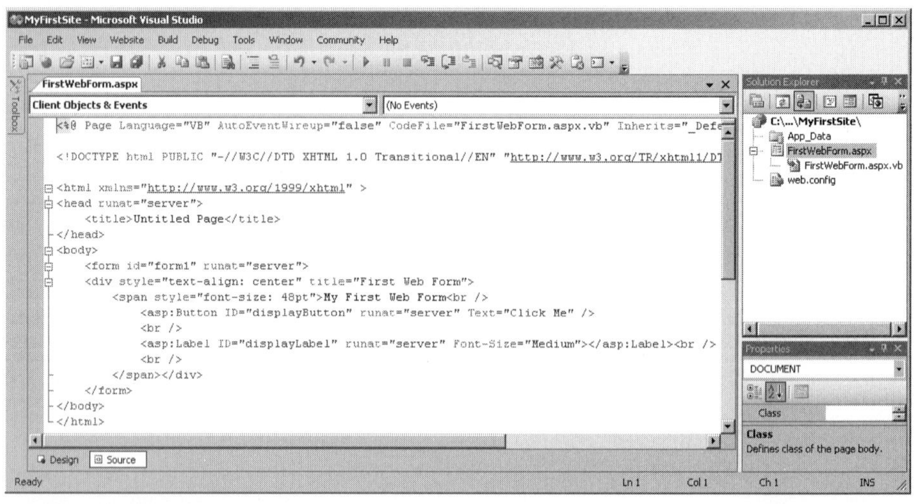

```
<%@ Page Language="VB" AutoEventWireup="false" CodeFile="FirstWebForm.aspx.vb" Inherits="_Defa

<!DOCTYPE html PUBLIC "-//W3C//DTD XHTML 1.0 Transitional//EN" "http://www.w3.org/TR/xhtml1/DT

<html xmlns="http://www.w3.org/1999/xhtml" >
<head runat="server">
    <title>Untitled Page</title>
</head>
<body>
    <form id="form1" runat="server">
    <div style="text-align: center" title="First Web Form">
        <span style="font-size: 48pt">My First Web Form<br />
            <asp:Button ID="displayButton" runat="server" Text="Click Me" />
            <br />
            <asp:Label ID="displayLabel" runat="server" Font-Size="Medium"></asp:Label><br />
            <br />
        </span></div>
    </form>
</body>
</html>
```

FIGURE 9.14 Code view of FirstWebForm.aspx

The `body` element contains several new items. The `form` element (with `id="form1"`), which contains many other elements, also has the attribute `runat="server"`. The `div` element (`div` stands for "logical division") contains text (`My First Web Form`), a button, and a label. The `div` element is used to create separate sections in a Web page to which special style formatting can be added. Note that the `div` element has the attribute `style="text-align: center"`, which causes everything between the tags `<div>` and `</div>` to be centered on the form.

The text on the Web page ("My First Web Page") is contained within a `span` element. Here, the `span` element has an attribute and a value that formats the text to display in 48pt font size. The `span` element is an inline element and formats text only within the body of a paragraph. The `div` element is an example of a block-level element, one that generates a blank line before and after the element, similar to pressing the Enter key twice on the keyboard. The `br` (line break) element is used to end a line short of the right margin, similar to pressing the Enter key once on the keyboard, as you would if you were typing a name and an address in a letter.

You will also notice two special ASP.NET elements, `<asp:Button>` and `<asp:Label>`, in Figure 9.14. These are Web controls that add both form and function to a Web form and are executed on the server. The intent of the `Button` in Figure 9.13 is to cause a message to be displayed in the `Label` when clicked. We will say more about Web server controls later in this chapter.

When FirstWebForm.aspx is saved and run (see Steps 10 and 11 in Figure 9.12), the Web form shown in Figure 9.15 displays. Nothing happens when the button is clicked because an event procedure for the button has not been created. You will see how to do that in the next section.

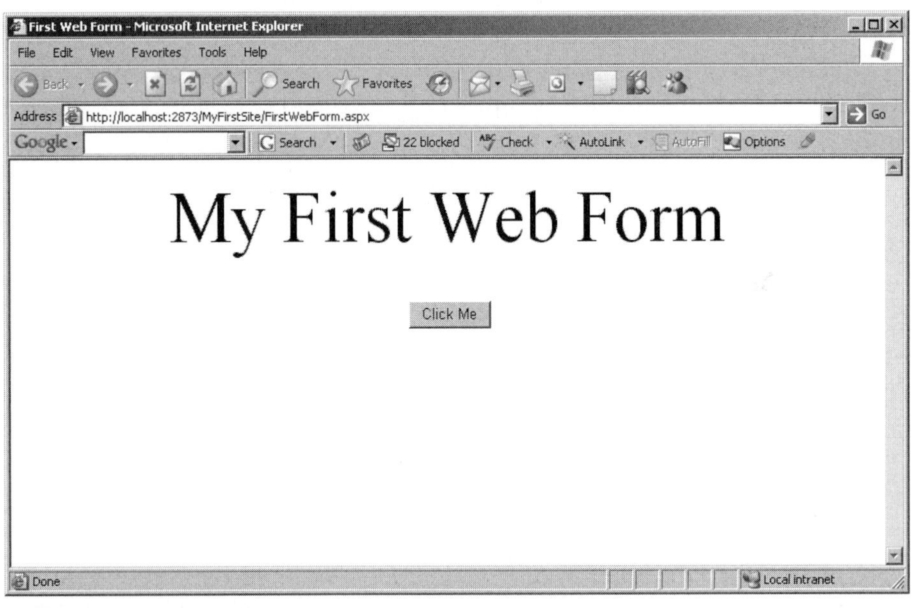

FIGURE 9.15 Sample run of FirstWebForm.aspx

Adding an Event Procedure to a Control

Web sites are much more interesting and useful when they are interactive—that is, when users can provide input and the site can provide responses that meet user needs. One way to accomplish this is through the event-driven programming model with which you are already familiar. The same model can be applied to Web sites by combining ASP.NET with Visual Basic, as Figure 9.16 demonstrates.

HOW TO...

Add an Event Procedure to a Web Form

1. To add a `Page_Load` procedure to a Web form, double-click an empty area of the Web form. This procedure executes every time the page is loaded from the server.
2. After adding a Web control (such as a button) to a Web form (see Figure 9.12), double-click the control. The code-behind file appears with the code for the event procedure displayed.
3. Add the required Visual Basic code within the event procedure to complete the event procedure and provide the desired response to the event.
4. Click the Save All button in the toolbar to save changes.
5. To test the Web page, click the Start Debugging button in the toolbar (or press F5).

FIGURE 9.16 How to add an event procedure to a Web page

Figure 9.17 shows the code for a button click event procedure in the FirstWebForm.aspx file shown in Figure 9.13. The "Click Me" button in the Design view was double-clicked, which opened the FirstWebForm.aspx.vb file (the code-behind file) with the declaration of the `displayButton_Click` event procedure added automatically. The code `displayLabel.Text = "You clicked the button"` was added to make the `Label` in Figure 9.13 display the desired text. A sample run of FirstWebForm.aspx is shown in Figure 9.18 (after clicking the button).

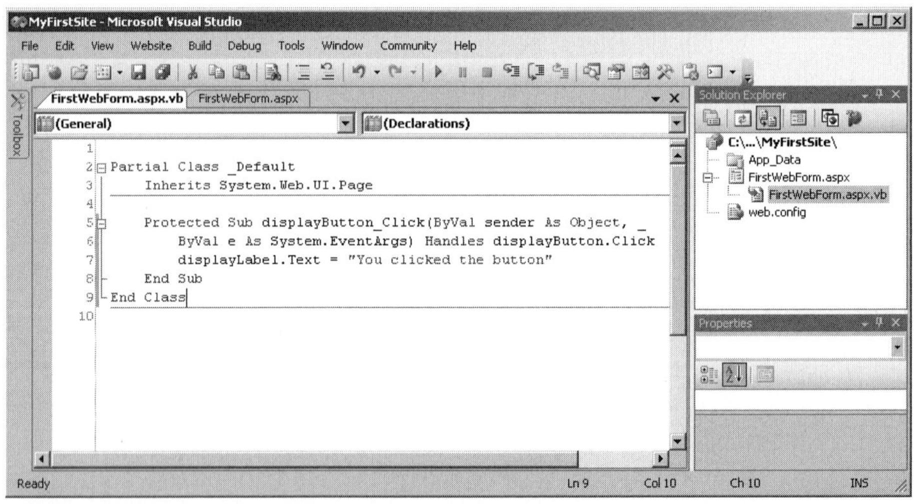

FIGURE 9.17 Event procedure in FirstWebForm.aspx.vb

FIGURE 9.18 Sample run of FirstWebForm.aspx with event procedure

The sample run in Figure 9.18 used an event procedure in the code-behind file FirstWebForm.aspx.vb (Figure 9.17). It is interesting to note, however, that the code-behind file is not absolutely essential. The same functionality of FirstWebForm.aspx can be achieved by placing this same event procedure within a script element in FirstWebForm.aspx. Figure 9.19 shows the code for FirstWebForm.aspx, which will produce the same output shown in Figure 9.18, even when FirstWebForm.aspx.vb is not present. The advantage of using the code-behind file is that it completely separates the presentation tier (that is, the user interface represented by FirstWebForm.aspx) from the logic tier (that is, the application logic contained within FirstWebForm.aspx.vb), making the application easier to understand and maintain.

Event procedure within `script` *element*

Code for text, `Button` *and* `Label`

```
<%@ Page Language="VB" AutoEventWireup="false" CodeFile="FirstWebForm.aspx.vb" Inherits="_Defa

<!DOCTYPE html PUBLIC "-//W3C//DTD XHTML 1.0 Transitional//EN" "http://www.w3.org/TR/xhtml1/DT

<html xmlns="http://www.w3.org/1999/xhtml" >
<head runat="server">
    <title>First Web Form</title>

    <script runat="server">
        Protected Sub displayButton_Click(ByVal sender As Object, _
            ByVal e As System.EventArgs) Handles displayButton.Click
            displayLabel.Text = "You clicked the button"
        End Sub
    </script>

</head>
<body>
    <form id="form1" runat="server">
    <div style="text-align: center" title="First Web Form">
        <span style="font-size: 48pt">My First Web Form<br />
            <asp:Button ID="displayButton" runat="server" Text="Click Me" />
            <br />
            <asp:Label ID="displayLabel" runat="server" Font-Size="Medium"></asp:Label><br />
            <br />
        </span></div>
    </form>
</body>
</html>
```

FIGURE 9.19 FirstWebForm.aspx with event procedure included

Adding a Web Form to a Site

When you first create an ASP.NET Web site, ASP.NET creates the Default.aspx file for you. However, nearly all Web sites will have more than one page. As you know, Web pages have hyperlinks to open new pages. A **hyperlink** (contraction of "hypertext link") is a graphic or text in a Web page that, when clicked, opens a new Web page or jumps to a new location in the current page. Figure 9.20 explains how to add a new Web form to a site.

HOW TO...

Add a New Web Form to a Site

1. With the Web site open in Visual Studio, click Web Site and click Add New Item in the Visual Studio menu. The Add New Item dialog box appears, similar to the one in Figure 9.21.
2. Click the Web Form icon in the Templates section.
3. Type the complete file name in the Name text box and click Add. The new .aspx file and its corresponding code-behind file are displayed in the Solution Explorer.

FIGURE 9.20 How to add a new Web form to a site

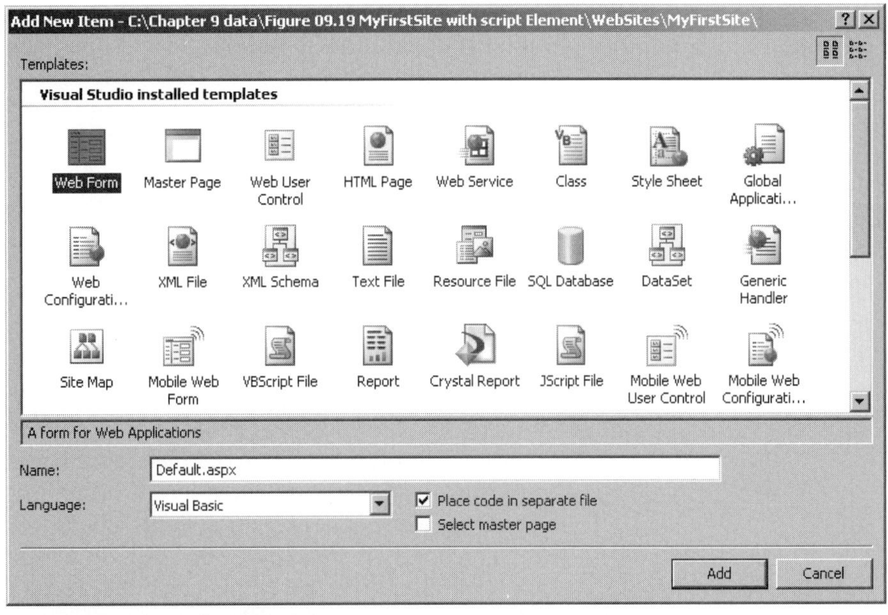

FIGURE 9.21 The Add New Item dialog box

Notice in the Add New Item dialog box (Figure 9.21) that there are many kinds of files that you can add to a Web site, including some that should be familiar to you (such as HTML Page, Class, and SQL Database) and some not so familiar (such as Web Service, Style Sheet, and XML File). Some of these file types will be covered in the following chapters while others are beyond the scope of this text. Next, you will learn about specific kinds of controls that can be added to Web forms in your site.

USING WEB SERVER CONTROLS

In the previous section, you learned how to create an ASP.NET Web form that included two Web server controls, `Button` and `Label`. In this section, you will learn more about how to use these and many other Web server controls.

Overview of Web Server Controls

You are already very familiar with Windows Forms controls, such as `Label`, `TextBox`, and `Button`, which you studied in the first six chapters of this text. Web server controls in ASP.NET (also referred to as ASP.NET server controls or just Web controls) are similar to typical Windows Forms controls because they are defined by classes and have many of the same properties, such as `Text`, `Enabled`, `Font`, and `TabIndex`. However, instead of the `Name` property, Web controls use the `ID` property. Most importantly, as with Windows Forms controls, Web controls can respond to events (such as `Click` or `TextChanged`) by executing the corresponding event procedure in the code-behind file.

A Web form typically contains a variety of controls, such as text boxes, check boxes, radio buttons, and drop-down lists. Each of these controls can have its own event procedure created in the code-behind file when the Web control is double-clicked. However, you often create just one event procedure in a Web form for a single button that submits the Web form to the Web server for processing.

Many Web controls have an AutoPostBack property, which has a default value of False. This is an important property because the value of AutoPostBack can affect the performance of a Web application. If AutoPostBack is True, then whenever the contents of an individual control (such as TextBox or RadioButtonList) changes, the entire Web form is automatically posted back to the Web server for processing. If AutoPostBack is False, the Web form is posted back to the Web server only when the user clicks a Submit button. You should set AutoPostBack to True only when such updates are really necessary. Frequent postbacks can slow the Web application's performance. In most cases, you will simply use a Submit button to post all information contained in the Web controls of a Web form to the Web server for processing.

Types of Web Controls

This section provides more detailed information about the various types of Web controls available in ASP.NET. Most Web controls are nearly identical to their Windows Forms counterparts. Remember, however, that every Web control has an ID property instead of a Name property. (That is a carryover from HTML.) Like the Name property, the ID property should be set to a meaningful value, such as submitButton or costTextBox.

The following discussion will give you a brief introduction to some of the more common Web controls, many of which will be demonstrated in the following examples and in the Programming Example at the end of this chapter.

Label Control

In a Web form, you can simply type text onto the page to provide information to the user. However, in some situations it's better to use a Label, which can provide useful functionality. For example, the Label content may need to change at runtime, or you may need to use its Visible property or ToolTip property. You also have easier control over style issues with a Label than with entering plain text because a Label has properties such as Font and BorderStyle.

TextBox Control

A TextBox control allows for user input. Its TextMode property has the following values: SingleLine (only one line of input is allowed), MultiLine (multiple lines of input are allowed), and Password (typed characters are masked as solid circles instead of the actual human-readable characters). To make your Web page compatible with a wider variety of Web browsers, you should use the Columns and Rows properties to set the size of a TextBox.

Button Control

You have already seen how to use the Button control in the application presented in Figures 9.17 and 9.18, but you may not realize that there are two kinds of buttons. The first is a Submit button. By default, a Button control is a Submit button that simply posts the Web form to the Web server for processing. You can also create an event procedure for the Click event to programmatically perform additional actions (besides a postback) when the Submit button is clicked. You will see an example of this shortly.

The second kind of button is a command button. A command button, like a Submit button, has a CommandName property. However, a Submit button has no value assigned to this property because it needs to function only as the sole Submit button for the Web form. A command button is a button that has a text value assigned to its `CommandName` property, such as Sort. Accessing the value of this property allows the programmer to write more specialized program code to respond to the state of specifically named buttons (for example, whether or not they have been clicked). This property also allows the programmer to place several buttons on a Web form, each with different `CommandName` values, but all using one event procedure.

`HyperLink` Control

You use the `HyperLink` control to create text or an image, which the user can then click to open a new page in the Web site or a page on an external Web site. The following list summarizes some important properties of the `HyperLink`:

- The `Text` property contains the text that is displayed as the hyperlink (such as "About Us" or "Visit Course Technology").
- The `NavigateUrl` property contains the URL of the Web page that will be opened in the browser when the user clicks the hyperlink. By clicking the value column for this property in the Properties window, you can navigate to the Web page located within the Web site or you can type the URL of the external page (such as *http://www.course.com/*).
- The `ImageUrl` property allows you to use a graphic as the hyperlink (instead of text). By clicking the value column for this property in the Properties window, you can navigate to an image file (such as company_logo.jpg) located within the Web site. The image is then displayed on the Web form and serves as a hyperlink.
- The `Target` property controls how the new page appears. One setting, `self`, displays the page in the current browser window. Another setting, `blank`, opens the page in a new browser window.

TIP

Do not place image files in the project's App_Data folder. If you do, they will not display correctly. The App_Data folder is for data stores (database files, XML files, etc.), which are discussed in the next chapter. Many developers store images for a Web site in a folder named images.

`ImageButton` Control

The `ImageButton` control behaves like a standard `Button` control, but it uses a graphic that is stored within the Web site instead of the standard `Button` style.

`LinkButton` Control

The `LinkButton` control behaves like a standard `Button`, but it uses plain text instead of the standard `Button` shape.

`ListBox` Control

The `ListBox` control is similar to the Windows Forms `ListBox` control with an `Items` collection and a `SelectedIndexChanged` event. Adding a `ListBox` control to a Web form is a little more involved than adding other controls to a Web form. You start by dragging this control from the Toolbox to a Web form, at which point an empty `ListBox` appears along with a set of tasks for the list, as shown in Figure 9.22. Clicking Edit Items in the set of options for the `ListBox` smart tag displays the ListItem Collection Editor dialog box, also shown in Figure 9.22. Notice the check box in the set of options for Enable AutoPostBack. This important feature was discussed earlier in this chapter.

Clicking the Add button in the ListItem Collection Editor and typing the values for the `Text` and `Value` properties creates the list. The `SelectedIndex`, `SelectedItem`, and `SelectedValue` properties of the list allow you to execute Visual Basic code based on user selections from the list, as you will soon see.

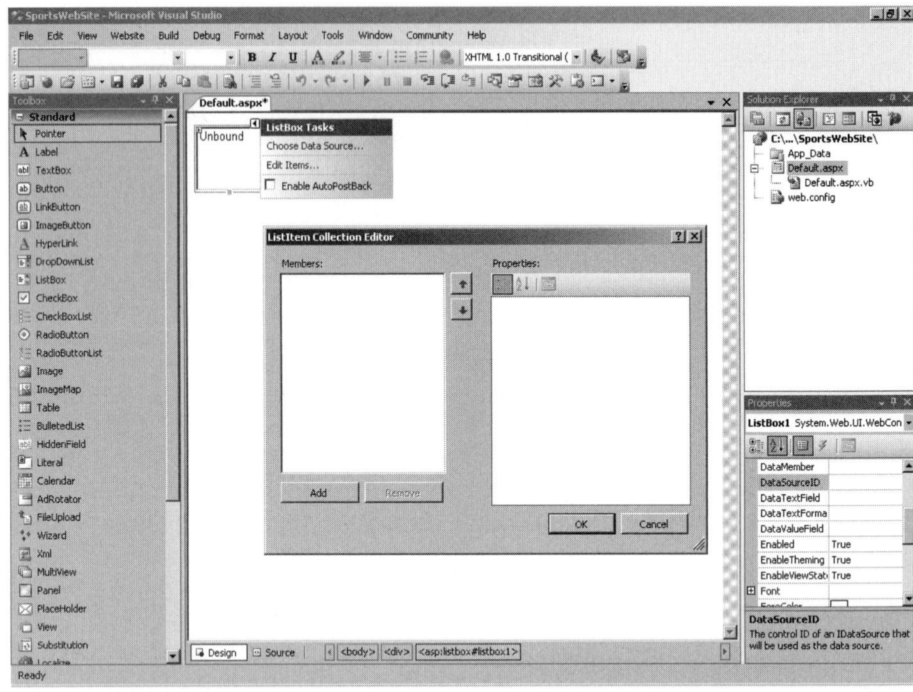

FIGURE 9.22 Adding a `ListBox` control to a Web form

As an example of using the `ListBox` control, Figure 9.23 shows the Web form Sports.aspx in the Web site SportsWebSite. The Web form begins with some explanatory `Label` controls, a `ListBox` control with `ID sportsListBox`, a `TextBox` with `ID sportsTextBox`, and a `Button` control with `ID submitButton`. The `SelectionMode` property of the `sportsListBox` is set to `Multiple`, thus allowing the user to select more than one item in the list using the Ctrl key plus a mouse click. The `TextMode` property of the `sportsTextBox` is set to `Multiple`, allowing multiple lines of text to be displayed. The `ReadOnly` property of `sportsTextBox` is set to `True` because the `TextBox` is for output only.

Next, the `submitButton` was double-clicked to create an event procedure in the code-behind file Sports.aspx.vb. Additional code was then added to this event procedure to iterate through all the `Item` objects in the `ListBox` object, as shown in Figure 9.24. A sample run of Sports.aspx is displayed in Figure 9.25.

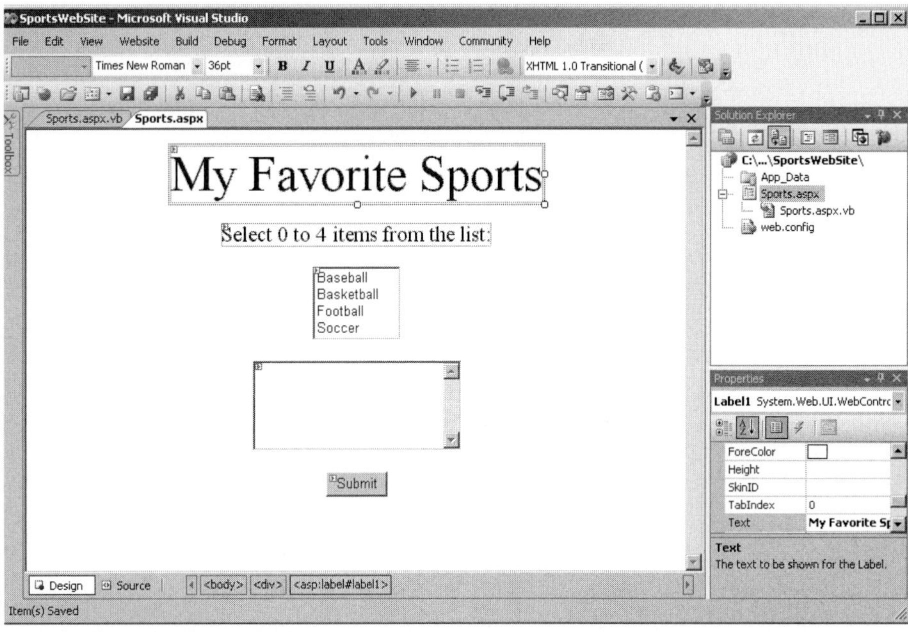

FIGURE 9.23 The Design window for Sports.aspx

```
Partial Class _Default
    Inherits System.Web.UI.Page

    Protected Sub submitButton_Click(ByVal sender As Object, _
        ByVal e As System.EventArgs) Handles submitButton.Click

        Dim item As ListItem
        Dim selection As String = Nothing

        For Each item In sportsListBox.Items
            If item.Selected Then
                selection += item.Text & ControlChars.CrLf
            End If
        Next

        If selection = Nothing Then
            selection = "None of the above"
        End If

        sportsTextBox.Text = "My favorite sport(s): " & _
            ControlChars.CrLf & selection

    End Sub
End Class
```

FIGURE 9.24 Program code for Sports.aspx.vb

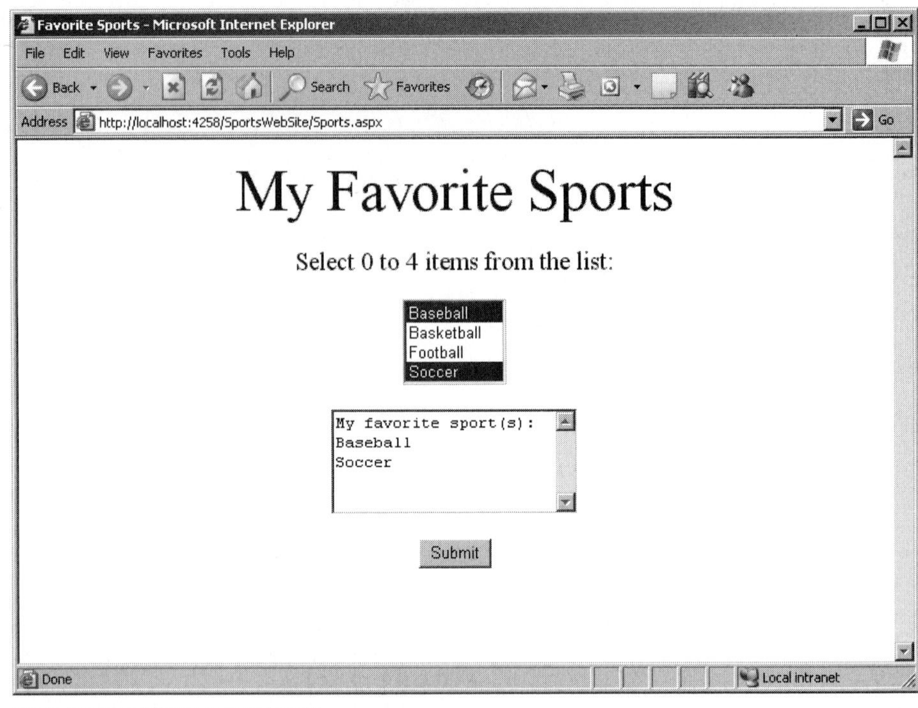

FIGURE 9.25 Sample run for Sports.aspx

As you can see in the Standard section of the Toolbox in Figure 9.22, there are many other Web controls that you can use in a Web form, such as `DropDownList`, `CheckBoxList`, and `RadioButtonList`. You are already familiar with most of these controls from your experience with Windows Forms applications. It is a relatively straightforward process to add these controls to a Web form, set their properties, and use them to provide information for the logic tier contained in a code-behind file. Remember that when the user clicks a Submit button, the Web form is posted to the Web server, which executes the code-behind file and returns the resulting HTML page to the browser.

USING TABLES FOR FORM LAYOUT

The previous section discussed a wide variety of Web controls that you can place on a Web page. You can simply drag controls from the Toolbox to the page, resulting in (by default) a flow layout where controls simply follow each other on the page (for example, see Figure 9.23). You can affect the location of controls somewhat by using the alignment buttons in the toolbar and the `Style` property of the document, and by using line breaks (which adds the `<br />` tag). However, these techniques are fairly limited.

A better way of organizing controls on a page is by using the HTML table control. This is a simple HTML control (or HTML element), not a Web control. (There is a table Web control, but it is not as well suited for form layout purposes.) A table, with its rows and columns, is useful for organizing Web controls such as labels, text boxes, lists, and buttons. Figure 9.26 explains how to add a table to a Web form and then add Web controls to a table.

HOW TO...

Create a Table Layout for a Form

1. With a Web form open in Visual Studio, drag a Table control from the HTML section of the Toolbox (not the Standard section) to the desired location on the page. An empty three-row, three-column table appears on the page. The `table` element also appears in the Properties window, as shown in Figure 9.27.
2. In the Properties window for the `table` element, set the `Width` property to the desired value (such as 50% to fill 50% of the Web form or an integer such as 100 for 100 pixels).
3. In the Properties window for the `table` element, set the `Border`, `CellPadding`, and `CellSpacing` properties to the desired number of pixels. `Border` is the width of the grid lines that appear for the table. (The default is 0 for no grid lines.) `CellPadding` is the minimum space between the cell border and the cell's contents, while `CellSpacing` is the distance between cells. (0 is the default for each.)
4. Click the Source tab at the bottom of the Designer. You see the HTML code for this initial table with the `<table></table>` tags. There are also attributes such as `width` and `border` if you added these. Within the table element are three sets of `<tr></tr>` tags. (The code `tr` stands for "table row.") Within each `tr` element are three sets of `<td></td>` tags. (The code `td` stands for "table data," but these are actually columns or cells within each row.) Figure 9.29 shows the HTML code for the three-row, three-column table shown in Figure 9.28.
5. Click the Design tab at the bottom of the Designer to return to the Design window (as shown in Figure 9.28).
6. You often need to select an entire table or just parts of the table to adjust a layout. To select the entire `table` element, move the cursor to the top edge of the table until the all-directions pointer appears and then click the table. To select an entire row, move the cursor to the left edge of a row and click the arrow. To select an entire column, move the cursor to the top edge of a row and click the arrow. To select a cell, click inside the cell. To select multiple rows, columns, or cells, point to a row, column, or cell, then click and drag.
7. Determine the exact number of rows and the maximum number of columns that the table needs for a given layout of controls (labels, text boxes, buttons, and so on). Then determine the exact number of columns (cells) needed in each individual row of the table. For example, the first row of a layout table may need just one cell to hold one control, but the second row may need two cells to hold two different controls.
8. To insert or delete rows or columns, select the rows or columns. In the Visual Studio menu, click Layout and point to Insert or Delete as necessary.

(Figure is continued on next page)

9. To merge two or more cells into a single cell, select the cells. In the Visual Studio menu, click Layout and click Merge Cells.
10. After the table design is complete, type text in individual cells and/or drag controls from the Toolbox (labels, text boxes, lists, buttons, and so on) to individual cells within the table. Then set the properties for each of the controls as necessary.

FIGURE 9.26 How to create a table layout for a form

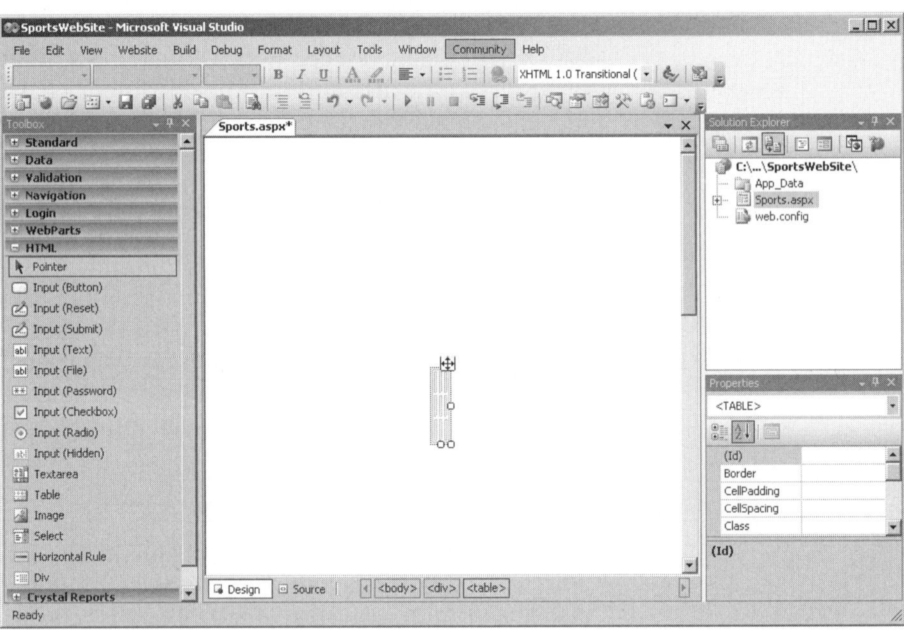

FIGURE 9.27 An HTML `table` control in a Web form

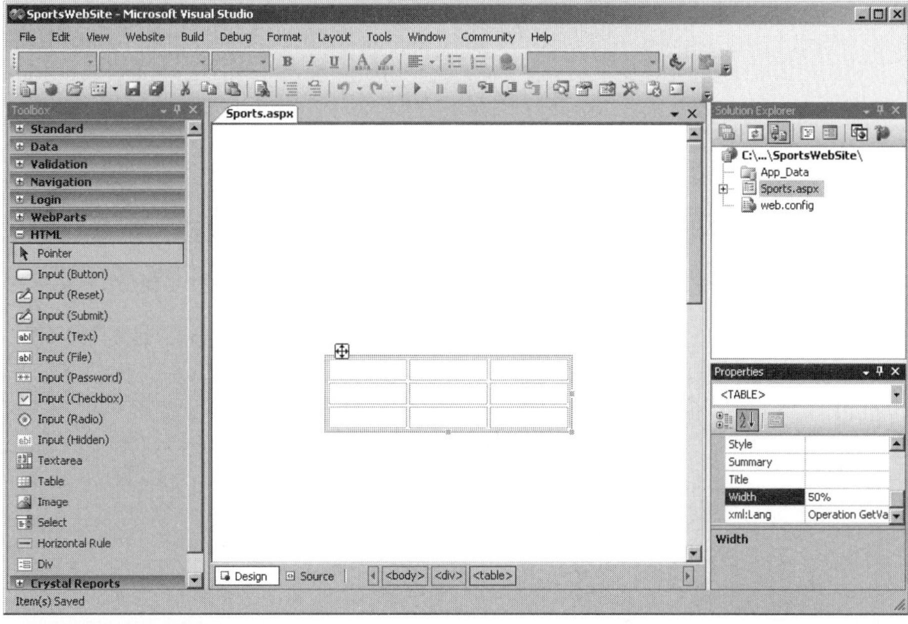

FIGURE 9.28 Adjusting the `Width` property of a `table` control

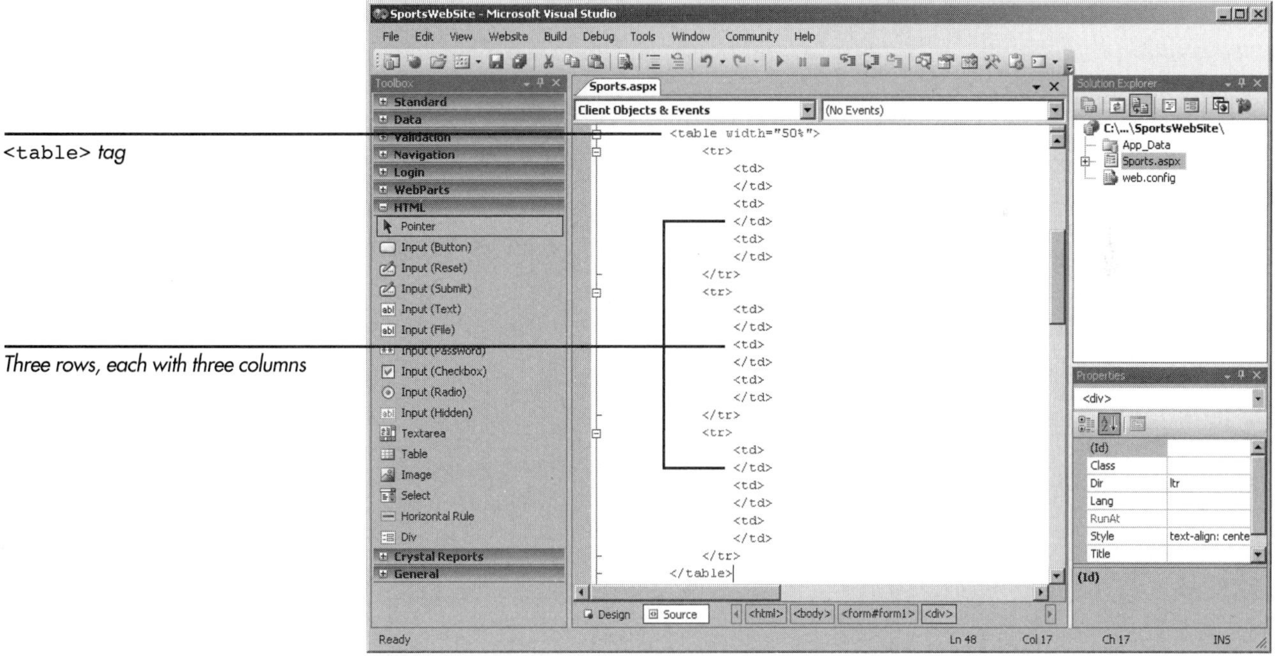

FIGURE 9.29 HTML code for a three-row by three-column `table` element

Figure 9.30 shows the design for a modified SportsWebSite that uses a table for the layout of the controls in the Sports.aspx Web form. Originally, a four-row by two-column table was added to the Web form. Then the two cells in the first row were merged into one cell, as were the two cells in the second row. The two cells in the third row were left unchanged, while the two cells in the fourth row were merged into one. Then the two `Label` controls, the `ListBox`, the `TextBox`, and the `Button` were placed in the appropriate cells.

Figure 9.31 shows the source code for Sports.aspx. It is instructive to view this code and see its relationship to the design in Figure 9.30, but it is not critical to understand all the details of the ASP.NET code at this point. Figure 9.32 shows a sample run of the modified Sports.aspx file.

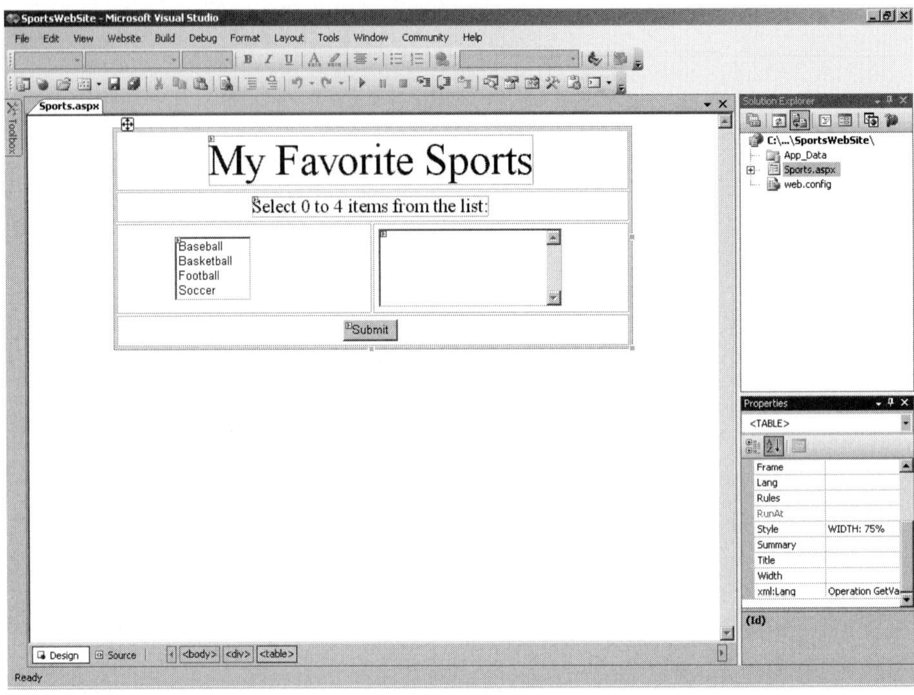

FIGURE 9.30 Design of Sports.aspx using a table layout

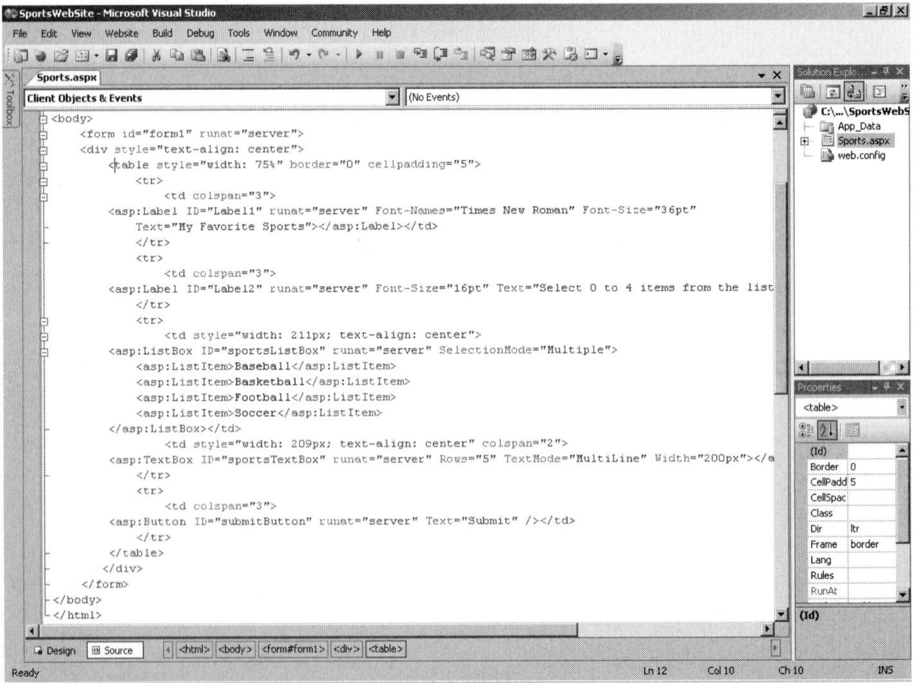

FIGURE 9.31 HTML code for Sports.aspx using a table layout

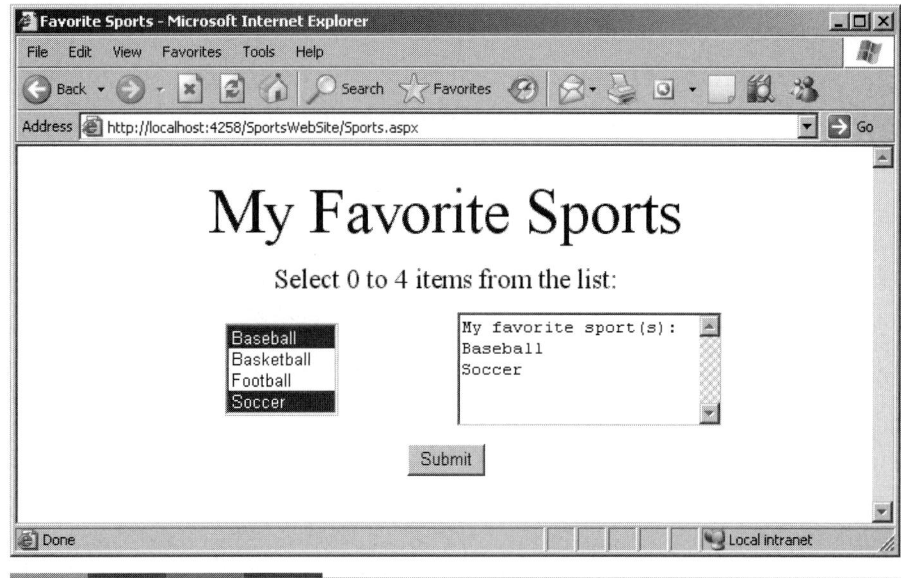

FIGURE 9.32 Sample run of Sports.aspx

In this chapter you have learned how to create an ASP.NET Web site, create Web forms, add controls to Web forms using a table layout, and write Visual Basic code to create event procedures. In the following Programming Example, you will apply these techniques and learn to use some additional Web controls.

PROGRAMMING EXAMPLE

Cars Web Site

This application creates an ASP.NET Web site with two Web forms, Default.aspx and PaymentCalculator.aspx. The Default.aspx form (the home page of the Web site as shown in Figure 9.33) has the following characteristics:

1. The document title "Cars Home Page"
2. The page heading "Cars"
3. An image hyperlink that navigates to *http://www.chevrolet.com*
4. A text hyperlink that navigates to PaymentCalculator.aspx

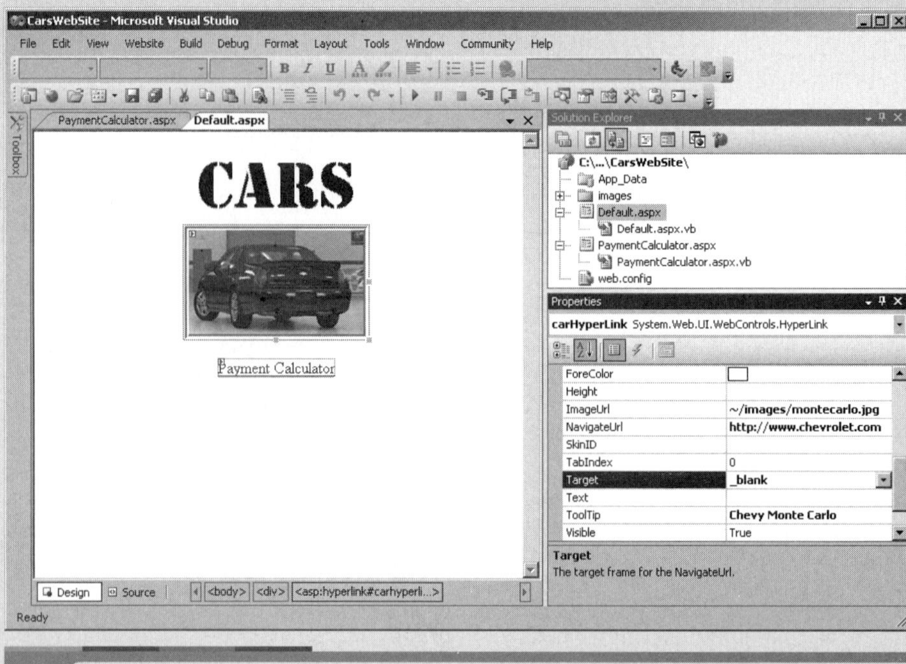

FIGURE 9.33 Design of Default.aspx

The PaymentCalculator.aspx form (Figure 9.34) has the following characteristics:

1. The document title "Payment Calculator"
2. The page heading "Payment Calculator"
3. A table with five rows and two columns containing text, `TextBox` Web controls for the loan amount, interest rate, number of months, monthly payment, and a Calculate button
4. A text hyperlink that navigates to Default.aspx

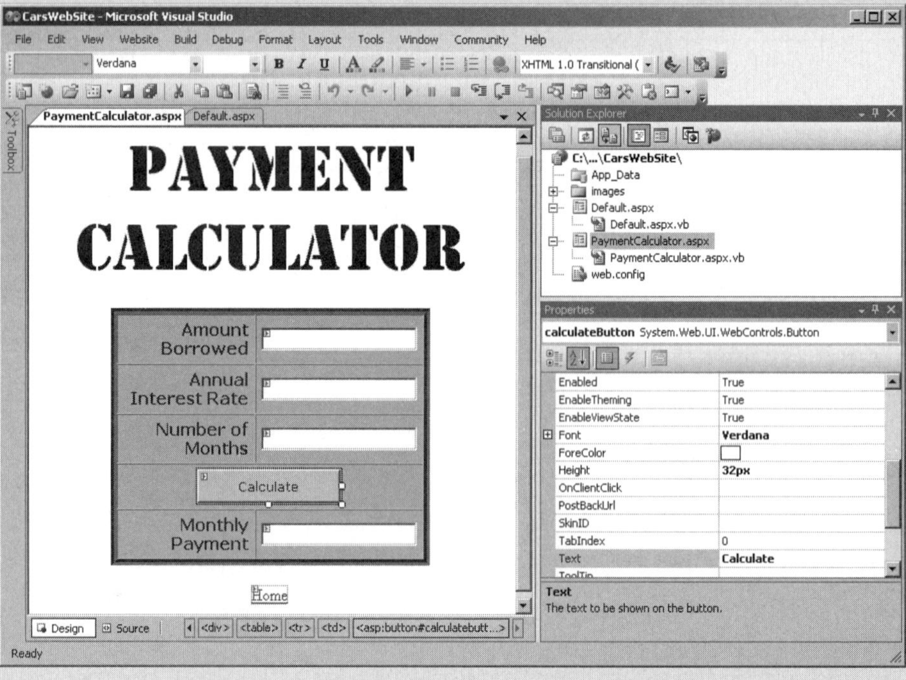

FIGURE 9.34 Design of PaymentCalculator.aspx

Pseudocode

`calculateButton Click` ***event procedure***

1. declare `Double` variables for loan amount, annual interest rate, and monthly payment
2. declare an `Integer` variable for the number of months
3. declare a `String` variable for money format
4. get the loan amount
5. get the annual interest rate
6. if the annual interest rate is greater than 1, divide it by 100
7. get the number of months
8. calculate the monthly payment using the `Pmt` function
9. display the monthly payment

Code

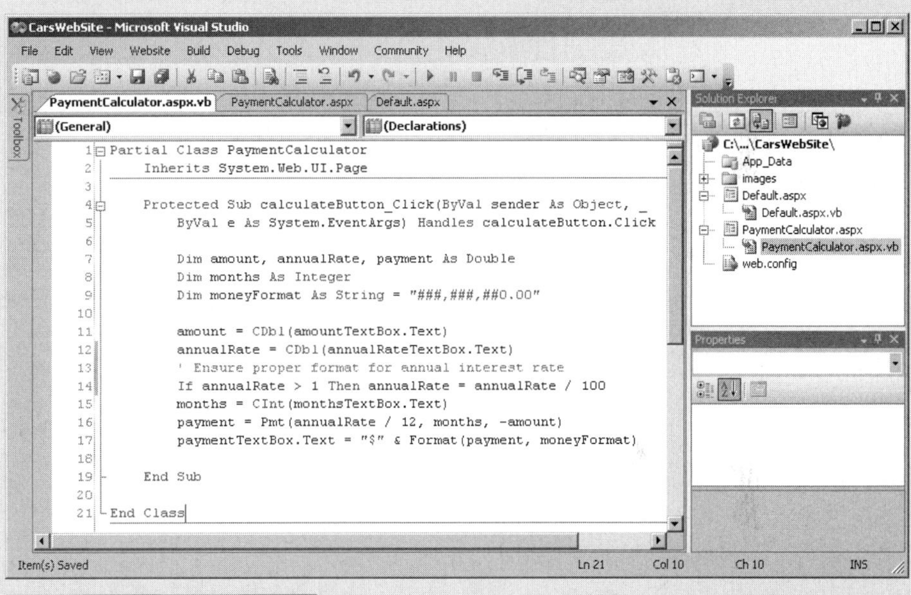

FIGURE 9.35 Program code for PaymentCalculator.aspx.vb

Input/Output

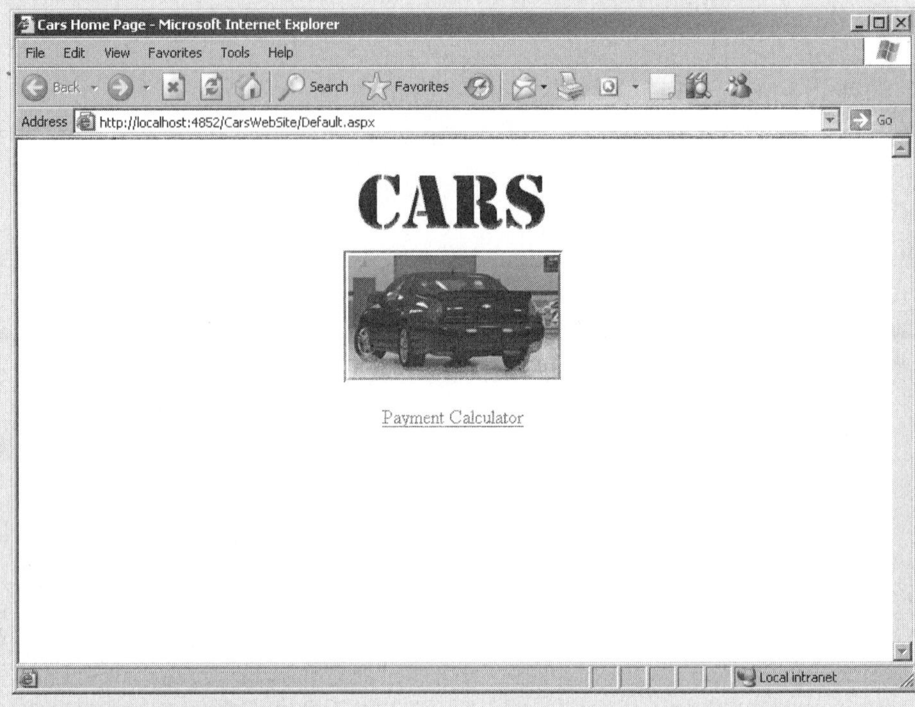

FIGURE 9.36 Sample run for Default.aspx in the CarsWebSite application

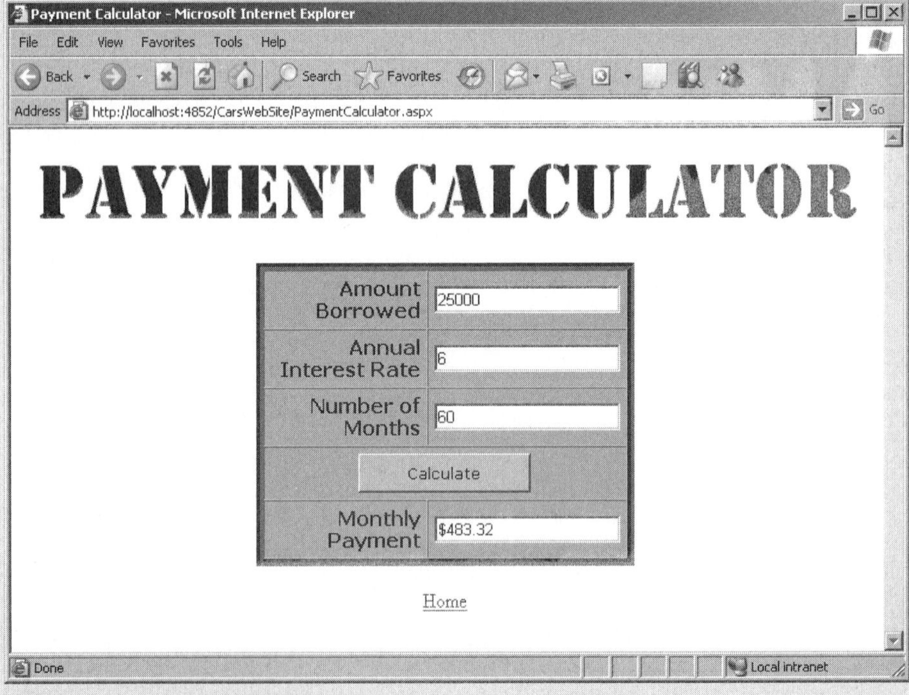

FIGURE 9.37 Sample run for PaymentCalculator.aspx in the CarsWebSite application

Quick Review

- A Web page is a text file written in Hypertext Markup Language (HTML). An HTML document has a file extension of .htm or .html.
- A simple Web page contains several HTML elements, which are sections within a Web page that define the page's structure, content, and functionality. An element usually consists of a start tag, element content, and an end tag. An example of an element is `<p>Hello World!</p>`.
- An Internet browser, such as Microsoft Internet Explorer, is used to open an HTML file located on the same computer, on an intranet (a private network that uses Internet technology), or on the Internet. The browser downloads the HTML file, reads it line by line, interprets the tags, and displays the page content accordingly.
- In a client/server system, software is distributed across networked hardware components consisting of clients, which send requests for services, and a server, which responds to the requests. In the case of Web applications, the client is a Web browser on the user's computer and the server is a Web server, a computer with special software that stores Web pages and is connected to the Internet.
- A URL, such as *http://courses.missouristate.edu/raj127f/HelloWorld.htm*, starts by specifying the protocol (http) used to request and send Web pages. Following the protocol is the domain name of the Web server, which is the text name (such as courses.missouristate.edu) corresponding to the unique numeric IP address of a computer on the Internet. Following the domain name is the path to the file, such as /raj127f/HelloWorld.htm.
- A Web application can use a simple client/server architecture or a multi-tier architecture (also called *n*-tier architecture). An *n*-tier architecture places different basic components of the application on *n* distinct software layers or tiers. A common three-tier architecture has the presentation tier, the logic tier, and the data tier.
- JavaScript is a scripting language, a programming language that can be used within a Web page. With a scripting language, code is embedded within a Web page using a special `<script>` tag. The Web browser is capable of interpreting the JavaScript code to define variables, execute if...then logic, create arrays, perform loops, and so on.
- Embedding scripting code in (or referencing scripting code from) Web pages on a Web server, and downloading these scripts to the browser (client) for execution, is known as client-side scripting. The disadvantages of client-side scripting include long download times and insecure program code.
- In server-side scripting, program code is embedded in a Web page but executed on the server instead of on the client. The most common server-side scripting technologies (all released in the mid-1990s) are PHP, ASP, and JSP.
- ASP.NET is the latest Microsoft technology for developing highly interactive Web applications. An ASP.NET file has a .aspx file extension and is called a Web form instead of a Web page. Web forms can contain ordinary HTML controls and special ASP.NET server controls. Web server controls are similar to HTML controls but are objects that have many properties and that can call complex event procedures.
- A code-behind file is a Visual Basic class containing the event procedures that accompany controls placed on an ASP.NET Web form, such as text boxes, lists, and buttons.

- A Web form can contain a variety of controls, such as text boxes, check boxes, radio buttons, and drop-down lists. Each of these controls can have its own event procedure in the code-behind file created when the Web control is double-clicked. However, you often create just one event procedure in a Web form for a single button that submits the Web form to the Web server for processing.
- A better way of organizing controls on a page is by using the HTML table control. Note that this is a simple HTML control (element), not a Web control. A table, with its rows and columns, is useful for containing Web controls such as labels, text boxes, lists, and buttons.

Key Terms

client-side scripting— The process of embedding scripts in a Web page and executing them on the client.

code-behind file— A Visual Basic class containing the event procedures that accompany controls (such as text boxes, lists, and buttons) placed on an ASP.NET Web form.

data tier—Data, often stored in a relational database management system, within a multi-tier architecture.

document type declaration—A formal declaration that begins with the keyword DOCTYPE, followed by the name of the base element of the document, followed by the specification of the markup language to be used.

domain name—The text name corresponding to the unique numeric IP address of a computer on the Internet.

element content—Some text or other HTML elements contained within an HTML element.

end tag—The same special code used in the start tag, preceded by a forward slash, enclosed in angle brackets, and placed at the end of an HTML element.

HTML element—A section within a Web page that defines the page's structure, content, and functionality.

HTTP transaction—The process in which a Web client requests a file and a Web server responds to the request using HTTP.

hyperlink—A contraction of "hypertext link"; a graphic or text in a Web page which, when clicked, opens a new Web page or jumps to a new location in the current page.

Hypertext Markup Language (HTML)—The language used to create Web pages.

Hypertext Transfer Protocol (HTTP)—The set of rules for exchanging files on the World Wide Web.

intranet—A private network that uses Internet technology.

logic tier—Programs that execute the logic of the application and communicate with the other tiers in a multi-tier architecture.

multi-tier architecture—An *n*-tier architecture that places different basic components of the application on *n* distinct software layers or tiers.

presentation tier—The user interface in a multi-tier architecture.

render block—A section of code in an ASP or ASP.NET file, between the delimiters `<%` and `%>`, that is run on the server.

script—A set of instructions interpreted by another program rather than the computer processor.

scripting language—A programming language that can be used within a Web page.

server-side scripting—The process of embedding scripts in a Web page and executing them on the server instead of on the client.

start tag—A special code enclosed in angle brackets that begins the definition of an HTML element.

Web application—A computer application that uses a Web browser as the user interface.

Web server controls—Objects that have many properties and that can call complex event procedures. Web server controls are similar to HTML controls. Also called ASP.NET server controls.

Web server—A computer with special software that stores Web pages and is connected to the Internet.

XML namespace—A collection of names, identified by a URI reference, that is used in XML documents as element types and attribute names.

Review Questions

1. ASP.NET server controls are part of HTML.
   a. True
   b. False
2. .htm is a valid file extension for an HTML file.
   a. True
   b. False
3. An HTML element can contain other HTML elements.
   a. True
   b. False
4. A Web application uses a Windows form for the user interface.
   a. True
   b. False
5. An HTTP transaction involves a Web server requesting information from a Web client.
   a. True
   b. False
6. The code-behind file in an ASP.NET application contains HTML code.
   a. True
   b. False
7. A client/server architecture is an example of an *n*-tier architecture.
   a. True
   b. False

8. A script in a Web page is compiled, not interpreted.
   a. True
   b. False
9. An HTML control is capable of executing an event procedure.
   a. True
   b. False
10. It is better to set the `AutoPostBack` property for most Web controls to `False`.
    a. True
    b. False
11. HTTP stands for Hypertext Transfer ____.
    a. Portal
    b. Protocol
    c. Program
    d. Project
12. The code-behind file in an ASP.NET application is associated with the ____ tier in a multi-tier system.
    a. presentation
    b. logic
    c. data
    d. user interface
13. Which of the following is not an advantage of ASP.NET?
    a. object-orientation
    b. interpreted code
    c. support of ADO.NET
    d. supported by the CLR
14. What is the file extension of an ASP.NET file?
    a. .aspx
    b. .asp
    c. .net
    d. .htm
15. Which of the following is the attribute that causes an HTML element to execute on the server?
    a. `execute`
    b. `compile`
    c. `goto`
    d. `runat`
16. Which HTML element creates a logical division in a Web page followed by a blank line?
    a. `br`
    b. `div`
    c. `span`
    d. `body`
17. The code-behind file has a file extension of ____.
    a. .asp
    b. .aspx
    c. .htm
    d. .vb

18. Which HTML element is used to represent a table column?
    a. `td`
    b. `tr`
    c. `col`
    d. `tablecol`

19. Which property of the Hyperlink Web control affects where a page opens?
    a. `Text`
    b. `NavigateUrl`
    c. `Target`
    d. `ImageUrl`

20. The App_Data folder in an ASP.NET Web site should not contain what type of file?
    a. .mdb
    b. .xml
    c. .jpg
    d. .mdf

Computer Exercises

All of the following exercises involve creating a Web application corresponding to a Windows application described in previous chapters. Follow all directions given in the previous exercise, but use ASP.NET to create a virtually identical Web application. Use tables in the design of all user interfaces. Also follow all conventions for writing HTML, ASP.NET, and Visual Basic code. Your instructor may also request that you use TOE charts, pseudocode, flowcharts, and/or UML diagrams as planning aids. Save all applications in the \VBReloadedAdvanced\Chap09 folder.

1. Re-create the application presented in Chapter 1's Programming Example, except create a Web application instead of a Windows application.
2. Follow the instructions for Computer Exercise 1 in Chapter 1, except create a Web application instead of a Windows application.
3. Follow the instructions for Computer Exercise 4 in Chapter 1, except create a Web application instead of a Windows application.
4. Follow the instructions for Computer Exercise 3 in Chapter 2, except create a Web application instead of a Windows application.
5. Re-create the application presented in Chapter 3's Programming Example, except create a Web application instead of a Windows application.
6. Re-create the application presented in Chapter 4's Programming Example, except create a Web application instead of a Windows application.
7. Follow the instructions for Computer Exercise 7 in Chapter 5, except create a Web application instead of a Windows application.

Case Projects

A Personal Web Site

Using ASP.NET, create a personal Web site with a home page, a resume page, and a personal page. The home page should have a picture of you, some brief information about you, and links to the other two pages. The resume page should have a professional-looking resume covering your education and work experience. The personal page should contain information and images about your hobbies and interests.

Net Present Value

Visit *http://msdn.microsoft.com/* and search for Financial.Rate. Create an application that allows the user to enter all the required and optional values specified in the Financial.Rate method in an organized user interface. If required values are not entered, use a text box to inform the user that they must be entered. If optional values are entered, use these in the calculations. The interface should display the return value, that is, the interest rate per period for an annuity. (This project is based on the Net Present Value project in Chapter 1.)

DVD Collection

Create a Web application called **DVD Collection**. Design an interface that allows the user to enter the ID for a DVD, the title of a DVD, and the total running time (in minutes) of the DVD. When the Add DVD button is clicked on the interface, the data should be added to a sequential file. When the Display button is clicked, the DVDs in the file should be displayed in a text box. Use structured exception handling to handle all types of possible exceptions, including at least one type of programmer-defined exception. (This project is adapted from the DVD Collection project in Chapter 5.)

CHAPTER

More ASP.NET: Database, XML, and Web Services

After studying Chapter 10, you should be able to:

- Add a database to a Web application
- Display a database table or query in a Web application
- Perform update, insert, and delete operations on a database in a Web application
- Create an XML file and display it in a Web application
- Produce a Web service using ASP.NET
- Consume a Web service in a Web application

The previous chapter introduced you to ASP.NET, the latest Microsoft technology for developing Web applications. As is the case with most computer applications, accessing data is a key element. This chapter introduces you to the techniques for creating Web applications that access data using ASP.NET. This is accomplished with two different types of data sources: database and XML. This chapter will also show you how ASP.NET is used to produce and consume (utilize) Web services. You will learn how to produce a Web service for your Web application (or someone else's) and how to consume a Web service (perhaps created by someone else) within your Web application.

ACCESSING DATA IN A WEB APPLICATION

Chapter 7 covered the subject of relational databases and SQL, while Chapter 8 concerned ADO.NET, a data access API (application program interface) used in Windows applications. The techniques of accessing databases and using SQL were applied to Windows applications through ADO.NET. As you will see, these same techniques are applied to Web applications through ASP.NET.

Adding a Database to a Web Application

Before your Web application can access a database, it needs a copy of the database within the project. Figure 10.1 explains how to do this.

HOW TO...

Add an Existing Database to a Web Application

1. Launch Visual Studio 2005. In the Visual Studio menu, click File and then click New Web Site. The New Web Site dialog box opens.
2. Click the ASP.NET Web Site icon and then click Browse. The Choose Location dialog box opens. Select the folder location for the Web site and then click Open. (If the folder does not already exist, a Microsoft Visual Studio dialog box will open and ask if you want to create the folder. Click Yes.) Then click OK in the New Web Site dialog box.
3. If the Solution Explorer window is not already displayed, click View and then click Solution Explorer in the Visual Studio menu.
4. In the Solution Explorer, click the App_Data folder.
5. In the Visual Studio menu, click Web Site and then click Add Existing Item. The Add Existing Item dialog box opens.
6. Navigate to the desired database file on your computer, select the database file, and then click Add.

FIGURE 10.1 How to add an existing database to a Web application

After following the steps in Figure 10.1, an SQL Server database called pubs (filename PUBS.MDF) was added to the Publications ASP.NET Web site, as shown in Figure 10.2.

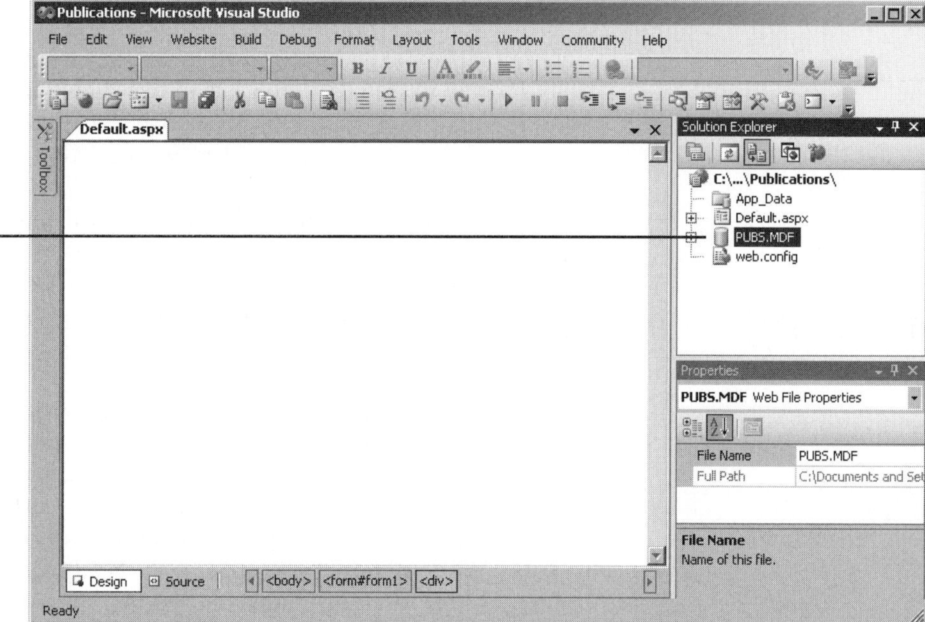

pubs database added

FIGURE 10.2 The Publications application with the pubs database added

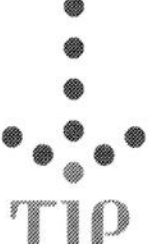

TIP

You can search your computer for Microsoft Access database files (with file extension .mdb) or SQL Server database files (with file extension .mdf). You can download the Northwind and pubs SQL Server database files by following the instructions in Figure 7.27. You can also find out how to download Microsoft databases by searching *http://www.microsoft.com* using keywords such as download, northwind, and pubs.

Displaying a Table with a GridView

After you add a database to a Web site, you can begin using it in the application. The simplest way to do this is to display the contents of a database table in a Web form. Figure 10.3 explains how to do this.

HOW TO...

Display a Table with a `GridView`

1. After adding a database to a Web application (see Figure 10.1), open a Web form (such as Default.aspx) in Design view within the Visual Studio IDE.
2. Drag a `GridView` control from the Data section of the Toolbox to the Web form. A `GridView` control appears in the Web form (see Figure 10.4).
3. Click the Smart Tag (the small arrow in a box) near the upper-right corner of the `GridView` control to display the GridView Tasks menu.
4. Click the arrow in the Choose Data Source drop-down list and click New data source. The Data Source Configuration Wizard opens.
5. On the Choose a Data Source Type page of the Data Source Configuration Wizard, click the Database icon and enter an ID for the data source in the text box, such as PubsSqlDataSource (see Figure 10.5). Click OK.
6. On the Choose Your Data Connection page of the Configure Data Source Wizard, click the New Connection button. The Add Connection dialog box opens.

(Figure is continued on next page)

7. If the Data Source shown in the Add Connection dialog box is correct, skip to Step 8. If the Data Source shown in the Add Connection dialog box is not correct, click Change. Then select the correct type of Data Source in the Change Data Source dialog box and click OK. You return to the Add Connection dialog box. Continue to Step 8.
8. In the Add Connection dialog box, click Browse. The Select SQL Server Database File dialog box opens. Navigate to the database file that is located in the App_Data folder in your project. Click the database file and click Open. You return to the Add Connection dialog box. Click OK and then click Next on the Choose Your Data Connection page of the Configure Data Source Wizard.
9. On the Save the Connection String to the Application Configuration File page of the Configure Data Source Wizard, click Next.
10. On the Configure the Select Statement page of the Configure Data Source Wizard, click the option Specify columns from a table or view. Select a table from the Name drop-down list (see Figure 10.6).
11. While still on the Configure the Select Statement page, click the check boxes for the columns of the table you want to display. (Clicking the check box by the asterisk selects all columns.) Click the WHERE, ORDER BY, and/or Advanced buttons to add a filter to the data, sort the data, and/or generate INSERT, UPDATE, and DELETE statements, respectively (see Figure 10.6). Click Next.
12. On the Test Query page of the Configure Data Source Wizard, click Test Query to test the resulting query. If the results are incorrect, click Previous to reconfigure the data source; otherwise, click Finish.

FIGURE 10.3 How to display a table with a `GridView`

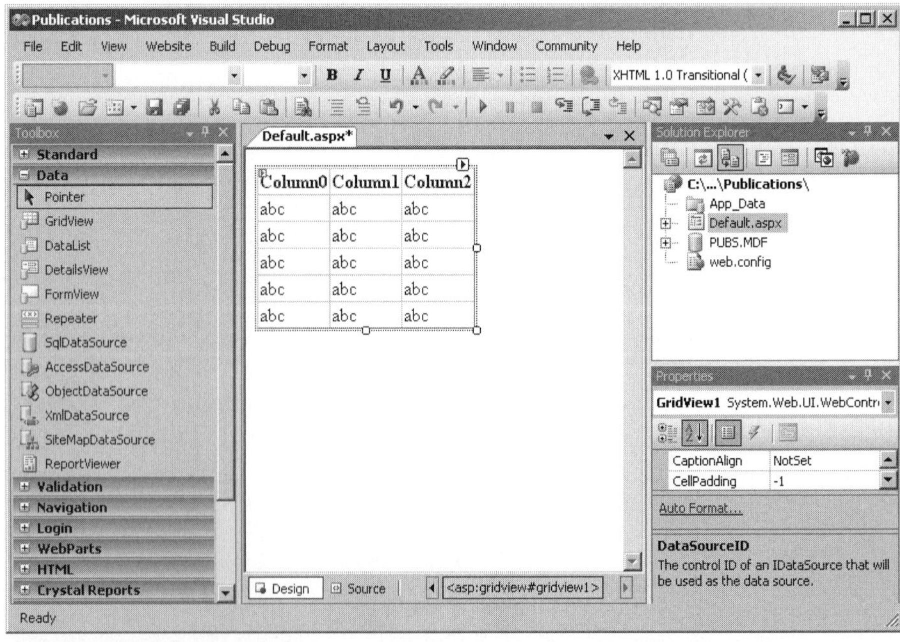

FIGURE 10.4 A `GridView` control in a Web form

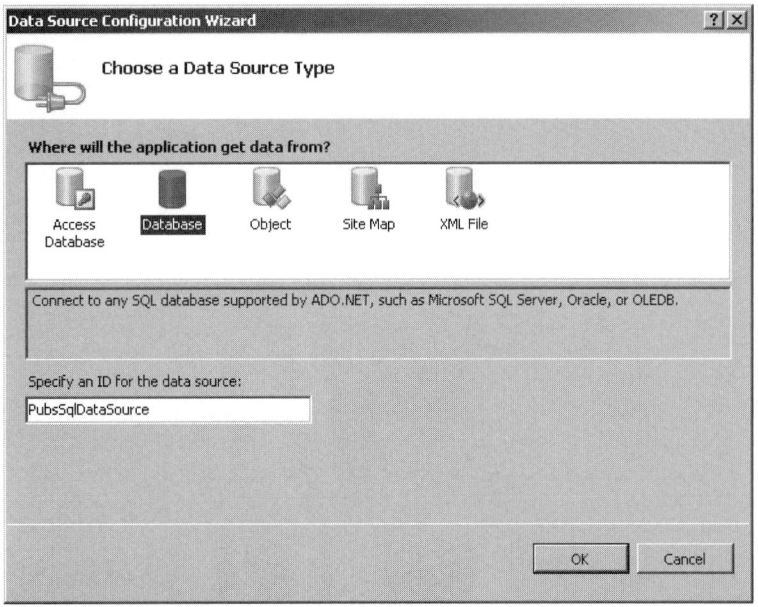

FIGURE 10.5 The Data Source Configuration Wizard

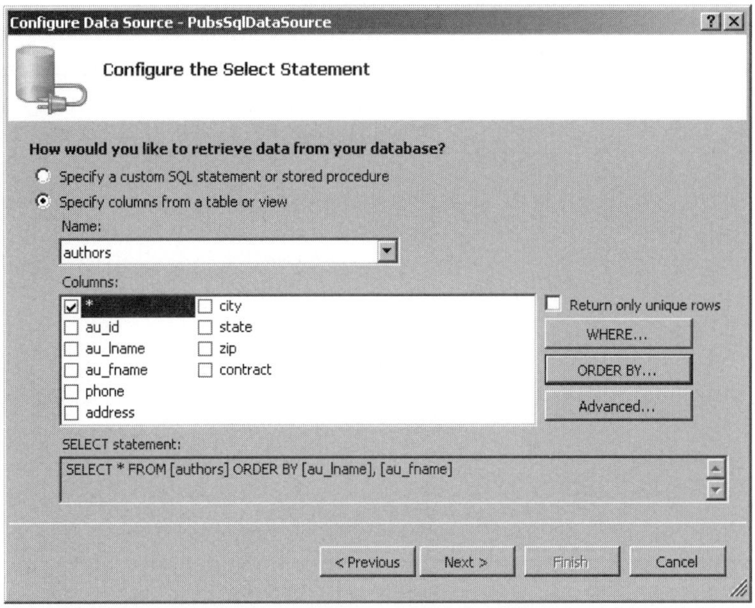

Configure Data Source - PubsSqlDataSource

Configure the Select Statement

How would you like to retrieve data from your database?

Specify a custom SQL statement or stored procedure

Specify columns from a table or view

Name:

authors

Columns:

* | city | au_id | state | au_lname | zip | au_fname | contract | phone | address

Return only unique rows

WHERE...

ORDER BY...

Advanced...

SELECT statement:

SELECT * FROM [authors] ORDER BY [au_lname], [au_fname]

< Previous | Next > | Finish | Cancel

FIGURE 10.6 The Configure the Select Statement page

Figure 10.7 shows the result of following the steps in Figure 10.3 for the Publications Web site. Note that the `SqlDataSource` object (`PubsSqlDataSource`), which binds the `GridView` to the pubs database, appears on the Web form. In this example, the authors table from the pubs database was selected in Step 10. In Step 11, the asterisk (*) was checked to select all columns. Then the ORDER BY... button was clicked and the `au_lname` and `au_fname` fields (author last name and author first name) were selected for sorting.

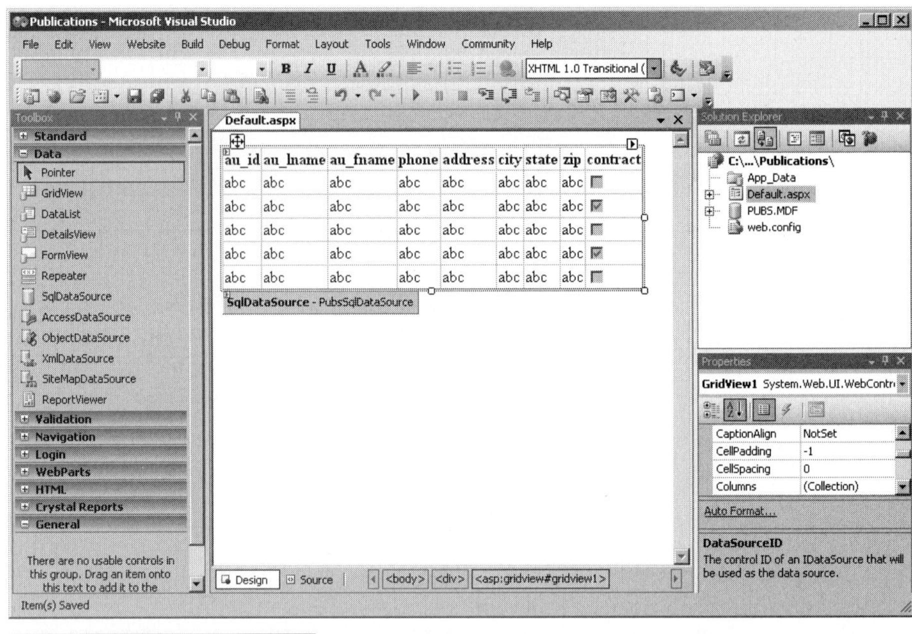

FIGURE 10.7 The Publications application with a `GridView`

Figure 10.8 displays the HTML code for the Default.aspx Web form. Carefully compare the Design view in Figure 10.7 with the Code view in Figure 10.8. Recall that the `form` element (within the `body` element) in Figure 10.8 represents the Web form. Within the form element is a `div` element, which in turn contains the Web controls `GridView` and `SqlDataSource`. The `GridView` control contains `BoundField` controls (fields that display text) and a `CheckBoxField` control that are bound (linked) to individual database columns. Finally, the `SqlDataSource` control connects the grid to the database and populates the grid based on the `SelectCommand` attribute (an SQL statement generated from the Data Source Configuration Wizard).

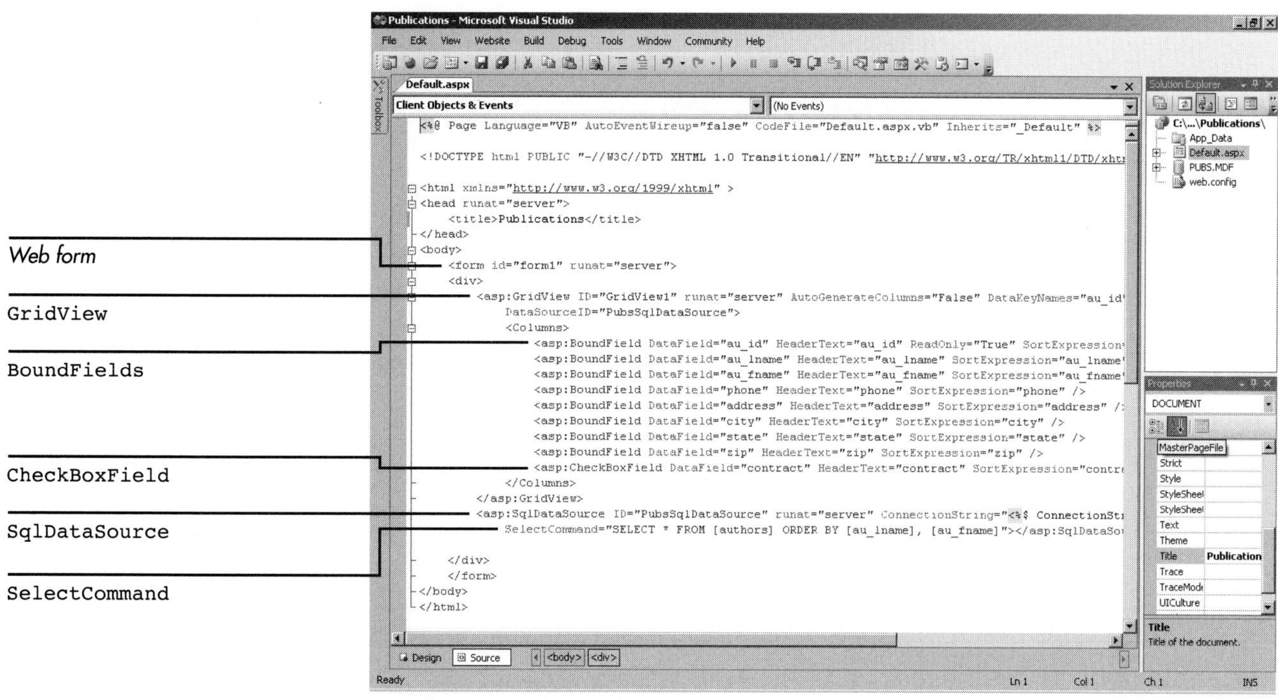

FIGURE 10.8 HTML code for the Default.aspx Web form

The result of a sample run of Default.aspx is shown in Figure 10.9. Note that you can add more HTML code to this page to provide additional content (such as a heading for the page) or special formatting. For example, adding the attribute `style="font-family: arial"` to the `<div>` tag that contains the `GridView` control changes the font from the default Times New Roman font to an Arial font.

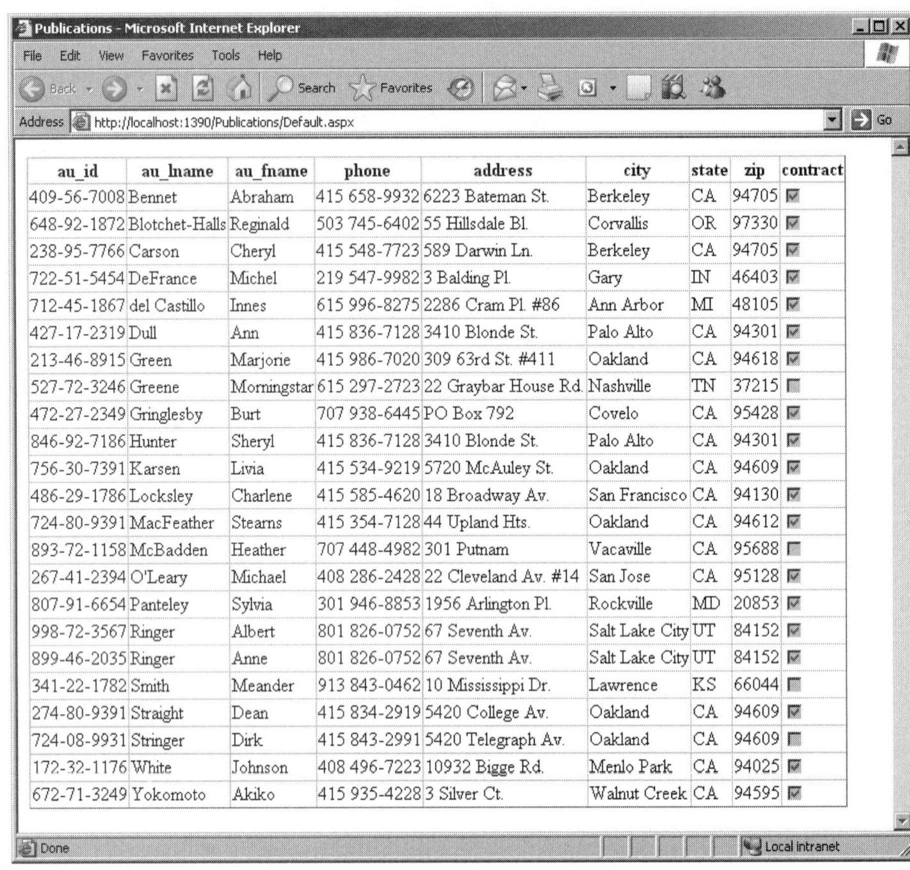

au_id	au_lname	au_fname	phone	address	city	state	zip	contract
409-56-7008	Bennet	Abraham	415 658-9932	6223 Bateman St.	Berkeley	CA	94705	☑
648-92-1872	Blotchet-Halls	Reginald	503 745-6402	55 Hillsdale Bl.	Corvallis	OR	97330	☑
238-95-7766	Carson	Cheryl	415 548-7723	589 Darwin Ln.	Berkeley	CA	94705	☑
722-51-5454	DeFrance	Michel	219 547-9982	3 Balding Pl.	Gary	IN	46403	☑
712-45-1867	del Castillo	Innes	615 996-8275	2286 Cram Pl. #86	Ann Arbor	MI	48105	☑
427-17-2319	Dull	Ann	415 836-7128	3410 Blonde St.	Palo Alto	CA	94301	☑
213-46-8915	Green	Marjorie	415 986-7020	309 63rd St. #411	Oakland	CA	94618	☑
527-72-3246	Greene	Morningstar	615 297-2723	22 Graybar House Rd.	Nashville	TN	37215	☐
472-27-2349	Gringlesby	Burt	707 938-6445	PO Box 792	Covelo	CA	95428	☑
846-92-7186	Hunter	Sheryl	415 836-7128	3410 Blonde St.	Palo Alto	CA	94301	☑
756-30-7391	Karsen	Livia	415 534-9219	5720 McAuley St.	Oakland	CA	94609	☑
486-29-1786	Locksley	Charlene	415 585-4620	18 Broadway Av.	San Francisco	CA	94130	☑
724-80-9391	MacFeather	Stearns	415 354-7128	44 Upland Hts.	Oakland	CA	94612	☑
893-72-1158	McBadden	Heather	707 448-4982	301 Putnam	Vacaville	CA	95688	☐
267-41-2394	O'Leary	Michael	408 286-2428	22 Cleveland Av. #14	San Jose	CA	95128	☑
807-91-6654	Panteley	Sylvia	301 946-8853	1956 Arlington Pl.	Rockville	MD	20853	☑
998-72-3567	Ringer	Albert	801 826-0752	67 Seventh Av.	Salt Lake City	UT	84152	☑
899-46-2035	Ringer	Anne	801 826-0752	67 Seventh Av.	Salt Lake City	UT	84152	☑
341-22-1782	Smith	Meander	913 843-0462	10 Mississippi Dr.	Lawrence	KS	66044	☐
274-80-9391	Straight	Dean	415 834-2919	5420 College Av.	Oakland	CA	94609	☑
724-08-9931	Stringer	Dirk	415 843-2991	5420 Telegraph Av.	Oakland	CA	94609	☐
172-32-1176	White	Johnson	408 496-7223	10932 Bigge Rd.	Menlo Park	CA	94025	☑
672-71-3249	Yokomoto	Akiko	415 935-4228	3 Silver Ct.	Walnut Creek	CA	94595	☑

FIGURE 10.9 Sample run of the Publications application

Modifying the Appearance of a `GridView`

The sample run in Figure 10.9 simply displays the data in a table (read only), but it doesn't provide any attractive formatting, nor does it give the user the ability to manipulate the data (such as by sorting the display). You can modify the GridView to improve its format and functionality by using the GridView Tasks menu as explained in Figure 10.10.

HOW TO...

Modify the Form and Function of a `GridView`

1. To access the `GridView` Smart Tag, point to the `GridView` in the Design window.
2. Click the Smart Tag on the `GridView` (the small boxed arrow in the upper-right corner of the control) to display the GridView Tasks menu.
3. To apply a preset format to a table, click Auto Format in the GridView Tasks menu. Click a scheme from the list (such as Rainy Day) and click Apply. If the new scheme is acceptable, click OK (see Figure 10.11).
4. To create a new data source for the `GridView` (such as a new table), click the drop-down arrow in the Choose Data Source option in the GridView Tasks menu and then click New data source.

(Figure is continued on next page)

5. To reconfigure the data source for the `GridView`, click the Configure Data Source option in the GridView Tasks menu. This option allows you to select new tables and columns, create new SQL statements, and implement update, insert, and delete capabilities in the `GridView`.
6. To incorporate any changes in the schema (design) of the data source (perhaps new tables or columns have been added to the data source by the database administrator), click the Refresh Schema option in the GridView Tasks menu.
7. To make changes in the columns displayed in the `GridView`, click the Edit Columns option in the GridView Tasks menu. The Fields dialog box appears. Within the Fields dialog box, you can change the header text displayed for the columns, as shown in Figure 10.12. Double-click a field in the Available fields list in Figure 10.12 to display its properties. Then change the Header Text property (for example, change au_id to the more readable Author ID). You can also use the Fields dialog box to make certain columns read-only, make certain columns invisible, delete certain columns from the `GridView`, and add new columns not in the data source. The Add New Column option in the GridView Tasks menu also allows you to add new columns, but this function is already included within the Edit Columns option.
8. To enable paging, sorting, and selection, click the appropriate check boxes in the GridView Tasks menu. Paging displays only a fixed number of records per Web page. (The default is 10, but this can be changed.) Sorting allows the user to sort a particular column (ascending or descending) by clicking its header text. Selection allows the user to select a row for customized processing.

FIGURE 10.10 How to modify the form and function of a `GridView`

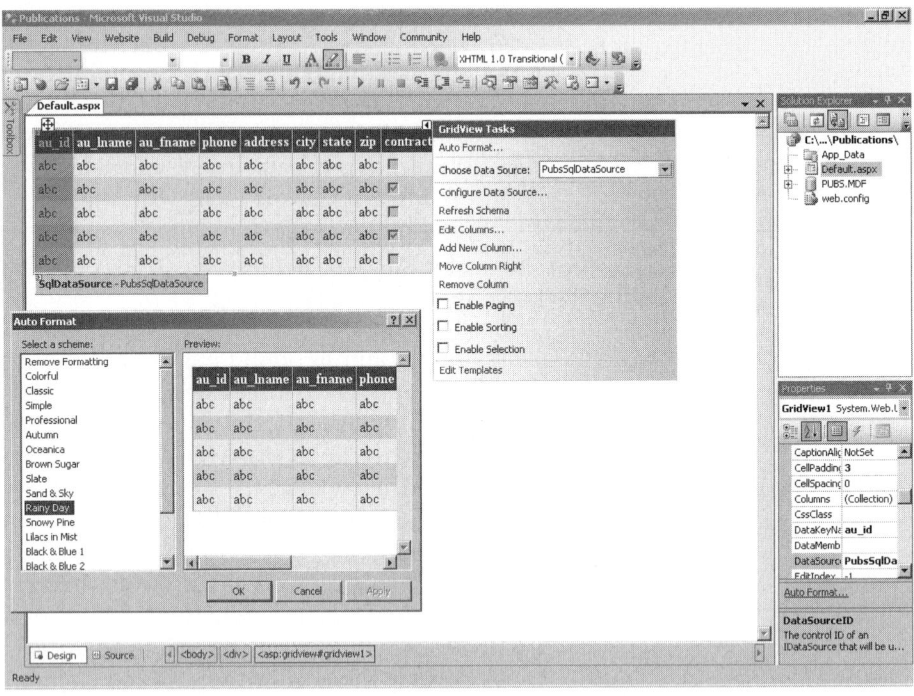

FIGURE 10.11 The `GridView` Auto Format option

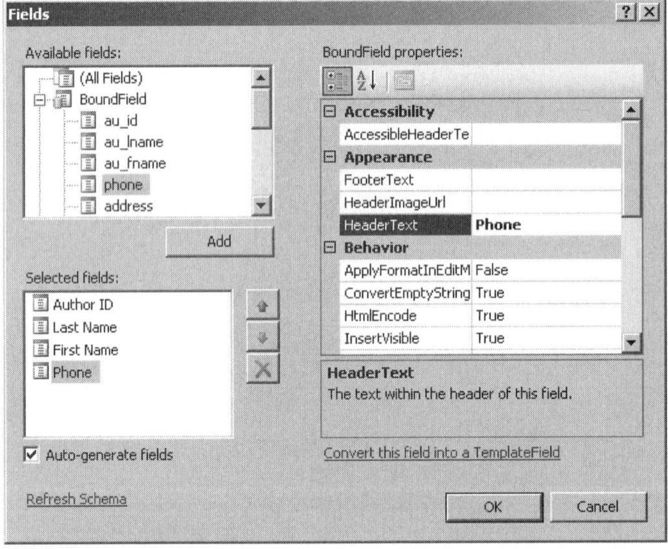

FIGURE 10.12 The Fields dialog box for editing columns

Figure 10.13 shows the result of renaming the column header text (Step 7 in Figure 10.10) and checking the options for paging, sorting, and selection in the GridView Tasks menu (Step 8 in Figure 10.10). The page numbers (1 and 2) at the bottom of the GridView control allow the user to navigate to different pages in the dataset. The column headers are also underlined, signifying that they can be clicked to perform an ascending or descending sort. Finally, the Select command appears at the extreme left of each row. Clicking Select allows the row to be selected for additional processing, such as changing data values or deleting an entire row.

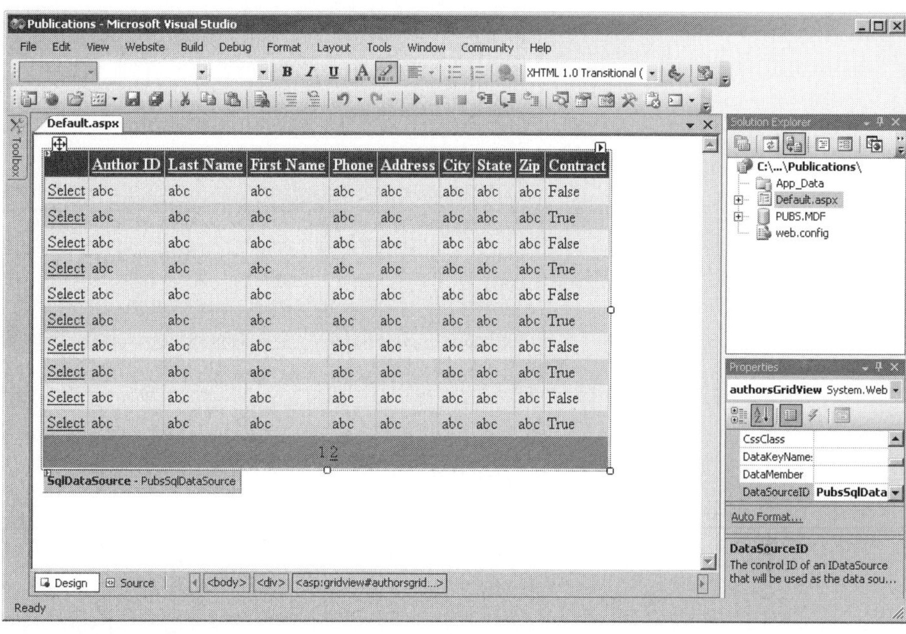

FIGURE 10.13 The `GridView` with Paging, Sorting, and Selection options checked

Figure 10.14 presents a sample run of Default.aspx in the Publications Web site with the Rainy Day scheme, new header text, sorted by Author ID, page 2, and Dirk Stringer's record selected. Notice that the appearance of the `GridView` in Figure 10.14 is much improved over that in Figure 10.9. Also, the `GridView` has additional functionality compared with the one in Figure 10.9 (particularly paging, sorting, and selection). However, the data in Figure 10.14 are read-only. The next section explores how to add update and delete capabilities to a `GridView`.

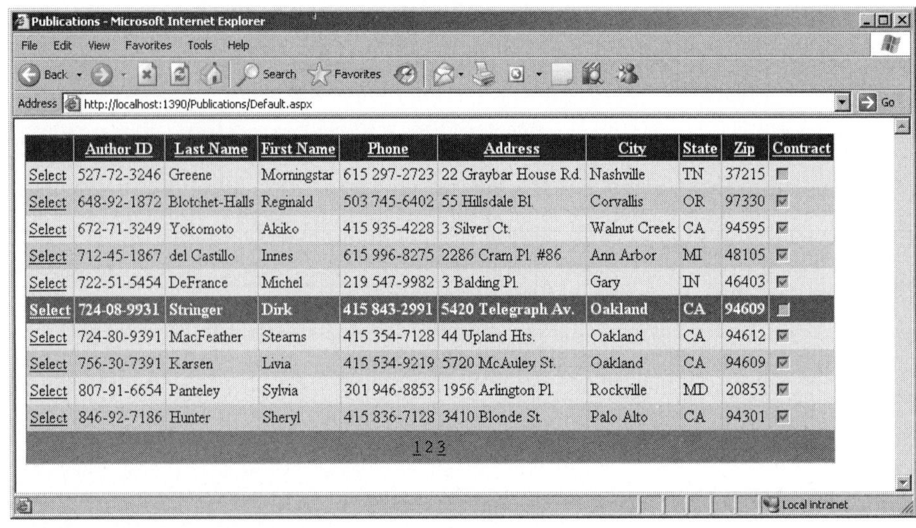

	Author ID	Last Name	First Name	Phone	Address	City	State	Zip	Contract
Select	527-72-3246	Greene	Morningstar	615 297-2723	22 Graybar House Rd.	Nashville	TN	37215	☐
Select	648-92-1872	Blotchet-Halls	Reginald	503 745-6402	55 Hillsdale Bl.	Corvallis	OR	97330	☑
Select	672-71-3249	Yokomoto	Akiko	415 935-4228	3 Silver Ct.	Walnut Creek	CA	94595	☑
Select	712-45-1867	del Castillo	Innes	615 996-8275	2286 Cram Pl. #86	Ann Arbor	MI	48105	☑
Select	722-51-5454	DeFrance	Michel	219 547-9982	3 Balding Pl.	Gary	IN	46403	☑
Select	724-08-9931	Stringer	Dirk	415 843-2991	5420 Telegraph Av.	Oakland	CA	94609	☐
Select	724-80-9391	MacFeather	Stearns	415 354-7128	44 Upland Hts.	Oakland	CA	94612	☑
Select	756-30-7391	Karsen	Livia	415 534-9219	5720 McAuley St.	Oakland	CA	94609	☑
Select	807-91-6654	Panteley	Sylvia	301 946-8853	1956 Arlington Pl.	Rockville	MD	20853	☑
Select	846-92-7186	Hunter	Sheryl	415 836-7128	3410 Blonde St.	Palo Alto	CA	94301	☑

1 2 3

FIGURE 10.14 Sample run of Default.aspx in the Publications application

Adding Update and Delete Capabilities to a `GridView`

In the previous section you learned how to use options on the GridView Tasks menu to change the appearance of a data table and add paging, sorting, and selection capabilities. Another option on the GridView Tasks menu, the Configure Data Source option, allows the user to make permanent changes to the underlying data source. As Figure 10.15 explains, this is accomplished by incoporating update, insert, and delete capabilities.

HOW TO...

Update and Delete in a `GridView`

1. Click the Smart Tag on the `GridView` (the small boxed arrow in the upper-right corner) to display the GridView Tasks menu.
2. Click the Configure Data Source option in the GridView Tasks menu to open the Configure Data Source Wizard.
3. The Choose Your Data Connection page of the wizard allows you to change the data source (for example, a different database) if necessary. Click Next.
4. The Configure the Select Statement page of the wizard (see Figure 10.6) can be used to specify a custom SQL statement or stored procedure. However, the default selection is the option button for Specify columns from a table or view. In this case, clicking Advanced (after selecting columns) opens the Advanced SQL Generation Options dialog box, as seen in Figure 10.16. Click both check boxes to allow for update, insert, and delete using optimistic concurrency. (Optimistic concurrency was discussed in Chapter 8.) Click Next and then click Finish.
5. In the GridView Tasks menu, click the Enable Editing and Enable Deleting check boxes.

FIGURE 10.15 How to update and delete in a `GridView`

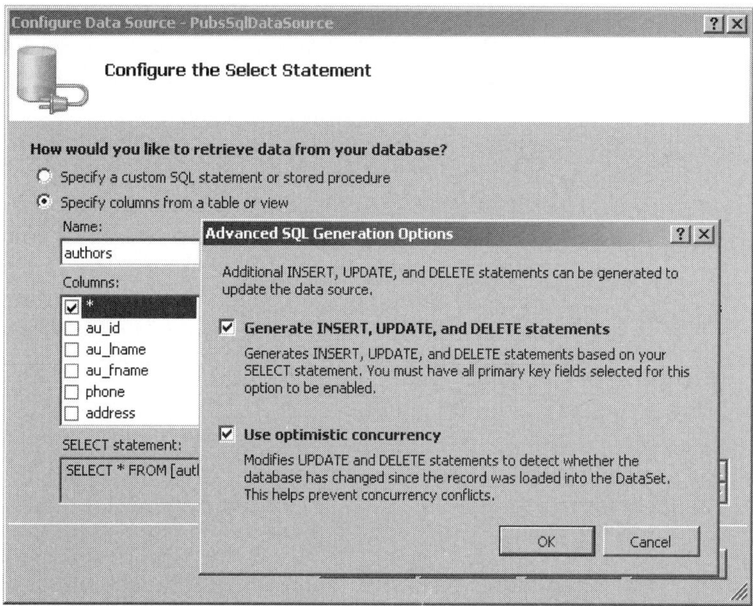

FIGURE 10.16 Advanced SQL Generation Options dialog

Figure 10.17 shows the results of running the Default.aspx Web form in the Publications Web site. In this figure, the user is in the process of editing the record for Ann Dull by changing "Dull" to "Bright". The editing process began when the user clicked Edit (on the left side of the record). Clicking Edit causes the fields that are not `ReadOnly` to display in text boxes. (Note that Author ID is a primary key, so it is `ReadOnly` by default and cannot be changed by the application.) Clicking the Update button saves the change to the authors table in the pubs database. As you might expect, clicking Cancel cancels the change.

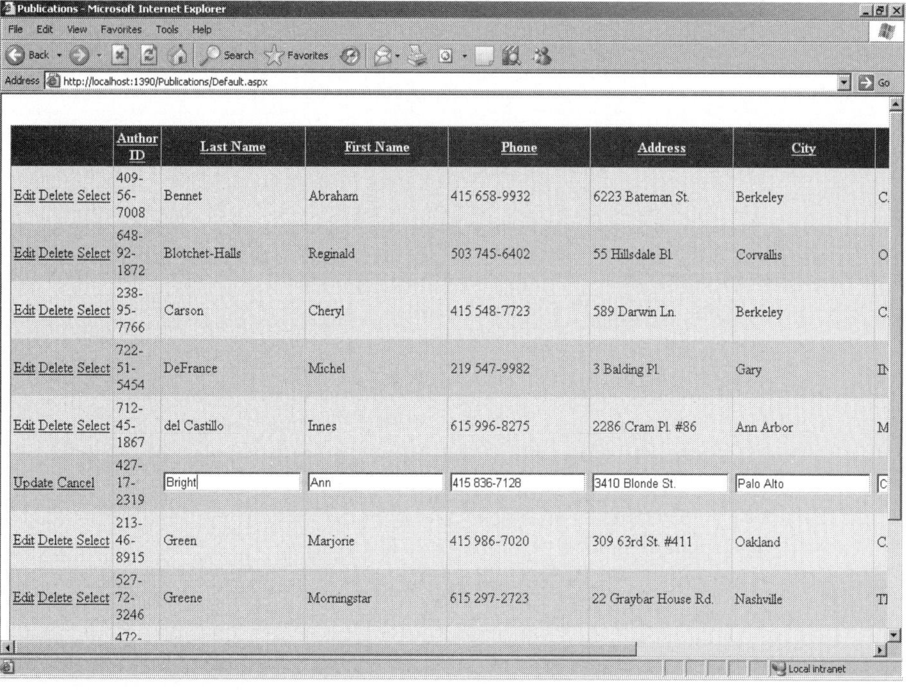

FIGURE 10.17 Sample run of Default.aspx in the Publications application

You might have noticed that there is no way to insert a record from the `GridView`. However, you can insert a record using the `DetailsView` control, discussed in the next section.

Using a DetailsView Control

The `GridView` control, discussed in the previous sections, displays table or query data in a grid format with rows and columns. The `DetailsView` control displays records in a table or query one at a time. Some users may prefer the `DetailsView` to the `GridView`. The procedure for adding and configuring a `DetailsView` is very similar to that for a `GridView`. Figure 10.18 explains how to add a `DetailsView` to a Web form.

HOW TO...

Add a `DetailsView` to a Web Form

1. After adding a database to a Web application (see Figure 10.1), open a Web form (such as Default.aspx) in Design view within the Visual Studio IDE.
2. Drag a `DetailsView` control from the Data section of the Toolbox to a Web form. A `DetailsView` control appears in the Web form (see Figure 10.19) with column headers appearing on the left and data fields appearing on the right for a single table record.
3. Point to the `DetailsView` control. Click the Smart Tag (the small arrow in a box) near the upper-right corner of the `DetailsView` control to display the DetailsView Tasks menu.
4. Click the Auto Format option in the DetailsView Tasks menu. Select a scheme from the list (such as Rainy Day) and click OK.
5. To change the formatting properties of the `DetailsView` control, open the Properties window. (In the Visual Studio menu, click View and click Properties Window.) Click the `DetailsView` control and change the values of formatting properties such as `BorderStyle`, `Font`, `GridLines`, `HeaderText`, and `Width`. You can also right-click the DetailsView control and click Style to set many additional formatting options.

FIGURE 10.18 How to add a `DetailsView` to a Web form

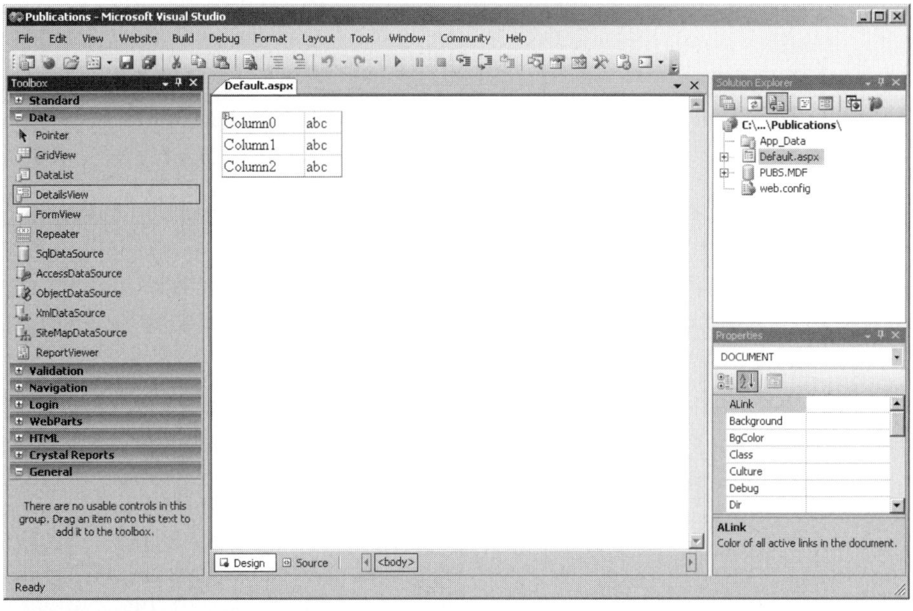

FIGURE 10.19 A `DetailsView` control in a Web form

After adding a `DetailsView` control to a Web form and performing some initial formatting, you can select and configure a data source as detailed in Figure 10.20.

HOW TO...

Configure a Data Source for a `DetailsView`

1. Click the `DetailsView` control and click the Smart Tag (boxed arrow in upper-right corner).
2. Click the arrow in the Choose Data Source drop-down list and click New data source. The Data Source Configuration Wizard opens.
3. In the Data Source Configuration Wizard, click the Database icon and enter an ID for the data source in the text box (if one other than the default name is desired). Click OK.
4. On the Choose Your Data Connection page of the Configure Data Source Wizard, click the New Connection button. The Add Connection dialog box appears.
5. If the Data Source shown in the Add Connection dialog box is not correct, click Change. Then select the correct Data Source in the Change Data Source dialog box and click OK.
6. In the Add Connection dialog box, click Browse. The Select dialog box opens. Navigate to the database file that is located in your project. Click the database file and click Open. You return to the Add Connection dialog box. Click the Test Connection button to test the connection to the database. If the connection is successful, click OK. If not, repeat the previous steps to ensure a valid database is added to the application.
7. Click Next on the Choose Your Data Connection page of the Configure Data Source Wizard.
8. On the Save the Connection String page of the Configure Data Source Wizard, click Next.

(Figure is continued on next page)

9. On the Configure the Select Statement page of the Configure Data Source Wizard, click Specify columns from a table or view. Select the table from the Name drop-down list.
10. While still on the Configure the Select Statement page, click the check box(es) for the columns to be displayed from the table. (Click the check box marked with the asterisk to select all columns in the table.)
11. While still on the Configure the Select Statement page, click the WHERE and ORDER BY buttons to open the Add WHERE Clause dialog box and the Add ORDER BY Clause dialog box. These dialog boxes enable you to configure the SELECT statement to add a filter to the data and sort the data.
12. While still on the Configure the Select Statement page, click the Advanced button to open the Advanced SQL Generation Options dialog box. This dialog box enables you to generate INSERT, UPDATE, and DELETE statements and use optimistic concurrency (recommended). Click Next when you are finished with the Configure the Select Statement page of the Configure Data Source Wizard.
13. On the Test Query page of the Configure Data Source Wizard, click Test Query to test the resulting query. If the results are incorrect, click Previous as required to reconfigure the data source and/or SQL statements; otherwise, click Finish.
14. In the DetailsView Tasks list, click the check boxes for Enable Paging, Enable Inserting, Enable Editing, and Enable Deleting.
15. To enter new values for the column headers in the `DetailsView` (and to set field properties, such as `ReadOnly`), click the Smart Tag and click the Edit Fields option. Select each field in the Selected fields: list and change the `HeaderText` property (or other properties) as desired. Click OK.
16. To complete formatting for paging (moving from one record to another in the `DetailsView`), click the `DetailsView` control and expand the `PagerSettings` property in the Properties window. You can add images for paging (such as arrow graphics) or modify the default text for paging (for example, using "Next" instead of ">" for the next record) by setting properties such as `NextPageImageUrl` and `NextPageText`. The `Mode` property under `PagerSettings` determines the kinds of paging that can be performed, such as `Numeric` or `NextPreviousFirstLast`.

FIGURE 10.20 How to configure a data source for a `DetailsView`

The steps of Figure 10.20 were applied to a `DetailsView` for the authors table in the pubs database. The Professional scheme was selected, with an Arial font. Header text was added to the `DetailsView` and the field names were changed to be more readable (for example, Author ID instead of au_id). Paging, inserting, updating, and deleting capabilities were added.

The end result of these changes is the sample run of the Publications Web application with a `DetailsView` control, as shown in Figure 10.21. The normal view of the Web form is shown in Figure 10.21(a) with the application in read mode. At the bottom of the form, the user can click First, Previous, Next, or Last to move from record to record. If the user clicks Edit, the form appears as in Figure 10.21(b). Only those fields that are not `ReadOnly` become editable. (Note that Author ID, the primary key, is `ReadOnly`.) When changes are made, the user can click Update to accept the changes, or the user can click Cancel to cancel the changes. When the user clicks New at the bottom of the form, the form appears as in Figure 10.21(c). Here, all fields are blank and editable for a new record. After data are entered, the user can click Insert to store the new record or Cancel to cancel the operation.

(a) Read mode of `DetailsView` control

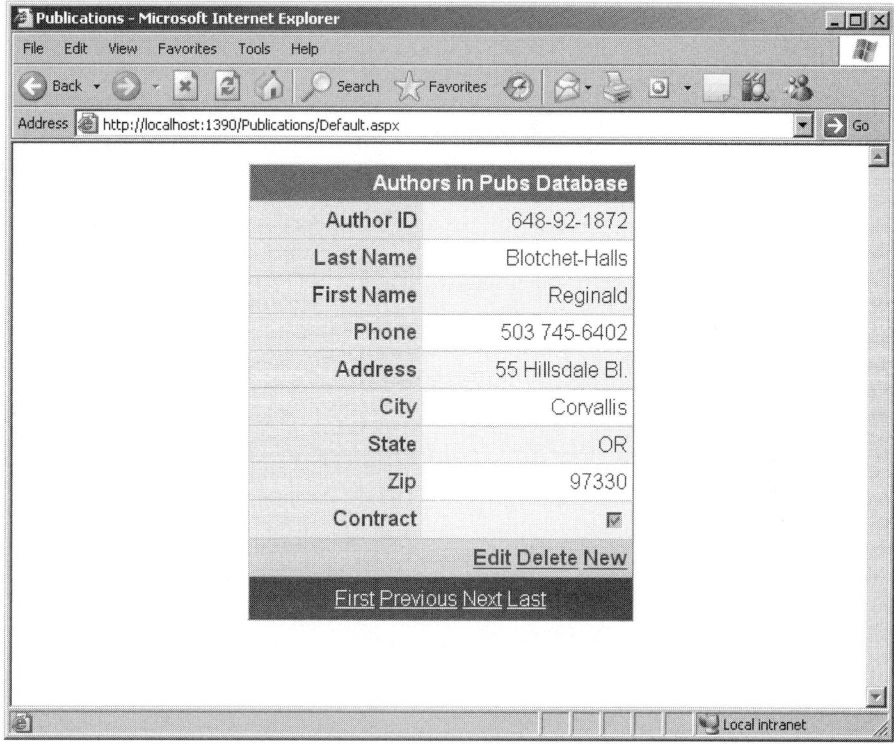

(b) Edit mode of `DetailsView` control

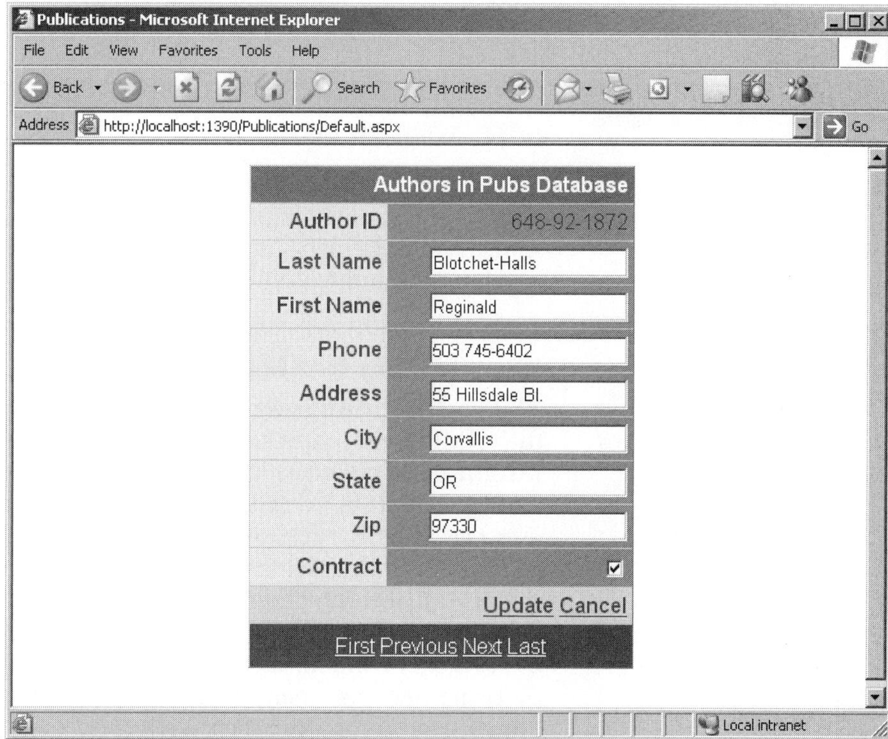

(c) Insert mode of `DetailsView` control

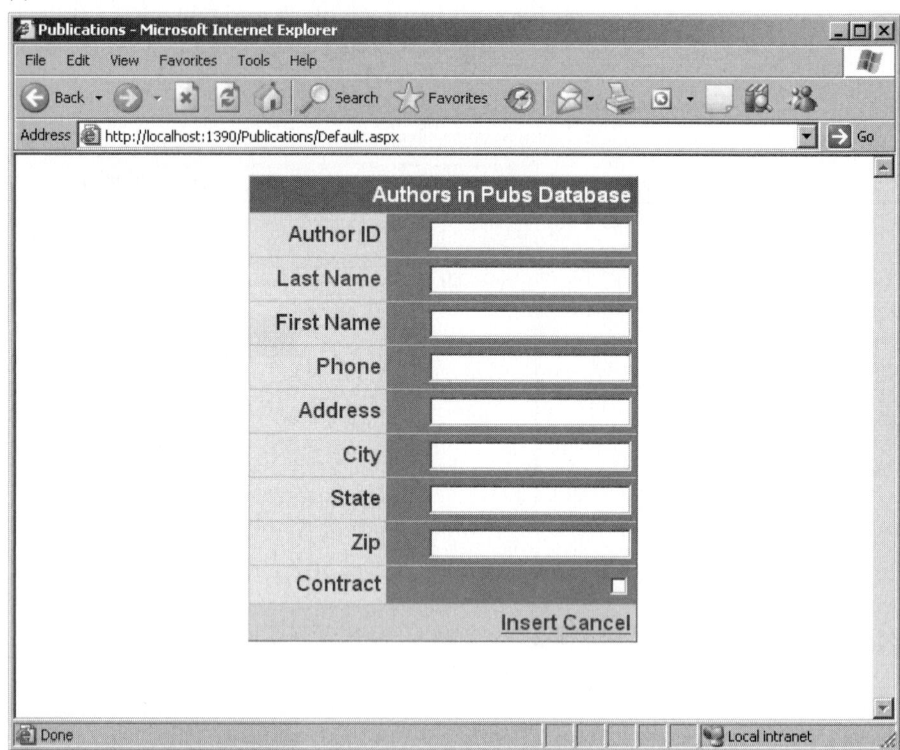

FIGURE 10.21 Sample run of a `DetailsView` for the Publications application

This section has discussed how to display data from a database using a `GridView` or `DetailsView` control in a Web form. The next section also discusses how to display data, but using an XML file instead.

INTRODUCTION TO XML

As you learned in Chapter 9, **XML** (eXtensible Markup Language) is a standard for creating markup languages that describe the structure of data. As you will see, XML is an extremely important technology associated with Web application development and ASP.NET.

Introduction to XML

XML is a **metalanguage**—that is, a language about a language. This means that XML contains the standards or rules for creating your own **markup language** (a language that uses tags to describe the structure and content of its files). HTML is a markup language with which you are already familiar. It uses tags such as `<html></html>`, `<form></form>`, and `<div></div>`. These HTML tags have specific, predefined meanings that Web browsers can understand. XML, on the other hand, uses tags that you, the programmer, define to describe and contain data. The tags in an XML file can be anything to describe the data they contain, such as `<car>`, `<book>`, or `<friend>`.

Using XML has many benefits. XML is textbased, so it is readable by both humans and computers. Also, XML is an open standard, meaning that any kind of computer or software will find it easy to use. (In other words, it is platform independent.) Because it is easy to use, XML is becoming an important standard for information exchange among diverse systems across the Internet. You can get additional information about XML from Web sites such as *http://www.w3.org/XML/*, *http://www.xml.com*, and *http://www.xml.org*.

Creating XML Files

You have already created simple HTML files. Creating an XML File is very similar because HTML and XML are both markup languages. The main difference is that you create your own custom tags in XML. Also, you will find that XML adheres to a stricter set of rules than HTML. (For example, XML is case sensitive and HTML is not.) Figure 10.22 explains how to create an XML file.

HOW TO...

Create an XML File

1. Begin in an ASP.NET Web site. In the Visual Studio menu, click Website and then click Add New Item.
2. In the Add New Item dialog box, click the XML File icon, type the name of the file (with an .xml extension), and click Add. The file opens and ASP.NET supplies the first line of code, the XML declaration, which identifies the file as an XML document. (The XML file is automatically saved in the App_Data folder of the Web site.)
3. Type the XML elements and their content following the syntax of XML 1.0.
4. Save the file.

FIGURE 10.22 How to create an XML file

Following the steps in Figure 10.22, the XML file named pubs.xml (shown in Figure 10.23) was created. Note that the first line is the XML declaration for this file. The root element is `pubs`, identified by the start tag `<pubs>` and the end tag `</pubs>`. Note that in XML, every start tag must have an end tag, which is not true of HTML (e.g., `<br />`). All XML documents require exactly one **root element**, which is the single element in an XML file that contains all other elements. The root element basically defines what the XML document is about (in this case, pubs or publications). In Figure 10.23, the root element `pubs` contains `author` elements, described by the tags `<author>` and `</author>`. (You could say that the `author` element is nested within the `pubs` element.) You can have as many `author` elements as you like in this XML document. Note that each `author` element has an `au_id` attribute (a Social Security number). Such an ID attribute is often used to uniquely identify an element.

Within the `author` element are elements for last name, first name, phone, and address. The `address` element contains other elements (`street`, `city`, `state`, and `zip`). As you can see, these custom tags allow for a very logical organization of the data.

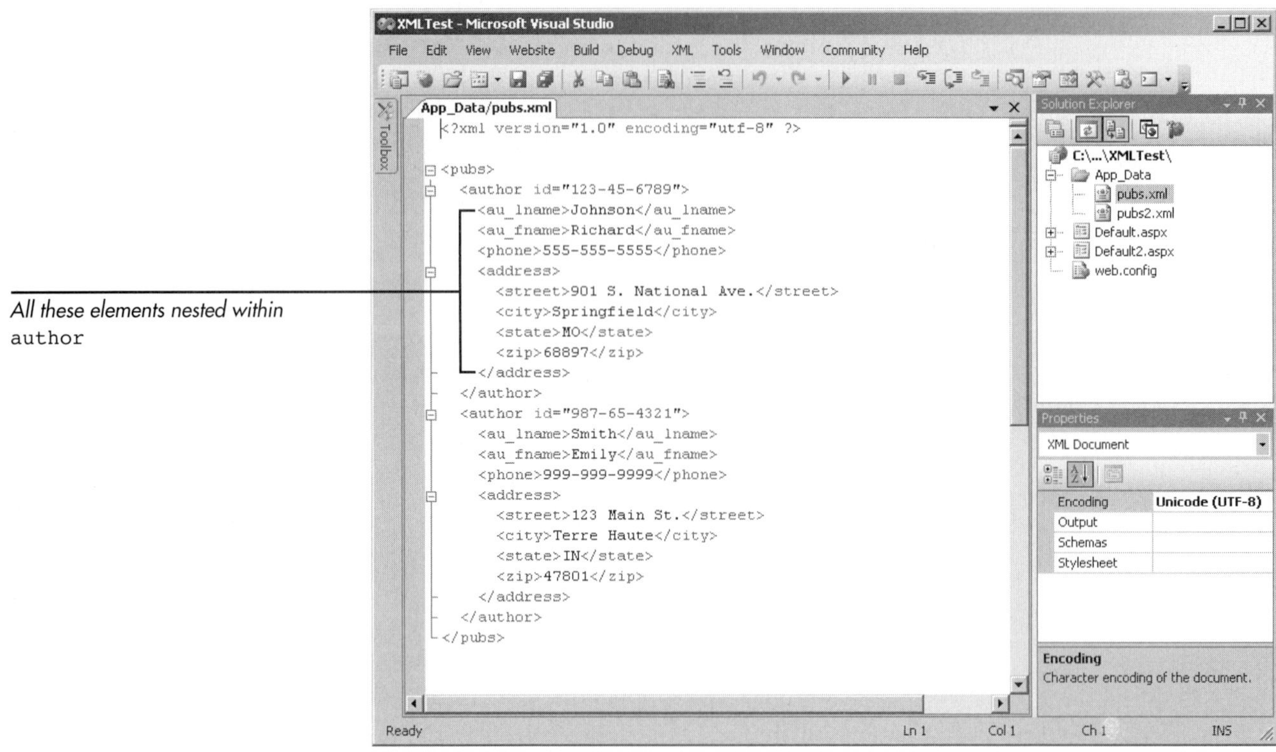

FIGURE 10.23 The pubs.xml file

As an example of how easy it is for software to understand the data in an XML file, you can quickly view the XML data in a grid within Visual Studio. Figure 10.24 shows a Data Grid view of pubs.xml (obtained by simply clicking View and clicking Data Grid in the Visual Studio menu).

(a) View of authors

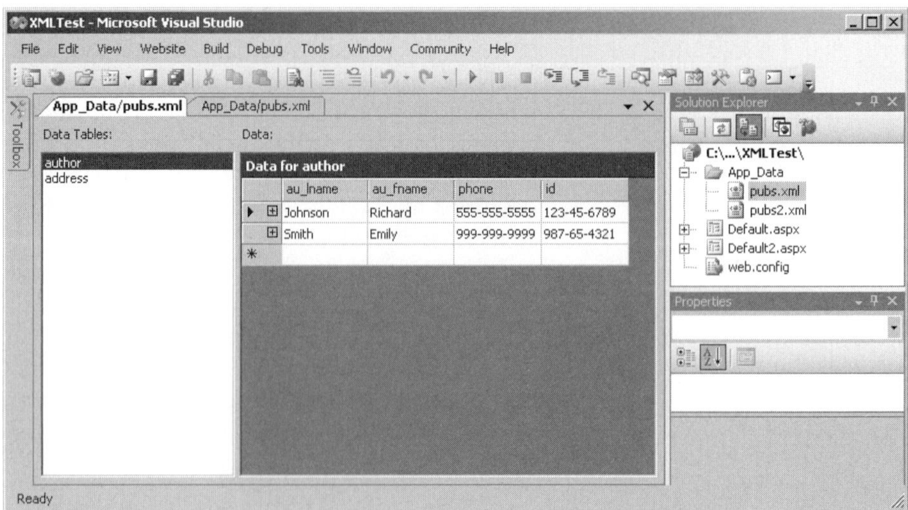

(b) View of author address

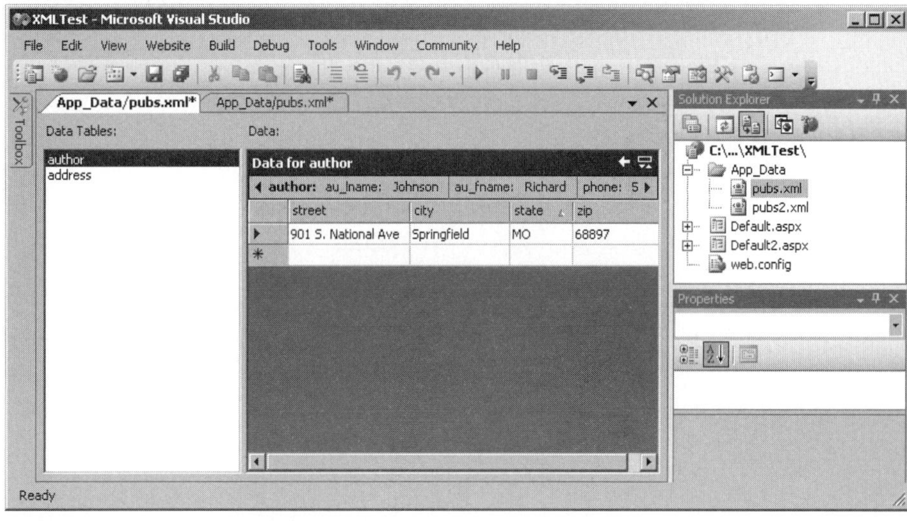

FIGURE 10.24 Data Grid view of the pubs.xml file

The existence of the Data Grid view option (not to be confused with the `GridView` control) in the Visual Studio menu demonstrates that XML files are considered very important for Web applications. Figure 10.24(a) shows the authors' last names, first names, phones, and IDs. Expanding the first author (clicking the plus sign just left of `au_lname`) and clicking the address option reveals that author's address data in Figure 10.24(b).

Software that understands how to interpret XML files is called an **XML parser**. As another example of the importance of XML, Internet Explorer uses an XML parser to display XML files. If you execute the pubs.xml file within Visual Studio (open the pubs.xml file and click the Start Debugging button or press F5), the file is displayed as shown in Figure 10.25.

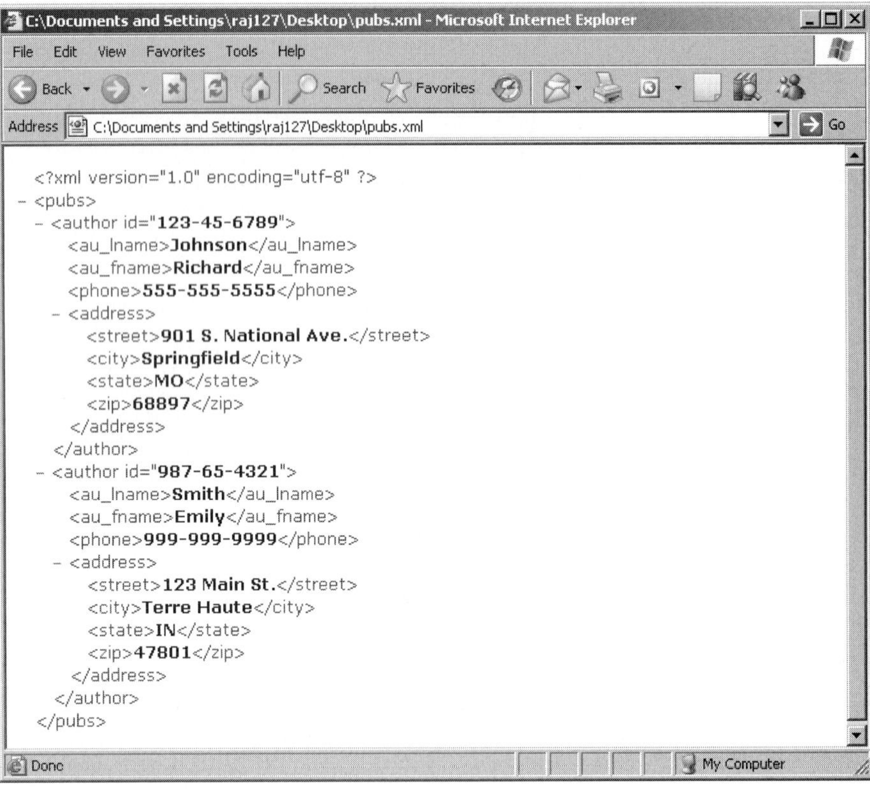

FIGURE 10.25 pubs.xml viewed in Internet Explorer

TIP

You can click the minus signs shown in Figure 10.25 to collapse elements in an XML file that contain other elements. After collapsing, they become plus signs that can be expanded.

Figure 10.25 looks almost identical to Figure 10.23. But, of course, a Web browser such as Internet Explorer is very different from Visual Studio. The point is that many kinds of software include parsers and can therefore interpret XML files. In fact, XML files are so important that Internet Explorer is capable of finding errors and reporting errors in such files, as shown in Figure 10.26, when an element name is misspelled.

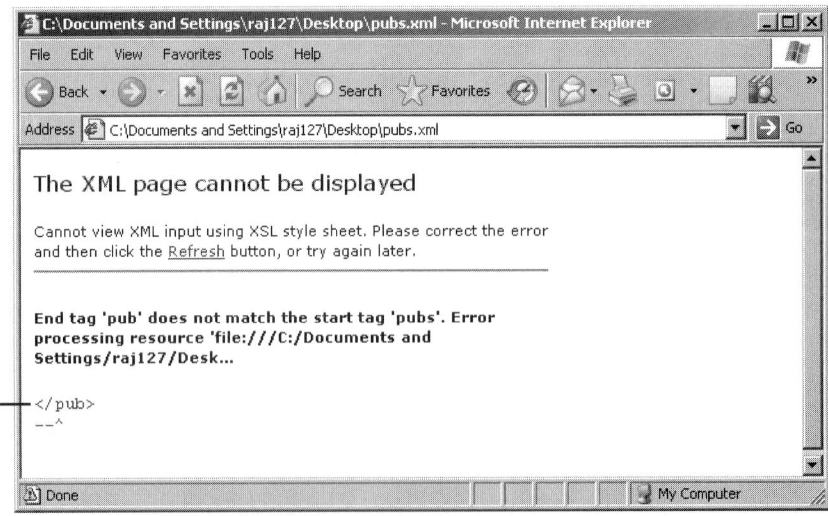

Closing pubs *tag misspelled*

FIGURE 10.26 pubs.xml with an error viewed in Internet Explorer

Displaying XML Files in a Web Form

Earlier in this chapter, you learned how to display data from a database file with either a `GridView` or a `DetailsView` control. You can also display data from an XML file in a `GridView` or a `DetailsView`. However, before doing so, you must structure the XML file in a certain way. The idea is to use an XML element to represent an entity (such as an author) and use attributes of the XML element to represent the attributes of the entity (such as author ID, last name, first name, etc.). Thus, the author element becomes analogous to an author table in a relational database and the author element attributes become analogous to the columns in an author table. An address element for an author (which has its own attributes such as street, city, state, and ZIP code) should be structured in a similar way. Figure 10.27 shows a new XML file called pubs2.xml with this new structure that is required for `GridView` and `DetailsView` controls. Figure 10.28 explains how to display such an XML file in a Web form with a `GridView` control.

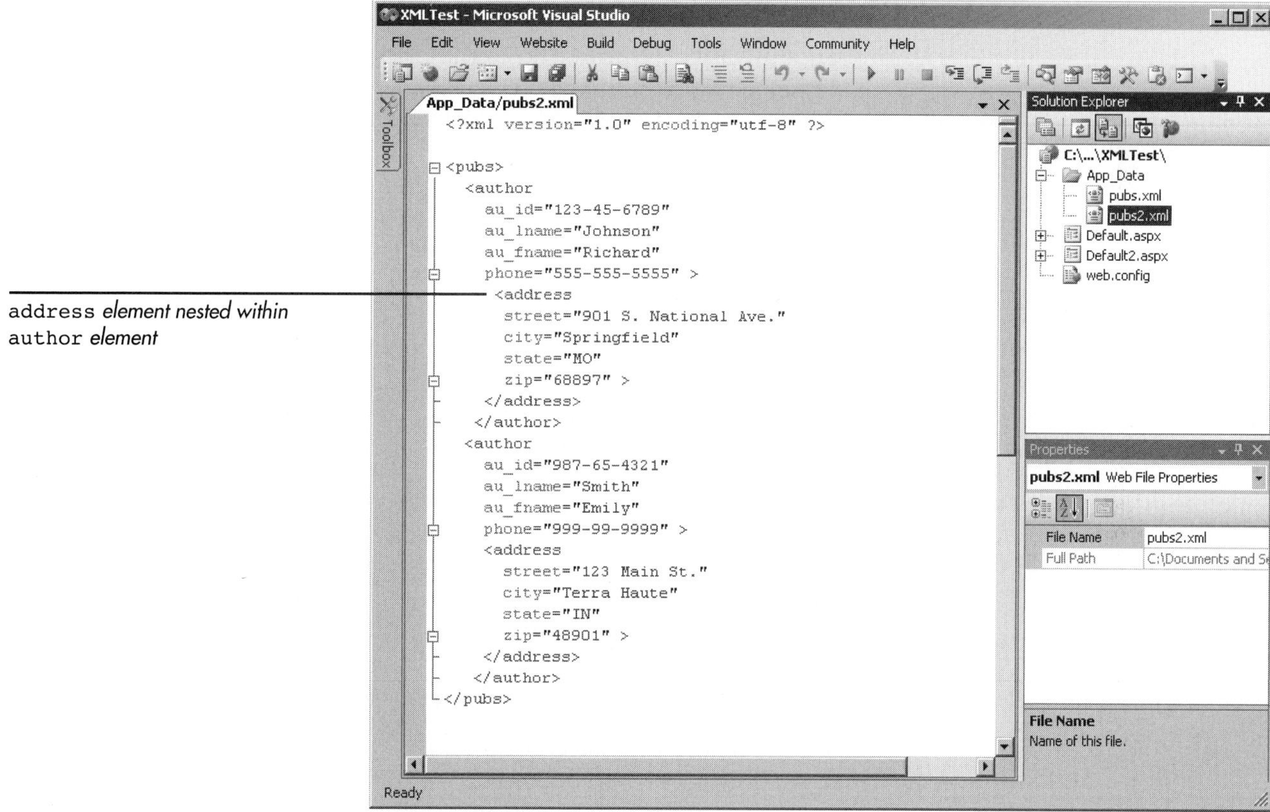

FIGURE 10.27 The pubs2.xml file

HOW TO...

Display an XML File in a GridView

1. After creating a valid XML file, store it in the App_Data folder of the ASP.NET Web site. You can drag and drop or cut and paste an existing XML file to the Visual Studio Solution Explorer or you can create a new XML file within Visual Studio (see Figure 10.22). The XML file can be located anywhere in the application, but the App_Data folder is recommended.
2. With a Web form open in the Web site, drag a `GridView` control from the Data section of the Toolbox to the Web form.
3. Click the Smart Tag on the `GridView` and select New data source from the Choose Data Source list.
4. Click the XML File icon in the Data Source Configuration Wizard. Use the ID for the data source provided (`XMLDataSource1`) or type a different ID if desired. Click OK. The Configure Data Source dialog box appears.
5. Click the Browse button next to the Data file text box and select the desired XML file in the App_Data folder, as shown in Figure 10.29.
6. Click OK in the Configure Data Source dialog box.
7. Save the Web form.

FIGURE 10.28 How to display an XML file in a `GridView`

TIP

In Figure 10.29 the Transform file and XPath expression text boxes deal with the topics of XSL Transform and XPath, which will be briefly discussed later in this chapter. For more information on these topics, see other Course Technology texts, such as *New Perspectives on XML, Second Edition—Comprehensive*, for more information on XSL Transform and XPath.

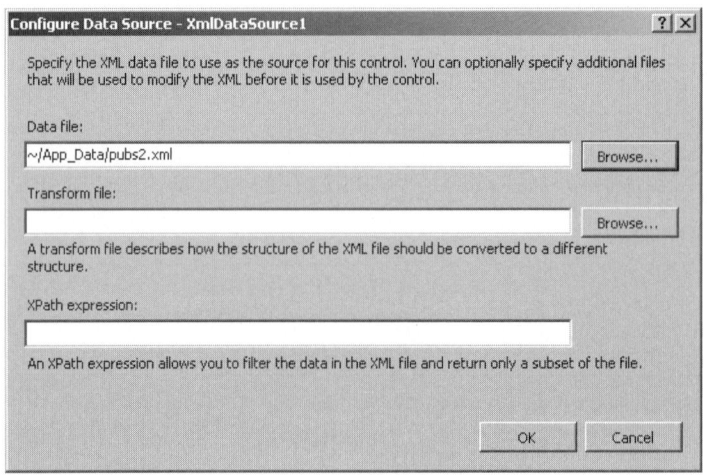

FIGURE 10.29 The Configure Data Source dialog box

The steps outlined in Figure 10.28 were applied to the pubs2.xml file in the XMLTest application. Also, the Gridview Tasks menu (displayed by clicking the Smart Tag on the GridView control) and the Properties window for the GridView control were used to apply an Auto Format, edit columns, and provide additional custom formatting, as described earlier in Figure 10.10. The resulting Design view and sample run of the XMLTest application are shown in Figure 10.30.

(a) Design view of the XMLTest application

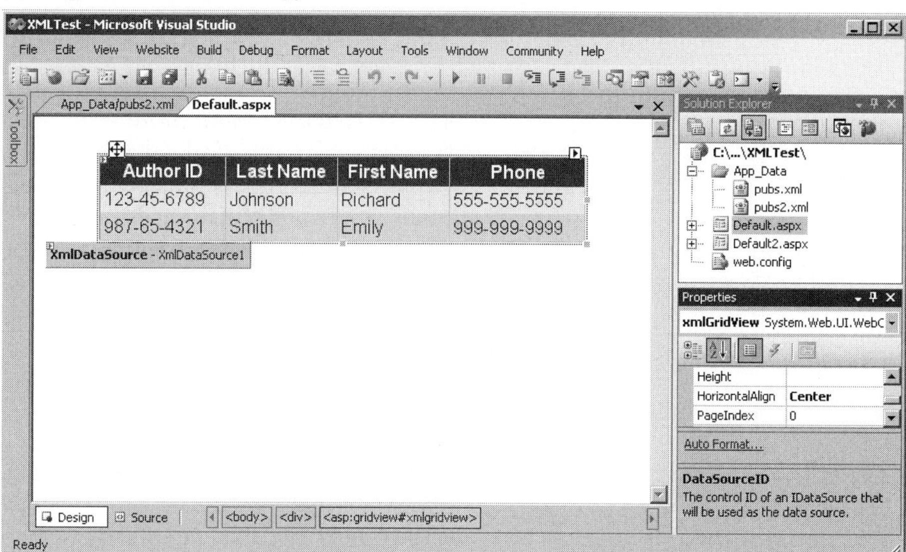

(b) Sample run of the XMLTest application

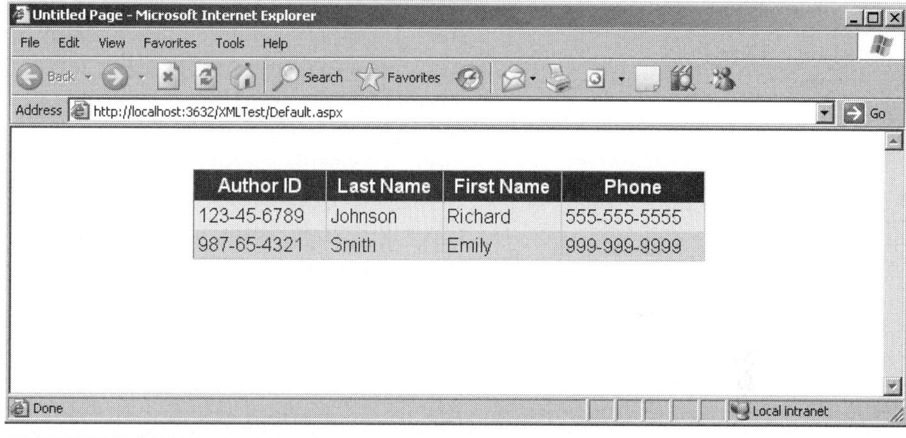

FIGURE 10.30 Design view and sample run of Default.aspx in the XMLTest application

Displaying Nested XML Elements

Note in Figure 10.30 that the address information for the `authors` is not visible. This is because the `address` element in pubs2.xml represents a separate, self-contained entity (similar to a table in a relational database) with its own attributes. The `address` element is nested within the `author` element, which indicates that a given address belongs to a specific author. (In a relational database, a foreign key in an address table would be used to enforce such a relationship.)

Some additional special processing is required to display the XML data contained within a nested element. Retrieving and displaying related data in a relational database is accomplished using an SQL statement that includes a JOIN operation. Retrieving and displaying related data in an XML file is a little more challenging. Figure 10.31 explains, in general terms, how this is done.

HOW TO...

Display Data in Nested XML Elements

1. Assume you have an XML file (pubs2.xml in this case) with one XML element (having one or more attributes) nested within another XML element (also having one or more attributes). In this example, the `address` element is nested within the `author` element.
2. As described in Figure 10.28, drag a `GridView` control (called `GridView1`) to a Web form and bind it to an XML file (pubs2.xml) as a data source (called `XmlDataSource1`).
3. In the GridView Tasks menu for `GridView1`, click the check box for Enable Selection. This causes a Select button to appear in each row of `GridView1`, allowing the user to select a record in `GridView1` for which the address data is to be displayed.
4. In the Properties Window for `GridView1`, click the value column for the `DataKeyNames` property. In the Data Fields Collection Editor dialog box, double-click `au_id` in the Available data fields list to move it to the Selected fields list and click OK. This configures the `GridView` control to treat `au_id` as the primary key for each author element in pubs2.xml.
5. Repeat the process in Step 1, dragging another `GridView` control (called `GridView2`) to the Web form. In the Configure Data Source dialog box, select the same data source (pubs2.xml in this case) for this `GridView`. However, this time type `/pubs/author/address` in the XPath expression text box (as shown in Figure 10.32) and click OK. (This sets the `XPath` property for `XmlDataSource2` to `/pubs/author/address` and causes this `GridView` to traverse to the address element in the XML file to get its data.)
6. In the Design window, click `GridView2` and change its `Visible` property to `False`. This will initially hide `GridView2` until the user clicks the Select button in `GridView1`. The Design window for this configuration now appears in Figure 10.33.
7. Open the code-behind file for Default2.aspx (named Default2.aspx.vb). Enter the code shown in Figure 10.34. Save all files.
8. Test the application. Clicking the Select button for Emily Smith's record produces the output shown in Figure 10.35.

FIGURE 10.31 How to display data in nested XML elements

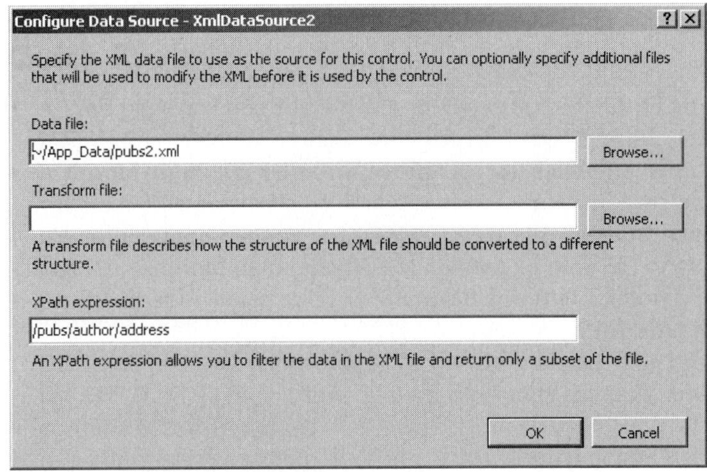

FIGURE 10.32 Configure Data Source dialog for `XmlDataSource2`

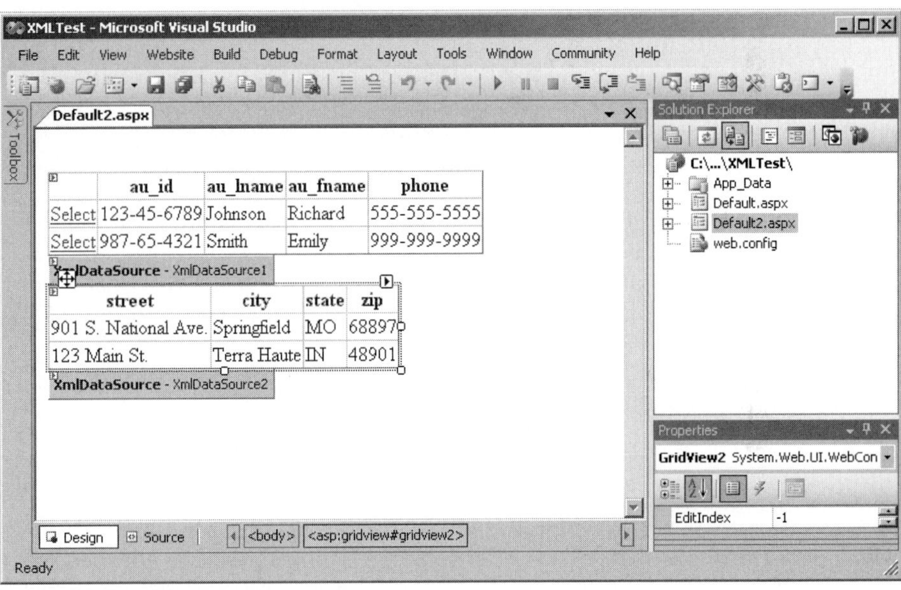

FIGURE 10.33 Design view for `GridView` controls belonging to nested XML elements

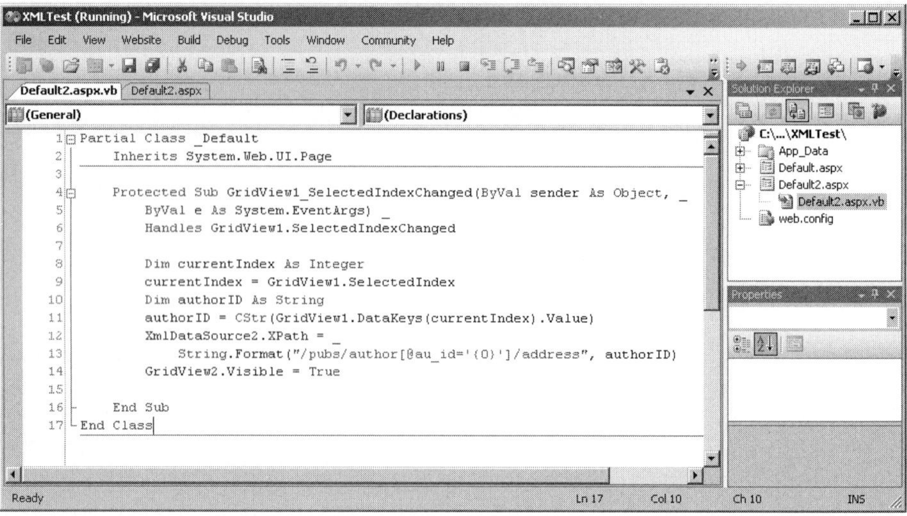

FIGURE 10.34 Code-behind file Default2.aspx.vb

Additional information about Emily Smith after clicking her Select link

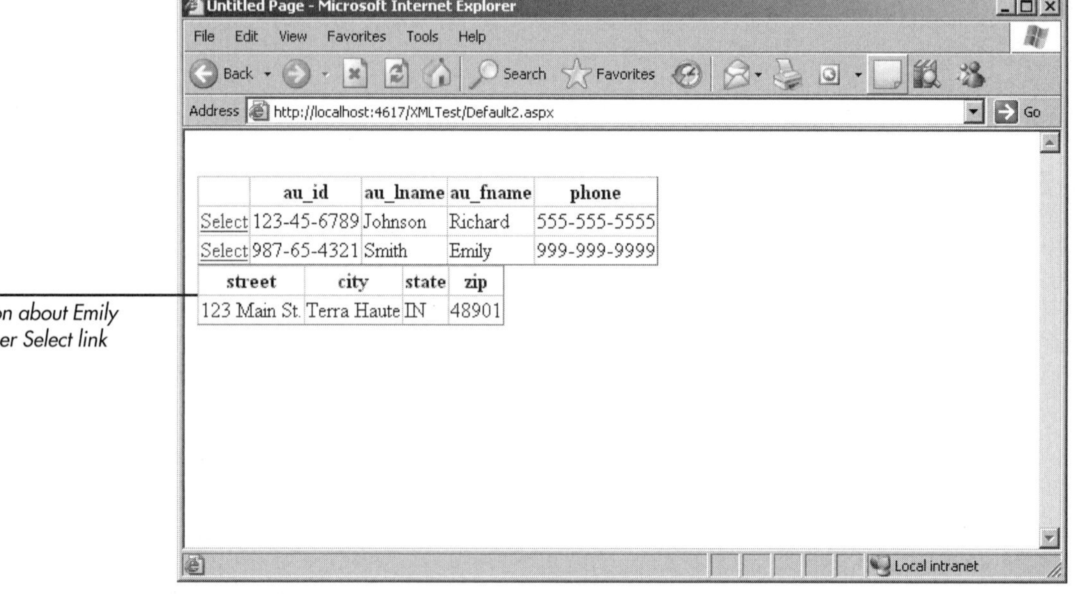

FIGURE 10.35 Sample run of Default2.aspx in the XMLTest application

The sample run in Figure 10.35 works as expected. Of course, the display could use a great deal of extra formatting to improve its appearance (a format scheme, new header text, explanatory text, etc.). The key to understanding how the display in Figure 10.35 is produced is in the code in Figure 10.34, which we will now explain.

When Default2.aspx loads, only the `GridView1` control is visible because the `Visible` property of `GridView2` is originally set to `False` by default. Line 9 of the code in Figure 10.34 sets the value of `currentIndex` to the `SelectedIndex` of `GridView1` on the `SelectedIndexChanged` event. (The initial value of `SelectedIndex` is `-1` and changes when the user clicks a Select link in `GridView1`.) Line 11 uses the value of `currentIndex` to return the `Value` of the

DataKeys property of GridView1, which is the value of au_id for the selected record. Note that au_id is the primary key, the Value of the DataKeyNames property of GridView1. In Lines 12–13, the value of the XPath property of XmlDataSource2 (the data source for GridView2), which was previously set in general to /pubs/author/address (see Figure 10.32), is now set specifically for the address belonging to the author with au_id equal to authorID. Then Line 14 makes the address information in GridView2 visible, but only for the specific author selected in GridView1, as shown in Figure 10.35.

You would probably agree that this is a long way around to display the data in Figure 10.35. It may seem much easier to display data in a GridView using a database as the data source and an SQL statement to extract specific information (and you would be correct). This example illustrates some of the disadvantages of XML when compared with databases. However, recall that XML does have many advantages over databases, such as a simple, standard, open format that makes it easier for organizations to share data. The usefulness of both XML and databases is the ability of organizations to convert data from a database to XML format for transferring, and then to convert data from XML format to a database for processing.

INTRODUCTION TO WEB SERVICES

The previous section introduced you to the important topic of XML. This section focuses on another critical technology related to ASP.NET Web sites: Web services.

Overview of Web Services

A **Web service** is a class (including its methods) that is available over a network (such as the Internet or an intranet). Thus, an ASP.NET application that you create and run on one computer can use a Web service (particularly, its methods) located on another computer via the Internet or an intranet. Using Web services, your application can access some very useful and sophisticated code made available by other developers over the Internet. In addition, Web services make extensive use of XML files. This section explores how to create and run Web services.

The uses of Web services are practically endless. In a typical arrangement, an organization places important parts of an application, such as business logic or database processing, on a Web server to be used by the organization's client computers, which are connected to the Web server via either the Internet or the organization's intranet. This is sometimes referred to as an intra-organizational use of Web services. The interorganizational use of Web services, in which multiple organizations share their applications via Web services, is also an option. For example, in order to enable automatic ordering, a supplier could make its inventory available as a Web service to a customer application. Alternatively, a customer could make its production plans available as a Web service to a supplier application to enable automatic production scheduling, thus minimizing costly human interaction.

Web services are based on three primary standards: WSDL (Web Services Description Language), UDDI (Universal description, discovery, and integration), and SOAP (Simple Object Access Protocol). **WSDL** is an XML-formatted language used to completely describe a Web service. **UDDI** is an XML-based standard that businesses use to publish and find Web services. **SOAP** is a protocol (data communications standard) for exchanging XML-based messages over a computer network, normally using HTTP (that is, via the Web). Thus, WSDL describes a Web service, UDDI makes Web services known to potential users, and SOAP makes Web services accessible. Now you will learn how to create a Web service.

Creating a Web Service Project

To create a Web service, you begin by creating a new Web site in Visual Studio. However, unlike other Web sites you create, this Web site is designed primarily as a Web service project, as Figure 10.36 explains.

HOW TO...

Create a Web Service Project

1. Launch Visual Studio. In the Visual Studio menu, click File and then click New Web Site.
2. In the New Web Site dialog box, click the ASP.NET Web Service icon. The Location list box should be set at File System and the Language list box at Visual Basic. Type the path (or browse) to the folder on your computer where you want to store the new Web service project and then click OK. A Web service class opens in the Code Editor (see Figure 10.37).
3. In the Visual Studio menu, click File and then click Save App_Code/Service.vb as. Change the Visual Basic class name to something more descriptive.
4. In the `WebService` attribute (beginning with the code `<WebService`), change the default namespace (`http://tempuri.org/`) to a unique URL.
5. In the `WebService` attribute, add a short but meaningful `Description` of this Web service.
6. Add additional Web methods to the class as necessary by adding code similar to Lines 12–15 in Figure 10.37. (A `WebMethod` is a function or operation that the Web service will perform.) Save this class.
7. Open the Service.asmx file in the Solution Explorer and change the name of the file in the `CodeBehind` attribute to match the new name of the .vb class file for the Web service. Also change the class name in the `Class` attribute (within the .asmx file) to match the name of the class in the .vb file. Finally, save the .asmx file and rename it to match the name of the .vb file (but keep the .asmx extension).

FIGURE 10.36 How to create a Web service project

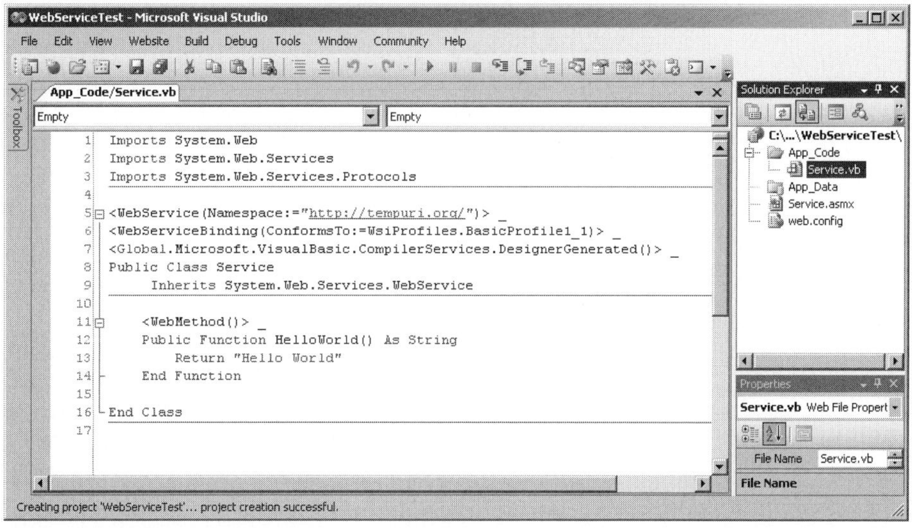

FIGURE 10.37 The default Web service class Service.vb

The default Web service class shown in Figure 10.37 was modified according to the steps in Figure 10.36. Its name was changed to `HelloWorld`. Its namespace was changed to `http://course.com/johnson/webservicetest`. (Any unique URL will do.) Finally, a description (`"Displays a Hello World greeting"`) was added to the `WebService` attribute. The Web service file (with the .asmx extension) was also modified according to the steps in Figure 10.36. The end result is the Web service class HelloWorld.vb shown in Figure 10.38 with the Web service file HelloWorld.asmx shown in Figure 10.39.

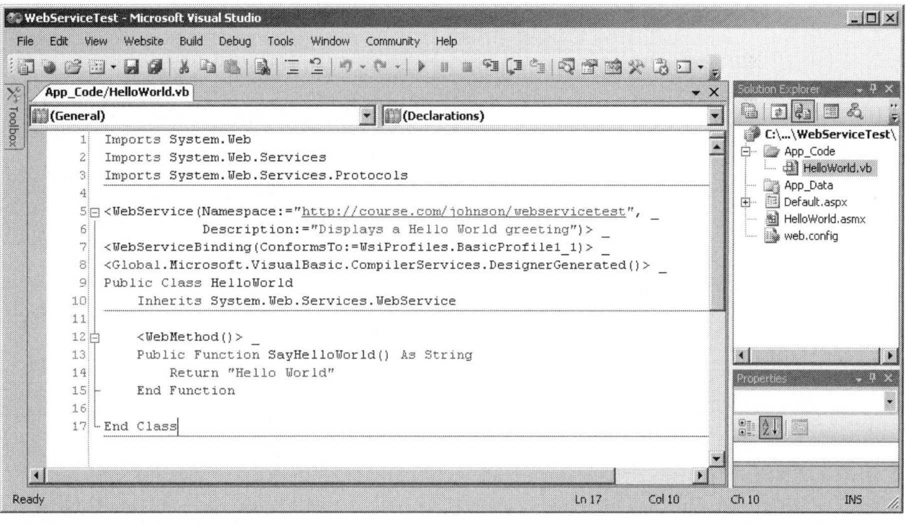

FIGURE 10.38 The Web service class HelloWorld.vb

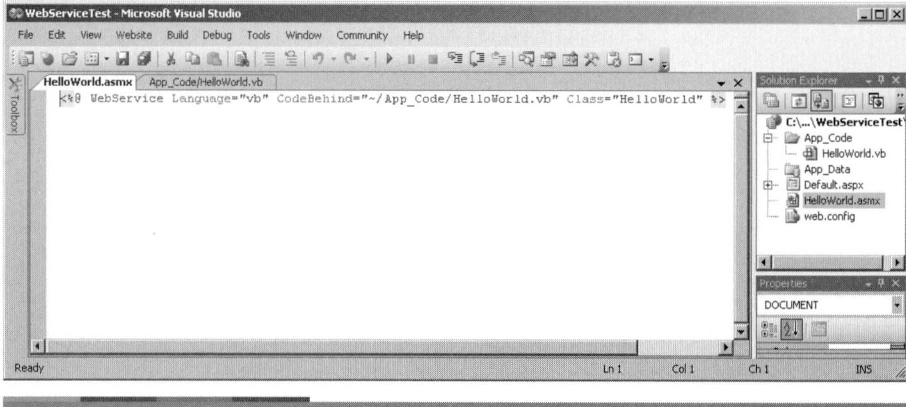

FIGURE 10.39 The Web service file HelloWorld.asmx

In Figure 10.38, the `HelloWorld` class (beginning in Line 9) contains the `WebMethod` attribute followed by a Visual Basic `Function` called `SayHelloWorld`, which simply returns the text `"Hello World"`. It is the code in the Web service file HelloWorld.asmx that will be executed when the Web service is invoked. The HelloWorld.asmx file uses the HelloWorld.vb code-behind file to provide the functionality of its Web methods.

Testing a Web Service

You can test the Web service from within Visual Basic without creating an actual client application that uses the Web service. Running the Web service application WebServiceTest within Visual Studio results in the Service help page displayed in Figure 10.40.

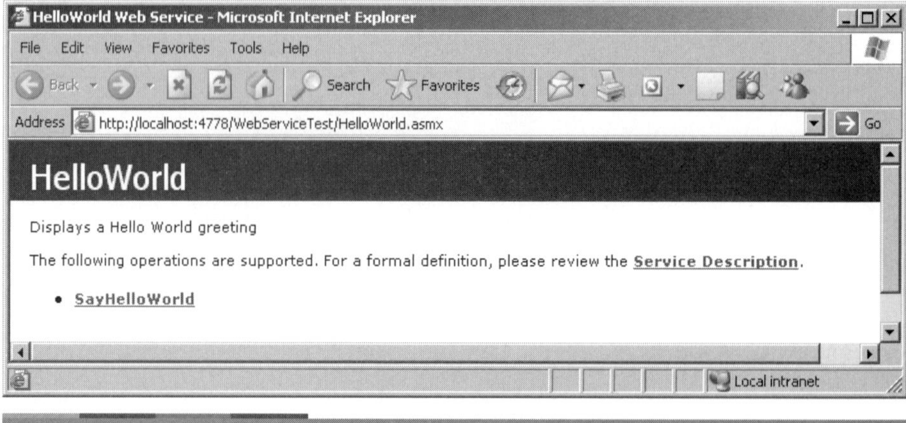

FIGURE 10.40 Sample run of the WebServiceTest application

The Service help page begins with the name of the Web service, HelloWorld. Directly below the Web service name is the description that was specified in the `WebService` attribute (Figure 10.38, Line 6). Following this description is some text that introduces the operations (functions) provided by the Web service. This text also discusses the formal definition of the Web service, providing a link to the service description, which is the complete WSDL document that the client uses to execute the Web service. As you can see, this WSDL document is written using XML.

Finally, the Service help page includes a link to the `SayHelloWorld` Web method. Clicking this link produces the Service Method help page in Figure 10.41, which contains additional information for someone considering using the `SayHelloWorld` Web method. Clicking the Invoke button in Figure 10.41 provides the XML code that is returned by the method, as shown in Figure 10.42. The remainder of the Web page in Figure 10.41 provides the potential Web service client with sample SOAP and HTTP POST requests and responses that could be of use to a developer who is planning to use the Web service.

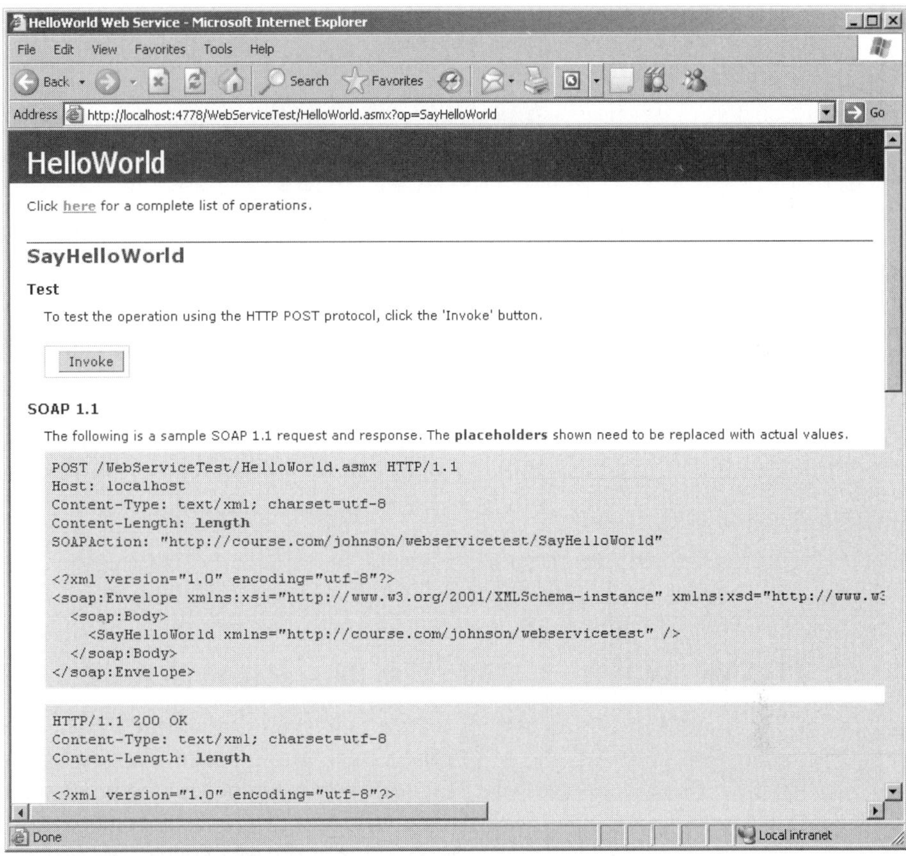

FIGURE 10.41 Service Method help page for the `SayHelloWorld` Web method

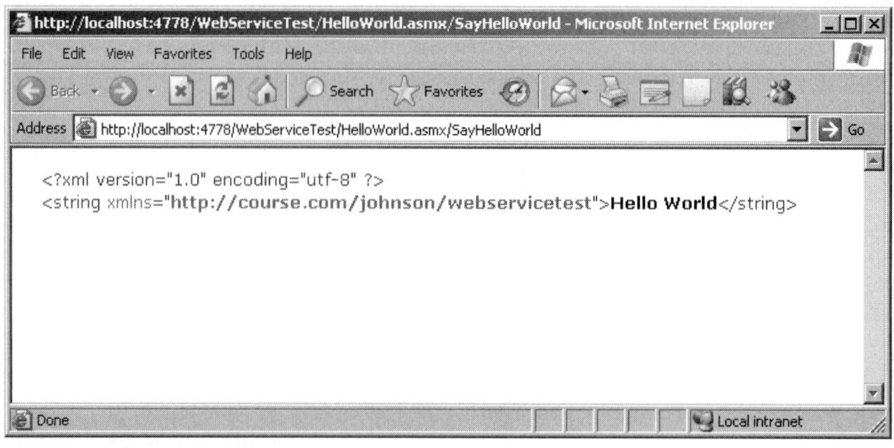

FIGURE 10.42 Testing the `SayHelloWorld` Web method

Consuming a Web Service

Now that you have produced and tested a Web service, you are ready to learn how to use or consume a Web service in an application. The first step in consuming a Web service is to add a Web reference to the Web service. Note that a Web service is simply a program with the .asmx extension, which has a code-behind file (a class) with a .vb extension. The Web service to which you want to add a Web reference can be located within your application (if you create it there), on a local network, or on the Internet. Figure 10.43 explains how to add a Web reference to a Web service.

HOW TO...

Add a Web Reference to an Application

1. Create a new Web site with ASP.NET (see Figure 9.8 for review).
2. In the Visual Studio menu, click Website and click Add Web Reference. The Add Web Reference dialog box appears as shown in Figure 10.44.
3. In the Add Web Reference dialog box, you can type the URL to a known Web service in the address bar, or you can use the links provided to search for a Web service. (Figure 10.45 shows the Service help page in the Add Web Reference dialog box after a Web service is located.)
4. In the Add Web Reference dialog box, click the Add Reference button. The project now contains a reference to the Web service in the App_WebReferences folder (Figure 10.46).

FIGURE 10.43 How to add a Web reference to an application

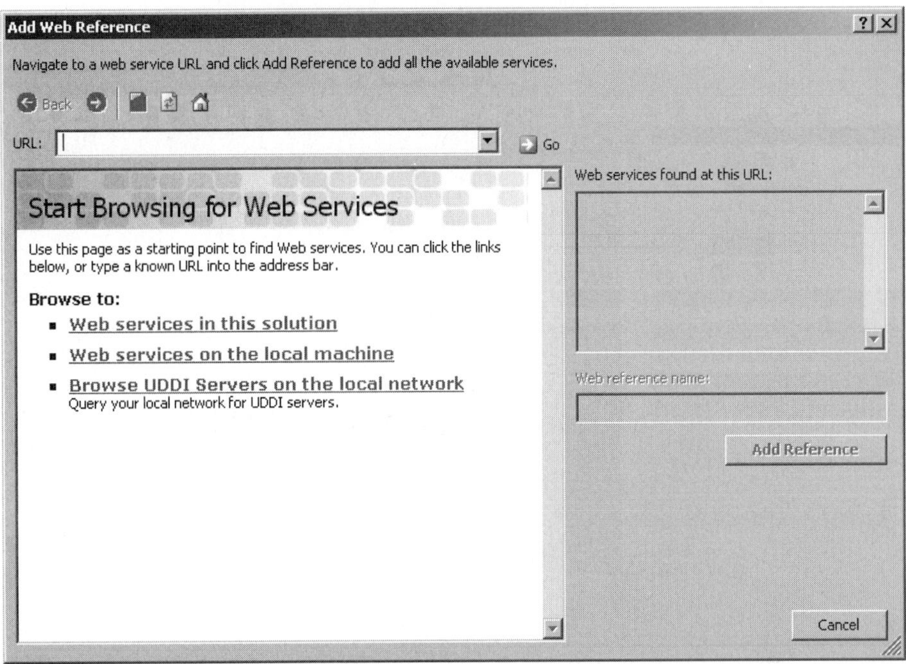

FIGURE 10.44 The Add Web Reference dialog box

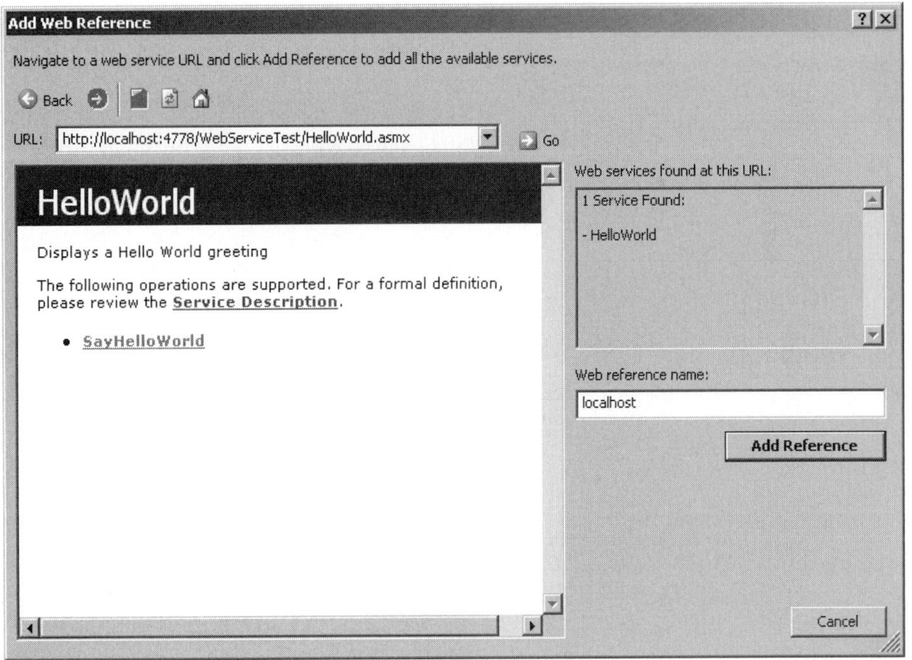

FIGURE 10.45 Add Web Reference dialog showing a Web service

FIGURE 10.46 The ConsumeWebService application with Web reference added

TIP

The Internet is a source of available Web services that you can include in your Web applications. For example, see *http://www.uddi.org* or *http://www.xmethods.com*.

Note in Figure 10.46 that the Web reference is contained within the App_WebReferences folder. Within this folder is the localhost folder, which represents the URL where the Web service is located. (The WebServiceTest project, created earlier in this section, was copied to the Web server on the local machine, so the URL for this Web service is localhost.) If the Web reference is added from an external Web server, the folder name would be that URL beginning with http://.

Within the localhost folder are the Web service files created by Visual Studio. The DISCO (Discovery of Web Services) files are used to locate the Web service on the Internet or intranet. The WSDL file is the Web service description file discussed earlier in this chapter. (WSDL is a complete description of the Web service in XML format.) You do not need to understand the contents of these files in order to use the Web service.

Now that the Web reference to the Web service is in place, the application can put it to use, as discussed in Figure 10.47.

HOW TO...

Consume a Web Service

1. Beginning with an application that has an added Web reference to a Web service (for example, the ConsumeWebService application in Figure 10.46), complete the design of the Web form (.aspx file) with the desired text and Web server controls (such as labels, text boxes, and buttons).
2. In the code-behind file (.vb file) belonging to the Web form, create the appropriate event procedure (e.g., for a button click). This can be done by double-clicking the Web server control in the Web form.

(Figure is continued on next page)

3. Within the event procedure in the code-behind file, complete the required code, calling the appropriate Web method in the Web service. You first create an instance of the Web service and then use this Web service object to call one of its methods.
4. Test the application, correct, and save.

FIGURE 10.47 How to consume a Web service

Figure 10.48 shows the design of a simple Web form (Default.aspx) in the ConsumeWebService application, which uses the `HelloWorld` Web service. The Web form has some explanatory text, a `greetingButton`, and a `greetingLabel`. Clicking the `greetingButton` should display the text "Hello World" in the `greetingLabel` using the `SayHelloWorld` Web method in the `HelloWorld` Web service. The HTML and ASP.NET code for Default.aspx is shown in Figure 10.49.

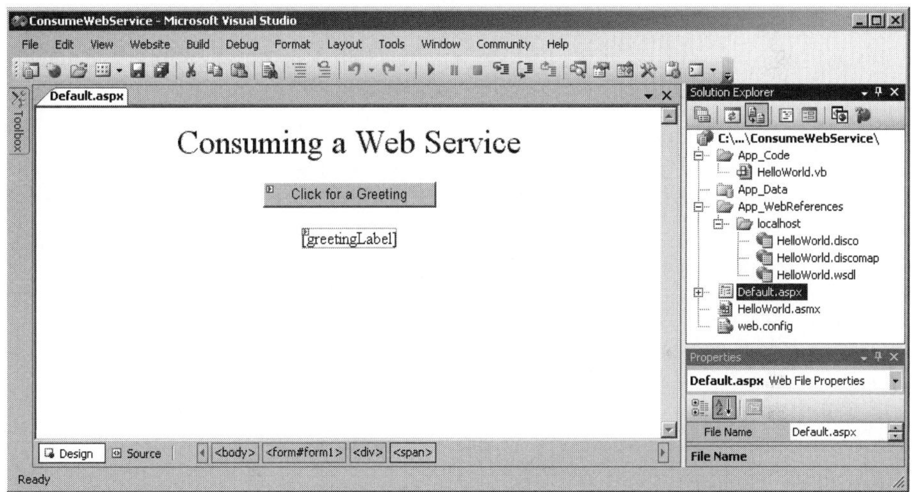

FIGURE 10.48 Design of Default.aspx in the ConsumeWebService project

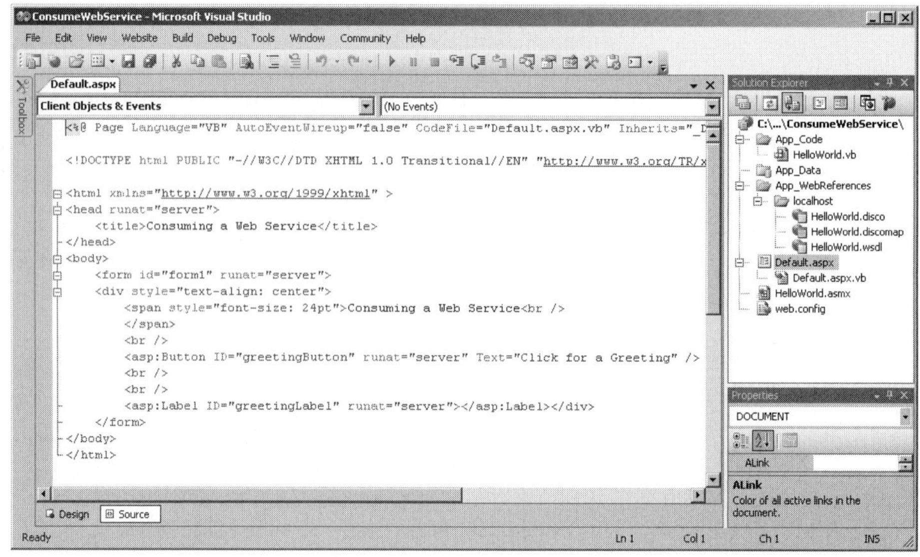

FIGURE 10.49 HTML and ASP.NET code for Default.aspx

The file that directly accesses the Web service is Default.aspx.vb, which is the code-behind file for Default.aspx. The code for this file is shown in Figure 10.50.

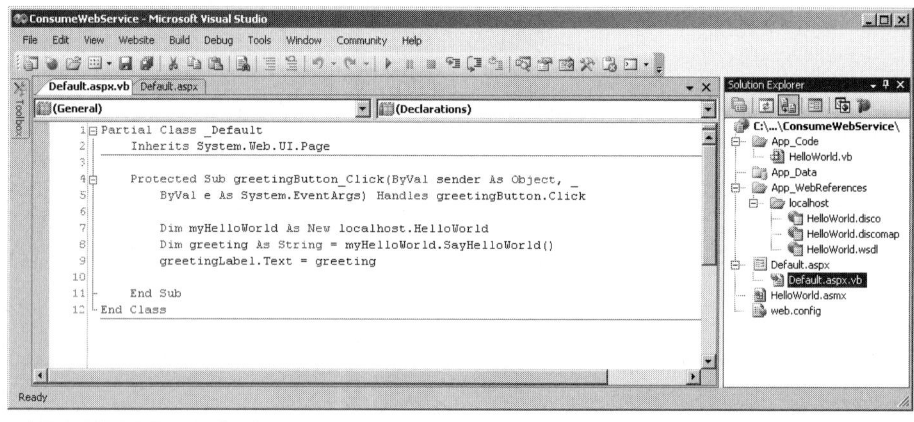

FIGURE 10.50 Program code for Default.aspx.vb in the ConsumeWebService application

The program code in Figure 10.50 is very nearly the same as most other Visual Basic code that you have written. The key difference is in Line 7:

```
Dim myHelloWorld As New localhost.HelloWorld
```

The variable `myHelloWorld` is an instance of the `HelloWorld` Web service class, but this class is referenced by `localhost`, the specific location of the Web service. Line 8 then uses the Web service object `myHelloWorld` to call the Web method `SayHelloWorld`, storing the result in the `String` variable `greeting`. Line 9 then displays the contents of `greeting` in the `greetingLabel`. A sample run of the ConsumeWebService application is shown in Figure 10.51.

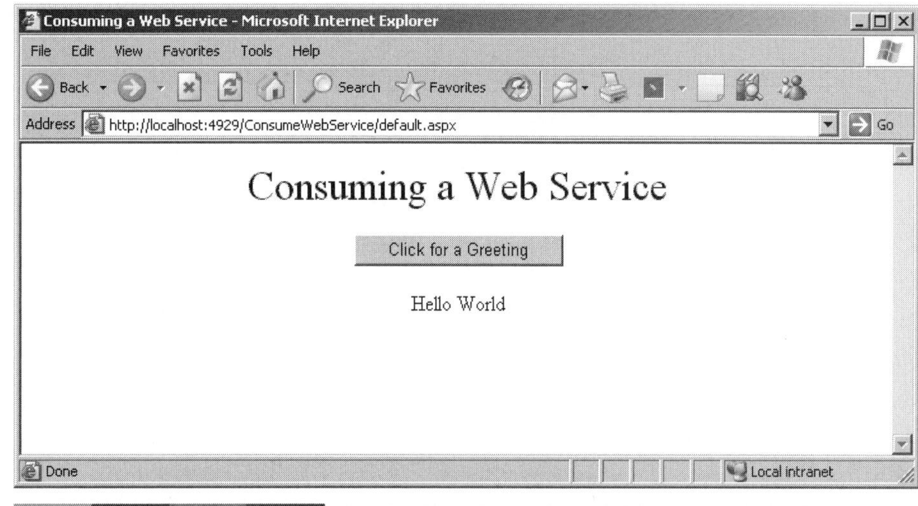

FIGURE 10.51 Sample run of the ConsumeWebService application

PROGRAMMING EXAMPLE

Loan Payment

This application creates an ASP.NET Web site with a Web form, Default.aspx, that consumes a Web service, PaymentService.asmx. The Default.aspx Web form displays certain loan information, collects additional needed data from the user, and outputs the monthly loan payment.

Web Form

The Web form for the Loan Payment application, Figure 10.52, has the following characteristics:

1. A document title, "Payments"
2. A page heading, "Loan Payment"
3. A table that contains some explanatory text and these components:
   a. A `GridView` control `bankGridView` that displays the bank IDs and names, and the loan fees that they charge. (These data come from an Access database within the project.)
   b. A `TextBox` control `amountTextBox` that receives the desired loan amount
   c. A `TextBox` control `yearsTextBox` that receives the number of years planned for repayment
   d. A `ListBox` control `rateListBox` that displays various annual interest rates from an XML file
   e. A Button control `calculateButton` with a `Click` event procedure that calls a Web method `CalculatePayment` in a Web service `PaymentService`
   f. A Label control `paymentLabel` that displays the calculated monthly loan payment

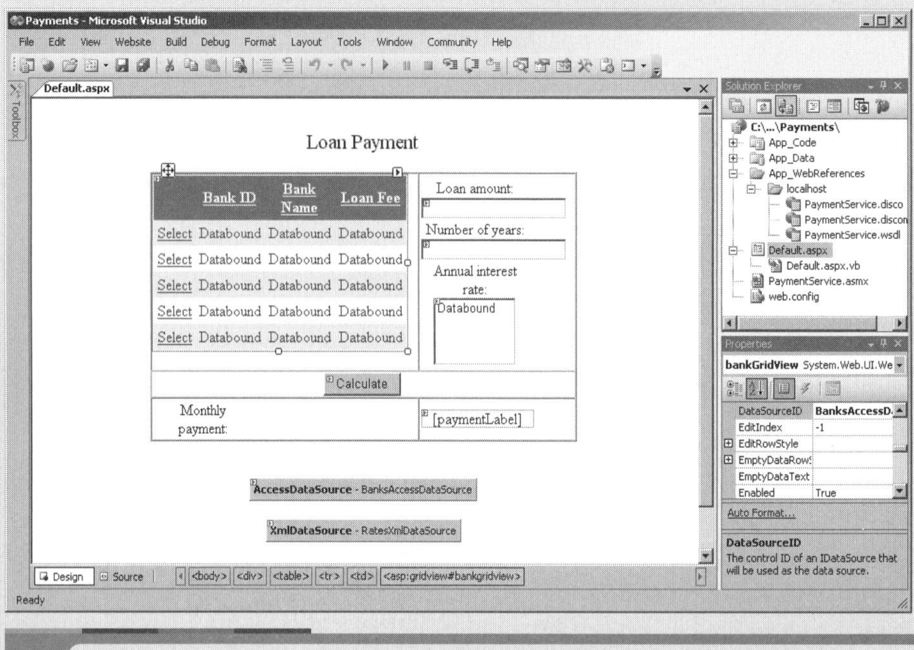

FIGURE 10.52 Design view of Default.aspx

To operate the Web application, the user selects a bank from the `GridView` and enters the loan amount and the number of years for repayment. Then the user selects an interest rate from the `ListBox` and clicks the `Button`. The monthly payment for the total loan amount (original loan amount plus the bank fee) is displayed in the `Label`.

Web Service

The Web service contains one Web method, `CalculatePayment`. This Web method receives data from the application and uses the `Financial.Pmt` method to calculate and return the monthly loan payment. The Service help page is shown in Figure 10.53.

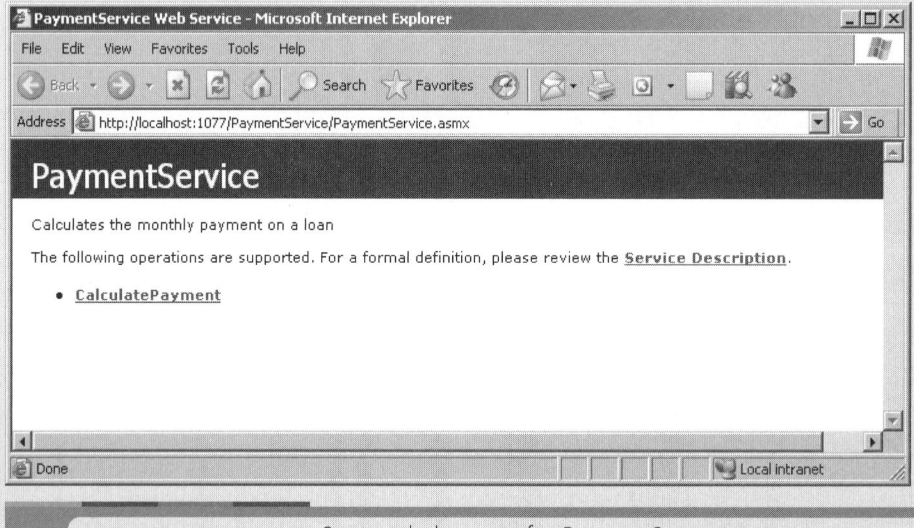

FIGURE 10.53 Service help page for PaymentService.asmx

Data

The Microsoft Access database banks.mdb contains data for three banks, as shown in Figure 10.54.

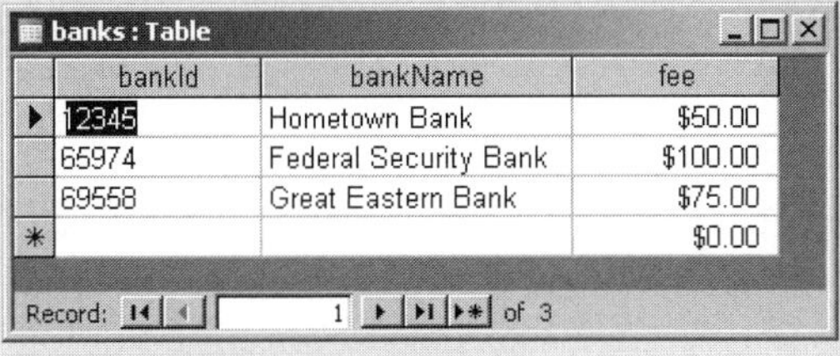

banks : Table

bankId	bankName	fee
12345	Hometown Bank	$50.00
65974	Federal Security Bank	$100.00
69558	Great Eastern Bank	$75.00
		$0.00

Record: 1 of 3

FIGURE 10.54 Access database banks.mdb

The XML file rates.xml contains available annual interest rates, as shown in Figure 10.55.

```
<?xml version="1.0" encoding="utf-8" ?>

<interest_rates>
    <rate value="5"></rate>
    <rate value="10"></rate>
    <rate value="15"></rate>
    <rate value="20"></rate>
</interest_rates>
```

FIGURE 10.55 XML file rates.xml

Pseudocode

`calculateButton Click` ***event procedure***

1. get the row in `bankGridView` selected by the user
2. get the fee from the `bankGridView` row
3. get the loan amount
4. calculate the total amount (loan amount + fee)
5. get the number of years
6. calculate the number of months = years * 12
7. get the selected annual interest rate
8. calculate the monthly interest rate = annual rate / 100 / 12
9. call the `CalculatePayment` Web method in the `PaymentService` Web service
10. display the monthly payment

Code

```
Partial Class _Default
    Inherits System.Web.UI.Page

    Protected Sub calculateButton_Click(ByVal sender As Object, _
        ByVal e As System.EventArgs) Handles calculateButton.Click

        ' get the selected row
        Dim theRow As GridViewRow = bankGridView.SelectedRow
        ' get the fee in the selected row
        Dim fee As Double = Convert.ToDouble(theRow.Cells(3).Text)
        ' get the values for payment parameters
        Dim totalAmount = Convert.ToDouble(amountTextBox.Text) + fee
        Dim months = Convert.ToInt16(yearsTextBox.Text) * 12
        Dim monthlyRate = Convert.ToDouble(rateListBox.SelectedValue) / 100 / 12
        'consume web service
        Dim myPaymentService As New localhost.PaymentService
        Dim monthlyPayment As Double = _
            myPaymentService.CalculatePayment(monthlyRate, months, totalAmount)
        paymentLabel.Text = FormatCurrency(monthlyPayment)

    End Sub
End Class
```

FIGURE 10.56 `_Default` class in Default.aspx.vb

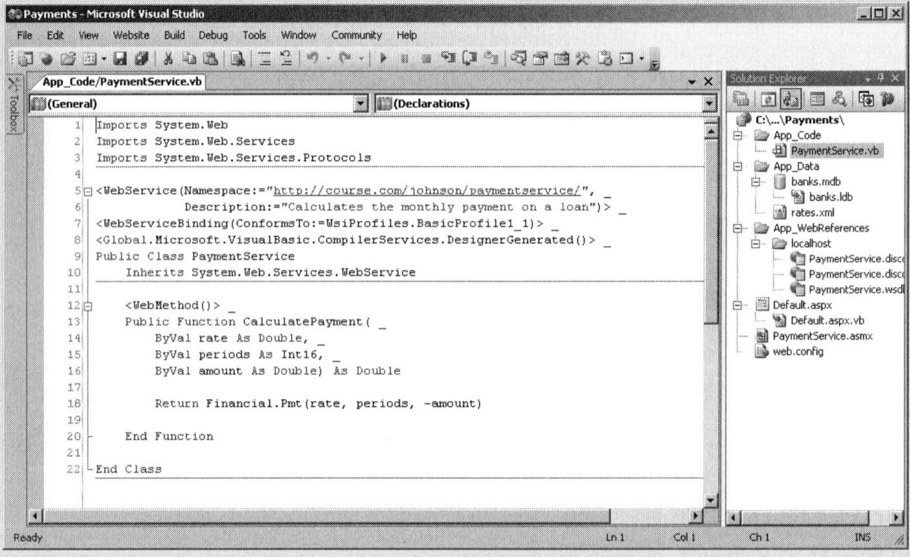

```
Imports System.Web
Imports System.Web.Services
Imports System.Web.Services.Protocols

<WebService(Namespace:="http://course.com/johnson/paymentservice/", _
            Description:="Calculates the monthly payment on a loan")> _
<WebServiceBinding(ConformsTo:=WsiProfiles.BasicProfile1_1)> _
<Global.Microsoft.VisualBasic.CompilerServices.DesignerGenerated()> _
Public Class PaymentService
    Inherits System.Web.Services.WebService

    <WebMethod()> _
    Public Function CalculatePayment( _
        ByVal rate As Double, _
        ByVal periods As Int16, _
        ByVal amount As Double) As Double

        Return Financial.Pmt(rate, periods, -amount)

    End Function

End Class
```

FIGURE 10.57 `PaymentService` class in PaymentService.vb

Input/Output

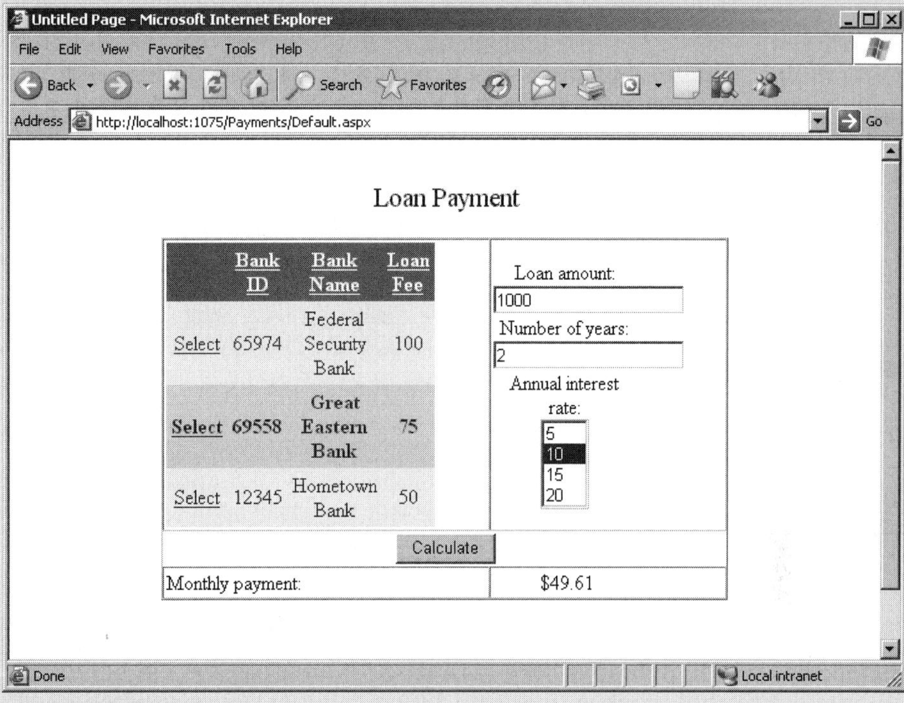

FIGURE 10.58 Sample run for Default.aspx in the Loan Payment application

Quick Review

- You can apply the techniques of accessing databases and using SQL to Windows applications through ADO.NET. You can apply these same techniques to Web applications through ASP.NET.
- The `GridView` control displays table or query data in a grid format with rows and columns. The `DetailsView` control displays records in a table or query one at a time.
- XML is a standard for creating markup languages that describe the structure of data. It is an extremely important technology associated with Web application development and ASP.NET.
- XML is a metalanguage—that is, a language about a language. This means that XML contains the standards or rules for creating your own markup language. (A markup language uses tags to describe the structure and content of its files.) The tags in an XML file can be anything that describes the data they contain, such as `<car>`, `<book>`, or `<friend>`.
- One of the major benefits of XML is that it is text based, so it is readable by both humans and computers. Also, XML is an open standard, meaning that any kind of computer or software will find it easy to use (that is, it is platform independent). Because of its ease of use and simplicity, XML is becoming an important standard for information exchange among diverse systems across the Internet.

- All XML documents require exactly one root element, which is the single element that contains all other elements. The root element defines what the XML document is about.
- In Visual Studio 2005, some additional special processing is required to display the XML data contained within a nested element. You can retrieve and display related data in a relational database using an SQL statement that includes a JOIN operation. Retrieving and displaying related data in an XML file is a little more challenging.
- A Web service is a class (including its methods) that is available over a network such as the Internet or an intranet. Thus, an ASP.NET application that you create and run on one computer can use a Web service (particularly, its methods) located on another computer. Using Web services, your application can access useful and sophisticated code made available by other developers over the Internet. Note that Web services make heavy use of XML files.
- In an intra-organizational use of Web services, an organization places important parts of an application, such as business logic or database processing, on a Web server to be used by many client computers that have Internet or intranet access. In an interorganizational use of Web services, multiple organizations share their applications via Web services.
- Web services are based on three primary standards: WSDL (Web Services Description Language), UDDI (Universal description, discovery, and integration), and SOAP (Simple Object Access Protocol). WSDL describes a Web service, UDDI makes Web services known to potential users, and SOAP makes Web services accessible.

Key Terms

markup language—A language that uses tags to describe the structure and content of its files.

metalanguage—A language about a language.

root element—The single element in an XML file that contains all other elements.

SOAP (Simple Object Access Protocol)—A protocol for exchanging XML-based messages over a computer network, normally using HTTP.

UDDI (Universal description, discovery, and integration)—An XML-based standard that businesses use to publish and find Web services.

Web service—A class that is available over a network.

WSDL (Web Services Description Language)—An XML-formatted language used to completely describe a Web service.

XML parser—Software that understands how to interpret XML files.

XML (eXtensible Markup Language)—A standard for creating markup languages that describe the structure of data.

Review Questions

1. ADO.NET is used for database access in Web applications.
   a. True
   b. False
2. In an ASP.NET Web site, databases are usually stored in the App_Data folder.
   a. True
   b. False
3. The Configure Data Source Wizard for a `GridView` allows for both optimistic and pessimistic concurrency.
   a. True
   b. False
4. A primary key field in a `GridView` control will automatically be read-only.
   a. True
   b. False
5. A `DetailsView` control shows more detailed information than a GridView control.
   a. True
   b. False
6. Displaying nested XML elements in a GridView requires an XPath expression.
   a. True
   b. False
7. Web services should have many business-to-business applications.
   a. True
   b. False
8. An ASP.NET Web service file has an extension .asmx.
   a. True
   b. False
9. To access a Web service called WebService1 on a different computer would require the code `localhost.WebService1`.
   a. True
   b. False
10. When ASP.NET adds a Web reference for a Web service, it creates a DISCO file.
    a. True
    b. False
11. Which technology is primarily responsible for transmitting Web services?
    a. SOAP
    b. FTP
    c. WSDL
    d. UDDI
12. The ASP.NET `GridView` control is in the ____ section of the Toolbox.
    a. Standard
    b. Data
    c. HTML
    d. WebParts

13. Which option from the GridView Tasks menu should be selected in case the structure of a database has changed?
    a. Auto Format
    b. Choose Data Source
    c. Configure Data Source
    d. Refresh Schema
14. Which of the following options is not automatically available for a `GridView` control?
    a. sort rows
    b. edit rows
    c. insert rows
    d. delete rows
15. To change the header text displayed by a `GridView` control, which GridView Tasks menu should be selected?
    a. Refresh Schema
    b. Choose Data Source
    c. Auto Format
    d. Edit Fields
16. XML stands for extensible _____ language.
    a. meta
    b. markup
    c. messaging
    d. multimedia
17. How many root elements can a valid XML file contain?
    a. 0
    b. 1
    c. 2
    d. unlimited
18. A Web service is basically a(n) _____.
    a. HTML document
    b. method
    c. function
    d. class
19. Which technology is primarily responsible for publishing Web services?
    a. SOAP
    b. FTP
    c. WSDL
    d. UDDI
20. What is normally used for a Web service namespace?
    a. e-mail address
    b. IP address
    c. URL
    d. telephone number

Computer Exercises

Exercises 1–3 assume that you have installed Microsoft SQL Server 2005 Express Edition on your computer. When creating user interfaces, follow all conventions for an attractive, organized form with meaningful names for controls. Also follow all conventions for writing Visual Basic code and SQL statements. Your instructor may also request that you use TOE charts, pseudocode, flowcharts, ER diagrams, and/or UML diagrams as planning aids.

1. In this exercise you create a Web application that displays the contents of the Products table in the Store database using a `GridView` object.
   a. Create a Web site called **Store Products GridView Display**. Save the application in the \VBReloadedAdvanced\Chap10 folder.
   b. Design and create a Web form that uses a `GridView` control to display the contents of the Products table in the Store database.
   c. Add explanatory text to the Web form and give the `GridView` an attractive format.
   d. Add sorting capability to all columns in the `GridView`.
   e. Save the solution, test the application, and modify as necessary.

2. In this exercise you create a Web application that displays the contents of the Products table in the Store database using a `GridView` object with update and delete capabilities.
   a. Create a Web site called **Store Products GridView Update**. Save the application in the \VBReloadedAdvanced\Chap10 folder.
   b. Design and create a Web form that uses a `GridView` control to display the contents of the Products table in the Store database.
   c. Add explanatory text to the Web form and give the `GridView` an attractive format.
   d. Add sorting capability to all columns in the `GridView`.
   e. Add update and delete capabilities to the `GridView`.
   f. Save the solution, test the application, and modify as necessary.

3. In this exercise you create a Web application that displays the contents of the Products table in the Store database using a `DetailsView` control with update, insert, and delete capabilities.
   a. Create a Web site called **Store Products DetailsView Update**. Save the application in the \VBReloadedAdvanced\Chap10 folder.
   b. Design and create a Web form that uses a `DetailsView` control to display the contents of the Products table in the Store database.
   c. Add header text to the `DetailsView` control and give it an attractive format.
   d. Add update, insert, and delete capabilities to the `GridView`.
   e. Save the solution, test the application, and modify as necessary.

4. In this exercise you create an XML file and create a Web application to view it.
   a. Create an XML file called **CdCollection.xml**. Save the file in the \VBReloadedAdvanced\Chap10 folder.
   b. Use a root element called `cdcollection`. The root should contain a `cd` element with attributes `cd_id`, `cd_title`, and `cd_artist`. The `cd` element should contain a `track` element with attributes `track_title`, `track_artist`, and `track_time`.
   c. Save the file and view it in a Web browser. Modify as necessary.
   d. Create a Web site called **Display CDs**. Save the application in the \VBReloadedAdvanced\Chap10 folder.

e. Design a Web form that uses a `GridView` to display only the basic CD information from CdCollection.xml.
f. Add explanatory text to the Web form and give the `GridView` an attractive format.
g. Add sorting capability to all columns in the `GridView`.
h. Save the solution, test the application, and modify as necessary.

5. In this exercise you modify the solution to Exercise 4 so that the track data of a CD are displayed.
   a. Copy the project Display CDs folder in the \VBReloadedAdvanced\Chap10 folder and rename it **Display CD Tracks**.
   b. Add the capability to click a Select button for a CD row in the GridView and display the track data for that CD.
   c. Give the GridView an attractive format and add explanatory text to the Web form.
   d. Save the solution, test the application, and modify as necessary.

6. In this exercise you create a Web service that calculates the number of days until a specified date.
   a. Create a Web service project called **DaysUntilService**. Save the project in the \VBReloadedAdvanced\Chap10 folder.
   b. Using the `Date` data type and the `DateDiff` function, create a Web service that determines the number of days between the current date (Now) and a specific future date.
   c. Save and test the Web service from within Visual Studio and modify as necessary.
   d. Copy the Web service project to the Personal Web Server on your local machine (within C:\Inetpub\wwwroot\) or an external Web server that is available to you.
   e. Test the Web service on the Web server.

7. In this exercise you create a project that uses the Web service created in Exercise 6.
   a. Create an ASP.NET project called **Days Until**. Save the application in the \VBReloadedAdvanced\Chap10 folder.
   b. Create an attractive Web form that collects a future date from the user in the format mm/dd/yyyy using a TextBox Web control.
   c. When the user clicks a Button Web control, the number of days until that date should be displayed in a Label Web control, using the Web service you created in Exercise 6. (Note: The Web service should be on your localhost or an external Web server.)
   d. Save the solution, test the application, and modify as necessary.

Case Projects

The Northwind Customers Web Site

Using ASP.NET, create a Web site called **Northwind Customers** that allows the user to display, update, and delete records in the Customers table of the Northwind database using a `GridView` control. Add an attractive format to the `GridView` control.

Northwind Customers with XML

Create an XML file called northwind.xml that contains several records from the Customers table in the Northwind database. Use `northwind` as the root element, which contains nested elements for `customer`, `address`, and `phonenumbers`. Display these records in the XML file using a `GridView` control in an ASP.NET Web site called **NorthwindXML**.

Days Until Your Birthday

Create a Web application called **Days Until Your Birthday**. The Web application uses an ASP.NET Web form in which the user enters her name and birthdate. Create a Web service called **Days Between Dates** that calculates the number of days between two dates. The Web application uses this Web service to display a message to the user that includes the user's name and the number of days until the user's next birthday.

CHAPTER

11 Arrays, Collections, and Generics

After studying Chapter 11, you should be able to:

- Use several different methods in the `Array` class
- Create and use a variety of classes in the `System.Collections` namespace
- Use predefined generic classes in the `System.Collections.Generic` namespace
- Create and use programmer-defined generic classes and procedures

MORE ABOUT ARRAYS

In a programming context, a **collection** is simply an object that contains a set of related items. In your study of Visual Basic, you have already encountered a collection called an array, which can store items with data types known as value types (such as `Integer`, `Double`, `Char`, `Boolean`, and `Date` data types) or references types (such as `String` or data types that you define with classes). A **value type** is a data type of a variable for which the variable contains the actual value. A **reference type** is a data type of a variable for which the variable contains a reference to the memory location that stores the actual value. The distinction is important because some of the methods for manipulating collections (such as `Sort`) depend on whether they contain value types or reference types.

An array is just one kind of **data structure** (a way of organizing data in computer memory). Recall that an array is a simple data structure consisting of a fixed set of sequentially indexed items (beginning with index 0), all having the same data type. One of the key characteristics of an array is that it has a fixed size, which limits its flexibility and applicability for various programming needs. For example, it is very difficult to add or delete items from an array. However, if you know beforehand exactly how many items a data structure needs to hold, and that all the items have the same data type, an array is very efficient. Chapter 2 covered a few basic features of arrays, but now you will take a closer look at some of their more advanced features. This will also set the stage for a study of other kinds of collections, such as `ArrayList`, `Stack`, and `Queue`.

Creating a One-Dimensional Array

As discussed in Chapter 2, a simple one-dimensional array is usually declared as a variable with parentheses. Figure 11.1 shows the ArrayTest application that creates and resizes an array.

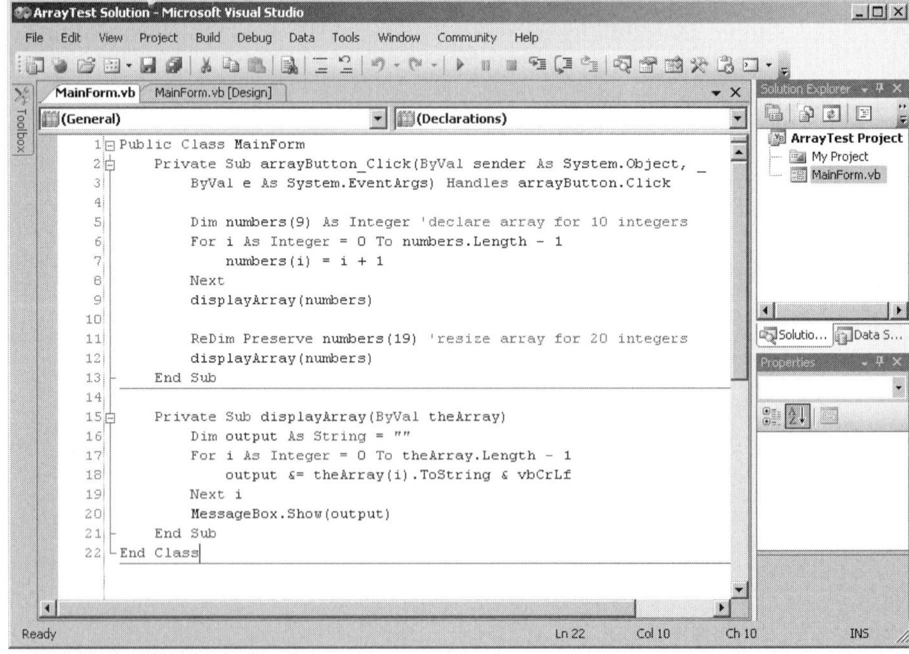

FIGURE 11.1 Program code for the ArrayTest application

In Figure 11.1, the `arrayButton_Click` procedure declares the `numbers` array and populates it with values 1 through 10. The `displayArray` procedure (Line 9) is called to display the array contents in a `MessageBox`. Then, the array is redimensioned to size 20 using the `ReDim` statement and `Preserve` keyword (Line 11). Using the `Preserve` keyword preserves the existing values in the array. (Without `Preserve`, all existing values would be lost when the array is redimensioned.) A sample run of the ArrayTest application is shown in Figure 11.2.

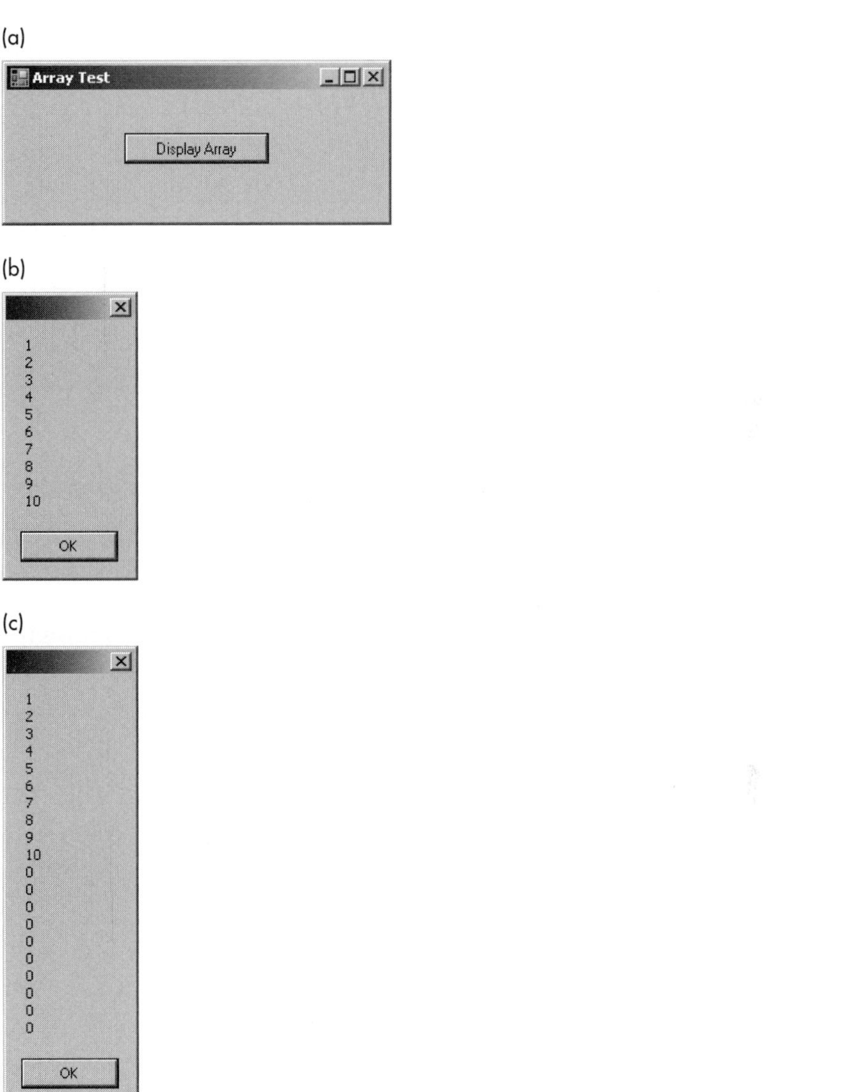

FIGURE 11.2 Sample run of the ArrayTest application

Basic Methods of the `Array` Class

The application in Figure 11.1 simply created an array, which is an instance of the `Array` class. The `Array` class contains many methods for creating, manipulating, searching, and sorting arrays that may be new to you. Some of these methods are very basic and easy to use, while others require additional programming support. Figure 11.3 explains how to use several of the basic methods of the `Array` class.

HOW TO...

Use Basic Methods of the `Array` Class

1. To create an array:

Syntax

`Array.CreateInstance(`*itemType*`,` *length*`)`

Examples

```
'create array that can hold 10 integers
Dim numbers As Array = Array.CreateInstance( _
    GetType(Int32), 10)

'create array that can hold 5 Person objects
Private presidents As Array = Array.CreateInstance( _
    GetType(Person), 5)
```

2. To set or get the item in an array:

Syntax

arrayName`.SetValue(`*item*`,` *index*`)`
arrayName`.GetValue(`*index*`)`

Examples

```
numbers.SetValue(15, 0)
presidents.SetValue(New Person("George", "Washington"), 1)

numbers.GetValue(3)
presidents.GetValue(2)
```

3. To get the length of a particular dimension of an array:

Syntax

arrayName`.GetLength(`*dimension*`)`

Examples

```
' use 0 for first dimension, 1 for second, etc.
numbers.GetLength(0)
```

4. To reverse the items in a one-dimensional array:

Syntax

`Array.Reverse(`*arrayName*`[,` *index*`,` *length*`])`

Examples

```
' reverse all items in presidents
Array.Reverse(presidents)

' beginning with index 5, reverse the next 6 items
Array.Reverse(numbers, 5, 6)
```

FIGURE 11.3 How to use basic methods of the Array class

Item 1 in Figure 11.3 shows how to create an instance of the `Array` class (in other words, an array). Figure 11.1 demonstrates the shortcut syntax for creating an array of 10 integers (`Dim numbers(9) As Integer`), but the code in Item 1 in Figure 11.3 works as well. The `GetType` method is used to establish the data type of the items that are to be stored in the array. The *length* parameter determines the number of items the array can contain. For example, the array `numbers` can hold 10 integers and the array `presidents` can contain five `Person` objects. The `CreateInstance` method is an alternative to the usual shorthand technique for declaring arrays. There is no particular advantage of using `Array.CreateInstance`, other than that it is more firmly grounded in the object-oriented paradigm, which may be desirable to some object-oriented purists.

Item 2 in Figure 11.3 demonstrates how to set or get items in an array. To set an *item*, you specify the item and the position (based on the value of *index*) where it is to be stored. (Recall that array indexes begin with 0.) To get an item, you simply specify the *index*.

Item 3 in Figure 11.3 shows how to determine the size of a particular dimension in an array. The argument 0 is used to get the length of the first dimension, 1 for the second dimension, and so on. (Recall from Chapter 2 that arrays can have one or more dimensions, just as a table can have one or more rows, each of which can have different lengths.) Note that the `Length` property of an array (`arrayName.Length`) can also be used to return the combined total number of items in all dimensions of an array.

Item 4 in Figure 11.3 presents the `Array.Reverse` method, which simply reverses the order of the items in a one-dimensional array. You can either reverse all items or specify just some items for reversal. Reversing items in an array is often used in connection with sorting array items, a technique discussed in upcoming sections.

Advanced Methods of the Array Class

There are many other important methods in the `Array` class, some of which are shown in Figure 11.4. Some of these methods are considered more advanced because they require additional supporting program code.

HOW TO...

Use Advanced Methods of the `Array` Class

1. To get the index of the first occurrence within a one-dimensional array that contains items of a value type or `String`:

Syntax

`Array.IndexOf(`*arrayName*`,` *value* `[,` *startIndex*`,` *count*`])`

Examples

```
'get index of first occurence of 52 in numbers array
Array.IndexOf(numbers, 52)

'get index of first occurence of 52 starting with index 5
Array.IndexOf(numbers, 52, 5)

'get index of first occurence of 52 starting with index 5 for
'for the next 6 items
Array.IndexOf(numbers, 52, 5, 6)
```

2. To get the index of the first occurrence within a one-dimensional array that contains items of a reference type (such as `Person`):

Syntax

`Array.IndexOf(`*arrayName*`,` *object* `[,` *startIndex*`,` *count*`])`

(Figure is continued on next page)

Example of overriding the `Object.Equals` method in the `Person` class

```
Public Overrides Function Equals(ByVal anObject As Object) _
    As Boolean
    'object to which Me will be compared converted to Person
    Dim otherPerson As Person = DirectCast(anObject, Person)

    'represent both objects as strings and call String.Equals
    Return String.Equals(Me.ToString, otherPerson.ToString)
End Function
```

Example of calling the `Array.IndexOf` method

```
  Dim targetIndex As Integer
  Dim targetPerson As Person = New Person( _
      firstNameTextBox.Text, lastNameTextBox.Text)
  targetIndex = Array.IndexOf(presidents, targetPerson)
```

3. To sort a one-dimensional array that contains items of a value type (numeric or `String`):

Syntax

`Array.Sort(`*arrayName***`)`**

Example

`Array.Sort(numbers)`

4. To sort a one-dimensional array that contains items of a reference type (such as `Person`), the class that defines the type must implement the `IComparable` interface and must define a `CompareTo` method for comparing objects of that type.

Syntax

`Array.Sort(`*arrayName***`)`**

Example of implementing the `IComparable` interface in the `Person` class

```
Public Class Person
    Implements IComparable
```

Example of implementing the `CompareTo` method in the `Person` class

```
Public Function CompareTo(ByVal anObject As Object) As Integer _
    Implements System.IComparable.CompareTo

    'object to which Me is compared converted to Person
    Dim otherPerson As Person = DirectCast(anObject, Person)

    'represent both objects as strings
    Return String.Compare(Me.ToString, otherPerson.ToString)
End Function
```

Example of calling the `Array.Sort` method

```
Array.Sort(presidents)
```

(Figure is continued on next page)

5. To perform a binary search for an item in a one-dimensional array (`Array.Sort` must be called before calling `Array.BinarySearch`):

Syntax

`Array.BinarySearch(`*arrayName*`,` *value*`)`

Examples

```
Array.BinarySearch(numbers, 52)
Array.BinarySearch(presidents, "Jefferson, Thomas")
```

FIGURE 11.4 How to use advanced methods of the `Array` class

Item 1 in Figure 11.4 is very straightforward. If the array contains items with value types (such as `Integer`, `Double`, and `Char`), `Array.IndexOf` simply returns the index of the first occurrence of the item in the array (either in the entire array or in specified subsections of the array). Remember that the indexes of an array begin with 0, not 1. If the item is not found, `Array.IndexOf` returns a negative integer.

Item 2 in Figure 11.4 shows how to find the index of array values for items with reference types (such as `String` or `Person`). The `Array.IndexOf` method uses the `Object.Equals` method to compare *object* with each item in the array. However, for reference types, `Object.Equals` determines only whether two variables actually refer to the same object in computer memory, not whether two different objects simply contain the same data values. Therefore, for reference types, the class defining the data type (`Person` in the example) must override the `Object.Equals` method in order to determine whether two different objects have the same value. By converting both objects to strings (using the `ToString` method in the class), the string representations of the objects (that is, their values) can be compared using `String.Equals`. If the string representations are the same, `String.Equals` returns `True`; otherwise, `String.Equals` returns `False`.

Item 3 in Figure 11.4 shows how to sort a one-dimensional array of value types, a very simple proposition. However, if an array contains reference types (such as items of type `Person`), the process of sorting is more involved, as demonstrated in Item 4 of Figure 11.4. First, the class that defines the reference type (`Person`) must implement the `IComparable` interface, which is a unit of Visual Basic code in the .NET Framework that contains just one member, the `CompareTo` method. The `CompareTo` method is a method that compares two objects, and is already defined for objects of predefined reference types, such as `String`. However, for programmer-defined objects, you must override `CompareTo` within the programmer-defined class. In Item 2 (Figure 11.4), the object that is sent to `CompareTo` for comparison is first converted to an object of the required type using the `DirectCast` keyword. (You can compare apples only to apples—that is, you can only compare objects of the same type.) Then the `Return` statement in the `CompareTo` method converts both objects, `Me` (the current object) and `otherPerson` (the object to which `Me` is being compared), to strings using the `ToString` method in the `Person` class. Finally, you call the `String.Compare` method to compare these two string representations of `Person` objects.

Finally, Item 5 in Figure 11.4 demonstrates how to search an array using the `Array.BinarySearch` method. Visual Basic uses an efficient **binary search algorithm** to search the contents of an array. This algorithm compares the target item with the middle value of an array to eliminate half of the array from the search, and repeats this process during each pass of the search. This technique is much faster than a simple sequential search (used by the `Array.IndexOf` method) that compares the target item with every item in the array from first to last. (This is especially true if the array is very large,) Obviously, using `Array.BinarySearch` requires first sorting the array using `Array.Sort`. If the target item is found, `Array.BinarySearch` returns the index of the item (0, 1, 2, ...); otherwise, `Array.BinarySearch` returns a negative integer.

The ArrayMethodsTest application in Figure 11.5 (consisting of the `MainForm` class and the `Person` class) demonstrates many of the methods of the `Array` class, and Figure 11.6 displays the results of a sample run.

(a) `MainForm` class

```
Public Class MainForm
    Private presidents As Array = Array.CreateInstance( _
        GetType(Person), 5)

    Private Sub MainForm_Load(ByVal sender As System.Object, _
        ByVal e As System.EventArgs) Handles MyBase.Load
        'populate array
        presidents.SetValue(New Person("Abraham", "Lincoln"), 3)
        presidents.SetValue(New Person("George", "Washington"), 0)
        presidents.SetValue(New Person("Thomas", "Jefferson"), 1)
        presidents.SetValue(New Person("Andrew", "Jackson"), 2)
        presidents.SetValue(New Person("Theodore", "Roosevelt"), 4)
    End Sub

    Private Sub arrayButton_Click(ByVal sender As System.Object, _
        ByVal e As System.EventArgs) Handles arrayButton.Click
        '0 for a one-dimensional array
        MessageBox.Show("The array contains " & _
            presidents.GetLength(0) & " presidents", "GetLength")
        'display array with caption
        displayArray(presidents, "Presidents")
        Array.Reverse(presidents)
        displayArray(presidents, "Reversed")
    End Sub

    Private Sub searchButton_Click(ByVal sender As System.Object, _
        ByVal e As System.EventArgs) Handles searchButton.Click
        Dim targetIndex As Integer
        Dim targetPerson As Person = New Person( _
            firstNameTextBox.Text, lastNameTextBox.Text)
        targetIndex = Array.IndexOf(presidents, targetPerson)
        MessageBox.Show(targetPerson.ToString & _
            " found at index " & targetIndex, "IndexOf")

        Array.Sort(presidents) 'sort the array before BinarySearch
        displayArray(presidents, "Sorted")

        Dim theCaption As String = "BinarySearch"
        targetIndex = Array.BinarySearch(presidents, targetPerson)
        If targetIndex >= 0 Then
            MessageBox.Show(targetPerson.ToString & _
                " found at index " & targetIndex, theCaption)
        Else
            MessageBox.Show("President not found in list", theCaption)
        End If
    End Sub
```

(Figure is continued on next page)

```
    Private Sub displayArray(ByVal theArray, ByVal theCaption)
        Dim output As String = ""
        For i As Integer = _
            theArray.GetLowerBound(0) To theArray.GetUpperBound(0)
            output &= theArray(i).ToString & vbCrLf
        Next i
        MessageBox.Show(output, theCaption)
    End Sub
End Class
```

(b) `Person` class

```
Public Class Person
    Implements IComparable 'required for Array.Sort

    'instance variables
    Private _firstName As String
    Private _lastName As String

    'constructor
    Public Sub New(ByVal firstName As String, _
        ByVal lastName As String)
        _firstName = firstName
        _lastName = lastName
    End Sub

    Public Overrides Function ToString() As String
        Return _lastName & ", " & _firstName 'last name first
    End Function

    Public Overrides Function Equals(ByVal anObject As Object) _
        As Boolean
        'object to which Me is compared converted to Person
        Dim otherPerson As Person = DirectCast(anObject, Person)
        'represent both objects as strings
        Return String.Equals(Me.ToString, otherPerson.ToString)
    End Function

    Public Function CompareTo(ByVal anObject As Object) As Integer _
        Implements System.IComparable.CompareTo
        'object to which Me is compared converted to Person
        Dim otherPerson As Person = DirectCast(anObject, Person)
        'represent both objects as strings
        Return String.Compare(Me.ToString, otherPerson.ToString)
    End Function
End Class
```

FIGURE 11.5 Program code for the ArrayMethodsTest application—(a) `MainForm` class and (b) `Person` class

(a)

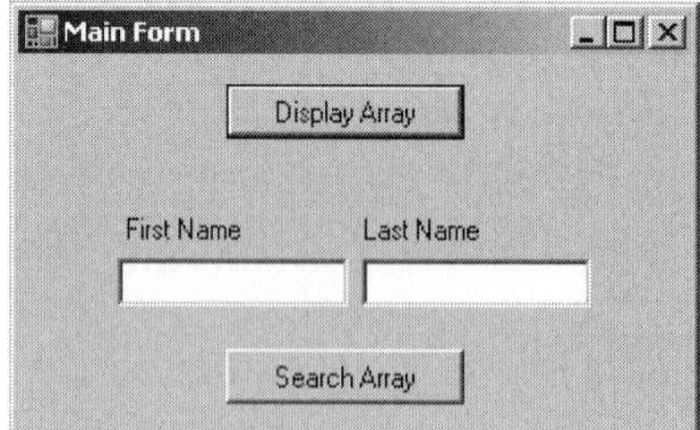
Main Form
Display Array
First Name
Last Name
Search Array

(b)

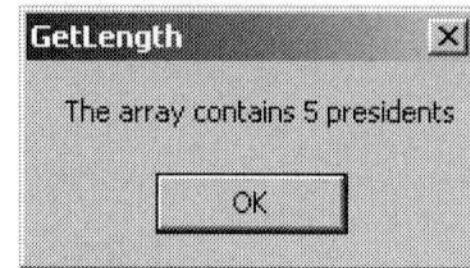
GetLength
The array contains 5 presidents
OK

(c)

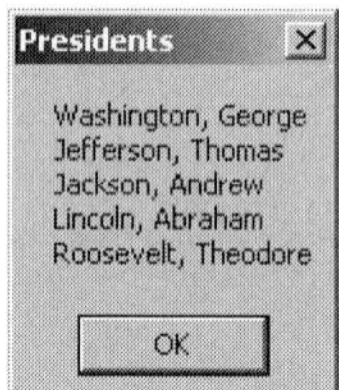
Presidents
Washington, George
Jefferson, Thomas
Jackson, Andrew
Lincoln, Abraham
Roosevelt, Theodore
OK

(d)

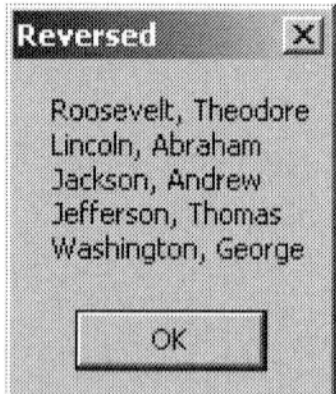
Reversed
Roosevelt, Theodore
Lincoln, Abraham
Jackson, Andrew
Jefferson, Thomas
Washington, George
OK

(e)

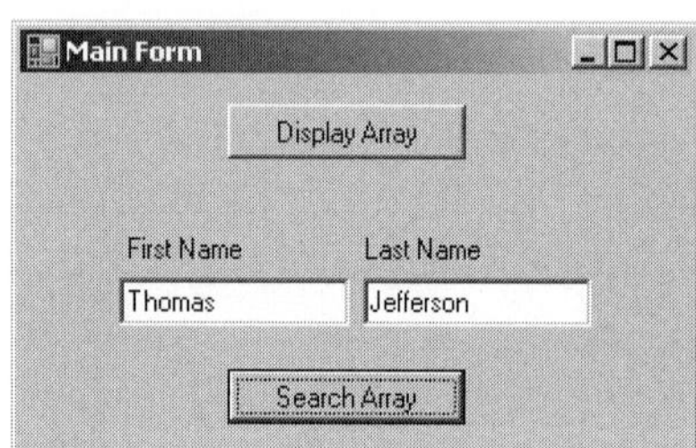
Main Form
Display Array
First Name
Last Name
Thomas
Jefferson
Search Array

(f)

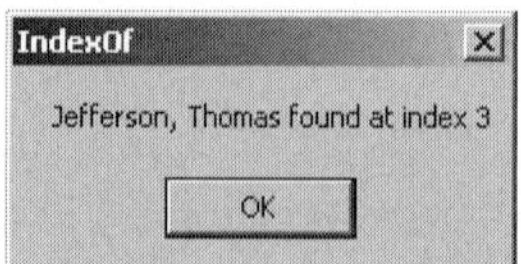
IndexOf
Jefferson, Thomas found at index 3
OK

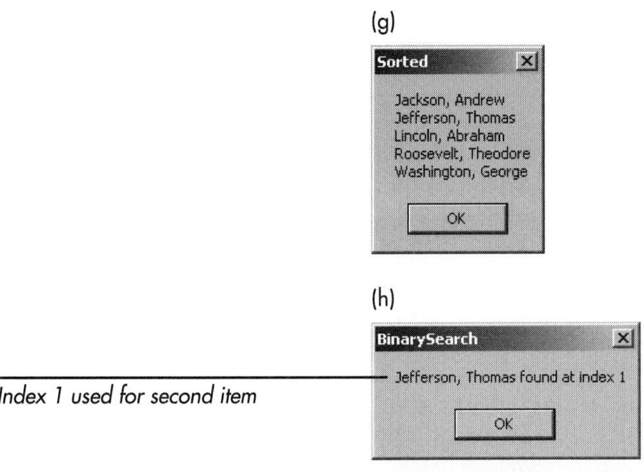

FIGURE 11.6 Sample run of the ArrayMethodsTest application

The `MainForm` class in Figure 11.5(a) begins by creating the `presidents` array (Lines 2–3). The `MainForm_Load` procedure populates the array with `Person` objects (Lines 8–12). Note that the indexes are in the chronological order of the presidencies. The `arrayButton_Click` procedure (called when the Display Array button in Figure 11.6(a) is clicked) displays the `Length` of the array, the array contents, and the reversed contents (Figures 11.6(b), (c), and (d), respectively). Note that the `displayArray` procedure in Figure 11.5(a) is used to display the array contents.

The `searchButton_Click` procedure in Figure 11.5(a) gets the first and last names entered by the user (see Figure 11.6(e)) and creates the `Person` object called `targetPerson` (Lines 29–30). Then the `Array.IndexOf` method uses the `presidents` array and the `targetPerson` object to find the index for Thomas Jefferson (Figure 11.6(f)). Note that the index for Jefferson is 3 (position 4 in Figure 11.6(d), since indexes begin at 0). Then the array is sorted and displayed (Figure 11.6(g)). Finally, a binary search is performed (Line 39) for `targetPerson` (after the sort), which is found at position (not index) 2.

COLLECTIONS

In addition to basic arrays, you can create collections of objects that possess special capabilities that can make your applications easier to create as well as more functional. These special collections are represented by classes in the `System.Collections` namespace of the .NET Framework.

The System.Collections Namespace

The `Array` class discussed in the previous section is in the `System` namespace of the .NET Framework and inherits directly from the `Object` class, also in the `System` namespace. While the array is a very simple and efficient data structure, it also represents a very old and inflexible technology for storing objects. For this reason, the .NET Framework contains the `System.Collections` namespace, which includes interfaces and classes that define various collections of objects, such as lists, queues, bit arrays, hash tables, and dictionaries. These collections have a wide variety of purposes to meet the needs of various kinds of applications. Table 11.1 provides a listing of certain classes in the `System.Collections` namespace and a brief description of each, taken from http://msdn.library.com. Some of the specialized terms in Table 11.1 (such as `Hashtable`, hash code, `Queue`, FIFO, `Stack`, and LIFO) will be explained later in this section.

Class	Description
`ArrayList`	Implements the `IList` interface using an array whose size is dynamically increased as required.
`Hashtable`	Represents a collection of key/value pairs that are organized based on the hash code of the key.
`Queue`	Represents a first-in, first-out (FIFO) collection of objects.
`SortedList`	Represents a collection of key/value pairs that are sorted by the keys and are accessible by key and by index.
`StringCollection`	Represents a collection of strings.
`Stack`	Represents a simple last-in, first-out (LIFO) nongeneric collection of objects. (Generics are discussed later in this chapter.)

TABLE 11.1 Selected classes in the .NET Framework `System.Collections` namespace

The `ArrayList` Class

While the `Array` class is in the `System` namespace of the .NET Framework, the `ArrayList` class is in the `System.Collections` namespace. An `ArrayList` collection is basically a resizable array. This means you can easily add new items at the end of the list, insert items anywhere within the list, and remove existing items from the list, along with a host of other interesting operations.

An `ArrayList` can store any number of different kinds of objects (such as `Integer`, `String`, `Array`, or even `ArrayList`) and can also contain duplicates. If an `ArrayList` does contain objects that are all the same type (such as `String`), you can use the `ArrayList.Sort` method, assuming that the class representing the data type of the `ArrayList` items implements the `IComparable` interface and a `CompareTo` method as discussed earlier in this chapter. The ArrayListTest application in Figure 11.7 demonstrates many of the properties and methods of the `ArrayList` class. You should examine this application carefully to learn many interesting techniques associated with `ArrayList`. A sample run of the ArrayListTest application is displayed in Figure 11.8.

An `ArrayList` Example

```
Public Class MainForm
    Private anArray As Array = Array.CreateInstance( _
        GetType(Integer), 3)

    Private Sub MainForm_Load(ByVal sender As System.Object, _
        ByVal e As System.EventArgs) Handles MyBase.Load
        'create an array of integers
```

(Figure is continued on next page)

```
            anArray.SetValue(1, 0)
            anArray.SetValue(2, 1)
            anArray.SetValue(3, 2)
        End Sub

        Private Sub arrayListButton_Click(ByVal sender As System.Object, _
            ByVal e As System.EventArgs) Handles arrayListButton.Click

            Dim output As String = Nothing
            Dim anArrayList As New ArrayList ' create an ArrayList

            anArrayList.Capacity = 10 ' set capacity of anArrayList to 10
            anArrayList.Add("Hello")
            anArrayList.Add(3.14159)
            anArrayList.Add(anArray) 'add an array to the ArrayList
            anArrayList.Add(anArrayList) 'add an ArrayList to the ArrayList
            displayArrayList(anArrayList, "Original ArrayList")

            anArrayList.Insert(1, "World")
            displayArrayList(anArrayList, "World Inserted")

            anArrayList.Remove(anArray)
            displayArrayList(anArrayList, "anArray Removed")

            output = _
                "Capacity of anArrayList: " & _
                anArrayList.Capacity & vbCrLf & _
                "Number of items in anArrayList: " & _
                anArrayList.Count & vbCrLf

            MessageBox.Show(output)
            anArrayList.TrimToSize()

            anArrayList.Add(anArray)
            displayArrayList(anArrayList, "anArray Added")

            output = _
                "Capacity of anArrayList: " & _
                anArrayList.Capacity & vbCrLf & _
                "Number of items in anArrayList: " & _
                anArrayList.Count & vbCrLf

            If anArrayList.Contains(anArray) Then
                output &= "Index of anArray: " &
                          anArrayList.IndexOf(anArray)
            End If
            MessageBox.Show(output)
        End Sub

        Private Sub displayArrayList(ByVal theArrayList As ArrayList, _
            ByVal theCaption As String)

            Dim output As String = Nothing
            Dim dataType As Type

            For i As Integer = 0 To theArrayList.Count - 1
                dataType = theArrayList(i).GetType
                If dataType.ToString.EndsWith("[]") Then ' an array
                    For j As Integer = 0 To theArrayList(i).Length - 1
                        output &= "The ArrayList item(" & i & ", " & _
                            j & "): " & theArrayList(i)(j) & vbCrLf
                    Next
```

(Figure is continued on next page)

```
            ElseIf _
                dataType.ToString.EndsWith("ArrayList") Then
                For k As Integer = 0 To theArrayList(i).Count - 1
                    output &= "The ArrayList item(" & i & ", " & _
                    k & "): " & theArrayList(i)(k).ToString & vbCrLf
                Next
            Else
                output &= "The ArrayList item(" & i & "): " & _
                theArrayList(i).ToString() & vbCrLf
            End If
        Next
        MessageBox.Show(output, theCaption)
    End SubEnd Class
```

FIGURE 11.7 Program code for the ArrayListTest application

(a)

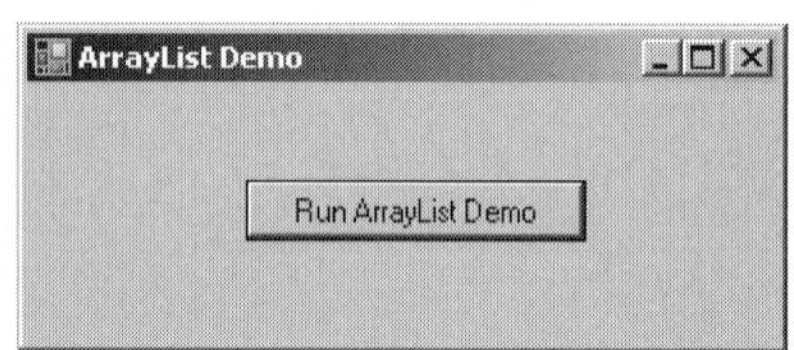

(b)

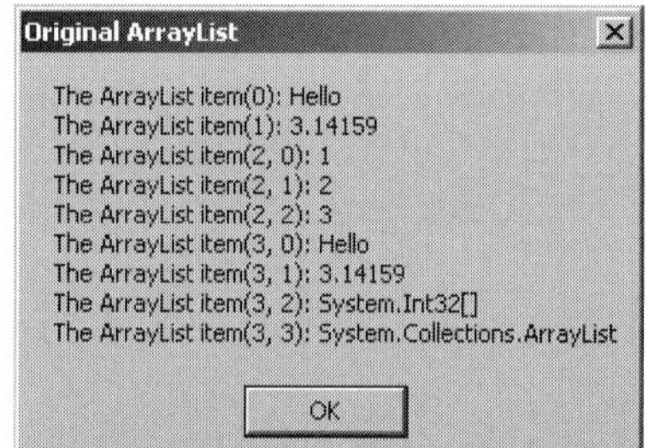

(c)

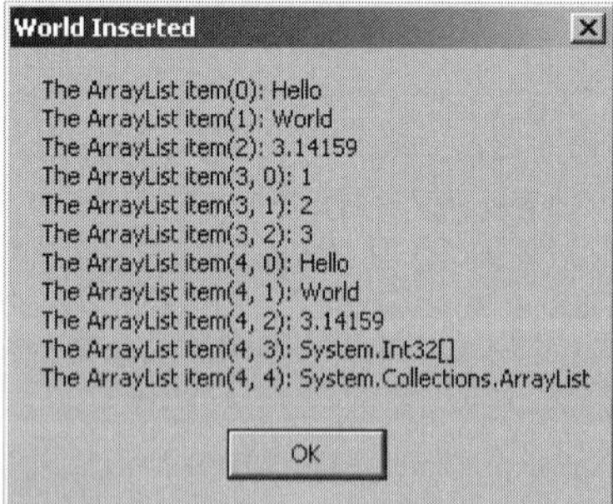

(d)

(e)

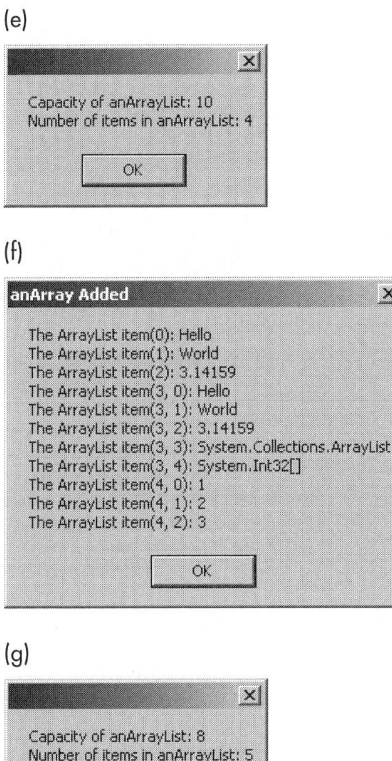

FIGURE 11.8 Sample run of the ArrayListTest application

The user interface in Figure 11.8(a) contains a button to begin the demonstration. Next, turn your attention to the program code in Figure 11.7. When the application runs, `anArray` is created to hold three integers (Lines 2–3). When `MainForm` loads, the `SetValue` method stores 1, 2, and 3 in `anArray` (Lines 8–10). When the `arrayListButton` is clicked, `anArrayList` is created (Line 17) with a `Capacity` of 10. Then, a `String`, a `Double`, an `Array`, and an `ArrayList` (all different types of objects) are added to `anArrayList` (Lines 20–23). The programmer-defined method `displayArrayList` is called to display `anArrayList` (Line 24) with the result shown in Figure 11.8(b).

You should examine the output in Figure 11.8(b) very carefully. The `displayArrayList` method (Lines 57–82) is defined to display `ArrayList` items that contain single values (such as the string `"Hello"` or the number `3.14159`) or the individual items of an array (where `dataType` ends with `"[]"`) or of an `ArrayList` (where `dataType` ends with `"ArrayList"`). Thus, Figure 11.8(b) displays `anArrayList(0)` as `Hello`, `anArrayList(1)` as `3.14159`, `anArrayList(2)` as the contents of `anArray` (`1`, `2`, `3`), and `anArrayList(3)` as the contents of `anArrayList` (`Hello`, `3.14159`, `System.Int32[]`, and `System.Collections.ArrayList`).

After Figure 11.8(b) is displayed, the `MainForm` class in Figure 11.7 inserts the string `"World"` in `anArrayList` at index 1 (Line 26) and displays the output in Figure 11.8(c). Then `MainForm` removes `anArray` from `anArrayList` (Line 29) and displays the output in Figure 11.8(d). The `Capacity` and `Count` properties of `anArrayList` are utilized (Lines 32–36) to display the output in Figure 11.8(e). The `Count` of `anArrayList` is 4 because it contains two strings, a number, and an `ArrayList` object.

Next, `MainForm` calls the `TrimToSize` method (Line 39); this method reduces the `Capacity` of `anArrayList` from 10 to its `Count`, which is 4. Then, `anArray` is added back to `anArrayList` at the end of the array using the `Add` method (Line 41), resulting in the output displayed in Figure 11.8(f). The `Contains` method is called (Line 50) to determine whether `anArrayList` contains the object `anArray`. If so, the `IndexOf` method is called to determine the index of `anArray`. Finally, the output string is displayed in Figure 11.8(g). Note that the `Capacity` has increased from 4 to 8, a seemingly unusual result due to the addition of `anArray` to `anArrayList`. However, Visual Basic is assuming that when `anArray` is added, the `Capacity` should increase by one (for the `anArray` object) plus three (for the three items contained within `anArray`).

The `StringCollection` Class

An `ArrayList` is a **weakly typed data structure**—that is, a data structure that is not checked at compile time for consistency of its items' data types. This is because an `ArrayList` can contain any and all kinds of objects, as evidenced in Figure 11.7 where a `String`, `Double`, `Array`, and `ArrayList` are all stored in an `ArrayList`.

A data structure that is identical to an `ArrayList`, but can contain only strings, is represented by the `StringCollection` class. A `StringCollection`, as the name implies, is a collection of strings (and only strings). Thus, `StringCollection` is a **strongly typed data structure**—that is, a data structure that is checked at compile time for consistency of the items' data type. If you need a collection that will contain only strings, you should use `StringCollection` instead of `ArrayList` because it is strongly typed and will provide extra type checking. Otherwise, all the properties and methods of the `ArrayList` class apply equally to `StringCollection`.

The `Stack` Class

An `ArrayList` is simply a collection of objects that can be manipulated in certain predefined ways (added, inserted, removed, sorted, etc.). However, there is no additional special meaning associated with an `ArrayList`.

In some applications, it is desirable to have data structures that can be manipulated only in very special ways. One of these is called a stack. A **stack** is a data structure that operates on the principle of last-in, first-out (or, LIFO, pronounced "life-o"). This means that the last item added to the data structure must be the first item removed from the data structure.

When discussing the LIFO principle, it's common to say that items are pushed onto a stack and popped off of a stack. The usual analogy is a spring-loaded stack of plates that you might find at your buffet restaurant. Workers must ordinarily add clean plates to the top of an existing stack, while customers can likewise remove such plates only from the top of the stack. Thus, the last plate pushed onto the stack is always the first plate popped off the stack. For example, if you are writing an application that simulates the operation of an elevator, you might want to use a stack data structure because the last person in the elevator is often the first person out of the elevator.

In Visual Basic, a stack data structure is defined by the `Stack` class in the `System.Collections` namespace. The `Stack` class has many of the same properties and methods as the `ArrayList` class (such as `Count`, `Clear`, `Contains`, `CopyTo`, `ToArray`, and `ToString`), but it also has many properties and methods that are unique (such as `Peek`, `Pop`, and `Push`). Note that the `Push` and `Pop` methods in the `Stack` class are used in a manner similar to the `Add` and `Remove` methods in the `ArrayList` class. The difference is that items are added to an `ArrayList` at the end by default (or can be inserted anywhere) and can be removed from anywhere in the `ArrayList`, but items in a `Stack` can be added or removed (never inserted) only according to the LIFO rule.

A `Stack` Example

Figure 11.9 presents the program code for the StackTest application. This application allows the user to enter one or more words in a `TextBox` and then displays the words in reverse order. It does so by utilizing a stack data structure. The string of words is dissected into individual words that are placed (pushed) onto a stack. When all words are in the stack, the application removes (pops) each word off the stack, adding each one to an output string. Thus, the output string contains the original words in reverse order.

```
Public Class MainForm
    Private wordStack As New Stack 'create stack

    Private Sub executeButton_Click(ByVal sender As System.Object, _
        ByVal e As System.EventArgs) Handles executeButton.Click
        'get string from text box and trim leading/trailing separators
        Dim restOfString As String = stringTextBox.Text.Trim
        Dim displayString As String = displayLabel.Text & " "
        Dim aWord As String = Nothing
        Dim separator As String = " " 'space is the separator
        Dim beginningIndex As Integer = 0
        'use String.IndexOf method to find separator (delimiter)
        Dim indexOfNextSeparator = restOfString.IndexOf(separator)

        If restOfString <> String.Empty Then 'user entered something
            If indexOfNextSeparator < 0 Then 'only one word entered
                wordStack.Push(restOfString)
            Else 'more than one word was entered
                While indexOfNextSeparator > 0 'while separator exists
                    'get first word in string using String.Substring
                    aWord = restOfString.Substring(beginningIndex, _
                        indexOfNextSeparator)
                    wordStack.Push(aWord) 'push aWord onto stack
                    'get rest of string, trim leading/trailing spaces
                    restOfString = restOfString.Substring( _
                        indexOfNextSeparator).Trim
                    'get next index of separator
                    indexOfNextSeparator = _
                        restOfString.IndexOf(separator)
                End While
                wordStack.Push(restOfString) 'push last word onto stack
            End If
            'for all stack items
            For i As Integer = 0 To wordStack.Count - 1
                'peek into the stack
                MessageBox.Show("The next item on the stack is " & _
                    wordStack.Peek())
                aWord = wordStack.Pop() 'pop the first item from stack
                displayString &= aWord & " " 'append aWord
            Next
            displayLabel.Text = displayString 'display reversed words
            MessageBox.Show("Finished with the current string")
            'reset
```

(Figure is continued on next page)

```
44             displayLabel.Text = "Result: "
45             stringTextBox.Text = String.Empty
46         Else
47             MessageBox.Show("No string was entered")
48         End If
49     End Sub
50 End Class
```

FIGURE 11.9 Program code for the StackTest application

The `MainForm` class in Figure 11.9 begins by creating the `Stack` object called `wordStack` (Line 2). When the user clicks the `executeButton`, the application uses the `Trim` method in the `String` class to remove any leading or trailing spaces from the string (stored in the variable `restOfString`) entered by the user in the `stringTextBox` (Line 7). The output from the application is stored in `displayString` (initialized in Line 8). Individual words from the original string are stored in the variable `aWord` (initialized in Line 9). The separator (a.k.a. delimiter) for the words in the original string is defined as the space, or `" "` (Line 10). The `Substring` method in the `String` class is used repeatedly in this application, so the variable `beginningIndex` is initialized (Line 11). The `IndexOf` method of the `String` class is used to find the index of the next separator (actually, the first separator at this point in the application) in `restOfTheString` (Line 13).

The If/Else selection structure (Lines 15–48) in Figure 11.9 begins by examining whether a string has been entered by the user. If so, a nested `If...Else...End If` structure (Lines 16–32) tests whether `indexOfNextSeparator` < 0. (This means a separator character was not found, implying that the user entered only one word.) If not, a `while` loop extracts `aWord`, pushes it onto the `wordStack`, removes `aWord` from the string, and finds the index of the next separator (Lines 19–30). This `while` loop continues as long as the next separator is found. When there are no more separators, flow leaves the `while` loop and the last word is pushed onto the stack (Line 31). The `For...Next` statement (Lines 34–40) uses the `Peek` method to look at the object on top of the stack (without removing it) and then uses the `Pop` method to remove `aWord` from the top of the stack and add it to `displayString`, which is then exhibited in `displayLabel`. A sample run of the `StackTest` application is presented in Figure 11.10.

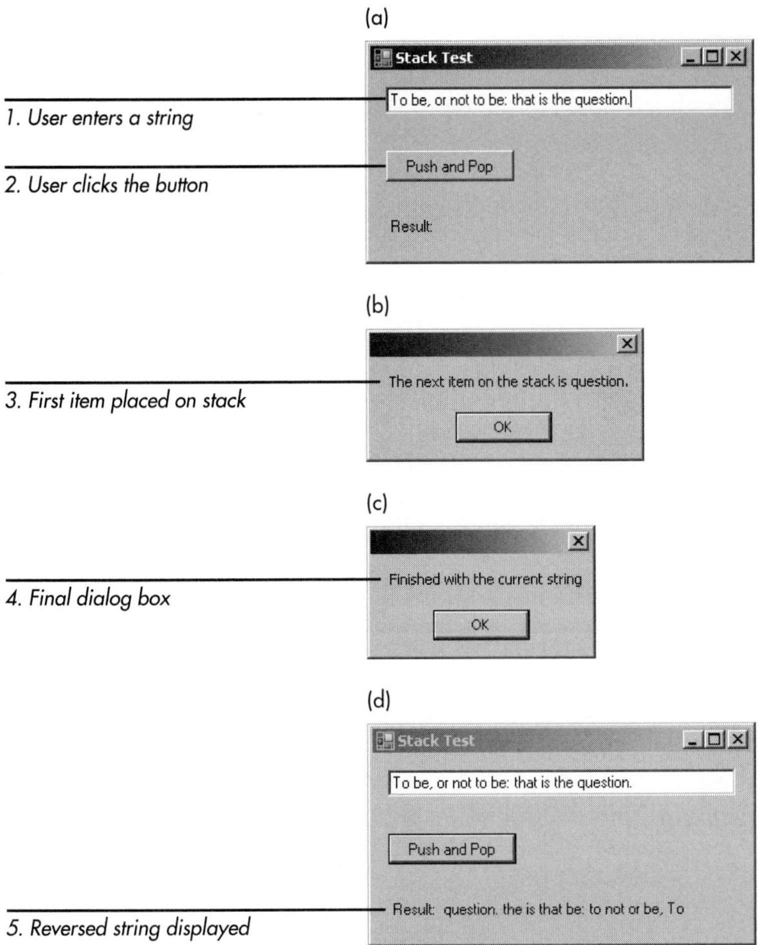

FIGURE 11.10 Sample run of the StackTest application

Note in Figure 11.10(a) that the user entered a famous Shakespeare quote, complete with punctuation: "To be, or not to be: that is the question." The application uses the space (" ") as a separator, so "To" is a word and "be:" is also considered a word. After the user clicks the `executeButton` (the "Push and Pop" button on the user interface) for the first time, the word "question." is displayed as the next (first) item on top of the stack, as Figure 11.10(b) demonstrates. As the user clicks OK on each of the subsequent dialog boxes, the next item on the top of the stack is displayed until all words in the string have been added to the stack (Figure 11.10(c)) and the resulting string appears in `displayLabel`: "question. the is that be: to not or be, To", as shown in Figure 11.10(d).

The `Queue` Class

While a stack data structure represents a collection of objects that follows the last-in, first-out (LIFO) rule, a queue data structure represents a collection of objects that follows the first-in, first-out (FIFO, pronounced "fife-o") rule. In general, a **queue** (any kind of first-in, first-out waiting list) is especially applicable to real-world waiting-in-line situations. If you get in line (or as the British would say, "join the queue"), you will wait (seemingly forever) and eventually (hopefully) leave the line ("exit the queue").

The class `Queue` in the .NET Framework is virtually identical to the class `Stack` with the exception of how objects are added or removed. For a `Stack`, you use the `Push` and `Pop` methods to add and remove objects, respectively. When you call `Push`, an object is added to the top of the stack, and when you call `Pop`, the object currently on top is removed. For a `Queue`, the method `Enqueue` adds an object to the end of the queue and the method `Dequeue` removes an object from the front of the queue. To enforce FIFO, these are the only ways to add and remove objects for a `Queue`. The `Queue` class also has a `TrimToSize` method (as does `ArrayList`) to trim excess capacity. (Visual Basic automatically increases the capacity of a `Queue` as objects are added.) In all other respects, `Queue` and `Stack` are identical. The data structure you choose depends on the requirements of the application.

Figure 11.11 shows a sample run of the QueueTest application, which is interesting because it is essentially identical to the StackTest application. All references to `Stack` have simply been changed to `Queue` (for example, `Queue` replaces `Stack`, `Enqueue` replaces `Push` and `Dequeue` replaces `Pop`). Note in Figure 11.11 that the resulting string is exactly the same as the original string because of FIFO. The details of making the conversion are left as an exercise at the end of this chapter.

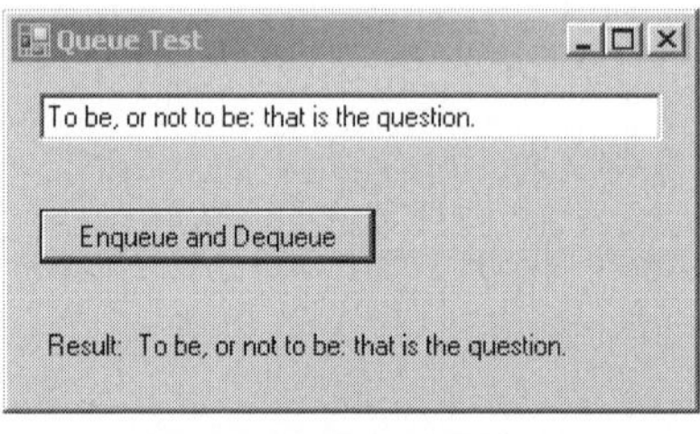

FIGURE 11.11 Sample run of the QueueTest application

The `HashTable` Class

Conceptually, a **hash table** is a data structure with two columns, the first containing a hash code and the second containing an object. Each object is identified by a **key**, which is a field belonging to the object that serves as its unique identifier for storage in a hash table. The **hash code** is a value derived from the key using a **hash function**, which is an algorithm that creates a hash code using the key. The hash function often generates an otherwise meaningless random number that serves as a reference for the object. The value of a hash table is in performing a rapid lookup of objects based on the value of the hash code.

In practice, a hash table is simply an array that contains the objects where the index values of the array items are hash codes (instead of the normal array index values of 0, 1, 2, ..., *n*). Thus, a hash table contains hash codes and objects. Given the key for an object, the hash code can be generated from the hash function. Objects can then be stored or retrieved using the hash code (instead of the key). With a hash table, a very large number of objects in a collection can be accessed much more quickly by searching through relatively few hash codes than by searching through a much larger number of key values directly.

A Hash Table Example

As an example of a hash table, suppose you want to reference a collection of thousands of employees. A common key for employees is the Social Security number (SSN), but a company could create its own unique employee ID number. A hash function for this application could be one that returns that last two digits of the SSN. Therefore, there are exactly 100 hash codes that can be used (00, 01, 02, ..., 99). Suppose an employee Jack Jones has an SSN of 123-45-6789 and employee Mary Maples has a SSN of 987-65-4321. The hash function returns the hash code 89 for Jack Jones and the hash code 21 for Mary Maples. Further, suppose employee Rodney Roberts has an SSN of 658-84-2589. The hash code for this SSN is also 89 (same as Jack Jones). This example is illustrated in Figure 11.12.

Hash Code	Employee
00	
01	
02	
...	
20	
21	Mary Maples (SSN=987-65-4321)
...	
88	
89	Jack Jones (SSN=123-45-6789), Rodney Roberts (SSN =658-84-2589)
...	
99	

FIGURE 11.12 A hash table for storing employees

For a hash table, a **collision** occurs when more than one object has the same hash code (as in the case of Jack Jones and Rodney Roberts). When this happens, **collision resolution** (a process for distinguishing objects that have the same hash code) is required. Collision resolution is often accomplished by storing multiple objects within a **linked list**, another kind of data structure in which each item in the list points to the next item in the list. Thus, each hash code in the hash table can be associated with a linked list (also referred to as a **hash table bucket**) that can contain multiple objects.

Using a hash table, a search for one employee among thousands is executed much faster by first looking through a few hundred hash codes and then performing a linear search within the correct bucket (linked list). Modern databases use techniques similar to hash tables to improve the efficiency of table lookups and queries.

The `HashTable` Class

Visual Basic uses the `HashTable` class to implement the hash table data structure. A `HashTable` contains key-and-value pairs that are organized based on the hash code of the key. The HashTableTest application in Figures 11.13 through 11.15 demonstrates several uses of `HashTable` class members.

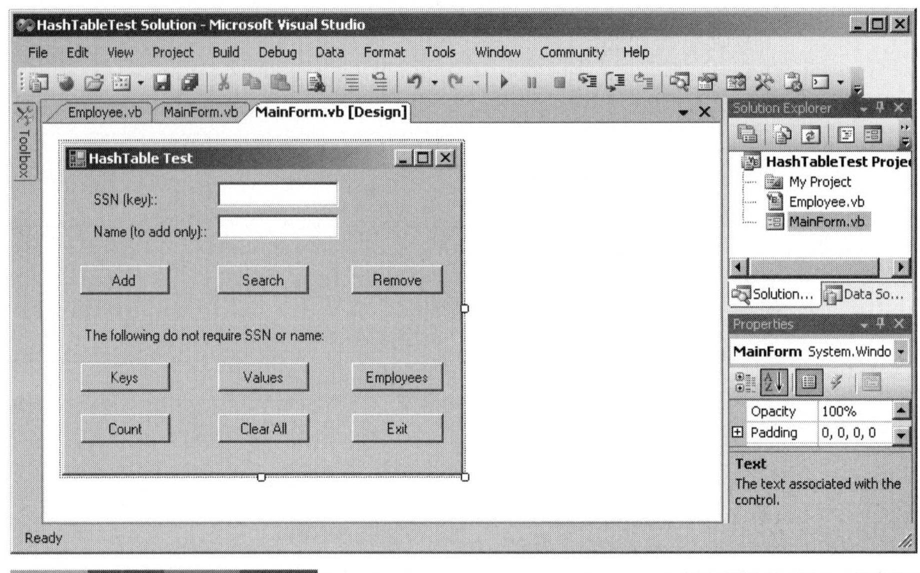

FIGURE 11.13 User interface for the HashTableTest application

The user interface for the HashTableTest application allows the user to enter an SSN and name for an employee, as shown in Figure 11.13. When the application runs, clicking the Add button creates an `Employee` object and adds the SSN and name to a `HashTable` (the SSN is the key and the name is the value). Other buttons in the interface allow the user to enter an SSN and search the `HashTable` for an employee or to enter an SSN and remove the employee from the `HashTable`.

Additionally, buttons exist to display all keys, all values, or all employee data (key-and-value pairs). The interface also allows the user to display the count of employees in the `HashTable` and to clear all entries from the `HashTable`. An Exit button is also provided.

Figure 11.14 shows the program code for the `Employee` class, which has two instance variables (`_employeeSsn` and `_employeeName`). The `ToString` function returns the employee's SSN and name.

Figure 11.15 provides the program code for the `MainForm` class. The `HashTable` called `employeeTable` is created when the application runs (Line 2). Each button in the interface has an event procedure. The `addbutton_Click` procedure (Lines 4–13) takes data from the text boxes, creates an `Employee` object, and adds employee data to the `employeeTable`. The `searchButton_Click` procedure (Lines 15–26) creates the object `foundEmployee` using the `Item` method in the `HashTable` class, which returns the item in `employeeTable` using the key entered in `ssnTextBox`. If `foundEmployee` exists, it is converted to a string and displayed. The `removeButton_Click` procedure (Lines 28–40) uses the `Remove` method (Line 34) to remove the `HashTable` entry with the specified key.

Several buttons in Figure 11.13 do not require any data entry. The `keysButton_Click` procedure (Lines 42–52) declares an item as a `DictionaryEntry` object. The `DictionaryBase` class provides the abstract base class for a strongly typed collection of key-and-value pairs, so an item in a `HashTable` can be declared as a `DictionaryEntry` object. Within a `For Each...Next` statement, each item accesses its `Key` property to display the keys (SSNs) within the `employeeTable`. Likewise, the `valuesButton_Click` procedure (Lines 54–64) displays the values in `employeeTable` (employee names). The `employeesButton_Click` procedure displays both the key and value for the items in `employeeTable`.

Finally, the `countButton_Click` procedure (Lines 77–80) simply displays the count of the items in `employeeTable` using the `Count` property of `HashTable`. The `clearButton_Click` procedure (Lines 82–86) clears all items from the `HashTable` using the `Clear` method. A sample run of the HashTableTest application is shown in Figures 11.16 through 11.18.

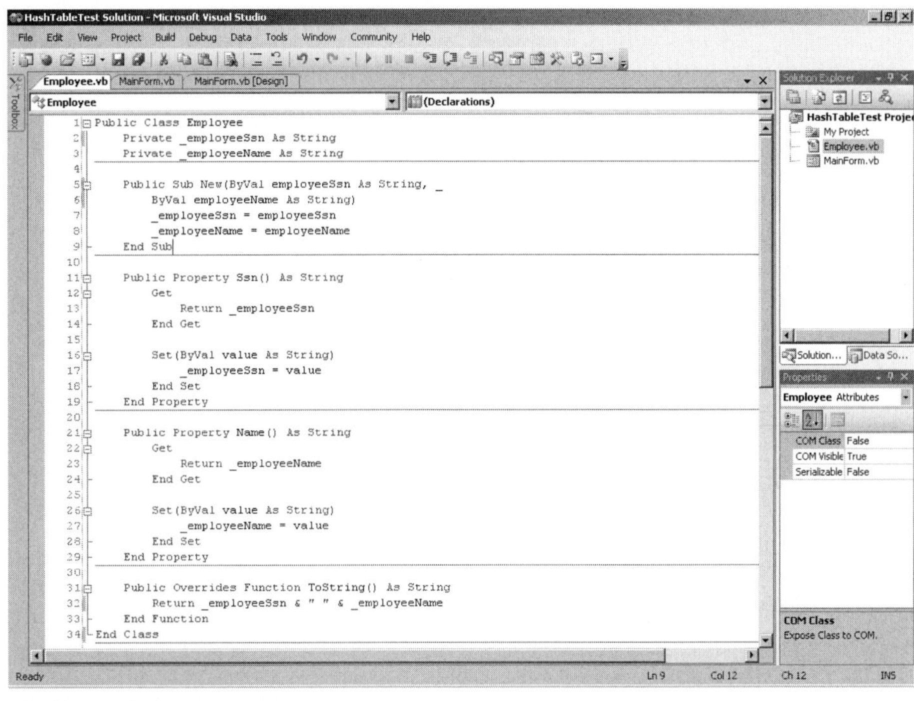

FIGURE 11.14 `Employee` class in the HashTableTest application

```
1  Public Class MainForm
2      Private employeeTable As Hashtable = New Hashtable
3
4      Private Sub addButton_Click(ByVal sender As System.Object, _
5          ByVal e As System.EventArgs) Handles addButton.Click
6          'create Employee object
7          Dim anEmployee As New Employee( _
8              ssnTextBox.Text, nameTextBox.Text)
9          'add anEmployee to HashTable
10         employeeTable.Add(anEmployee.Ssn, anEmployee.Name)
11         MessageBox.Show(anEmployee.ToString, "Added")
12         clearTextBoxes()
13     End Sub
14
15     Private Sub searchButton_Click(ByVal sender As System.Object, _
16         ByVal e As System.EventArgs) Handles searchButton.Click
17         'get entry from HashTable based on SSN key
18         Dim foundEmployee As Object = _
19             employeeTable.Item(ssnTextBox.Text)
20         If Not foundEmployee Is Nothing Then 'object found
21             MessageBox.Show(foundEmployee.ToString, "Search")
```

(Figure is continued on next page)

```
        Else 'object not found
            MessageBox.Show("Employee not found", "Search")
        End If
        clearTextBoxes()
    End Sub

    Private Sub removeButton_Click(ByVal sender As System.Object, _
        ByVal e As System.EventArgs) Handles removeButton.Click
        'get entry from HashTable based on SSN key
        Dim foundEmployee As Object = employeeTable(ssnTextBox.Text)

        If Not foundEmployee Is Nothing Then 'object found
            employeeTable.Remove(ssnTextBox.Text)
            MessageBox.Show(foundEmployee.ToString, "Remove")
        Else 'object not found
            MessageBox.Show("Employee not found", "Remove")
        End If
        clearTextBoxes()
    End Sub

    Private Sub keysButton_Click(ByVal sender As System.Object, _
        ByVal e As System.EventArgs) Handles keysButton.Click

        Dim element As DictionaryEntry
        Dim outputString As String = Nothing

        For Each element In employeeTable
            outputString &= element.Key & vbCrLf
        Next
        MessageBox.Show(outputString, "Keys")
    End Sub

    Private Sub valuesButton_Click(ByVal sender As System.Object, _
        ByVal e As System.EventArgs) Handles valuesButton.Click

        Dim element As DictionaryEntry
        Dim outputString As String = Nothing

        For Each element In employeeTable
            outputString &= element.Value & vbCrLf
        Next
        MessageBox.Show(outputString, "Values")
    End Sub

    Private Sub employeesButton_Click(ByVal sender As System.Object, _
        ByVal e As System.EventArgs) Handles employeesButton.Click
        Dim element As DictionaryEntry
        Dim outputString As String = Nothing
        For Each element In employeeTable
            outputString &= _
                element.Key & ControlChars.Tab & element.Value + vbCrLf
        Next
        MessageBox.Show(outputString, "Employees")
    End Sub

    Private Sub countButton_Click(ByVal sender As System.Object, _
    ByVal e As System.EventArgs) Handles countButton.Click
        MessageBox.Show(employeeTable.Count, "Count of Employees")
    End Sub
```

(Figure is continued on next page)

```
    Private Sub clearButton_Click(ByVal sender As System.Object, _
        ByVal e As System.EventArgs) Handles clearButton.Click
        employeeTable.Clear()
        MessageBox.Show("Employee table cleared", "Clear")
    End Sub

    Private Sub exitButton_Click(ByVal sender As System.Object, _
        ByVal e As System.EventArgs) Handles exitButton.Click
        Me.Close()
    End Sub

    Private Sub clearTextBoxes()
        ssnTextBox.Text = String.Empty
        nameTextBox.Text = String.Empty
    End Sub
End Class
```

FIGURE 11.15 `MainForm` class in the HashTableTest application

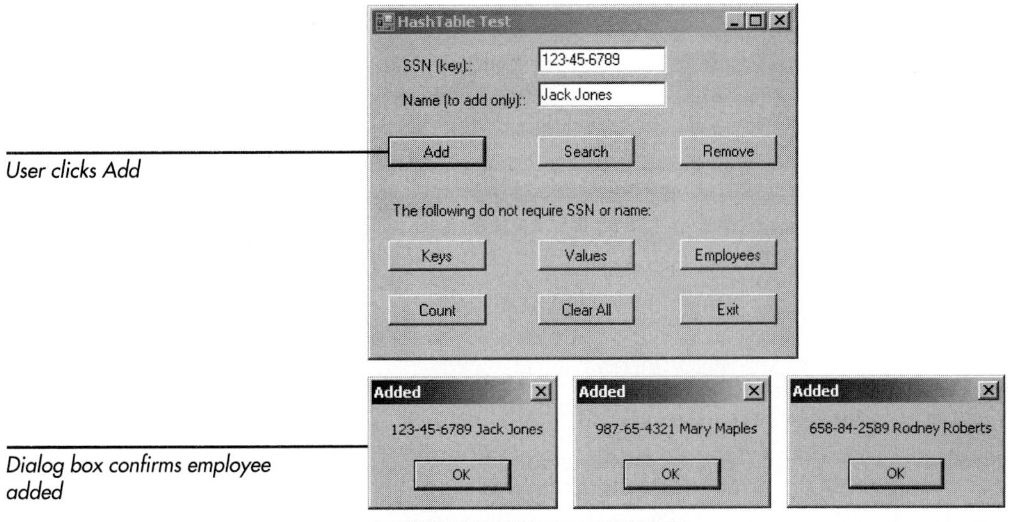

FIGURE 11.16 Adding three employees in the HashTableTest application

(a)

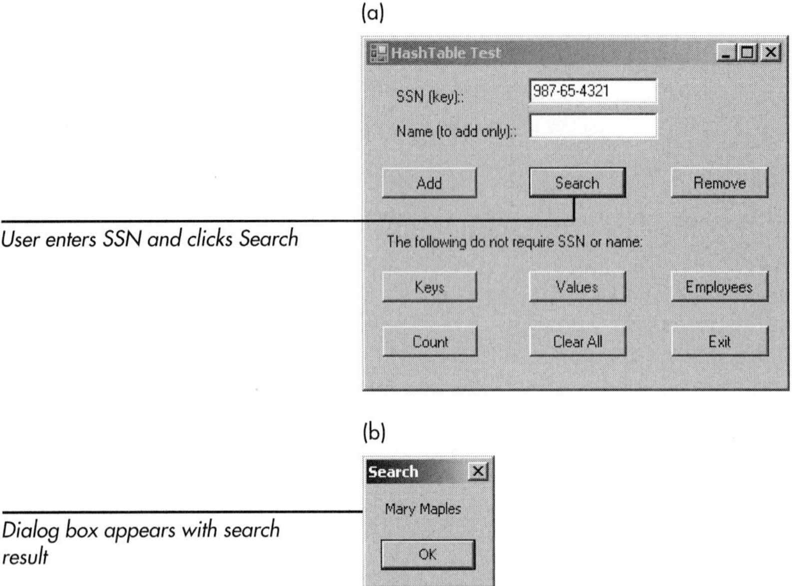

FIGURE 11.17 Searching for an item in the HashTableTest application

(a)

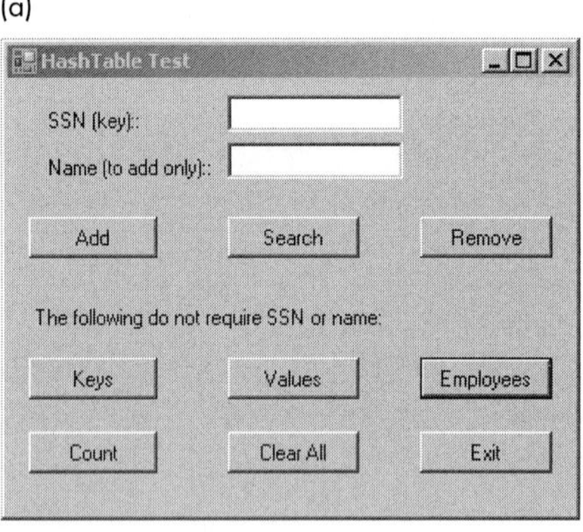

(b)

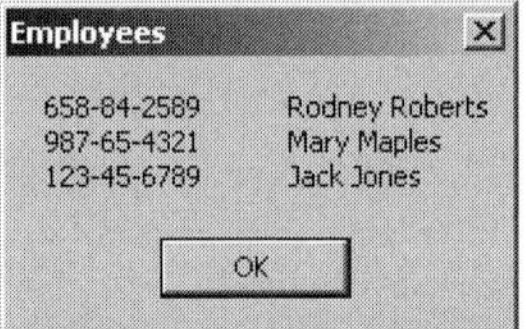

FIGURE 11.18 Displaying all employees in the HashTableTest application

GENERICS

In the dictionary, the term generic means "relating to or characteristic of a whole group or class." Generic items are more general (less specific) than non-generic items. Generic drugs contain the basic, general active ingredient without the specific brand name. (For example, acetaminophen is generic, Tylenol is brand specific). A multipurpose pocketknife (Figure 11.19) is one tool that can perform a wide variety of tasks; it is a generic tool.

FIGURE 11.19 A mulitpurpose pocket knife—a generic tool

In a programming context, **generics** refers to programming elements that can accommodate variables of a wide variety of data types rather than only one specific data type. For example, when you create a procedure in Visual Basic, it is ordinarily defined to accept only variables of specific data types. Likewise, when you create a class, it defines only one specified data type. Then that class can contain only constructors and methods that work for that specific data type. On the other hand, a generic method could conceivably perform the same set of tasks using the same logic on variables of a wide range of data types, or a generic class could define constructors and methods that work for a wide range of data types. Thus, a **generic type** is a single programming element that adapts to perform the same functionality for a variety of data types. This section will explore the versatility offered by generics in Visual Basic.

Advantages of Generics

As a programmer, you can use predefined generic classes or procedures that belong to the .NET Framework and you can create your own programmer-defined generic classes or procedures. Either way, the primary advantage of using generics is code reuse. You can use one class that works with any data type instead of working with a large number of classes that perform similar tasks, one for each different data type (such as `String`, `Integer`, or `Employee`).

Another major advantage is that a generic class defined to use a specific data type becomes strongly typed. For example, a generic `Queue` class defined for `Customer` data types can accept only `Customer` types (not `String` or `Employee`). Strong typing ensures that objects of the wrong type are not allowed to enter the queue, thus helping to avoid programming errors. Also, strong typing with generic classes eliminates the need for Visual Basic to continuously convert items to and from the `Object` data type (known as **boxing**). For example, without strong typing, using the `Enqueue` method to add a `Customer` object to the `Queue` requires conversion from type `Customer` to type `Object`, and the `Dequeue` method requires conversion from type `Object` to type `Customer`. Using generics that are strongly typed can dramatically improve application performance.

The `System.Collections.Generic` Namespace

One important application of generics is that of generic collections. The .NET Framework includes the `System.Collections.Generic` namespace, which contains classes, interfaces, and structures that define generic collections. Some of the more important generic classes in this namespace are listed and briefly described in Table 11.2.

Class Name	Description
Comparer	Provides a base class for implementations of the `IComparer` generic interface.
`Dictionary`	Represents a collection of keys and values.
`LinkedList`	Represents a doubly linked list.
`List`	Represents a strongly typed list of objects that can be accessed by index. Provides methods to search, sort, and manipulate lists.
`Queue`	Represents a first-in, first-out (FIFO) collection of objects.
`SortedDictionary`	Represents a collection of key-and-value pairs that are sorted on the key.
`SortedList`	Represents a collection of key-and-value pairs that are sorted by key based on the associated `IComparer` implementation.
`Stack`	Represents a variable-size last-in, first-out (LIFO) collection of instances of the same arbitrary type.

TABLE 11.2 Selected generic classes in the `System.Collections.Generic` namespace

You will notice in Table 11.2 that there are generic versions of many non-generic collections classes discussed in the previous section of this chapter. For example, the `List` class is the generic version of the nongeneric `ArrayList` class. There are also generic versions of `Stack` and `Queue`.

The `System.Collections.Generic` namespace also contains several interfaces that work with the collection classes. Recall that an interface is a unit of program code that contains methods that are automatically made available to those classes that implement the interface. For example, the generic `IDictionary` interface is the base interface for generic collections of key-and-value pairs, the generic `IComparer` interface defines a method that a type implements to compare two objects, and the `IEnumerator` interface supports a simple iteration over a generic collection. In addition to interfaces, the `System.Collections.Generic` namespace contains structures (that is, data type definitions) to work with generic classes, such as `KeyValuePair` (defines a key-and-value pair object used by the `IDictionary` interface) or `List.Enumerator` (enumerates the items of a `List` used by the `For Each...Next` statement in Visual Basic). The usage of several of these generic classes, interfaces, and structures will now be explored.

Using Predefined Generic Classes

As mentioned earlier, there are generally two ways of using generic classes. One is to use a predefined generic class (such as `List`, `Stack`, or `Queue`) and the other is to define your own programmer-defined generic class. The general syntax for using the generic class `List` to create a specific `List` object is as follows.

```
Dim|Private listName As New List(Of typeParameter)
```

The *typeParameter* is a placeholder for a data type you supply when you declare the type. For example, the following code uses the generic `List` class to create a list called `stringList` that can contain only items of type `String`.

```
Private stringList As New List(Of String)
```

The GenericListTest application uses the generic `List` class to manipulate a list of strings. The user interface for this application is shown in Figure 11.20 and the program code for the `MainForm` class is provided in Figure 11.21.

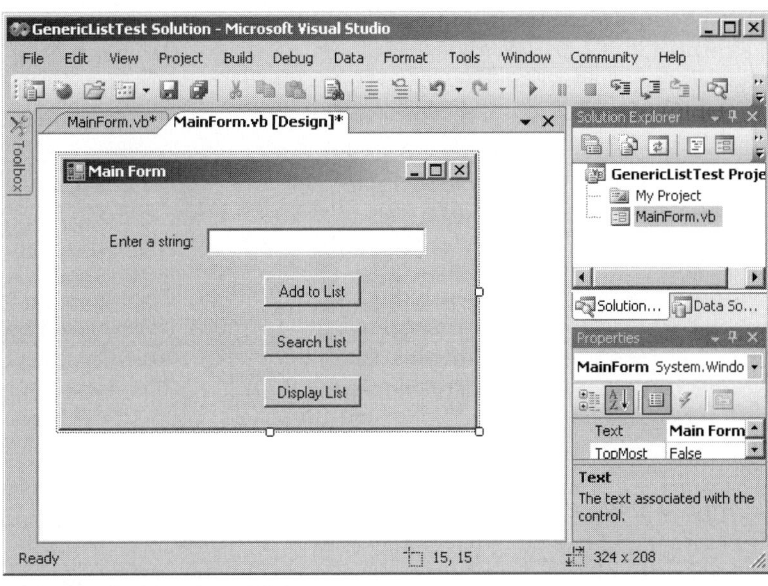

FIGURE 11.20 Interface design for the GenericListTest application

```
Public Class MainForm
    Private stringList As New List(Of String) 'use generic List

    Private Sub addButton_Click(ByVal sender As System.Object, _
        ByVal e As System.EventArgs) Handles addButton.Click
        stringList.Add(stringTextBox.Text)
        'display the last item added to the list
        MessageBox.Show(stringList.Item(stringList.Count - 1), _
            "Added...")
    End Sub

    Private Sub searchButton_Click(ByVal sender As System.Object, _
    ByVal e As System.EventArgs) Handles searchButton.Click
        'stringList.Sort() 'must sort before search
        Dim searchString = stringTextBox.Text
        Dim indexOfString As Integer = _
            stringList.BinarySearch(searchString) 'binary search
        If indexOfString < 0 Then
            MessageBox.Show("'" & searchString & _
                "' not found", "Search")
        Else
            MessageBox.Show("'" & searchString & _
```

(Figure is continued on next page)

```
23                 "' found at position " & indexOfString + 1, "Search")
24             End If
25         End Sub
26 
27         Private Sub displayButton_Click(ByVal sender As System.Object, _
28             ByVal e As System.EventArgs) Handles displayButton.Click
29             Dim outputString As String = String.Empty
30             'For Each uses IEnumerator and List.Enumerator
31             '(behind the scenes)
32             For Each stringElement As String In stringList
33                 outputString &= (stringList.IndexOf(stringElement) + 1) & _
34                 " " & stringElement & vbCrLf
35             Next
36             MessageBox.Show(outputString, "String List")
37         End Sub
38     End Class
```

FIGURE 11.21 Program code for the **MainForm** class in the GenericListTest application

In Figure 11.21, the generic `List` class is used to create `stringList`, a list that can contain only items of type `String` (Line 2). The remainder of the code should be fairly straightforward because of your prior experience with the `ArrayList` class. (Recall that the `List` class is simply the generic version of the `ArrayList` class.) The `addButton_Click` event procedure uses the `Add`, `Item`, and `Count` methods in the `List` class. The `searchButton_Click` event procedure uses the `Sort` and `BinarySearch` methods to display the result of a search for a particular string. (Remember that the `Sort` method must be called prior to `BinarySearch`.) Finally, the `displayButton_Click` event procedure uses the `IndexOf` method (as well as the `IEnumerator` interface and the `List.Enumerator` structure) to display all items in the list. A sample run of the GenericListTest application is shown in Figure 11.22.

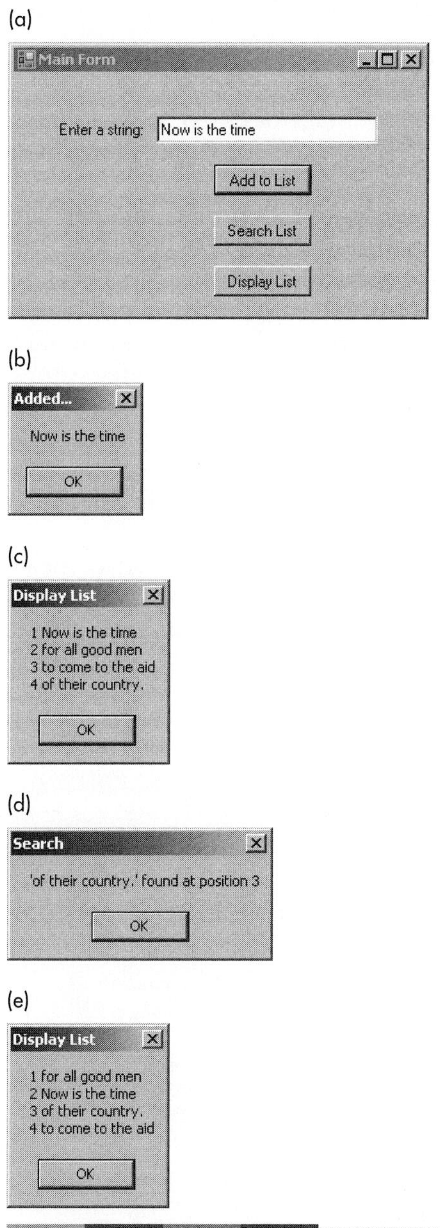

FIGURE 11.22 Sample run of the GenericListTest application

To explain the output shown in Figure 11.22, note the `MainForm` class in Figure 11.22(a). The user has entered a string "Now is the time" and clicked the Add to List button, resulting in the `MessageBox` in Figure 11.22(b). Then the user entered three more strings and clicked the Display List button, resulting in the `MessageBox` in Figure 11.22(c). To search for the string "of their country." the user entered that exact string and clicked the Search List button. The `searchButton_Click` event procedure first must sort the list and then perform a binary search, resulting in the `MessageBox` in Figure 11.22(d). That string is in position 3 (index = 2, since indexes begin with 0) in the list after sorting, as shown in Figure 11.22(e).

Programmer-Defined Generic Classes

The previous section explained how to use Visual Basic predefined generic classes. However, you can also create your own programmer-defined generic classes. The advantage of doing so is that the generic class can be used with a variety of data types (`String`, `Integer`, `Employee`, etc.), allowing for code reuse and strong typing.

Before creating a programmer-defined generic class, consider the GenericListTest application of Figure 11.21. This application uses the predefined generic `List` class to maintain a list of strings. Suppose you want to define a class that maintains the top three items added to a list, regardless of what kind of items they are (`String`, `Integer`, `Employee`, etc.). "Top three" here means the three largest. For example, the top three strings would be the three largest strings in terms of how strings are normally compared (that is, alphabetically). However, the top three employees would need to be defined by a `CompareTo` procedure in the `Employee` class that implements the `IComparable` interface. (Employees can be compared in a variety of ways, such as years of service or annual sales commission.)

Figure 11.23 presents the user interface for a modification of the GenericListTest application (Figures 11.20 through 11.22). This new GenericClassTest application is designed to accept strings from the user as before, but the user interface has a Display Top Three button that displays the three largest strings (the top three in reverse alphabetical order).

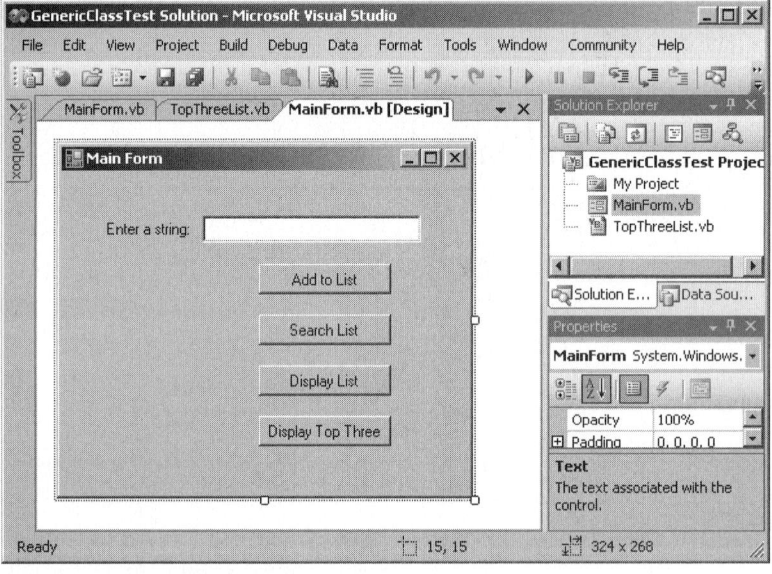

FIGURE 11.23 Interface design for the GenericClassTest application

The difference in the GenericListTest and GenericClassTest applications is that, as strings are added to the `stringList`, they are also added to an object called `topThree`, which is a `List` created from a new generic class called `TopThreeList`. This class is shown in Figure 11.24. Note that `TopThreeList` is a generic class with a type parameter called `ItemType`. `ItemType` can be any value type or reference type (`String`, `Integer`, `Employee`, etc.). This class creates a `List` of `ItemType` objects called `theTopThreeList`. It also defines the `Item` property, which gets or sets items in the list.

Finally, class `TopThreeList` has an `Add` procedure, which does several things. First, if the item is already in `theTopThreeList`, it is removed. (No duplicates are allowed in `theTopThreeList`, although they are allowed in `stringList`.) Then, the new string is added to `theTopThreeList`. Next, `theTopThreeList` is sorted (alphabetically) and then reversed. Last, if there are more than three items in `theTopThreeList`, they are removed using the `RemoveRange` procedure, beginning with index 3 for a total of `theTopThreeList.Count - 3` items.

```
Imports System.Collections.Generic

Public Class TopThreeList(Of ItemType)
    Private theTopThreeList As New List(Of ItemType)

    Public Property Item(ByVal index As Integer) As ItemType
        Get
            Return theTopThreeList(index)
        End Get
        Set(ByVal value As ItemType)
            theTopThreeList(index) = value
        End Set
    End Property

    Public Sub Add(ByVal value As ItemType)
        'no duplicates allowed in topThree
        If theTopThreeList.Contains(value) Then
            theTopThreeList.Remove(value)
        End If
        theTopThreeList.Add(value)
        theTopThreeList.Sort()
        theTopThreeList.Reverse()
        If theTopThreeList.Count > 3 Then
            theTopThreeList.RemoveRange(3, theTopThreeList.Count - 3)
        End If
    End Sub
End Class
```

FIGURE 11.24 Program code for the **`TopThreeList`** class in the GenericClassTest application

The program code for the `MainForm` class in the GenericClassTest application is shown in Figure 11.25. There are only a few differences between this `MainForm` class and the one in Figure 11.21. First, a `TopThreeList` object called `topThree` is instantiated (Line 4), which has `theTopThreeList` as an instance variable, a generic `List`. The next difference is in the `addButton_Click` procedure (Line 9), where the string in `stringTextBox` is added to `theTopThreeList`. Recall that the `Add` procedure in the `TopThreeList` class handles the details of maintaining the three largest strings. The only other difference in `MainForm` is the addition of the `displayTopThreeButton_Click` procedure (Lines 42–51). This procedure simply uses a `For...Next` loop to display the contents of `theTopThreeList`.

```
Public Class MainForm
    Private stringList As New List(Of String) 'use generic List
    'create programmer-defined generic list
    Private topThree As New TopThreeList(Of String)

    Private Sub addButton_Click(ByVal sender As System.Object, _
        ByVal e As System.EventArgs) Handles addButton.Click
        stringList.Add(stringTextBox.Text)
        topThree.Add(stringTextBox.Text) 'add to top three
        'display the last item added to the list
        MessageBox.Show(stringList.Item(stringList.Count - 1), _
            "Added...")
    End Sub

    Private Sub searchButton_Click(ByVal sender As System.Object, _
    ByVal e As System.EventArgs) Handles searchButton.Click
        stringList.Sort() 'must sort before search
        Dim searchString = stringTextBox.Text
        Dim indexOfString As Integer = _
            stringList.BinarySearch(searchString) 'binary search
        If indexOfString < 0 Then
            MessageBox.Show("'" & searchString & _
                "' not found", "Search")
        Else
            MessageBox.Show("'" & searchString & _
                "' found at position " & indexOfString + 1, "Search")
        End If
    End Sub

    Private Sub displayButton_Click(ByVal sender As System.Object, _
        ByVal e As System.EventArgs) Handles displayButton.Click
        Dim outputString As String = String.Empty
        'For Each uses IEnumerator and List.Enumerator
        '(behind the scenes)
        For Each stringElement As String In stringList
            outputString &= (stringList.IndexOf(stringElement) + 1) & _
            " " & stringElement & vbCrLf
        Next
        MessageBox.Show(outputString, "Display Entire List")
    End Sub

    Private Sub displayTopThreeButton_Click( _
        ByVal sender As System.Object, _
        ByVal e As System.EventArgs) _
        Handles displayTopThreeButton.Click
        Dim outputString As String = String.Empty
        For i As Integer = 0 To 2
            outputString &= ((i + 1) & " " & topThree.Item(i) & vbCrLf)
        Next
        MessageBox.Show(outputString, "Display Top Three")
    End Sub
End Class
```

FIGURE 11.25 Program code for the `MainForm` class in the GenericClassTest application

A sample run of the GenericClassTest application is shown in Figure 11.26. The new user interface is shown in Figure 11.26(a). The same strings that were added in Figure 11.22 are also added here, so the output for this application would be the same as in Figure 11.22(b)–(e). The difference is apparent when the Display Top Three button is clicked, resulting in the `MessageBox` shown in Figure 11.26(b). Note that the three "largest" strings (the top three in reverse alphabetical order) are displayed. The key is that this generic `TopThreeList` class can work for strings or any other kind of value types or reference types.

(a)

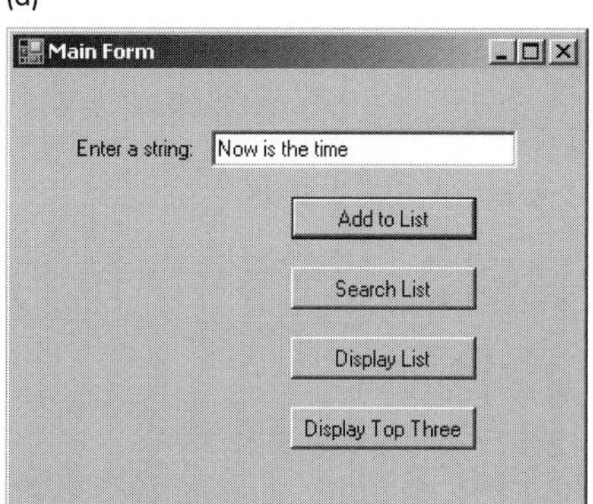

(b)

Display Top Three
1 to come to the aid
2 of their country.
3 Now is the time
OK

FIGURE 11.26 Sample run of the GenericClassTest application

Generic Procedures

Not only can you create generic classes, but you can also create generic procedures. Again, the primary advantage is code reuse—you write one procedure that can work with many different data types. The secondary advantage is strong type checking. Using generic procedures is a two-step process. First, you must specify the type parameter when you define the procedure:

```
Public Sub procedureName(Of T)(ByVal param As T)
    (procedure code goes here)
End Sub
```

In this example, `T` represents the type parameter (the placeholder for an actual data type) and `param` is the procedure's parameter. The second step is the procedure call:

```
procedureName(Of actualDataType)(argument)
```

Thus, the procedure is defined to accept a *param* of data type `T`. When the procedure is called, the *actualDataType* is specified and the argument (having that data type) is passed. An example of this process is provided by the GenericProcedureTest application, which contains a `displayArray` procedure that can display arrays of any data type. The user interface is given in Figure 11.27, program code in Figure 11.28, and a sample run in Figure 11.29. Make sure you study this application carefully.

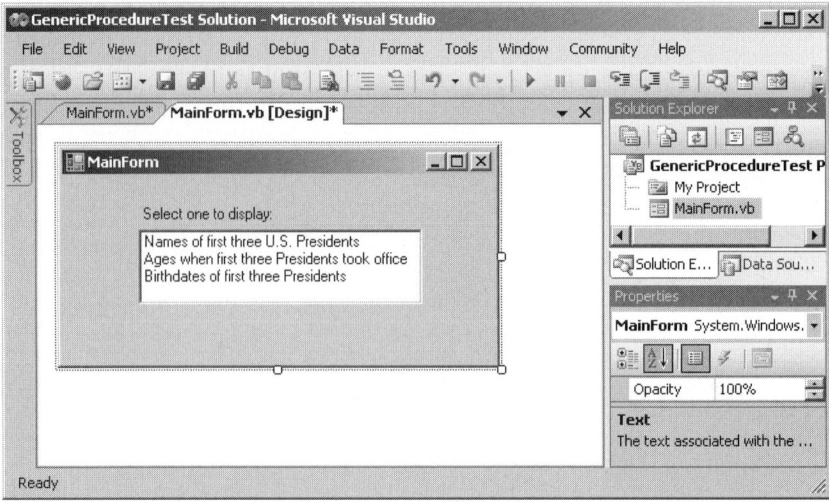

FIGURE 11.27 User interface for the GenericProcedureTest application

```
Public Class MainForm
    Private Sub choiceListBox_SelectedIndexChanged( _
        ByVal sender As System.Object, _
        ByVal e As System.EventArgs) _
        Handles choiceListBox.SelectedIndexChanged

        Select Case (choiceListBox.SelectedIndex)
            Case 0
                Dim theArray() As String = _
                    {"George Washington", _
                     "John Adams", _
                     "Thomas Jefferson"}
                displayArray(Of String)(theArray)
            Case 1
                Dim theArray() As Integer = {57, 62, 57}
                displayArray(Of Integer)(theArray)
            Case 2
                Dim theArray() As DateTime = _
                    {#2/22/1732#, #10/30/1735#, #4/13/1743#}
                displayArray(Of DateTime)(theArray)
        End Select
    End Sub

    Public Sub displayArray(Of T)(ByVal anArray As T())
        Dim outputString As String = ""

        For i As Integer = 0 To anArray.GetUpperBound(0)
            outputString &= Convert.ToString(anArray(i)) & vbCrLf
        Next

        MessageBox.Show(outputString, "Display Array")
    End Sub
End Class
```

FIGURE 11.28 Program code for the `MainForm` class in the GenericProcedureTest application

(a)

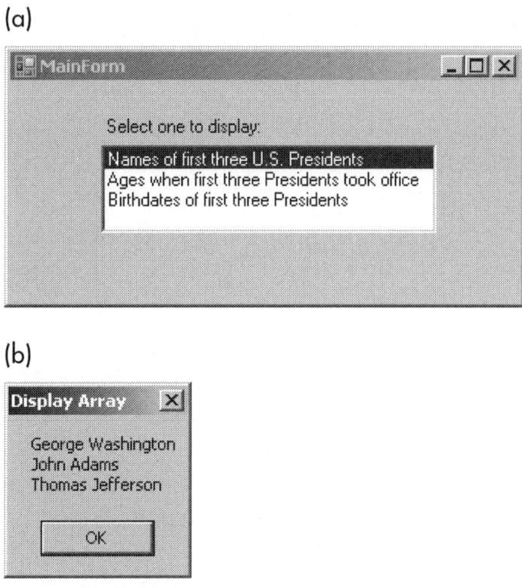

FIGURE 11.29 Sample run of the GenericProcedureTest application

PROGRAMMING EXAMPLE

Palindrome Primes

The PalindromePrimes application determines a set of prime numbers (less than a given number) that are also palindromes. A prime number is a number that is divisible by only itself and 1. The first few prime numbers are 2, 3, 5, 7, 11, 13, ... A palindrome is a word, phrase, or number that reads the same in either direction, such as "abba", 191, or "Madam, in Eden I'm Adam." Punctuation is usually ignored. The details of the PalindromePrimes application follow.

Pseudocode for `palindromePrimesButton` event procedure:

1. get maximum number from text box
2. call `FindPalindromePrimes` procedure

Pseudocode for `FindPalindromePrimes` procedure

1. get first prime number (= 2)
2. add to prime palindrome list
3. get next potential prime number (next integer)
4. while next potential prime number is less than maximum number

```
      for each previous prime number
            if next potential prime number is divisible by previous prime
                  exit for loop (potential prime number not a prime)
            else
                  call DetermineIfPalindrome
      get next potential prime number
```

5. display all palindrome primes

Pseudocode for `DetermineIfPalindrome` procedure:

Pseudocode

```
1. for each digit in potential palindrome prime
       push digit onto prime digits stack
       add digit to end of prime digits list
       for each digit in potential palindrome prime
           if digit on top of stack <> digit at end of list
               return (not a palindrome)
           else
               pop digit off of stack
2. add palindrome prime to palindrome prime list
```

FIGURE 11.30 Pseudocode for PalindromePrimes application

Code

```
Public Class MainForm
    Private max As Integer
    Private palindromePrimeList As New List(Of Integer)

    Private Sub palindromePrimesButton_Click( _
        ByVal sender As System.Object, _
        ByVal e As System.EventArgs) _
        Handles palindromePrimesButton.Click
        max = Convert.ToInt16(maxNumberTextBox.Text)
        FindPalindromePrimes(max)
    End Sub

    Public Sub FindPalindromePrimes(ByVal maxNumber As Integer)
        'declare variables
        Dim i, newNumber, lastPrime, countOfList As Integer
        Dim outputString As String = String.Empty
        palindromePrimeList.Clear()

        'algorithm for finding prime numbers
        palindromePrimeList.Add(2) 'first known prime number is 2
        countOfList = palindromePrimeList.Count
        lastPrime = palindromePrimeList.Item(0)
        newNumber = lastPrime + 1

        While newNumber < maxNumber
            For i = 0 To countOfList - 1
                lastPrime = palindromePrimeList.Item(i)
                If newNumber Mod lastPrime = 0 Then 'not a prime
                    Exit For
                Else                                'is a prime
                    If i = countOfList - 1 Then
                        'call procedure to determine if palindrome
                        DetermineIfPalindrome(newNumber)
                        countOfList = palindromePrimeList.Count
                        lastPrime = newNumber
                    End If
                End If
```

(Figure is continued on next page)

```
            Next
            newNumber += 1 'get next number for testing
        End While

        'output
        For i = 0 To countOfList - 1
            outputString &= palindromePrimeList.Item(i) & vbCrLf
        Next
        MessageBox.Show(outputString, "Palindrome Primes")
    End Sub 'FindPalindromePrimes

    Public Sub DetermineIfPalindrome(ByVal primeNumber As Integer)
        Dim primeDigitsStack = New Stack
        Dim primeDigitsList = New ArrayList
        Dim primeNumberStr As String = Convert.ToString(primeNumber)
        Dim isPalindromePrime = True
        Dim numberOfDigits As Integer = primeNumberStr.Length

        For i As Integer = 0 To (numberOfDigits - 1)
            primeDigitsStack.Push(CInt(primeNumberStr.Substring(i, 1)))
            primeDigitsList.Add(CInt(primeNumberStr.Substring(i, 1)))
        Next

        For i As Integer = 0 To primeDigitsStack.Count - 1
            If primeDigitsStack.Peek <> primeDigitsList.Item(i) Then
                Return
            Else
                primeDigitsStack.pop()
            End If
        Next
        palindromePrimeList.Add(primeNumber)
    End Sub 'DetermineIfPalindrome

End Class
```

FIGURE 11.31 Program code for the PalindromePrimes application

Input/Output

(a)

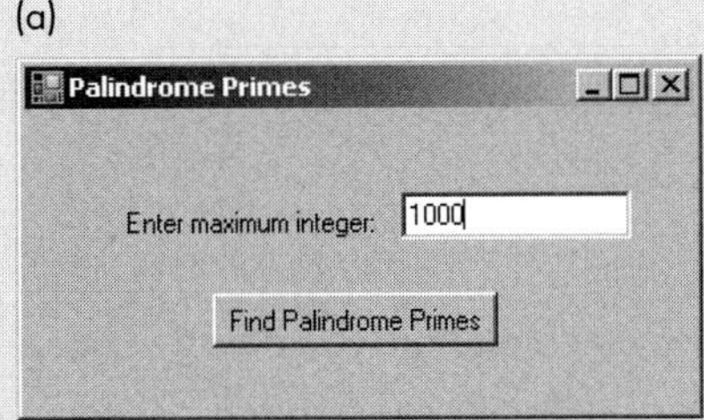

(b)

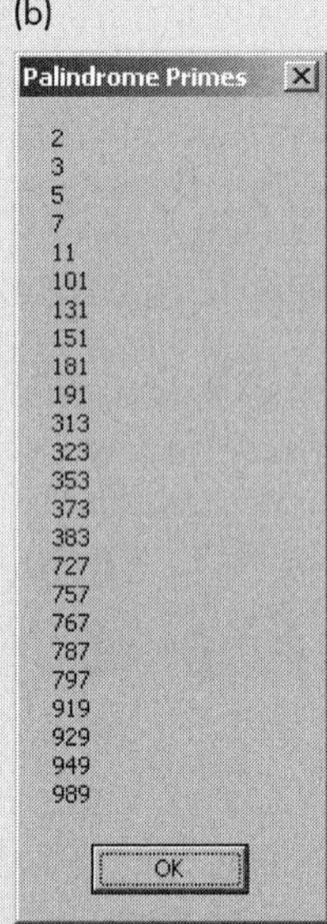

FIGURE 11.32 Sample run of the PalindromePrimes application

Quick Review

- In a programming context, a collection is simply an object that contains a set of related items. You have already studied a collection called an array, which can store items with data types known as value types or references types.
- A value type is a data type for a variable where the variable contains the actual value. A reference type is a data type for a variable where the variable contains a reference to the memory location that stores the actual value.
- The `Array` class contains many methods for creating, manipulating, searching, and sorting arrays that may be new to you. Some of these methods are very basic and easy to use while others require additional programming support.
- Visual Basic uses an efficient binary search algorithm to search the contents of an array. This algorithm compares the target item with the middle value of an array to eliminate half of the array from the search, and repeats this process during each pass of the search.
- In addition to basic arrays, you can create collections of objects that possess special capabilities that can make your applications easier to create as well as more functional. These special collections are represented by classes in the `System.Collections` namespace of the .NET Framework.
- An `ArrayList` collection is basically a resizable array. This means you can easily add new items at the end of the list, insert items anywhere within the list, and remove existing items from the list (along with a host of other interesting operations).
- An `ArrayList` is a weakly typed data structure, which is a data structure that is not checked at compile time for a consistent data type of its components. This is because an `ArrayList` can contain any and all kinds of objects.
- The `StringCollection` class is a data structure that is identical to an `ArrayList` but can contain only strings. A `StringCollection`, as the name implies, is a collection of strings (and only strings). Thus, `StringCollection`

is a strongly typed data structure, which is a data structure that is checked at compile time for consistent data types of its items.

- A stack is a data structure that operates on the principle of last-in, first-out (LIFO, pronounced "life-o"). This means that the last item added to the data structure must be the first item removed from the data structure. You commonly say that items are pushed onto a stack and popped off of a stack.
- In Visual Basic, a stack data structure is defined by the `Stack` class in the `System.Collections` namespace. The `Stack` class has many of the same properties and methods as the `ArrayList` class (such as `Count`, `Clear`, `Contains`, `CopyTo`, `ToArray`, and `ToString`), but it also has many properties and methods that are unique (such as `Peek`, `Pop`, and `Push`).
- While a stack data structure represents a collection of objects that follows the last-in, first-out (LIFO) rule, a queue data structure represents a collection of objects that follows the first-in, first-out (FIFO, pronounced "fife-o") rule. Thus a queue is especially applicable to real-world waiting-in-line situations.
- The class `Queue` in the .NET Framework is virtually identical to the class `Stack` with the exception of how objects are added or removed. For a `Queue`, the method `Enqueue` adds an object to the end of the queue and the method `Dequeue` removes an object from the front of the queue. To enforce FIFO, these are the only ways to add/remove objects for a `Queue`.
- Conceptually, a hash table is a data structure with two columns, the first containing a hash code and the second containing the object. Each object is identified by a key, which is a field belonging to the object that serves as its unique identifier. The hash code is a value derived from the key using a hash function, which is an algorithm that creates a hash code from the key.
- In a hash table, a collision occurs when more than one object has the same hash code. When this happens, collision resolution (a process for distinguishing objects stored in the same hash table bucket) is required. A collision resolution is often accomplished by storing multiple objects within a linked list, another kind of data structure where each item in the list points to the next item in the list.
- Visual Basic uses the `HashTable` class to implement the hash table data structure. A `HashTable` contains key-and-value pairs that are organized based on the hash code of the key.
- In a programming context, generics refers to programming elements that can accommodate variables of a wide variety of data types rather than only one specific data type. Thus, a generic type is a single programming element that adapts to perform the same functionality for a variety of data types.
- The primary advantage of using generics is code reuse. You can use one class that works with any data type instead of working with a large number of classes that perform similar tasks, one for each different data type. Another major advantage is that a generic class defined to use a specific data type becomes strongly typed.
- One important application of generics is that of generic collections. The .NET Framework includes the `System.Collections.Generic` namespace, which contains classes, interfaces, and structures that define generic collections.
- You can also create your own programmer-defined generic classes. The advantage of doing so is that the generic class can be used with a variety of data types allowing for code reuse and strong typing.
- You can also create generic procedures. Again, the primary advantage is code reuse—you write one procedure that can work with many different data types. The secondary advantage is strong type checking. To use generic procedures, you must first declare the procedure to be generic using a type parameter and then call the generic procedure by specifying the particular data type being used.

Key Terms

binary search algorithm—A programmed procedure that compares the target item with the middle value of an array of values to eliminate half of the array from the search, and repeats this process during each pass of the search.

boxing—The process of converting values to and from the `Object` data type.

collection—An object that contains a set of related items.

collision—In relation to a hash table, a condition that occurs when more than one object has the same hash code.

collision resolution—A process for distinguishing objects that have the same hash code.

data structure—A way of organizing data in computer memory.

generic type—A single programming element that adapts to perform the same functionality for a variety of data types.

generics—Programming elements that can accommodate variables of a wide variety of data types rather than only one specific data type.

hash code—A value derived from the key using a hash function.

hash function—An algorithm that creates a hash code from the key.

hash table—A data structure with two columns, the first containing a hash code and the second containing the object.

hash table bucket—A linked list used to store objects in a hash table when the objects have the same hash code.

key—A field belonging to the object that serves as its unique identifier for storage in a hash table.

linked list—A data structure in which each item in the list points to the next item in the list.

queue—A first-in, first-out (FIFO) waiting list.

reference type—A data type of a variable for which the variable contains a reference to the memory location that stores the actual value.

stack—A data structure that operates on the principle of last-in, first-out (LIFO).

strongly typed data structure—A data structure that is checked at compile time for consistency of the items' data type.

value type—A data type of a variable for which the variable contains the actual value.

weakly typed data structure—A data structure that is not checked at compile time for consistency of the items' data type.

Review Questions

1. The `String` data type is a value type.
   a. True
   b. False
2. The `Length` of an array cannot be changed after it is created.
   a. True
   b. False

3. Elements in an array must have the same data type.
   a. True
   b. False
4. The `BinarySearch` procedure for an array must be called before the `Sort` procedure can be called.
   a. True
   b. False
5. The `Array` class is in the `System.Collections` namespace.
   a. True
   b. False
6. An `ArrayList` is a weakly typed data structure.
   a. True
   b. False
7. A `StringCollection` is a weakly typed data structure.
   a. True
   b. False
8. A `Queue` uses a FIFO process for adding and removing items.
   a. True
   b. False
9. A disadvantage of generics is that they are strongly typed.
   a. True
   b. False
10. An advantage of generics is code reuse.
    a. True
    b. False
11. An array begins with an index value of _____.
    a. –1
    b. 0
    c. 1
    d. `Nothing`
12. Which of the following collections stores key-and-value pairs?
    a. `ArrayList`
    b. `Hashtable`
    c. `Queue`
    d. `Stack`
13. Which of the following collections uses a LIFO process for adding and removing items?
    a. `ArrayList`
    b. `Hashtable`
    c. `Queue`
    d. `Stack`
14. Which of the following collections is used for waiting-in-line situations?
    a. `ArrayList`
    b. `Hashtable`
    c. `Queue`
    d. `Stack`

15. Which of the following collections is not in the `System.Collections.Generic` namespace?
    a. `ArrayList`
    b. `Dictionary`
    c. `Queue`
    d. `Stack`
16. Which of the following generic classes stores key-and-value pairs?
    a. `List`
    b. `LinkedList`
    c. `Queue`
    d. `Dictionary`
16. Which of the following Array procedures requires the implementation of the `IComparable` interface?
    a. IndexOf
    b. SetValue
    c. Sort
    d. Reverse
17. Which of the following collections has an `Insert` procedure?
    a. `ArrayList`
    b. `Hashtable`
    c. `Queue`
    d. `Stack`
18. Which of the following collections is a strongly typed version of `ArrayList`?
    a. `Queue`
    b. `Hashtable`
    c. `SortedList`
    d. `StringCollection`
19. Which of the following collections uses the `Push` and `Pop` procedures?
    a. `ArrayList`
    b. `Hashtable`
    c. `Queue`
    d. `Stack`

Computer Exercises

In the following exercises, follow all conventions for creating organized, user-friendly console or GUI applications. Your instructor may also request that you use TOE charts, pseudocode, flowcharts, and/or UML diagrams as planning aids.

1. In this exercise, you modify the StackTest application (Figure 11.9) to create the QueueTest application that produces the output shown in Figure 11.11.
    a. Copy the StackTest Solution folder in the \VBReloadedAdvanced\Chap11 folder and rename it QueueTest Solution.
    b. Open the application in the QueueTest Solution folder.
    c. Modify the program code in the QueueTest application to use the `Queue` class instead of the `Stack` class (and make all other necessary changes).
    d. Save the solution, test the application, and modify as necessary.
2. In this exercise, you create the BookArray application.
    a. Create the BookArray project in a BookArray solution.
    b. In the BookArray project, create a `Book` class with instance variables

_isbn (a book's ID number) and _bookTitle.

c. Create a user interface that allows the user to enter his or her five favorite books and store them in an array. Use the CreateInstance method of the Array class to create the array.
d. Add buttons to the user interface to display all books sorted by ISBN and by title. Output should be provided in a MessageBox.
e. Save the solution, test the application, and modify as necessary.

3. In this exercise, you create the EmployeeArray application.
   a. Create the EmployeeArray project in an EmployeeArray solution.
   b. In the EmployeeArray project, create an Employee class with instance variables _ssn (an employee's Social Security number), _lastName, and _firstName.
   c. Create a user interface that allows the user to enter a maximum of 10 employees. Use the CreateInstance method of the Array class to create the array.
   d. Add buttons to the user interface to display all employees sorted by SSN and by last name. Output should be provided in a label within the user interface.
   e. Add a button that allows the user to search for an employee's last name, displaying the employee's data in a label within the user interface.
   f. Add a button that allows the user to search for an employee's SSN, displaying the employee's data in a label within the user interface.
   g. Save the solution, test the application, and modify as necessary.

4. In this exercise, you create the MP3ArrayList application to store an MP3 collection in an ArrayList.
   a. Create the MP3ArrayList project in an MP3ArrayList solution.
   b. In the MP3ArrayList project, create an MP3 class with instance variables _mp3Id (a sequential ID number that the application automatically generates for each new MP3), _mp3Title, and _mp3Artist.
   c. Create a user interface that allows the user to enter new MP3s, display existing MP3s in a ListBox (sorted by title or artist), and delete MP3s by selecting them in a ListBox.
   d. Save the solution, test the application, and modify as necessary.

5. In this exercise, you create the PalindromeTest application, which tests a string to determine if it is a palindrome. (A palindrome is a word, phrase, or number that reads the same in either direction, such as "abba", 191, or "Madam, in Eden I'm Adam." Punctuation is usually ignored.) Use a stack data structure.
   a. Create the PalindromeTest project in a PalindromeTest solution.
   b. Create a user interface that allows the user to enter a string and then click a button to test whether the string is a palindrome, ignoring spaces, case, and punctuation.
   c. Save the solution, test the application, and modify as necessary.

6. In this exercise, you create the JobSchedulingTest application. A job is represented as a word. Longer words represent jobs that require more time. Use the ArrayList class to place each string in the list of jobs based on its length (in case of a tie, order the strings alphabetically).
   a. Create the JobSchedulingTest project in a JobSchedulingTest solution.
   b. Create a user interface that allows the user to enter a word (no spaces). When a button is clicked, the word is placed in the ArrayList in its proper position.
   c. Add a button that displays the entire list of jobs (words).
   d. Save the solution, test the application, and modify as necessary.

7. In this exercise, you create the GenericJobSchedulingTest application. A job is represented as a word (string of nonnumeric characters) or an integer. Longer words and larger integers represent jobs that require more time. Use the `List` class to place each string in either a list of word jobs or a list of integer jobs (in case of a tie, order words alphabetically).
   a. Create the GenericJobSchedulingTest project in a GenericJobSchedulingTest solution.
   b. Create a user interface that allows the user to enter a word (no spaces) or an integer in a text box.
   c. When a button is clicked, the "job" is placed in either a `List` of words or a `List` of integers, but only one generic `List` class is used to accomplish this. The jobs are placed in the lists in order from smallest to largest.
   d. Add two other buttons. One button converts the list of word jobs to an array and prints the array in a `MessageBox`. The other button does likewise for the list of integer jobs. Only one generic `printArray` procedure is used to display either list of jobs.
   e. Save the solution, test the application, and modify as necessary.

Case Projects

Friends

Create a **MyFriends** project that uses a `Friend` class to describe friends. Use instance variables such as `_lastName`, `_firstName`, `_gender`, and `_dateOfBirth`. Also include an array called `_hobbies` as an instance variable. Create a user interface that stores friends in an `ArrayList` and displays your friends and their hobbies.

Fast Food

Create a **FastFood** project that simulates people waiting in line at a fast-food restaurant. Each time a button is clicked in the user interface, a customer object is created and added to a `Queue`. Use the `Timer` class to assign a random service time for each customer (the time it takes the customer to get his or her order). When the service time is up, the customer should be removed from the queue. Also, each time the button is clicked, a list of all the customers in the queue (and their service times) should be displayed in a `MessageBox`.

Books Hash Table

Create a **BooksHashTable** project that creates a hash table for books using the book's ISBN as the key and a Book object as the value. Use an interface similar to Figure 11.13, but instead of just a Name text box, use a Title text box, a Year of Publication text box, and an author `ListBox` to create the `Book` object. All authors should be stored in an `ArrayList` for each book.

CHAPTER

12 Multithreading in Visual Basic

After studying Chapter 12, you should be able to:

- Explain how multithreading works
- Create a console multithreading application with `Sleep` and `Priority`
- Enforce thread synchronization using the `Monitor` class
- Create a console multithreading application with `Join` and `Interrupt`
- Create a thread-safe multithreading Windows Forms application

Multithreading is a very important, but sometimes difficult, programming technique about which all software developers should be aware. You are probably already quite familiar with the concept of multitasking. Generally, the term **multitasking** refers to the perceived ability to perform several different tasks at the same time. Actually, a person can't do several things at the same time, but he can appear to perform tasks at about the same time by switching from one to another very quickly. You might say that a juggler is multitasking, but he is actually handling only one object (a ball, bowling pin, or flaming sword) at a time in rapid succession.

TIP

Several programming examples of multithreading are included in this chapter. Because there is an element of randomness in the time that the CPU assigns to various program threads and because the speed of different computers may vary, the results you get by running these programs may be different than those shown.

Similarly, you might say that a computer processor multitasks by running several programs at the same time. In fact, however, a computer processor that appears to run multiple programs concurrently is actually switching its attention at lightning speed from one program to another. The slight lag time that occurs when your computer is running multiple programs is a result of the computer processor switching its attention from one program to another. Most computer users are willing to tolerate this side effect of multitasking, because the benefits of multitasking are so great. For example, you are probably quite pleased when you can print a document and download music while you are also browsing the Internet. Without multitasking, you would have to wait until the entire document printed, then wait until the music downloaded, before you could begin to browse the Web.

In this chapter, you will learn about a special kind of multitasking called multithreading.

OVERVIEW OF MULTITHREADING

While multitasking involves a processor running several programs at the same time, **multithreading** involves one processor executing several parts (or threads) of a single program at the same time (or, rather, quickly switching its resources from one program thread to another). A **thread** (short for "thread of execution") is that part of a larger process or program on which the processor is working at any one time. Multithreading is usually accomplished through the technique of **time slicing**, where the processor gives a small slice of its time to one thread after another until all threads are completed. When execution of multiple threads is performed by more than one processor, multithreading is called **multiprocessing**.

Advantages and Disadvantages of Multithreading

Within a computer, the processor's time is a valuable commodity. Just as a factory owner can't afford to let machinery sit idle for long, a computer system can't afford to let its processor remain idle. If a processor could work on only one thread from start to finish, it would have to sit idle for relatively long periods of time while other, nonprocessing operations (commonly input/output operations) took place. If the processor could do nothing else during that idle time, the computer would run very slowly, frustrating the user.

A major benefit of multithreading is that when a processor is idle (usually because of input/output operations), it can be used by the next thread in line. For example, suppose you want to watch a video clip of a news broadcast or a sporting event on the Internet. When you click the play button, you may wait a few seconds while the multimedia application downloads enough of the video for you to start watching. Then the application displays the beginning of the video while it continues to download more of the video. This is all possible because the processor is switching back and forth between the playing thread and the downloading thread of the application. If users had to wait a long time for some applications to work, many would just decide not to use the applications.

Note that to ensure that the video isn't played faster than it can be downloaded, synchronization is required. The term **synchronization** refers to communication between threads for the purpose of controlling the order of thread execution and access to program code. A streaming video application that is properly synchronized switches back and forth between playing and downloading with just the right timing so that the video does not appear broken or choppy.

Another benefit of multithreading is that it can improve application **scalability**, which is the ability of an application to adapt to increasing demands without significant changes in the computer system's architecture (such as adding more processors). Threads can be added to an application, thereby giving a greater number of users access to the application at the same time and making more efficient use of the already available processing power.

While the advantages of multithreading can be significant, multithreading can add to the complexity of developing the application. As the programmer, you must know what your application and all its threads are doing at all times. The rest of this chapter enables you to do just that.

THREAD STATES, PRIORITY, AND SYNCHRONIZATION

A proper understanding of multithreading can be challenging. This section provides a simple analogy that may help.

A Race Car Analogy

Imagine a race car training track that is designed to accommodate only one car at a time. As Figure 12.1 illustrates, this track is analogous to a single computer processor that can really do only one thing at a time. Each new car (including its driver) that arrives in the pit area represents a new thread created in a program. After each car is created, a test driver is given a special set of instructions explaining how to perform a designated series of tests (acceleration, handling, braking, and so on). These instructions represent methods or procedures that each thread is supposed to execute. All these tests for each car must be completed before the car finally ends its practice run, although the total practice run may be interrupted several times by cars of higher priority.

Now imagine several different new race cars (cars that have just been built) waiting in the pit area to access the track in order to perform their respective sets of instructions. The track manager has a great deal of control over these race cars. In fact, she controls when each car is built, when each car is granted access to the test track, and how long each car can remain on the track to perform its set of instructions. In computer terms, the track manager is analogous to the computer program.

In terms of actual threads in a computer program, the `Thread` constructor is used by the program to create the thread. A **`ThreadStart` delegate** (a specific method that executes on a particular thread) contains the instructions for the thread. Throughout the following discussion, keep in mind that the track is the processor, a car (and its driver) is a thread, the set of instructions given to a driver is a method, and the track manager is the controlling program.

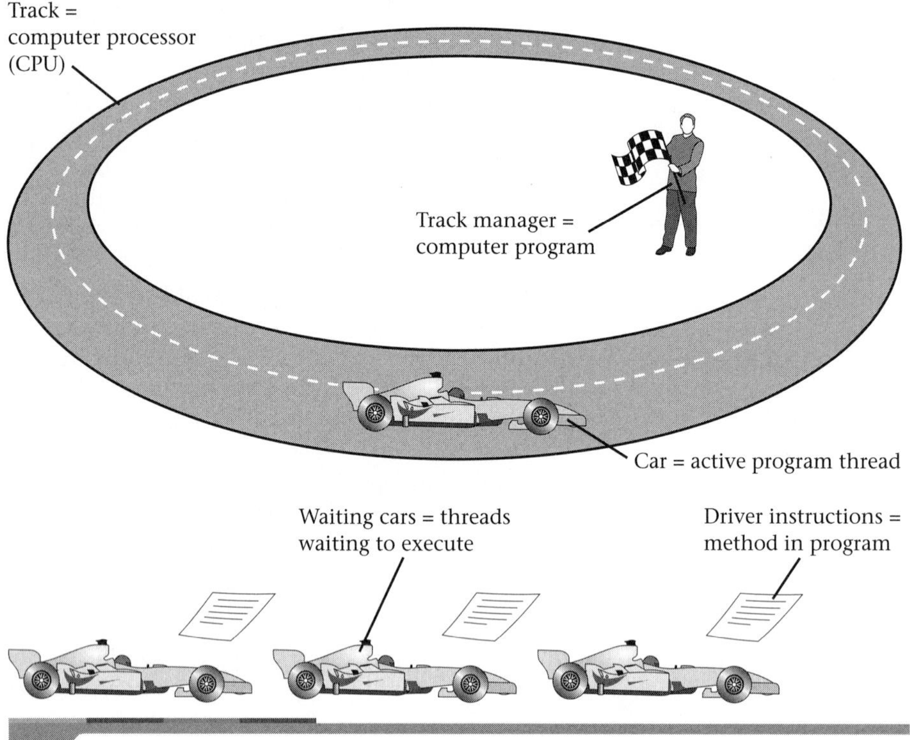

FIGURE 12.1 A race car analogy for multithreading

Race Car States

A race car whose engine is not yet started is said to be in an Unstarted state. A race car whose engine has been started is said to be in a Started state. The other possible states for a race car (and a thread) are Running, Blocked, or Stopped. A car can move from one state to another, such as from Unstarted to Started, or Running to Stopped. A car moves from one state to another when the track manager issues a special command, such as `Start` or `Wait`. In terms of actual threads, a **thread state** is the condition or status of a thread at any one time, while a **thread transition** is the act of changing from one thread state to another.

Leaving the Unstarted State

At first, all cars under the control of the track manager are in the **Unstarted state** (engines are off). In programming terminology, the Unstarted state is the initial thread state for threads that have been created by a program but never executed. Then the track manager issues the command `Start` for one or more cars to "start their engines" and they enter the **Started state**, the state in which a thread is capable of executing. (A car can't speed onto the track if its engine has not yet been started.) Once one or more cars are in the Started state, the car with the highest priority (as predetermined by the track manager) automatically takes the track, thus entering the **Running state**, the state where a thread is executing. If several cars in the Started state have the same priority, the track manager gives each car a fixed amount of time during which the car takes turns in the Running state (is on the track). When the fixed amount of time expires, the car reenters the Started state by leaving the track and giving way to the next car of equal priority. For threads in a program, the fixed amount of time that a thread is granted access to the CPU (as little as a few milliseconds) is called a **quantum**.

Leaving the Running State

A car in the Running state can be interrupted before it completes its training program (or its quantum) in one of several ways. A car can enter the **Blocked state** if, for example, the car needs gas or tires or the driver needs to make an important phone call. (In terms of real threads, a thread might enter such a state of inactivity after it issues an input/output request.) When a car is in the Blocked state, the track manager will direct another car, already in the Started state, to take the track so that the track's utilization is maximized. (This is why several cars are placed in the Started state initially, so that they are warmed up and ready to take the track at a moment's notice.) When the car in a Blocked state completes its input/output operations, it returns to the Started state to await directions from the track manager.

Another state of thread inactivity is the **WaitSleepJoin state**, which occurs when the `Wait`, `Sleep`, or `Join` methods are called on a thread. In the race car analogy, there are three ways that a car in the Running state can enter the WaitSleepJoin state. First, the track manager can direct the running car to get off the track and wait, possibly due to unavailable resources. (Perhaps the track's safety crew is taking a coffee break or is attending to a broken-down car on the track.) When the track manager determines that conditions for the waiting car are again acceptable, the car is signaled to get back in the Started state. (It does not return to Running, because another car has taken the track during the wait.) A thread in the WaitSleepJoin state can be returned to the Started state using the `Pulse` method; all threads that are waiting for a resource can be returned to the Started state using the `PulseAll` method.

A car can also enter the WaitSleepJoin state when the track manager determines that the driver needs a nap and forces him to sleep for a designated period of time, after which the car returns to the Started state. (Again, during sleep another car has taken the track.) A sleeping thread can be awakened using the `Interrupt` method. A sleeping thread will also return to the Started state when its designated sleep time expires.

The third way a car can enter the WaitSleepJoin state is if it is joined with another car. These two cars become something of a tag team. Suppose Car B is in the Running state, but it is joined to Car A. If Car A is suddenly given the green light to use the track, Car B must enter the WaitSleepJoin state until Car A finishes the entirety of its practice run (terminates).

Terminating a Trial Run

Finally, when a car has finished its trial run on the track, it enters the **Stopped state**, never to return to the test track again. This is the state for threads that have completed their assigned tasks. A car can also enter the **Aborted state** for something like a blown engine, never to return to the test track again. This state is for threads terminated due to abnormal conditions. Threads entering the Stopped or Aborted state cannot be restarted.

Figure 12.2 illustrates these thread states and their transitions. Note that code font is used for actual Visual Basic methods that are called to place threads in various states. As you can see, the program is very critical in controlling the functions of threads.

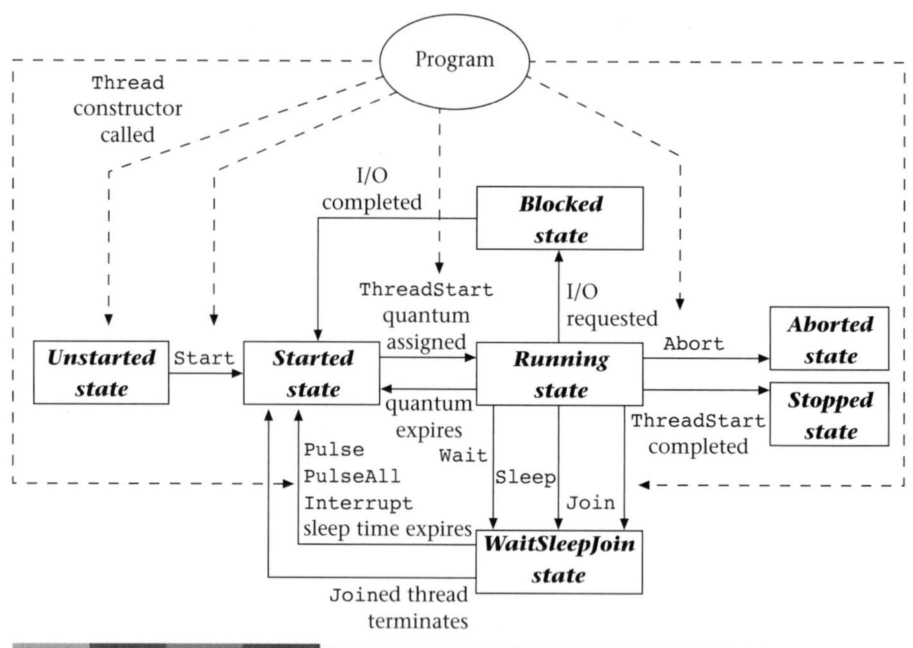

FIGURE 12.2 Thread states and transitions

Thread Priorities and Thread Scheduling

Several threads in a program can all begin in the `Unstarted` state. Every thread is assigned a priority. Possible priority values range between `Lowest`, `BelowNormal`, `Normal` (the default), `AboveNormal`, and, finally, `Highest`. A special component of the operating system, called the thread scheduler, determines which thread enters the Running state based on priorities, which are assigned by the program. Of a group of threads, the one with the highest priority is executed first and continues to run to completion unless it enters the WaitSleepJoin, Blocked, or Aborted state. In that case, a thread with the next highest priority executes. However, once a higher-priority thread reenters the Started state, it will regain its Running state.

If two or more threads have the same priority, then the scheduler repeatedly gives each thread a time slice (quantum) on the processor, usually several milliseconds. A thread will continue to execute until its quantum expires or it enters a Stopped, Aborted, Blocked, or WaitSleepJoin state, or until another thread with higher priority is placed in the Started state.

Thread Synchronization

Earlier you learned that thread synchronization is the communication between threads for the purpose of controlling the order of thread execution. The idea is that only one thread should control a key resource of the application. To use the race car analogy, only one race car should be granted access to a key resource of the test track at a time. For example, the track has a safety crew, which can give its attention to only one car at a time. Allowing several cars to use a key resource of the test track at the same time could have unpredictable or even disastrous consequences. Likewise, a multithreaded application should grant only one thread access to a key data source (such as a variable, an array, or a file) at a time. Special techniques are available to enforce synchronization among threads, as you will see in the following examples.

MULTITHREADING EXAMPLES IN A CONSOLE APPLICATION

Now that you understand the basic operation of threads in a program, you will explore various examples of multithreading with many interesting features. All of the examples in this section are written as console applications (applications that execute in the command prompt rather than in Windows forms) because the flow of multithreaded console applications is much easier to follow than in multithreaded Windows applications. Multitasking in Windows Forms applications is discussed in the following section.

Multithreading with a Single Added Thread

This section presents an example of multithreading in an application called SimpleThreadTest. This application contains a module called `SimpleThreadTest` in the file SimpleThreadTest.vb and a class called `PrimeNumberFinder` in the file PrimeNumberFinder.vb. The module `SimpleThreadTest` is used to start the application and will run in the application's main thread. The class `PrimeNumberFinder` is used by a separate thread to find prime numbers.

Figure 12.3 shows the class `PrimeNumberFinder` that contains the `ThreadStart` delegate (method) `FindPrime`. The program in Figure 12.3 begins with importing the `System.Threading` namespace (Line 1), which provides classes and interfaces that enable multithreaded programming. The `PrimeNumberFinder` constructor (Lines 5–7) is used to create an instance of this class. The job of `FindPrime` (Lines 9–52) is to find and display all prime numbers less than a given maximum value (`maxNumber`). (A prime number is a number whose only factors are itself and 1, such as 2, 3, 5, 7, 11, ...) The algorithm for finding prime numbers in `FindPrime` begins (Line 24) with the known first prime (2), adding it to a list of integers. The `numberInList`, `lastPrime`, and `newNumber` variables are then initialized (Lines 25–27).

The `FindPrime` method then takes the next integer (`newNumber`), trying to divide it by all the previous prime numbers (Lines 29–45). If `newNumber` cannot be evenly divided by any of the previous primes (using the `Mod` operator in Line 32), then it is a prime and is added to the `List` (Line 37) called `primeList`, where it becomes the `lastPrime`. This process continues in the `while` loop until `newNumber` exceeds `maxNumber`. The empty constructor `New` in Figure 12.3 is used to create an instance of `PrimeNumberFinder`, which can then be used to call the delegate `FindPrime`, which in turn creates a thread.

```
1  Imports System.Threading
2
3  Public Class PrimeNumberFinder
4
5      Public Sub New()
6          'constructor
7      End Sub
8
9      Public Sub FindPrime()
10         'declare variables
11         Dim i, maxNumber, newNumber, lastPrime As Integer
12         Dim numberInList As Integer
13         Dim current As Thread = Thread.CurrentThread
```

(Figure is continued on next page)

```
        Dim someText As String
        Dim primeList As New List(Of Integer)
        maxNumber = 50

        someText = _
            "Finding prime numbers less than " & maxNumber & _
            " in " & current.Name
        Console.WriteLine(someText)

        'algorithm for finding prime numbers
        primeList.Add(2) 'first prime number is 2
        numberInList = primeList.Count
        lastPrime = primeList.Item(0)
        newNumber = lastPrime + 1

        While newNumber < maxNumber
            For i = 0 To numberInList - 1
                lastPrime = primeList.Item(i)
                If newNumber Mod lastPrime = 0 Then 'not a prime
                    newNumber += 1
                    Exit For
                Else                                'is a prime
                    If i = numberInList - 1 Then
                        primeList.Add(newNumber)
                        Console.WriteLine(primeList.Item(i))
                        numberInList = primeList.Count
                        lastPrime = newNumber
                        newNumber += 1 'get next number for testing
                    End If
                End If
            Next
        End While

        'closing remarks
        someText = vbCrLf & current.Name & " completed"
        Console.WriteLine(someText)
        Console.WriteLine(vbCrLf & "Press any key to quit" & vbCrLf)
        Console.ReadLine()
    End Sub 'FindPrime

End Class
```

FIGURE 12.3 Class `PrimeNumberFinder` with a `ThreadStart` delegate `FindPrime`

The module `SimpleThreadTest` that begins the application is shown in Figure 12.4. Method `Main` will run in the application's main thread. In method `Main`, a `PrimeNumberFinder` object, called `finder`, is created (Line 6). Then a thread called `aThread` is created (Line 8). When started, this new thread called `aThread` will begin execution at the address of the `FindPrime` delegate (method); hence the name of the operator `AddressOf`. Note that Visual Basic knows where the `FindPrime` delegate is located because it is called by the object `finder`, an instance of the `PrimeNumberFinder` class.

After `aThread` is created, the thread is named using the `Name` property (Line 10). After sending an explanatory message to the console (Lines 12–13), the thread is started using the `Start` method (Line 14). The output from running the SimpleThreadTest console application is shown in Figure 12.5.

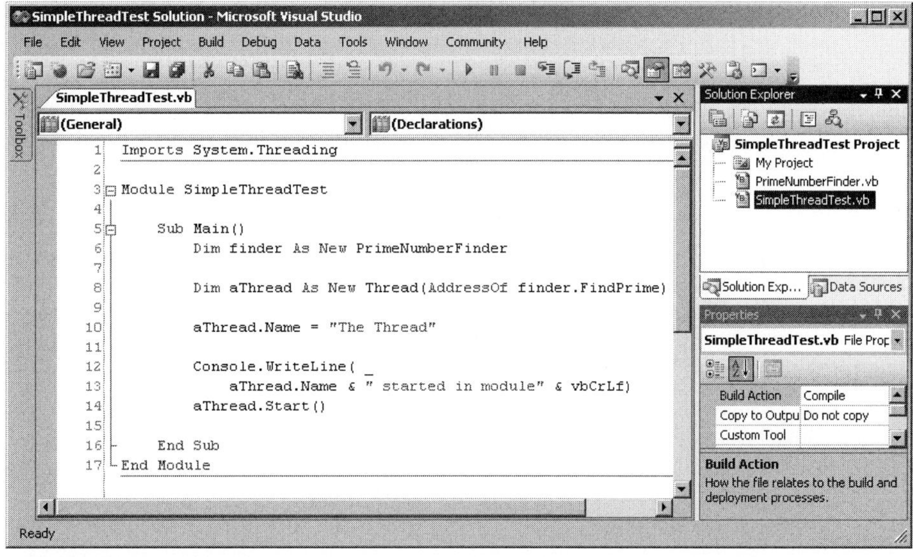

FIGURE 12.4 Module `SimpleThreadTest` for console application

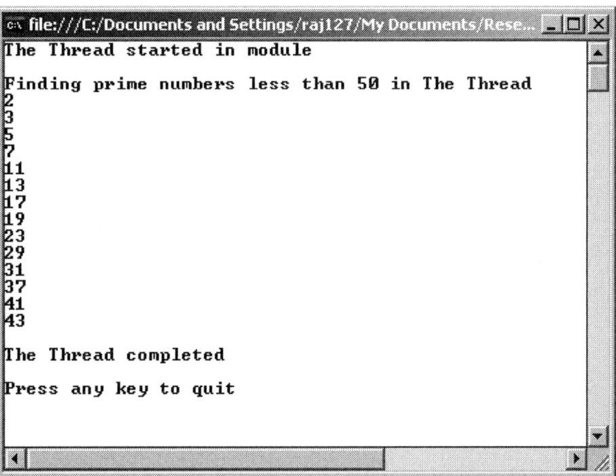

FIGURE 12.5 Sample run of the SimpleThreadTest console application

The output in Figure 12.5 demonstrates that the application begins in the main thread (the `Main` method in the module) and then shifts to the thread named `"The Thread"` where the primes are found and displayed.

Multithreading with Two Created Threads

The example in Figures 12.3 and 12.4 is very simple. The application (executing in the main thread) creates another thread, which in turn finds and displays prime numbers. While the new thread is busy finding prime numbers, the main thread could have continued to get additional input from the user, access a database, and perform other useful tasks. Often, applications need several threads to perform tasks independently. This section illustrates what happens when two new threads are created by an application called DualThreadTest.

Figure 12.6 displays the code for a new `PrimeNumberFinder` class that contains two delegates, `FindPrime1` (Lines 9–54) and `FindPrime2` (Lines 56–101). These two delegates are used to create two different threads, `finder1` and `finder2`. The code in Figure 12.6 is essentially the same as that in Figure 12.3 with the exception that an identical delegate is added.

```
1  Imports System.Threading
2
3  Public Class PrimeNumberFinder
4
5      Public Sub New()
6          'empty constructor
7      End Sub 'New
8
9      Public Sub FindPrime1()
10         'declare and initialize variables
11         Dim i, maxNumber, newNumber, lastPrime As Integer
12         Dim numberInList As Integer
13         Dim randomNumber As New Random()
14         Dim current As Thread = Thread.CurrentThread
15         Dim someText As String
16         Dim primeList As New List(Of Integer)
17         maxNumber = 50
18
19         someText = vbCrLf & "Finding prime numbers less than " & _
20             maxNumber & " in " & current.Name
21         Console.WriteLine(someText)
22
23         Console.WriteLine(vbCrLf & "Prime numbers in " & current.Name)
24
25         'algorithm for finding prime numbers
26         primeList.Add(2) 'first prime number is 2
27         numberInList = primeList.Count
28         lastPrime = primeList.Item(0)
29         newNumber = lastPrime + 1
30
31         While newNumber < maxNumber
32             For i = 0 To numberInList - 1
33                 lastPrime = primeList.Item(i)
34                 If newNumber Mod lastPrime = 0 Then 'not a prime
35                     newNumber += 1
36                     Exit For
37                 Else                              'is a prime
38                     If i = numberInList - 1 Then
39                         primeList.Add(newNumber)
40                         Console.WriteLine(primeList.Item(i))
41                         numberInList = primeList.Count
42                         lastPrime = newNumber
43                         newNumber += 1 'get next number for testing
44                     End If
45                 End If
46             Next
47         End While
48
49         'closing remarks
50         someText = vbCrLf & current.Name & " completed"
51         Console.WriteLine(someText)
52         Console.WriteLine(vbCrLf & "Press any key to quit" & vbCrLf)
53         Console.ReadLine()
54     End Sub 'FindPrime1
55
```

(Figure is continued on next page)

```
    Public Sub FindPrime2()
        'declare and initialize variables
        Dim i, maxNumber, newNumber, lastPrime As Integer
        Dim numberInList As Integer
        Dim randomNumber As New Random()
        Dim current As Thread = Thread.CurrentThread
        Dim someText As String
        Dim primeList As New List(Of Integer)
        maxNumber = 50

        someText = vbCrLf & "Finding prime numbers less than " & _
            maxNumber & " in " & current.Name
        Console.WriteLine(someText)

        Console.WriteLine(vbCrLf & "Prime numbers in " & current.Name)

        'algorithm for finding prime numbers
        primeList.Add(2) 'first prime number is 2
        numberInList = primeList.Count
        lastPrime = primeList.Item(0)
        newNumber = lastPrime + 1

        While newNumber < maxNumber
            For i = 0 To numberInList - 1
                lastPrime = primeList.Item(i)
                If newNumber Mod lastPrime = 0 Then 'not a prime
                    newNumber += 1
                    Exit For
                Else                                'is a prime
                    If i = numberInList - 1 Then
                        primeList.Add(newNumber)
                        Console.WriteLine(primeList.Item(i))
                        numberInList = primeList.Count
                        lastPrime = newNumber
                        newNumber += 1 'get next number for testing
                    End If
                End If
            Next
        End While

        'closing remarks
        someText = vbCrLf & current.Name & " completed"
        Console.WriteLine(someText)
        Console.WriteLine(vbCrLf & "Press any key to quit" & vbCrLf)
        Console.ReadLine()
    End Sub 'FindPrime2
End Class
```

FIGURE 12.6 Class `PrimeNumberFinder` with `ThreadStart` delegates `FindPrime1` and `FindPrime2`

The module `DualThreadTest` in Figure 12.7 is also very similar to the `SimpleThreadTest` module in Figure 12.4 except that two different threads, `thread1` and `thread2`, are created and started. Figure 12.8 shows a sample run of the DualThreadTest application.

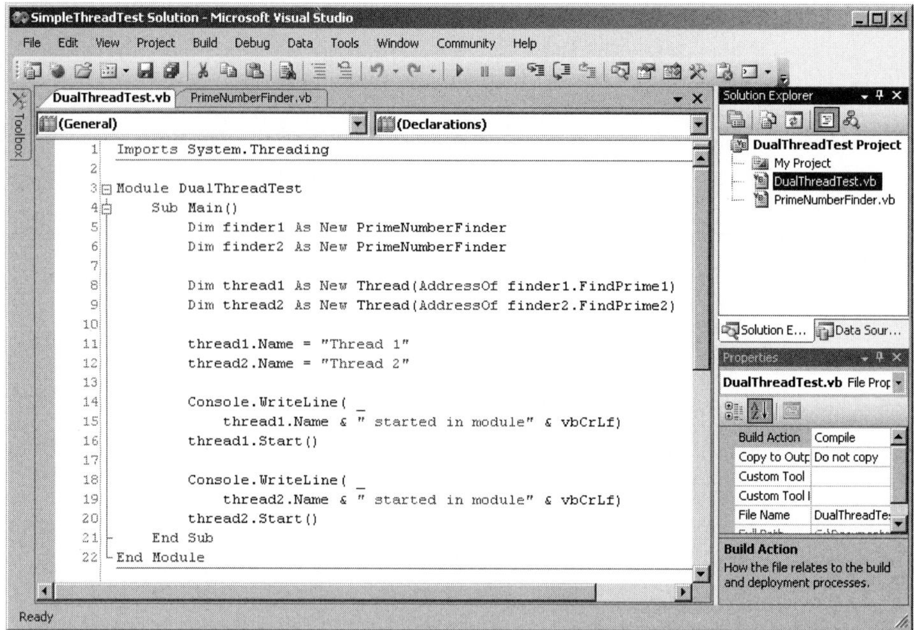

FIGURE 12.7 Module `DualThreadTest` for console application

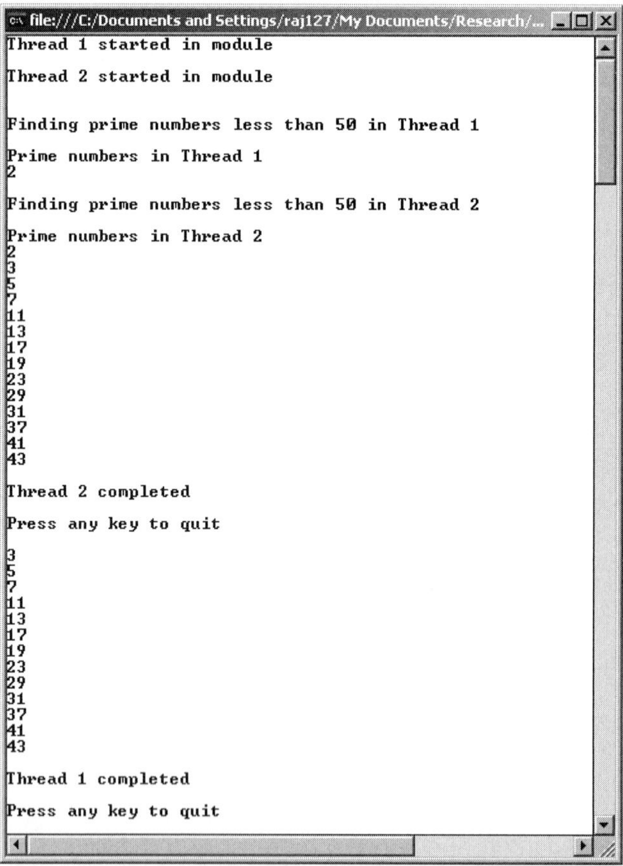

FIGURE 12.8 Sample run of the DualThreadTest console application

The sample run of the DualThreadTest application in Figure 12.8 is very interesting. As expected, Thread 1 is started, followed by Thread 2. Since Thread 1 goes first, it starts listing prime numbers. However, after finding the prime number 2 in Thread 1, the CPU switches from Thread 1 to Thread 2, giving Thread 2 a time slice (quantum) of a few milliseconds, during which Thread 2 displays all the prime numbers less than 50. After Thread 2 is finished, it is terminated and Thread 1 is restarted, producing the remainder of its primes less than 50. The next section discusses another concept related to multithreading: sleep.

Multithreading with Sleep

You can manipulate application threads in a variety of ways. One option is to temporarily halt a thread, or put it to sleep, so that other threads can execute. To illustrate this technique, the program code in Figure 12.6 is altered slightly. The following code is added immediately after the class declaration for `PrimeNumberFinder` (Line 3) and before the constructor `New` (Line 5):

```
Private sleepTime As Integer
```

This code declares the variable `sleepTime`. The following code then generates a random number, which in turn dictates the amount of sleep time (in milliseconds) for a thread. This code is located within both delegates `FindPrime1` and `FindPrime2`, just before the algorithms that generate prime numbers (inserted at Lines 25 and 72 in Figure 12.6):

```
Dim randomNumber As New Random()
sleepTime = randomNumber.Next(5001) 'sleep time from 0 to 5 sec

someText = "Sorry, " & current.Name & _
    " is going to sleep now for " & sleepTime / 1000 & " sec"
Console.WriteLine(someText)

Thread.Sleep(sleepTime) 'this thread goes to sleep

someText = vbCrLf & "OK, " & current.Name & _
    " is awake now" & vbCrLf
Console.WriteLine(someText)
```

In the preceding code, the object `randomNumber` is first declared. Then `randomNumber` calls the `Next` method (with an argument of `5001`) to generate a random integer between 0 and 5000, representing a number of milliseconds, which is stored in the variable `sleepTime`. After printing some explanatory text to the console, the statement `Thread.Sleep(sleepTime)` puts the current thread to sleep for 0 to 5 seconds. When the thread awakens, more explanatory text is printed to the console. A sample run of the resulting SleepThreadTest application is shown in Figure 12.9.

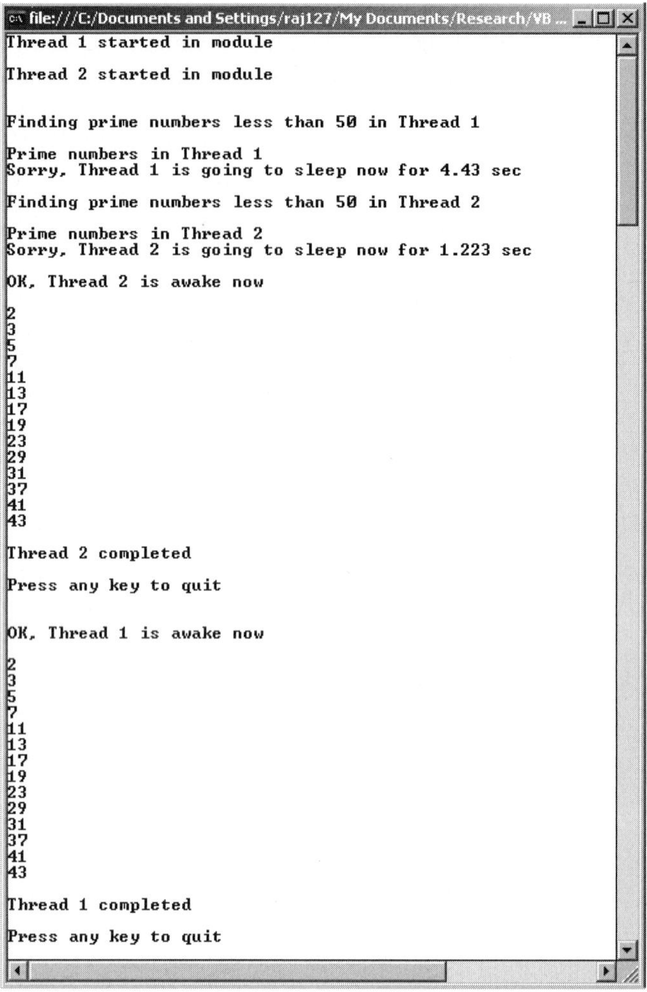

FIGURE 12.9 A sample run of the SleepThreadTest console application

Figure 12.9 indicates that Thread 1 is created first, Thread 2 second, as expected. Then, Thread 1 is put to sleep for 4.43 seconds. Immediately, Thread 2 is put to sleep for 1.223 seconds. We can expect Thread 2 to wake up before Thread 1, which indeed turns out to be the case. When Thread 2 wakes up, Thread 1 will still be sleeping for another 4.43 – 1.223 = 3.207 seconds, plenty of time for Thread 2 to generate all its prime numbers and then terminate. Then, Thread 1 wakes up and displays its prime numbers.

In the previous examples, all threads were created with equal priority by default, so the CPU assigns quanta (time slices) to each equally. Next, you will learn how to assign threads different levels of priority, allowing more important threads to complete their tasks first.

Multithreading with Priority

You can assign threads different priorities, and even have your program change those priorities while the application is running. This allows more important threads to execute ahead of less important threads, which may indeed make users of the application more satisfied.

To add priorities to threads, add the following code to the `PrimeNumberFinder` class in Figure 12.6 just after the class declaration (Line 3) and before the constructor `New` (Line 5):

```
Const THREAD_PRIORITY_HIGHEST = 2
Private Declare Function SetThreadPriority Lib "kernel32" ( _
    ByVal hThread As Integer, ByVal nPriority As Integer) _
    As Integer
Private Declare Function GetCurrentThread Lib "kernel32" () _
    As Integer
```

The first statement declares a constant `THREAD_PRIORITY_HIGHEST` and sets it equal to a value of 2. Recall that the normal default priority of all threads is 0. The second statement declares the `Function SetThreadPriority`. It uses the file kernel32.dll, which is the 32-bit dynamic link library found in the Windows operating system kernel that handles memory management, input/output operations, and interrupts. The arguments of `SetThreadPriority` are `hThread` (an integer variable of type `HANDLE` that gives the application access to a numbered thread in an application) and `nPriority` (an integer variable representing the priority of a thread). The final statement declares a `Function GetCurrentThread`, which returns the integer value that the operating system assigns to a thread.

The following statement is also added to the `PrimeNumberFinder` class in Figure 12.6, within the PrimeFinder2 method, immediately after the variable declarations (Line 64):

```
SetThreadPriority(GetCurrentThread, THREAD_PRIORITY_HIGHEST)
```

This statement calls the `SetThreadPriority` function, which in turn calls the `GetCurrentThread` function and uses the `THREAD_PRIORITY_HIGHEST` constant to set the priority of the `FindPrime2` thread to 2. Note that doing so will cause Thread 2 in the DualThreadTest application to have a higher priority than Thread 1 (which is normal, or 0).

When this code is added to the DualThreadTest application (referred to now as the PriorityThreadTest application), the sample run in Figure 12.10 results.

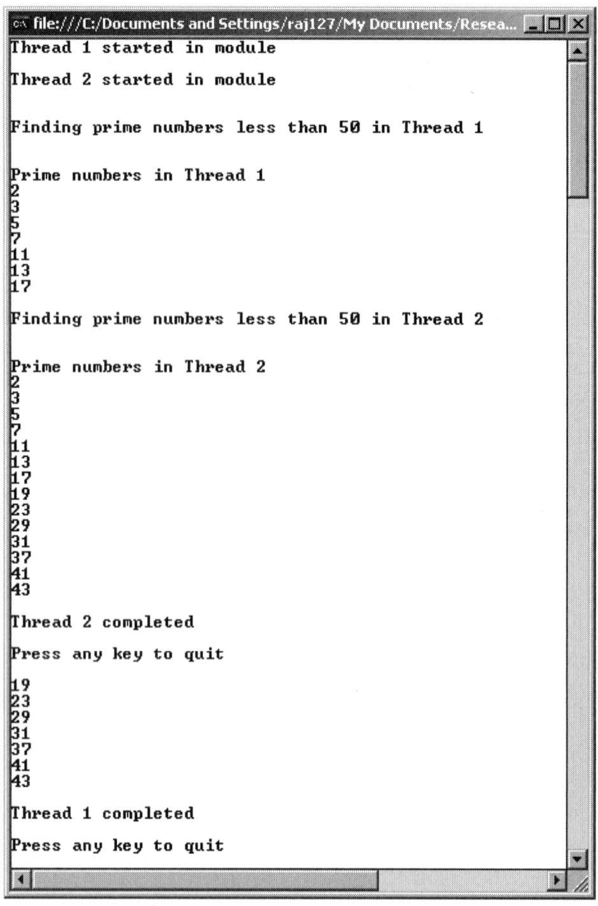

FIGURE 12.10 Sample run of the PriorityThreadTest console application with priorities

Figure 12.10 indicates that Thread 1 and Thread 2 begin as expected. Thread 1 is started and a message displays in the console. Then Thread 2 is started (it has a higher priority than Thread 1), but in the time that it takes the computer to display the message "Thread 2 started in module" (an input/output operation that requires extra time), Thread 1 begins finding primes. (See the code in Figure 12.7—Thread 1 is started, then the message is printed, and then Thread 2 is started.) Thread 1, taking advantage of the delay in starting Thread 2, jumps the gun and begins generating prime numbers. Thread 1 actually makes it through 17. However, once Thread 2 starts (after the message has been printed to the console), it has priority, and the CPU gives it all the time it needs to display all of its primes. When Thread 2 is complete, the CPU switches back to Thread 1, which then finishes.

Multithreading with `Monitor`, `Join`, and `Interrupt`

The previous examples in this section have dealt with basic multithreading involving sleep and priority. The example presented in this section represents a major overhaul of these previous examples in order to demonstrate other important multithreading techniques using the class `Monitor` and the methods `Join` and `Interrupt`.

An Example of a Thread Synchronization Problem

Several threads in an application can safely attempt to read from one source of data (such as an array); because the processor gives each thread a turn, no conflicts arise. However, if different threads attempt to modify a shared data resource, conflicts can occur.

To illustrate, suppose three threads are running in an application: `thread1`, `thread2`, and `thread3`. It is the job of `thread1` and `thread2` to update the same data structure, `anArray`, which contains three elements, `anArray(0)`, `anArray(1)`, and `anArray(2)`. Each element initially has a value of 0. The task of `thread3` is to read the data from the array. If `anArray` is not carefully monitored by the application, the CPU will grant access to `anArray` to the three threads in a simple round-robin fashion, giving a quantum (time slice) to each equally.

Suppose `thread1` has new information and wants to update `anArray` with values 10, 20, and 30 for `anArray(0)`, `anArray(1)`, and `anArray(2)`, respectively. Also, `thread2` has even more up-to-date information than this and needs to store the values 40, 50, and 60 in `anArray`. Say that the CPU lets `thread1` begin its update, which stores 10 and 20, but it then gives `thread2` access to `anArray` (perhaps due to a quantum expiration), which stores 40, 50, and 60 in `anArray` and finishes. The CPU then gives `thread3` access to `anArray` with just enough time to read the 40 and 50 before giving control back to `thread1`, which updates `anArray(2)` with the value of 30 and finishes. Finally, `thread3` is given access to `anArray` to read the final value, which is now 30. So, `thread3` has incorrectly read the values 40, 50, and 30 from `anArray`.

Enforcing Thread Synchronization with the `Monitor` Class

To solve the problem described in the previous section, the application needs to give a thread exclusive access to an object (such as `anArray`) until it completes its update before the application gives access to other threads. This is an example of thread synchronization. Visual Basic .NET uses the class `Monitor` to lock objects so that a thread has exclusive access while other threads are kept waiting. Table 12.1 explains some of the key methods of the `Monitor` class.

Method	Action
`Monitor.Enter(`*object*`)`	Acquires an exclusive lock on the specified object.
`Monitor.Pulse(`*object*`)`	Moves the next thread in line for the object to the ready state.
`Monitor.PulseAll(`*object*`)`	Moves all threads in line for the object to the ready state.
`Monitor.Wait(`*object*`)` or `Monitor.Wait(`*object*, *interval*`)`	Releases the lock on an object and blocks the current thread until it reacquires the lock. If the specified time-out interval elapses, the thread enters the ready queue.
`Method.Exit(`*object*`)`	Releases an exclusive lock on the specified object.

TABLE 12.1 Key methods in the `Monitor` class

The Monitor.Enter method gives the current thread access to the object and locks out all others. The thread can then update the object as necessary. The Monitor.Pulse method gets the next thread in line ready to acquire the object, while the Monitor.PulseAll gets all waiting threads ready. As with the Thread.Sleep method, the WaitSleepJoin state of a thread (where a thread is blocked) is entered when the Monitor.Wait method is called. Thus, Monitor.Wait blocks the current thread, giving other waiting threads access to the object. Finally, Method.Exit releases the lock imposed by the current thread. An example of using the Monitor class is provided later in this section.

Enforcing Thread Synchronization with SyncLock

Instead of using Method.Enter and Method.Exit to block threads from accessing a particular object, synchronization can also be implemented using the SyncLock statement as follows:

```
Dim codeKey = New Object()
SyncLock codeKey
      'code to be executed by different threads
End SyncLock
```

The variable codeKey is a reference type that acts like a key to the SyncLock statement. Objects within the SyncLock statement (such as an array) block access to other threads until the executing thread that has possession of the codeKey finishes running the code. You'll have a chance to learn more about the SyncLock statement in the Programming Example at the end of the chapter.

Join and Interrupt

A thread can also enter the WaitSleepJoin state via the Thread.Join method. The Join method is called by a particular thread object and works as follows. Suppose the delegate (the code that defines what a thread does) for thread1 contains the code thread2.Join(). This means that when thread1 is started (and calls its delegate), the code thread2.Join() will be executed. That statement causes thread1 to join thread2, implying that thread1 is blocked until thread2 completes. (This is something like a tag team at a professional wrestling match.) Code such as thread2.Join(5000) implies that thread1 joins thread2 and is blocked until thread2 terminates or 5000 milliseconds (5 seconds) elapses, whichever comes first.

When a thread is blocked in the WaitSleepJoin state, the Thread.Interrupt() method places it in the Running state. For example, if thread1 is blocked, thread1.Interrupt() removes it from the WaitSleepJoin state. If a thread is not currently blocked, it will be interrupted when it next begins to block. Calling the Interrupt method always causes an exception to be thrown. Examples of Join and Interrupt are given in the following application.

Examples of Monitor, Join, and Interrupt

The thread test applications presented earlier in this chapter will now undergo a major overhaul to illustrate the Wait, Join, and Interrupt methods. The new console application, WaitJoinInterruptThreadTest, consists of a module that contains a Main method and a PrimeNumberFinder class, all in a single file, PrimeNumberFinder.vb, as shown in Figure 12.11.

```
Imports System.Threading

Module PrimeNumberModule
    Private finder1 As New PrimeNumberFinder
    Private finder2 As New PrimeNumberFinder
    Private finder3 As New PrimeNumberFinder
    Private thread1 As New Thread(AddressOf finder1.FindPrime1)
    Private thread2 As New Thread(AddressOf finder2.FindPrime2)
    Private thread3 As New Thread(AddressOf finder3.FindPrime3)
    Private aQueue = New Queue
    Private waitTime As Integer
    Private maxNumber As Integer = 40

    'program starts in main thread
    Public Sub Main()
        thread1.Name = "Thread 1"
        thread2.Name = "Thread 2"
        thread3.Name = "Thread 3"

        Console.WriteLine( _
            thread1.Name & " started in module")
        thread1.Start()

        Console.WriteLine( _
            thread2.Name & " started in module")
        thread2.Start()

        Console.WriteLine( _
            thread3.Name & " started in module")
        thread3.Start()

        Console.WriteLine("Main thread completed")
    End Sub 'Main

    Private Class PrimeNumberFinder
        Public Sub New() 'constructor
        End Sub

        Public Sub FindPrime1()
            waitTime = 5000 '5000 milliseconds, or 5 seconds
            EnterTheQueue(thread1, waitTime)
            FindAndDisplayPrimes(thread1, maxNumber)
        End Sub 'FindPrime1

        Public Sub FindPrime2()
            waitTime = 1000 '1000 milliseconds, or 1 second
            EnterTheQueue(thread2, waitTime)
            Try
                Console.WriteLine(thread2.Name & _
                    " going to sleep indefinitely")
                Thread.Sleep(Timeout.Infinite)
            Catch ex As ThreadInterruptedException
                Console.WriteLine(thread2.Name & " interrupted")
            End Try
            FindAndDisplayPrimes(thread2, maxNumber)
        End Sub 'FindPrime2

        Public Sub FindPrime3()
            Console.WriteLine(thread3.Name & _
                " joined to Thread 1")
            thread1.Join() 'this thread (thread3) joins thread1
            thread2.Interrupt() 'interrupt thread2 from infinite sleep
```

(Figure is continued on next page)

```
63            FindAndDisplayPrimes(thread3, maxNumber)
64        End Sub 'FindPrime3
65
66        Public Sub EnterTheQueue(ByVal theThread, ByVal timeInQueue)
67            Monitor.Enter(aQueue)
68            Console.WriteLine(theThread.Name & _
69                " waiting in queue for " & timeInQueue / 1000 & _
70                " second(s)")
71            Monitor.Wait(aQueue, timeInQueue) 'wait in queue
72            Monitor.Pulse(aQueue) 'activate next in line
73            Monitor.Exit(aQueue) 'exit the queue
74            Console.WriteLine(theThread.Name & _
75                " is out of queue")
76        End Sub
77
78        Public Sub FindAndDisplayPrimes( _
79            ByVal aThread, ByVal maximumPrime)
80            Dim i, newNumber, lastPrime As Integer
81            Dim numberInList As Integer
82            Dim primeList As New List(Of Integer)
83            Console.WriteLine("Finding prime numbers less than " & _
84                maximumPrime & " in " & aThread.Name)
85            'algorithm for finding prime numbers
86            primeList.Add(2) 'first prime number is 2
87            numberInList = primeList.Count
88            lastPrime = primeList.Item(0)
89            newNumber = lastPrime + 1
90            While newNumber < maximumPrime
91                For i = 0 To numberInList - 1
92                    If newNumber Mod primeList.Item(i) = 0 Then
93                        Exit For 'not a prime
94                    Else 'is a prime
95                        If i = numberInList - 1 Then
96                            lastPrime = newNumber
97                            primeList.Add(lastPrime)
98                            numberInList = primeList.Count
99                            Console.WriteLine(lastPrime)
100                       End If
101                   End If
102               Next
103               newNumber += 1 'test next number
104           End While
105           Console.WriteLine(vbCrLf & aThread.Name & " completed")
106           Console.WriteLine("Press any key to continue")
107           Console.ReadLine()
108       End Sub 'FindAndDisplayPrimes
109   End Class 'PrimeNumberFinder
110 End Module 'PrimeNumberModule
```

FIGURE 12.11 Module `PrimeNumberModule` in the WaitJoinInterruptThreadTest application

The application begins by importing the namespace `System.Threading`, which contains classes such as `Thread` and `Monitor` (Line 1). It then declares the module `PrimeNumberModule` (Line 3). Following the module declaration are several `Private` variable declarations (Lines 4–12). These include three `PrimeNumberFinder` objects, three `Thread` objects, a `Queue` object, and two integers. The `Main` method (Lines 15–33) simply names the three threads, starts the three threads, and prints a message to the console that the `Main` thread has completed its tasks.

Following the `Main` method is the `PrimeNumberFinder` class (Lines 35–109). It contains an empty constructor (Lines 36–37), which is simply used to create three objects, `finder1`, `finder2`, and `finder3`. These three objects are used in `Main` to call the delegates `FindPrime1`, `FindPrime2`, and `FindPrime3`, which are defined in the `PrimeNumberFinder` class. `FindPrime1` (Lines 39–43) is the delegate that represents the actions of `thread1`. It sets `waitTime` to 5 seconds and then calls the `EnterTheQueue` method (Lines 66–76), which will be explained shortly. After this thread exits the queue, it calls the `FindAndDisplayPrimes` method (Lines 78–108), with which you are already familiar. This method finds and displays all prime numbers less than `maxNumber`. The arguments of `FindAndDisplayPrimes` are (1) the thread and (2) the upper limit of prime numbers.

The delegate `FindPrime2` (Lines 45–56, representing `thread2`) also calls `EnterTheQueue` with a wait time of 1000 milliseconds (1 second). Then a `Try` statement (Lines 48–54) is used to put `thread2` to sleep indefinitely. (Recall that the `Sleep` method blocks a thread, putting it in the WaitSleepJoin state.) The `Try` statement is required because waking a sleeping thread throws a `ThreadInterruptedException`, which must be handled. The `Interrupt` is performed by `thread3` (Line 62). `FindPrime2` finishes by calling `FindAndDisplayPrimes` (Line 55).

The delegate `FindPrime3` (Lines 58–64, representing `thread3`) joins (Line 61) with `thread1`, which blocks `thread3` until `thread1` completes. Then `thread3` interrupts (awakens) `thread2` (Line 62). After that, `thread3` calls `FindAndDisplayPrimes` (Line 63).

The `EnterTheQueue` method (Lines 66–76) deserves some explanation. It receives a thread and an integer as parameters. It then uses the `Monitor` class to call certain methods. First, `Monitor.Enter(aQueue)` locks the object `aQueue` to prevent access by any threads other than the current thread. Then, `Monitor.Wait(aQueue, timeInQueue)` places the thread in the WaitSleepJoin state for the specified `timeInQueue`. Note that while a thread is thus blocked, other threads do have access to `aQueue`. After the thread waits, the `Monitor.Pulse(aQueue)` method executes, which makes the next thread in line ready to acquire `aQueue`. Finally, the current thread executes `Method.Exit(aQueue)` to remove the thread from `aQueue`.

The last method in the `PrimeNumberFinder` class is `FindAndDisplayPrimes` (Lines 78–108). You are already familiar with the algorithm in this method from earlier examples in this chapter. In Figure 12.11, the algorithm is placed here within a method for convenience. A sample run of this application is shown in Figure 12.12.

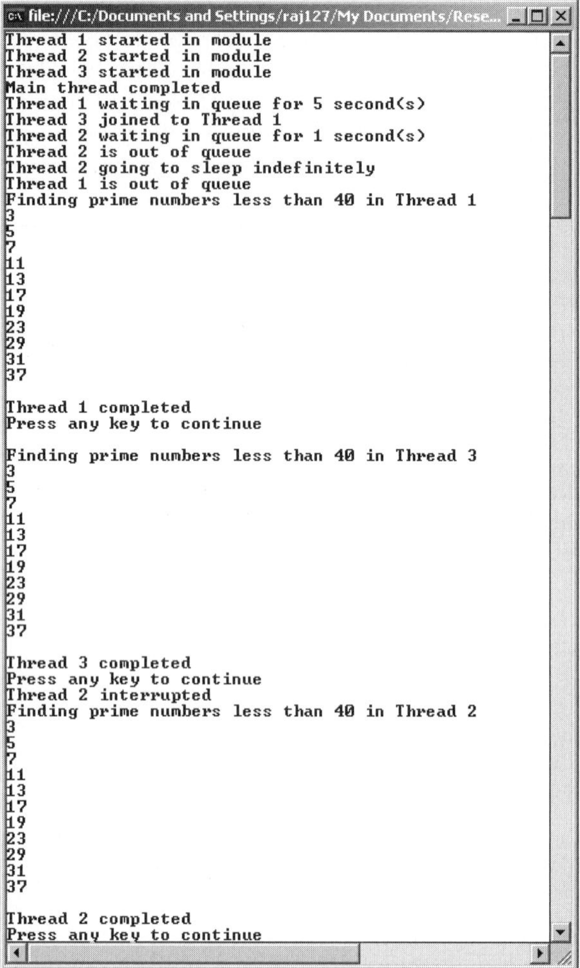

FIGURE 12.12 Sample run of the WaitJoinInterruptThreadTest console application

Following the flow of execution in Figure 12.12, Thread 1, Thread 2, and Thread 3 are started and the main thread completes its tasks. Since Thread 1 was started first, it appears next in the display, but it immediately waits in the queue for 5 seconds. (See the `FindPrime1` delegate in Figure 12.11.) While Thread 1 is waiting, the CPU next gives its attention to Thread 2, which also immediately enters the queue, but only for 1 second. While Thread 2 is now in the queue, Thread 3 grabs the CPU and is immediately joined to Thread 1. This means that Thread 3 must wait until Thread 1 completes before it can proceed.

Figure 12.12 now indicates that Thread 2 is out of the queue after remaining there for 1 second. (Thread 1 still has 4 more seconds to wait in the queue.) We know that as soon as Thread 2 is out of the queue, it goes to sleep indefinitely.We also know that Thread 3 must wait for Thread 1 to complete before it can run. So the only other possible event is that Thread 1 exits the queue. (Thread 3 must wait for Thread 1 to complete and Thread 2 is asleep.) Therefore, Thread 1 will display all of its prime numbers under 40 and complete.

After Thread 1 terminates, that leaves only Thread 3 ready for action, since Thread 2 is still asleep, Thread 3 can now execute because it was joined to Thread 1, which is finished. The very next thing that Thread 3 does is an

`Interrupt` of Thread 2. Note that the `Interrupt` method throws a `ThreadInterruptedException` and Thread 2 wants to display the message "Thread 2 interrupted" to the console. This is an I/O operation that causes Thread 2 to be blocked momentarily, so Thread 3 takes advantage of the available CPU and has just enough time to call the `FindAndDisplayPrimes` method, displaying the values 3 and 5. At this point, Thread 2's I/O operation is complete and it grabs the available CPU, displaying all of its primes. With Thread 2 complete, Thread 3 can now display its primes. This is a fairly dizzying but interesting display of multithreaded events.

MULTITHREADING WITH WINDOWS FORMS

The previous section presented many multithreading examples in a console application. You can also create a multithreaded Windows Forms application (an application that uses forms for input and output). In that case, various threads of the application will ordinarily need to access certain controls in the form. For example, a form may contain a `ListBox` control whose items may be added or deleted by various threads. However, multithreading in a Windows Forms applications presents problems.

As it turns out, Windows Forms applications that grant multithreaded access to controls do not inherently contain **thread-safe code** (code that will execute properly when run in a threaded environment). Two or more threads manipulating the state of a single control may force the control into an **inconsistent state** (a condition in which the properties of a control have unpredictable values). An inconsistent state is caused by a **race condition**, which means that the outcome of a program depends on which of two or more threads accesses a control first. Thus, if a race condition exists for a control (such as a `ListBox` whose values are determined by an array), it is very likely that the control will enter an inconsistent state, producing unpredictable results. Another possible result of multithreading in a Windows Forms application is a **deadlock**, a condition where two or more processes are blocked, each waiting on a lock held by the others. (A deadlock is also known as a deadly embrace.) Whether the problem is an inconsistent state or a deadlock, multithreading with forms can yield applications that fail to meet user needs.

The problem is that Windows Forms do not automatically enforce synchronization among threads. When your application creates a Windows form, that form is executed in its own special GUI thread. A Windows application can contain many different forms, each running in its own GUI thread. When the Windows application has sole control over creating threads, method calls made by component events (such as clicking a button) are always made within the GUI thread that created the form. Therefore, no conflicts can occur.

However, when the programmer assumes control over creating threads in a Windows Forms application, **cross-threading** occurs. Cross-threading is a method call made to a control by a thread that did not create the control, and it is not thread safe. Such cross-threading will result in an error message while you are debugging the application. If you decide to disable this error message during debugging, the same error message may occur while the application is running. The next section provides an example of Windows Forms cross-threading, along with a solution to this problem.

Example of Unsafe Threading in a Windows Forms Application

Figure 12.13 provides the design and the program code for `MainForm` and Figure 12.14 provides the same for `FibonacciForm`, both part of the UnsafeThreadTest application. This application is designed to display numbers in a Fibonacci sequence, a mathematical sequence of numbers obtained by adding the two previous numbers in the sequence to get the next number in the sequence (0, 1, 1, 2, 3, 5, 8, 13, 21, ...). However, it will not run due to cross-threading, as explained in the discussion to follow.

(a) Design for `MainForm`

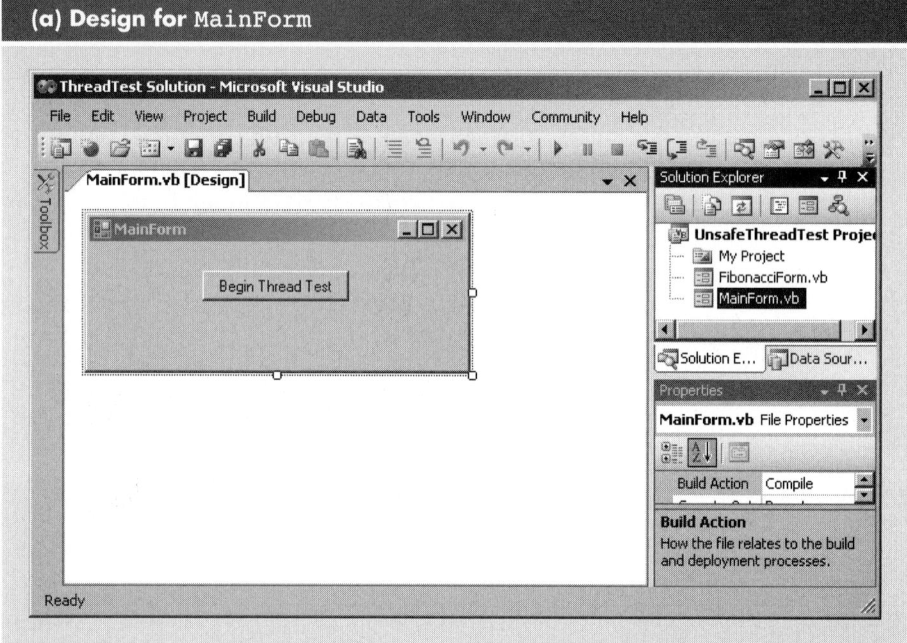

(b) Code for `MainForm`

```
Imports System.Threading

Public Class MainForm
    Private Sub beginButton_Click(ByVal sender As System.Object, _
        ByVal e As System.EventArgs) Handles beginButton.Click

        Dim finder1 As New FibonacciForm
        Dim thread1 As New Thread(AddressOf finder1.FindFibonacci)

        finder1.Show()
        thread1.Start()
        mainLabel.Text = "Thread started"
    End Sub
End Class
```

FIGURE 12.13 Design and code for `MainForm` in the UnsafeThreadTest application

(a) Design for `FibonacciForm`

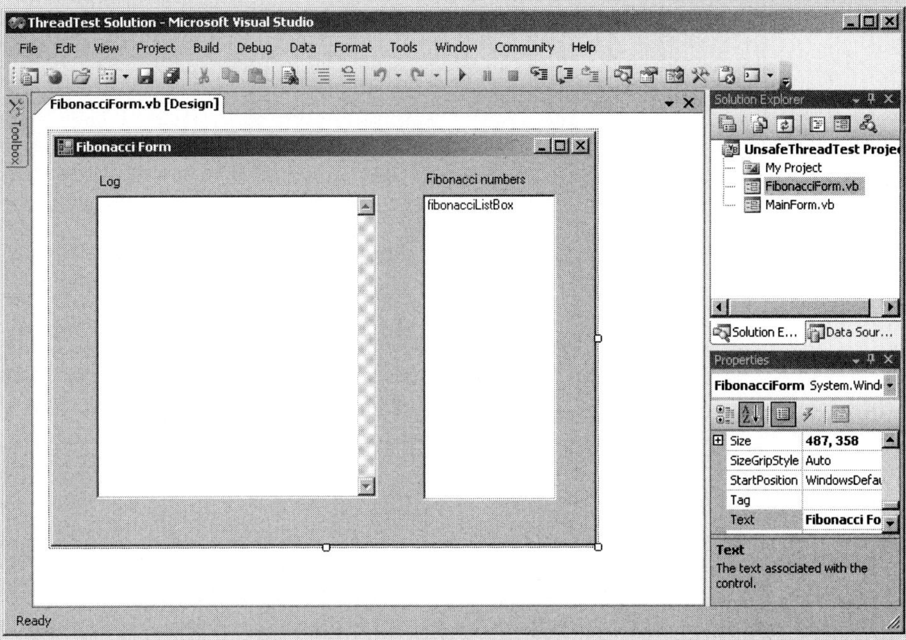

(b) Code for `FibonacciForm`

```
Imports System.Threading

Public Class FibonacciForm

    Public Sub New()
        InitializeComponent()
    End Sub 'New

    Public Sub FindFibonacci()
        Dim maxNumber As Integer = 10
        Dim lastFibonacciNumber, nextToLastFibonacciNumber As Integer
        Dim newFibonacciNumber, numberInListBox As Integer
        Dim current As Thread = Thread.CurrentThread

        Me.fibonacciTextBox.Text = _
            "Finding Fibonacci numbers less than " & maxNumber & vbCrLf
        'algorithm for finding Fibonacci numbers
        Me.fibonacciListBox.Items.Add(0) 'first Fibonacci number is 0
        Me.fibonacciListBox.Items.Add(1) 'second Fibonacci number is 1
        numberInListBox = fibonacciListBox.Items.Count
        lastFibonacciNumber = _
            fibonacciListBox.Items.Item(numberInListBox - 1)

        While lastFibonacciNumber < maxNumber
            nextToLastFibonacciNumber = _
                fibonacciListBox.Items.Item(numberInListBox - 2)
            newFibonacciNumber = _
                lastFibonacciNumber + nextToLastFibonacciNumber
            lastFibonacciNumber = newFibonacciNumber
```

(Figure is continued on next page)

```
30             If lastFibonacciNumber < maxNumber Then
31                 Me.fibonacciListBox.Items.Add(newFibonacciNumber)
32                 numberInListBox = fibonacciListBox.Items.Count
33             End If
34         End While
35 
36         Me.fibonacciTextBox.Text = "Finished finding Fibonacci numbers"
37     End Sub 'FindFibonacci
38 End Class 'FibonacciForm
```

FIGURE 12.14 Design and code for `FibonacciForm` in the UnsafeThreadTest application

The code for MainForm.vb in Figure 12.13(b) imports the `System.Threading` namespace and declares the `MainForm` class, which contains a `beginButton_Click` event procedure. When `beginButton` is clicked, the object `finder1` (an instance of `FibonacciForm`) is declared (Line 7). It is important to note that it is this main GUI thread that creates `finder1`. Then, a new thread called `thread1` is declared (Line 8) that will execute the delegate `FindFibonacci`, located in class `FibonacciForm`. Finally, `finder1` calls the `Show` method to display `FibonacciForm` (Line 10) and `thread1` is started (Line 11). A brief message is then displayed in `mainLabel` (Line 12). Note that `MainForm` runs in the main GUI thread of the application.

The code for FibonacciForm.vb in Figure 12.14(b) contains the constructor `New`, which creates the form by calling the method `InitializeComponent` (Lines 5–7). The delegate `FindFibonacci`, which is called by `thread1` in the class `MainForm`, contains the code for finding the Fibonacci numbers (Lines 9–37).

Within the delegate `FindFibonacci`, several variables are declared and initialized (Lines 10–13). Then, the apparently simple task of displaying a message in `fibonacciTextBox` is performed (Lines 15–16). The remainder of the code in the delegate represents the algorithm for finding Fibonacci numbers. It is this method call to display text in Line 16 that is critical for this application. The output of Figure 12.15 results when the application runs in the debugger.

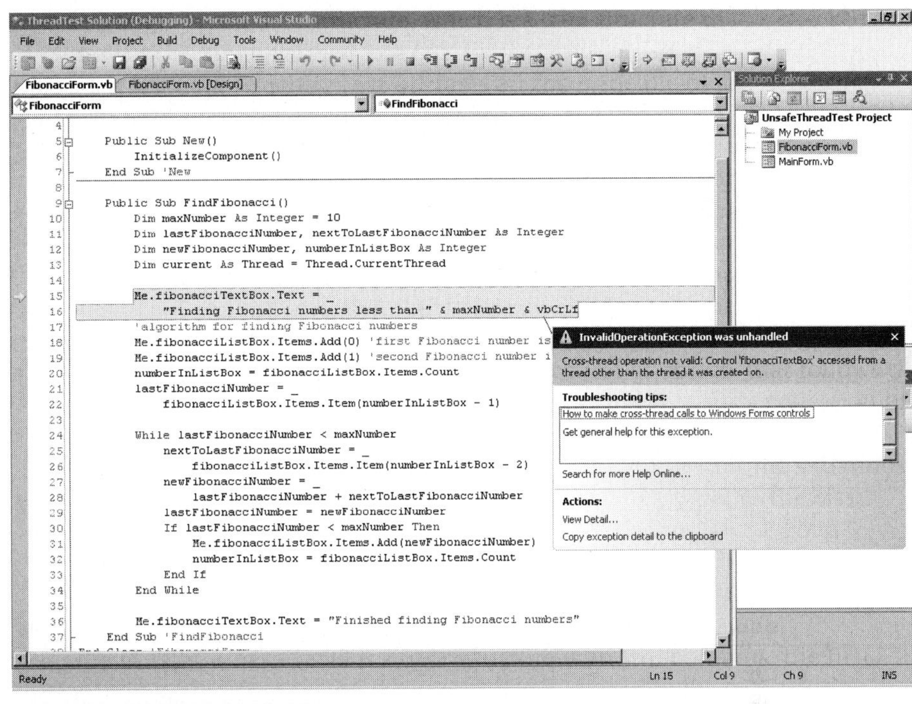

FIGURE 12.15 Sample run of the UnsafeThreadTest application

As Figure 12.15 indicates, the error message "Cross-thread operation not valid: Control 'fibonacciTextBox' accessed from a thread other than the thread it was created on." results during the sample run. This error message signifies that `fibonacciTextBox` was created in the main thread of the application, but it is being accessed by the newly created thread, `thread1`. This is a case of cross-threading which Visual Basic does not inherently allow and which must be addressed by the addition of program code, as explained in the next section.

Performing Thread-Safe Operations in a Windows Forms Application

The problem with cross-threading is that code in one thread (one that your program code creates) is attempting to access a control created by the application's main GUI thread. Doing so is not inherently thread safe in Visual Basic. To address this problem, your program needs to determine if a call to a given control is being made from a thread other than the one that created the control. For this purpose, controls have a property called `InvokeRequired` that has a value of `True` if the caller is on a different thread. If `InvokeRequired` is `True`, then this program code from an outside thread can't access the control in a normal way because that is not thread safe.

A thread-safe way of accessing a control is through the use of a delegate. You are already familiar with the term "delegate" in the context of creating a thread. It was rather loosely defined then as the method that a thread will execute, such as thread `thread1` executing the delegate (method) `finder1.FindFibonacci` in Figure 12.13(b). In fact, you won't see the actual delegate object in the code of Figure 12.13(b) because Visual Basic creates it for you behind the scenes.

However, in a cross-threading context, you will need a more precise definition of a delegate. In this context, a **delegate** is an instance of the `Delegate` class that holds a reference to a method. Thus, executing a delegate becomes an indirect way of calling a method. This is really the same as the delegate discussed in a thread creation context because in that case, a delegate is an object (instantiated by Visual Basic when the thread is created) that the new thread uses to execute a particular method. For example, the delegate for `thread1` in Figure 12.13(b) contains the method reference `AddressOf finder1.findFibonacci`.

Here is the key point: Using delegates in a cross-threading context is very important because the delegate is called by the same thread that created the control, thus making the call thread safe. Synchronization is automatically enforced for calls to GUI controls made from the GUI thread. The same Fibonacci number–generating application that was presented in Figures 12.13 and 12.14 is now revamped using delegates in a thread-safe manner.

Example of Safe Threading in a Windows Forms Application

Recall that the problem in Figure 12.15 is caused by attempting to access `fibonacciTextBox`, created in the main GUI thread, from the method `FindFibonacci`, executed in `thread1`. To solve that problem, access to `fibonacciTextBox` should be made through a delegate. Figure 12.16 explains how this is done.

HOW TO...

Use a Delegate for Safe Cross-Threading

1. Declare the `Delegate` object within the form that contains the control to which access is required. The method signature for the delegate must exactly match the signature of the method to which the delegate refers.
2. Create a separate `Sub` procedure to access the control (the method to which the delegate will refer).
3. Within this `Sub` procedure, create an `If...Else...End If` structure with the following logic: If the `InvokeRequired` property for the control is `True` (the call to the control is made by a thread other than the thread that created the control), create the `Delegate` object and then apply the delegate with the `Invoke` method; otherwise, access the control in the normal direct manner.

FIGURE 12.16 How to use a delegate for safe cross-threading

The `Invoke` method above is simply the method used to execute a delegate. The Fibonacci sequence problem will be used to illustrate safe threading for Windows Forms in the SafeThreadTest application. The code for `MainForm` in this application is the same as that shown in Figure 12.13(b). However, the code for `FibonacciForm` in the SafeThreadTest application will be different than that for the UnsafeThreadTest application, as shown in Figure 12.17. The new code in Figure 12.17 is shaded.

```
Imports System.Threading

Public Class FibonacciForm
    Delegate Sub SetTextBoxCallBack(ByVal someText As String)
    Delegate Sub SetListBoxCallBack(ByVal aNumber As Integer)
```

(Figure is continued on next page)

```
    Private someText As String

    Public Sub New()
        InitializeComponent()
    End Sub 'New

    Public Sub FindFibonacci()
        Dim maxNumber As Integer = 5000
        Dim lastFibonacciNumber, nextToLastFibonacciNumber As Integer
        Dim newFibonacciNumber, numberInListBox As Integer
        Dim current As Thread = Thread.CurrentThread
        someText = "Finding Fibonacci numbers less than " & _
            maxNumber & vbCrLf
        SetTextBox(someText)

        'algorithm for finding Fibonacci numbers
        SetListBox(0) 'first Fibonacci number is 0
        SetListBox(1) 'second Fibonacci number is 1
        numberInListBox = fibonacciListBox.Items.Count
        lastFibonacciNumber = _
            fibonacciListBox.Items.Item(numberInListBox - 1)

        While lastFibonacciNumber < maxNumber
            nextToLastFibonacciNumber = _
                fibonacciListBox.Items.Item(numberInListBox - 2)
            newFibonacciNumber = _
                lastFibonacciNumber + nextToLastFibonacciNumber
            lastFibonacciNumber = newFibonacciNumber
            If lastFibonacciNumber < maxNumber Then
                SetListBox(newFibonacciNumber)
                numberInListBox = fibonacciListBox.Items.Count
            End If
        End While

        someText += "Finished finding Fibonacci numbers"
        Me.SetTextBox(someText)
    End Sub

    Private Sub SetTextBox(ByVal someText As String)
        If Me.fibonacciTextBox.InvokeRequired Then
            Dim aDelegate As New _
                SetTextBoxCallBack(AddressOf SetTextBox)
            Me.Invoke(aDelegate, New Object() {someText})
        Else
            Me.fibonacciTextBox.Text = someText
        End If
    End Sub

    Private Sub SetListBox(ByVal aNumber As Integer)
        If Me.fibonacciTextBox.InvokeRequired Then
            Dim aDelegate As New _
                SetListBoxCallBack(AddressOf SetListBox)
            Me.Invoke(aDelegate, New Object() {aNumber})
        Else
            Me.fibonacciListBox.Items.Add(aNumber)
        End If
    End Sub
End Class
```

FIGURE 12.17 Code for `FibonacciForm` in the SafeThreadTest application

In Figure 12.17, two `Delegate` objects are declared, one for calling the `SetTextBox` method and one for calling the `SetListBox` method (Lines 4 and 5, respectively). These delegates have names `SetTextBoxCallBack` and `SetListBoxCallBack`. The term "callback" is customarily used because it implies that a method call will be performed indirectly through a delegate. Then these two methods (`Sub` procedures) are defined (in Lines 45–53 and 55–63, respectively). Within each of these methods, an `If. . .Else. . .End If` structure is coded. If `fibonacciTextBox.InvokeRequired` is `True` (a call is being made from a thread other than the thread that created `fibonacciTextBox`), `aDelegate` is created that contains a reference (a pointer) to the address of the `SetTextBox` method. Next, this delegate is executed using the `Invoke` method by the control that owns `fibonacciTextBox` (`Me`, or `FibonacciForm`). This indirect call to the `SetTextBox` method, using a delegate, is thread safe because the call is made by the same thread that created `fibonacciTextBox`. Exactly the same conditions are set up for `fibonacciListBox`. A sample run of the SafeThreadTest application is shown in Figure 12.18.

(a) `MainForm`

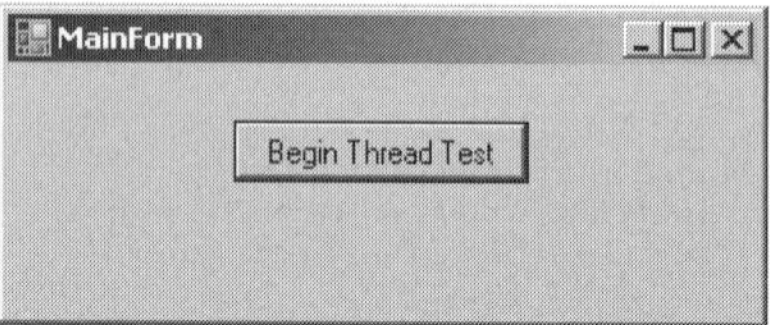

(b) `FibonacciForm`

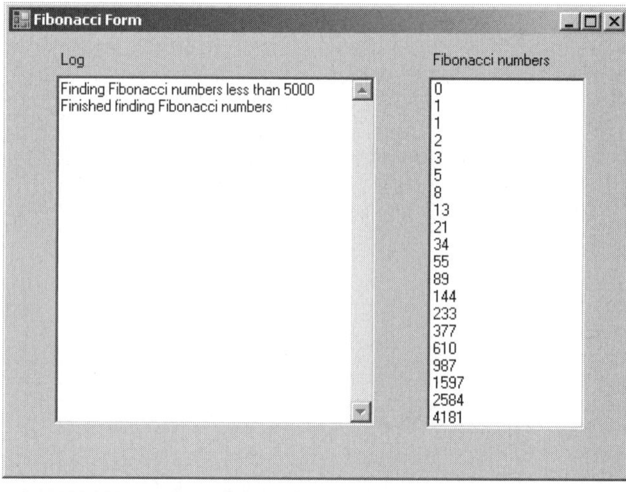

FIGURE 12.18 Sample run of the SafeThreadTest application

PROGRAMMING EXAMPLE

Checking Account

This application creates a console application called Account Balance that creates a checking account and performs transactions on that account (a deposit and a withdrawal). The module `AccountBalance` uses a separate thread for each transaction, which is essential to keeping the balance of the checking account accurate. For example, if a husband and wife have a joint account, one might be making a deposit at roughly the same time another is making a withdrawal. In that case, the first transaction should be allowed to complete before another transaction is allowed to begin, and threading enables this kind of logic.

The module `AccountBalance` contains a `Main` method that drives the application, a `CheckingAccount` class, and a `Transaction` class. The details of the Account Balance application follow.

Class Diagram

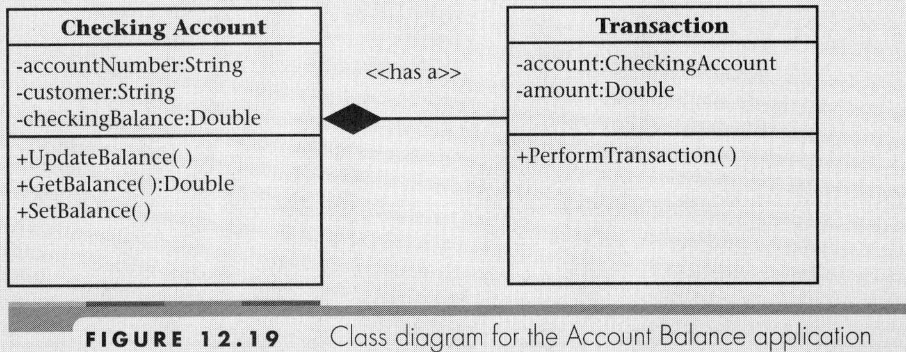

FIGURE 12.19 Class diagram for the Account Balance application

Pseudocode for `Sub Main`

Pseudocode

1. create a new `CheckingAccount` object with an initial balance
2. create two Transaction objects (one deposit, one withdrawal)
3. create two Thread objects, one for each Transaction object
4. start the two Thread objects
5. join the main thread with the two created threads

FIGURE 12.20 Pseudocode for Account Balance application

Code

```
Imports System.Threading

Public Module AccountBalance
    Sub Main() 'main thread of console application
        'create two new checking accounts
        Dim account1 As CheckingAccount = _
            New CheckingAccount("111", "Customer 1", 500)

        'create two transactions
        Dim transaction1 As Transaction = _
            New Transaction(account1, 2000)
        Dim transaction2 As Transaction = _
            New Transaction(account1, -1000)

```

(Figure is continued on next page)

```
        'create two threads, one for each transaction
        Dim thread1 As Thread = New _
            Thread(AddressOf transaction1.PerformTransaction)
        Dim thread2 As Thread = New _
            Thread(AddressOf transaction2.performTransaction)

        'perform the transactions
        thread1.Start()
        thread2.Start()
        Try
            'main thread is joined to other two threads
            thread1.Join()
            thread2.Join()
        Catch e As Exception
            Console.Write(e.ToString())
        End Try

        Console.Write("Press any key to continue" & vbCrLf)
        Console.ReadLine()
    End Sub

    Public Class CheckingAccount
        Private accountNumber As String
        Private customer As String
        Private checkingBalance As Double

        Public Sub New(ByRef accountNumber As String, _
            ByVal customer As String, ByVal checkingBalance As Double)
            'set instance variables
            Me.accountNumber = accountNumber
            Me.customer = customer
            Me.checkingBalance = checkingBalance
        End Sub

        Public Sub UpdateBalance(ByVal amount As Integer)
            Dim typeOfTransaction As String
            Dim reportedAmount As Double
            If amount > 0 Then
                typeOfTransaction = "depositing"
                reportedAmount = amount
            Else
                typeOfTransaction = "withdrawing"
                reportedAmount = -amount
            End If

            Monitor.Enter(Me)
            Console.WriteLine(customer & " previous balance: $" & _
                GetBalance()) 'report
            Console.WriteLine(customer & " " & typeOfTransaction _
                & " $" & reportedAmount)
            checkingBalance += amount 'calculate new balance
            SetBalance(checkingBalance) 'set balance
            Console.WriteLine(customer & " new balance: $" & _
                GetBalance()) 'report
            Monitor.Exit(Me)

            Console.WriteLine()
        End Sub

        Private Function GetBalance() As Integer
            Try
                Thread.Sleep(1000) 'delay for processing
```

(Figure is continued on next page)

```
            Catch e As Exception
                Console.Write(e.ToString())
            End Try
            Return checkingBalance
        End Function

        Private Sub SetBalance(ByVal amount As Integer)
            Try
                Thread.Sleep(1000) 'delay for processing
            Catch e As Exception
                Console.Write(e.ToString())
            End Try
            checkingBalance = amount
        End Sub
    End Class

    Public Class Transaction
        Private account As CheckingAccount
        Private amount As Integer

        Public Sub New(ByRef account As CheckingAccount, _
            ByVal amount As Integer)
            'set instance variables
            Me.account = account
            Me.amount = amount
        End Sub

        Public Sub PerformTransaction()
            account.UpdateBalance(amount)
        End Sub
    End Class 'Transaction
End Module
```

FIGURE 12.21 Program code for Account Balance application

Input/Output

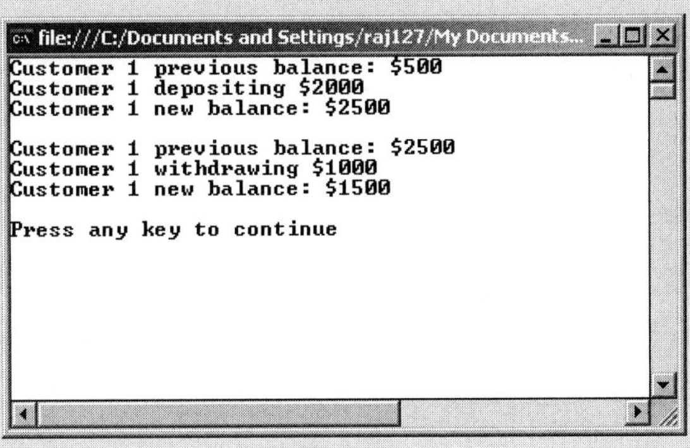

FIGURE 12.22 Sample run of the AccountBalance application

Quick Review

- In general, multitasking is the perceived ability to perform several different tasks more or less at the same time. Actually, a person can't do several things at the same time, but he can appear to perform tasks at about the same time by switching from one to another very quickly.
- A thread (short for thread of execution) is that part of a larger process or program on which the processor is working at any one time.
- While multitasking involves a processor running several programs at the same time, multithreading is the condition in which one processor executes several parts (or threads) of a single program at the same time. It actually switches its resources quickly from one program thread to another.
- Multithreading is usually accomplished by the technique of time slicing, where the processor gives a small slice of its time to one thread after another until all are completed. When more than one processor executes multiple threads, multithreading is called multiprocessing.
- A major benefit of multithreading is that it ultimately enables a single program to run faster because any idle processor time on one thread is utilized by another thread. Another benefit of multithreading is that it can make applications more scalable. While the advantages of multithreading can be significant, multithreading also significantly adds to the complexity of developing the application.
- Threads can exist in the following states: Unstarted, Started, Running, Blocked, WaitSleepJoin, Stopped, and Aborted. These states are controlled with Visual Basic methods such as `Start`, `Wait`, `Sleep`, `Join`, `Interrupt`, and `Abort`.
- Every thread has a priority with a value of `Lowest`, `BelowNormal`, `Normal` (the default), `AboveNormal`, or `Highest`. The operating system has a thread scheduler that determines which thread enters the Running state based on a thread's priority. Of a group of threads, the one with the highest priority is executed first and continues to run to completion unless it enters the WaitSleepJoin, Blocked, or Aborted state.
- If more than one thread has the same priority, then the scheduler repeatedly gives each thread a time slice (quantum) on the processor, usually several milliseconds. A thread will continue to execute until its quantum expires or it enters a Stopped, Aborted, Blocked, or WaitSleepJoin state, or another thread with higher priority is placed in the Started state.
- Synchronization is communication between threads for the purpose of controlling the order of thread execution. A multithreaded application should grant only one thread access to a key data source (such as a variable, an array, or a file) at a time. Visual Basic enforces synchronization using the `Monitor` class or the `SyncLock` statement.
- Thread-safe code is program code that executes properly when run in a threaded environment.
- Windows Forms applications that grant multithreaded access to controls do not inherently contain thread-safe code. Two or more threads manipulating the state of a control may force the control into an inconsistent state due to a race condition or a deadlock. This problem is addressed using a `Delegate` object to access form controls in a synchronized and thread-safe manner.

Key Terms

Aborted state—The state a thread enters when it has been terminated due to abnormal conditions.

Blocked state—The state of thread inactivity, due to occurrences such as an input/output request.

cross-threading—A method call made to a control by a thread that did not create the control.

deadlock—A condition in which two or more processes are blocked, each waiting on a lock held by the others. Also known as a deadly embrace.

delegate—An instance of the `Delegate` class, which holds a reference to a method.

inconsistent state—A condition in which the properties of a control have unpredictable values.

multiprocessing—The execution of multiple threads by more than one processor.

multitasking—The perceived ability to perform several different tasks at the same time.

multithreading—The condition in which one processor executes several threads of a single program at the same time.

quantum—A fixed amount of time during which a thread is granted access to the CPU.

race condition—A condition in which the outcome of a program depends on which of two or more threads accesses a control first, resulting in unpredictable results.

Running state—A state a thread enters when it is executing.

scalability—The ability of an application to adapt to increasing demands without significant changes in the computer system's architecture.

Started state—The state a thread enters when it is capable of executing.

Stopped state—The state a thread enters after it has completed its assigned tasks.

synchronization—The communication between threads for the purpose of controlling the order of thread execution and access to program code.

thread—Short for thread of execution, that part of a larger process or program on which the processor is working at any one time.

thread state—The condition or status of a thread at any one time.

thread transition—The act of changing from one thread state to another.

thread-safe code—Code that will execute properly when run in a threaded environment.

`ThreadStart` **delegate**—A specific method that executes on a particular thread.

time slicing—The process by which the processor gives a small slice of its time to one thread after another until all are completed.

Unstarted state—The initial thread state for threads that have been created by a program but never executed.

WaitSleepJoin state—A state of thread inactivity that occurs when either the Wait, Sleep, or Join methods are called on a thread.

Review Questions

1. A thread is the combination of several programs.
   a. True
   b. False
2. A thread can transition directly from the Started to the Running state.
   a. True
   b. False
3. A thread with priority `Highest` will never be required to wait.
   a. True
   b. False
4. The `SyncLock` statement should be used with the `Monitor.Enter` method.
   a. True
   b. False
5. Calling the method `Interrupt` throws an exception.
   a. True
   b. False
6. Multithreading in a Windows Forms application is automatically thread safe.
   a. True
   b. False
7. A race condition is also known as a deadly race.
   a. True
   b. False
8. A deadlock is also known as a deadly embrace.
   a. True
   b. False
9. Access to a Windows Forms control should always be made from a thread that created the control.
   a. True
   b. False
10. The `Start` method belongs to the `Thread` class.
    a. True
    b. False
11. Which term refers to executing multiple programs?
    a. multithreading
    b. multiprocessing
    c. multitasking
    d. none of the above
12. Which term refers to the ability of an application to adapt to increasing demands?
    a. responsibility
    b. extensibility
    c. multithreading
    d. scalability

13. The term "time slice" relates most directly to which of the following terms?
    a. second
    b. millisecond
    c. nanosecond
    d. quantum
14. Which of the following thread states is entered when a thread encounters I/O operations?
    a. Stopped
    b. Aborted
    c. Blocked
    d. WaitSleepJoin
15. Which of the following thread states is entered when a thread completes its process?
    a. Stopped
    b. Aborted
    c. Blocked
    d. WaitSleepJoin
16. Which of the following thread states involves the `Monitor` class?
    a. Stopped
    b. Aborted
    c. Blocked
    d. WaitSleepJoin
17. Which of the following is not a method of the `Monitor` class?
    a. `Wait`
    b. `Sleep`
    c. `Pulse`
    d. `Enter`
18. The `AddressOf` operator is most closely associated with which of the following?
    a. console
    b. delegate
    c. thread state
    d. form
19. `InvokeRequired` is a property of which of the following classes?
    a. `Exception`
    b. `Monitor`
    c. `Thread`
    d. `Delegate`
20. `PulseAll` is a method of which of the following classes?
    a. `Exception`
    b. `Monitor`
    c. `Thread`
    d. `Delegate`

Computer Exercises

In the following exercises, follow all conventions for creating organized, user-friendly console or GUI applications. Your instructor may also request that you use TOE charts, pseudocode, flowcharts, and/or UML diagrams as planning aids.

1. In this exercise, you modify the SimpleThreadTest application to find Fibonacci numbers instead of prime numbers.
   a. Copy the SimpleThreadTest Solution folder in the \VBReloadedAdvanced\Chap12 folder and rename it FibonacciThreadTest Solution.
   b. Open the application in the FibonacciThreadTest Solution folder.
   c. Open the application in the SafeThreadTest Solution folder in the \VBReloadedAdvanced\Chap12 folder.
   d. Replace the code for the prime number algorithm in the FibonacciThreadTest application with code from the Fibonacci algorithm in the SafeThreadTest application so that the FibonacciThreadTest application finds Fibonacci numbers instead of prime numbers.
   e. Save the solution, test the application, and modify as necessary.
2. In this exercise, you modify the DualThreadTest application to utilize three threads instead of two.
   a. Copy the DualThreadTest Solution folder in the \VBReloadedAdvanced\Chap12 folder and rename it TripleThreadTest Solution.
   b. Open the application in the TripleThreadTest Solution folder.
   c. Modify the application so that it creates three threads and uses three different delegates.
   d. Modify the application so that the prime number algorithm exists in only one method.
   e. Save the solution, test the application, and modify as necessary.
3. In this exercise, you modify the SleepThreadTest application to utilize one delegate instead of two.
   a. Copy the SleepThreadTest Solution folder in the \VBReloadedAdvanced\Chap12 folder and rename it ModifiedSleepThreadTest Solution.
   b. Open the application in the ModifiedSleepThreadTest Solution folder.
   c. Modify the application so that it uses one delegate called FindPrime instead of using FindPrime1 and FindPrime2.
   d. Save the solution, test the application, and modify as necessary.
4. In this exercise, you modify the PriorityThreadTest application to utilize three threads with different priorities.
   a. Copy the PriorityThreadTest Solution folder in the \VBReloadedAdvanced\Chap12 folder and rename it ModifiedPriorityThreadTest Solution.
   b. Open the application in the ModifiedPriorityThreadTest Solution folder.
   c. Modify the application so that it uses three threads, each of which has a different priority.
   d. Save the solution, test the application, and modify as necessary.

5. In this exercise, you modify the WaitJoinInterruptThreadTest application to utilize three threads with different priorities.
   a. Copy the WaitJoinInterruptThreadTest Solution folder in the \VBReloadedAdvanced\Chap12 folder and rename it ModifiedWaitJoinInterruptThreadTest Solution.
   b. Open the application in the ModifiedWaitJoinInterruptThreadTest Solution folder.
   c. Add code for a third thread that utilizes all of the following: `SyncLock` with `Wait`; `Join`; and `Sleep`.
   d. Save the solution, test the application, and modify as necessary.

6. In this exercise, you modify the SafeThreadTest application to utilize two threads instead of one.
   a. Copy the SafeThreadTest Solution folder in the \VBReloadedAdvanced\Chap12 folder and rename it ModifiedSafeThreadTest Solution.
   b. Open the application in the ModifiedSafeThreadTest Solution folder.
   c. Add a PrimesForm class that displays prime numbers.
   d. Modify the MainForm so that it creates and executes two threads, one for FibonacciForm and one for PrimesForm.
   e. Save the solution, test the application, and modify as necessary.

7. In this exercise, you modify the AccountBalance application to utilize two threads instead of one.
   a. Copy the AccountBalance Solution folder in the \VBReloadedAdvanced\Chap12 folder and rename it ModifiedAccountBalance Solution.
   b. Open the application in the ModifiedAccountBalance Solution folder.
   c. Add a thread for a new customer with a separate account.
   d. Modify the Main method so that more multiple deposits and withdrawals are made for both accounts.
   e. Save the solution, test the application, and modify as necessary.

Case Projects

Checking Account

Modify the AccountBalance project in this chapter so that it runs as a Windows Forms application. Call the project **GuiAccountBalance**. The form should have a text box for a transaction amount with a deposit and a withdrawal button. A label should display the current balance. Create two different threads for two different customers.

Fast Food

Create a **FastFood** project that simulates the experiences of two different customers (threads) that must wait in line for a clerk, order their food, wait for their orders, and leave the restaurant. Use random times for order preparation.

Library

Create a **Library** project that simulates the experiences of three different library patrons that try to check out one of two different magazines that the library owns. Create a Patron class with instance variables patronId and patronName. Create a Magazine class with magazineId and magazineName. A patron should be able to check out a magazine for a random amount of time from 0 to 60 minutes. A patron's visit to the library should be represented as a thread in the application.

APPENDIX

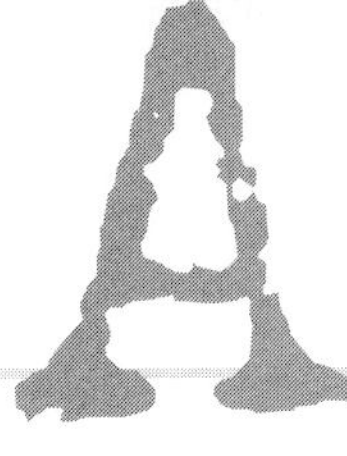

A Deployment

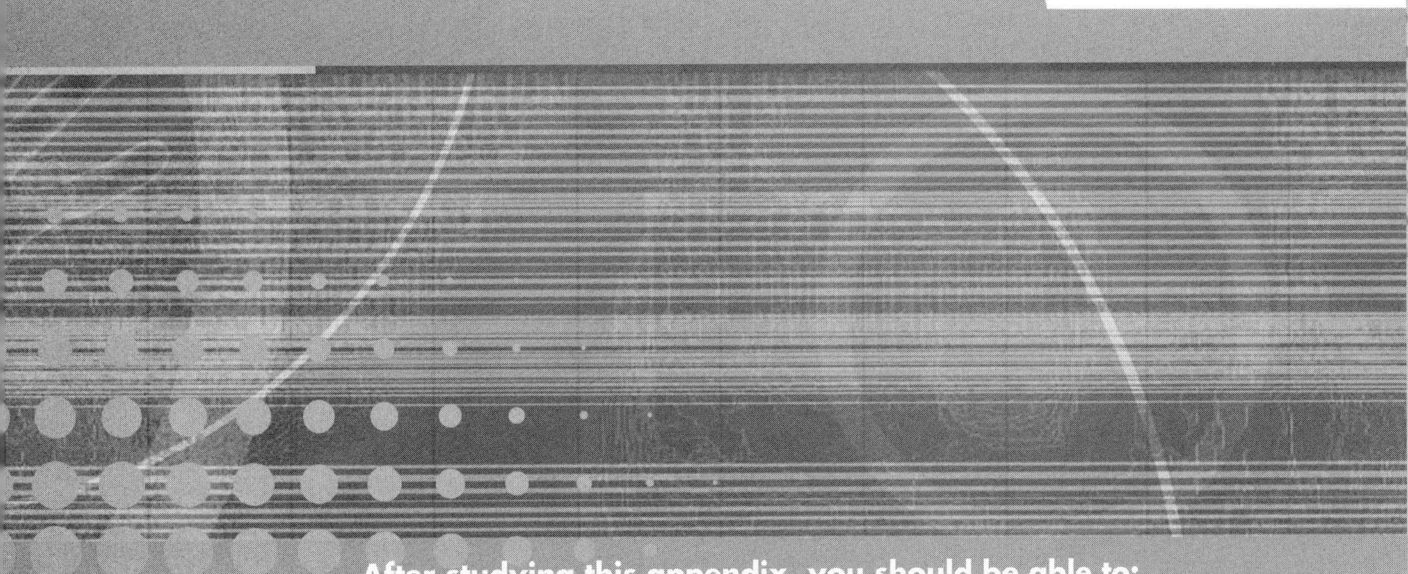

After studying this appendix, you should be able to:

- Deploy a Visual Basic application using ClickOnce technology.

OVERVIEW OF CLICKONCE DEPLOYMENT

Creating an application is one thing; deploying the finished application (placing an application in the production environment) is something else. Deployment usually involves many steps, such as setting up databases, placing files on servers, and configuring options. Not only does deployment involve the initial installation of software, but it includes handling changes and upgrades to the application.

Microsoft Visual Studio .NET offers many deployment options. However, Visual Studio 2005 makes it especially easy to deploy an application by using a special new feature called ClickOnce deployment. ClickOnce eliminates many of the details required with deployment of applications in previous versions of Visual Basic. A ClickOnce application is any Windows Presentation Foundation, Windows Forms, or console application published using ClickOnce technology. You can publish a ClickOnce application in three different ways: from a Web page, from a network file share, or from a medium such as a CD-ROM. A ClickOnce application can be installed on an end user's computer and run locally even when the computer is offline, or it can be run in an online-only mode without permanently installing anything on the end user's computer.

ClickOnce applications can be self-updating; that is, they can check for newer versions as they become available and automatically replace any updated files. The developer can specify the update behavior; a network administrator can also control update strategies, for example by marking an update as mandatory. Updates can also be rolled back to a previous version by the end user or by an administrator.

Because ClickOnce applications are inherently isolated, installing or running a ClickOnce application cannot break existing applications. ClickOnce applications are completely self-contained, thus eliminating the need for installing cooperating files separately. The following sections describe how to publish a ClickOnce application in various ways.

PUBLISHING A CLICKONCE APPLICATION TO THE WEB

The first way of publishing a ClickOnce application is described in Figure A.1. Publishing to the Web allows the end user to run the application either from his or her local computer, from a Web server, or both.

HOW TO...

Publish a ClickOnce Application to the Web

1. Open an existing Visual Basic application project, either by double-clicking the solution file for the project (the file with the .sln extension) or by launching Visual Studio, clicking File in the Visual Studio menu, clicking Open Project, navigating to and clicking the solution file for the project, and clicking Open.
2. Open the Solution Explorer window by clicking View and then clicking Solution Explorer in the Visual Studio menu (see Figure A.2).
3. Right-click the project node in the Server Explorer window and click Publish. The Publish Wizard appears (see Figure A.3).

(Figure is continued on next page)

4. On the **Where do you want to publish the application?** page, enter a valid URL using the format ***http://www.microsoft.com/*** *foldername* (see Figure A.4), then click Next.
5. In the **Will the application be available offline?** page (see Figure A.5), click the appropriate option:
   a. If you want to enable the application to run when the user is disconnected from the network, click **Yes, this application will be available online or offline**. A shortcut on the Start menu will be created for the application.
   b. If you want to run the application directly from the publish location, click **No, this application is only available online**. A shortcut on the Start menu will not be created.
6. Click Next to continue. The **Ready to Publish!** page of the Publish Wizard appears (see Figure A.6).
7. Click Finish to publish the application. The installation Web page appears as seen in Figure A.7.

FIGURE A.1 How to publish a ClickOnce application to the Web

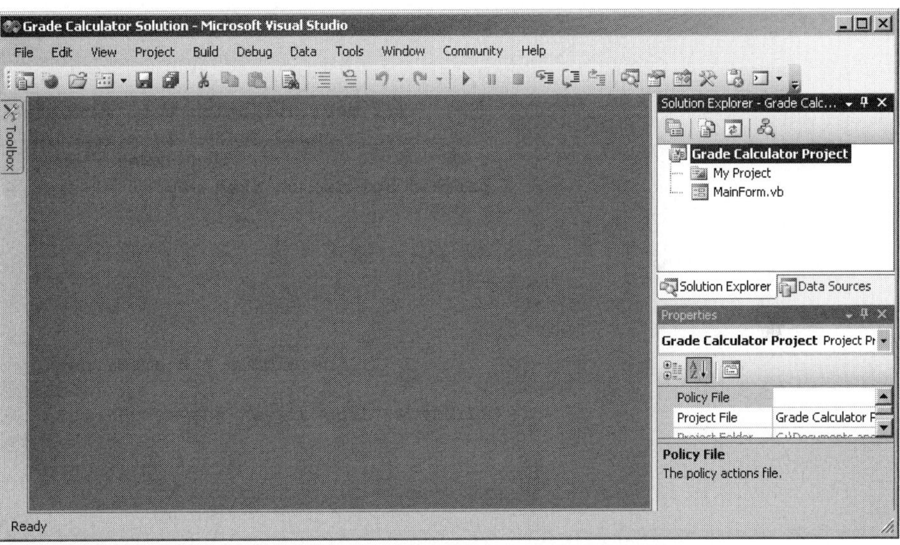

FIGURE A.2 The Grade Calculator solution with the Grade Calculator project

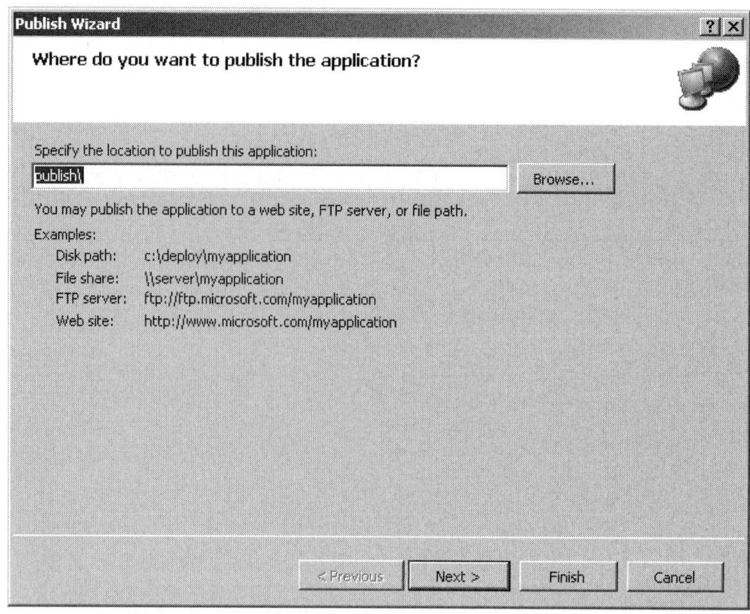

FIGURE A.3 The Add Project Output Group dialog box

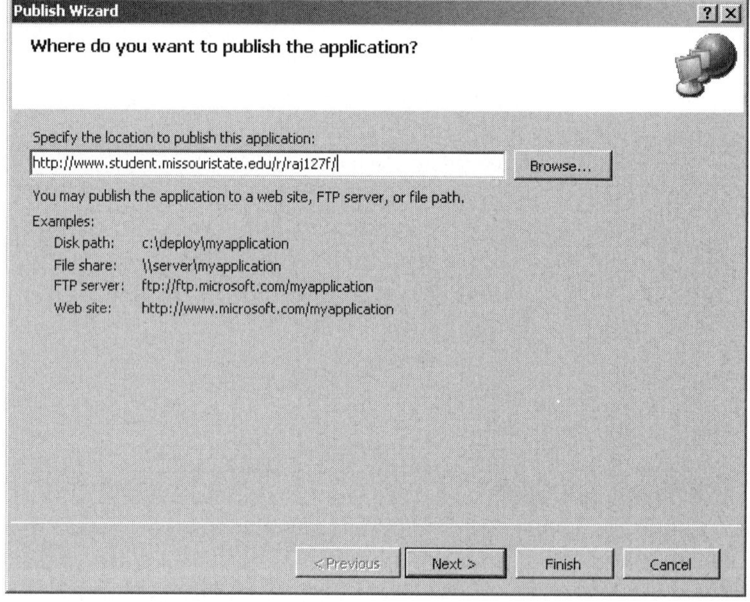

FIGURE A.4 Where do you want to publish the application? page of the Publish Wizard

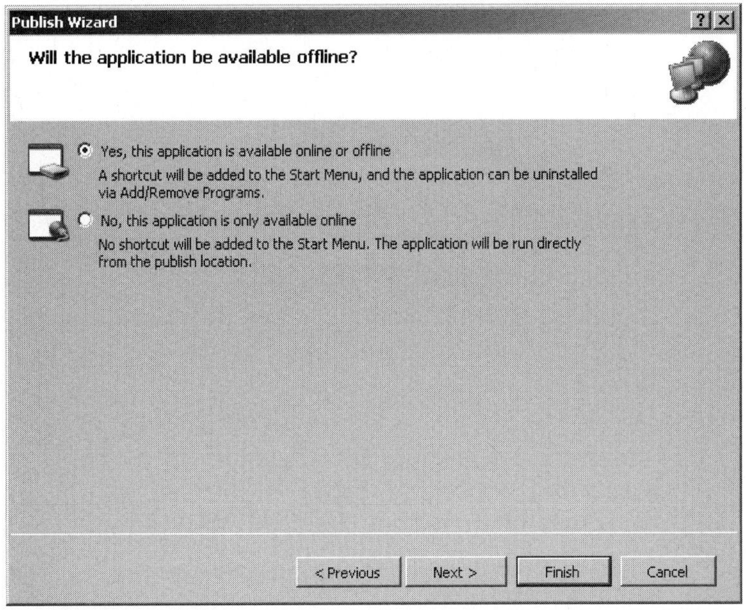

FIGURE A.5 Will the application be available offline? page of the Publish Wizard

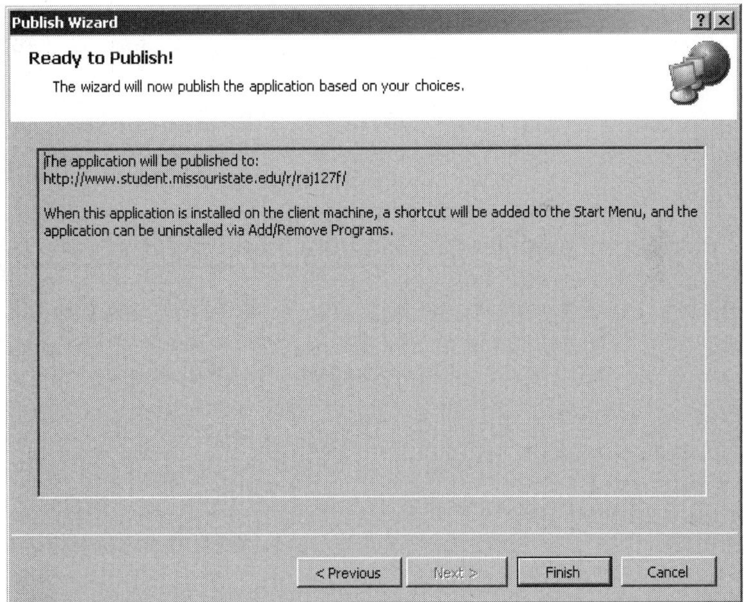

FIGURE A.6 Ready to Publish! page of the Publish Wizard

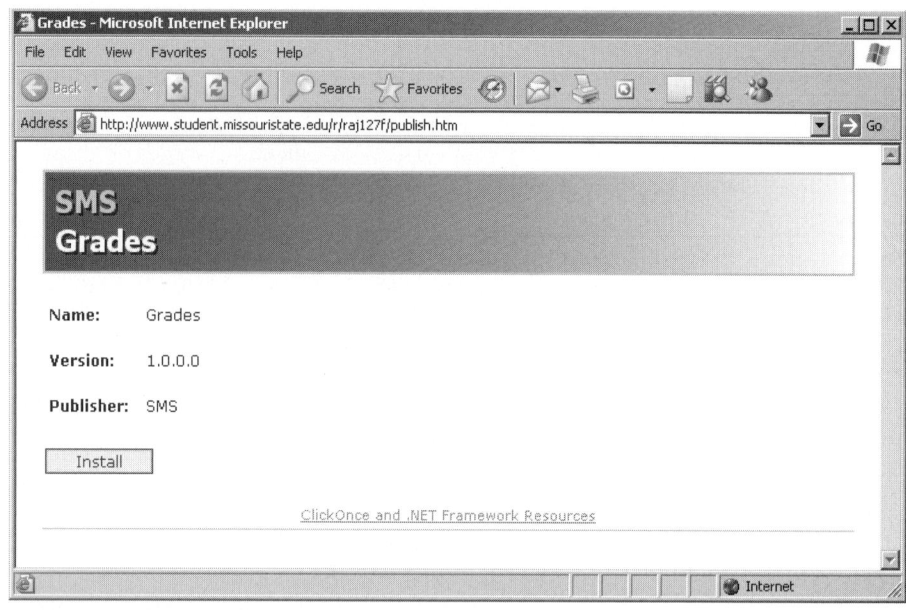

FIGURE A.7 Installation Web page for the Grades application

Figure A.7 shows the installation Web page for the Grades application. (The Grades application is identical to the Grades Calculator application found in Figure 1.64 in Chapter 1 of this text.) Note that this Web page identifies the organization to which Visual Studio was licensed (SMS in this case) and the name of the application (Grades). Clicking the Install button on this installation page begins the simple installation process for the application. The user can then run the application offline by clicking Start, pointing to the SMS group, and clicking Grades.

The user can also run the application online directly from the Web server to which the application was published. When a ClickOnce application is created as described in Figure A.1, several files are placed in the specified directory (\raj127 in this case). One of those files is Grades.application. The developer can create a Web page, such as grades.htm, that contains a link to the file Grades.application on the Web server. When a user downloads the grades.htm page and clicks the link to the Grades.application file, the application will run from the Web server (not the user's computer).

PUBLISHING A CLICKONCE APPLICATION TO A FILE SHARE

Another option for deploying a ClickOnce application is to publish to a file share (also known as a file server). This option is best when the application is not intended to be made easily available over the Internet. Figure A.8 demonstrates how to publish to a file share. (The steps are very similar to those in Figure A.1 with a few differences.)

HOW TO...

Publish a ClickOnce Application to a File Share

1. Open an existing Visual Basic application project, either by double-clicking the solution file for the project (the file with the .sln extension) or by launching Visual Studio, clicking File in the Visual Studio menu, clicking Open Project, navigating to and clicking the solution file for the project, and clicking Open.
2. Open the Solution Explorer window by clicking View and then clicking Solution Explorer in the Visual Studio menu (see Figure A.2).
3. Right-click the project node in the Server Explorer window and click Publish. The Publish Wizard appears (see Figure A.3).
4. In the **Where do you want to publish the application?** page, enter a valid file path using the format **machinename****applicationname** (see Figure A.9), then click Next.
5. In the **How will users install the application?** page, the **From a UNC path or file share** option will be selected using the path entered in Step 4 (see Figure A.10). Click Next.
6. In the **Will the application be available offline?** page (see Figure A.5), click the appropriate option:
   a. If you want to enable the application to run when the user is disconnected from the network, click **Yes, this application will be available online or offline**. A shortcut on the Start menu will be created for the application.
   b. If you want to run the application directly from the publish location, click **No, this application is only available online**. A shortcut on the Start menu will not be created.
7. Click Next to continue. **The Ready to Publish!** page of the Publish Wizard appears (see Figure A.11).
8. Click Finish to publish the application. The installation Web page appears, as shown in Figure A.12.

FIGURE A.8 How to publish a ClickOnce Application to a file share

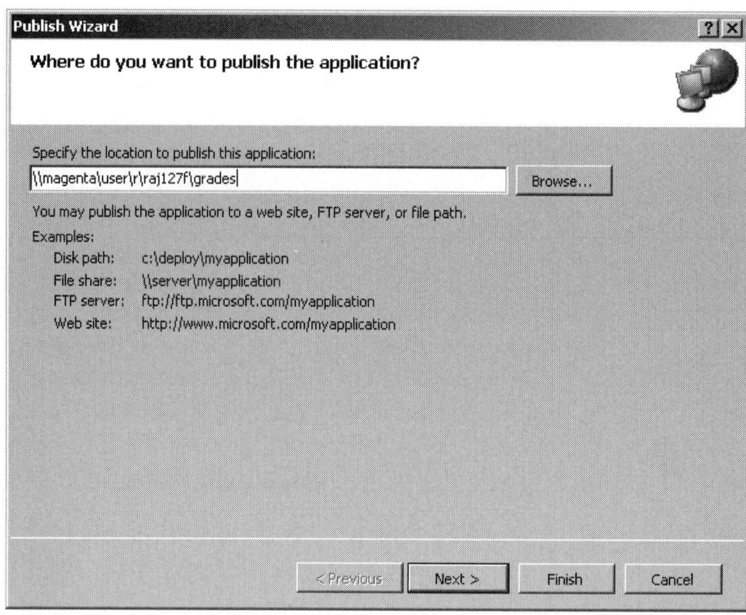

FIGURE A.9 Where do you want to publish the application? page of the Publish Wizard

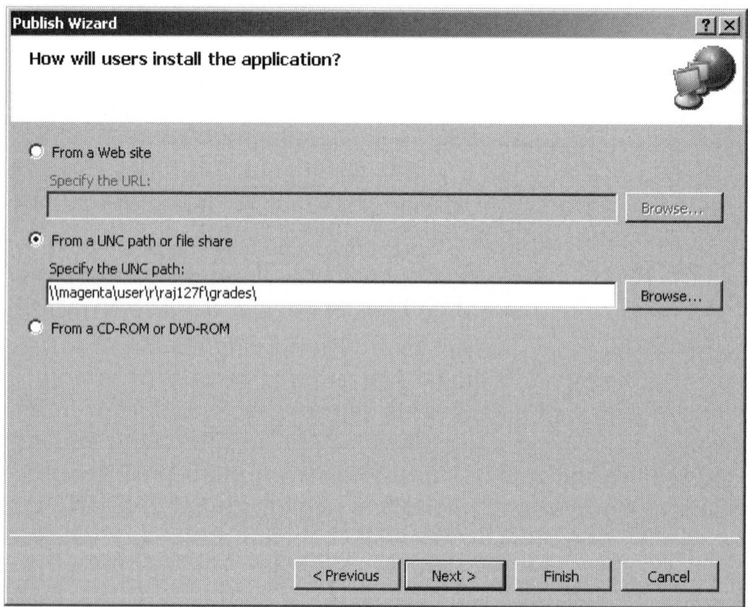

FIGURE A.10 How will users install the application? page of the Publish Wizard

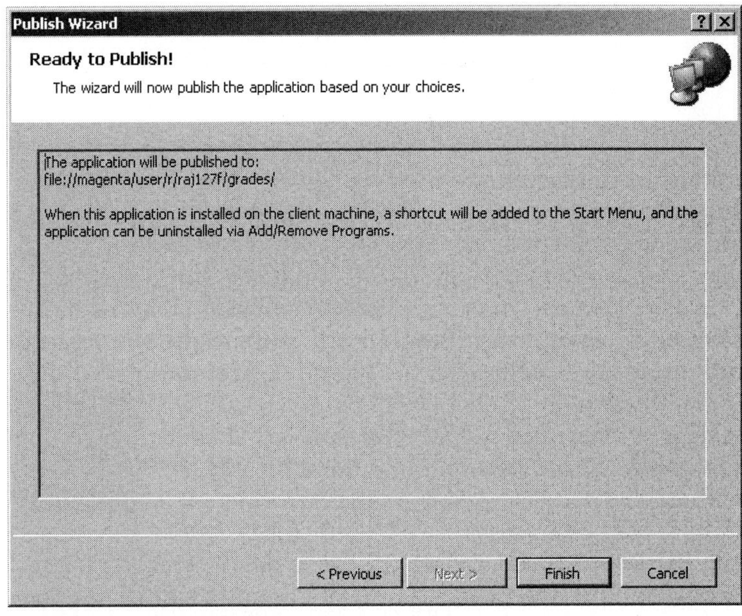

FIGURE A.11 Ready to Publish! page of the Publish Wizard

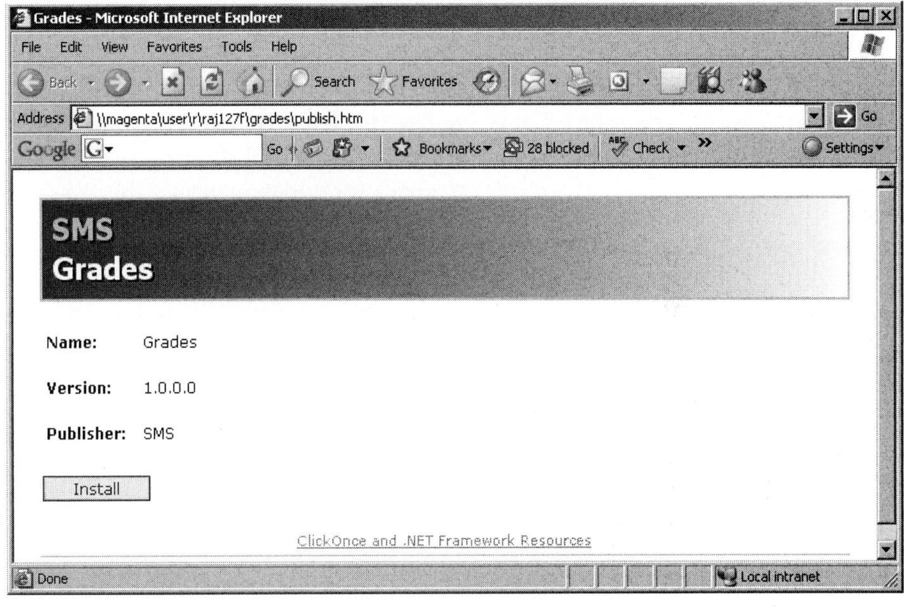

FIGURE A.12 Installation Web page for the Grades application

Again, after the deployment procedure of Figure A.8, the user can run the application offline by clicking Start, pointing to the SMS group, and clicking Grades. The user can also run the application online by logging onto the file share and double-clicking the file Grades.application.

PUBLISHING A CLICKONCE APPLICATION TO A CD-ROM OR A DVD-ROM

The final method of publishing a ClickOnce application is described in Figure A.13. This option is especially helpful for delivering an application where the Internet is not available. Again, many of these steps are similar to those provided earlier.

HOW TO...

Publish a ClickOnce Application to a CD-ROM or a DVD-ROM

1. Open an existing Visual Basic application project, either by double-clicking the solution file for the project (the file with the .sln extension) or by launching Visual Studio, clicking File in the Visual Studio menu, clicking Open Project, navigating to and clicking the solution file for the project, and clicking Open.
2. Open the Solution Explorer window by clicking View and then clicking Solution Explorer in the Visual Studio menu (see Figure A.2).
3. Right-click the project node in the Server Explorer window and click Publish. The Publish Wizard appears (see Figure A.3).
4. In the **Where do you want to publish the application?** page, enter the file path where the application will be published, for example c:\deploy (see Figure A.14). Then click Next to continue.
5. In the **How will users install the application?** page, the **From a CD-ROM or DVD-ROM** option will be selected using the path entered in Step 4 (see Figure A.15). Click Next.
6. In the **Where will the application check for updates?** page (see Figure A.16), click the appropriate option. If you want the application to check for updates, specify the Web site where the application is installed (see Figure A.1, Step 4).
7. Click Next to continue. **The Ready to Publish!** page of the Publish Wizard appears (see Figure A.17).
8. Click Finish to publish the application. The directory in which the application was published appears, as shown in Figure A.18.

FIGURE A.13 How to publish a ClickOnce Application to a CD-ROM or a DVD-ROM

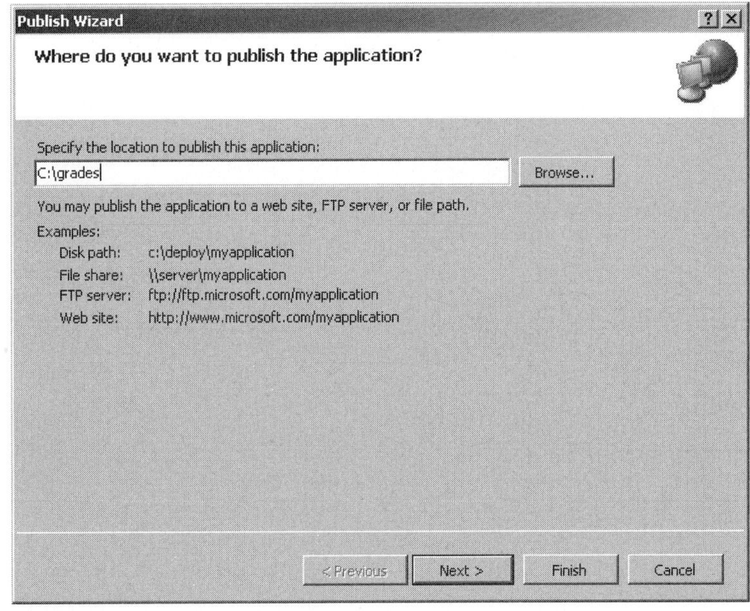

FIGURE A.14 Where do you want to publish the application? page of the Publish Wizard

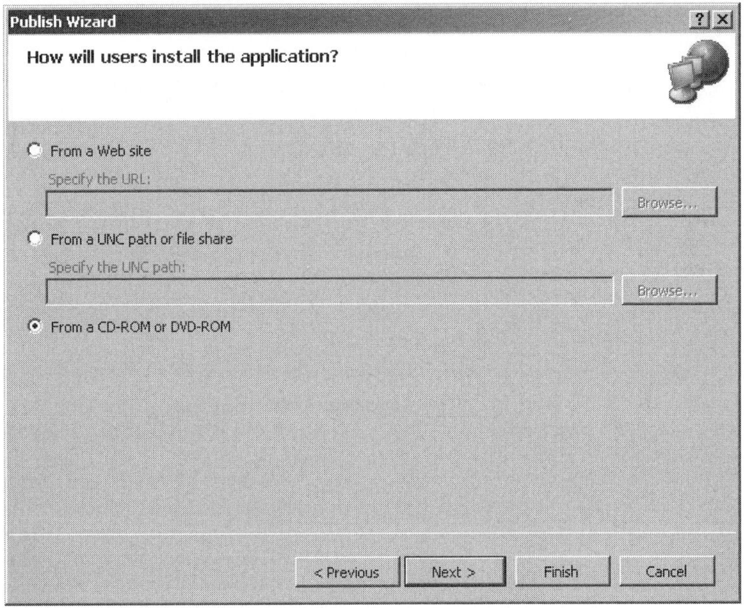

FIGURE A.15 How will users install the application? page of the Publish Wizard

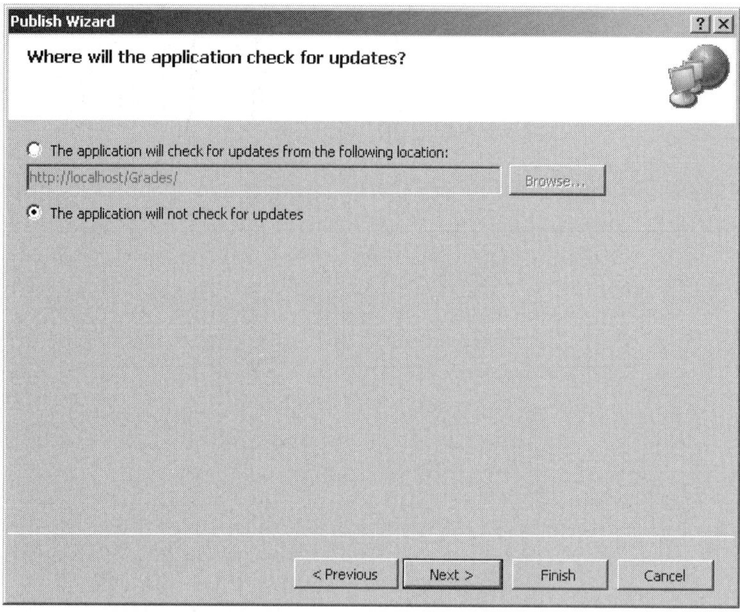

FIGURE A.16 Where will the application check for updates? page of the Publish Wizard

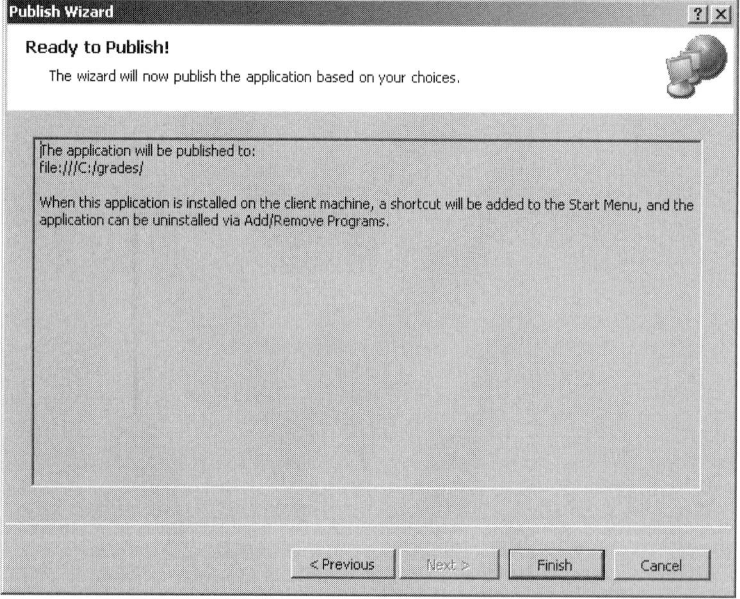

FIGURE A.17 Ready to Publish! page of the Publish Wizard

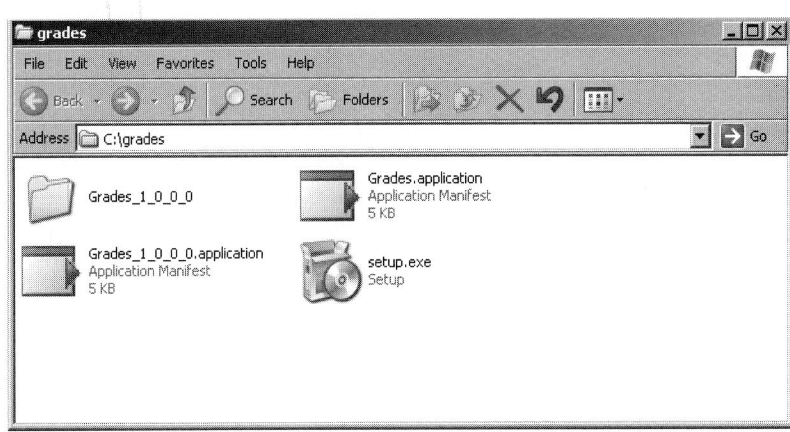

FIGURE A.18 Folder containing the ClickOnce application

Figure A.18 shows what the user sees when she opens the grades folder on the CD-ROM or DVD-ROM. Double-clicking the setup.exe file installs the application on the user's computer.

The developer can also publish a ClickOnce application by right-clicking the project in the Solution Explorer, clicking Properties, and then clicking the Publish tab in the Project Designer, as shown in Figure A.19. This window allows you to set many additional options for publishing an application using the Application Files, Prerequisites, Updates, and Options buttons. When you are ready to publish, you can click the Publish Now button or click the Publish Wizard button for additional guidance.

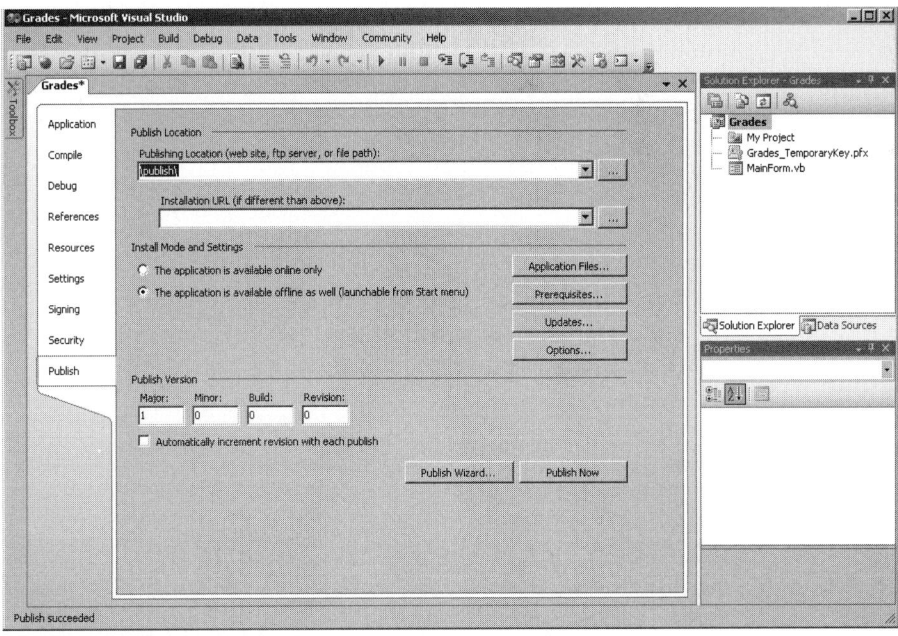

FIGURE A.19 Project Designer for the Grades application

APPENDIX

B Debugging

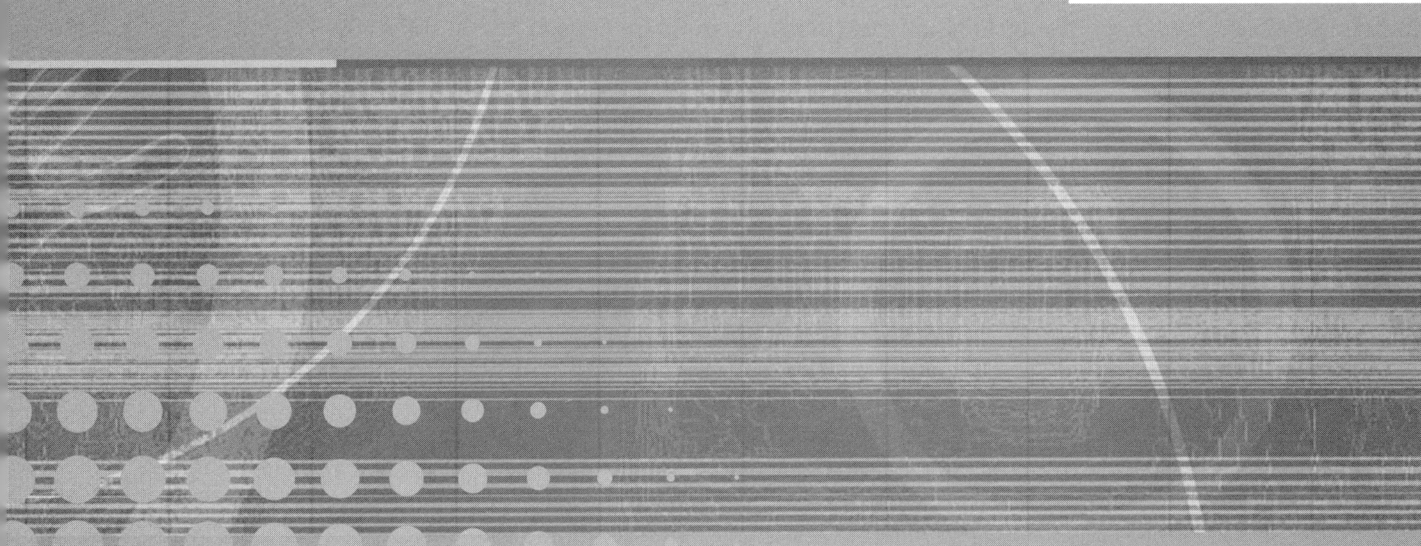

After studying Appendix B, you should be able to:

- Use the Visual Studio debugger in a variety of ways to uncover logic errors in a program.

ERRORS

Computer programs are created by humans and are thus subject to error. Errors can be classified as syntax errors, semantic errors, and logic errors. Syntax errors occur when the program code does not follow the syntax (rules) of the programming language (such as Visual Basic). Syntax errors are almost always caught by the compiler or interpreter. In Visual Studio, syntax errors are displayed in the Output window, which provides the location of the error in the program and a brief description of the error.

Semantic errors are more difficult to uncover. These occur when the syntax of the code is correct, but the semantics or meaning of the code deviates from what the programmer intended. A semantic error, such as an infinite loop, is not detected by the compiler or interpreter but can cause a program to behave abnormally. In colloquial terms, the program may crash (terminate unexpectedly) or hang (pause indefinitely).

Logic errors are similar to semantic errors. The syntax of the code is correct, but the code is not performing as intended. However, logic errors do not crash or hang a program—instead, the program appears to run normally. The problem is that variables may contain incorrect values or the program may take an incorrect path. The end result is incorrect output, which may or may not be detected by the user. Testing a program (running it under a wide variety of conditions) can determine if semantic or logic errors exist. However, testing only evaluates the correctness of a program's output. Debugging is the process of determining the cause of semantic or logic errors.

DEBUGGING

Debugging can be performed manually or with the aid of a debugger. Manual debugging usually involves adding code to a program (such as `printf` or `MessageBox` statements) to output information about the path that the program is taking and/or the values of certain key variables. This is a valid debugging technique, but it can be relatively hit-and-miss. It also requires that all the debugging code be removed once the problems are solved.

On the other hand, a debugger is a software tool that allows the programmer to observe the runtime performance of a program and investigate potential errors without adding extra code. With a debugger, you can set breakpoints in the code to pause execution and then view the contents of variables. Setting breakpoints does not add code to the program, and you can easily remove them. To use various features of the Visual Studio debugger, you must first enter debug mode, as explained in the next section.

STARTING AND STOPPING DEBUGGING

Using the debugger allows you to control the execution of a program for the purpose of finding and correcting errors. Figure B.1 explains how to start, break, and stop debugging.

HOW TO...

Start, Break, and Stop Debugging

1. Open an existing Visual Basic application project and display the Code window for the desired program.
2. To enter debug mode, click the Start Debugging icon in the Standard toolbar. The application begins running (see Figure B.2). (You can also click Debug and then click Start Debugging in the Visual Studio menu, or press F5.)
3. To break (halt or pause) the execution of the program, click the Break All icon in the Standard toolbar. (You can also click Debug and then click Break All in the Visual Studio menu, or press Ctrl-Break.) Program execution temporarily halts, allowing you to examine the state of the program. (How to do this will be explained later.) When a program breaks, it is said to be in break mode (see Figure B.3).
4. To exit debug mode, click the Stop Debugging icon in the Standard toolbar. The application terminates. (You can also click Debug and then click Stop Debugging in the Visual Studio menu.)

FIGURE B.1 How to start, break, and stop debugging

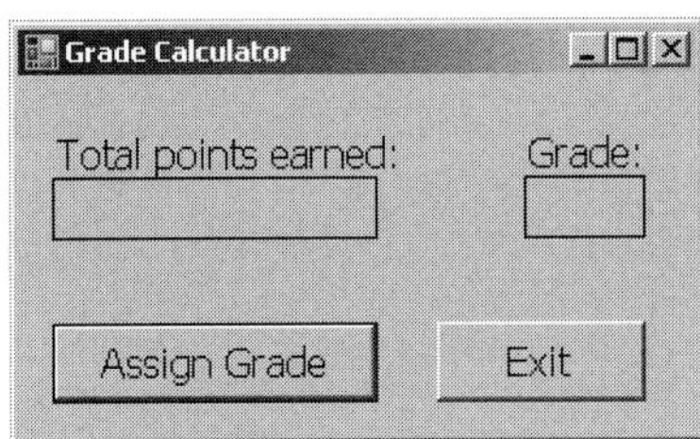

FIGURE B.2 The Grades application user interface

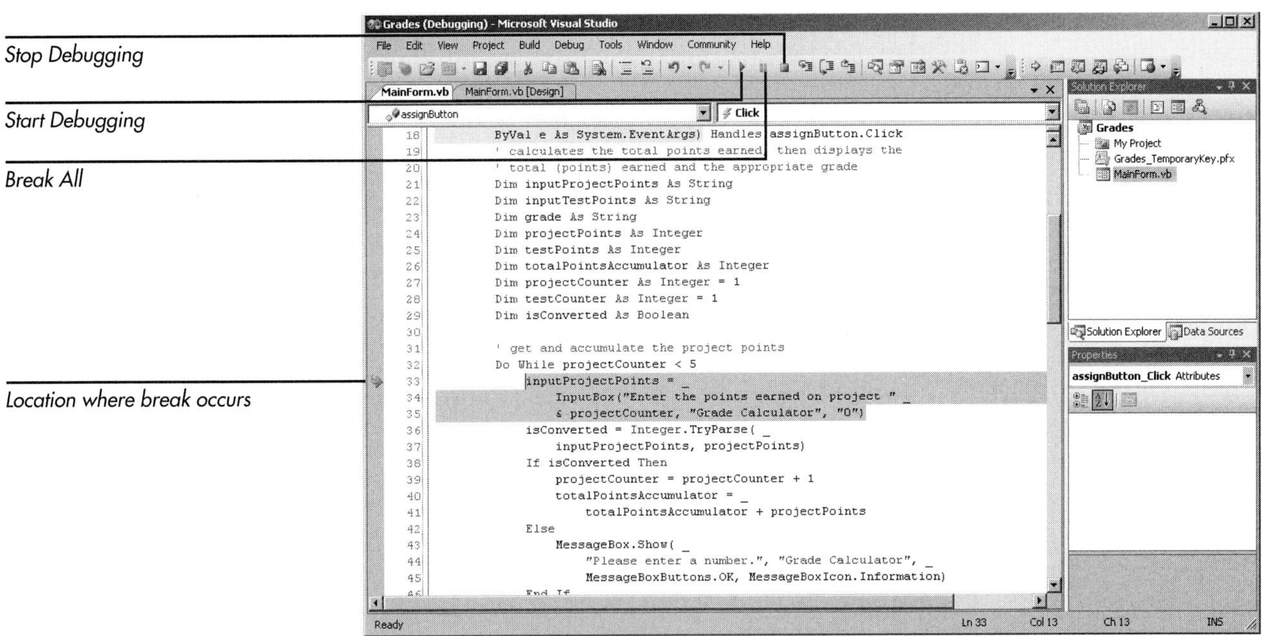

FIGURE B.3 The Grades application in break mode

The Grades application in Figure B.2 was launched by clicking the Start Debugging icon. The Assign Grade button in the user interface was then clicked to begin execution. However, the Break All icon was then immediately clicked, resulting in what you see in Figure B.3. This indicates that Line 33 is the next line waiting to be executed when the Start Debugging icon is clicked again. Clicking the Stop Debugging icon will terminate the application.

STEPPING THROUGH A PROGRAM

You can also step through a program line by line to better understand how the program flows and examine the state of the program at each step. Figure B.4 explains how to use the features Step Into, Step Over, and Step Out.

HOW TO...

Step Through a Program

1. Open an existing Visual Basic application project and display the Code window for the desired program.
2. To step into a program, click the Step Into icon in the Standard toolbar. (You can also click Debug and then click Step Into in the Visual Studio menu, or press F8.) Stepping into a program causes the program to break after each and every program statement is executed (see Figure B.5).
3. To step over a function, click the Step Over icon in the Standard toolbar. (You can also click Debug and then click Step Over in the Visual Studio menu, or press Shift-F8.) Step Over behaves the same as Step Into except when a function call is encountered. Step Into enters the function and breaks after each line of code in the function. Step Over executes the entire function and breaks at the first line of code following the function call.
4. To step out of a function, click the Step Out icon in the Standard toolbar. (You can also click Debug and then click Step Out in the Visual Studio menu, or press Shift-F8.) Once program execution is inside a function, Step Out causes the program to step out of a function (to execute the remainder of the current function and return to the first line of code following the function call).
5. To step into, step over, or step out while a program is running, first click Break All in the Standard toolbar.

FIGURE B.4 How to step through a program

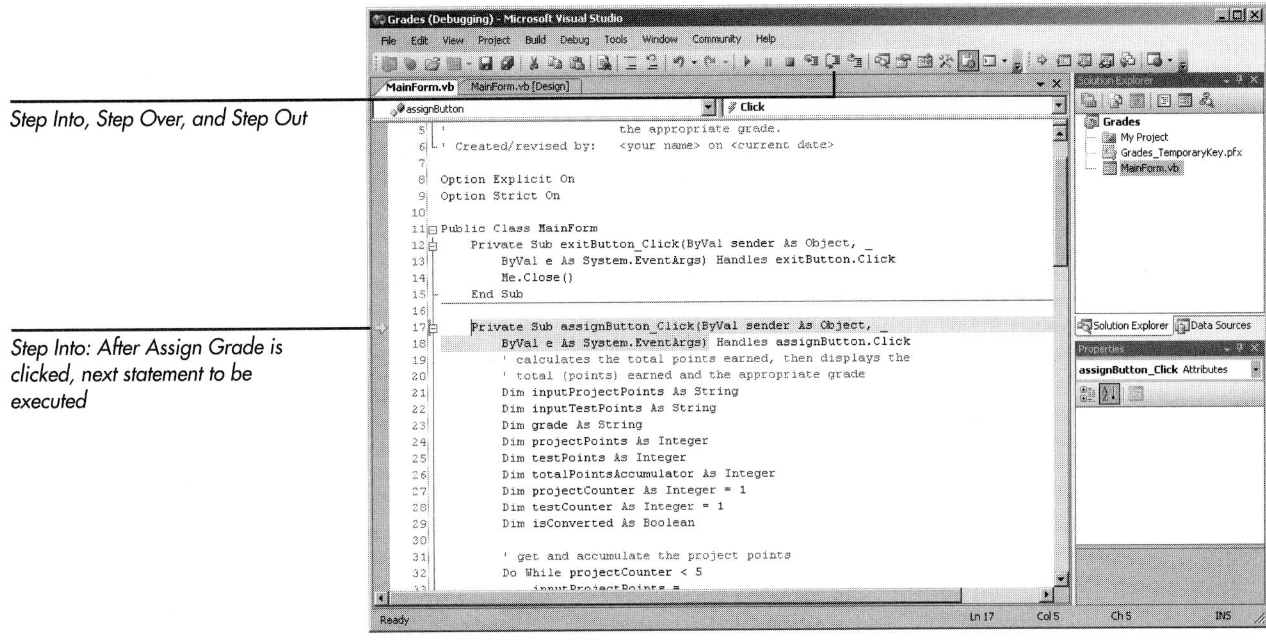

FIGURE B.5 Stepping into the Grades application

WORKING WITH BREAKPOINTS

Stepping through a program is a helpful way of debugging, but sometimes you want to pause an application at a specific location within the program code. You can accomplish this by setting breakpoints. Figure B.6 explains how to work with breakpoints.

HOW TO...

Work with Breakpoints

1. Open an existing Visual Basic application project and display the Code window for the desired program.
2. To set a breakpoint, place the cursor in the program code precisely where you want the program to pause.
3. Right-click the Code window, point to Breakpoint, and click Insert Breakpoint. A breakpoint icon (circle) appears and the breakpoint code is highlighted (see Figure B.7). When the breakpoint is hit, the program will pause at this location.
4. To add extra functionality to a breakpoint, right-click the breakpoint icon or the breakpoint code, point to Breakpoint, and click one of the options listed. These options allow you to perform such actions as disabling a breakpoint, setting conditions for a breakpoint hit, and printing messages when the breakpoint is hit.
5. To delete a breakpoint, right-click the breakpoint, point to Breakpoint, and click Delete Breakpoint.
6. Another way to break an application without setting a breakpoint is to position the cursor anywhere within the program code, right-click on the Code window, and click Run to Cursor. The application runs until it reaches the position of the cursor.

FIGURE B.6 How to work with breakpoints

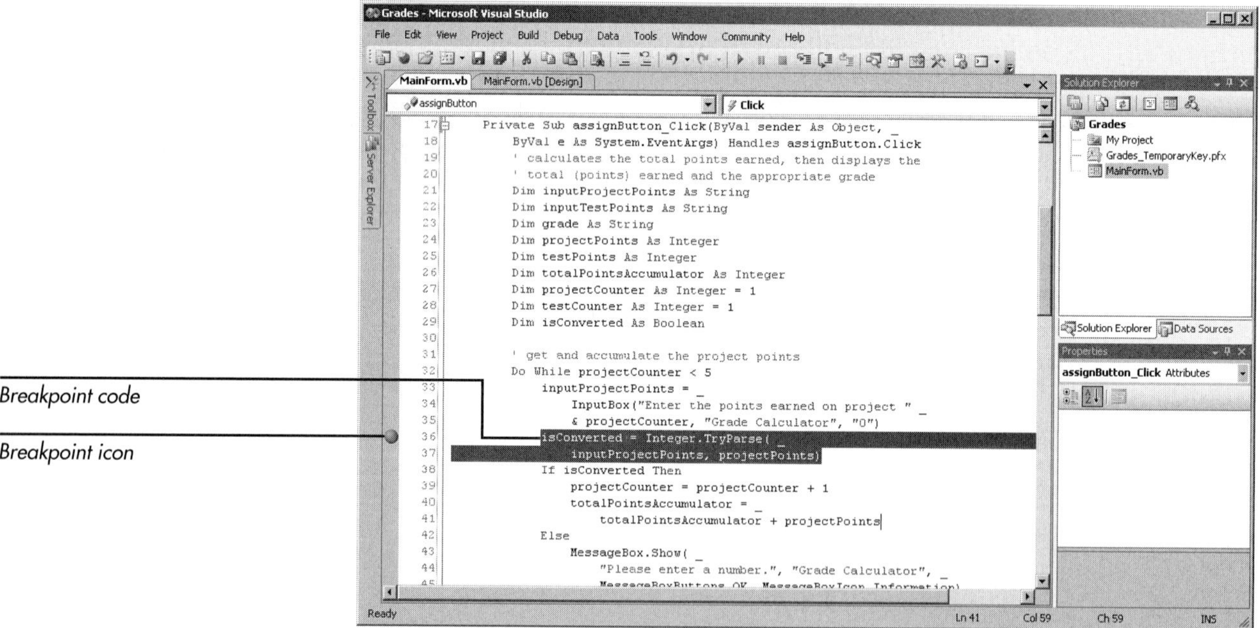

FIGURE B.7 A breakpoint in the Grades application

EXAMINING PROGRAM STATE

So far, you have learned how to enter and exit debug mode, step through a program, and work with breakpoints. However, these activities are only a means to an end. The purpose of debugging is to examine the state of a program (including the values of variables and the method call stack) in order to find possible logic errors. Figure B.8 explains how to examine the state of a program while in debug mode.

HOW TO...

Examine Program State in Debug Mode

1. Open an existing Visual Basic application project and display the Code window for the desired program.
2. Enter debug mode by clicking, for example, Start Debugging or Step Into (see Figures B.1 and B.4). The Debug toolbar will appear (see Figure B.9).
3. Break the application by clicking Break All or by having previously set one or more breakpoints (see Figures B.1 and B.6).
4. Click one or more of the icons in the Debug toolbar to examine the state of the program. For example, clicking the Immediate Window icon displays the Immediate Window in which the programmer can type code to reveal aspects of program state (see Figure B.10). For example, typing the code `?isConverted` and pressing Enter will display the value of the variable `isConverted`.
5. Clicking the Locals icon displays the Locals window where you can view the values of all local variables (see Figure B.11). Other icons in the Debug toolbar include Watch 1 (to enter specific variables to be watched), Call Stack (to view the current sequence of method calls), and Breakpoints (to view the status of all breakpoints).
6. Many other debugging options, such as Threads, Modules, Processes, and Registers, are also available by clicking the drop-down list in the Debug toolbar. Consult *http://msdn.microsoft.com/library/* for more information on these advanced features.

FIGURE B.8 How to examine program state in debug mode

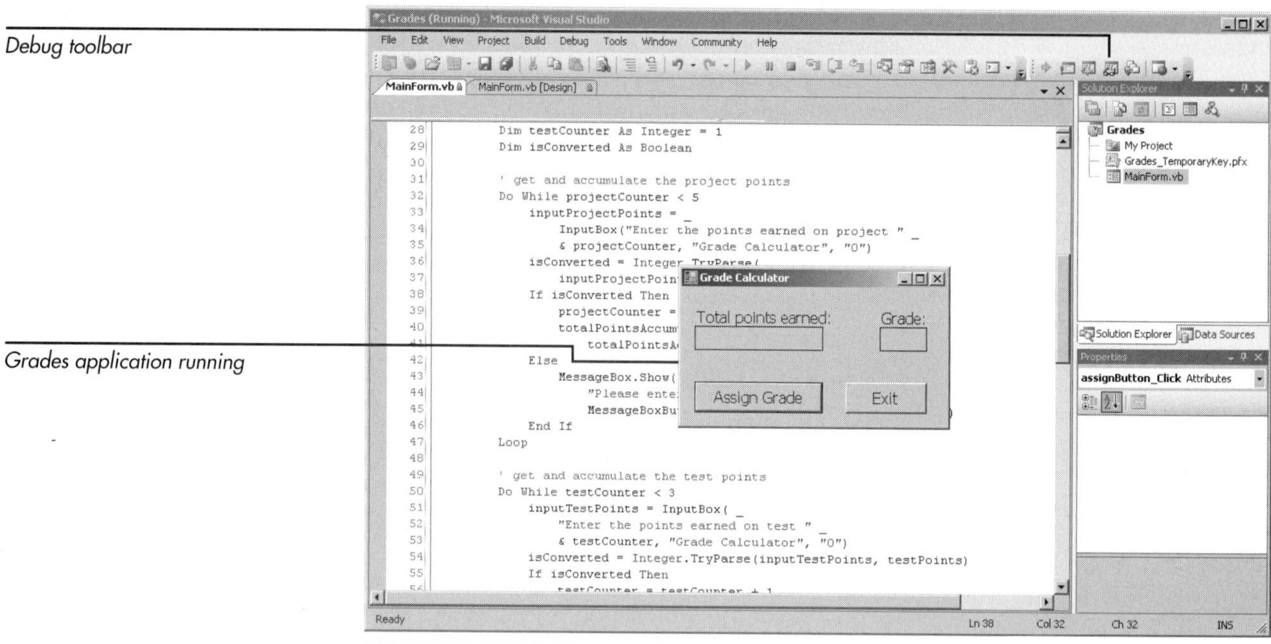

FIGURE B.9 Grades application in debug mode with the Debug toolbar

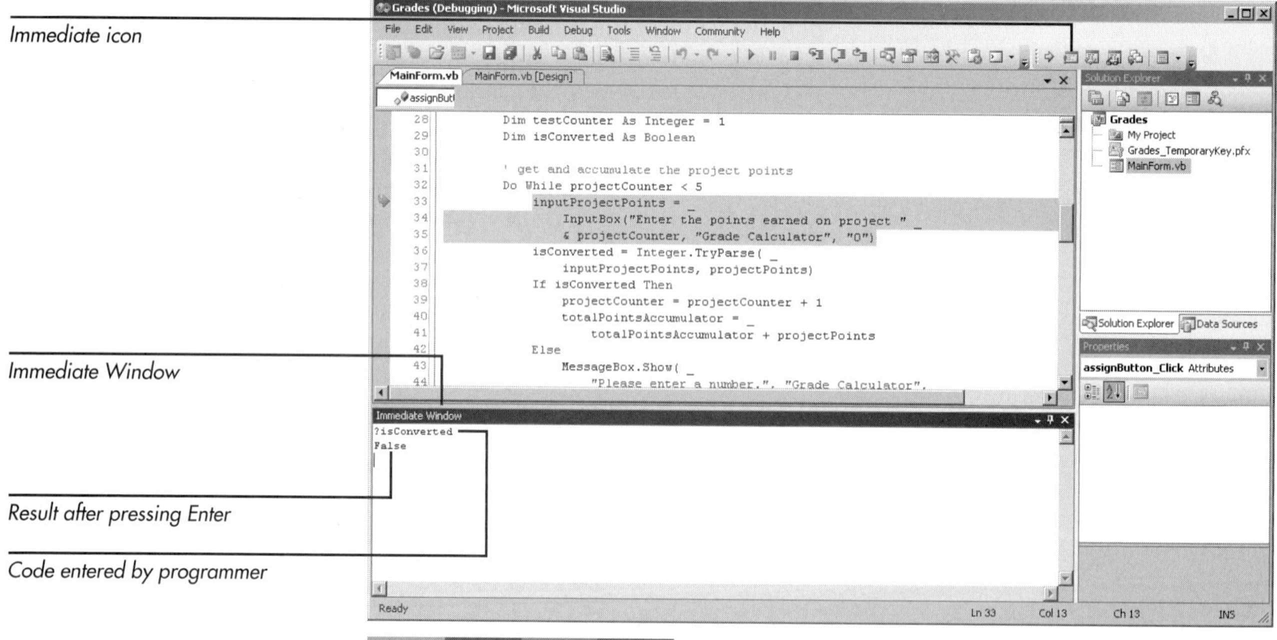

FIGURE B.10 The Immediate Window in the Grades application

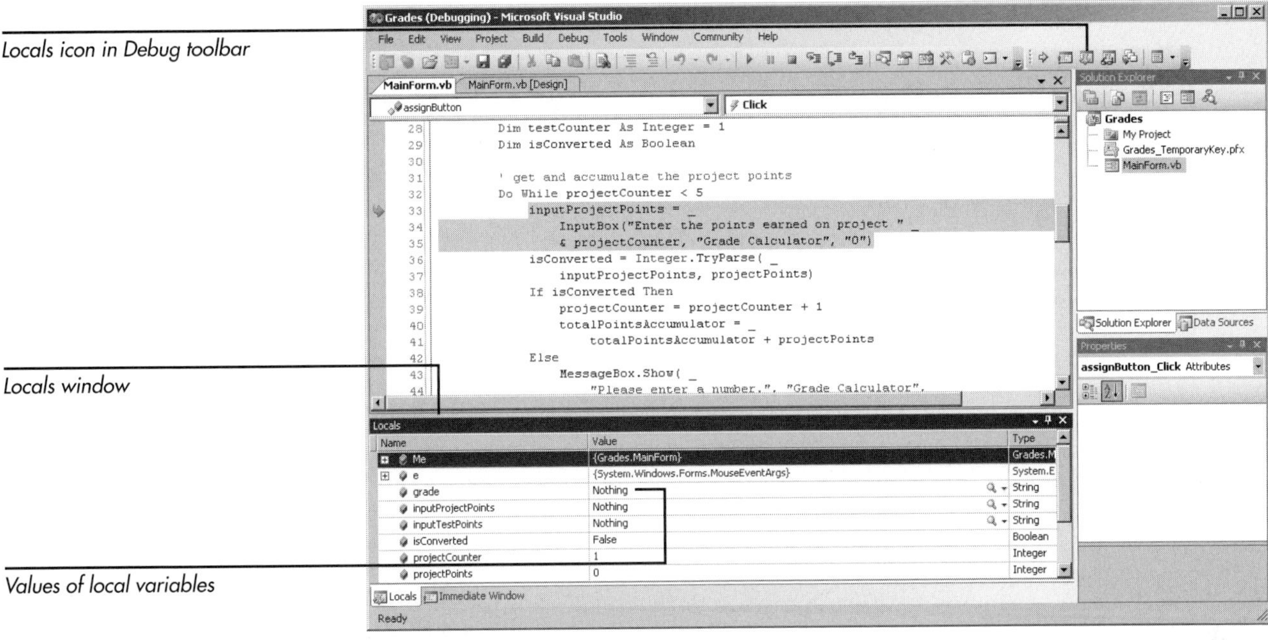

FIGURE B.11 The Locals window in the Grades application

Glossary

A

Aborted state The state a thread enters when it has been terminated due to abnormal conditions.

abstract class A class with data members and/or method members from which objects cannot be instantiated.

abstract data type (ADT) A programmer-defined type with a set of values and a collection of operations that may be performed on those values.

Abstract method A method that is declared in a base class but has no body or implementation in that base class.

abstraction The act of focusing only on the relevant aspects of something.

access key The underlined character in an object's identifying label or caption. An access key allows the user to select the object by pressing the Alt key in combination with the character.

accumulator A numeric variable used for accumulating (adding) items; it allows users to answer the question "How much?"

ActiveX Data Objects (ADO) A Microsoft technology for accessing data from a wide variety of data stores in both Windows applications and Web applications.

ADO (ActiveX Data Objects) The Microsoft data access API (released in 1996) that preceded ADO.NET (released in 2002).

ADO.NET An enhanced version of ADO designed specifically for Microsoft .NET applications.

application class A class that defines the application and that usually contains the user interface.

applications programmers Programmers who write and maintain programs that handle a specific task.

array A group of variables where the group is given a name, all variables in the group have the same data type, and the variables are accessed using the group name with a subscript.

assembly languages Programming languages that allow the programmer to use mnemonics in place of the 0s and 1s in a program.

assignment operator The equal sign (=) in an assignment statement.

association A relationship between classes in which one class contains variables that are references to objects of another class.

attributes The characteristics that describe an object.

B

base class A class from which another class (called the derived class) inherits `Public` members.

behaviors The operations (actions) that an object is capable of performing.

binary access file A file that contains data accessed by byte location in the file.

binary search algorithm A programmed procedure that compares the target item with the middle value of an array of values to eliminate half of the array from the search, and repeats this process during each pass of the search.

block scope Scope confined to the code block in which a variable is declared (using the keyword `Dim`).

Blocked state The state of thread inactivity, due to occurrences such as an input/output request.

Boolean operators See **logical operators**.

boxing The process of converting values to and from the `Object` data type.

C

cardinality When referring to a relationship between Tables A and B in a database, the number of rows in Table B that can be associated with each row in Table A.

catch To utilize a `Catch` block to handle or process an exception.

`Catch` block Code in a `Try...Catch...Finally` statement designed to catch and handle an exception object.

check box A control in an interface that allows the user to select any number of choices from a group of one or more choices.

child window The window within the parent window of an MDI program.

class A unit of program code that defines a category of objects.

Class Designer A visual design environment for the Common Language Runtime.

class members The data members and method members of a class.

class methods Method members that define classwide behaviors.

class variables Data members that define classwide attributes.

classic error handling The Visual Basic process for managing the error object `Err` generated by the program when standard runtime errors occur.

client program A program that uses the members of a class.

client/server system A system in which software is distributed across networked hardware components consisting of clients, which send requests for services; and a server, which provides responses to the requests.

client-side scripting The process of embedding scripts in a Web page and executing them on the client.

code-behind file A Visual Basic class containing the event procedures that accompany controls (such as text boxes, lists, and buttons) placed on an ASP.NET Web form.

collection An object that contains a set of related items.

collision In relation to a hash table, a condition that occurs when more than one object has the same hash code.

collision resolution A process for distinguishing objects that have the same hash code.

Common Language Runtime (CLR) The core runtime engine of the Microsoft .NET Framework.

compile-time error An error that occurs while the program is being compiled, usually due to a syntax error.

component An object (that is, an instance of a class) that is added to a form to provide the form with functionality.

Component Object Model (COM) A Microsoft technology for intersoftware communication using objects.

composition relationship A special type of association between two classes, in which the contained object would not normally exist apart from the containing class.

concrete class A class from which objects can be instantiated.

concurrency management A database management process for maintaining data consistency when two or more users access the same data simultaneously.

constructor A special method that performs instantiation.

control A visible component.

counter A numeric variable used for counting something; it allows users to answer the question "How many?"

crash In the context of program execution, an unexpected termination.

cross-threading A method call made to a control by a thread that did not create the control.

D

data The plural of datum; an entire collection of factual knowledge.

data access application programming interface (API) Software that provides an interface between the application and the database.

data members The variables defined within a class.

data provider A set of classes that provide the link between the dataset and the database.

data store Any organized collection of data.

data structure A way of organizing data in computer memory.

data tier Data often stored in a relational database management system in a multi-tier architecture.

data type The type of data a variable can store.

database A data store that has a special structure for facilitating computerized storage, retrieval, and manipulation of data.

database management system (DBMS) Software designed to create and access a database.

dataset A memory resident representation of only the part of a database that an application needs.

datum A single item of factual knowledge obtained from measurement or observation. The singular of data.

deadlock A condition in which two or more processes are blocked, each waiting on a lock held by the others. Also known as a deadly embrace.

debugging The process of locating errors in a program.

default constructor A constructor that contains no parameters.

delegate An instance of the `Delegate` class, which holds a reference to a method.

dependency relationship A relationship between two classes in which one class uses the members of another class (usually with method calls).

dialog box A window that supports and supplements a user's activities in the primary window.

dialog form A modal form that returns standard results using the `DialogResult` property.

document type declaration A formal declaration that begins with the keyword DOCTYPE, followed by the name of the base element of the document, followed by the specification of the markup language to be used.

domain name The text name corresponding to the unique numeric IP address of a computer on the Internet.

dot operator See **member access operator**.

E

element One of the variables in an array.

element content Some text or other HTML elements contained within an HTML element.

end tag The same special code used in the start tag, preceded by a forward slash, enclosed in angle brackets, and placed at the end of an HTML element.

entity-relationship diagram (ERD) A pictorial representation of the entities (tables), the entity attributes (fields), and the relationships between the entities in a relational database.

error handler Error-handling code that processes errors using classic error handling.

error-handling mode A state of a Visual Basic application that enables the features of classic error handling.

event A message announcing that a user action has occurred.

event driven The characteristic of an application whereby events control the application's functionality.

event procedure The set of instructions (program code) that tells the application what to do when an event occurs.

exception An exceptional, unusual, or abnormal condition that occurs during program execution; more specifically, an object that contains information about such a condition.

exception catcher See **exception handler**.

exception handler A method in a program that handles a thrown exception.

exception propagator See **exception thrower**.

exception thrower A method in a program that throws an exception.

F

fault tolerant Term used to describe a program that can tolerate user errors without crashing.

field A space reserved for a datum.

`Finally` block A section of code that performs final actions after a `Try` block or `Catch` block fully executes.

flat file A way of structuring data in simple records and fields that could be written on a flat (two-dimensional) piece of paper.

flowchart An arrangement of standard graphic symbols used to plan a procedure.

focus The ability of an object to accept user input.

foreign key A primary key of one table included as a field of another table.

form A window or dialog box that makes up an application's graphical user interface.

format specifier A letter (either uppercase or lowercase) that signifies the type of formatting. The possible format specifiers are: `C` for currency, `D` for decimal, `F` for fixed-point, `N` for number, or `P` for percent.

function A procedure that returns a value after completing its task.

G

generic type A single programming element that adapts to perform the same functionality for a variety of data types.

generics Programming elements that can accommodate variables of a wide variety of data types rather than only one specific data type.

get methods Methods that retrieve values of instance variables.

H

has-a relationship See **association**.

hash code A value derived from the key using a hash function.

hash function An algorithm that creates a hash code from the key.

hash table A data structure with two columns, the first containing a hash code and the second containing the object.

hash table bucket A linked list used to store objects in a hash table when the objects have the same hash code.

high-level languages Programming languages that allow the programmer to use computer instructions that more closely resemble the English language.

HTML element A section within a Web page that defines the page's structure, content, and functionality.

HTTP transaction The process in which a Web client requests a file and a Web server responds to the request using HTTP.

hyperlink A contraction of "hypertext link"; a graphic or text in a Web page that, when clicked, opens a new Web page or jumps to a new location in the current page.

Hypertext Markup Language (HTML) The language used to create Web pages.

Hypertext Transfer Protocol The set of rules for exchanging files on the World Wide Web.

I

IDE An acronym for integrated development environment (an example is Visual Studio 2005).

identifier The descriptive name given to an object.

implicit type conversion Automatically assigning values of one data type to variables of a different data type.

inconsistent state A condition in which the properties of a control have unpredictable values.

independent `Sub` procedure A procedure that can be invoked from one or more places in an application and that is independent of any object and event.

information Knowledge obtained by processing data.

information system A system designed to provide needed information.

inheritance A special relationship between two classes in which one class (called the base class) gives to another class (called the derived class) direct access to all of its `Public` members.

inheritance hierarchy A treelike structure showing inheritance relationships among classes.

initialize To assign an initial value to a variable when it is first declared.

input file A file that is read to provide data input to an application.

input validation The process of validating data entered by the user before the data are used by the program.

instance methods Method members that define the behaviors of class objects.

instance variables Data members that define the attributes of class objects.

instantiation The process of creating an object in computer memory.

intranet A private network that uses Internet technology.

is-a relationship See **inheritance**.

K

key A field belonging to the object that serves as its unique identifier for storage in a hash table.

L

lifetime The amount of time a variable remains in computer memory.

linked list A data structure in which each item in the list points to the next item in the list.

literal type character A suffix character that forces a literal constant to assume a data type other than the one its form indicates.

logic error A mistake made in the design and/or implementation of program logic that can result in incorrect output, which may not be apparent to the user.

logic tier Programs that execute the logic of the application and communicate with the other tiers in a multi-tier architecture.

logical operators Operators (also called Boolean operators) such as `Not`, `And`, and `Or`, that allow users to combine two or more conditions into one compound condition.

M

machine languages Computer instructions consisting of 0s and 1s.

`Margin` property A property of a control that determines the amount of space, in pixels, reserved around a control when calculating its automatic position in a `FlowLayoutPanel`.

markup language A language that uses tags to describe the structure and content of its files.

member access operator The period character (`.`) used to access a data member or call a method member of a class. Sometimes referred to as a dot operator.

metalanguage A language about a language.

method-call stack The sequence of method calls (or call chain), displayed in the exception's stack trace, that leads to the creation of an exception object.

method members The methods defined within a class.

method signature The combination of the method name and its parameter list.

method Part of a class that performs a task.

modal form A form that must be closed or hidden before the user can continue working with the application.

modeless form A form that is not modal.

module scope Scope confined to the module, class, or structure in which a variable is declared (using the keyword `Private`).

`MultiCastDelegate` A class that defines a data structure that can contain references to several different methods.

multiple-document-interface (MDI) application An application that allows many documents to be opened at once.

multiprocessing The execution of multiple threads by more than one processor.

multitasking The perceived ability to perform several different tasks at the same time.

multithreading The condition in which one processor executes several threads of a single program at the same time.

multi-tier architecture An *n*-tier architecture that places different basic components of the application on *n* distinct software layers or tiers.

MyBase A Visual Basic keyword that refers to the base class of the current object.

N

named constant A computer memory location whose contents cannot be changed while the application is running.

namespace A name given to a group of related classes.

nested selection structure A selection structure (the inner selection structure) within another selection structure (the outer selection structure).

O

object An instance of a class that consists of data and the operations associated with that data.

Object Management Group (OMG) A not-for-profit computer industry specifications consortium dedicated to the standardization of software-modeling techniques (*http://www.omg.org*).

object name The identifier of an object, which is a reference variable.

object-defining class A class used to define object attributes and behaviors.

object-oriented (OO) application An application in which the programmer uses an object-oriented programming language to create special classes that are used to represent objects in the real world for the purpose of solving a particular real-world problem.

object-oriented programming A method of programming in which the programmer concentrates on the objects that the program can use to accomplish its goal.

OLE DB (Object Linking and Embedding for Databases) A Microsoft technology for interfacing with data stores that comes under the umbrella of the Component Object Model (COM).

one-dimensional array An array that logically represents a single column (or row) that contains the array variables.

OO Abbreviation for "object-oriented."

optimistic concurrency A policy of concurrency management in which the first update is processed and other users are notified of a concurrency violation when multiple users are trying to update the same value in a database.

output file A file to which data from an application is written.

overloaded constructors Constructors within a single class (all having the same name, `New`) with different parameter lists.

overloaded method One of two or more methods in the same class or an inheritance hierarchy with the same name but different parameter lists.

overridden method A method in a base class with exactly the same signature as a method in a derived class.

P

`Padding` property A property of a container control that determines the amount of space, in pixels, reserved along the inside of containers.

parallel arrays Two or more arrays whose elements are related by their positions in the arrays.

parameter The data type and name of a variable within the parentheses of a procedure header.

parameterized constructor A constructor that has one or more parameters.

parent menu A menu item that is a menu for other menu items.

parent window The application window of an MDI program.

passing by reference Passing a variable's memory address from a procedure call to a receiving procedure.

passing by value Passing a variable's value from a procedure call to a receiving procedure.

pessimistic concurrency A policy of concurrency management in which a row of data retrieved by a user for possible updates is locked and cannot be retrieved by other users until the first user releases it.

polymorphism The object-oriented feature that enables one method to have several different implementations depending on the type of object calling the method.

precedence numbers The order in which the computer performs an operation in an expression.

presentation tier The user interface in a multi-tier architecture.

primary key One or more fields in a database table that, taken in combination, form a unique value and thus uniquely identify a record.

primary window The main user interface of an application.

priming read A program statement that initializes a variable used in the condition of a `Do...Loop`.

principle of least privilege A principle stating that elements in a computing environment should be granted only information and resources that are immediately necessary in order to enhance protection of data and functionality from faults and malicious behavior.

procedure A block of program code that performs a specific task.

procedure scope Scope confined to the procedure in which a variable is declared (using the keyword `Dim`).

procedure-oriented programming A method of programming in which the programmer concentrates on the major tasks that the program needs to perform.

programmer-defined exception A custom class created by the programmer to define an exception not already associated with a Visual Basic runtime error.

Properties window The window that displays an object's attributes (properties).

`Property` **procedure** A Visual Basic procedure designed to implement set and get methods.

pseudocode Text (which may look similar to programming code) that is used to plan a procedure.

pseudo-random number generator A device that produces a sequence of numbers that meet certain statistical requirements for randomness.

Q

quantum A fixed amount of time during which a thread is granted access to the CPU.

query A set of instructions for extracting data from a database.

queue A first-in, first-out (FIFO) waiting list.

R

race condition A condition in which the outcome of a program depends on which of two or more threads accesses a control first, resulting in unpredictable results.

radio button A control in an interface that allows the user to make only one choice in a group of two or more buttons.

random access file A file that contains data that are accessed directly using information stored with the file.

real-world class A category to which similar real-world objects belong.

real-world object A thing in the real world that has attributes and behaviors.

real-world system A system that exists in the real world.

record A complete set of data, usually consisting of several fields.

reference type A data type of a variable for which the variable contains a reference to the memory location that stores the actual value.

reference variable A variable that stores the memory address of an object.

relational database A database that follows the relational model.

relational model A way of organizing data in related tables based on strict mathematical principles.

render block A section of code in an ASP or ASP.NET file, between the delimiters `<%` and `%>`, that is run on the server.

repetition structure A basic programming structure (also called a loop) that allows the program to repeatedly process one or more program instructions until some condition is met.

robust A characteristic of a program that implies it is well constructed and performs reliably.

root element The single element in an XML file that contains all other elements.

Running state A state a thread enters when it is executing.

runtime error An error that occurs while a program is running, usually causing the program to terminate unexpectedly if not handled.

S

scalability The ability of an application to adapt to increasing demands without significant changes in the computer system's architecture.

scalable The characteristic of an application that makes it more capable of handling increasing demands from many users over time.

scalar variable See **simple variable**.

scope The part of a program where a variable is declared and can be used.

script A set of instructions interpreted by another program rather than the computer processor.

scripting language A programming language that can be used within a Web page.

selection structure A basic programming structure (also called the decision structure) that allows a program to make a decision or comparison and then select the appropriate path.

sequence structure A basic programming structure in which each statement is processed, one after another, each time the procedure is called.

sequential access file A file that contains lines of human-readable text that are accessed in sequence from the beginning of the file through the end of the file. Also called a text file.

server-side scripting The process of embedding scripts in a Web page and executing them on the server instead of on the client.

set methods Methods that assign values to instance variables.

shortcut key A key or combination of keys that execute a menu item.

signature The combination of the method's name and its parameter list.

simple variable A variable that is unrelated to any other variable. Also known as a scalar variable.

single-document-interface (SDI) application An application that supports only one open window or document at a time.

SOAP (Simple Object Access Protocol) A protocol for exchanging XML-based messages over a computer network, normally using HTTP.

software class Program code that defines and creates software objects.

software object A representation of a real-world object in computer memory.

Solution Explorer window The window in the Visual Studio 2005 IDE that displays a list of the projects contained in the current solution, and the items contained in each project.

stack A data structure that operates on the principle of last-in, first-out (LIFO).

start tag A special code enclosed in angle brackets that begins the definition of an HTML element.

Started state The state a thread enters when it is capable of executing.

startup form The form that is automatically displayed when an application is started.

statement block A set of statements terminated by an `Else`, `End If`, `Loop`, or `Next` statement.

static variable A special type of procedure-level variable that retains its value even when the procedure ends.

Stopped state The state a thread enters after it has completed its assigned tasks.

strongly typed data structure A data structure that is checked at compile time for consistency of the items' data type.

strongly typed objects Objects whose type can be checked at compile time.

structure A single data type consisting of a logical grouping of simple variables, each variable having possibly different data types. Also called a user-defined data type.

structure members The variables, constants, or procedures contained within a structure.

structure variables Structure members of which all members are variables.

structured exception handling A process for managing program exceptions that uses a special `Try...Catch...Finally` statement to handle specific exception objects.

structured query language (SQL) A standard language used to store, retrieve, and manipulate data within a relational database.

`Sub` procedure A procedure that does not return a value.

submenu A menu contained within another menu item.

subscript An integer, beginning with 0, that serves as an index number for all elements in an array.

substring A contiguous sequence of characters taken from a string.

synchronization The communication between threads for the purpose of controlling the order of thread execution and access to program code.

syntax The rules of a programming language.

syntax error An error resulting from violating the programming language's syntax.

system components The parts of a system that interact to meet system objectives.

systems programmers Programmers who write and maintain programs that help the computer carry out its basic operating functions.

T

text file See **sequential access file**.

thread state The condition or status of a thread at any one time.

thread transition The act of changing from one thread state to another.

thread-safe code Code that will execute properly when run in a threaded environment.

thread Short for thread of execution, that part of a larger process or program on which the processor is working at any one time.

`ThreadStart` delegate A specific method that executes on a particular thread.

throw To create or generate an exception.

time slicing The process by which the processor gives a small slice of its time to one thread after another until all are completed.

Toolbox window The window in the Visual Studio 2005 IDE that contains the tools you use when creating an application. Each tool represents a class.

Transact-SQL Microsoft SQL Server version of SQL.

`Try` block A continuous section of program code, beginning with the keyword `Try`, that could possibly create an exception including code that should not execute if an exception is thrown.

`Try...Catch...Finally` statement The combination of a `Try` block plus its associated `Catch` block(s) and `Finally` block.

two-dimensional array An array that logically represents a fixed number of rows and columns that contain the array variables.

U

UDDI (Universal description, discovery, and integration) An XML-based standard that businesses use to publish and find Web services.

uncaught exception An exception that is not caught by any `Catch` block in the application and is therefore processed by the Common Language Runtime, resulting in program termination.

Unified Modeling Language (UML) A standardized, graphical notation for specifying, visualizing, constructing, and documenting a software system.

Unstarted state The initial thread state for threads that have been created by a program but never executed.

user interface The means by which the user interacts with the application.

user-defined data type See **structure**.

user-defined exception See **programmer-defined exception**.

V

value type A data type of a variable for which the variable contains the actual value.

variable A computer memory location where the programmer can temporarily store data while an application is running.

W

WaitSleepJoin state A state of thread inactivity that occurs when either the Wait, Sleep, or Join methods are called on a thread.

weakly typed data structure A data structure that is not checked at compile time for consistency of the items' data type.

Web application A computer application that uses a Web browser as the user interface.

Web server A computer with special software that stores Web pages and is connected to the Internet.

Web server controls Objects that have many properties and that can call complex event procedures. Web server controls are similar to HTML controls. Also called ASP.NET server controls.

Web service A class that is available over a network.

Windows Form Designer window The window in the Visual Basic IDE that contains a Windows Form object (or form) that serves as the application's graphical user interface.

word sort rules A set of rules for comparing strings where numbers are considered less than lowercase letters, which are considered less than uppercase letters.

WSDL (Web Services Description Language) An XML-formatted language used to completely describe a Web service.

X

XML (eXtensible Markup Language) A simple, widely used, human-readable, text-based format for storing data using customized tags similar to the HTML code found in Web pages.

XML namespace A collection of names, identified by a URI reference, that is used in XML documents as element types and attribute names.

XML parser Software that understands how to interpret XML files.

Index

D

E

H

I

J

K

L

M

N

O

R

S